INDIAN AFFAIRS ANNUAL 2008

INDIAN AFFAIRS ANNUAL 2008

(In 9 Vols.)

Vol. 5

Chronology of Events

(11-09-2007 to 29-10-2007)

Shailendra Sengar

KALPAZ PUBLICATIONS

KALPAZ PUBLICATIONS

DELHI - 110052

Indian Affairs Annual 2008

Rs. 6300 (Set)

ISBN: 81-7835-693-7 (Set)
ISBN: 81-7835-698-8 (Vol. 5)

Published in 2008 in India by
Kalpaz Publications
C-30, Satyawati Nagar,
Delhi-110052
E-mail: kalpaz@hotmail.com
Phone : 9212729499

Laser Type Setting by: Quick Media, Delhi
Printed at : Singhal Print Media, Delhi

INDIAN AFFAIRS ANNUAL 2008

Chronology of Events

(11-09-2007 to 29-10-2007)

3221. (11-9-2007) NEW DELHI : The second annual conference of Heads of Indian Missions of six GCC countries, Malaysia, Jordan, Libya and Yemen has concluded in New Delhi today. On the Occasion, The Minister of Overseas Indian Affairs Shri Vayalar Ravi said that the conference was successful. Important issues related to the welfare and protection of Overseas Indian Workers and Housemaids were discussed in the Conference. He said that the Head of the Mission were suggested to evolve a method so that the Overseas Indian workers and Household Service Workers can easily access Embassy for help. He also said that the Ministry has been taking several important steps for the welfare and protection of Overseas Indian Workers. The two-day conference of Heads of ten Indian Missions of made following recommendations: A minimum level of Policy Coherence was reached and appropriate institutional arrangements established to ensure bench marked standards of living and working conditions for Overseas Indian Workers in all major destination countries. A package of policy measures for the protection and welfare of women emigrants approved. This will include specifying a minimum wage, a 24/7 help line, establishing shelters for runaway maids, legal assistance and health care support. These measures will be channelled through overseas workers resource centres to be outsourced.

3222. (11-9-2007) NEW DELHI : The Minister for Rural Development, Dr. Raghuvansh Prasad Singh has called for total transparency and accountability in implementation of National Rural Employment Guarantee Programme in 330 districts of the country. Dr. Singh was addressing the Consultative Committee meeting of the Ministry of Rural Development in New Delhi yesterday. Dr. Singh said that the Members of Parliament who are also the Chairmen of the District Vigilance and Monitoring Committee in their respective districts can play an active role in ensuring that the officials responsible for implementation of the programme are accountable and transparent in implementing the scheme. He said that the programme is progressing well and improving the daily lives of the common people in rural India. Dr. Singh informed the Members about the out-come of the programme so far, its various components, financial progress and future plans. He said people's participation is very important for the successful implementation of the programme in various districts of the country. He also asked the Members of Parliament to ensure strict vigilance and monitoring in every district of the country. He particularly requested the Members of the Consultative Committee to visit various works' sites and point out the shortcomings to the concerned officials on the spot. He appealed to the Members to randomly verify the muster rolls and inform the Ministry also if there are any flaws. The Minister said that the States have been directed that social audit of each and every work of NREGA should be completed and the Ministry be apprised of the result of the social audit which is very important for implementation of the programme. The Members of the Consultative Committee congratulated the Minister for successful implementation of the programme and also pointed out certain difficulties and shortcomings in the implementation process. The points made by the Members, particularly pertain to ensuring the payment of minimum wages in every State which differ from State to State, unemployment allowance, and also improving the work conditions at the works' sites. The Members also requested the Minister to increase the number of districts in the next phase and to cover the entire country with the programme. The meeting was also attended by the Union Minister of State for Rural Development, Shri Chandra Sekhar Sahu and senior officers of the Ministry.

3223. (11-9-2007) NEW DELHI : The Minister of Railways Shri Lalu Prasad presided over a meeting of Members of Parliament from Kerala and Tamil Nadu on the issue of the formation of Salem Division in the state of Tamil Nadu, here today. Also present at the meeting were the Minister for Transport, Highways & Shipping, Shri T.R.Baalu, the Minister of State for Railways, Shri R. Velu and leader of CPI(M), Shri Sitaram Yechury. The following decisions were taken at the meeting:-· The section between Palghat to Polachi (58 route kms) from Madurai Division will be given to Palghat Division.· The section between Polachi to Kinattukkadavu (21 ruote kms) from Madurai Division will also be given to Palghat Division. The MPs from Kerela who attended the meeting were; Su/Shri P.Karunakaran CPI(M), N.N.Krishnadas, CPI(M), Chandran Pillai, CPI(M), M.P.Virendrakumar, JD(S), P.J.Kurien, INC, C.K.Chandrappan, CPI and P.C.Thomas, IFDP. The MPs from Tamil Nadu who attended the meting were; Su/Shri K.V. Thangkabalu, Cong., N. Siva, DMK, A. Krishnasamy, DMK, D.R. Senthil, PMK, Mohan, CPM and Subbarayan.

3224. (11-9-2007) NEW DELHI : Congress spokesperson Smt Jayanti Natarajan said that the Unorganized Sector Workers' Social Security Bill, which was introduced in Parliament recently, reflects the commitment of the Government towards the needs of unorganized sector workers. It will provide legislative backing to all the social security schemes. The Hon'ble Prime Minister announced a package of three schemes on the 15th of August this year as we completed 60 years of independence. These Schemes are a part of the Schedule to the proposed Bill. Under the "Aam Admi Bima Yojana", all the rural landless households in the country will be provided life and disability insurance cover. This cover will be for Rs. 75,000/- on death due to accident and permanent disability due to accident. In case of partial disability due to accident, the insurance cover would be Rs. 37,500/-. Upon death of a member, prior to terminal date, Rs. 30,000/- is the insurance amount. The premium to be charged under the scheme will be Rs. 200 per annum per member of which 50% will be contributed by the Central Government and remaining by the State Governments. The Finance Minister has already committed Rs. 1000 crore for this scheme in the budget. The National Old Age Pension will be extended to all the persons Below Poverty Line above the age of 65 years. A pension of Rs. 200/- per month will be provided and states will be requested to add another Rs. 200/- to this Scheme. An amount of more than Rs. 4000/- crore per annum will be spent under the scheme, which will be administered by the Ministry of Rural Development. A Health Insurance Scheme has also been formulated for all the BPL workers and their families. These six crore families will be covered progressively in the next five years. In all, more than 30 crore workers will be benefited. A provision has been made for issuing smart card, carrying a unique identification number, to each of these families. Both public and private health facilities will be utilized for providing medical services and there would be cashless transactions to ensure that there is no harassment of the beneficiaries. Under the scheme, during the first year, there is estimated expenditure of more than Rs. 700/- crore and this will go upto more than Rs. 3500/- crore at the end of five years when all the six crore BPL families would be covered. The coverage of BPL families represents just a beginning. The objective is to cover all the workers in the unorganized sector including those Above Poverty Line as well in a phased manner. The Bill also envisages setting up of Advisory Boards at the National and the State level. There will be representation from all the stakeholders on these Boards and, on the basis of advice given by these Boards, programmes and schemes will be worked out in future as well. The State Boards and the State Governments will play a key role in implementing various schemes as well as in registration of workers and issue of smart cards. To a question whether the Congress Party was in election mode? Smt. Natarajan said that this is an important commitment in the Common Minimum Programme from the last election. To a question whether 123 Agreement was not in the CMP? Smt. Natarajan said that it is an ongoing discussion as you know that another important discussion is taking place elsewhere. To a question on the remarks made by Maharashtra Chief Minister and Textile Minister about the farmers of Vidharbha, Smt. Natarajan said that I would like to categorically condemn any derogatory remarks that have been made against the hard- working farmers of this country.

3225. (11-9-2007) NEW DELHI : India has followed a consistent and calibrated industrial policy over the last few decades which has yielded significant results and made it a role model for other developing countries, especially Africa. The process of continuity with change was brought out in a presentation on "Industrial Policy – The Indian Perspective" by Shri N.N. Prasad, Joint Secretary, Department of Industrial Policy and Promotion (DIPP), at the International Conference on India-Africa Cooperation in Industry, Trade and Investment, which has been organized here by the United Nations Industrial Development Organisation (UNIDO) in cooperation with the Government of India, under the banner of the UNIDO Centre for South-South Industrial Cooperation(UCSSIC), and was inaugurated yesterday by Shri Kamal Nath, Minister of Commerce and Industry. Known as the Sanjay Lall Memorial Conference, the five-day event is being attended by 42 delegates from 13 African countries – Cameroon, Ethiopia, Ghana, Kenya, Madagascar, Mozambique, Nigeria, Senegal, South Africa, Sudan, Tanzania, Uganda and Zambia. "We would like to continue to share our experience, our expertise, our technology with Africa", the Minister had said, adding that India had as much to learn as to teach. Shri Prasad in his presentation explained the three Ds that characterized India's industrial policy – viz., decontrol, deregulation and de-bureaucratisation. Whereas, earlier 100s of inspections had to be gone through for setting up a factory, there had since been a sea change with drastic simplification of procedures and end of the licence raj, Shri Prasad said while stressing importance of a holistic approach to industrialization covering all aspects of industry from capital flows and foreign direct investment (FDI) to technology transfer and intellectual property rights(IPRs). Addressing the inaugural session, Shri Ajay Shankar, Secretary(DIPP), said the Conference was a timely initiative which would help in carrying the south-south development process forward. Mr. J. Vinanchiarachi, Principal Adviser to the Director-General/UNIDO, described the late Professor Sanjaya Lall as a development-minded practical thinker, whose concepts on R & D and innovation-induced products as the drivers of global trade helped UNIDO in framing its industrial performance and capabilities index. Mr. Anthony de Sa, Director, UCSSIC, mentioned that the Centre would develop projects on leather, cotton, auto components, hand tools, low-cost building materials, renewable energy, pharmaceuticals and IT applications in industry. Mr. Philippe Scholtes, Representative and Regional Director of UNIDO/South Asia, underlined the importance of the Conference as the first event of its kind in the field of south-south cooperation. While there had been similar initiatives in the past, the UNIDO initiative was important as it would focus on various sectors, in line with UNIDO's 8 service modules (viz., industrial governance; investment and technology promotion; industrial competitiveness and trade; private sector development; agro-industry; sustainable energy and climate change; implementation of environmental agreements; and environmental management of industries) and its large network of field offices and experts. The event was not an end in itself, but the beginning of a long-term-partnership between India and Africa, he said.

3226. (11-9-2007) NEW DELHI : Shri Kamal Nath, Union Minister of Commerce & Industry, has called for maximization of bilateral trade potential between India and Bulgaria. Observing that the Indo-Bulgarian bilateral trade, which at present stands at US $ 79 million (exports-$ 40 million and imports-$ 39 million), Shri Kamal Nath stated that this needs to grow significantly, considering the vast potential that exists for increasing the trade. This was stated by the Indian Commerce and Industry Minister when Mr. Petar Dimitrov, Bulgarian Minister for Economy and Energy called on him here today. While congratulating Bulgaria on its accession to the European Union (EU), Shri Kamal Nath said: "we look forward to your cooperation and support in strengthening the India-EU strategic partnership in all its manifestations. We have begun negotiations on a broad based trade and investment agreement". The Bulgarian geographical location and membership of the EU offer new opportunities for Indian companies to sell to and invest in Bulgaria, Shri Kamal Nath added. Major items of exports to Bulgaria include machinery & instruments, drugs, pharmaceuticals & fine chemicals, manufactures of metals, non-ferrous metals etc. and major items of imports from Bulgaria are – inorganic chemicals, wheat, iron & steel, machinery except electric & electronic.

3227. (11-9-2007) NEW DELHI : Inaugurating the College of Nursing of the Lady Hardinge Medical College and Associated Hospital, today, the Union Minister for Health & Family Welfare, Dr. Anbumani Ramadoss said the concept of nursing has expanded over the years and is no longer confined to the hospitals and patient care alone. Today, the nurses are the sheet anchor of our total health care delivery system. Our main aim is to provide primary health care, including the preventive, promotive and rehabilitative services, as close to the doorsteps of the people as possible. Smt. Sheila Dixit, Chief Minister of Delhi, Smt. Panabaka Lakshmi, Minister of State for Health & Family Welfare, Shri Naresh Dayal, Secretary (HFW), Dr. R.K. Srivastava, DGHS, Dr. Deepak Pantal, Vice-Chancellor, Delhi University and other senior officials from the Ministry and Medical Institutions were also present. The following is the text of the Health Minister's speech: "Training school for Nurses in the LHMC started very modestly in 1916 with 11 probationers admitted to the school for training every year. This has been expanded to admit 55 pupil nurses each year. The school provides training facilities for diploma course in nursing. Keeping in mind to improve the quality of nursing services and need for training more graduate Nurses we have upgraded the School of Nursing into College of Nursing. We are in the process of upgrading 2 more Schools of Nursing into College of Nursing in RML Hospital and Safdarjung Hospital in Delhi. I would also like to congratulate the first batch of students who have just taken the admission in this prestigious institution. We are upgrading the Schools of Nursing, which are attached with Medical Colleges into Colleges of Nursing in the country. Nursing binds the human society with a silken bond of love and affection. We may take it as the best example of national integrity, as the nurses serve the humanity without prejudice of caste, colour, creed, region or language. The pioneers like Florence Nightingale and Mother Teressa have built the bridges of international understanding and cooperation with their sense of service and self-sacrifice. The nursing profession occupies a strategic position in the primary health care network. They are the mainstay of our health care delivery system who take the services to the doorsteps of the people in the villages, remote and tribal areas including economically weaker sections in cities and towns. Hence, nurses are being trained for unconventional roles that of promoting health practices, educating people about disease prevention, offering family welfare services, counselling and motivation. They are the ones who provide the most vital maternal and child health care services to the community. The role of nurses is very vital in this endeavour. A large number of nursing personnel are required under NRHM to serve at Primary Health Centres.

3228. (11-9-2007) NEW DELHI : Union Power Minister, Shri Sushilkumar Shinde has expressed confidence that the targets his Ministry has set out for the 11th Plan will be achieved. Delivering the inaugural address at the 10th Power Forum in New Delhi today he said that the capacity addition of over 78000 MW is not an ambitious target and can be achieved through various programmes and policies the Ministry has been following. Reiterating his commitment to electrify every village in the country by 2009 and provide electricity to every household by 2012, Shri Shinde emphasized the need for open access in power sector which is crucial for sustaining the growth of above 9 per cent. Speaking about the measures being taken to put power generation on fast track the Minister said that the loopholes in the bidding process of UMPPs have been corrected, problems related to merchant power plants of about 12000 MW have been sorted out. Speaking on the occasion, Secretary, Ministry of Power, Shri Anil Razdan said that the 11th Plan will not only bring huge opportunities for the industries active in power sector but also generate employment on a large scale in urban as well as rural areas. In his address, Member, Planning Commission, Shri B.K. Chaturvedi described theft of electricity as a major challenge and stressed the need to plug the leak. Sighting examples of telecom and insurance sectors where allowing access to private sector has been a win-win situation for both the public and private sectors, he said open access is a must. He also emphasized improvement in equipment delivery system and availability of fuel as other challenges. Shri C.P. Jain, former CMD, NTPC and Chairman Power Group, Indian Energy Forum and Shri P.S. Bami, President, IEF also spoke on the occasion. The theme of the day-long event organized by India Energy Forum (IEF) is "Power Sector-Driver of Growth".

3229. (11-9-2007) NEW DELHI : The Prime Minister Dr. Manmohan Singh has said that water conservation and management can be better served through appropriate incentives and penalties. Delivering inaugural address at the National Ground Water Congress – 2007 here today Dr. Singh said that we cannot continue to subsidize the economic and commercial use of water. There are related policies that must also be corrected to ensure water conservation, especially ground water. Providing free power to farmers has encouraged excessive use of pump sets and excessive drawing of ground water. If there is economic pricing of power, there would be some incentive for conserving ground water. The Prime Minister said that the Government has taken several steps in the past three years. We are in the process of formulating a scheme for Dug Well Recharge in hard rock regions of the country covering seven States. However, any strategy for water conservation, management and utilization cannot be imposed on the country from here in New Delhi. We need a community-based, region-specific strategy that is owned by the people who have to implement it. The Prime Minister said that our Panchayati Raj institutions and our municipalities and local bodies, along with civil society organizations, have a critical and vital role to play. He wanted each and every Panchayat and municipality to come forward with a water conservation strategy. The impressive example of Chennai city that had a city-based, neighbourhood-based strategy is before us. Every village, every locality, every neighbourhood, every town should have a rain water harvesting scheme. Panchayats must be actively engaged in ground water recharge and the renovation and maintenance of water bodies. Referring to National Rural Employment Guarantee Programme Dr. Singh said that it provides an opportunity to mobilize people for this purpose and hoped that State Governments and local bodies would take an active interest in utilizing these resources for water management, conservation and utilization. The Prime Minister said that the water especially potable water is finite and vulnerable resource. There is also wide consensus that water development and management should be based on a participatory approach, involving all stakeholders. The Dublin Conference on water and environment held in 1992 drew our attention to the central role of women in water management. Thereby it brought the gender dimension into focus. There was also recognition that water is both a public good and an economic good. Modern governments must base their policies pertaining to water on both criteria. The question before us-is have we paid adequate attention to these principles and priorities since 1992. I am afraid we have not done so, he added. The Prime Minister hoped that this Conference will impart a greater sense of urgency to the challenge of water conservation, groundwater recharge and rainwater harvesting. He urged that Advisory Council on Artificial Recharge of Ground Water to create widespread national awareness and a genuine national consensus on an equitable, efficient and environmentally sustainable water policy. Prof. Saifuddin Soz, the Union Minister of Water Resources in his welcome address said that Ground Water has been an important resource to meet our water requirements. It is of vital importance for sustaining life, health and agriculture. However, over the years, there have been instances of over-exploitation of ground water in some areas.

3230. (11-9-2007) NEW DELHI : The Union Minister of Shipping, Road Transport and Highways, Thiru T.R. Baalu has said that the East-West Corridor which, passes through the States of Assam, West Bengal, Bihar, Uttar Pradesh, Madhya Pradesh, Rajasthan and Gujarat, is likely to be substantially completed by 2009. Speaking at the Parliamentary Consultative Committee Meeting of the Ministry, Thiru T.R. Baalu said that on completion, this Corridor would open up new opportunities for the people residing in these States and lead to all round economic development of these States. The subject of the today's Consultative Committee Meeting was the progress of work on the East West Corridor. Thiru Baalu said that the main problems affecting the progress have been the delay in disbursement of compensation for land acquisition in Assam, Bihar, Madhya Pradesh and Uttar Pradesh. There has also been some delay in Uttar Pradesh due to the condition stipulated by the State Government for providing 10-metre wide strip of land for afforestation before allowing tree-cutting, the Minister said and added that law and order in Assam has also to some extent affected the work in that State. However, assuring the Members, Thiru Baalu said that all these issues are being pursued with the respective State Governments and efforts are being made to speed up the work. Giving details about the progress of the East-West Corridor, the Minister said that out of the total length of 3,443 kms, widening has already been completed in 765 kms and is in progress in a length of 2,446 kms and the work in a length of 232 kms remains to be awarded. This includes 201 kms in West Bengal from Siliguri on NH-31 to West Bengal/Assam Border where the alignment had to be changed due to Mahananda and Jaldapara Wild Life Sanctuaries and Buxa Tiger Reserve, Thiru Baalu said. The Minister informed the Members that the revised Detailed Project Report (DPR) on the alternate alignment which avoids wild life altogether, is expected in two months and thereafter action would be initiated on these projects. Similarly work in a length of 31 kms in Assam between Udarband and Harangajo also could not be awarded due to declaration of Burail Wild Life Sanctuary, he said and added that revised DPR for alternate alignment in this section is also being prepared for this stretch. Thiru Baalu also informed that in the East-West Corridor, some major bridges like the Second Brahamputra Bridge near Saraighat in Guwahati, Kosi Bridge on NH-57 in Bihar and the cable-stayed bridge on Kota Bypass in Rajasthan are likely to be completed in 2010.Participating in the discussion, the Members raised the issue of damaged roads due to recent floods in Bihar.

3231. (11-9-2007) NEW DELHI : The Prime Minister, Dr. Manmohan Singh, said that today's humankind faces a real danger of human conflict based on our need for water and "We must resolve together to ensure the equitable, efficient and environmentally friendly use of this life†giving natural resource." Speaking at the National Congress on Ground Water 2007 here today, the Prime Minister said that the Government has taken several steps to address the challenges in the past three years. A scheme for Dug Well Recharge in hard rock regions of the country covering seven States is under process. Any strategy for water conservation, management and utilization cannot be imposed on the country from New Delhi. "We need a community based, region specific strategy that is owned by the people who have to implement it," he added. The Prime Minister said that we cannot continue to subsidise the economic and commercial use of water. There are related policies that must also be corrected to ensure adequate emphasis on water conservation, especially ground water. Dr. Manmohan Singh appealed to each and every citizen of the country to make genuine and wholehearted efforts to conserve water, prevent its over exploitation and pollution of ground water, and adopt measures both individually and collectively, as a family, as a community and as a village and locality.

3232. (11-9-2007) NEW DELHI : One Kiran Mk-I trainer aircraft of Indian Air Force crashed near Hakimpet in Hyderabad on 11 Sep 07 at 02: 50 am. The aircraft had got airborne from Hakimpet air base and was on a routine training-flying mission by night. The pilots, instructor and the trainee, lost their lives in the accident. There was no damage to civil property as a result of air crash. An inquiry has been ordered to investigate the reasons for the accident.

3233. (12-9-2007) NEW DELHI : The Union Minister of Shipping, Road Transport & Highways, Thiru T.R. Baalu met the leaders of the five Labour Federations of the Port & Dock Workers here today and gave a patient hearing to the demands of the leaders of the Federations. After detailed deliberations, certain important decisions were taken. On the demand relating to enhancement of the retirement age of Port and Dock Employees/Workers, the five Federations agreed to unilaterally withdraw the two references pending before the Chief Labour Commissioner (Central) relating to restoration of the age of retirement of Port and Dock Employees and the notice of strike. On immediate withdrawal of these references by the Federation before the CLC, the Department will consider the enhancement of the age of retirement from 58 years to 60 years with effect from 1st October 2007. Thiru T.R. Baalu also constituted a Committee under the Managing Director, Indian Ports Association, to make a realistic assessment of vacancies in Ports in discussion with the Unions. The Committee will also examine the outsourcing of technical and specialised jobs through contracts by the Ports and submit its Report by 31st October 2007. The leaders of the Federations assured cooperation in the development of the Port sector.

3234. (12-9-2007) NEW DELHI : The President, Smt. Pratibha Devisingh Patil has congratulated the Indian Woman Cricketer, Ms. Jhulan Goswami on winning the International Cricket Council's, 'Cricketer of the Year' award. The President has said that the award will be a special milestone for women's cricket in India and the nation is proud of her achievement.

3235. (12-9-2007) NEW DELHI : By virtue of the provision of clause (d) of sub-section (1) section 115 WB, introduced by Finance Act, 2007, an employer is liable to pay Fringe Benefit Tax on any consideration for employment provided by way of any specified security or sweat equity shares allotted or transferred, directly or indirectly, by such employer free of cost or at concessional rate to his employees. The value of the fringe benefit is determined as the fair market value of the specified security or sweat equity share on the date on which the option vests with the employee as reduced by the amount actually paid, by or recovered from the employee in respect of such security or shares. The fair market value for this purpose is to be determined in accordance with the method prescribed by the Board. Since the method for determination of the fair market value was yet to be prescribed, the Central Board of Direct Taxes (CBDT) had earlier extended the date of payment of first instalment of Fringe Benefit Tax, which was to be paid on or before June 15, 2007, in respect of transfer or allotment of specified security or sweat equity shares to its employees, to 15th of September, 2007 (the date of second instalment). The Central Board of Direct Taxes (CBDT) is currently in the final stage of finalizing the method for determination of the fair market value. In the meantime, the extended first instalment and the second instalment of advance tax in respect of fringe benefit tax falls due on 15th of September. In the absence of a method for determination of the fair market value, it will not be possible for an employer to determine the value of these instalments of advance tax related to fringe benefit tax in respect of allotment or transfer of specified security or sweat equity shares to its employees. In order to mitigate this hardship, the CBDT has decided that the first instalment of Fringe Benefit Tax, which was to be paid on or before June 15, 2007, and the second instalment of Fringe Benefit Tax, which is to be paid on or before September 15, 2007, in respect of transfer or allotment of specified security or sweat equity shares to its employees, may be paid on or before the 15th of December, 2007 (the date of third instalment).

3236. (12-9-2007) NEW DELHI : Inaugurating the seminar on Impact of Preventive Healthcare on Indian Industry and Economy organized by Indian Council for Research on International Economic Relations (ICRIER), today, the Union Minister for Health & Family Welfare, Dr. Anbumani Ramadoss said preventive, as opposed to curative health care has become the preferred option in most developed countries as it allows employees to be more productive. However preventive healthcare in India is still at early stages. I think we need to confront this problem with more compassion, commitment and concentration. It is my belief that the Health Policy should be even more forthcoming on this point and take firm steps to achieve this objective. Shri Naresh Dayal, Secretary (HFW), Shri Parthasarathi Shome, Adviser to Union Finance Minister, Dr. Rajiv Kumar, Director and Chief Executive, ICRIER, and other senior officials of the Ministry of Health & Family Welfare and members of ICRIER were also present at the meeting. The following is the summary of the Health Minister's speech: The need for preventive versus curative healthcare is partly attributed to the changing corporate environment in India. In recent times with greater globalization and urbanization there is a greater amount of stress in companies leading to adverse lifestyle choices. There are individual and group level initiatives, which can improve business effectiveness and the quality of executive and employees lives. Companies can design programmes that help stimulate healthy work environments that people want to be in. The rising costs of healthcare are taking a significant toll on every company's profits. The leading contributor is lifestyle choices-and questions that corporates need to ask themselves is: are their employees sedentary, over their ideal weight, struggling with aging parents, growing children and a demanding career. There is an urgent need to adopt measures to reduce absenteeism, increase employee productivity and reduce healthcare expenditure. According to a study by the Journal of Occupational and Environmental Medicine reducing just one health risk, increases on-the-job productivity by 9% and cuts absenteeism by 2%. Today, stress is a part of everyday life and the workplace is definitely no exception. Deadlines need to be met, long hours at the office, rapidly changing technology affect how we work, and interpersonal conflicts are just some of the stresses coped with daily. There has to be greater play for private participation in the health sector. Several innovative financing mechanisms have to be institutionalized. India has the potential to be at the forefront of modern health care, given its strong base in quality health care professionals and cost effective research. India has the opportunity to harness these strengths to deliver quality health care not only for its people but to larger geographical regions as well. India has to see health not as a social cost but as an investment in human capital for economic growth. It is our national determination to make India a nation of healthy people. National Rural Health Mission (NRHM) was launched by Hon'ble Prime Minister on 12th April, 2005. Plan of Action includes, increased public expenditure on Health, reducing regional imbalances in Health, pooling resources, optimisation of Health Manpower, community participation and ownership, operationalizing Community Health Centres (CHCs) into functional hospitals. The Mission is an articulation of the commitment of the Government to raise public spending on Health from 0.9% of GDP to 2-3% of GDP. It aims to undertake architectural correction of the health system to enable it to effectively handle increased allocations as promised under the National Common Minimum Programme and promote policies that strengthen public health management and service delivery in the country. Seventy five percent of our health services is provided by private sector. Private-public partnership brings convergence of private sector interests and public sector goals. Aim is to optimally utilize and enable increased access to healthcare facilities for our vast rural poor. Today the Non Communicable Diseases (NCDs), especially Cardiovascular Diseases (CVD's), Diabetes Mellitus, Cancer, Stroke and Chronic Lung Diseases have emerged as major public health problems, due to an ageing population and environmentally driven changes in behaviour. Surveys in India reveal that about 10 % of adults suffer from hypertension.

3237. (12-9-2007) NEW DELHI : The Human Resource Development Minister, Shri Arjun Singh said that the number of National Awards for the Kendriya Vidyalaya is being increased. The Minister was speaking in New Delhi today after giving away incentive awards to teachers and non-teaching staff of Kendriya Vidyalayas (KVs). The Human Resource Development Minister expressed satisfaction over the performance of KVs in all fields. He remarked that unless "we have dedicated and committed teachers to take to teaching as a mission in their lives, a good educational system cannot be developed." Again and again he emphasized the basic educational necessity of fostering a strong relationship between teachers and students. Forty nine Kendriya Vidyalaya teachers and five non-teaching employees were presented with incentive awards at a glittering function, held here today. The Minister for Human Resource Development and the Chairman Kendriya Vidyalaya Sangathan, Shri Arjun Singh presented the awards. Out of 54 incentive awardees and 13 national awardees, 36 were women. Mohammad A.A. Fatmi, Minister of State (HRD) paid glowing tributes to teachers and averred that the next decade will be the decade of secondary education in which the role of KVs will definitely be of a pace-setter. Underlining the importance of education, he remarked that education only has the power to alleviate all the melodies India is being affected by. Speaking on the occasion, another Minister of State, Smt. Purandeshwari Devi asked that Kendriya Vidyalaya teachers to stand exemplary for the teaching community. The Commissioner, Kendriya Vidyalaya Sangathan, Shri Ranglal Jamuda gave details of the overall achievements of the KVs in academic as well as co-academic fields.

3238. (12-9-2007) NEW DELHI : A Tsunami alert has been issued for the Andaman & Nicobar Islands. The Islands administration has been advised to take all precautionary measures to alert the people in the coastal areas and be in the highest state of preparedness. Tamil Nadu, Kerala, Andhra Pradesh and Pondicherry have also been asked to maintain vigil. The Ministry of Home Affairs is constantly monitoring the situation. As per information received from the Indian National Centre for Ocean Information Services, Hyderabad (NCOIS) an earthquake of magnitude 8.0 occurred in southern Sumatra, Indonesia at about 4.41 p.m. IST today.

3239. (12-9-2007) NEW DELHI : Prof. Saifuddin Soz, the Union Minister for Water Resources has said that it is heartening to observe that the media agencies are associating themselves with issues related to environment, water and wildlife which are directly related to our well being. There is a very important role of media in creating awareness among the people. He was addressing at a function of the Fourth Centre for Media Studies Vatavaran Environment and Wildlife film Festival here today. He appreciated that entries in the festival have been invited for the theme "Water For All" which is indeed very topical. Prof. Soz said that the participation of all stakeholders in water management has been well recognized. It has been our policy to give due importance to the management of the water resources with active participation and involvement of the stakeholders at all levels-planning, development as well as management of water resources for diverse uses should incorporate a participatory approach; by involving not only the various governmental agencies but also the users and other stakeholders, in an effective and decisive manner, in various aspects of planning, design, development and management of the water resources schemes. Prof. Soz said that the traditional practices for water resources development and management have been adopted in many parts of our country. These practices are in complete harmony with the environment. The Film Media which has the capacity to reach and influence common people can contribute in a big way in popularizing sound traditional practices. Successful practices of water management being followed in various parts of the country can be brought out by the Film Media and thus help in populazing the cause of water conservation and environment and promote replication of best practices, he emphasized.

3240. (12-9-2007) NEW DELHI : Dr. Raghuvansh Prasad Singh, Union Minister for Rural Development has said that efforts are on to establish centres for proper packaging, branding and marketing for the rural products made by the rural artisans across the country. Inaugurating the fortnight long rural handicraft fair SARAS – 2007 here the minister said that rural employment is a key to eliminate poverty from the country. He said that under the Swarnajayanti Gram Swarozgar Yojana (SGSY), a pilot scheme of his Ministry to provide employment in the rural areas the BPL families and the women folks are being encouraged to form Self Help Groups. During the 11th five year plan it will be ensured that at least one member of every rural family is associated with a Self Help Group engaged in providing respectful earning to the rural masses across the country. Necessary training and financial help is also being provided to them. Till now handicrafts, food items and handloom products manufactured in the rural areas lags behind for want of proper publicity and marketing avenues, Dr. Singh added. Lauding the role of SARAS like avenues, the minister said that from seven SARAS fairs in 2003-04 benefiting 3174 SHGs in the country the number has now reached to 24,408 in the year 2006-07. The sales turnover of Rs.12,59,56,538 crore in 2003-04 has also taken a quantum leap to the tune of Rs. 21,45,40,472 crore during the last financial year. The sale of rural products during the current financial year (2007-08) is so far to the tune of Rs. 83,98,746 lakhs. Till now a total of 66 SARAS fairs have generated a sales turnover of Rs.76,19,49,623 crores, Dr. Singh added. He said that so far 11 States have provided necessary marketing infrastructure at State Capitals and the remaining States are also working in this direction. Besides the renovation work at the site of Annual trade fair at Pragati Maidan, New Delhi, shops for rural artisans at Rajiv Gandhi Bhawan, New Delhi and at the venue of sales emporia's at Baba Kharag Singh Marg New Delhi are also being established in addition the procurement of land at Pritampura and Jasola in Delhi, the minister added. He also appreciated Council for Advancement of People's Action and Rural Technology (CAPART) in providing necessary help to the rural artisans through a widespread network of NGOs.

3241. (12-9-2007) NEW DELHI : The floriculture industry has vast potential for generating income and employment and enhancing export earnings and this sector is growing at a fast pace, helped by recent initiatives launched by the Government. Stating this at the inauguration of the 3rd International Flora Expo here today, Agriculture Minister Shri Sharad Pawar mentioned the contribution of National Horticulture Mission launched last year and the Technology Mission for Integrated Development of Horticulture in the North Eastern States in 2001-

02. During the last two years, nearly Rs. 68 crore has been resulting to the states for expansion of area under flower cultivation, resulting in about 22,000 hectares of additional area coming under floriculture production. Centres for organized floriculture have emerged in many parts of the country, including Bangalore, Pune and Nasik. Mizoram, Meghalaya and Sikkim have entered export and domestic markets in this field. The domestic market of flowers and ornamental plants fetches nearly Rs. 10,000 million for cultivators, the Minister informed. Since there is no organized market for flowers at present, the increasing popularity of retail markets, particularly of perishables, is likely to provide a fillip to the domestic floriculture industry. Setting up of six Agri Export Zones for floriculture, besides a large number of flower clusters under NHM, is expected to provide further impetus to the domestic and international trade of floriculture products in the coming years, Shri Pawar said. Delineating the growth of floriculture exports, the Minister said that flower exports have recorded a robust growth from Rs. 188 million in 1993-94 to over Rs. 4000 million in 2006-07 and now India's share in floriculture export is about 2% of the total agri-export basket. Our fresh flowers are reaching about 87 countries with a significant share going to countries like Australia, UK, Japan, Netherlands and UAE. During the last ten years, there has been an exponential growth in the earning through the marketing of floriculture products, both in the domestic and international markets. This has been achieved despite stiff competition from many of the flower exporting countries and high domestic freight charges on floriculture products. The Minister also invited entrepreneurs from other countries to take advantage of the government's policies and take up commercial ventures in floriculture in India. He said that liberalization of industrial and trade policies has paved the way for export-oriented production of cut flowers. Besides, since 2006, the Government has permitted 100% Foreign Direct Investment in the floriculture sector.

3242. (12-9-2007) NEW DELHI : The Union Minister of Shipping, Road Transport and Highways, Thiru T.R. Baalu has approved the construction of Railway over Bridge (ROB) cum Flyover approach over river Subernrekha on NH-33 at Namkum in Jharkhand at a total cost of Rs. 26.30 crore. Existing bridge on NH-33 on Subernrekha river is of narrow width and in dilapidated condition. Due to high traffic volume of goods traffic, flyover is required over crossing of NH-33 with SH-1. The proposed grade-separated alignment corridors would provide relief to the traffic. The proposal is primarily aimed at achieving permanent closures of railway level crossing at Namkum and to provide through passage between Ranchi leg and Jamshedpur leg on NH-33 and Purulia side of SH-01. The Ministry of Railway will also provide Rs. 7.61 crore as its share of the ROB.

3243. (12-9-2007) NEW DELHI : The Ministry of Law and Justice has made a provision of Rs. 17.5 crore as grant-in-aid to National Legal Services Authorities (NALSA) during the current financial year (2007-08). The Central Government has provided grant-in-aid to NALSA amounting to Rs. 5 crore during 2004-05, and Rs. 10 crore each during 2005-06 and 2006-07. The NALSA utilizes the grant-in-aid provided by the Central Government and the grants and other amounts received from other sources for meeting the cost of legal services provided under the Legal Services Authorities Act, 1987.

3244. (12-9-2007) NEW DELHI : The employment of women in the organised sector has increased during the first half of this decade. According to the information collected by the Ministry of Labour and Employment under Employment Market Information Programme, the number of women employees in both public and private sectors has increased from 49.5 lakh in 2001 to 50.2 lakh in 2005. Women employment during the years 2002, 2003 and 2004 as on 31st March, was 49.4 lakh, 49.7 lakh and 49.3 lakh respectively. Employment of men in public and private sectors has declined from 228.4 lakh in 2001 to 214.4 lakh in 2005. Total employment in the organised sector, public and private combined, for both men and women has declined from 277.9 lakh as on March 31, 2001 to 264.6 lakh as on March 31, 2005.

3245. (12-9-2007) NEW DELHI : The Employees State Insurance Corporation (ESIC) has given in principle approval for setting up five new hospitals for workers. These hospitals would be located at Raipur in Chattisgarh, Baddi in Himachal Pradesh, Gurgaon in Haryana, Tirunelveli & Tiruupur in Tamil Nadu and Haldia in West Bengal. The ESI Corporation has also given approval for setting up of 10-bedded diagnostic centres at Dehradun in Uttaranchal and Raipur in Chattisgarh. At present there are 144 ESI hospitals all over the country.

3246. (12-9-2007) NEW DELHI : A broad based Rashtriya Sanskrit Parishad has been constituted in place of Kendriya Sanskrit Board by the Government to conserve, encourage and develop the rich heritage of Sanskrit language. The Parishad will advise the State Governments, University Grants Commission, Universities, Research Institutions, National Council of Educational Research & Training and National Council for Teachers Training. This was stated by the Human Resource Development Minister, Shri Arjun Singh while presiding over the second Convocation Ceremony of Rashtriya Sanskrit Sansthan (Deemed University, New Delhi), here today. Referring to the still alive tradition of Sanskrit studies in France, Germany, Japan, Poland, England, America, Italy, Russia and Thailand, Minister said Sanskrit not only unites India, it has strength to unite the world as well. Sanskrit is a scientific language and is being considered today the best computer language due to its perfection and practicality. Sanskrit has special space in galaxy of world languages. Among all the ancient languages, Sanskrit is the only oldest language which is still alive and in use. Sanskrit is a reservoir of knowledge and science, hence, research work be emphasized on untouched subjects, the Minister said. The Minister also released 12 books written/edited/translated by various scholars and unveiled 21 buildings of the Sansthan in four complexes of Jaipur, Lucknow, Puri & Shrangeri and also inaugurated the distance education courses of the Sansthan. Delivering the convocation address,

Prof. Sukhadeo Thorat, Chairman of University Grants Commission said that without the knowledge of Sanskrit, it is not possible to understand the culture and heritage of India. Presenting his reports, Vice Chancellor of Rashtriya Sanskrit Sansthan Acharya Vempati Kutumbshastri said that the Sansthan today owns 1, 06,000 sq. mtrs. built up area and 90 acre of land through out the country. The Sansthan has the hostel facilities to accommodate about 1800 students and libraries having 3,50,000 books and 72,000 manuscripts in the country.

3247. (12-9-2007) NEW DELHI : The Ministry of Women and Child Development is developing Gender Budgeting Manuals to ensure committed funds for women related schemes. The manuals will help in institutionalizing the concept of Gender Budgeting at all levels of governance. Gender Budgeting cells has been set up in 53 Ministries and Departments. The Ministry is making an assessment of impact of the Gender Budgeting by these Ministries. Remaining Ministries also being persuaded to set up the cells. This was disclosed by Smt. Renuka Chowdhury, Minister for Women and Child Development to the Members of the Parliamentary Consultative Committee here today. She said that her Ministry will approach the Finance Ministry to include the performance of the schemes separately in performance budget. Briefing about the various initiatives taken by her Ministry for the empowerment of women, the Minister said that sex disaggregated database and Gender Development Index were also being developed by the Ministry of Women and Child Development. Beside that intensive training and capacity building programme is being implemented which include dissemination of framework comprising of tools and strategies to enable Gender Budgeting Cells to conduct Gender Budgeting exercise, the Minister added. The Government has already brought out a Gender Budgeting Charter for all Ministries and Departments detailing the composition and functioning of their respective Gender Budgeting cells. Regional workshops with state Governments and training institutes are being conducted to develop a core group of trainers. Smt. Renuka Chowdhury said that her Ministry is also working on review of implementation of all legislations with the gender perspective to eliminate all forms of discrimination and violence against women. The Minister said that access of the women to the resources is very important to check disparities in important parameters like health, nutrition and literacy. "There are number of gender specific barriers, which prevent women from gaining access to their rightful share in the flow of public goods and services. Unless these gender requirements and their felt needs are incorporated in the planning and development process, it is apprehended that the fruits of economic growth are likely to completely bypass a significant section of the country's population", She said.

3248. (12-9-2007) NEW DELHI : The Prime Minister, Dr. Manmohan Singh, received a delegation of the Bharatiya Kisan Union and the Indian Coordination Committee of Farmers Movement led by Shri Mahendra Singh Tikait. Receiving their memorandum, the Prime Minister said that the welfare of the farmers was the top most priority for the UPA Government. He said that the government is committed to ensuring livelihood security for the farming community and food security for all. The Prime Minister told the delegation that in the past three years the UPA government has ensured remunerative prices and has affected significant increase in the Minimum Support Price, reversing the neglect of the farming community and the policy of minimal increase in MSP under the previous NDA government. The Prime Minister reiterated the government's commitment to offering insurance to farmers against risk and said that the government is considering a loan-insurance scheme to mitigate risk for indebted farmers. The Prime Minister also assured the farmers' delegation that the government is committed to increased investment in agricultural research so that the productivity of indigenous seeds and the productivity of land and water utilization can be increased. The Prime Minister also stated that the government will safeguard the interests of Indian farmers in the WTO negotiations and will not accept any obligations that will hurt our farmers' interests. The Prime Minister assured the delegation that he will draw the attention of the Union Agriculture Minister to the various demands of the farmers.

3249. (12-9-2007) NEW DELHI : Prof. Saifuddin Soz, the Union Minister for Water Resources presided over the second meeting of the Advisory Council for Artificial Recharge of Ground Water here today. The Union Minister of Water Resources Shri Jai Prakash Narayan Yadav and the Secretary, Ministry of Water Resources Smt. Gauri Chatterjee were also present. The Council has 38 Members. The Secretary Incharge Water Resources of the States/ UTs each from Eastern States, Western States, Northern States, Central States, North-Eastern States, Hilly States are also Member on rotational basis. The Members have been drawn from Farmer's representatives, NABARD, Rural Electrification Corporation, Industries/ Public Undertakings, NGOs in addition to Government officials. The Council members deliberated on a programme to make rainwater harvesting and water conservation as a national goal. A number of issues were discussed and a future programme of action was recommended. The key items discussed at the meeting are as follows:- 1. The Committee will work for wider dissemination and replication of the efforts made by the National Water Award winner so that other stakeholders get requisite motivation and can benefit from this success story. Similarly action would be taken regarding replication of the success of all other Puraskar winners also. 2. The Committee will further monitor and take steps to ensure success of village demonstration programmes for more crop per drop of water. For this purpose independent monitors will be selected in the six zones. 3. Coordinated efforts will be made to bring out a white paper on the impact of climate change on India's Hydrological Cycle. 4. Programmes will be implemented in selected blocks in coordination with the concerned State Governments with a view turning critical blocks to safe category. 5. The Directorate of Film Festivals will be requested to have a separate section on Water in the film festivals. 6. A special campaign will be mounted for dissemination of information on ground water recharge and rain water harvesting in educational institutions. 7. Central Ground Water Board will give greater attention to water quality issues in order to have focused interventions in this regard. The Board will prepare a National Ground Water Quality Hot Spot Map. 8. The Committee expressed happiness over the steps taken by the Central Ground Water Board for developing web enabled ground water information system. 9. The best practices adopted by various urban bodies in the country will be mapped and the information relating thereto will be shared with other stakeholders. The objective of the setting up of Artificial Recharge of Ground Water Advisory Council is to popularize the concept of artificial recharge amongst various stakeholders. The terms of reference of the Council includes prioritizing areas for recharging ground water, development of areas specific techniques of recharging, developing, coordination amongst Central and State Agencies and stakeholders, creating of awareness, education, capacity building in whole programme of rain water harvesting and recharging of ground water. The first meeting of the council was held on 22nd July 2006 in New Delhi. The issues discussed in the first meeting included need for ground water regulatory measures, setting u of Sub Committees, more crop and income per drop of water, and role of Pani Panchayats etc.

3250. (12-9-2007) NEW DELHI : The students of Prahar Vidyalaya, Nagpur, meet General JJ Singh, COAS on September 10, at the residence here. The students of the Vidyalaya presented a song and drama composition before the COAS. The Army chief presented the Army logo to all visiting students and a memento to school authorities. A brief introduction of the school and the society: The Prahar Samaj Jagruti Sanstha was founded by Lt Col (Retd) Sunil W Deshpande VSM (Ex CO 2 Maratha LI) in the year 1994 with the aim of spreading soldierly qualities in society namely discipline, courage, vigilance, values of life, service to mankind and patriotism. Prahar is non-political and a charitable trust registered with Charity Commissioner Nagpur.

3251. (12-9-2007) NEW DELHI : The Parliamentary Consultative Committee attached to the Ministry of Chemicals and Fertilizers has strongly supported the decision to revive the 8 closed plants of the Fertilizer Corporation of India and the Hindustan Fertilizer Corporation. The units are located at Gorakhpur, Sindhri, Durgapur, Barauni, Haldia, Talcher, Ramagundam and Kobra. The Committee which met here today under the chairmanship of the Minister for Steel, Chemicals and Fertilizers Shri Ram Vilas Paswan to discuss Pricing Policy for new Investment in the Urea Sector also congratulated the Department of Fertilizers for exploring various options. Members were of the opinion that in view of the large subsidy implications and its impact on the food security of the nation the department should work on formulating a urea pricing policy with a mix of existing cost based pricing policy with improvements to make it more investor friendly and option of selecting investors through a reverse bidding process for pre identified locations. Members were of the view that the urea pricing policy is inextricably linked with the gas pricing policy. Therefore the gas price should be decided in such a manner that it is made available to fertilizer sector at the lowest possible price. Shri Paswan pointed out there are four different options for increasing availability of fertilizer and attracting investment in the sector. They are-(i) modifying existing policy to make it more attractive to investors (ii) to adopt a pricing policy based on import parity benchmark for recognition of cost of production from new investments (iii) a procurement policy based on long term global bidding (iv) setting up of new plants on identified locations through reverse bidding procedure. The Minister said, the new plants should be set up in our country to ensure the availability of quality fertilizer at reasonable price. Shri Paswan hoped that Fertilizer sector will get top priority in supply of gas in terms of both availability and pricing.He said, the department of fertilizers has ensured the supply of 75 per cent of the requirement for the month at each district by the first of the month and another 25 per cent by the 15th of the month. He said, government is trying to address the issue of bottlenecks in the supply chain at the block and village level and ensure that hoarding does not take place. Shri Paswan said, revival of the 8 sick units and resumption of production will be in the national interest but it will depend upon the availability of gas. Members of Parliament who attended today's meeting are Shri Surendra Prakash Goyal, Shri Sunil Khan, Shri Madhusudhana Reddy Thakkala, Shri Chandrakant Bhaurao Khaire, Shri Bagun Sumbrui, Smt. Jhansi Lakshmi Botcha and Smt. K. Rani from the Lok Sabha and Shri Tapan Kumar Sen and Shri Banwari Lal Kanchhal from the Rajya Sabha.

3252. (12-9-2007) NEW DELHI : The Quick Estimates of Index of Industrial Production (IIP) with base 1993-94 for the month of July 2007 have been released by the Central Statistical Organisation of the Ministry of Statistics and Programme Implementation. The General Index stands at 252.2, which is 7.1% higher as compared to the level in the month of July 2006. The cumulative growth for the period April-July 2007-08 stands at 9.6% over the corresponding period of the pervious year. 2. The Indices of Industrial Production for the Mining, Manufacturing and Electricity sectors for the month of July 2007 stand at 159.5, 269.0, and 216.2 respectively, with the corresponding growth rates of 4.9%, 7.2% and 7.5% as compared to July 2006. The cumulative growth during April-July, 2007-08 over the corresponding period of 2006-07 in the three sectors have been 3.1%, 10.3% and 8.1% respectively, which moved the overall growth in the General Index to 9.6% 3. In terms of industries, as many as thirteen (13) out of the seventeen (17) industry groups (as per 2-digit NIC-1987) have shown positive growth during the month of July 2007 as compared to the corresponding month of the previous year. The industry group 'Wood and Wood Products; Furniture and Fixtures' have shown the highest growth of 21.1%, followed by 17.5% in 'Basic Metal and Alloy Industries' and 16.1% in 'Jute and other Vegetable Fibre Textiles (except cotton)'. On the other hand, the industry group 'Metal Products and Parts, except Machinery and Equipment' have shown a negative growth of 5.1% followed by 4.6% in 'Paper & Paper Products and printing, Publishing & Allied Industries' and 4.1% in 'Food products'. 4. As per Use-based classification, the Sectoral growth rates in July 2007 over July 2006 are 9.0% in Basic goods, 12.9% in Capital goods and 4.7% in Intermediate goods. The Consumer durables and Consumer non-durables have recorded growth of (-)3.2% and 8.4% respectively, with the overall growth in Consumer goods being 5.3%. 5. Alongwith the Quick Estimates of IIP for July 2007, the indices for June 2007 have undergone the first revision and those for April 2007 have undergone the second (final) revision in the light of the updated data received from the source agencies. There are no significant revisions in the indices for April 2007 and June 2007. 6. Statements giving Quick Estimates of the Index of Industrial Production at Sectoral, 2-digit level of National Industrial Classification (NIC)-1987 and by Use-based classification for the month of July 2007, along with the growth rates over the corresponding month of previous year, including the cumulative indices and growth rates, are enclosed.

3253. (12-9-2007) NEW DELHI : In a fast growing economy such as India's, public sector finance and expenditure plays a vital role in accelerating the economic development of the country. However, the public finance has to be backed by sound public financial management information systems for greater accountability, transparency and for improving the allocative efficiency of public money.Over the years, there has been substantial increase in the social sector outlay by the Government, both at the Central and the State level. As per the Union Budget 2007-08, the Central Plan outlay is Rs. 154, 939 Crores. It is pertinent to mention that the accounting and information regarding this outlay and expenditure is crucial for all stakeholders.State governments in India manage very sizable economies, and hence need a modern set of tools to provide financial managers with the information required to design appropriate fiscal responses for changing economic conditions. Several States have already developed a suite of automated information systems to assist in public financial management, and they have established a basic information systems capacity to record and process the main transactions related to budget management, expenditure and receipts processing. There are some other states which are still not at this level and are currently engaged in establishing this capacity. Therefore, a synergistic approach for coordinating all these efforts is essential at this time. The institutional arrangements for accounting and information systems in India are slightly different at the Central and State levels, due to which there is lack of commonality between the financial reporting systems of Central and State Governments. As an example, in centrally sponsored schemes, under which Central Government makes releases to the implementing agencies at the State level, reporting of consumption expenditure proves to be a predicament. The current accounting and reporting systems are not geared to provide MIS information about up to date expenditure vis-a-vis releases. This necessitates the requirement of a dynamic interface for information exchange between the financial systems of Central and State Governments. Such a system would entail:· Central Government making the segmented release position available to State Governments/ DRDAs/ Societies,· State Governments/ DRDAs/ Societies making the utilization position available to Central Government, and · A platform which can make release and utilization position available to all stakeholders.

3254. (13-9-2007) NEW DELHI : The Prime Minister, Dr. Manmohan Singh, chaired the full Planning Commission meeting here today. Following is the text of the Prime Minister's closing remarks on the occasion: "We have had a wide ranging discussion on a subject which is vital for the continued progress of our country. We have covered all the critical areas in education, although I believe that more work needs to be done to give a final shape to the Skill Development area. The approach presented by the note of the Planning Commission has received broad support. The proposed scale of Central Government funding for education in the 11th Plan amounts to almost Rs.2.5 lakh crores in constant prices, which is a four-fold increase over the 10th Plan. The share of education in the total Plan will correspondingly increase from 7.7% to 19.4%. This reflects the high priority being given to education by our Government and represents credible progress towards the objective of raising public spending of the Centre and the States combined to 6% of our GDP. The proposals discussed today are at varying degrees of conceptualisation. While some are ready to be operationalised in a few weeks, others will take longer to take final shape. The Planning Commission, the Ministry of Human Resource Development and other Ministries concerned with Skill Development must now move quickly to operationalise the approach agreed to today by preparing detailed programmes for each of the major new initiatives. I wish to emphasise a few points in particular: 1. Focus on Quality Education in Elementary Education. The Sarva Siksha Abhiyan has made breakthroughs in providing universal access in most parts of the country even though I recognise that the quality and quantity of high incidence of drop-out rates I think constitute, I think serious drawbacks. It must now move to a phase where the goal would be to extract the maximum value for the money being spent. It should rapidly move its focus to quality improvement. It should even be called the Second Phase of SSA. The Ministry of HRD should work out minimum standards which must be met by all schools, whether public or private, and also chalk out the details of how to ensure that the objective is actually achieved. Special attention needs to be paid to districts with concentrations of SC, ST and minority populations. The Mid Day Meals (MDM) scheme has to be rapidly expanded to cover 60 million additional children at the upper primary level by the end of year 2008-09 and I am glad to report that the Cabinet had today approved this ambitious proposal. 2. Secondary and Higher Secondary Education We are setting out a goal of universalising secondary education. This is clearly the next step after universalising elementary education. While the goal is laudable, much work needs to be done before we are in a position to launch the Scheme for Universalisation of Access for Secondary Education (SUCCESS). Its details need to be quickly spelt out and discussed with States so that we are fully ready to launch it from the year 2008-09. We must not underestimate the complexity of this task as the principles for universalising elementary education cannot be easily transferred to secondary education. The physical, financial, pedagogical and human resource needs are quite different. We also need to recognize the role currently being played by the private sector and the policy design must factor this in. Detailed strategies and plans would need to be worked out rapidly for each state. Special attention would need to be paid to Districts with SC/ST/OBC/Minority concentration. The points that are made by Shri Sharad Pawar when we are dealing with children from disadvantaged background I think their special needs need to be kept in mind. The recommendations of the Sachar Committee need to be seriously considered and factored into our planning processes while planning for this programme. To kick start the initiative, the proposal for setting up 6000 high quality model schools with costs to be shared by the Centre and the States needs to be finalised within the next few weeks. The mechanism for setting up and managing these schools – whether in the government sector or through private participation in some aspects-should be worked out by the Ministry of HRD, in consultation with the Planning Commission. It must be recognised that about 60% of secondary schools are under private management and the Ministry and the Planning Commission should focus on incorporating the role of the private sector wherever possible. An outline of the proposal should be available within two months. Expanding secondary education would run into capacity constraints on many fronts – in getting an adequate number of mathematics and science teachers, in ensuring better attendance of teachers, in ensuring a high quality of education and in ensuring accountability of schools. This would require attention to be paid to teacher training and managerial control aspects. The Ministry of HRD, there is no doubt that elaborate specific proposals for meeting this need. 3. Higher Education The Higher Education System has been relatively neglected in the past decade. It was the investment made in this system in the 50s and 60s which has given us a strong knowledge base in many fields. We are committed to rapidly expanding this sector as well. There is now general agreement on setting up 16 Central Universities in States which do not have a university, 14 Central Universities in other States, 8 IITs, 7 IIMs and 5 Indian Institute of Science, Education & Researches. I am already getting requests from a large number of states for locating these institutions in their states. I am sure that with the large number of institutions we are considering, we would be able to satisfy every state to some extent. Some of these universities/institutions should, ab initio, be targeted to achieve world class standards. For the Central Universities aimed at world class standards it will be necessary to be more ambitious in terms of infrastructure, especially if they are to include departments of science, medicine and engineering. This involves higher costs. The scope for private participation in these universities should therefore be systematically explored.

3255. (13-9-2007) AGARTALA: BJP National President Shri Rajnath Singh said that the Law Ministry's decision to file a supplementary affidavit before the Hon'ble Supreme Court proves that the government had indeed committed a mistake in filing the controversial affidavit. Shri Rajnath Singh said this while answering a question before the press at Agartala. The BJP President further said that mere acknowledgment of the mistake and the withdrawal of the current affidavit is not enough. The BJP demands an unconditional apology from the government for hurting the religious sentiments of the Hindus, he added. Shri Rajnath Singh pointed out that affidavits are not filed without formal approval. They are not documents filed on the whims and fancies of any one individual. Affidavits represent the considered view of the government and its unambiguous stand on an issue. This affidavit would have been filed by the Ministries of the Government of India only after due examination and necessary approval. Shri Rajnath Singh said that the BJP demands that responsibility be immediately fixed and action must be taken against all those officers and the concerned ministers who approved this affidavit.

3256. (13-9-2007) NEW DELHI : Following is text of the President, Smt. Pratibha Devisingh Patil's speech at the award presentation function for the outstanding parliamentarians here today: I am delighted to participate in this function and to congratulate Shri Sharad Pawar, Smt. Sushma Swaraj, Shri P. Chidambaram and Shri Mani Shankar Aiyar for being awarded the Outstanding Parliamentarian Awards for the year 2003, 2004, 2005 and 2006 respectively. All of them have made exceptional contributions to the debates and proceedings of Parliament. Each one of them has had very distinguished careers as Ministers as well. They richly deserve the recognition that is being bestowed on them today. In a democratic setup, Parliamentarians represent the will and the voice of the people. The people look up to their representatives for articulating their concerns and also meeting their aspirations. Parliamentarians are a link between the people and the Government. They carry the people's mandate to Parliament. To be faithful to the mandate of the electorate is, thus the primary responsibility of a Parliamentarian. Aptly describing the role of a Parliamentarian, Pandit Jawaharlal Nehru in his speech in the Lok Sabha on 28th March, 1957 said, and I quote 'there can be no higher responsibility or greater privilege than to be a member of this sovereign body, which is responsible for the fate of the vast number of human beings who live in this country.' Parliament symbolizes a national purpose and it should lead to stability and progress of the nation. The citizens of this country must have full faith and trust in their elected representatives. Any doubt or lack of confidence in their minds about their representatives will undermine the very basis of democracy and unity of our country. Their trust can be reinforced only through statesmanship and dedicated service as people's representatives. For this purpose, let us keep away from political recriminations and work together towards building a strong nation ready to meet the challenges of this century. Thus, the elected representatives could fulfil their leadership role to help achieve a better life for every citizen of this country. When change takes place it is natural that everyone asks the question as to how that change would impact their lives. Therefore, in today's rapidly changing world, it would be worthwhile for the Members of Parliament to examine how to meet the expectations of the people in a better manner. India's economy is growing at unprecedented high rates, but many sections of our society and many areas of our country are not seeing the fruits of this growth. It is important for Parliamentarians and society to ensure that benefits are equitably shared. Parliamentarians must look after the interests of the less privileged and the most vulnerable sections of society, who due to their very condition are the voiceless. It should be the duty of every Member of Parliament to stand in support of activities and policies that promote better health and education facilities as also better opportunities for all.

3257. (13-9-2007) NEW DELHI : President Pratibha Devisingh Patil today gave away the "Outstanding Parliamentarian Award" to Shri Mani Shankar Aiyar, Minister for Panchayati Raj, Youth Affairs & Sports and DoNER. Three other parliamentarians including Union Ministers, S/Shri Sharad Pawar, P.Chidambaram and BJP leader Ms. Sushma Swaraj were also given the award. Accepting the award Shri Aiyar said that the greatest achievement of our country in the last 60 years has been that we are a full-fledged democracy. He said it is a matter of great pride that today we have about 3.2 million elected representatives, 1.2 million of them being women; at various tiers of democracy. Congratulating the awardees on the occasion, Prime Minister Manmohan Singh said: " I am naturally delighted that three of the four awardees today are members of my Cabinet. All of them are not just good parliamentarians, but also have proved to be good administrators." The Prime Minister said "Aiyar has been an energetic spokesman of the third tier of democracy in this first tier reminding us that decentralization of power and development is essential for the success of our democracy". While Agriculture Minister Shri Sharad Pawar has been awarded for 2003. Ms. Sushma Swaraj has been awarded for the year 2004. Finance Minister Shri P.Chidambaram for 2005 and Panchayati Raj Minister, Shri Mani Shankar Aiyar for 2006. Vice President Hamid Ansari and Lok Sabha Speaker Somnath Chatterjee, were also present on the occasion. The outstanding Parliamentarian Award was first instituted in 1994.

3258. (13-9-2007) NEW DELHI : Domestic sewage is the major source of pollution of rivers besides industrial and other non-point sources of pollution. Interception and diversion of raw sewage and setting up of Sewage Treatment Plants have been among the main components of pollution abatement works undertaken in the River Conservation Plan. As regards pollution by industries, efforts taken include notifying industry specific effluent standards, promoting setting up of Effluent Treatment Plants and environmental surveillance by the Central/State Pollution Control Board under Environment Protection Act 1986 and Water (Prevention and Control of Pollution) Act, 1974. With the pollution abatement works completed so far in both the phases under Ganga Action Plan, the water quality of the river Ganga has shown improvement at major locations over its pre-GAP quality. In respect of river Yamuna, the quality of river water has not shown the desired improvement owing to the large gap between the demand and the availability of sewage treatment capacity particularly in Delhi, and the lack of availability of fresh water for ensuring minimum flow in the river. The works in respect of other rivers are at different stages of completion.Conservation of rivers is a dynamic activity with the ever increasing pollution load due to increase in population. Review of the strategies of conservation policy and identification of additional towns and rivers is a continuous process. Water being a State subject, Central Government supplements the efforts of the State Governments by providing one time grant for capital works for identified polluted stretches. The National River Conservation Plan is a major programme of the Government.

3259. (13-9-2007) NEW DELHI : The Cabinet Committee on Economic Affairs today gave its approval for expansion of Nigahi Opencast Project of Northern Coalfields Ltd. Of Coal India Ltd. From 10 Million tones per annum to 15 Mtpa with an additional investment of Rs.259.40 crore also incremental coal production capacity of 5 Mtpa by departmental operations and removal of corresponding overburden through outsourcing. CCEA also gave its approval for flexibility in the implementation stage within the approved cost estimates to respond to improvement profitability parameters. The project will provide an additional coal production of 5 Mtpa to meet the requirements of 3rd phase of Vindhyachal STPS of NTPC (2 x 500 MW).

3260. (13-9-2007) NEW DELHI : INS Jalashwa, the latest induction into the Indian Navy, arrived at Visakhapatnam on PM 12 Sep 07 after being commissioned at Norfolk, USA on 22 Jun 07. 'Jalashwa', (a Sanskrit name of the Hippopotamus), with its Motto 'The Fearless Pioneers', is an amphibious assault ship that can embark, transport and land various elements of an amphibious force to support operations ashore. This is the 1st ship to be transferred from the US besides being the 1st Landing Platform Dock (LPD) to be acquired by the Navy. The second largest ship in the Navy's inventory, INS Jalashwa is equipped with a Landing Craft Mechanized (LCM-8) along with Seaking helicopters, Radars and rapid firing guns to undertake amphibious operations, Maritime surveillance, Special operations, Search and Rescue, Medical support and also Humanitarian relief. The specialty of this ship is the 'Well Deck' housing the LCM-8 which can be launched by flooding the 'Well deck' and operating the hinged gate at the rear end of the ship. The ship's cargo space enhances the equipment carrying capability. Unlike regular warships, this ship has a flight deck for helicopter operations from which four medium helicopters can operate simultaneously. This deck can also be used to operate vertical take-off and landing (VTOL) aircraft like the Sea Harrier, in special circumstances. Since the ship is capable of embarking over 1000 troops, she is fully equipped with extensive medical facilities including four Operation Theatres, 12-bed ward, Laboratory and a Dental centre to ensure the health care of the embarked personnel. INS Jalashwa is commanded by Captain BS Ahluwalia, a helicopter pilot and manned by a crew of about 27 Officers and 380 sailors. With a length of about 175 metres and width of 32 metres, the ship is capable of doing speeds of 20 Knots. On arrival at Visakhapatnam, the ship was accorded a warm reception by senior officers of the Command and families of the crew. The Navy Band was in attendance. INS Jalashwa will now form part of the Eastern Fleet under the Eastern Naval Command.

3261. (13-9-2007) NEW DELHI : India's policies for its micro and small and medium enterprises (MSMEs) are most appropriate for developing countries and are viewed as a role model especially in Africa, participants said while responding to a presentation on "SMEs – The Indian Perspective" by Shri Jawahar Sircar, Additional Secretary and Development Commissioner, Ministry of Micro, Small and Medium Enterprises, at the first International Conference on "India-Africa Cooperation in Industry, Trade and Investment" here today. The five-day Conference, organized by the United Nations Industrial Development Organisation (UNIDO) in cooperation with the Government of India under the banner of the UNIDO Centre for South-South Industrial Cooperation (UCSSIC), was inaugurated by Shri Kamal Nath, Union Minister of Commerce & Industry, on 10th of September 2007. Shri Sircar said the MSMEs had emerged as a vibrant sector of the Indian economy, with the 12.5 million MSMEs employing over 30 million people and accounting for 50 % of the country's industrial production and 45 % of its exports. Total exports from Indian MSMEs were valued at US $ 56 billion (based on 2005 figures), he added. "MSMEs were expected to grow at the rate of 13% and generate additional 1.3 million jobs per annum during the Plan period 2007-2012", he said. In a detailed presentation, Shri Sircar pointed out that MSME development as a tool of Industrial policy aims at: generation of employment; dispersal of industry to reduce regional disparities; utilization of local skills and resources; and to meet local demands, as feasible. He referred to a new Act, which classified enterprises having investment up to US $ 55,000 as micro, US $ 60,000 to US $ 1.2 million as small, and US $ 1.2 million to US $ 2.5 million as medium enterprises. Changes in policy and support had been effected as per the emerging needs of globalization to enable Indian SMEs to gain a competitive edge, and these related to: WTO compatibility, availability of finance; technology upgradation; and skill development, he said. The support programmes and schemes for MSMEs listed out in the comprehensive presentation include: (1) assistance for entrepreneur development; (2) credit guarantee fund schemes; (3) micro finance programmes; (4) credit linked subsidy schemes for technology upgradation; (5) Tool Rooms for dies, moulds, jigs and fixtures; (6) testing stations for calibration; (7) cluster development programmes; (8) quality upgradation in small scale sector especially in the context of ISO 9000 and 14001 certification; (9) trade related entrepreneurship assistance for women; and (10) setting up of testing centre by industry associations.

3262. (13-9-2007) NEW DELHI : Following is the text of the speech of Finance Minister, Shri P. Chidambaram on accepting the outstanding Parliamentarian Award of the year 2005 received by him here today at a function organised in the Central Hall of Parliament House :-"I am grateful and deeply honoured to receive this Award for the year 2005. I accept the Award with humility. Standing here in 2007 and looking back, the year 2005 indeed appears to have been a good year for parliamentary democracy – when bills were passed and there were lively and enlightening debates on matters of great importance. Parliament, I submit with respect, has two major functions: to make laws and to debate issues. On the first, we may have a respectable score but the process is deeply flawed. On the second, we need to rediscover the art of reasoned debate. Democracy is well and alive in India – witness the millions who turn out at every election at every level. It is our recent experience with representative democracy that has cast a shadow of gloom. I remember the day when I first came to Parliament. I remember my leader, Shri Rajiv Gandhi. I recall the support and affection extended to me by my constituency, Sivaganga, in Tamil Nadu. I came with the belief that parliamentary democracy – especially representative democracy – is the apogee of humankind's urge to devise a model of governance that will reflect our aspirations – life, liberty and equality; also, the pursuit of learning, excellence and happiness. Despite doubts and discordant voices, I remain firm in that belief, and I promise you, especially my fellow parliamentarians, that as long as I continue as a Member of Parliament I shall contribute my mite to make that belief into a reality."

3263. (13-9-2007) NEW DELHI : The Ministry of Railways has decided to constitute a committee for fixing menu/tariff of standard meals served in Rajdhani/ Shatabdi trains and other Mail/Express trains. The committee will mainly focus on following aspects: · Study the present menu and tariff and point out the shortcomings and suggest scope for improvement or adopting an entirely new menu and tariff. Rotation of menu and multi menu should also be suggested. Committee may also recommend the low cost janta meals and matching tariff for poor travellers. Provision of free packaged potable water may also be considered and recommended.· In the study, due consideration should be made of regional variation of culinary trends, taste, recipe etc.· Separate tariff for mobile units and static units may be suggested, as service tax is applicable only on mobile units on Railways. Tariff for mobile units should include service tax as per laid down norms and VAT and these taxes should be reflected separately. Similarly, tariff for static units should include VAT.· Free food is provided to infants and children below five years of age in Rajdhani trains. Menu for such infants/child should be suggested separately. Similarly, a parallel diet menu and tariff and menu for diabetics and related tariff should also be suggested. And· Free light lunch/dinner is provided in Rajdhani/Shatabdi trains in cases of late running of these trains. The committee should suggest menu against late running of Rajdhani/Shatabdi trains. The committee will consist of Chief Commercial Manager (Northern Railways), Chief Commercial Manager (Southern Railway), Chief Commercial Manager (Central Railway), FA&CAO (Central Railway), Director, Catering Service (IRCTC), Dr., Jayshree Rana, CSS (Northern Railway, Central Hospital, New Delhi) and Shri Alok Shivpuri, Principal/IHM, Pusa Raod, New Delhi.

3264. (13-9-2007) NEW DELHI : The Cabinet Committee on Economic Affairs today gave its approval for continuation of the Centrally Sponsored "Livestock

Insurance Scheme" during 2007-08 of the 11th Plan with an outlay of Rs.35.00 crore as it was implemented during 2005-06 and 2006-07 of the 10th Plan. The Scheme will be implemented through the State Implementing Agencies (SIA) implementing the National Project on Cattle and Buffalo Breeding Programme. The Livestock Insurance Scheme will encourage the farmers and cattle rearers to go for genetically improved and high yielding animals, thus developing and establishing Animal Husbandry as an Industry. This would ultimately help in achieving qualitative improvement in livestock and their products. Further, there will be improved scope for employment generation through direct engagement as well as through allied activities.

3265. (13-9-2007) NEW DELHI : The Union Cabinet today approved a proposal to modify the eligibility criteria under NOAPS from one "who is 65 years or higher and a destitute" to one "who is 65 years or higher and belonging to a household below the poverty line according to the criteria prescribed by the Government of India" and also to make this modification of the eligibility criteria applicable during 2007-08 itself by making available the necessary resources. The scheme will be implemented in the light of the announcement made by the Prime Minister in his Independence Day speech made on 15-08-2007. The text of the announcement made by the Prime Minister is as under :-" We will provide an old age pension to all citizens above the age of 65 years and living below the poverty line". The decision for making modification will extend much needed financial support to the needy old persons who belong to households below the poverty line.

3266. (13-9-2007) NEW DELHI : Shri L.K. Advani said that, with the UPA government claiming in an affidavit before the Supreme Court that Lord Ram did not exist and that the Ramayana has no historical basis, it is clear that the Congress party's pseudo-secularism has degenerated into sadist-secularism. By filing this shocking affidavit before the country's highest court in the ongoing dispute over the Ram Setu in the Setusamudram Ship Canal Project near Tamil Nadu, the leadership of the Congress party and the UPA government has poured contempt on the religious sentiments of crores of Hindus all over the world. It is blasphemous and arrogant at worst, and insensitivity and recklessness at best, for a government claiming to be "secular" to trash the deepest and noblest sensiilities of the Hindus. In one stroke of its legal pen, the government has sought to negate all that the Hindus consider sacred in their faith. I would like to point out that the Ramayana, along with the Mahabharata, is also considered the bedrock of India's national culture and identity by all the great leaders of India's freedom movement – from Mahatma Gandhi to Lokamanya Tilak, and from Jawaharlal Nehru to Sardar Patel. By describing it as a pure myth and a work of fiction, the government has wounded the very Idea of India and sought to rewrite the civilizational identity of our ancient nation. Not even during the Ayodhya movement had anyone responsible in the government taken such a bizarre stand in the name of "secularism". It is true that some people who were opposed to the construction of the Ram Temple at Ram

Janmabhoomi did ask, "How can you prove that Ram was born here?" But none questioned the very existence Lord Ram. It is the present UPA government, which is politically steered by Smt. Sonia Gandhi and only nominally headed by Dr. Manmohan Singh, that has the dubious distinction of telling the Supreme Court that Lord Ram was never born The BJP deems the UPA government's anti-Hindu act to be a very grave development in the political and social history of India. I would like to warn the leadership of the Congress party and the government that, unless corrective action is taken immediately, it will face a massive, sustained and peaceful protest action all over the country. The BJP will participate in this agitation in full force.

3267. (13-9-2007) NEW DELHI : Shri Kamal Nath, Union Minister of Commerce & Industry, has called for a coordinated effort by all stakeholders so that SEZ Scheme can fulfil its objectives and is implemented efficiently by the State Governments by providing single window facilities and all other promised benefits. It is also important that SEZ Developers do their work at a faster pace so that the space in SEZs is actually made available to the SEZ units, he added. Highlighting the importance of the EOU Scheme that has played a very important role in last 25 years in creation of manufacturing facilities and generation of employment, Shri Kamal Nath informed that pursuant to the discussions with EPCES in various open houses, a number of issues relating to EOUs have been resolved. This includes implementation of Fast Track Scheme, exemption from Bank Guarantee, extending the facility of Cenvat Credit, reduction of basic customs duty to 25% on the DTA sale, simplified procedure of registration at the port etc. However, a major issue relating to EOU *i.e.* removal of Sunset Clause is yet to be resolved and had been discussed with the Prime Minister's Economic Advisory Council, Shri Kamal Nath informed. He was addressing the 4th Annual General Meeting of the Export Promotion Council for EOUs and SEZ Units (EPCES), here today. Shri T. Vasu, Chairman, EPCES; Shri L.B. Singhal, Director General, EPCES; Shri R. Gopalan, Additional Secretary, Department of Commerce; Shri Anil Mukhim, Joint Secretary, Department of Commerce besides representatives of the SEZ and EOUs were also present at the occasion. In his address on the occasion, Shri Kamal Nath informed that: "SEZ Policy is going to play a very important role in employment generation, increasing exports, creation of world class infrastructure and attracting Foreign Direct Investment in the country in the next one decade. SEZs are certainly going to play a very important role by providing inclusive growth in the country. At present SEZs-new and old are already providing direct employment to over 2,30,000 people. New Generation SEZs have already provided direct employment to over 45,000 people and I have been informed that over 1 lakh additional jobs will get created by December, 2007. Once all the 366 formally approved SEZs, become operational 4 million additional jobs are likely to be created. Manufacturing sector will also get a big boost. If you go and see the new SEZs, which have started functioning, you will find that most of the employment provided is to the rural youth from the nearby villages. Employment in the SEZs has completely changed the life of these employees and their family as well. I feel that this is the greatest contribution SEZs will make to the society. The huge investment being made by these SEZs is resulting in fast developments and as the SEZs become functional, the benefits will become more pronounced".

3268. (13-9-2007) NEW DELHI : The President, Smt. Pratibha Devi Singh Patil, presented "Outstanding Parliamentarian Award" to Shri Sharad Pawar, Smt. Sushma Swaraj, Shri P. Chidambaram and Shri Mani Shankar Ayiar at a function in the Central Hall of Parliament this morning. The Vice President, Mohd. Hamid Ansari, the Prime Minister, Dr. Manmohan Singh, Lok Sabha Speaker, Shri Somnath Chaterjee, were also present on the occasion. Following is the text of the Prime Minister, Dr. Manmohan Singh's remarks on the occasion: "I join all of you in complimenting the four distinguished Members of Parliament who have been selected for the Best Parliamentarians Awards. I am sure all of you will agree that each one of them deserves the award given the important contribution they have made, over the years, to the proceedings in Parliament and various walks of national life. They have done so both from the Treasury benches as well as from the Opposition. I am naturally delighted that three of the four awardees today are members of my Cabinet. I can vouch for the fact that they have not only contributed handsomely to the proceedings in Parliament, but also to the functioning of our Government. Sharad Pawarji has been a valued colleague, an experienced and mature guide and a steadfast ally for many years. Shri Chidambaram is an extremely gifted, talented and hard working member of my Cabinet who has contributed enormously to the implementation of our policies. Shri Mani Shankar Aiyar has been an energetic spokesman of the third tier of democracy in this first tier reminding us that decentralization of power and development is essential for the success of our democracy. Smt. Sushma Swaraj is not just a vocal Member of the Opposition but has been an effective Minister in the previous Government. All of them are not just good Parliamentarians but also have proved to be good administrators. Each one of them in their own rights has been a role model. This year we celebrate the 60th anniversary of our Independence. It is no mean achievement that our system of parliamentary democracy has withstood not just the test of time but also the test of our people's faith and conviction. We have much to be proud of. And the success of democratic institutions in India today gives hope to countries all over the world. I recall the words of President Hamid Karzai when I had visited Afghanistan some two years ago.

3269. (13-9-2007) NEW DELHI : The National Capital Territory of Delhi Laws (Special Provisions) Second Ordinance, 2007 received the concurrence of the Cabinet which includes to give statusquo in respect of the following categories of unauthorized developments: slum dwellers and jhuggi jhompri clusters, hawkers and urban street vendors, unauthorized colonies, existing farm houses, involving construction beyond permissible building limits and schools, dispensaries, religious institutions, cultural institutions and storages, warehouses and godowns used for agricultural inputs to produce (including dairy and poultry) in rural areas built on agricultural land, commercial establishments in unauthorized colonies.

3270. (14-9-2007) NEW DELHI : The Prime Minister, Dr. Manmohan Singh greets the people on the occasion of Ganesh Chaturthi. In his message, Dr. Manmohan Singh has said that no less than Lokmanya Balgangadhar Tilak used Ganesh Chaturthi for the cause of the freedom struggle. Let the festivities associated with Ganesh Chaturthi inspire us to recapture the spirit of the freedom struggle and to rededicate ourselves to the larger cause of nation building. On this auspicious occasion of Ganesh Chaturthi the Prime Minister extends his greetings and good wishes to the people of the country.

3271. (14-9-2007) NEW DELHI : The Vice President of India Mohd. Hamid Ansari has said that the macro-economic figures of the Indian economy appear good. We have had a real GDP growth of 9.4 % for 2006-07 and an exchange rate per capita GDP of $880; in Purchasing Power Parity terms, the per capita GDP climbed to around $4000. Addressing at the "Fifth India Today State of States Conclave" here today, he said that our savings and investment rates have increased, there was a gross FDI inflow of $19.5 billion in 2006-07 and good reasons exist to believe that there have been productivity and efficiency improvements. The Vice President said that while all citizens contribute to the national effort, in public perception there are two Indias-an India focused on wealth accumulation and another India focused on poverty reduction. We have a situation where the richest 10% of the population account for slightly less than 30% of the share of expenditure and the poorest 10% of the population account for less than 5%. Thus overall economic growth of the country has not yet translated itself into fair distribution of the fruits of development. Wealth accumulation at the top has been more impressive than poverty reduction at the bottom. The challenge is to accept that wealth accumulation and poverty reduction are two sides of the same coin and need to be addressed together.

3272. (14-9-2007) NEW DELHI : The President, Smt. Pratibha Devisingh Patil has greeted her fellow citizens in India and abroad on the occasion of Ganesh Chaturthi, which falls tomorrow. In her message she has said that Ganesh Chaturhti is a festival, which brings the people together in gaiety and happiness. The President has wished the people of the nation wisdom, prosperity and good fortune in the year ahead.

3273. (14-9-2007) NEW DELHI : Union Rural Development Minister, Dr. Raghuvansh Prasad Singh has said that closer and strict monitoring is the key for success of the rural development programmes. Dr. Singh was addressing the last interactive session of recent series on Rural Development Schemes with the Members of Parliament from Bihar and Jharkhand here yesterday. He emphasised the need of MPs active participation in the task and said monitoring and guidance are required in the implementation of all the rural development programmes with full enthusiasm and efficacy. Through district vigilance and monitoring committees, the government has attempted for effective implementation of rural schemes, Dr. Singh added. Eight central ministers and twenty one Parliament Members from Bihar and Jharkhand participated in this last interactive session of the current series. The ministers who attended the session are Shri Ram Vilas Paswan, Shri Subodh Kant Sahai, Smt. Kanti Singh, Shri Fatmi Mohammad Ali Ashraf, Shri Taslimuddin, Dr. Ahmad Shakeel, Shri Jay Prakash Narayan Yadav and Dr. Akhilesh Prasad Singh. Shri Chandrasekhar Sahu, Minister of State for Rural Development was also present. Shri Ram Vilas Paswan asked for powers to monitoring and vigilance committees' chairmen for better compliance of committees' proposals, unemployment wages to people who could not get under the NREG Act and centre funding the entire cost of Swajadhaara scheme. Almost all MPs' asked for houses to the flood affected people under the Indira Awas Yojana Scheme. They also pointed out discrepancies in the BPL lists and asked for a review to include those who have been left out from the list. The members called for further improvement in the quality of roads being constructed under the Prime Minister Gram Sadak Yojana (PMGSY). One member asked for increase the amount to Rs. 50,000 to construct each house under the Indira Awas Yojana. Some members asked for elevated tube wells in flood affected areas. The series of inter active sessions that commenced since 20th August,2007 was a unique initiative of Dr. Singh for a face-to-face interaction with the MPs in separate batches so as to ensure effective implementation of rural schemes through greater participation by the elected representatives and also to apprise the MPs about different provisions of the rural schemes, the progress of various programmes in the concerned states, physical and financial achievements and also to get members valuable feedback and suggestions.

3274. (14-9-2007) NEW DELHI : This year the world will celebrate the 20th anniversary of the signing of the Montreal Protocol, the landmark international treaty to protect the stratospheric ozone layer. The Montreal Protocol has been hailed as perhaps the most successful international treaty to date and provides a message of hope for working cooperatively to solve major environmental problems. The Montreal Protocol on Substances that Deplete the Ozone Layer was signed on 16th September, 1987 to protect the Ozone Layer. Since 1995, 16th September is celebrated every year as the International Day for Preservation of the Ozone Layer and commemorates the date of signing of Montreal Protocol. To date 191 countries have signed the protocol, which commits countries to phase out the production and consumption of Ozone depleting chemicals. The Protocol was the culmination of decades of research, which established that chemicals released in the atmosphere could damage the ozone layer. A depleted Ozone Layer in the stratosphere allows the Ultra Violet rays of the sun to reach the earth exposing mankind, flora and fauna to its harmful effects. According to the World Health Organization each year between 2-3 million skin cancers are detected would wide and upto 20% of these may be caused or enhanced by sun exposure. Initially on the basis of very definite empirical findings, the Protocol enjoined upon all the signatory nations to completely phase out harmful chemicals such as Chlorofluorocarbons (CFC), halons, Carbontetrachloride (CTC), Methylchloroform in a given time schedule. Later, other studies have brought more chemicals such as Hydrochlorofluorocarbons (HCFC) and Methyl bromide under the purview of the Protocol for phasing out within a given deadline. India, being a Party to the Vienna Convention and the Montreal Protocol, has been sharing the global concern for protecting the Ozone Layer and to phase out Ozone Depleting Substances (ODS) like CFC, halons, CTC, methyl chloroform, methyl bromide and HCFC.

3275. (14-9-2007) NEW DELHI : To a question on Smt. Sonia Gandhi's directive to the Prime Minister on Ramsethu controversy, Congress spokesperson Shri Abhishek Singhvi said that if I may adapt a saying that "to err is human but to rectify may perhaps be described as divine". When, immediately on coming to know of what had happened, immediate steps were taken to make a statement to tell the nation and to begin the process of filing a supplementary affidavit to clarify the stand, then I can only say that some parties are trying to needlessly further politicize the matter. The Government, the Congress Party, had itself been the first to say that this stand is unnecessary. It should be inquired into, responsibility should be fixed and rectification should occur. So I think we should realize that something constructive is being done and not just make brownie points based on politics. To a question on the ASI stand on Ramsethu, Shri Singhvi said that we don't know the facts. Kindly be patient for a short while. When the Government of India and the relevant agency have clarified their stand and the stand is that issue is not relevant to the proceedings and that issue need not be deposed either way in an affidavit then the matter ends. Now, the only thing is to set the record formally straight and that process you will see is completed in a couple of days. To a question that do you want to say that the ASI affidavit was wrong, Shri Singhvi said that if the ASI affidavit on this issue was right, we wouldn't be filing a supplementary affidavit replacing this paragraph. Obviously that paragraph is an erroneous reflection of a stand, which was not an issue before the Court and that, is precisely why it is being superseded and being replaced by a supplementary affidavit. Therefore as I said earlier the speed and the focus with which the moment this came to light the Government and the Congress Party acted, I think that deserves kudos and not criticism. To a question on the Congress Party's stand on the issue of authenticity of Lord Rama, Shri Singhvi said that it is a futile argument to raise here. It is not relevant to any Court proceedings. It does not require any affidavit either way and therefore it is completely foreign to the issue.

3276. (14-9-2007) NEW DELHI : The Ministry of Steel will institute three prizes for the Public Sector Undertakings under its control for excellent work in Hindi. This was stated by the Minister of State for Steel Dr. Akhilesh Das while addressing the officers and staff of the Ministry on the occasion of Hindi Day here today.

He said, besides being the national language, Hindi has served as a wonderful link language for the country. Dr. Das said, Hindi has gained popularity internationally through our movies and songs. Complementing the officers and staff on the Hindi Day, he urged them to take up more original work in Hindi. He said, Hindi speaking people should learn other Indian languages also to promote national integration.

3277. (14-9-2007) NEW DELHI : The area coverage of kharif crops as compared to 14th September last year has gone up considerably as per data compiled by Agriculture Ministry. The total coverage of kharif rice has gone up to 355.73 lakh ha as compared to 355.16 lakh hectare last year, the weekly Crop Weather Watch Group meeting of the Ministry of Agriculture was informed here today. Transplanting is at ending stage in the states of Gujarat, Haryana, Maharashtra, Punjab, Rajasthan, Uttar Pradesh, Uttarakhand and West Bengal. In rest of the states transplanting is at peak. The sowing of various coarse cereals has ended in almost all states. The area coverage under jowar, so far, is 33.92 lakh ha against 34.98 lakh ha during last year, under bajra 82.17 lakh ha against 78.23 lakh ha last year, maize 76.17 lakh ha against 71.74 lakh ha last year and total coarse cereals 213.33 lakh ha against 202.53 lakh ha during the corresponding period of last year. The area covered under cotton so far is 90.68 lakh ha against 86.89 lakh ha during the corresponding period of last year. Out of this 53.32 lakh ha is under Bt Cotton. The total coveage under sugarcane has been reported at 51.04 lakh hectare against 48.32 lakh ha during the corresponding period last year. The coverage under jute has been reported at 8.29 lakh ha against 8.18 lakh ha during the corresponding period of last year. Mesta has been sown in 1.48 lakh ha against 1.53 lakh ha during the corresponding period of last year. The total coverage of oilseeds so far has been 173.01 lakh ha as compared to 161.72 lakh ha on September 13, last year. Soyabean has been sown in 8 % and groundnut in 13% higher area as compared to that in 2006. Pulses cover an area of 121.25 lakh ha against 110.35 lakh ha up to this time last year.

3278. (14-9-2007) NEW DELHI : The Ministry of Steel will institute three prizes for the Public Sector Undertakings under its control for excellent work in Hindi. This was stated by the Minister of State for Steel Dr. Akhilesh Das while addressing the officers and staff of the Ministry on the occasion of Hindi Day here today. He said, besides being the national language, Hindi has served as a wonderful link language for the country. Dr. Das said, Hindi has gained popularity internationally through our movies and songs. Complementing the officers and staff on the Hindi Day, he urged them to take up more original work in Hindi. He said, Hindi speaking people should learn other Indian languages also to promote national integration.

3279. (14-9-2007) NEW DELHI : The Sardar Vallabhbhai Patel National Police Academy, Hyderabad is entering its Diamond Jubilee Year (60th Year) tomorrow. On this occasion, a Ceremonial Parade will be held at the Academy Parade Ground tomorrow. A series of events have been planned to mark the Diamond Jubilee Year. These include: organizing a National Seminar on IPS training, a Half Marathon in Hyderabad, release of a Postage Stamp, publication of a Coffee Table Book on the Academy, hosting of the All India Police Equestrian Meet, release of a Documentary Film on the Academy. The Academy is the premier training institution for the training of Indian Police Service Officers. Over the years, as many as 4100 IPS Officers have passed out of this Institution. The present Batch of trainee officers comprises 88 IPS Officers, including 18 Lady Officers (the highest so far), and 4 Officers each from Royal Bhutan Police and Maldivian Police. The Academy also conducts over 30 need-based thematic and refresher courses, every year, for senior police officers of different ranks. There are courses on topics like 'National Security', 'Day-to-Day Policing and Internal Security', 'Cyber Crimes', 'Economic Crimes', 'Organised Crimes', 'Crime against Women & Children', and 'Human Rights', etc. in the past five years, as many as 5000 officers have undergone various in-service courses. Established as the Central Police Training College (CPTC) at Mount Abu in Rajasthan, on September 15, 1948, it was rechristened as the Sardar Vallabhbhai Patel National Police Academy, in 1974. The Academy shifted to its premises in Hyderabad, in 1975.

3280. (14-9-2007) NEW DELHI : The following is the full text of the keynote Address by the External Affairs Minister, Shri Pranab Mukherjee at the Institute for Security and International Studies (ISIS), Chulalongkorn University on "India's Look East Policy: Implications for Thailand and South East Asia" : "Dr. Thitinan Pongsudhirak, Director of the Institute of Security and International Studies, Faculty and Students, Distinguished Guests, It gives me great pleasure to be here today to address this distinguished and knowledgeable gathering on "India's Look East Policy and its implications for Thailand and South East Asia". I am particularly happy to be doing so during the 60th Anniversary year of the establishment of diplomatic relations between India and Thailand. The Anniversary is, indeed, an opportune moment to share with each other our respective priorities and plans for the future. By doing so, I believe, we can craft a shared vision that would form the basis for cooperative action leading to progress and stability for the entire region.I would, at the outset, like to congratulate the Institute for Security and International Studies for their work in conducting independent research and disseminating knowledge on international issues. I am also happy that issues relating to this region and to Asia are of priority for the Institute. This is particularly important as our countries have too often in the past looked at each other through the eyes of others. As the 21st century begins and as Asian nations rise to take their proper place at the table of global affairs, we need a better understanding of each other, both at the level of states and of civil society. I, therefore, commend the ISIS for the work that they are doing to foster closer understanding in the region. I would, at the beginning, also like to say a few words about India and Thailand. Our two countries are no strangers to each other. The architecture, sculpture and mythology of both countries reflect our shared cultural and civilizational linkages. India and Thailand are also maritime neighbours. It is, perhaps, not so well known that India's Andaman & Nicobar Islands are much closer to Thailand's coast than to the Indian mainland. History and geography make our two countries natural partners and it, therefore, follows that Thailand occupies a central place in India's "Look East" policy. I have chosen to speak on this topic for a number of reasons. As many of you would be aware, India has undergone significant changes over the last decade and a half. During the same period, the international order has seen a profound structural transformation. Consequently, the foreign policy of India has had to re-formulate its priorities. When our "Look East" policy was initiated in 1991, it marked a strategic shift in our perspective of the world. It coincided with the beginning of our economic reform process and provided an opportunity for significantly enlarging our economic engagement. At the same time, it also encouraged a renewal of linkages with our civilizational neighbours in South East and East Asia. From sectoral dialogue partners in 1992, we became full dialogue partners in 1996 and, since 2002, we have annual Summits with ASEAN. India-ASEAN cooperation now covers a wide field, including trade and investment, science & technology, tourism, human resource development, transportation & infrastructure and health & pharmaceuticals. At the Third India-ASEAN Summit held in Vientiane in November 2004, we signed the "India-ASEAN Partnership for Peace, Progress and Shared Prosperity". The document contained a Plan of Action providing for enhanced political, economic, social and cultural cooperation, which is being implemented in a phased manner. In October 2003, India also signed the Treaty of Amity and Cooperation. A significant aspect of the cooperation, both bilateral and through multilateral institutions like the ASEAN Regional Forum (ARF), has been the growing collaboration on security issues fostered through dialogue and practical measures as well as through the establishment of legal frameworks. This cooperation has focused on many areas, notably maritime security and counter-terrorism, which are of vital interest to the security of States as well as commerce through the sea-lanes of communication in this region. On maritime security especially, India has entered into bilateral arrangements, including MoUs signed with Thailand and Indonesia, for joint coordinated patrols by the Navies of India, Indonesia and Thailand in the Bay of Bengal at the mouth of the Malacca Straits. We have also offered to contribute to capacity building of littoral states in this area. The participation of navies of Southeast Asian countries in the bi-annual MILAN exercises has also fostered closer regional cooperation on maritime security issues. India has also, for many years, consistently urged the ARF to take up discussions on international terrorism.

3281. (14-9-2007) NEW DELHI : Following is the text of the speech delivered by the Chief Guest, Minister of State for Defence Shri M M Pallam Raju to a seminar on "Network Security, Information Privacy and Lawful Monitoring" at ASSOCHAM House here today. "The operational stability and security of critical information infrastructure is vital for the existence and survival of any enterprise.

Advances in ICT (Information-Communication Technology) have given us facilities like mobiles, Short Message Serivce, Multimedia Message Service, e-mail, instant messaging, blogging etc. While these new means of communication help to increase our productivity, knowledge provide us entertainment, the same infrastructure makes it easier for anti-social elements, criminals and terrorists to plan and execute their activities. For example, in planning and executing the attack on Indian Parliament and numerous blasts in different parts of India, it is now well known that IT was very extensively used. The recent episode where a Swedish hacker apparently infiltrated some government websites and cracked important passwords is another example. The disturbing part is that apparently the said Swede not only hacked into various Indian embassy websites across Asia, but also some of the websites pertaining to Defence Organisations. Incidents of cyber attack have increased over the years. According the Indian Computer Emergency Response Team (CERT-in), around 200 cases related to computer security were reported this year. This has raised the question of reliability of security cover to corporate and government websites. The fast growing Telecom infrastructure is no exception for hackers, spammers and criminals to target the networks and through them the general public or even countries. Therefore, not only the security systems have to keep pace with the advances in technology to deal with the threats, but also the same need to be integrated, made foolproof & shared amongst various agencies. With complex applications now being run on the networks, there is growning realization to protect and secure data information. Lawful interception, monitoring, proactive & post event analysis etc, also need to be strengthened to track criminals and their activities. There is also an urgent need for increased awareness on security related issues in telecommunications services sector, requiring increased compliance.

3282. (14-9-2007) NEW DELHI : The Government of India has approved the National e-Governance Plan. This Plan comprises of 27 Mission Mode Projects; 100,000 Common Service Centres; State Wide Area Networks to provide connectivity up to block level with provision for wireless connectivity from the block level to the village level; and State Data Centres. This was stated by Shri A.Raja, Minister of Communications and Information Technology, while addressing the closing session of 7th Interpol Cyber Crime Conference here today. Following is the text of the speech of the Minister: “It gives me great pleasure to be here amidst you all on this important occasion; important because this conference has dealt with a fundamental responsibility of any State – that is providing security to its citizens. Today, when cyber world is becoming as relevant as the physical world, maintaining law and order and prevention and detection of crime in the cyber world has become a genuine need of people and a fundamental responsibility of Governments. Information and Communication Technology, which is the foundation stone of the cyber world, is likely to come under serious onslaught of cyber crimes. If left unchecked, Cyber Crimes are likely to pose a significant threat to the exploitation of full potential of Information and Communication

Technology for the benefit of the mankind. Information and Communication Technology has a great potential for improving the quality of life of citizens by lending transparency in Governance, cost-effectiveness of delivery of public services at a quick pace, informed decision-making, integration of remote areas with the business centres on the information highway, creation of wealth, creation of more jobs, etc. Information and Communication Technology revolution holds a great hope for a better tomorrow and therefore, all out efforts need to be made to facilitate its furtherance. Realizing the great potential of e-Governance, the Government of India has approved the National e-Governance Plan in May 2006. The vision of this plan is to 'make all Government services accessible to the common man in his locality, through common service delivery outlets and to ensure efficiency, transparency & reliability of such services at affordable costs to realize the basic needs of the common man'. This Plan comprises of 27 Mission Mode Projects; 100,000 Common Service Centres; State Wide Area Networks to provide connectivity up to block level with provision for wireless connectivity from the block level to the village level; and State Data Centres.

3283. (14-9-2007) NEW DELHI : Vice President of India Mohd. Hamid Ansari has greeted the people of our country on the auspicious occasion of the beginning of the holy month of 'Ramzan'. In his message the Vice President has said that Ramzan marks the beginning of the holy month. The fasting associated with the auspicious period gives spiritual strength to promote the tradition of compassion, brotherhood and harmony in the society. Vice President has said that the noble ideals of Ramzan fill our lives with peace, prosperity, happiness and social harmony and unite us all in a common brotherhood of humanity.

3284. (14-9-2007) NEW DELHI : The Home Minister has called for a much wider use of Hindi in official work. Speaking at the 'Hindi Diwas' function here today, Shri Shivraj Patil said that although a lot of progress has been achieved in this regard, much more remains to be done. He said that use of simple Hindi would lead to its wider and faster spread. The Home Minister also called for promoting the use of modern technology to enable people to learn Hindi more quickly and easily. A total of 44 awards in the form of shield/cash were given away on this occasion. These included Rajiv Gandhi National Award for Original book writing on Ghyan Vigyan, Indira Gandhi Rajbhasha Award and awards for Original Book Writing in Hindi. A special issue of the quarterly magazine of the Department of Official Language, "Rajbhasha Bharti" on technology was released at the function. The latest edition of "compilation of orders regarding the use of Hindi" was also released. The last edition of the compilation was published over 10 years back in 1996. To modernize the training system and language learning process, different computer software have been developed with the assistance of C-DAC, Pune. These are primarily in the fields of Hindi Teaching through various regional languages (Lila series), translation from English to Hindi (Mantra) and automatic typing out of Hindi dictation/speech (Shrutlekhan) on the computer. The

Lila-Rajbhasha software for learning Hindi through Punjabi, Gujarati, Nepali and Kashmiri and Mantra –Rajbhasha software for Information Technology and Health Care were launched on the world wide web. The Beta version of Vachantar-Rajbhasha based on Mantra-Rajbhasha were released on the occasion. Those who attended the function included the Ministers of State, S/Shri Manikrao H. Gavit and Sriprakash Jaiswal, Home Secretary, Shri Madhukar Gupta and Secretary, Department of Official Language, Shri Ranjeet Issar.

3285. (14-9-2007) NEW DELHI : As per the 2005 Environmental Sustainability Index (ESI) the ranking of India is at 101 position out of 146 countries. The Central Pollution Control Board (CPCB) is executing a nationwide programme of ambient air quality monitoring known as National Air Quality Monitoring Programme (NAMP). Based on the monitoring of ambient air quality, fifty-one (51) non-attainment cities have been identified in the country in which the prescribed Respirable Particulate Matter (RSPM) levels, specified under the National Ambient Air Quality Standards (NAAQS), are not met. The list of cities and their pollution level is annexed.

3286. (14-9-2007) NEW DELHI : India doubled its financial contribution to the International Telecommunication Union from five 'contributory units' to ten, amounting to CHF 3.18 million per annum. Announcing the increase at the ITU Council meeting in Geneva, Mr. D.S. Mathur, Secretary, Ministry of Communications and Information Technology, Government of India said, "India fully supports the mission of the International Telecommunication Union to connect the world and, in particular, to develop online resources and strengthen cybersecurity. The Global Cybersecurity Agenda launched by ITU this year is a significant step in ensuring confidence and security in the use of information and communication technologies around the world." Mr. Mathur added that India would support ITU not only financially but with human resources as well. "India is at the forefront of ICT development in the world owing largely to its wealth of human capacity, which is based on our top-class educational system," said the Secretary. "We will use our growing global presence in this sector to promote ITU's work in reaching the benefits of ICT to all inhabitants of the world." Mr. Mathur expressed India's confidence in ITU's management and the launch of new global initiatives, including the series to Connect the World. ICT is the driver of economic growth and employment around the world and the catalyst for improved services such as health care and education. Dr. Hamadoun Touré, Secretary-General of ITU, welcomed India's increased contribution and said it was a reflection of the spectacular growth of telecommunications in the country. He said, "I thank the Government of India for the increased financial contribution that will support ITU's commitment to connect people everywhere, especially in remote and underserved regions. By doing so, we will be able to accelerate the process of meeting the broader development goals." Dr. Touré said that a Marshall Plan for ICT is needed if we are to meet the 2015 connectivity targets of the Millennium Development Goals

(MDGs). "India's increased financial support must be emulated by other Member States and stakeholders who have made commitments to connect the world in the Millennium Declaration and at the World Summit on the Information Society."

3287. (14-9-2007) NEW DELHI : The quantity of the carbon dioxide has increased tremendously in the atmosphere and as a result thereof the temperature of earth has been increasing. The quantity, increased during the last three years, year-wise and country-wise shows gradual increase in this trend. The Government of India made efforts to reduce this quantity to keep the earth in a normal atmosphere. According to Fourth Assessment Report of the three Working Groups of the Inter-governmental Panel on Climate Change, the global atmospheric concentration of carbon dioxide has increased at the rate of 2.5 parts per million (ppm) by volume per year since the year 2000. The atmospheric concentrations of carbon dioxide during three years, viz. 2005, 2004 and 2003, were 379 ppm, 376.5 ppm and 374 ppm respectively. The country-wise estimates of atmospheric concentration are not recorded. The updated 100 years linear trend of increase of average global surface air temperature is 0.74 degree Celsius. The Government of India is a Party to the Kyoto Protocol to the United Nations Framework Convention on Climate Change (UNFCCCC) and has set up the National Clean Development Mechanism Authority to accord Host Country Approvals (HCA) to eligible Clean Development Mechanism (CDM) projects. India also has the largest number of projects under the CDM of the Kyoto Protocol, which reduce net emissions of greenhouse gases. Even though India as a developing country does not have any mitigation commitments, nevertheless, a sustainable development path is being followed through a range of policies and programmes to mitigate climate change: (i) ensuring energy conservation and improved energy efficiency in various sectors as well as setting up of Bureau of Energy Efficiency (ii) promoting use of renewable energy (iii) power sector reforms and active renewable energy programme (iv) use of cleaner and lesser carbon intensive fuel for transport (v) fuel switching to cleaner energy (vi) afforestation and conservation of forests (vii) promotion of clean coal technologies (viii) reduction of gas flaring (ix) encouraging Mass Rapid Transport systems (x) environmental quality management for all sectors.

3288. (14-9-2007) NEW DELHI : The Vice President Mohd. Hamid Ansari has greeted the people of our country on the auspicious occasion of Ganesh Chaturthi which is celebrated across the country with religious fervour and enthusiasm. In his greetings, the Vice President said that this festival celebrates the birth of Lord Ganesha, who symbolizes wisdom, prosperity and happiness. Lord Ganesha is invoked before any auspicious work begins and for removing obstacles on the path of spiritual and material success. Ganesh Chaturthi reminds us of the importance of imbibing the sublime and eternal values in our lives to usher in a humane society. The Vice President said that this festival bring peace, prosperity and happiness in our lives.

3289. (14-9-2007) NEW DELHI : (i) Legal protection has been provided to wild animals against hunting and commercial exploitation under the provisions of the Wild Life (Protection) Act, 1972.(ii) Several rare and endangered species of wild animals have been included in the Schedules of Wild Life (Protection) Act, 1972, thereby giving it highest degree of protection. (iii) The Wild Life (Protection) Act, 1972 has been amended and made more stringent. The punishment in cases of offences has been enhanced. The Act also provides for forfeiture of any equipment, vehicle or weapon that has been used for committing any wild life offence. (iv) Central Bureau of Investigation (CBI) has been empowered under the Wildlife (Protection) Act, 1972 to apprehended and prosecute wildlife offenders. (v) Government of India has set up Regional and Sub-regional Offices for wildlife preservation in major export and trade centres of the country to prevent smuggling of wild animals and their products. (vi) Financial and technical help is provided to the States under various Centrally Sponsored Schemes, viz. Project Tiger, Project Elephant and Development of National Parks and Sanctuaries for enhancing the capacity and infrastructure of the States for providing effective protection to wild animals. (vii) A National Wildlife Action Plan 2002-16 was adopted by the Indian Board for Wild Life under the chairmanship of Prime Minister in January 2002. The plan outlines the strategy for conservation and protection of wildlife in the country. (viii) Government of India is a signatory to many international conventions concerning biodiversity conservation and control of illegal trade in wild flora and fauna. (ix) Bilateral agreements have been signed with Nepal and Republic of China for controlling trans-boundary illegal trade in wildlife. (x) A Global Tiger Forum of Tiger Range Countries has been created for addressing international issues related to tiger conservation. (xi) creation of Tiger Task Force and National Wildlife Crime Control Bureau.

3290. (14-9-2007) NEW DELHI : The Union Minister of Shipping, Road Transport and Highways, Thiru T.R. Baalu has approved a sum of Rs. 1116.97 lakh for road repair works in the state of Andhra Pradesh. An amount of Rs. 743.56 lakh has been sanctioned for Improvement to riding quality from Km. 160/0 to 181/0 of Chennai-Chittor-Bangalore road on NH-4. This road serves as a link road between NH 46 and NH 7. This road passes through important Mandal Headquarters like Gudipala, Chittoor, Bangarupalem, Palamaner besides touching commercial towns like Chittoor, Palamaner, Kolar etc. Most of the agricultural products from these commercial towns is being transported to district headquarters and the two cities, Chennai and Bangalore through this road only. Therefore, the proposal to strengthen the riding surface has been approved by Thiru Baalu. Further, an amount of Rs. 373.41 lakh has been sanctioned for the work of strengthening the existing carriageway from km 190/0 to km 199/0 of NH 16 (Nizamabad-Jagdalpur road) in the state of Andhra Pradesh. This is an old National Highway connecting Nizamabad in Andhra Pradesh with Jagdalpur in Chattisgarh State. This road is an important link to Mancheriyal coal mines to various parts of the State. Due to increase, in traffic volume, there is an immediate necessity to strengthening the existing carriageway to cater for the needs of present day traffic. Therefore, this proposal has also been approved by the Minister.

3291. (14-9-2007) NEW DELHI : An IAF Placement fair would be hosted at Air Force Auditorium premises in Subroto Park New Delhi on 22 & 23 Sep 07 for its Air warriors who have left the service. The IAF placement fair is being conducted under the auspices of Air Force Records Office (AFRO), New Delhi. Every year a large numbers of highly multi-skilled personnel retire from the service after completing their terms of engagement at a relatively younger age group of 35-54 years. These ex-air warriors are hardworking and dedicated and form a pool of highly trained human resources from which the corporate world can benefit immensely. Finding or assisting suitable placements for these ex-air warriors is the main purpose of this 'Placement Fair'. Every year about five to six thousand air warriors superannuate and approximately equal number of persons joins the IAF. Those who leave the IAF have at least about 15-20 years experience in Flying, Navigation, Air Traffic Controlling, aeronautical engineering, technology management and engineering work experience, education management, finance and logistics management, security, driving, catering etc. This experience would be of colossal use in the corporate world. ICICI as the lead sponsor for the IAF Placement Fair is participating with five of its companies. Kalinga Commercial, Ahmedabad Aviation and Aeronautics Ltd and Godrej & Boyce Mfg Co Ltd have become the Associate sponsors for the IAF Placement Fair. Other important companies are Tata Steel, WIPRO, Bajaj Capital, Vishal Retail Ltd, Bhaskar Power Project, Relcom group and HCL infinet just to name a few. As on date 36 companies have registered. Companies engaged in infrastructure, technology, software, aviation etc are coming forward to tap the talent, experience, dedication and loyalty of air warriors. Air India Express and Pawan Hans have signed MOUs with the Indian Air Force and have already absorbed experienced personnel from the IAF. A unique seminar on 'corporate acclimatization' would be taking place in the sidelines of the fair.

3292. (14-9-2007) NEW DELHI : Providing rural connectivity is an important component of time-bound targeted ambitious BHARAT NIRMAN Programme of the Central Government. Under Rural Connectivity programme, all villages of 1000+ population (500+ in case of hilly and tribal areas) are to be provided with all-weather connectivity by the year 2009. The Ministry of Rural Development, while reviewing the performance of Pradhan Mantri Gram Sadak Yojana (PMGSY) in the States of Assam, Chattisgarh, J&K, Jharkhand, Orissa, Tripura, UP, Uttaranchal and West Bengal has expressed concern over slow progress in implementatioin of this programme, despite availability of sufficient funds and proper and effective support by Government of India. In the State of Assam, as against the eligible 5641 villages, so far only 1150 villages have been provided with connectivity and Ministry has cleared proposals to connect only 1598 habitations. During the year 2006-07, as against the target of providing connectivity to 1998 habitations, only

804 habitations have been provided with connectivity. As against the target of construction of new roads of 2864 K.m., only 1552 km. have been constructed. In the State of Chattisgarh, as against the eligible 4728 villages, so far only 1129 villages have been provided with connectivity and Ministry has cleared proposals to connect only 1954 habitations. During the year 2006-07, as against the target of providing connectivity to 1310 habitations, only 632 habitations have been provided with connectivity. As against the target of construction of 4368 km., only 2645 km. have been constructed. In the State of J&K, as against the eligible 1468 villages, so far only 19 villages have been provided with connectivity and Ministry has cleared proposals to connect only 373 habitations. During the year 2006-07, as against the target of providing connectivity to 352 habitations, only 16 habitations have been provided with connectivity. As against the target of construction of 1059 km., only 49 km. have been constructed. In the State of Jharkhand, as against the eligible 3877 villages, so far only 209 villages have been provided with connectivity and Ministry has cleared proposals to connect only 490 habitations. During the year 2006-07, as against the target of providing connectivity to 1295 habitations, only 108 habitations have been provided with connectivity.

3293. (15-9-2007) NEW DELHI : The Thirteen International Ozone Day will be celebrated tomorrow. It is to commemorate the date of signing of Montreal Protocol on Substance that depletes the Ozone Layer. The Montreal Protocol was signed on 16th September 1987. Since then, 191 countries have signed the Montreal Protocol which share the global concern for phasing out of Ozone depleting substances. This Protocol was the culmination of decades of research which established that chemicals released in the atmosphere could damage Ozone layer. A depleted Ozone layer in the stratosphere allows the ultra violate rays of the sun to reach exposing mankind, flora and fauna to its harmful effects which each year between 2-3 million kin cancers are detected. The Government of India has taken a number of policy measures, both fiscal and regulatory to encourage early adaption of new technologies by existing and new enterprises. The Ozone Depleting Substances (Regulation and Control Rules 2000 Regulating OSD production, consumption and trade have been put into place. These rules are imposed under the Environment Protection Act 1986 with effect from 19th July 2000. Three amendments have been made in 2001, 2003,2004 and 2005 to the rules thereafter. India will receive the Montreal Protocol Implementers Award on 17th September 2007 at Montreal, Canada to mark the 20th Anniversary of the Protocol. Through out the year various competitions *e.g.* poster design, painting viz. on Ozone Science, Skit, Model Making and Slogan Writing were organized to create awareness among people. The winners of this competition will receive their prizes tomorrow at the function to celebrate Ozone Day.

3294. (15-9-2007) NEW DELHI : The President, Smt. Pratibha Devisingh Patil presented the 53rd National Film Awards to winners of different categories at a function, late last evening. The legendary film director Shyam Benegal received the Dada Saheb Phalke Award for the year 2005. Instituted in 1969, the Dada Saheb Phalke Award is given every year to a film personality for outstanding contribution to the growth and development of Indian cinema. The Award consists of a Swarna Kamal, a Shawl and cash prize of Rs two lakhs. In her speech, the President exhorted the Indian film industry to be socially responsible and committed to the cause of upholding human values. Cinema is the art of story telling and it should give expression to the many untold stories that reside in the heart of our great nation that is India. Full text of President's speech available on website *i.e.* http://presidentofindia.nic.in. As suggested by the Hon'ble President, the Minister of Information and Broadcasting and Parliamentary Affairs, Shri P.R. Dasmunsi announced that the cash amount of awards would be raised five fold from next year. In his address, Shri Dasmunsi said that Indian cinema is gaining ground and recognition amongst the film viewers of the world, especially those of Europe and Africa. Indian movies can made a major break-through, in our cultural tie-up with the rest of the world in a positive dimension. In the fields of camera operation and photography some more competitive understanding and advanced skills are required, if we compare us with Hollywood, he added. Keeping this in view we signed a Joint Cooperation Agreement with Germany and our Ministry is engaged in giving a final shape to the agreement with UK, the Minister said. With a view to boost film exports, it is time now to have a Film Export Development Council, which is to be constituted by the initiatives of FICCI and with the Ministry of Commerce.

3295. (15-9-2007) NEW DELHI: In fresh submissions in the Sethusamudram case, the Central Government on Friday told the Supreme Court, "It is alive [to] and conscious of religious sensibilities, including the unique and holy text Ramayana." The Centre said it had "taken note of the wide-ranging public sentiment, which has been expressed in respect of the decision to proceed with the construction of the Sethusamudram shipping channel." It said, "The Central Government has total respect for all religions and Hinduism in particular, in the context of the present case. Having regard to the public sentiment, and having regard to the fact that representations, including additional material, are being brought to the attention of the Government since the filing of this affidavit [the one filed by the Culture Ministry in response to Subramanian Swamy's petition], the Central government without any reservation, in a spirit of inclusiveness and high democratic tradition, to consider a different point of view, withdraws the present affidavit, to re-examine the entire matter." The government clarified that the affidavit did not, at any point of time, intend to touch upon the freedom/articles of faith or belief of any section. "The Central Government respects the sentiments of each and every citizen within the parameters of the Constitution, and acknowledges every citizen's fundamental right to feel a part of the composite cultural and religious heritage of the country."

3296. (15-9-2007) NEW DELHI : The Second Meeting of SAARC Finance Ministers held here today. Shri P. Chidambaram, Union Finance Minister was elected as the Chairperson of the meeting. Following is the text of inaugural address by Shri P. Chidambaram: "It is my pleasure to welcome all of you to this meeting of the Finance Ministers of the SAARC countries. Let me take this opportunity to welcome His Excellency, Dr. Anwarulhaq Ahadi, the Finance Minister of Afghanistan. As you know, Afghanistan is attending for the first time a meeting of SAARC Finance Ministers. I am confident that the deliberations today would pave the way for a quick transition from the declaration stage to the implementation stage of the objectives of SAARC. This was the dominant theme of the 14th Summit held at Delhi in April this year. It is our sincere and earnest desire to make a concerted move in that direction. The economies of the SAARC countries have been maintaining sustained high rates of growth. This is an encouraging sign. It is necessary to work together to develop closer regional cooperation so that the adverse effects of cyclical fluctuations on our economies is reduced to a large extent. For developing countries, growth is an imperative. Hence, growth – by itself – is a desirable goal. But it has to be inclusive and every citizen must enjoy the fruits of high growth. Our countries, therefore, need to work towards achieving the goal of a broad based and inclusive growth. The development of infrastructure in our countries is one of the major challenges facing us today. In my view, it is also a huge opportunity for investment and creation of jobs and expansion of our respective economies. In the last informal meeting of the Finance Ministers, there was a consensus on greater connectivity among SAARC countries. The meeting of the SAARC Transport Ministers that concluded recently has outlined the way forward to implement this resolve. Connectivity is heavily dependent on development of infrastructure. In India, the high growth witnessed in recent years has made our infrastructure deficiencies more visible. Since the total requirement of the infrastructure sector cannot be met from public funds alone or by the public sector alone, we have decided to promote Public Private Partnerships (PPPs) in this sector. India would be happy to share its experience in PPPs and learn from your experience as well.

3297. (15-9-2007) NEW DELHI : The President of India said here today that, it gives me immense pleasure to be amidst such an impressive gathering this evening on the occasion of the 53rd National Film Awards presentation ceremony. I would like to congratulate this year's award winners for their contribution towards enriching the world of Indian Cinema. Films in our country are enormously popular with the masses and, therefore, it is not surprising that India ranks high amongst cinema-loving nations of the world. The love for films unites people across the country as well as those Indians who reside overseas. The upsurge in the popularity of Indian cinema worldwide is a testimony to the talent and creativity of our artists and directors. However, there still is a lot of untapped potential in our country and it is important that the Indian Film Industry accommodates and harnesses this potential in order to ensure that India claims its rightful place in world cinema. With increasing popularity and commercial success of Indian cinema arise questions about its responsibilities. Cinema does not exist in an isolated vacuum, removed from reality. Cinema expresses the social, political, economic and cultural ethos of the society in which it is produced and in turn cinema also has an impact on societies. The Indian film industry must ensure that it is socially responsible and committed to the greater cause of upholding human values.

3298. (15-9-2007) NEW DELHI : The Prime Minister, Dr. Manmohan Singh underwent surgery today at the All India Institute of Medical Sciences. The procedure (Trans Urethral Resection of the Prostate gland) was performed to treat Benign Prostatic Hypertrophy of the Prostate (benign enlargement of the prostate gland). The surgery was performed by a team of doctors led by Prof. N.P. Gupta, Head of the Department of Urology at AIIMS. The Prime Minister is convalescing after the surgery and has had a stable post-operative course. After two days of rest at AIIMS the Prime Minister will return home on Monday, the 17th September.

3299. (16-9-2007) NEW DELHI : The thirteenth international day for preservation of the ozone layer was celebrated today to commemorate the date of signing the Montreal Protocol on Substances that Deplete the Ozone Layer. The Montreal Protocol is a landmark international agreement to protect the ozone layer. The Protocol was negotiated under the framework of the Vienna Convention for the Protection of the Ozone Layer (1985), which outlines governments' responsibilities for protecting human health and the environment against the adverse effects of ozone depletion. The treaty was first signed in 1987 and substantially amended in 1990 and 1992. The Montreal Protocol stipulates that the production and consumption of compounds that deplete ozone in the stratosphere-chlorofluorocarbons (CFCs), halons, carbon tetrachloride, and methyl chloroform-are to be phased out by 2000 (2005 for methyl chloroform). These compounds significantly deplete the stratospheric ozone layer that shields the planet from damaging UV-B radiation. To date, 191 countries have signed the Protocol. The United Nations Environment Programme (UNEP)'s theme for 2007 is Celebrating 20 Years of Progress of the Montreal Protocol's goals. The Montreal Protocol has been hailed as perhaps the most successful international treaty to date and provides a message of hope for working cooperatively to solve major environmental problems. In recognition of the importance of the Montreal Protocol and its works, various activities are being planned by regions/countries world-wide to celebrate this event and to further raise awareness on ozone layer protection. Shri Namo Narayan Meena, Minister of State for Environment and Forests, in a message said that India became a party to the Montreal Protocol in 1992 and has been sharing the global concern for phasing out Ozone Depleting Substances. India has emerged as a global leader in promoting smooth transition for phasing out Ozone Depleting Substances (ODS). Mr. Meena said that India is continuing dedicated efforts for generating awareness among all stakeholders on the importance of the Protocol. Mr. Meena further said that the Ministry has specifically focused on small and medium scale enterprises by encouraging them to actively participate in the phase-out process. India has fulfilled all the commitments of the Montreal Protocol and has significantly reduced chlorofluorocarbon production and consumption. Expressing immense satisfaction at the honour of being bestowed the Montreal

Protocol Implementers Award, Mr. Meena said that India has taken a number of policy measures, both fiscal and regulatory.

3300. (16-9-2007) NEW DELHI : Himalayan Warrior, a joint UK-India exercise comprising specialist high altitude training, will be held in the Ladakh region 17 September-11 October including a period of acclimatisation. This is a unique opportunity to share best practice between elite soldiers of both British and Indian Armed Forces. This specialist environmental training is the culmination of three years interaction between the Royal Marine (RM) mountain leaders and the Indian Army High Altitude Warfare School. Emphasis will be given to survival and basic infantry skills in order to improve their ability to operate above 5000 metres. The RM welcome the opportunity to train alongside the Indian Army in one of the most challenging environments in the world that will test their specialist high altitude and mountain leadership skills. The RM are the amphibious infantry of the UK and, along with the Royal Navy and Royal Fleet Auxiliary form the Naval Service. They are also the UK's amphibious force and specialists in mountain and Arctic warfare. A core component of the country's Rapid Deployment Force, the Corps is able to operate independently in all types of terrain and is highly-trained as a commando force designed to be able to quickly deploy and fight in any terrain in the world. The Indian airborne forces who are taking part in this Exercise 'HIMALAYAN WARRIOR', are especially trained high altitude warfare troops capable of operating independently in varied snow-bound mountainous regions. They are well equipped and experienced for conduct of all types of operations in all environments.

3301. (16-9-2007) NEW DELHI : The blueprint of an action plan to promote south-south cooperation with countries of Africa will be drawn up soon by the UNIDO Centre For South-South Industrial Cooperation (UCSSIC), following deliberations of the 5-day International Conference on India-Africa Cooperation on Industry, Trade and Investment, jointly organized by the United Nations Industrial Development Organisation (UNIDO) in cooperation with the Government of India, under the aegis of the recently established UCSSIC, which concluded here on 14th September. The selected industry sectors for cooperation would include cluster development, pharmaceuticals, low cost housing and building materials, renewable energy, leather, ICT applications in industry, food processing and traditional knowledge and traditional medicines. Participants from 13 African countries said they had learnt a lot about India's industrial experience over the last five days, and evinced particular interest in cluster development of small and medium enterprises (SMEs), while participating in the valedictory session of the Conference dedicated to the memory of Prof. Sanjaya Lall which was chaired by Shri Ajay Shanker, Secretary, Department of Industrial Policy & Promotion (DIPP), Government of India and addressed by Shri N.N. Prasad, Joint Secretary/DIPP; Mr. Philippe Scholtes, Representative and Regional Director of UNIDO; Shri Anthony de Sa, Director/UCSSIC; representatives of UNCTAD/ITC, and participating civil servants and private sector business representatives of the 13 countries of Africa. Describing the deliberations as productive and useful, Shri Ajay Shanker said it had helped create a critical mass of interaction and personal relationships which needed to be built upon to carry the process of south-south cooperation forward. He also underlined the need and space for creative industrial policies and programmes, which would lead to results. Shri Prasad stressed the need for developing on the momentum generated by the event through country-specific action plans and monitoring of the progress. Mr. Scholtes spoke of the interest being expressed by developing countries to share best practices for industrial development and said that UNIDO was setting up a global network of south-south centres, which included the UCSSIC set up earlier this year in India, as well as the centre proposed to be established soon in China. He said the Conference marked the first step in the road to stronger trade and industrial relations with Africa, brokered by UNIDO.

3302. (16-9-2007) NEW DELHI : Nine tea gardens out of 17 closed ones in Kerala have reopened consequent to the rehabilitation package announced by the government recently. The owners of the closed tea gardens were asked to avail the package by the end of August 2007 and reopen the gardens expeditiously. Five gardens are in the process of settling their accounts and would open soon. In West Bengal one garden, out of 14 closed tea gardens, has reopened and started functioning. Three gardens are in the process of being taken over by the new management. Two gardens have been negotiating with the banks for restructuring of the outstanding dues. Two more garden owners have indicated that they intend to sell the gardens and are on the look out for prospective entrepreneurs. All these are expected to reopen soon. The two closed tea gardens in Assam have got new management who is in the process of restarting the garden. A rehabilitation was announced by the Government of India on 29th June, 2007 for 33 tea gardens which were closed as on 1st April, 2007. More than 30,000 workers employed in these gardens were affected due to their closure. The package provides for restructuring of the outstanding bank dues, provision of fresh working capital with interest subsidy from Government, waiver of outstanding loan dues to Tea Board and settlement of Provident Fund dues in instalments. Once the accounts of these gardens are regularized, they will become eligible for term loan for replanting under the Special Purpose Tea Fund, and upfront subsidy for the machinery items under the Quality Upgradation Scheme of Tea Board.

3303. (17-9-2007) NEW DELHI : The Prime Minister, Dr. Manmohan Singh, has approved the appointment of a high level committee to coordinate the development of new road links between Delhi and Gurgaon. The committee will be chaired by the Member Secretary of the Planning Commission with the following members. 1) Secretary, Department of Road Transport and Highways 2) Secretary, Ministry of Finance 3) Chief Secretary, Government of NCT Delhi 4) Chief Secretary, Government of Haryana. The committee will facilitate development and establishment of new road links between Delhi and Gurgaon. It will be free to co-opt other secretaries as and when necessary.

3304. (17-9-2007) NEW DELHI : The following is the full text of the Address by the External Affairs Minister, Shri Pranab Mukherjee at the Institute of Foreign Affairs and National Security, Republic of Korea on "India's Look East Policy. "Chancellor Lee Ju-heum of the Institute of Foreign Affairs and National Security (IFANS), Excellencies, Distinguished Guests I am delighted to be here today to address this distinguished gathering on India's growing engagement with East Asia. Many decades back our first Prime Minister, Jawaharlal Nehru, prophesized that the "emergence of Asia in world affairs will be a powerful influence for the world peace". It has taken some time for Asia to make that journey from a colonized continent to being the world's economic power-house. The character of the economy today, its demographics and active diplomacy reveal that the balance is shifting to Asia. As the international order witnesses this significant structural transformation, we are engaged in our own process of enabling change and in reformulating our external priorities. It began when India launched its "Look East Policy" in the early 1990s. That fundamental new step was not merely the outcome of economics; it was a strategic shift in India's vision of the world in the 21st century. We were aware of the achievements of our neighbours to the East who, by emerging as economic powerhouses, also provided us with a message that enriching the flower bed of enterprise fires rapid economic growth. The Republic of Korea stood tall among the achievers and it is not a coincidence that the first visit by a Prime Minister from India was in 1993. It is not as if we suddenly discovered Korea in 1990. The legend of the Princess of Ayodhya who travelled to Korea in the Ist century AD to marry King Suro is symbolic of the common cultural and spiritual values that we shared as Indians and Koreans.

3305. (17-9-2007) NEW DELHI : The Ministry of Rural Development has set up a High Powered Technical Expert Group (TEG) under the Chairmanship of Shri Gourishankar Ghosh, founder Mission Director of the Rajiv Gandhi National Drinking Water Mission (RGNDWM). This Technical Expert Group will analyze the status of the ongoing programmes and identify issues and emerging challenges in enabling the rural community to have access to adequate safe drinking water and sanitation on a sustainable basis in all parts of the country; identify critical linkages with other sectors for optimal impact on poverty reduction and better health for the poor through increased impact on access to safe drinking water and sanitation/ hygiene facilities and recommend improved operational and institutional linkages with other programmes like National Rural Health Mission (NRHM), Watershed Development and Management, Housing and Industrial Development, new research areas in science & technology, rural employment & National Rural Employment Guarantee Act (NREGA), etc. TEG will also review and recommend steps for better integration between drinking water supply, sanitation and hygiene with health at the grass root level and recommend a strategy to channelise the efforts and resources properly to achieve the universal goal of safe drinking water and sanitation to all by 2012 in India; and identify existing gaps in water and sanitation technologies and its usage, new R&D efforts and latest advances; integrated water and sanitation management; surface, ground and rainwater management; technological advances and, adoption and formulation of suitable strategies to bridge these gaps; and also suggest methodology/ agencies/ structures which can address issues to bring in technology information and knowledge translated for the people after assessing the capacity in the states as well as PRIs. Taking into consideration of all existing relevant legal/ regulatory aspects/ issues involved in water quality, drinking water standards, sanitation, public health, prevention of pollution of drinking water sources, withdrawal of water for other purposes affecting drinking water availability, preservation of drinking water sources, etc. and recommend necessary steps to rectify the same, if necessary; suggest mechanisms for control/ regulation and enforcement of public health and pollution control requirements. TEG will further review the activities and the contribution of international and bilateral agencies and recommend possible areas of their activities to increase impact of their limited support to help best the efforts of the ministry/ mission and recommend better coordination mechanism for improved interventions for increasing regional and international collaboration, any new mechanism for betterment of the partnership with bilateral and multilateral agencies, civil society, NGO/ CBO, private sector, State Governments, R&D institutions and PRIs; and identify areas for private sector partnership especially for promotion of small private entrepreneur participation and for sector development as well as for local level economic activity for income generation.

3306. (17-9-2007) NEW DELHI : The world's hunger for energy is growing, but our resources are dwindling. The pressure on conventional energy source is enormous, which are 'finite' sources, once consumed-gone forever. Will our world run out of energy then? Will the progress of civilization come to a stop? The sustainable solution for this ever-hungry planet and advancing nation is new and renewable energy. India realized the importance of new, renewable and non-polluting energy sources more than two and a half decades ago and has found an answer in hydrogen, which is a clean energy source. There are questions regarding this source. Will Hydrogen provide clean, reliable and sustainable energy? Will it meet our growing needs for transportation and power generation? Can it be used directly as fuel cell to generate electricity for various applications? Does it have potential to replace liquid fossil fuels in the future? There are many more questions and doubts in people's mind.

3307. (17-9-2007) NEW DELHI : The Union Minister of Shipping, Road Transport and Highways, Thiru T. R. Baalu has approved 21 proposals for road improvement works on various stretches of State roads and four proposals for the construction of high level bridges (HLB) in the State of Rajasthan at a total cost of Rs. 86.81 crore (Rs. 8681.14 lakh). The approved proposals have a total length of 350.83

km at various stretches of the State Roads spread across different districts of Rajasthan. Some of the approved stretches include portions of Jhalawar-Bhawani Mandi-Dug-Agar Road (SH-19 A), Kota-Sangod-Chhabra road (SH-51), Churu-Bhaleri road (SH-69), Alanpur-Bansur-Tala Dhola road (SH-52), Nadoti-Shri Mahaveerji-Kheda road, Bharatpur-Deeg-Alwar Road, Ramgarh-Govindgarh-Sikri Road (SH-45), Mertacity-Gotan-Asop road. The total expenditure on improvement of 21 such stretches has been approved at a cost of Rs. 6563.37 lakh. The approved four high level bridges (HLB) are : construction of HLB on river Parwan on Aklera-Maharajapura Road, construction of HLB in km 2nd on Reodar-Jaswantpura-Bhinmal-Bagoda, construction of HLB with approaches on river Newaj in km 11 of Aklera-Maharajpur road and construction of Cross Drainage works across Chawali river in km 35 of Surya-Sunail-Pirawa-Soyat Road. An amount of Rs. 2117.77 lakh has been approved for these works.

3308. (17-9-2007) NEW DELHI : Kumari Selja, Minister of State (Independent Charge) for Housing & Urban Poverty Alleviation, has emphasized the need for creation of a strong database and Management Information System (MIS) on urban poverty, slums, housing, construction and other urbanization related statistics for effective policy making, planning, project formulation, implementation and monitoring. The Minister was speaking while inaugurating National Consultation on "Database & MIS on Urban Poverty, Slums and Housing" here, today. A day long event is being organized by the National Building Organization (NBO) and attended by representatives from the Central and State Governments and Union Territories and representatives from urban local bodies. On the occasion, the Minister also released the guidelines for a new Plan Scheme namely "Urban Statistics for HR and Assessments (USHA)" and user manual for Building Related Information And Knowledge Systems (BRIKS), in the presence of Shri G.K. Vasan, Union Minister of State for Statistics & Programme Implementation, Prof. Suresh Tendulkar, Chairman, National Statistical Commission (NSC) and Dr. H.S. Anand, Secretary, Ministry of Housing and Urban Poverty Alleviation. Kumari Selja stated that the new Plan Scheme "USHA" will go a long way to develop a national system on data and MIS on urban poverty, slums, housing and construction. It will also assist the network of knowledge resource centres and various forums in the implementation of the capacity building programmes relating to Database and MIS on urban poverty, slums and housing, he added. Under the new scheme one time Grants-in aid to the State Governments would be given for Hardware and Software, procurement of statistical and electronic tools, establishment of a Knowledge Centre on urban poverty and slums etc, the Minister added. While drawing the attention the some of findings of NSSO's 61st round of survey estimates, Kumari Selja stressed the need to carefully plan and design programmes for "poverty-free" and "slum-free" cities and towns. There is an estimated shortage of urban housing to the tune of 24.7 million in the country at the beginning of the 11th Plan. More than 99% of the shortage pertains to economically weaker sections and low income group categories.

3309. (17-9-2007) NEW DELHI : India's external debt stock stood at US$155.0 billion as on March 31, 2007 accounting for 16.4 per cent of Gross Domestic Product (GDP). The debt accumulation of US$ 28.5 billion during the year represents an increase of 22.6 per cent. Almost 10 per cent of the addition in total external debt during the year was ascribed to a valuation change as a result of the weakening US dollar vis-a-vis other major international currencies. This has been stated in 'India's External Debt : A Status Report' released, here today by the Department of Economic Affairs, Ministry of Finance. In terms of rupees, India's external debt at end-March 2007 stood at Rs. 675,857 crore. Component-wise, as much as 56 per cent of the increase was accounted for by commercial borrowings, followed by Non-Resident Indian (NRI) deposits (16 per cent), short-term debt (12 per cent) and multilateral debt (11 per cent). Sovereign debt at US $48.6 billion at end-March 2007 accounted for around 31.4 per cent of total external debt stock and 5.3 per cent in relation to GDP. While the total external debt stock rose during the year, the movement in critical external debt indicators showed a mixed trend. Debt service ratio showed a perceptible improvement, declining from 9.9 per cent during 2005-06 to 4.8 per cent during 2006-07. Besides, the foreign exchange reserves accounted for a cover of as much as 129 per cent to total external debt stock. However, other indicators, such as debt to GDP ratio rose, though marginally, to 16.4 per cent, short-term debt to GDP ratio to 1.3 per cent, short-term debt to total debt to 7.7 per cent, and short-term debt to foreign exchange assets to 6.2 per cent. According to the latest Global Development Finance, 2007 of the World Bank, which contains data for 2005, the ratio of external debt to Gross National Income was the second lowest for India after that for China. The concessional loan component in India's debt portfolio was the highest amongst the top ten indebted developing countries. Likewise, the ratio of short-term debt to foreign exchange reserves was the lowest for India and the share of short-term debt in total debt was the second lowest. India accumulated the least amount of external debt between 1990 and 2005. The present volume of the Status Report, the thirteenth in the series, presents developments in India's external debt during 2006-07 and provides the picture of the country's external debt position since 1990. Besides containing an analysis and presentation of India's external debt, the Report also carries an international comparison of India's external debt position vis-a-vis other indebted developing countries.

3310. (17-9-2007) NEW DELHI : Ground Water quality monitoring is being carried out through analysis of ground water samples collected mostly from the dugwells tapping the phreatic aquifers. The samples are collected during pre-monsoon period from nearly 15000 wells distributed through out the country. In addition, ground water samples are also collected during the ground water management studies, ground water exploration and special studies. The samples are analyzed for the major cations and anions for evaluating the ground water quality and its suitability for various uses. The data of the ground water quality are being computerized in the dedicated software. The quality data along with the analysis are represented the form of graphs, maps, tables and are being produced in Ground Water Year books prepared by al the regional offices. In general ground water quality in shallow aquifers is suitable for use for different purposes, except few areas in which high concentration of some of the constituents are reported. The quality in deeper aquifers varies from place to place and exploration work is going on to assess the suitability of water for various uses. High incidence of the constituents such as Arsenic, Fluoride, and Iron has been reported from some of the areas which has been mostly attributed to geogenic reasons. Similarly salinity both in the inland and coastal areas has been reported from various parts of the country.

3311. (17-9-2007) NEW DELHI : The Ministry of Women and Child Development is implementing a scheme named Kishori Shakti Yojana (KSY) using the infrastructure of Integrated Child Development Scheme (ICDS). The Scheme targets adolescent girls in the age group of 11 to 18 years, for addressing their needs of self-development, nutrition and health status, literacy and numerical skills, vocational skills etc. in 2006-07, the scheme has been expanded from 2000 ICDS projects to all the 6118 ICDS projects. Under KSY, various programmatic options are available to the States/ UTs to selectively intervene for the development of the adolescent girls on the basis of specific needs of the area. This scheme also seeks convergence with schemes of the Health Department in order to improve the nutritional and health status of the Adolescent Girls.

3312. (17-9-2007) NEW DELHI : India's external debt stock stood at US$155.0 billion as on March 31, 2007 accounting for 16.4 per cent of Gross Domestic Product (GDP). The debt accumulation of US$ 28.5 billion during the year represents an increase of 22.6 per cent. Almost 10 per cent of the addition in total external debt during the year was ascribed to a valuation change as a result of the weakening US dollar vis-a-vis other major international currencies. This has been stated in 'India's External Debt : A Status Report' released, here today by the Department of Economic Affairs, Ministry of Finance. In terms of rupees, India's external debt at end-March 2007 stood at Rs. 675,857 crore. Component-wise, as much as 56 per cent of the increase was accounted for by commercial borrowings, followed by Non-Resident Indian (NRI) deposits (16 per cent), short-term debt (12 per cent) and multilateral debt (11 per cent). Sovereign debt at US $48.6 billion at end-March 2007 accounted for around 31.4 per cent of total external debt stock and 5.3 per cent in relation to GDP. While the total external debt stock rose during the year, the movement in critical external debt indicators showed a mixed trend. Debt service ratio showed a perceptible improvement, declining from 9.9 per cent during 2005-06 to 4.8 per cent during 2006-07. Besides, the foreign exchange reserves accounted for a cover of as much as 129 per cent to total external debt stock. However, other indicators, such as debt to GDP ratio rose, though marginally, to 16.4 per cent, short-term debt to GDP ratio to 1.3 per cent, short-term debt to total debt to 7.7 per cent, and short-term debt to foreign exchange assets to 6.2 per cent. According to the latest *Global Development Finance, 2007* of the World Bank, which contains data for 2005, the ratio of external debt to Gross National Income was the second lowest for India after that for China. The concessional loan component in India's debt portfolio was the highest amongst the top ten indebted developing countries. Likewise, the ratio of short-term debt to foreign exchange reserves was the lowest for India and the share of short-term debt in total debt was the second lowest. India accumulated the least amount of external debt between 1990 and 2005. The present volume of the Status Report, the thirteenth in the series, presents developments in India's external debt during 2006-07 and provides the picture of the country's external debt position since 1990. Besides containing an analysis and presentation of India's external debt, the Report also carries an international comparison of India's external debt position *vis-a-vis* other indebted developing countries.

3313. (17-9-2007) NEW DELHI : According to the Chairman, Medical Expert Panel for the Prime Minister, Professor K. Srinath Reddy, the Prime Minister, Dr. Manmohan Singh, is convalescing after his surgery and is doing well. After completing post surgical tests the Prime Minister will be discharged from All India Institute of Medical Sciences on Tuesday, September 18, 2007 and will return home.

3314. (17-9-2007) NEW DELHI : Railways have proposed to install about 57000 Anti-Collision Device (ACDs) over the entire Broad Gauge (BG) Network of Indian Railways by 2013-14. So far about 2,300 ACDs have been supplied by M/s Konkan Railway Corporation Limited (KRCL) in association with M/s Kernex Microsystems (India) Ltd during the last about three years. Installation of ACDs on Katihar-New Jalpaiguri-Guwahati-Tinsukia-Dibrugarh-Ledo section of Northeast Frontier Railway (NFR) has been completed and is operational. Survey for expanding the system to another 10,000 route kilometres falling on the critical and busy sections of the network is almost completed. The installation of this device will go a long way in preventing accidents due to collision, which is more fatal in nature. The application of this device has been refined to not only prevent mid section collisions but also to pre-empt their occurrences in station yards. The newly engineered solution is integrated with the signalling systems and interlocking to react appropriately in case collision like conditions are perceived at the time of reception and dispatch of trains from a station. Despite the phenomenal increase in traffic, the numbers of consequential train accidents have come down from 464 in 2000-01 to 234 in 2005-06, a reduction of almost 50 per cent. In the year 2006-07, the numbers of accidents have further come down to 195, which is ever lowest since sixties. Safety is the prime concern of Indian Railways and all possible measures are being taken to ensure the safety of passengers.

3315. (17-9-2007) NEW DELHI : To a question on the resignation of Union Minister of Culture Smt. Ambika Soni on the Ramsethu affidavit congress spokesperson Shri Abhishek Singhvi said that like you, we have seen and taken note of the different statements in respect of the Ramsethu issue. Let me make it clear that the Congress is a large and democratic party unlike several others. What you have heard and seen is the expression of personal views in nature. Indeed most of them have said that it is their personal view. What you are seeing is a spectrum of shades of personal opinion, which is not at all surprising in the vibrancy of the democratic culture of a democratic party. However, since the issue of the Ramsethu affidavit has been settled with speed utmost expedition by the process of withdrawal announced within hours of coming to know of the filing of the original affidavit, it is but natural that the less different persons would speak on the matter, the better it is, because the main issue stands settled, the stand of the Government is clear, and therefore, there should be no occasion to speak about this issue at different points of time. To a question regarding the accountability being fixed about this error, Shri Singhvi said that I stand by the statement. The process of fixing responsibility for what I have already said was an error and what I have already said that to correct an error is divine and that process is on, that's an administrative inquiry. Give it some time and we have no hesitation in saying that when we get the facts we'll take action accordingly. To a question on the action being taken against the ASI officials, Shri Singhvi said that the suspension is an interim measure but naturally prima facie it has some responsibility there and that will be decided in the final outcome of the inquiry.

3316. (17-9-2007) NEW DELHI : The 26th Conference of State and UT Ministers of Information and Cinematography, SIMCON XXVI, begins in New Delhi tomorrow. On the first day of the two-day Conference, Secretary level deliberations will be held. The ministerial proceedings will be conducted under the Chairmanship of Minister of Information & Broadcasting and Parliamentary Affairs, Shri P. R. Dasmunsi on the second day. On the agenda are, the major issues in the broadcast sector like proposed 'Broadcasting Services Regulation Bill', role of State Governments in CAS roll out in the country, popularizing community radio and appointment of district level monitoring committees on broadcasting content. Measures to curb piracy of films and rationalization of entertainment tax are high on the agenda in the film sector issues whereas amendments to the Press and Registration Books (PRB) Act 1867 and further felicitation of newspapers at the Central and the State level are the major topics in the information sector. Various proposals made by the State Governments and UT Administrations on different issues would also be taken up for wider deliberations. Chief Ministers of Haryana, Delhi, Lt. Governors of Arunachal Pradesh, Andaman & Nicobar Islands, and Information Ministers from various States are expected to take part in the discussions besides presence of high-level officials at the Secretary level discussions. SIMCON XXV was held in April 2005.

3317. (17-9-2007) NEW DELHI : Exports from Indian micro, small and medium enterprises (MSMEs) is estimated to have reached a record level of US $ 50 billion during 2006-07, amounting to 40 % of India's total merchandise exports. There are 12.5 million MSMEs in India, providing employment to 30 million people, and contributing around 50 % of the country's industrial production. The major MSME export products include ready made garments, chemicals and pharmaceuticals, engineering goods, processed foods, leather products, and marine products. Small scale industries in the country have consistently maintained a growth rate higher by about 1.5 to 2 than the overall industrial growth rate. The availability of policy and development support has enabled the rapid development of MSMEs in India. This was has been indicated in a presentation on MSMEs– The Indian Scenario, by Shri Jawahar Sircar, Additional Secretary and Development Commissioner, Ministry of Micro, Small and Medium Enterprises, at the recent International Conference on India-Africa Cooperation in Industry, Trade and Investment, which was organized by the United Nations Industrial Development Organisation (UNIDO) in cooperation with the Government of India under the banner of the UNIDO Centre for South-South Industrial Cooperation established earlier this year. Changes in policy and support have been effected in tune with the emerging needs of globalization to enable SSIs to maintain and improve their competitive edge by ensuring WTO compatibility; availability of finance; technology upgradation; and skill development. Support programmes and schemes for MSMEs in India include : assistance for entrepreneurship development; credit guarantee fund scheme for small industries, micro finance programmes; credit linked subsidy scheme for technology upgradation; tool rooms for dies, moulds, jigs and fixtures; testing stations for calibration; cluster development programmes; quality upgradation in small scale sector through incentives for ISO 9000 and 14001 certification; trade-related entrepreneurship assistance for women; and setting up of testing centres by industry associations.

3318. (18-9-2007) NEW DELHI : National Buildings Organisation (NBO) under the Ministry of Housing and Urban Poverty Alleviation has launched a software "Building related Information & Knowledge System" (BRIKS) for online transmission of data relating to housing and building construction activities in the country. The software is bi-lingual *i.e.* English & Hindi. An e-unit in NBO will be up-linked to the State Government departments/Bureau of Economics and Statistics, Municipal Administration and Urban Development, Municipal Corporations, Municipalities, Urban Development Authorities and Research and Training Institutions. BRIKS will enable the NBO to set up National Data Centre and MIS on Urban Poverty, Slums, Housing, Building Construction and related urbanisation statistics under the plan scheme "Urban Statistics for HR and Assessments (USHA)" launched yesterday by the Minister of State for Housing & Urban Poverty Alleviation, Kumari Selja.

3319. (18-9-2007) NEW DELHI : The National Highways Authority of India (NHAI) has signed the Concession Agreement for four laning of Chattisgarh / Maharashtra Border –Wainganga Bridge Section of NH – 6 from Km 405.000

to km 485.000 in the State of Maharashtra on Build, Operate and Transfer (BOT) basis under National Highways Development Project (NHDP) Phase III at a total project cost of Rs. 424 Crore. The Agreement was signed here today in the presence of Dr. Jivtesh Singh Maini, Chairman, NHAI with M/s Ashoka Highways (Bhandara) Limited, an SPV formed by M/s Ashoka – IDFC Consortium. The 80 km project will have a Concession Period of 20 years (including 30 months of construction period).

3320. (18-9-2007) NEW DELHI: External Affairs Minister Pranab Mukherjee has said he does "not visualise any constraints" on the development of "bilateral relations" between India and the U.S. in the present context. At the same time, India is "confident" that its "Strategic and Cooperative Partnership" with China "will mature and steadily develop." Addressing the Seoul-based Institute of Foreign Affairs and National Security on Monday, Mr. Mukherjee outlined India's policy of such a diplomatic balance as between the U.S. and China. He was responding to a question from the audience about the "implications" of the India-U.S. civilian nuclear energy deal "for regional stability" in East Asia and about the "concerns of some people whether that kind of rapprochement will continue." He was also asked whether he would foresee "any other kinds of constraints or issues of contention between your country and the U.S." Mr. Mukherjee said: "I do not visualise any constraints in our bilateral relations [with the U.S.]. It is expanding very fast. In fact, we [have] had good relations with the U.S. from the very beginning. And now, it has assumed new dimensions, new angularities. ... And, the latest ... civilian nuclear cooperation, if it is finally materialised, would be a landmark agreement for bilateral cooperation in the context of the multilateral framework. Because... the implication would be the involvement of a large number of NSG [Nuclear Suppliers Group] countries and also India-specific arrangements with the IAEA [International Atomic Energy Agency] in [the] future... In every individual relations, there may be certain areas of divergences of views on certain aspects in a particular context. But, it is not necessary that it [the divergence] stands in the way of the overall expansion of relationship with any country." The Minister did not, however, indicate categorically whether he had in his mind the current political "divergences" within India over the nuclear deal. Nor was it clear from the question whether the "concerns" of some people related just to the continuance of the ongoing India-U.S. rapprochement. Asked about the possible impact of the emerging U.S.-India equation on China's ties with New Delhi, Mr. Mukherjee said: "There is no question of cooperation between India and the U.S. to act as some sort of containment of any country, including China."

3321. (18-9-2007) NEW DELHI : India is committed to the Montreal Protocol and have already achieved the control targets as per the protocol. Addressing the 19th Meeting of the Parties to the Montreal Protocol on substances that deplete the Ozone layer at Montreal, Canada, Shri Namo Narayan Meena, Minister of State for Environment and Forests said that production phase-out of cholrofluoro carbons (CFCs) are progressing as per the agreed schedule to meet the reduction targets specified in the Protocol. Shri Meena also informed that India has phased out the use of CFCs in manufacturing aerosol products excluding metered dose inhaler, foam and all types of refrigeration equipments. Shri Meena urged other countries to follow phasing out process at the earliest as it would check trade in equipment containing ODSs specifically CFCs and Halons. The Minister said technical assistance need to be provided for destruction of ODSs to prevent emissions in the atmosphere. Giving more details about the phase out programme, Shri Meena said India has ratified all the amendments to the Montreal Protocol. Periodically review is carried out for preparedness in various sectors under the protocol. The National Regulatory Measures have been designed in a manner which encourages enterprises using non-ODSs based technologies through fiscal incentives. He said that we provide for licensing regime for imports and exports of ODSs. Referring to the consumption of Carbon Tetra Chloride (CTCs) and CFCs in servicing sector, he said that it is largely represented by small and micro enterprises, which provide livelihood to thousands of people. India is taking pro-active steps for creating awareness and providing adequate training to customs and other officials. Shri Meena said that to freeze HCFCs in 2016 for which the Body would recommend to the TEAP to determine the financial requirement for the next replenishment of the Multilateral Fund (MLF) for the period 2009-2011. He appealed that adequate funding availability of environmentally safe substitutes and expeditious transfer of related technologies under fair and favourable conditions need to be ensured. This will assist developing countries in preparing strategies for taking action to meet the first target for HCFCs control measures under this Protocol.

3322. (18-9-2007) NEW DELHI : The President, Smt. Pratibha Devisingh Patil has congratulated Tania Sachdev for winning the Women's Chess Championship held in Tehran, Iran. The President has said that the victory will be a source of inspiration to budding chess players who adopt sports as a career.

3323. (18-9-2007) BHUBANESWAR: Train services across Orissa were affected following a 'rail roko' organised by activists of Communist Party of India (CPI) in protest against the alleged assault of their leaders by personnel of Railway Special Protection Force. Several long-distance trains were stranded at different places as CPI workers squatted on railway tracks at places such as Bhubaneswar, Sambalpur, Berhampur and Rourkela. The train movement was affected from morning to noon. CPI leader Dibakar Nayak was allegedly assaulted by RSPF jawans and TTE at Bhubaneswar Railway Station on Saturday. Following the incident, CPI workers staged demonstration and demanded action against RSPF jawans. Subsequently, the 'culprits' were identified in test identification parade. But CPI workers accused that no action was taken against security personnel and they were let off. A two-member delegation of the party on Monday submitted a memorandum to Railway Minister Lalu Prasad through the Bhubaneswar Station

Manager, demanding dismissal of the railway personnel involved in the assault. Owing to the bandh, the Puri New Delhi Neelachal Express, Guwahati-Bangalore Express, Sambalpur-Puri Intercity Express Jodhpur-Puri Express, Falknama Express and Kharagpur-Puri passenger were detained at Bhubaneswar, while Visakha Express at Berhampur, Rourkela-Puri passenger at Rengali, Titlagarh-Jharsuguda passenger at Baragarh were halted for around an hour.

3324. (18-9-2007) NEW DELHI : Based on the result of the Indian Economic Service/Indian Statistical Service Examination, 2006 held by the UPSC in November, 2006, 35 candidates, in order of merit, have been recommended for appointment to the Indian Economic Service/Indian Statistical Service. The list for the Indian Economic Service contains names of 08 candidates, including 02 belonging to the Other Backward Classes, 01 to the Scheduled Castes and 01 to the Scheduled Tribes and that for the Indian Statistical Service contains names of 27 candidates including 09 belonging to the Other Backward Classes, 04 to the Scheduled Castes and 01 to the PH-I.

3325. (18-9-2007) NEW DELHI : Within the framework of their bilateral relations, both Indian and the French Navy are taking part in "Varuna 07", a sea and air military exercise that commenced on 11 Sep 07 offshore Somali coast and in the Gulf of Aden. Aiming at increasing the two navies' interoperability, it plans various manoeuvres such as the visiting of ships by airborne and seaborne means, commando projection and air to surface exercise as well as a maritime patrol the in the abovementioned maritime zones. The exercise will terminate on 19 Sep 07. The French contribution in the forthcoming exercise comes from the Djibouti based units (six Mirage 2000 and two Pumas helicopters) as well as from those placed under Alindien's (the Admiral commanding the Indian Ocean maritime zone) command; a maritime patrol aircraft, a corvette ("Commandant Blaison") and the "La Motte Picquet" frigate, which spearheaded the conduct of exercise from the French side. The Indian Navy participated through the destroyer "Rajput", guided missile frigate "Beas", supply ship – the "Jyoti" – two helicopters as well as several commando units. "Varuna 07" is a continuation of the yearly-organized exercise, such as Varuna 06" held in March and April 2006 offshore the Indian state of Goa. The French contribution was then centered on the aircraft carrier group "Charles de Gaulle". It is also consistent with the Garuda biennial exercises (carried out last February, "Garuda III" associated Indian and French Air Force squadrons). India and France have been establishing a solid and ever –strengthening partnership that has been formalised since the Indian Prime Minister and French President signed a comprehensive defence agreement between the two countries in 2006. "Varuna 07" is as such very much significant of this common will to develop and strengthen an ambitious cooperation between the two countries.

3326. (18-9-2007) NEW DELHI : The ratification process for Indo-Chile Preferential Trade Agreement (PTA) has been completed in New Delhi recently after the visit of the Chilean President to India. This is based on the PTA signed between India and Chile earlier last year. Both sides have also issued customs notifications. The PTA provides tariff concessions ranging from 10% to 50% on 178 tariff lines at the 8 digit level to Chile and similar range of tariff concessions on 296 tariff lines at the 8 digit level to India. Tariff concessions offered by Chile inter-alia include agriculture products, chemicals and pharmaceuticals, dyes and resins, plastic, rubber and miscellaneous chemicals, leather products, textiles and clothing, footwear and some industrial products. Tariff concessions offered by India inter-alia include meat and fish products, rock salt, iodine, copper ore and concentrates, chemicals, leather products, newsprint and paper, wood and plywood articles, industrial products, shorn wool & noils of wool etc. Chile has been India's major trading partner in Latin America and India accords a great deal of significance in promoting bilateral commercial relations. Trade statistics show that bilateral trade between India and Chile has increased from US $ 163.68 million in 1996-97 to US $ 582.60 million in 2005-06. The PTA is expected to give further impetus to the growing bilateral trade.

3327. (18-9-2007) NEW DELHI : Shri Kamal Nath, Union Minister of Commerce & Industry, has expressed hope that the outstanding issues relating to the operationalisation of TRQ of vanaspati including bakery shortening and margarine and import of marble and copper from Sri Lanka to India would be negotiated soon to further increase the Indo-Sri Lankan bilateral trade. Observing that the bilateral trade has increased from US $ 1497 million in 2004-05 to US $ 2590 million in 2005-06 and has been valued at US $ 2462.28 million in 2006-07, Shri Kamal Nath hoped that the increase in the coming years would be substantial. This was stated by the Indian Commerce Minister when Dr. Sarath Amunugama, Minister of Enterprise Development and Investment Promotion of Sri Lanka, called on him here today. India is the dominant partner in the bilateral economic relations with Sri Lanka, as almost 15%-20% of total Sri Lankan imports are accounted for by India. With an investment of US $ 400-500 million in FDI, India is also amongst the fourth largest investor in Sri Lanka. During the ongoing negotiations, India has already agreed to prove Sri Lankan garment industry a TRQ of 3 million pieces of garments without any condition of sourcing of fabrics and port restrictions. Further cooperation between the two countries include bilateral cooperation agreement (MOU) on product, quality, certification and testing that has been signed between Sri Lankan Standards Institute and Bureau of Indian Standards. This is expected to benefit both the countries in areas related to standardization, quality and certification of products.

3328. (18-9-2007) NEW DELHI : The Ministry of Civil Aviation vide an order dated 18th September 2007 has announced the names of the persons who would constitute the Board of the National Aviation Company of India Ltd., (NACIL). As per the order Shri V. Thulasidas will be the Chairman and Managing Director of NACIl, Shri Vishwapati Trivedi the Joint Managing Director, Shri V.K. Verma, Director (Commercial), Shri Anup Srivastava, Director (Personnel), Shri S.

Chandrashekhar, Director (Finance), Shri S. Punhani (SBU Head) – Ground Handling, Shri Amod Sharma (SBU Head) – Related Business, Shri K.M. Unni (SBU Head) – MRO (Airframe), Shri V.K. Sharma (SBU Head) – MRO (Eng. & Comp.), Ms. Anita Khurana (SBU Head) – Cargo, Shri N. Vaghul, Chairman ICICI, Non-Official Director, Shri Raghu Menon, Addl. Secretary & Financial Advisor, M/o. Civil Aviation, Government Director and Shri R.K. Singh, Joint Secretary, Ministry of Civil Aviation, Government Director. Other than Shri V. Thulasidas, Shri V. Trivedi, Shri Raghu Menon and Shri R.K.Singh all the other Directors have been appointed to the Board of NACIL for the balance period of their tenure as Directors on the respective Boards of erstwhile Air India/ Indian Airlines.

3329. (18-9-2007) NEW DELHI : The two-day National Conference on Agriculture for Rabi Campaign-2007 got underway here today with a call for increasing production by way of increased area coverage and productivity. Dr. P.K. Mishra, Secretary, Department of Agriculture and Cooperation in his opening remarks complimented the farming community for realising newer landmarks in production performance during 2006-07. The rabi foodgrain production of 105.6 million tonne surpassed the previous record production of 104.2 million tonne achieved in 1999-2000 as well as the target set for 2006-07, he pointed out. However, there is little room for complacency on these achievements, as the production level has not been maintaining the pace with demand, particularly in respect of oilseeds and pulses causing substantial import dependence. Dr. Mishra added that the stimulation of agricultural growth would necessitate special efforts for reversing the trend of growth deceleration with short-term to medium and long term perspective to achieve the targeted 4.1% annual growth rate during 11th Five Year Plan.Dr. N.B. Singh, Agricultural Commissioner, Department of Agriculture and Cooperation in his presentation on National Food Security Mission informed that the scheme would be implemented in 16 states of the country. The Mission seeks to increase the production of rice by 10 million tonnes, wheat by 8 million tonnes and pulses by 2 million tonnes by end of 11th Plan.Dr. J.S. Samra, Chief Executive Officer, National Rainfed Area Authority also addressed the session. The business session of the Conference will have presentations by States on subjects like Kharif assessment and Rabi Prospects, National Food Security Mission, Rashtriya Krishi Vikas Yojana, Extension, Marketing, Availability of Seeds and Fertilizers, Best Practices adopted by the states etc. Vice Chancellors of State Agricultural Universities, State Agriculture Secretaries, and Commisioners and representatives from different Ministries and Departments and agricultural research organisations are attending the two-day conference.

3330. (18-9-2007) NEW DELHI : The Government today came out with a Draft Policy for Price Preference under Section 11 of the Micro, Small & Medium Enterprises Development Act 2006. It was presented at the Second Meeting of National Board for Micro, Small & Medium Enterprises here today. The salient features of Price Preference Policy for MSEs, interalia say: (1) the Central Government Ministries, its Departments, aided Institutions and PSUs under it shall procure at least 20% of the value of their total annual purchases from Micro & Small Enterprises for the products or services produced and provided by such enterprises or National Small Industries Corporation (NSIC) as Supplier; (2) At least 22.5% of the purchases mentioned above will be procured by Central Government Ministries or Departments from MSEs owned by Scheduled Caste and Scheduled Tribes; (3) at least 10% of purchases will be procured by the Central Government Ministries or Departments from such micro and small enterprises which are owned by women entrepreneurs; (4) the Micro & Small Enterprises registered with NSIC under its Single Point Registration Scheme shall be entitled to various benefits and facilities like exemption from payment of earnest money, issue of tender sets free of cost etc.; (5) the existing reservation of 358 items for exclusive purchases from micro and small enterprises will be dispensed with.; (6) NSIC as supplier engaged in selling goods by Micro and Small Enterprises and rendering services which are provided by such enterprises would provide the required help in procuring and executing tenders for bulk supplies for micro and small enterprises individually or by forming consortia. Besides, it has also been proposed to extend the benefit of Purchase Preference Policy of the Ministry of Heavy Industries, Department of Public Enterprises for purchases from Public Sector Undertakings, shall be made available to NSIC as Supplier under this Procurement Policy of MSEs. Further, it has been suggested that the Central Government Ministries/Departments shall not impose the restricted conditions for MSEs in their tenders. The minimum turnover as one of the eligibility criteria for MSEs shall not be incorporated in tenders because it restricts MSEs participation. The participants deliberated upon the Action Taken Report of the first meeting of the Board held on June 20, 2007. They also came out with various suggestions to be incorporated in the Draft Procurement Preference Policy. Earlier, inaugurating the meeting the Minister for Micro, Small & Medium Enterprises Shri Mahabir Prasad said, in various countries including the United States of America, the Government gave preference in purchasing from the Micro & Small Enterprises. He said although there was a Non-statutory Executive Policy for Price Preference in our country, but the same was not being implemented properly. Hence it was felt to prepare a Draft Price Preference Policy in consultation with all the stakeholders. The Minister assured that after taking into consideration the suggestions from the Members and the Associations, a final Draft would be prepared, which would be sent to other Ministries for comments. Dr. Syeda Hameed, Vice-Chairperson of the Board and Shri Jawahar Sircar, Addl. Secretary & Development Commissioner, MSME also spoke on this occasion.

3331. (18-9-2007) NEW DELHI : The second meeting of the National Board of Micro, Small & Medium Enterprises was held in New Delhi under the chairmanship of the Minister of Micro, Small & Medium Enterprises, Shri Mahabir Prasad today. The main topic of the agenda related to the consideration of a draft

Procurement Preference Policy for Micro and Small Enterprises. Currently, the Government of India implements a non-statutory executive policy which extends price preference of 15 per cent and certain other facilities including reserving 358 products manufactured by Micro and Small Enterprises. A proposal to have a statutory Government of India policy was discussed by Ministers from State Governments, Member Planning Commission Mrs. Syeda Hameed, Dr. M.K. Pandhe, President of Centre for Indian Trade Unions (CITU), representatives of MSME Associations from all over the country and Secretaries to the Government of India from the Departments of Commerce and Labour & Employment Ministries. The proposal involved making 20 per cent of the purchases by Ministries, Departments and CPSUs, etc., of the Government of India from the products and services provided by MSE mandatory. The proposal also includes provision of 22.5 per cent reservation for the products manufactured and services rendered by MSEs owned or managed by SCs/STs and 10 per cent from those owned/managed by women entrepreneurs. It makes it mandatory for the Central Ministries/ Departments and CPSUs to mention the percentage of purchases effected from Micro and Small Enterprises in their Annual Reports to be laid in Parliament. During the meeting, several important suggestions were received from the Members. The Minister of MSME decided that these suggestions received from the Members of the National Board and the special invites would be considered by the Ministry of MSME before finalizing a draft policy, which would then be circulated for consultations with other Ministries before finalisation.

3332. (19-9-2007) NEW DELHI : Since Minister of Tourism and Culture, Smt. Ambika Soni has not yet been able to meet the Prime Minister (as he is indisposed following his return from hospital), she has decided not to go to New York for the IncredibleIndia@60 festival from September 23-26, 2007. She has asked Secretary (Tourism), Shri Sheelbhadra Banerjee to represent the Ministry of Tourism at the event.

3333. (19-9-2007) NEW DELHI : To coincide with the September session of UN General Assembly, the Ministry of Tourism, Ministry of Culture and Confederation of Indian Industry (CII) are organizing IncredibleIndia@60 – a four day celebration starting from 23rd September 2007, that will take India's extraordinary energy and cultural diversity to New York. The focus of IncredibleIndia@60 would be on cherishing democracy and celebrating diversity. Celebrating the 60th anniversary of India's independence in New York provides a unique opportunity to capture the minds of global leaders by projecting the best of India's economy, culture, heritage and art forms during the UN General Assembly session. IncredibleIndia@60 has been conceptualized as a complete experience to showcase India's economic dynamism and highlight its growth and vibrancy. The Celebrations comprise a sand sculpture of Taj in Manhattan, cultural performances from the different regions of India, demonstration and display of Indian handicrafts, handlooms and textiles, fashion shows, music concerts, art exhibition, Indian food festivals, panel discussion on "Women and Global leadership" with Yale University; an interaction on "Brand India" at Harvard Club and a conference on Water: Challenges and Options with the Earth Institute, Columbia University. The entire event is being supported by a multi pronged publicity campaign in the TV, Radio and a number of outdoor sites in Manhattan/ New York which include, six fully wrapped buses, 150 taxi tops, 150 bus shelters in Manhattan, four panels at Times Square, 120 panels at the Grand Central Railway Station, Street banners and hoarding near the UN Headquarters, hoarding at the Rockefeller Centre, etc. In addition, massive publicity for the event is also given at Haarlem and Queens, adjoining Burroughs of New York, through advertising in 200 bus shelters. The creatives used in the campaign showcases a wide range of themes/subjects, depicting the progress and achievements made by India in various field in the last 60 years. The American market is the most important source market for India and this event would provide an effective platform for promoting India as a tourist destination.

3334. (19-9-2007) NEW DELHI : The term Indian Systems of Medicine & Homoeopathy, currently known as AYUSH (acronym for Ayurveda, Yoga & Naturopathy, Unani, Siddha and Homoeopathy) systems of medicine covers both the systems which originated in India and outside and got official recognition in course of time. The systems that originated in India are Ayurveda, Siddha, Yoga and Naturopathy. Homoeopathy originated in Germany and came to India in early part of 18th century. Unani system of medicine originally emanated from Greece, developed in Arabian countries and came to India around 9th Century after exchange of Indian and Persian thoughts of Medicine. Unani system assimilated into Indian Medicine with passage time and is much popular here, than anywhere else.

3335. (19-9-2007) NEW DELHI : Dr. Arjun Sengupta, Chairman of the National Commission for Enterprises in the Unorganized Sector (NCEUS) under the Ministry of Micro, Small & Medium Enterprises has been elected as the new Chairperson of the Inter-Governmental Working Group of the Human Rights Council on the Right to Development. The Working Group on the Right to Development is one of the Inter-Governmental Working Groups on Human Rights and was established in 1998. Dr. Sengupta has been associated with the issues relating to Right to Development for a long time and has been serving as the Indian expert on Human Rights and Extreme Poverty. He is well known internationally in the field of human rights and obtained strong endorsement for his election to the Working Group from all countries in the world. His candidature was proposed in the Human Rights Council by the Asian Group, recorded by the African Group and supported by Cuba, on behalf of NAM, Honduras on behalf of G-77 plus China and Brazil. The Industrial countries also supported his election. The Working Group on the Right to Development holds particular importance to India as this is the only Inter-governmental mechanism in the Human Rights machinery that focuses on the issue of Development. Dr. Sengupta was earlier Member Secretary of the Planning Commission and Economic Adviser (Secretary) to the former Prime Minister, Smt. Indira Gandhi.

3336. (19-9-2007) NEW DELHI : Shri Rakesh Mehrotra, Managing Director, Container Corporation of India Ltd. (CONCOR) presented a dividend cheque of Rs.45.10 crore to the Minister of Railways, Shri Lalu Prasad here today, representing dividend at the rate of 10 per cent on the equity paid-up share capital of Rs. 64.99 crore. Ministry of Railways holds 63.08 per cent of the equity share capital of CONCOR. Member Traffic, Railway Board & Chairman, CONCOR and other officials were also present on the occasion. CONCOR's shareholders in its 19th Annual General Meeting held on 22nd August 2007, declared Dividend at the rate of 220 per cent (inclusive of interim dividend at the rate of 10 per cent already paid) on the paid-up equity share capital for the financial year 2006-07 as against total dividend at the rate of 180 per cent for the financial year 2005-06. So far CONCOR has paid to its shareholders a total dividend of Rs.722.94 crore, out of which the share of Indian Railways has been Rs.464.15 crore.

3337. (19-9-2007) NEW DELHI : The Jammu and Kashmir Light Infantry (JAK LI) Regiment has conducted a successful mountaineering expedition to Mt Nun (23410 ft). The expedition was undertaken as part of numerous activities planned to commemorate the Diamond Jubilee of the Regiment. The expedition led by Col Vinay Khosla set a new record of maximum numbers summiting the peak wherein a total of 3 Officers, 2 JCOs and 17 other ranks submitted the peak over a period of three days, with the last batch being successful in late hours yesterday. JAK LI draws its troops from J & K. In this expedition five belonged to Srinagar, three to Kargil, five to Poonch, three to Doda region while others were from Jammu region. Scaling of Mt Nun demands very high standards of technical expertise, courage, physical fitness and mental robustness to scale it. Lt Gen PR Gangadhran, Military Secretary and Colonel of the JAK LI Regiment congratulated the team on this outstanding feat.

3338. (19-9-2007) NEW DELHI : Shri P. R. Dasmunsi, Minister of Information & Broadcasting and Parliamentary Affairs, today inaugurated the 26th SIMCON. In his address, he said that this Conference provides us all an opportunity to understand each other's point of view on the issues that impinge upon the information and entertainment industry of our country. Shri Dasmunsi hoped that "Monitoring Committee mechanism at the district and local levels for the Programmes and Advertisements Telecast by TV Channels" as proposed in last SIMCON would have yielded the desired results. The Minister underlined that the powers conferred upon the Authorized Officers have to be exercised with due care and caution. No cable operator should feel that he or she is being targeted arbitrarily without any justifiable grounds. This is particularly imperative because the Act has been given teeth by including imprisonment for a term that may extend upto two years, which may extend to five years for subsequent offence. The Minister said, a free and

Independent media is one of the corner stones of our democracy. There is not even a remotest thinking in the Government to interfere with the programming or the news or the editorial desk of any newspaper or electronic channel. Of course, the ultimate choice is left to the people but a democratic governance must ensure that the public has a wider choice via fair competition of the media in a level playing field. It is in this context, that the issue of cross media ownership restrictions need to be addressed. Even our modest attempt for the preparation of the draft broadcasting related bill, evoked a lot of hue and cry and an impression that the rights and freedom of the media were being curtailed, he added. Shri Dasmunsi said that the Government does not wish to dictate terms vis-a-vis functioning of any channel but is striving to develop the system where accountability and responsibility could be adhered to in the true sprit of the programme code and advertisement code. A free society does not mean that there could be a scenario of "go as you like" and the people have no choice. The Government has to be equally be sensitive to the cause of society, dignity of women, interest of children and our secular amity, to be able to justify our accountability to the nation through a system. My endeavour has been to set up a transparent regulatory mechanism, which is acceptable to the people and the stakeholders, the Minister said. Shri Dasmunsi said that there has been a great demand for allowing news and current affairs in the private FM channels. The Government did not allow it since there is no effective and established system to monitor the FM stations, though we are not against it straightaway, he said. He said, liberalization of the Community Radio policy is an achievement of the UPA Government. The Government has so far received 95 applications and permission has been granted to five organizations.

3339. (19-9-2007) NEW DELHI : The Information and Broadcasting Minister said that, I am extremely happy to welcome you all again to this important Conference, being held after two years. I am sure that the two-year period must have given ample time to the State Governments and Union Territories to initiate steps for the implementation of the decisions taken at the last SIMCON conference held in April 2005. This Conference provides us all an opportunity to understand each others points of views on the issues that impinge upon the information and entertainment industry of our country. It also enables us to determine our line of action for taking steps to protect the interests of the consumer – the common man. The presence here of a large number of Information Ministers from the States as well as the Union Territories, amply demonstrates the willingness of us all to take effective and constructive steps in dealing with the menace of piracy, implementation of CAS, regulation of broadcasting media, creating an environment to catalyze the healthy growth of this sector and framing laws to create an enabling framework to achieve this end-besides tackling other issues. Taking cognizance of the fact that the implementation of the Cable Television Networks (Regulation) Act, 1995, had not been satisfactory due to lack of knowledge or mechanism to enforce the same, the last SIMCON conference had recommended that an enforcement mechanism be constituted to implement the provisions of the said Act. In pursuance of that decision, a "Monitoring Committee for the Programmes and Advertisements Telecast by TV Channels" was proposed to be constituted at the State, district and local levels to oversee the implementation of the Cable Television Network (Regulation) Act. I am sure this step would have yielded the desired results. I want to underline here that the powers conferred upon the Authorized Officers have to be exercised with due care and caution. It must be ensured that the decisions taken by these officers should strictly be in conformity with the provisions of the Act so that they can withstand any amount of judicial scrutiny. No cable operator should feel that he or she is being targeted arbitrarily without any justifiable grounds. This is particularly imperative because the Act has been given teeth by including imprisonment for a term that may extend upto two years, or a fine up to one thousand rupees, or both. Further, for subsequent offences, the prison term may extend to five years, or with a fine up to five thousand rupees, or both. Therefore exercising a great deal of caution is the watchword for all Authorized Officers.At present, the entire electronic media is guided by the Cable Television Networks (Regulation) Act, 1995, which includes the programme code and the advertising code. During the recent times, we have received several directions from the Court that the downlinking and uplinking guidelines did not have legislative backing, whereby we were compelled to enact the legislation pertaining to the Sports Signals Mandatory Sharing Rights, in public interest.

3340. (19-9-2007) NEW DELHI : The BJP is in the midst of an existential crisis. The lotus is wilting. They are not just downwardly mobile – they are in an irreversible decline. This blind and meaningless attack on the Congress Party is nothing more than an expression of the dysfunctional incoherence of the BJP, and we reject their remarks with contempt. The party went into shock after their electoral contradictions, internal squabbles and lack of ideas began. The BJP is struggling to find direction. Controversies, Scandals and open rebellions destroyed its image. The BJP has failed as an opposition although 20 to 26 years has been spent in Opposition. The BJP is divided and confused on all issues whether the Nuclear deal or Economic Reforms or even Hindutva. All their NDA allies have left them and they stand all alone. They have a leadership crisis. They can't even make up their minds whether the leader of the Opposition should become Prime Minister or not. The issue becomes even more laughable when it is not even certain how many seats they can win. In order to divert attention from their identity crisis, they have been making dire prediction about the imminent collapse of the UPA. Any attempt to forge ideology and common purpose have crumbled against the onslaught of venality and vaulting ambitions. The contrary perceptions within the BJP – calculations and compulsions have brought it to this state of incoherence. The double standards that BJP has used in the past will not serve them any purpose as they now face demoralization and defeat stares them in the face. To a question that Prakash Karat has asked that the Nuclear deal be put on hold for six months, Smt. Natarajan said that as you are aware there is a mechanism which has been set up between the Left and the UPA to discuss all aspects of the Indo-US nuclear agreement. I have no doubt that this too will be discussed within that panel. To a question on the dispute between Left and UPA, Smt. Natarajan said that as far as the dispute is concerned, we in the Congress Party are very sure that all differences will be ironed out within the panel that has been set up for the purpose. To a question about the threat to the deal because of Left's role, Smt. Natarajan said that the interests of India and the people of India are paramount as far as Congress Party is concerned. Talking with allies does not amount to capitulation. It will be our constant endeavour and I have confidence that the government will take every step to bring all our allies on board. It is important and historic initiative. To a question about the attack on Tamil Nadu Chief Minister's daughter in Bangalore and DMK asking government to go ahead with the Setu Samundram project, Smt. Natarajan said that first I would like to strongly condemn the attack made allegedly by certain sections of the VHP upon the residence of the daughter of the Chief Minister of Tamil Nadu. These authoritarian tactics in a democracy should be put down with a very strong hand. We find it both highly unfortunate and condemnable that these attacks should have been made against a person who is not even in politics. I will call upon the government of Karnataka to provide security for all Tamils within Karnataka to prevent such incidents in future. Regarding the statement made by Mr. Baloo, Smt. Natarajan said that this is for the government to answer. The Congress Party naturally, feels that whatever government has said in support of the project in the court will ensure that the sentiments of the public at large are not affected by any move of the government. To a question that is the US is dictating the Indian government, Smt. Natarajan said that the UPA government at the Centre and the people of India do not require favour or remarks made by anybody. The American Ambassador has made certain remarks but we have our views, we have our process that will be followed. To a question that Left is making preconditions, Smt. Natarajan said that nobody dictates to the Congress Party, nobody can dictate to the people of India, nobody can dictate to our government. We will do what is in the best interest of the people.

3341. (19-9-2007) NEW DELHI : The two-day National Conference on Agriculture for Rabi Campaign 2007 ended here today. The strategy to be adopted to maximize farm production in the coming rabi season was finalized in consultation with States and the first advance estimates for the year 2007-08 were firmed up. Agriculturre Minister, Shri Sharad Pawar also addressed the Conference.The Conference was inaugurated by Dr. P.K. Mishra, Secretary, Department of Agriculture & Cooperation (DAC). The Conference was also addressed by Dr. J. S. Samra, CEO, National Rainfed Area Authority (NRAA). The participants at the Conference included Principal Secretaries/State Agricultural Production Commissioners, Vice-Chancellors of State Agriculture Universities, Officers of Department of Agriculture & Cooperation, Scientists from the ICAR, NIC, Department of Earth Sciences, Space Application Centre and others. In his inaugural address Dr. P.K. Mishra highlighted some of the recent achievements in the agriculture sector. He pointed out that the record production of 216 million tonnes of foodgrains, 22.7 million bales of cotton, 345 million tonnes of sugarcane during 2006-07 renews the confidence to further accelerate the rate of growth of the agriculture sector. The Rabi production of 105.6 million tonnes during 2006-07 surpassed the previous record of 104.3 million tonnes achieved in 1999-2000. The pro-active response to initiatives under the National Horticulture Mission and the Technology Mission for Integrated Development of Horticulture in the North Eastern States including Sikkim reaffirms the enterprising zeal of our farming community. The agricultural situation during the current Kharif season appears to be excellent. There has been increase in the area under pulses, oilseeds and maize. It appears that concerted efforts are showing better outcomes during the current Kharif season as was the case during the last Rabi season. However, there is, he continued, no room for complacency on these achievements because the agriculture sector continues to be susceptible to spatial and temporal climatic aberrations. Furthermore, there is a need to focus on enhancing income of farmers and making farming activity more viable. Dr. Mishra informed the gathering that in pursuance of the resolution adopted in the 53rd National Development Council (NDC) meeting the Government has approved "Rashtriya Krishi Vikas Yojana" with an allocation of Rs. 25,000 crores for the 11th Plan. The NDC had also resolved to enhance production of rice, wheat and pulses by 10, 8 and 2 million tonnes respectively by 2011. In fulfilment of this resolution, the Government has launched a Centrally Sponsored Scheme "National Food Security Mission" with proposed Plan Outlay of Rs. 4882.48 crores. He also highlighted the importance of agricultural statistics being compiled and provided by the State Governments to the Ministry of Agriculture which is very crucial for policy decisions and therefore requested them to verify and validate the statistics for consistency with reference to weather, prices and other parameters. The Conference was also addressed by Shri Sharad Pawar, Union Agriculture Minister on 19th September 2007.

3342. (20-9-2007) NEW DELHI : Ground Water has played crucial role for food production, drinking water supply, irrigation, drought mitigation and economic development of the country. However, unscientific development and inefficient management of ground water resources in some parts has resulted in deleterious effect in terms of steep decline in ground water levels, dwindling yield/ drying up of wells and water quality deterioration. The challenge can be effectively met by taking up programmes of artificial recharge to ground water in a big way throughout the country. There is a scope of artificial recharge in the country through recharging of surplus monsoon runoff of 36.4 BCM in an area of about 4.5 lakh sq. km identified in various parts of the country.

3343. (20-9-2007) NEW DELHI : Following is the text of speech of the Minister of Corporate Affairs, Shri Prem Chand Gupta, delivered on the occasion of 35th national convention of Company Secretaries in Jaipur, today: "I feel delighted to be here this afternoon in the mega gathering of professionals. I compliment the Institute of Company Secretaries of India for organizing such an event to deliberate upon a very topical theme-'Excellence Through Business Value Addition' which is of paramount importance in today's business arena. It gives me immense pleasure to recognize that the Institute of Company Secretaries, through its sustained efforts over decades, has created a huge base of competent professionals, which is adding sustainable value to the corporate India. It is also heartening to note that the Institute has been continuously upgrading its programmes, so that these are comparable with the best in the world and the professionals qualifying the CS course are not only able to make a global career for themselves but also take forward the Indian corporates in this highly competitive world. In this context, the Government has been keen to extend all possible help and we want our professionals to seize the opportunities emerging today in view of globalization of the market place. In order to achieve these objectives, it has been necessary to take steps to bring greater transparency and accountability in functioning of the professional institutes like yours while ensuring and promoting their functional autonomy. The comprehensive amendments made to the laws governing the ICSI, ICAI and ICWAI last year, should be seen in this background. Friends, a company is the creation of law. It is called artificial legal person. You know it better that it has several attributes of living persons. The law gives it the birth. However, it is the professionals like you who act as the nurses, doctors, gurus and guides of such artificial legal persons. Their behaviour is moulded by the guidance given by you. Many a times, their existence is dependant on you. If you nourish them well, guide them positively, they become good corporate citizens. In absence of such nourishing, they are likely to stray. Such is the importance of yours and the responsibility on your shoulders is quite huge. If you discharge this responsibility successfully, you create value. By doing this you not only serve your profession better but also serve the nation in true sense. We know there are different kinds of persons in our society. Some are extremely good, others simply good and a few are bad also.

3344. (20-9-2007) NEW DELHI : A group of experts form the Steel Authority of India Limited (SAIL) and the Rashtriya Ispat Nigam Limited (RINL) will visit Australia soon to negotiate acquisition of coking coal assets. SAIL, which is in touch with at least three coking coal companies there, is focusing on Australia while RINL is also looking at assets in Indonesia. The Minister for Steel, Chemicals and Fertilisers Shri Ram Vilas Paswan was informed about the visit during a meeting to review the functioning of SAIL here today. The Minister had led a high power delegation to Australia earlier this year to explore opportunities to acquire cocking coal assets there. Both Public Sector Steel giants depend on imports for a major part of their coking coal requirement. During the review, the Minister praised the financial performance of SAIL in FY 07 and the first quarter of FY 08. He said, those units whose year-on-year and quarter-on-quarter performance has improved must be given some incentives while those units lagging behind must be pulled up. Shri Paswan said, someone has to take responsibility for the slippages either at the corporate head quarters or at the plant level. He said, plants wher the growth rate is below last years level for no justifiable reason or whose performance on Techno Economic Parameters is not favourably comparable with their peers, should try to improve their performance in the second half of this year. He reiterated that all the expansion and modernization programmes must be completed on time and a suitable penal clause should be included in all the contracts to avoid delay in implementation. The Minister also asked SAIL to prepare a comprehensive policy proposal for promotions and that all the backlog of vacancies for SC/ST and other weaker sections should be filled up at the earliest. He also asked the company to implement the Corporate Social Responsibility programme as per the plan for which the company has earmarked nearly 2 per cent of its net profit.

3345. (20-9-2007) NEW DELHI : Shri Murli Deora, Minister for Petroleum & Natural Gas has said that in spite of rising crude oil prices, the Government has ensured that additional cost is not passed on to the consumers and common man. Inaugurating XIV Refinery Technology Meet at Thiruvananthapuram today, he informed that the Government is bearing almost 85% of the increased cost burden. He further said that the continued shortage and shortfall in crude oil supplies, rise in crude oil prices, increased use of sour and heavy crude oil, stringent environmental stipulations, other geo-political factors, globalization, etc. are the most daunting challenges to the country's energy security today. The Minister also emphasized that the Government is totally committed to accelerate the growth of this crucial sector and has taken adequate initiatives for sustainable development of the Hydrocarbon Sector. The Government has adopted various short term and long term measures, like demand restraint through efficient conservation practices, increasing production and use of bio-fuels, increased fuel substitution through utilization of natural gas, increasing emergency stocks for strategic reserve, energy efficiency improvement, etc. "Exploration and coverage of domestic resources through New Exploration Licensing Policies (NELP), intensive efforts for investment for acquisition of oil and gas equity abroad, enhancing availability of natural gas / LNG, Coal Bed Methane (CBM), underground Coal Gasification, development of Alternative Fuels, initiative for Hydrogen production for use as clean fuel, etc. are being encouraged for development in long term", he added. Stating that climate change is the most severe concern for the mankind today, Shri Deora informed that the Government has initiated measures and taken appropriate steps for clean development and climate. India has a sustainable energy policy and road map for energy security as well as emission mitigation. The hydrocarbon sector has taken up massive investments to improve the Auto Fuel Quality as per the policy formed by the Government and maximizing supplies of CNG for automobile and other applications as fuel. Along with fuel quality improvement, 5% ethanol blending in petrol has been introduced to minimize auto exhaust emissions. Energy optimization and environment management in the hydrocarbon sector in general and refining sector in particular is one of the major thrust areas to sustain growth and derive maximum benefits through successful application of strategies. Centre for High Technology (CHT), a body under the Ministry of P&NG, along with MRPL has organized the 3 Day Conference to address various technical, environmental, safety and other energy related issues. Various aspects of refining, like refinery configuration, up-gradation and process technology, refinery optimization, environment management, safety & reliability, fuel quality improvement, alternative fuels, refinery integration, refinery case studies, energy options, etc. will be covered during the conference.

3346. (20-9-2007) NEW DELHI : The All-India Consumer Price Index for Agricultural and Rural Labourers (Base 1986-87 = 100) increased by four points each during August 2007 to stand at 408 points for both the series. The rise and fall in index varied from state to state. In case of Agricultural Labourers 18 states reflected an increase in indices ranging between 1 to 10 points, in one state the indices went down by 2 points while in one state the index remained constant. In case of Rural Labourers, 18 states reflected an increase in indices ranging between 1 to 9 points while in one state the indices fell by two points. The Indices remained constant in one state. Bihar experienced the highest increase of 10 points and 9 points respectively for Agricultural Labourers and Rural Labourers. The rise has been mainly due to increase in the prices of Rice, Wheat Atta, Masur Dal, Mustard Oil, Onions, Vegetables & Fruits and Anacin. On the other hand, the indices in respect of Manipur showed a decrease of two points each for Agricultural Labourers and Rural Labourers mainly due to decrease in the prices of RICE. PUNJAB with 437 points for Agricultural Labourers and 438 points for Rural Labourers figured at the top of the index table. Manipur with 360 points for Agricultural Labourers and 361 points for Rural Labourers remained at the bottom of the index. Point to point rate of inflation based on CPI-AL increased from 8.60% during July 2007 to 8.80% during August, 2007 and in respect of CPI-RL it went up from 8.02% to 8.51% during the same period. Respective rates of inflation during August 2006 were 6.53 % and 6.21%.

3347. (20-9-2007) NEW DELHI : Shri Sharad Pawar, Minister of Agriculture, Consumer Affairs, Food and Public Distribution has said that contract farming can empower farmers with technology and provide them better market access. Inaugurating the National Conference on Emerging Platform for Agriculture Marketing here today he expressed the hope that pricing arrangements through contract farming can significantly reduced the risk and uncertainty of market place. The Minister stated that emergence of organized retailing in recent years has led to demand for quality produce and thereby private investment in supply chain infrastructure is getting a boost. Modern food retailing will lower marketing costs and lead to lower prices for consumers and higher realization for farmers. Concerns being expressed about the impact of contract farming and organized retail chains for rural India and the small farmers need to be addressed, he added. Shri Pawar pointed out that the establishment of Modern Terminal Market complexes would ensure both backward and forward linkages to farmers. The newly proposed electronic spot markets can provide a viable alternative to the existing practice of the mandi system, by improving the decision making capability of the farmers and strengthening their bargaining power. The Minister called for an in-depth analysis of how marketing development infrastructure can be catalyzed in public-private partnership mode.

3348. (20-9-2007) NEW DELHI : The Centre has made Rs.70.55 crores available to the Gujarat Government for providing additional ex-gratia assistance to the victims of the communal violence of 2002 in the State. In case of death, involving 1169 cases, an ex-gratia assistance of Rs.3.5 lakh would be paid in addition to the assistance already given by the State Government. In case of injury, involving 2548 cases, an ex-gratia assistance of Rs.1.25 lakh would be paid minus the assistance given by the State Government. The entire expenditure on payment of ex-gratia in case of death and injury would be borne by the Central Government. Only those who received ex-gratia earlier will be eligible for the enhanced additional ex-gratia amount. All the claims will be verified by the local administration or agency of the State Government. In a letter sent last week, the Centre has asked the State Government to ensure that the claims are settled and the utilization certificates are sent to the Ministry of Home Affairs within 45 days.

3349. (20-9-2007) NEW DELHI: All organisations of the Rashtriya Swayamsevak Sangh (RSS) have been directed to work together and in a coordinated manner to take forward the campaign related to Ramar Sethu. A Ramar Sethu Raksha Samiti has been set up for this purpose with representatives of various RSS organisations on it. Bharatiya Janata Party (BJP) and Vishwa Hindu Parishad (VHP) leaders confirmed here on Wednesday that there was no contradiction between what the BJP and the VHP wanted to do. While Murli Manohar Joshi and Gopal Vyas, both Rajya Sabha MPs, represent the BJP on this Samiti, its general secretary is working president of the VHP S. Vedantam. Against the backdrop of the experience of the Ayodhya agitation, when the Sangh seemed to have lost the plot, the RSS, it seems, is wary of the Ramar Sethu agitation going the Ayodhya way. It does not want it to be hijacked by the BJP, turned into a political agitation, and then discarded when the party is in power due to "political compulsions," with consequent loss of face for the RSS and its other organisations such as the VHP.

3350. (20-9-2007) NEW DELHI : The Engineering Units of Central Public Sector Enterprises (CPSEs) achieved a turnover of Rs.1582.54 crore against a target of Rs.1422.69 crore during August 2007. The turnover of Non-Engineering Units for the month was Rs.149.11 crore against a target of Rs.128.61 crore, while the turnover of Consultancy/Contract Units was Rs.119.06 crore against a target of Rs.113.96 crore. The CPSEs that achieved or exceeded their targets during the month were Bharat Heavy Electricals Ltd.(BHEL), Bharat Heavy Plates & Vessels Ltd (BHPV), Heavy Engineering Corporation (HEC), Cement Corporation of India (CCI), Hindustan Salts Ltd. (HSL), Tyre Corporation of India Ltd.(TCIL), Engineering Projects (India) Ltd. (EPIL), Hindustan Paper Corporation Ltd. (HPC),

Rajasthan Electronics & Istruments Ltd.(REIL), Sambhar Salts Ltd. (SSL) and Nepa Ltd.(NEPA).

3351. (20-9-2007) NEW DELHI : Stressing the need for creating more players in the area of power equipment manufacturing Union Power Minister Shri Sushilkumar Shinde has said that this would be one of the major areas of his initiatives in the coming few months. Delivering the keynote address after inaugurating the "India Electricity-2007" at Pragati Maidan, New Delhi today, he said lack of adequate domestic manufacturing capacity for generation equipment has been a major bottleneck in the way of timely completion of generation projects, therefore, creating more players in this field is the only way to increase capacities, bring in cost-competitiveness and accountability to timelines. The Minister expressed confidence that the Rajiv Gandhi Grameen Vidyutikaran Yojana (RGGVY) under which 42,000 villages have already been electrified, and more than 12 lakh BPL connections already provided will change the very face of rural India within a short time. The rural electrification backbone that is being created will not only cater to domestic demand for electricity, but can also be augmented by States to cater to requirements of agriculture, small industry and other applications of electricity. Shri Shinde said that the capacity addition of 78,000 MW in the next five years is not too ambitious a target as various projects of a total capacity of 50,000 MW are already under implementation and the balance orders are expected to be placed by the end of this year.

3352. (20-9-2007) NEW DELHI : Retail prices of essential commodities monitored by the Department of Consumer Affairs at four metropolitan cities have remained stable or shown mixed trend in the week ending 14.9.2007. Prices of rice, wheat, atta, gram, groundnut oil, vanaspati, tea, milk and salt were stable over the week. Prices increased in respect of tur dal by 50 paise/kg at Delhi, sugar by 50 paise/kg at Mumbai and mustard oil by Rs 2 /kg at Kolkata. Prices declined in the case of potato by 50 paise/kg at Delhi and onion by Rs 3/ kg at Mumbai. In Delhi, prices of rice, wheat and atta remained steady over six months and that of sugar, mustard oil, vanaspati, milk and salt remained steady over the month.

3353. (20-9-2007) NEW DELHI : Shri Kamal Nath, Union Minister of Commerce and Industry, has stressed on constructing more rail lines and improving their gauges for the development of industrial nodes being taken up under the Delhi-Mumbai Industrial Corridor (DMIC) Project. In his communication sent to the Railway Minister here today, Shri Kamal Nath has focused on the crucial need for the development of rail networks especially in Madhya Pradesh where the rail route kilometer length is much less than the neighbouring states. This is needed to ensure that the DMIC Project gets on stream as per the schedule and benefits reach to the stakeholders, he added. Shri Kamal Nath has urged the Railway Minister to get these works sanctioned and expedited. The Commerce and Industry Minister has identified the following rail works that need to be sanctioned or the work expedited through higher allocation of funds: 1. Starting work on the Indore–Dhar–Chotta Udaipur route: To improve the connectivity of the Indore and Shajapur-Dewas regions through Vadodara and Mumbai, this broad-gauge line need to be completed for benefitting the entire West and South Madhya Pradesh, Maharashtra and Gujarat. 2. Expediting the new line work from Indore to Dahod: Connectivity of the Pithampur – Dahod – Mhow – Mega Industrial Region near Indore to the Western ports in Gujarat will improve if this broad gauge new line work is completed soon. This will improve connectivity to the Shajapur Dewas Industrial Regions, which is proposed to be taken up through Phase-II of the DMIC project. 3. Linking Indore to Khandwa on a broad gauge route: The survey work on Indore-Khandwa section needs to be completed early and work sanctioned for providing faster connectivity from Indore to Hyderabad as well as to Mumbai via Khandwa, Bhusawal.

3354. (20-9-2007) NEW DELHI : The Information & Broadcasting Ministry has prohibited the transmission/re-transmission of satellite channel 'Janmat' (assumed name Live India) on all platforms throughout the country. The ban effective from today will be up to 20.10.2007. The prohibition has been imposed in terms of the Sub-Section (2) of Section 20 of the Cable Television Networks Regulation Act, 1995. It had come to the notice of the Central Government that some Cable Operators in the country through their Cable Television Networks had been transmitting/re-transmitting the satellite channel namely 'Janmat' (assumed name Live India), which telecast an admittedly doctored sting operation on Smt. Uma Khurana, teacher, Sarvodaya Kanya Vidyalaya in Darya Ganj, Delhi. The telecast of said sting operation was defamatory, deliberate, false and contained suggestive innuendos and half-truths; incited violence and contained content against maintenance of law and order. It criticized, maligned and slandered an individual in person and it denigrated children and was irresponsibly aired by the channel without exercise of due diligence in preliminary verification of the facts of the case. Therefore, the Central Government thought it necessary to prohibit transmission or re-transmission of the said channel throughout the country.

3355. (20-9-2007) NEW DELHI : India has called upon Australian companies to make India their investment destination. Addressing the Australia-India Business Council Investors' Meeting in Sydney today, Shri Pawan Kumar Bansal, Minister of State for Finance said that India's growing and stable investment climate present immense opportunities for Australian companies, particularly in energy and infrastructure sector. He said India offers a huge market and enormous business potential with a growing middle class in the country. It has also the potential to become trade and business centre of South Asia and East Asia with its proposed regional trade agreements with several countries and trade blocks in the near future. He expressed the hope that Australia would find India as an attractive destination for business expansion plans mutually rewarding for both the countries. Shri Bansal said that trade between the two countries has been continuously expanding. The bilateral goods trade between India and Australia has seen a growth of 34.51% between 2005-06 and 2006-07. The total bilateral trade during 2006-07 was US $ 7.7 billion making India 11th largest trading partner of Australia. Shri Bansal said that Indian investments in Australia are now well over 1 billion US dollars, mostly in IT sector. On the other hand, Australia ranks 10th and accounts for only about 2.37% of total FDI approvals with US$ 1.92 billion. Of this the inflow of FDI investment from 1991 to May 2007 has been US $ 208.8 millions. FDI investment from Australia reflect neither the potential of Australia to invest, nor the absorptive capacity of India. He urged the Australian Investors to explore the natural complementarities between the two economies to achieve optimum levels of economic engagement between the two countries. Shri Bansal said that investment by Foreign Institutional Investors in Indian stock markets also reaffirms the confidence which the investors have in India's potential. The FII investment was 10.9 billion US dollars in the year 2003-04, 8.6 billion US dollars in the year 2004-2005 and 9.2 billion US dollars in the year 2005-06. In 2006-07 the net investments were US$ 6.14 billion upto Feb. 2007. To further widen and diversity the investor base, the limit of FII investment in corporate debt in India has been increased from US$ 1.5 billion to US $ 2 billion in April, 2006. Investment cap on Government securities has also been increased from US$ 1.5 billion to US$ 2 billion in April 2006. This positive trend reflects the strong economic fundamentals of the country as well as the confidence of the foreign investors in the growth and stability of the Indian market. Shri Bansal added that India's GDP has shown a growth rate of 9.4% in 2006-07. Higher domestic savings and accelerated FDI inflows have contributed to this growth in investment. He emphasized that that India offers one of the safest investment opportunities in terms of country risk also.

3356. (21-9-2007) NEW DELHI : Government of India have announced the issue of "8.13 per cent Government Stock 2022" for an aggregate amount of Rs. 2,495.28 crore (nominal), "8.28 per cent Government Stock 2027" for an aggregate amount of Rs.1,252.24 crore (nominal) and "8.33 per cent Government Stock 2032" for an aggregate amount of Rs. 1,522.48 crore (nominal) to 19 nationalized banks on September 21, 2007. The Government Stocks are issued in lieu of outstanding amount of the following securities held by these nationalized banks.

3357. (21-9-2007) NEW DELHI : The Prime Minister's Office celebrated Hindi week from September 14 to September 20, 2007 as part of the programme to promote the use of Rajbhasha, Hindi, in official work. During the week the Officers used Hindi for their official work to the extent possible. Hindi essay, Hindi noting and drafting and Hindi typing competitions were held as part of the celebrations. The winners will be given cash awards. The competitions were held in two categories for Hindi speaking and non-Hindi speaking officers and staff. Hindi speaking and non-Hindi speaking officers and officials participated in these competitions, that aimed at promoting the use of Hindi, with great enthusiasm.

3358. (21-9-2007) NEW DELHI : The Union Minister of Railways Shri Lalu Prasad said that all possible steps will be taken for the upgradation and modernization/strengthening of Railway Protection Force (RPF) of Indian Railways. Addressing a gathering at the foundation stone laying ceremony for the construction of residential block of 'Vaatika', the RPF Officers' mess here today, the Minister said that the Railways have witnessed a quantum jump in the traffic volumes during the recent years and RPF has played a significant role in the turnaround of Indian Railways by ensuring a safe environment for transportation of freight and passengers. 'Vaatika' is a 20-room residential block of RPF officers' mess to be constructed at Brar Square, New Delhi with a cost of Rs.1.70 crore. The Minister said that even today there are unfortunate incidents of theft, burglaries and lootings of train passengers by drugging them. The incidents of explosions by terrorists in trains are also a matter of grave concern. He urged RPF to take appropriate action in this regard and make all out efforts to ensure safe, fearless and comfortable journey of train passengers. Commending the RPF for performing their job with full responsibility especially during difficult circumstances and with limited resources, Shri Lalu Prasad said that Indian Railways face tough competition with road transport for carrying freight traffic and hoped that RPF would further develop strong faith among the people to attract more and more clients towards Rail transport network by providing adequate protection and security to goods, passengers and railway property. The Minister also assured the RPF that the Ministry of Railways is committed to take all possible steps to modernize/strengthen RPF with latest security equipment and priority is being given to fulfil the vacant posts. Efforts are also being made for the creation of news posts in RPF in view of increasing security requirements. The Minister directed the department to take up a proposal for construction of a mess for RPF staff also. In his welcome address, Shri M.K.Sinha, Director General, RPF explained in detail the various works and initiatives undertaken taken by the RPF like 'RPF Mitra Yojana', 'Anti-Drugging Cells', 'Public Information Campaign' etc. Also present on the occasion were Shri V.N.Mathur, Member Traffic, Railway Board, General Manager, Northern Railway, Shri Shri Prakash, and other senior officials of the Ministry of Railways and RPF.

3359. (21-9-2007) NEW DELHI : Minister of State for Defence Shri MM Pallam Raju, inaugurated the first meeting of Defence Information Technology Consultative Committee (DITCC) in New Delhi today. The meeting was organised by HQ Integrated Defence Staff (IDS) for the easy and joint interaction between Armed Forces, Academia, Industry and Govt Officials in the area of Information Technology. HQ IDS being a Tri Services organization, is been tasked to synergies the efforts put in individually by three arms so as to harness the maximum potential and march towards more integrated approach. The quantum jump in the IT and its entry into every discipline of science and technology has a strong influence in the future war fighting capability of a nation state. Fortunately India is a world leader in this technology and it is pertinent to leverage this strength to enhance our defence capability. The three services have been independently developing their capability to augment their operational, logistic, administrative and management functions. This developmental process is further expected to grow exponentially necessitating phenomenal budget support. These efforts, however, need to be synergised for effective capability building and optimum utilisation of resources taking benefit of the commonality among the three forces, MoD and its other departments. It is perceived that in order to achieve synergy amongst the three services and to derive maximum benefits from the technology it is imperative that the correct advice and direction be provided to the conceived plans. Towards this end the Ministry of Defence has decided to formulate a Defence IT Consultative Committee comprising members from the three Services, DRDO, Industry and Academia under the Chairmanship of the Chief of Integrated Staff Committee (CISC), HQ IDS. DITCC being advisory in nature will help Armed Forces in synchronizing the efforts with the rapidly changing Information and Communication Technologies.

3360. (21-9-2007) NEW DELHI : The hearing in the Delhi High Court in the matter of "Air India Cabin Crew Association" Vs. Union of India was held on September 20, 2007. The Division Bench comprised of the Chief Justice of the Delhi High Court and Mr. Justice Sanjeev Khanna. The Division Bench during the course of the hearing and while passing the order has stated that any decision taken by the respondents pursuant to the amalgamation or merger and formation of a new company, called National Aviation Company of India Ltd., (NACIL), shall be subject to the final decision of the writ petition before them. The Bench has in no manner put on hold any administrative decision or decisions on the merger/amalgamation of Air India Ltd., and Indian Airlines Ltd., with NACIL. Further the Division Bench of the Delhi High Court has taken on record the statement of NACIL's counsel that the agreements of the Petitioner Association with Air India and Indian Airlines shall be honoured by NACIL in terms of Scheme of Amalgamation. The Bench has further observed that it is open to NACIL to have negotiation and talks with the Petitioner Association. The Court has granted the Respondents three weeks time to file the reply and the rejoinder, if any. The matter is slated to be next listed for final hearing on 30, October 2007.

3361. (21-9-2007) NEW DELHI : The Rural Development Minister, Dr. Raghuvansh Prasad Singh has asked the State Governments to organise rural development specific programmes on the occasion of the 138th birth anniversary of Mahatma Gandhi on 2nd October, 2007. In a letter addressed to the Rural Development Ministers of all the States/ UTs, Dr. Singh has urged to observe the day by organising functions as under: Organising functions at least at one place in the district for distribution of house sites to the homeless under the Indira Awaas Yojana (IAY) and create awareness by reading the name of all the beneficiaries. The selection of beneficiaries for the year 2007-08 under IAY should also be completed by then; Convening of Gram Sabhas on the day in all Panchayats for social auditing of National Rural Employment Guarantee Schemes (NREGS) where the details of employment provided under NREGS during the financial year must be spelled out. The day should also be observed as 'Cleanliness Day' to give impetus to the Total Sanitation Campaign. In this regard construction of sanitary latrines has to be started in the so far uncovered villages along with the appraisal of progress under TSC. An action plan is also to be worked out for construction of individual households latrines, school toilets, anganwadi toilets and community toilets. A pledge to follow the 8-point programme for sanitation as advised by the former President of India, Dr. A.P.J. Abdul Kalam during the award giving ceremony of Nirmal Gram Puraskar held in May 2007 to be under taken in Gram Sabha to mark the ocassion. In addition, all the Self Help Groups formed so far should be requested to convene a meeting to hold discussions on implementation of various rural development programmes. This year Gandhi Jayanti is being observed as the `National Day of Dedication'. This decision follows the United Nations Declaration of Mahatma Gandhi birth anniversary as `International Day of Non-Violence.'

3362. (21-9-2007) NEW DELHI : The area coverage of kharif crops as compared to 21st September last year has gone up considerably as per data compiled by Agriculture Ministry. The total coverage of kharif rice has gone up to 363.15 lakh ha as compared to 361.65 lakh hectare last year, the weekly Crop Weather Watch Group meeting of the Ministry of Agriculture was informed here today. Transplanting is at ending stage in almost all the states except Andhra Pradesh, Karnataka, Kerala, Orissa and Tamil Nadu where transplanting is at peak. The sowing of various coarse cereals has ended in almost all states. The area coverage under jowar, so far, is 34.36 lakh ha against 36.64 lakh ha during last year, under bajra 83.11 lakh ha against 91.81 lakh ha last year, maize 76.40 lakh ha against 72.42 lakh ha last year and total coarse cereals 215.47 lakh ha against 220.95 lakh ha during the corresponding period of last year. The area covered under cotton so far is 90.68 lakh ha against 86.89 lakh ha during the corresponding period of last year. Out of this 53.32 lakh ha is under Bt Cotton. The total coveage under sugarcane has been reported at 51.04 lakh hectare against 48.32 lakh ha during the corresponding period last year. The coverage under jute has been reported at 8.29 lakh ha against 8.18 lakh ha during the corresponding period of last year. Mesta has been sown in 1.48 lakh ha against 1.53 lakh ha during the corresponding period of last year. The total coverage of oilseeds so far has been 174.98 lakh ha as compared to 162.63 lakh ha on September 20, last year. Soyabean has been sown in 8 % and groundnut in 14% higher area as compared to that in 2006. Pulses cover an area of 121.40 lakh ha against 111.35 lakh ha up to this time last year.

3363. (21-9-2007) NEW DELHI : The Minister of State for Defence Shri MM Pallam Raju has called for extending NCC Services to the remote and rural areas of the country. Inaugurating the 17th Joint State Representatives and Deputy Directors General (JSR&D) Conference of NCC in New Delhi today, the Minister said, there are over 5000 institutions waiting to enroll as members of the NCC family. He said it is for this reason that the Defence Ministry is considering a proposal to increase the strength of NCC by another 2 lakh cadets. The Minister informed the conference that the proposal of NCC to increase the overall coverage of the students by way of reducing the enrolment period of senior wing / senior division cadets by one year has been sanctioned. Shri Raju emphasised the need to focus on enhancement of incentives for NCC cadets both in education and employment. Earlier the DG NCC Lt Gen Prakash Choudhary gave a detailed power-point presentation. He informed the conference that NCC has taken up an adult girl literacy programme with the assistance from UNICEF. This programme will be implemented as a pilot project in some districts of the country. The one day Conference was attended by representatives of all the States. The conference was held with the aim of evolving and formulating policies based on past experience for eliminating the inadequacies for further refinement and improvements in the training methods and organizational matters. The issues like increase in NCC cadet strength, provisioning of adequate infrastructural support to NCC by the states and restructuring of NCC came up for discussion during the day-long conference.

3364. (21-9-2007) NEW DELHI : The Department of Science & Technology has proposed to bring in a new legislation to enforce uniform and effective standards of Medical Devices throughout the country. This will ensure that substandard devices are not exported, especially to developing countries, which do not have medical devices regulation in place. The Government has also proposed to create a Regulatory Authority that will seek to establish and maintain a national system of certification relating to quality, safety, efficacy and availability of medical devices. Shri Kapil Sibal, Union Minister for Science & Technology and Earth Sciences informed this at a press conference here today. He said, as of today, medical device regulation is managed by the application of quality systems in Design, Development and Manufacture and Conformity with various standards. Medical Device Regulations have become NON-TARRIF barriers in international trade. Hence promotion and growth of Medical Devices industry in the country requires effective and prudent regulation incorporating the current accepted principles of Global Harmonizing Task Force (GHTF). Even within the country, the Central Government is responsible for pre-market approval whereas post market surveillance is the responsibility of State Government. This was not applicable to Medical Devices, since Medical Devices would require uniform quality throughout the country, he added. The Minister explained that a very wide and diverse range of medical devices were in use today, ranging from very simple devices with low risks (*e.g.* steel implants) to very sophisticated devices (*e.g.* heart valves) with significant risks. They use a variety of technologies and are manufactured from Small and Medium Enterprises (SMEs) to multinationals. Their duration of use of also vary from a few minutes to permanent nature. Most devices have to be sterile, some are for single use and some are reusable. Shri Sibal further stated that failure of medical devices could be fatal. Complex implantable devices can be handled only by a professionally qualified multidisciplinary team. Some medical devices may emit or be affected by electromagnetic interferences and need to be adequately safeguarded. Disposal of medical devices also poses special problems in view of environmental issues. Hence, some sort of regulatory mechanism was required to put in place, the Minister said.

3365. (21-9-2007) NEW DELHI : The Union Minister for Steel, Chemicals & Fertilizers, Shri Ram Vilas Paswan today dedicated to the nation the Coke Oven Battery at Bokaro Steel Plant. The five meter tall Battery no. 5 has been successfully rebuilt by MECON Limited on EPC basis with all pollution control facilities to meet stringent emission norms as stipulated by Ministry of Environment and Forests. The scope of work included design, engineering, manufacture, inspection, supply, erection, testing at site, trial runs, heating-up and commissioning. To meet the pollution norms stipulated by Government of India and to maintain healthy operational practice, several unique features like Air-Cooled diaphragm type doors with spring loaded latches, water sealed ascension pipe lids, computerized combustion control system and process automation etc. have been implemented in the battery. To improve the life and performance of the battery, MECON has innovated in-house designs in certain systems.

3366. (21-9-2007) NEW DELHI : Under Bharat Nirman Programme, 536 VPTs were provided in the month of July 2007. Thus, out of the targeted 66,822 villages, a total of 49240 villages have been provided with VPTs till July 2007. A total of 2271 VPTs have been provided in this financial year. The expansion of the telecom sector was accelerated with a record increase of 81.52 lakh in the number of telecom subscribers during the month of August 2007. As a result, the total number of telephones in the country is more than 2410.17 lakh, as compared to 1640.92 lakh as on August 2006, *i.e.*, a growth of 47% during August 2006 – July 2007.The GSM segment has shown an increase of 62.36 lakh during the month of August 2007, the CDMA segment of 20.75 lakh while the fixed segment has decreased by 1.59 lakh. The overall teledensity improved further to 21.2% in August 2007 as compared to 14.6% as on August 31, 2006. In the GSM segment, Tamilnadu telecom circle added more than 6.05 lakh subscribers during August 2007. In the CDMA segment, Maharashtra added more than 2.58 lakh subscribers during the period. Andhra Pradesh and Maharashtra telecom circles have added more than 7 lakh subscribers each. The growth of broadband connections improved further and at the end of July 2007, about 25.02 lakh broadband connections were provided and coverage of broadband connectivity by public sector service providers has reached 1037 cities. Further, the total number of existing ISP licencees is 372.

3367. (21-9-2007) NEW DELHI : A dedicated unit has been set up in the Business Development Directorate of the Department of Posts for designing and implementing new IT based business packages in the rural areas. It is also proposed to set up a separate Division in the Postal Directorate with the primary objective of strengthening the rural postal network and to build capacity for extending IT enabled services in the rural areas. This was stated by Shri A.Raja, Minister of

Communications and Information Technology at a meeting of the Parliamentary Consultative Committee attached to his Ministry last evening. Shri Raja said that the changing economic and technological environment has stimulated the beginning of the process of transformation of India Post also. This is manifested in the consistent growth registered in the field of business development, insurance, small savings and rapid technology induction to support all spheres of postal activities. From Rs.563.64 crore in 2002-03, revenues from premium products have gone up to Rs.1,507.55 crore in 2006-07 registering a growth of 167.47%. Premium collected from Postal Life Insurance has gone up from Rs.590.84 crore in 2002-03 to Rs.1,211.79 crore in 2006-07 registering an annual average growth of 26.27%. Premium from Rural Postal Life Insurance has also shown a consistent growth from Rs.171.35 crore in 2002-03 to Rs.601.02 crore in 2006-07 registering an annual average growth of 62.68%. Agency commission received from the Ministry of Finance for small savings business generated in the Post Offices has gone up from Rs.1,693.03 crore in the year 2002-03 to Rs.2,246.95 crore in the year 2005-06 registering a growth of 30.5%. He said that 8,263 Post Offices have been computerized including 2,403 in the rural areas up to the Tenth Plan. Computerized banking is operational in more than 4,500 Post Offices. This wide spread and strong ICT base has enabled India Post to launch a series of IT enabled services aimed at enhancing the quality of services both in the rural and urban areas. Some of the services are: Designed to bridge the digital divide. A network of 907 e-Post operational centres make it possible to send handwritten or typed messages and greetings electronically from and to any part of the country. More than 500 Instant Money Order (iMO) Centres have revolutionalized money transfer in the country. It is a web based on-line domestic money transfer service. More than 5500 Post Offices across the country are providing an IT based bill / fee / tax collection facility called e-payment which will immensely benefit both rural and urban populations by making it possible for them to deposit bills / fees / taxes in a nearby Post Offices.

3368. (21-9-2007) NEW DELHI : The total approximate earnings of Indian Railways on originating basis during the period 1st September – 10th September 2007 were Rs. 1768.95 crore compared to Rs. 1553.87 crore during the same period last year, registering an increase of 13.84 per cent. The total goods earnings have gone up from Rs. 1023.05 crore during 1st September – 10th September 2006 to Rs. 1149.95 crorc during 1st September – 10th September 2007, showing an increase of 12.40 per cent. The total passenger revenue earnings during the period 1 – 10 September 2007 were Rs. 553.94 crore compared to Rs. 467.96 crore during the same period last year, reflecting an increase of 18.37 per cent. The revenue earnings from other coaching amounted to Rs. 47.59 crore during this period compared to Rs. 41.14 crore during the same period last year, showing an increase of 15.68 per cent. The total approximate number of passengers booked during the period 1 – 10 September 2007 were 187.37 million compared to 170.47 million during the same period last year, showing an increase of 9.91 per cent.

In the suburban and non-suburban sectors, the number of passengers booked during 1 – 10 September 2007 were 104.21 million and 83.16 million compared to 96.61 million and 73.86 million during the same period last year, registering an increase of 7.87 per cent and 12.59 per cent respectively.

3369. (21-9-2007) NEW DELHI : Investor Helpline launched by the Minister of Corporate Affairs, Shri Prem Chand Gupta on September 08 last year, has been playing an important role towards restoring investor confidence in the Indian corporate sector. Investor Helpline has achieved good results in the first year of it's operations. Out of the 2415 valid investor grievances received by it (after rejection of 695 grievances) it has been able to get 956 (40%) of them resolved and 528 (22%) are under redressal. In the balance 38% grievances, there is not much the investor helpline can do as 667 (27%) grievances relate to companies where quasi or judicial process is already on and 264 (11%) relate to companies which are physically not available at the last address known to the stock exchanges or authorities. Numerous grievances resolved, after intervention by investor helpline, were more than five years old. Mukund Joshi of Pune received 1000 shares certificates-after 12 years of allotment-of Sterling Biotech Ltd. Refund of deposits were received by the investors in Llyods Finance Ltd., Escorts Finance Ltd., www.investorhelpline.in is, free of charge, internet based service to the investors for assistance in redressal of their grievances. This innovative project is sponsored by Investor Education & Protection Fund (IEPF), under the Ministry of Corporate Affairs and conceived, developed and run by Midas Touch Investors Association. Investor Helpline is another step forward towards e-governance, directed to regain and retain small investors' confidence. Investor helpline received grievances from investors spread over 200 cities of the country, besides some foreign countries. There were over 1000 companies, including Mutual Funds, manufacturing and NBFCs, against whom the investors lodged their grievances. Nearly 90% of these companies are listed on the stock exchanges.

3370. (21-9-2007) NEW DELHI : The Dugwell Recharge Scheme aims to increase the recharge to the ground water reservoir by utilizing the runoff generated in the agriculture fields, which otherwise goes as waste. The scheme has large potential not only because of its capacity to recharge shallow aquifers but also it is economically affordable for local people. The Central Ground Water Board (CGWB) and State Ground Water Departments will provide technical guidance for optimum benefit and creating awareness amongst beneficiaries. It is proposed that owners of the dugwells belonging to small and marginal farmers may be considered for 100% subsidy, while for others the component of subsidy could be 50% of the cost. The dugwell recharge scheme is proposed in 1180 over-exploited, critical and semi critical blocks in seven states namely Andhra Pradesh, Maharashtra, Karnataka, Rajasthan, Tamil Nadu, Gujarat, & Madhya Pradesh which are predominantly underlain by hard rocks at total cost of Rs. 1723.87 crores. The scheme will be implemented in 75 identified areas of various States, particularly in Over-exploited and Dark blocks, drought prone and water scarcity areas, coastal areas & islands affected by saline water ingress, areas of inland salinity, urban areas showing steep decline in ground water levels and in sub-mountainous / hilly areas of the country. The proposal costing Rs. 100 crores has been included in the XI Five Year Plan of CGWB.

3371. (21-9-2007) NEW DELHI : As per monthly monitoring report of the "20 Point Programmes" of the Government being brought out by the Ministry of Statistics and Programme Implementation, Integrated Child Development Services Scheme of the Ministry of Women and Child Development has achieved more than 90% targets during April, 2007. The scheme has been appraised as very good, (90% or above the targets). The report indicates 99% achievement for ICDS blocks operational and 95% for functional Anganwadis. This performance is in connection with 5976 operational ICDS Blocks during April, 07. On the other hand, the Ministry achieved 862946 numbers of functional Anganwadis against the monthly target of 908414 (annual target 1017952). Statewise performance of the Ministry concerning ICDS operational Blocks is by and large above 100% except Dadra & Nagar Haveli (50%) and Bihar (77%) and for functional Anganwadis, the progress among the states ranges from 93% to 133% except the states of Himachal Pradesh (44%) and Bihar (77%). The best performance for both the indicators is made by Assam (133% for operational blocks and 102% for Anganwadis), Tripura (108 & 106%) and Arunachal Pradesh (105% for the both items).

3372. (21-9-2007) NEW DELHI : The Government has withdrawn the permission of M/s. Jeevan Telecasting Corporation Ltd. to uplink their TV channel "Jeevan TV" with effect from 11.9.2007. "Jeevan TV" channel was also carrying News & Current Affairs programme. Therefore, M/s. Jeevan Telecasting Corporation Ltd. had applied to conform to the revised guidelines. But Ministry of Home Affairs did not grant security clearance to the company to uplink a news & current affairs TV channel. Accordingly, no DTH service provider & cable operator is to carry this channel on their DTH/Cable network. The company was permitted to uplink this channel from India on 18.7.2002 as per uplinking guidelines at that time. Subsequently, Government had introduced separate guidelines for permission for uplinking of news & current affairs TV channels from India and all existing channels, which were carrying news & current affairs in their programme content were asked to conform to these guidelines.

3373. (21-9-2007) NEW DELHI : Turnover and profit after tax (PAT) of RITES Ltd, a Government of India Enterprise under the Ministry of Railways, registered a growth of 32.9% and 19.2% respectively in the financial year ended March 31,2007. Turnover and PAT at Rs 566 crore (previous year Rs.426 crore) and Rs.118 crore (previous year Rs99 crore) respectively, is the highest ever achieved by the Company. Turnover from export of locomotives and rolling stock including leasing was the highest ever of Rs.266 crore. Export was made to a number of new countries for the first time including Angola, Senegal and Mali. RITES has been declared as a schedule 'A' company. RITES, the first PSU, under the Ministry of Railways, was established in 1974 as schedule 'C' company with the initial capital of Rs.10 lakh, was upgraded to schedule 'B' in 1987.

3374. (21-9-2007) NEW DELHI : Insurance Sector in India is poised for tremendous expansion. This was hinted by Shri Pawan Kumar Bansal, the Minister of State for Finance while addressing a meeting of Insurance Australia Group in Sydney today. Shri Bansal said the banks also have entered the insurance sector in the form of corporate agencies or under referral arrangements to utilize the extensive and broad reach for marketing of insurance products. He said that IRDA has also notified Micro Insurance regulations facilitating insurers to tap the potential of rural markets. As per these regulations like Non-Government Organizations (NGO), Micro Finance Institutions (MFI) and Self Help Groups (SHG) have been recognized as micro insurance agents. It is envisaged that micro insurance would facilitate penetration of insurance to rural and remote areas. He said that Micro Insurance being an integral part of overall insurance system, attempts to offer the target specific insurance products at a relatively lower cost, for a lower coverage of amount. The Minister said foreign equity upto 26% is allowed in the insurance sector. The entry of foreign partners has resulted in the sector attracting FDI of US 543 million as on 31 st March, 2007.

3375. (21-9-2007) NEW DELHI : Department of Posts will be issuing a postage stamp commemorating the 53rd Commonwealth Parliamentary Conference on Sunday September 23, 2007. The stamp will be released by the Vice-president Shri Mohd. Hamid Ansari.

3376. (21-9-2007) NEW DELHI : Congress spokesman Shri Abhishek Singhvi was accompanied by Smt. Bhattal, CLP leader from Punjab who brought to light the Akali misrule and highhandedness in which five Congress Party supporters were killed in mysterious circumstances in police custody. Shri Singhvi said that coming to power in the state of Punjab for the Akalis meant a licence to run goonda raj. The Akali government in Punjab has unleashed a reign of lawlessness of terror, of complete callousness, gross harassment and full apathy. I have with me names of five respectable persons of civil society whose crime was that they were voters and supporters of the Congress Party and that they are no more. They were subjected to torture and continuous harassment. The Sarpanch Malkiat Singh along with another member committed suicide. Malkiat Singh left a suicide note in which he alleged that the relative of an Akali minister along with members of the Akali party harassed them to such an extent that they were forced to take this step. All this because they were supporters and loyal Congress Party workers. False cases were filed against them. Kewal Singh a victim against whom false cases were filed was jailed and was found dead in the cell and his body bore torture marks all over. In the other case some persons were killed in cold blood. Till date no action has been taken against the guilty. Smt. Bhattal came along with a delegation of those persons whose family members were done to death. She accompanied the delegation to have an audience with Smt. Sonia Gandhi, the Home Minister and the Prime Minister to press their demand for Central intervention. Of the five persons killed four were dalits and the fifth was an OBC. To a question whether the Congress Party is demanding a CBI enquiry, Shri Singhvi said that this is something so basic and something so related to human rights that we have to demand first, that the authorities do their job. We reserve our right to demand all of the things. It is very convenient to transfer the blame, to transfer the responsibilities to other agencies. Certainly, the CBI option remains but I want to ask that an ordinary Sarpanch, an ordinary worker, an ordinary person in a district is found dead and their entire families have repeatedly represented their case to the authorities. Can the state be so supine, so apathetic, so callous so as not to take the skeleton of an action against the accused. To a question that UPA ally Shri Karat was backing Karunanidhi's views on Ramsethu, Shri Singhvi said that the Congress Party's stand is clear and we have articulated before and it is for the others to decide whether they share our views or not. Our view does not change from day to day. We believe that as far as the affidavit issue is concerned, it is closed and over with promptitude and alacrity we have taken steps to immediately rectify the mistake. We also hold the stand that on issues regarding Ramsethu are completely and totally issues of personal belief and personal faith. This was not an issue before the court, this was not an issue asked for by the court. As far as the project is concerned the matter is now completely, comprehensively and totally subjudice and it will be decided only on the outcome of the Supreme Court directions. No person and no authority can act contrary to those directions because the matter is pending in the Supreme Court. To a question that your alliance partner is continuing to hurt the faith of the people, Shri Singhvi said that the Congress Party is entitled to speak to its members, which it has done recently and there is no question of giving unasked for advice. Certainly, if any party or political entity ask for advice, we are ready to give it. My stand is at variance with the stand of other parties quoted to me. So it is obvious that the Congress Party stand is different. It therefore, should be obvious that our stand is not the same.

3377. (21-9-2007) NEW DELHI : The Union Government has increased the number of seats in MBBS course from 75 to 100 at Jawaharlal Institute of Post Graduate Medical Education and Research (JIPMER) from the academic year 2007-08. This decision was conveyed to the Registrar Puducherry University on 20th September 2007 by the Ministry of Health & Family Welfare.

3378. (21-9-2007) NEW DELHI : The Prime Minister, Dr. Manmohan Singh, had a telephonic conversation with the US Astronaut, Ms. Sunita Williams. The Prime Minister congratulated her on her unique achievement and her contribution to the human quest for a better understanding of our Universe. The Prime Minister invited Ms. Williams to meet him and said that she is a role model for Indian children and a source of inspiration for Indian women and that India feels proud of her achievement, even though she is a citizen of the United States of America.

3379. (21-9-2007) NEW DELHI : NFDC will conduct a co-production market at Goa Marriott Resort from 24th to 26th November, 2007. This initiative is undertaken by the NFDC as a part of the Film Bazaar to be held alongside the International Film Festival of India in Goa. The co-production market aims to offer selected directors/producers the opportunity to present their feature film projects (in all languages and at any state of production) to co producers, bankers, funds, sales agents, distributors, TV stations and other potential financers from India and abroad. The feature film projects, which the producers & distributors of various languages will present at the market will be in English language version. The objective is to promote the "Cinemas of India". Entry in this market would be by invitation only and a maximum of 15 projects would be pre-selected for the same for 2007 edition of the market. NFDC will set up meetings by the organizers between the presenters of the selected projects and the industry delegates. The deadline for submitting a project to NFDC is 28th September, 2007. The main criteria for selection are the viability and quality of the project submitted and the demonstrable talent of the directors and/or producers. The projects can be all phases of pre semi finished undergoing production or post production stage, project can be in all stages of production, from script to rough cut but they have to be new or recent in their nature. The projects should have the potential of an international market. Directors or producers should submit a complete screenplay along with their application for the same. There is no entry fee for applications & none of the submitted materials will be returned to the sender. Once a project has been selected, one representative from the respective project would be present during all the three days of the market. Projects can be submitted (online entry form + required materials) along with 1-2 pages of synopsis in English. A brief treatment of the story of 8-10 pages in English, budget outline and finance plan & a DVD/VHS of previous work. For projects, which are in different stages of progress two production stills & a DVD/HS with material already shot will have to be submitted. All entries can be sent to Ms. Usha Nair, DGM (Film Festivals), National Film Development Corporation Ltd., Discovery of India Bldg., 6th Floor, Nehru Centre, Dr. A. B. Road, Worli, Mumbai – 400018. Further details/information can be checked up with her or through filmbazaar@nfdcindia.com.

3380. (22-9-2007) NEW DELHI : The Nation today suffers an era of political instability. The breakdown of the relationship between the partners of the UPA and the Left are threatening to reduce the Central Government to a minority. The possibility of a mid term poll appears imminent. Policy disagreements between the UPA and its allies have paralysed the decision –making process in the government. The credibility of the leadership of the UPA has been shaken. Slanging matches between supporting parties, hurling accusations and even ministerial clashes have become the order of the day. The UPA Government is in power but it is devoid of any governance. The government is rudderless, directionless and merely sticking to office to complete a few extra days. The political environment is one on the eve of cracking up of the Raj. Each party which is a part of the

UPA-Left combine is now positioning to strengthen itself in a possible election. Policy decision making in matters relating to the economy are the worst sufferers. The momentum which the Indian economy gained in the NDA rule in last few years would have been strengthened further if policy decision making had continued. Unfortunately, the government is preoccupied with the primary task of managing its own survival. The government is a complete failure in a matter of controlling prices of essential commodities and in management of the farm economy. The intensity of farmers' suicide continue unabated. Faced with the imminent possibility of elections, the UPA Government is today concentrating not on serious governance and policy issues but trying to consolidate its vote banks by damaging the social fabric of the country. Each one of its decisions is intended to pursue the politics of minoritism intended to use the Muslims electorate as an instrument of political power. Infiltration into the country both on Western and Eastern borders has increased. Terrorism continues unabated; terrorist attacks have been happening mostly in States ruled by the Congress and other pseudo secular parties. This is primarily because the signal to the police administration in these States is to go slow on searches, intelligence and cracking up of terrorist modules. The UPA government has chosen the path of trying to tackle terrorism not from the standpoint of national security but with the desire of consolidating vote bank politics. It is disturbing that infiltration is on the increase. India can no longer claim to be free from Al-Qaida. Logistical support to terrorists by a section of the local population is freely available. Arms, ammunitions and explosives have increased the ability of the terrorists to strike at will at destinations chosen by them. The country is without an effective anti-terror law. An anti-terror law would have enabled the prosecuting agencies to detect terrorist activities more effectively and to convict terrorists under a tough regime. After repealing POTA the Union Government has withheld consent to laws which requires to deal with organized crimes in States such as Gujarat and Rajasthan. It is significant that terrorist attacks in BJP ruled States have been minimal essentially because of tough signalling and authority being given to police agencies to deal with terrorists modules. The ability of our intelligence agencies and security agencies to resolve terrorist crimes has been seriously eroded. The attitude of the Central government while insisting on the demolition of the Ram Setu has shaken the faith of the people of India with regard to the UPA government's intentions. The Ram Setu is a symbol of faith. Its references are found in history, mythology and religion. The UPA and its allies wanted to dismantle the Setu even when alternative alignments were possible essentially with the object of onslaughting the Hindu mind.

3381. (22-9-2007) NEW DELHI : Shri Murli Deora, Minister of Petroleum and Natural will be leaving on a two day visit to Myanmar, tomorrow. He would be accompanied by Petroleum Secretary Shri M. S. Srinivasan and MD ONGC Videsh Ltd (OVL) Shri R S Butola. After his arrival at Nay Pyi Taw, Myanmar on 23rd September, Shri Deora will meet his counterpart Brigadier General Lun Thi, Minister of Energy, Myanmar to discuss possibilities of enhancing bilateral cooperation in hydrocarbon sector. Shri Deora will also attend the signing of Production Sharing Contracts (PSCs) for 3 Deep Water exploration Blocks between OVL, and Myanmar Oil and Gas Enterprise (MOGE), a Govt of Myanmar enterprise. OVL succeeded in acquiring 100% participating interests in these 3 Deep Water Blocks AD-2, AD-3 and AD-9 in Myanmar Offshore. The aerial extent of the blocks AD-2, AD-3 and AD-9 is 8,100sq. km, 9,900sq.km, and 7,800sq.km respectively. Water depth in the block areas ranges from 1500m up to 3000m off the Rakhine coast of Myanmar. Prior to these three blocks, Oil PSUs OVL and GAIl have participated in the exploration activities in A-1 and A-3 blocks in Myanmar. In Block A-1 OVL and GAIL have 20% and 10% Participating Interests respectively. Gas discovery was made in 2004 and 2005 from Shwe and Shwe Phyu in block A1 which is estimated at 3.34 and 0.5 tcf respectively. In Block A-3 also OVL and GAIL have Participating Interests of 20% and 10% respectively. Gas discovery was made in this block in January 2006 and the Consortium has established a gas reserve of 1.52 tcf in the Mya Gas field. The total recoverable reserves of gas from A1 and A3 blocks are estimated to be about 4tcf (final study is in progress). The first gas is anticipated in early part of 2011. Attempts are being made to acquire oil and gas assets in Myanmar. Currently, total oil and gas production of Myanmar is about 10,000 barrel oil per day (bopd) and 820 Million Standard Cubic Feet Per Day (MMSCFD) respectively. The total oil and gas reserves are estimated at 50 Million Barrel (MMBL) and 10 trillion cubic feet (tcf) respectively. Myanmar Oil and Gas Enterprise, the National Enterprise produces about 10,000bopd and 120 MMSCFD gas from onshore oil and gas fields. In order to enhance energy security of the country, India is pursuing the option of acquiring equity in oil & gas assets overseas apart from developing our indigenous production. Oil Sector PSU's and joint ventures have acquired blocks/participating interest in Vietnam, Iraq, Russia, Myanmar, Iran, Libya, Sudan, Syria, Nigeria, Egypt, Qatar, Brazil, Cuba, Colombia, Ivory Cost, Gabon, Yemen and Oman. rcj/deora visits Myanmar 22-09-07

3382. (22-9-2007) NEW DELHI : The Bharatiya Janata Party expresses its grave concern over the manner in which the UPA Government has completely bungled in handling the Ram Setu issue. First, it ignored the sane advice of the Acharyas, Tsunami experts, scientists, environmentalists, scholars and rejected the appeals from eminent persons like former Justice Krishna Aiyer and former Justice Padma Bhushan K.T. Thomas and consigned to dustbin the 3.6 million signatures submitted by all sections of society demanding a change in the alignment of the SSCP because it would result in the destruction of the Setu. The government also failed even to recognize that during the debate on this issue in Rajya Sabha important party leaders had demanded that the Ram Setu be declared as a national heritage monument. The UPA government should take note of the statements of various political leaders across the party lines recognising Rama as a great national hero and even incarnation of the Devine. Secondly, when the matter was raised in the Supreme Court, the Government filed an affidavit unabashedly denying the very existence of Sri Rama. This was an affront to the nation, its traditions, and was infact an insult to the freedom struggle which according to Mahatma Gandhi was aimed at establishing Ram Rajya. The U.P.A. government has no respect to the sentiments of the people - Hindu, Muslims and Christians – who revere the bridge as Setu Mandir, Rama Setu, Adampul, Adam's bridge, Adi Setu etc. Thirdly instead of totally withdrawing that blasphemous affidavit and apologizing from the Nation the UPA government has failed even to identify as to who drafted the affidavit and at what level was it approved. Infact the government should have owned the responsibility for this sacrilege. The government should immediately stop all dredging and take steps to assuage the hurt caused to millions of countrymen. On the other hand it is now trying to submit a supplementary affidavit and the Shipping Ministry wants to file an appeal against the stay granted by the Supreme Court. The utter confusion prevailing on this issue in Congress Party has been reflected in the war of attrition going on between various leaders blaming each other for this fiasco. A government displaying such complete ignorance about its history, culture, tradition, literature and not accepting the contribution of the great heroic characters like Rama and great saints like Valmiki who had shaped the ethos of the nation from times immemorial does not deserve to stay in the office. The B.J.P. congratulates all sections of society who have stood solidly in opposing the destruction of the Setu and demanding its preservation as a NATIONAL HERITAGE. The BJP reiterates its demand for declaring the Ram Setu as a world heritage and stopping all activities which will or are likely to destroy the bridge. The BJP strongly condemns all attempts to describe those who want to seek a realignment of the project as antinational. The party also disapproves the diversionary tactics adopted by certain groups by raising slogans and arguments which tend to divide the people on the basis of geographical, linguistic and racial theories which have long been rejected by scholars and the people as well. India is one People and one Nation and the BJP will not allow the divisive forces to play their mischief. It the constituents of the UPA government continue to insult Sri Ram then the inescapable conclusion would be that the Congress led UPA government also approves such statements and is conniving with such acts of national shame.

3383. (22-9-2007) NEW DELHI : Defence Attaches of 30 countries including the United States, Brazil, Greece, the Czech Republic and Saudi Arabia were briefed yesterday on various arrangements relating to the conduct of Military World Games 2007 at Hyderabad and Mumbai. The Games are scheduled to be held from 14 to 21 October, 2007. These Defence Officials were told that preparations for the MWG were going on in full swing and India is fully prepared to host the Games in a befitting manner. DAs of prominent member countries from Asia, Europe, Americas and Africa were thoroughly briefed about all the aspects about the conduct of the games *e.g.*, arrival formalities, reception of their contingents, location of stay, movement in the city and security arrangements. Defence officials of these countries were briefed by senior members of the Military World Games Organising Committee. Defence Attaches were impressed with the meticulous planning of Organising Committee and reposed full faith in the abilities in the Indian Armed Forces to host the Games.94 countries have already confirmed their participation for the Games and it is excepted that this figure could cross the 100 mark. More than 5000 sports persons are going to compete in the 13 events in the eight day event. The Games are slated to be biggest ever congregation of countries for any sporting event in India. Besides sportspersons, several countries have intimated that their Defence Ministers, Chiefs of Armed Forces and top Defence officialswill be coming over to Hyderabad to attend the 4th MWG. Armed Forces are gearing up to host these dignitaries in a befitting manner. A high level protocol committee has been created to look after the complex task of handling so many defence ministers, heads of armed forces besides the Indian VIPS which include President of India and Chiefs of Indian Armed Forces. Defence Ministers of the countries which have already confirmed their participation include Italy, Burundy, Latvia and Slovakia. This is for the first time the Defence Ministers of so many countries are arriving for attend the single event at the same time in India. Ministry of Defence is going to utilise the opportunity to build bonds between Armed Forces of India and these countries. ***Sitanshu Kar Chairman, Media & Publicity Committee Military World Games-2007

3384. (23-9-2007) NEW DELHI : A postage stamp to commemorate the 53rd Commonwalth Parliamentary Conference being held in New Delhi was released by the Vice President Shri M. Hamid Ansari today. The Conference was inaugurated by the Vice President here today. Speaking at the function, Shri A. Raja, Minister of Communications and Information Technology said that in the last decade more than 50 new Parliaments and Legislatures joined or rejoined the CPA. The growth of CPA is a testimony of the resurgence of Parliamentary democracy. A multi-racial, multi-lingual, multi-cultural and multi-religious Association of Sovereign nations spread across all the continents, the Commonwealth is a well knit international organisation. It fosters belief in international cooperation being the way to remove causes of war, combating injustice and securing development among the peoples of the world. This august gathering of the 53rd Commonwealth Parliamentary Conference has eminent Parliamentarians from across the Commonwealth who will deliberate and evolve consensus on issues confronting us today like managing effects of globalization on small countries. Shri Raja said that the Department of Posts is privileged to release a stamp to commemorate the 53rd Commonwealth Parliamentary Conference. This stamp is a tribute to the Commonwealth's spirit of parliamentary democracy.

3385. (23-9-2007) NEW DELHI : Shri P. R. Dasmunsi, Minister of Parliamentary Affairs and Information & Broadcasting shall be the leader of Indian Parliamentary delegation in the Commonwealth Parliamentary Association's (CPA) Conference in New Delhi. Indian delegation shall take part in various workshops on the matters related to Women Empowerment, Global Warming, Environment, Women's Role in Parliament, Sustainable Water Development, Opposition's Role in Parliamentary

System etc. Indian delegates shall take part in all such workshops along with other Commonwealth delegates. The CPA deliberations will conclude on September 28, 2007.

3386. (23-9-2007) NEW DELHI : Following is the text of inaugural address by Vice-President of India and Chairman, Rajya Sabha Mohd. Hamid Ansari at the "27th Small Countries Conference" here today: "I am happy to be here today amongst friends from the Commonwealth family. Since its inception in Fiji in 1981, this gathering has emerged as the world's longest continuing forum dedicated to the concerns of small states. On a conceptual plane, it would be difficult to argue that size and beauty necessarily stand in inverse proportion to each other. Humankind has, nevertheless, traditionally bestowed certain virtues on smallness. These may or may not stand geo-strategic scrutiny; the fact remains that small states have and continue to play a significant role in history. The Commonwealth Parliamentary Association was the first international organisation to focus on the specific concerns of small states. This is indicative of far sightedness. Today, in a fast changing global scenario, the need of the hour is to address new questions that confront or may confront small states. I hope the deliberations at this conference will address these issues. This is the second time that India is hosting the Small Countries Conference, the last being in 1991. The world has changed since then; the concerns and issues that affect parliamentarians and common people alike have been transformed during the past sixteen years. In the context of a country's size, 'small' is a comparative rather than an absolute concept. Each country has its own set of concerns and vulnerabilities arising from the interplay of economic, environmental and social factors. This is more pronounced in the context of small countries as they have limited resources and limited capacity to withstand and manage adversity and crises. Ladies and Gentlemen, the Commonwealth has good reasons for its interest in small states. The overwhelming majority of the members of the Commonwealth are developing countries; 49 of the 53 members to be precise. Around 60% of the membership of the Commonwealth represents small states. Thus, your concerns and problems, while being unique to the small and developing states, represent the concerns of the majority of the members of the Commonwealth. Distinctiveness, nevertheless, is partial.

3387. (24-9-2007) NEW DELHI : The President, Smt. Pratibha Devisingh Patil has congratulated the Indian Cricket team for its victory in the finals of the T20 World Cup in Johannesburg to clinch the title. In her message to Mahender Singh Dhoni and his team, Smt. Patil said, " I congratulate you and your team for becoming the 20-20 Cricket World Champions. Your team played positive cricket and the victory is an inspiration for our youth."

3388. (24-9-2007) NEW DELHI : The first ever placement fair for Air Warriors who have retired or about to retire from service concluded yesterday, on 23 Sep 07 having turned out to be a roaring success. The placement fair was hosted at Air Force Auditorium, New Delhi on 22 & 23 Sep 07 under the auspices of Air

Force Record Office.More than 48 leading Corporate companies such as ICICI, Godrej, WIPRO, Bajaj Capital, Tata Steel, HCL, Kalinga Commercial, Air India Express, Relcom, Pawan Kans, Ahmedabad Aviation & Aeronautics registered for the fair and over 20,000 cvs were collectively picked up by these companies. It is estimated from the participating companies projections that more than 1500 appointment letters would be issued to the participants within a month. A unique feature of the fair was a workship/seminar on corporate acclimatization conducted for the ex-Air Warriors. Appreciating the effort the Vice Chief of Air Staff Air Marshal BN Gokhale said "IAF is a potent combatant force and its personnel are trained to deliver against all odds. It is necessary that the Corporate world makes full use of this opportunity". He also said "Air Warriors during their stay in IAF achieve such versatility in job handling that it is time corporate does not stereo type them in security and administrative duties." Mr. Krishnaswamy Ram Kumar, HR Head of ICICI said "here are people (Air Warriors) who have dealt with life and various difficult issues. This is unique opportunity for industry to capitalize. The age does not matter in time where knowledge and information is the mantra". He also said that ICICI had already recruited 130 ex-air warriors in leading banking process and said that they were very fast to pick up the profession. Every year about five to six thousand Air Warriors superannuate and approximately equal number of persons joins the IAF. Those who leave the IAF have at least about 15-20 years experience in Flying, Navigation, Air Traffic Controlling, aeronautical engineering, technology management and engineering work experience, education management, finance and logistics management, security, driving, catering etc. This experience would be of colossal use in the corporate world.

3389. (24-9-2007) NEW DELHI : The first meeting of the Group of Power Ministers, constituted in pursuance of the Resolution adopted at the Conference of the Chief Ministers on Power Sector was held today in New Delhi. Setting the Agenda for the meeting, the Union Power Minister, Shri Sushilkumar Shinde said that 'Power' related issues are at centre stage now as the sector is the key driver of economic growth. There is, he said, an urgent need to substantially enhance power availability at a rapid pace which is crucial for the development and prosperity of the country.

3390. (24-9-2007) NEW DELHI : Government of India have announced the sale (re-issue) of "5.48 percent Government Stock, 2009" under Market Stabilization Scheme for a notified amount of Rs. 5,000 crore (nominal). Government of India have also announced the sale (re-issue) of "5.87 percent Government Stock, 2010" under Market Stabilization Scheme for a notified amount of Rs. 5,000 crore (nominal). The Government Stocks will be sold through price based auction using multiple price method. The auctions will be conducted by the Reserve Bank of India, Mumbai Office, Fort, Mumbai on September 26, 2007(Wednesday)

3391. (24-9-2007) NEW DELHI : Direct tax collections maintained a growth of over 40% up to the period 21st September 2007. Net tax collections stood at

Rs.1,06,095 crore, up from Rs.75,510 crore during the same period last fiscal. Corporate tax recorded a growth of 42.37% at Rs.67,207 crore, up from Rs.47,207 crore during the previous fiscal. Personal income tax (including FBT, STT and BCTT) grew by 37.47% at Rs.38,819 crore, up from Rs.28,238 crore. The growth in Securities Transaction Tax (STT) was 45.52% and Banking Cash Transaction Tax (BCTT) was 21.36%. Fringe Benefit Tax (FBT) also jumped 87.41%. In terms of payment types, advance tax increased by 32% and tax deducted at source (TDS) by 48% indicating all-round buoyancy in taxes. Self-assessment tax grew by 81%, indicating better tax compliance levels.

3392. (24-9-2007) NEW DELHI : With a view to enabling institutional and retail investors to plan their investment in a better manner and also for providing transparency and stability in the Government securities market, it has been decided to continue with the system of releasing an indicative calendar for issuance of Government of India securities. Accordingly, an indicative issuance calendar for issue of dated securities for the second half of the year 2007-2008 covering the period from October 1, 2007 to March 31, 2008 (as given below) is being issued in consultation with the Reserve Bank of India.

3393. (24-9-2007) NEW DELHI : Direct tax collections maintained a growth of over 40% up to the period 21st September 2007. Net tax collections stood at Rs.1,06,095 crore, up from Rs.75,510 crore during the same period last fiscal. Corporate tax recorded a growth of 42.37% at Rs.67,207 crore, up from Rs.47,207 crore during the previous fiscal. Personal income tax (including FBT, STT and BCTT) grew by 37.47% at Rs.38,819 crore, up from Rs.28,238 crore. The growth in Securities Transaction Tax (STT) was 45.52% and Banking Cash Transaction Tax (BCTT) was 21.36%. Fringe Benefit Tax (FBT) also jumped 87.41%. In terms of payment types, advance tax increased by 32% and tax deducted at source (TDS) by 48% indicating all-round buoyancy in taxes. Self-assessment tax grew by 81%, indicating better tax compliance levels.

3394. (24-9-2007) NEW DELHI : Rear Admiral (Retd.) A K Handa, Chairman and Managing Director of Goa Shipyard Limited (GSL), a public sector company under the Ministry of Defence presented a dividend cheque of Rs. 4,16,26,746 to the Defence Minister Shri A K Antony, here today. The company has declared a dividend of Rs. 815 lakh equal to 28% of the paid up share capital for the fiscal year 2006-07 against a dividend of RS. 640 lakhs equal to 22% of the paid up capital for the financial year 2005-06. This is in addition Bonus share issued in the ratio of 1:2 on 16th February, 2006. Receiving the Dividend cheque, Defence Minister Shri Antony congratulated GSL for its excellent performance and wished them good luck in the future. During the financial year 2006-07, the company registered its highest ever Value of Production (VoP) of Rs. 267.07 crore since its inception and earned a operating profit of 36.83 crore as compared to Rs. 9.62 crore last year. The net profit after tax stood at Rs. 40.69 crore in 2006-07 as against Rs. 16.72 crore in the previous year. With a healthy order book position of Rs. 3116 crore, the company is confident of achieving the production target or Rs. 270.99 crore for the fiscal year 2007-08 as per the Memorandum of Understanding (MoU) signed by the company with the Government. The company has bagged Raksha Mantri's excellence award for "Best Performing Shipyard" for the financial year 2005-06. It was formally conferred the Mini Ratna Category – I status in March 2007.

3395. (24-9-2007) NEW DELHI : Rear Admiral (Retd.) T S Ganeshan, Chairman & Managing Director, Garden Reach Shipbuilders & Engineers (GRSE) Ltd., Kolkata, presented a cheque of Rs. 14.76 crore towards dividend for the Financial Year 2006-07 to the Defence Minister Shri A K Antony in New Delhi today. This is in addition to an amount of Rs. 10.00 crore paid as interim dividend on February 20, 2007.GRSE has declared a record Net Profit of Rs. 120.14 as compared to Rs. 65.33 crore in the previous year – an increase of 83.90%. The company's net worth has gone up to Rs. 438.16 crore from Rs. 347.06 crore in 2005-06 – an increase of 26.25%. GRSE has now embarked upon ambitious expansion / modernization plan and has already acquired the Raja Bagan Dockyard (RBD) as a first step in this direction. The acquisition of RBD and modernization will contribute significantly to the growing needs of the country's maritime security, especially the warships for the Indian Navy and the Coast Guard.

3396. (24-9-2007) NEW DELHI : The public sector undertakings (PSUs) under the administrative control of the Ministry of Steel signed Memoranda of Understanding (MoU) with Transparency International India here today during a Vigilance Conclave organised by the Ministry of Steel. These PSUs include Steel Authority of India Limited (SAIL), National Mineral Development Corporation, Manganese Ore India Limited, Metal Scrap Trading Corporation, Kudremukh Iron Ore Company Limited, Metallurgical and Engineering Consultants India Limited, Hindustan Steel Works Construction Limited, Ferro Scrap Nigam Limited and Bharat Refractories Limited. The MOUs aim at improving fairness and transparency in procurement and contracts pertaining to these PSUs. This will substantially improve the systems and reduce corruption in public dealings and incidentally go a long way in enhancing the image of the organisations as well as the nation. Shri Pratyush Sinha, Chief Vigilance Commissioner who was the chief guest on the occasion, commended the Ministry and its PSUs for taking this initiative. In his address, he emphasised that vigilance should not be perceived as having an adversarial relation with management functions and must be seen as a tool to enhance the efficiency and effectiveness of the organisation. He requested the PSUs to build institutional frameworks to enhance preventive vigilance. Secretary, Ministry of Steel, Shri R.S. Pandey in his address remarked that by signing the MoUs, the PSUs were extending the frontiers of transparency. He said the MOUs demonstrates our commitment to improve the ambience of transparency in the business of governance of PSUs". He, however, cautioned about the imbalances the 'Integrity Pact' might cause if not implemented in the right spirit. Admiral R.H.

Tahiliani (Retd), Chairman, Transparency International India, spoke about the origin and development of his organisation and the significance of public perception of countries and companies as far as adoption of fair practices is concerned. He gave examples from India and abroad as to how the signatories to an Integrity Pact could benefit in financial terms in the long run. In the afternoon, two panel discussion were held on the topics 'Transparency and fairness in procurements and contracts' and 'Operationalising the Integrity Pact'. The panelists were from the top management of the PSUs and senior Vigilance Department officials.

3397. (24-9-2007) NEW DELHI : Shri Kamal Nath, Minister of Commerce and Industry, has called for upgradation of educational standards so as to develop skills in industrial sectors. He was speaking at the first Pravasi Bharatiya Divas held outside India with the theme of 'Engaging the Diaspora: The way forward', organised jointly by the Confederation of Indian Industry, Ministry of Overseas Indian Affairs and the Overseas Indian Facilitation Centre in New York.Addressing the session on Investing in India, Shri Kamal Nath, Minister of Commerce and Industry, said that there has been a huge difference in perception of India, and the diaspora represents the intellectual and entrepreneurial talent of India. India is valued in the world for its arts and culture and its ethos of unity and harmony, said the Minister. The most important aspect of India's growth trajectory is its credibility of laws and institutional strengths which scores over other countries. Lauding the Indian diaspora, the Minister said that the community has made its mark across the world and is the face of India. Mr. Nandan M Nilekani, Co-Chairman of Infosys Technologies Limited, emphasized the opportunities for the diaspora in the services sector. The IT sector will double to $ 50-60 billion in 3-4 years, doubling employment as well. Its larger social purpose in education, urban governance, healthcare, etc will increase. A special session on India@75 was held featuring Professor CK Prahalad, Paul and Ruth McCracken Distinguished University Professor, Ross School of Business, University of Michigan. Sharing his vision for India in 2022, he stated that the country has the potential to actively shape the world order through economic strength, technological vitality and moral leadership. For this India needs to balance its aspirations and resources, the mismatch of which creates innovation. India should fold the future rather than extrapolate the past, and take small clear steps. The emerging issues will be about income inequality rather than poverty, and about lifestyles, universality of aspirations, impact on world prices, moving from 'bottom of the pyramid' to 'straddling the pyramid' and the environmental impact of development. The session on education and health partnerships was addressed by Mr. Sam Pitroda, Chairman National Knowledge Commission, and Chairman, CII Indian American Council, Rajat Kumar Gupta, Senior Partner Worldwide, McKinsey and Co. and Chairman, Public Health Foundation of India, B Ramalinga Raju, Founder and Chairman, Satyam Computer Services Ltd, Mr. Thomas Abraham, Chairman, Global Organisation of People of Indian Origin, Hemant Patel, President, American Association of Physicians of Indian Origin, and Mr. Analjit Singh, Chairman, Max

India Group of Companies and Chairman, CII International Council. They outlined their experiences in the social sectors and the lessons arising from them for Indian Americans keen to take part in the sectors.

3398. (24-9-2007) NEW DELHI : It has been decided that new applications for Unified (Telecom) Access Services (UAS) Licences will not be accepted by Department of Telecommunications (DoT) after 01.10.2007 till further orders. New Delhi, Asvina 02, 1929, September 24, 2007 Department of Telecommunications

3399. (24-9-2007) NEW DELHI : Shri Murli Deora, Minister of Petroleum and Natural returned today from a successful two day visit to Myanmar. He was accompanied by Petroleum Secretary Shri M. S. Srinivasan and MD ONGC Videsh Ltd (OVL) Shri R S Butola. After his arrival at Nay Pyi Taw the new capital of Myanmar, Shri Deora held wide ranging discussions, late in the afternoon yesterday, with his counterpart Brigadier General Lun Thi, Minister of Energy, Myanmar to explore possibilities of enhancing bilateral cooperation in the hydrocarbon sector. They also reviewed the progress achieved so far. Shri Deora invited Brig Gen Lun Thi to visit India to see the Indian capabilities in refining crude oil and training facilities in the oil and natural gas sector. Brig Gen Lun Thi conveyed his thanks to the Government of India for $20 million Line of Credit offered for Myanmar and added that they have already imported machinery and allied assemblies for revamp of one of their refineries. He requested Shri Deora for another Line of Credit for revamp of their second refinery. Shri Deora assured him of following it up with the External Affairs Ministry. Shri Deora also extended an offer to his Myanmar counterpart for training their oil and gas personnel in the world class training facilities available in India, in both upstream and downstream. Brig. Gen. Lun Thi thanked Shri Deora for this offer and directed his Ministry's officials to follow this up quickly with the local Indian Mission. Shri Deora also attended the signing of Production Sharing Contracts (PSCs) for 3 Deep Water exploration Blocks between OVL, and Myanmar Oil and Gas Enterprise (MOGE), a Govt of Myanmar enterprise. Speaking on the occasion, he noted that the signing of these contracts between OVL and MOGE is a happy development and augurs well for expanding the cooperation between two neighbours. He added that the synergies between the two countries need to be harnessed to the full potential for mutual benefit. PSCs were signed by Shri R S Butola, Managing Director on behalf of OVL and Mr. U, Myint Htay, Managing Director on behalf of MOGE. The blocks have been awarded to OVL on the basis of mutual understanding and cooperation between India and Myanmar in the hydrocarbon sector. All the 3 blocks are believed have good hydrocarbon potential as they lie in proximity to shallow water blocks A-1 & A-3 where OVL is part of the Consortium which is developing the gas find in these two blocks. OVL has succeeded in acquiring 100% participating interests in these 3 Deep Water Blocks AD-2, AD-3 and AD-9 in Myanmar Offshore. The aerial extent of the blocks AD-2, AD-3 and AD-9 is 8,100sq. km, 9,900sq.km, and 7,800sq.km respectively.

Water depth in the block areas ranges from 1500m up to 3000m off the Rakhine coast of Myanmar.

3400. (24-9-2007) NEW DELHI : The year 2007 has been one of expansion, consolidation and constant reform for Central Reserve Police Force. The force has grown in size to 201 Battalions, which translates to over two and a half lakh personnel. The primary focus of the force is to assist the state governments in maintaining law and order, which is an essential condition for economic growth and social harmony. To effectively check the disruptive forces in the country, the force has to constantly evolve and adapt-which is the exact focus of its activities this year.

3401. (24-9-2007) NEW DELHI : Large scale urbanization in India has put severe strain on urban infrastructure which includes water supply, road and transport, sewerage and sanitation, drainage and solid waste management. If momentum of economic growth is to be maintained, challenges thrown up by large-scale urbanization will have to be addressed without delay. This was stated by Shri S.Jaipal Reddy, Minister of Urban Development here today after signing Memorandum of Cooperation with the United States in the fields of Public Transportation, Intermodal Transportation, Safety Transportation, Transportation for persons with Disabilities, Intelligent Transportation Systems, Traffic Information Centre, capacity building and training in public transportation and other fields of mutual interest. The MoC will facilitate the following: Exchange of scientific and technical information on subjects of mututal interest; exchange of specialists, delegations, and scientific and technical personnel; joint organization of symposia, seminars, training programmes and other meetings; joint research in urban transportation science and technology; other forums of cooperation as mutually agreed. Ms Sherry Little, Deputy Administrator, US Federal Transit Administration led a delegation of five officers. Shri M.Ramachandran, Secretary, Urban Development led the Indian delegation.

3402. (24-9-2007) NEW DELHI : India Posts presents a fine and unique blend of technology and human intervention in all its spheres of activities. Here lies the inherent strength of India Posts *i.e.*, riding high on technology and at the same time retaining that bit of human touch which provides the customer ease and confidence. This was stated by Shri A.Raja, Minister of Communications and Information Technology while presenting the Meghdoot Awards, 2006 here today. He said that it is this strength of India Posts which makes it most capable for implementing the vision of e-Governance of Government of India which has its focus on: Delivery of public services, Radically changing the way Government deliver services and Integrating service delivery through common service centres *e.g.* Post Offices. The list of awardees is given below: Smt.Amrik Kaur, Shri T.Lalnunpuia, Shri Kompithra Philip Zacharia, Shri Ve Chennakkeshavalu, Shri Harshad Kumar Chimanlal Joshi, Shri Niyaz Ahmed, Shri Ch.Siva Rama Krishna.

3403. (24-9-2007) NEW DELHI : The Prime Minister Dr. Manmohan Singh watched the India Pakistan twenty-20 World Cup Final Cricket match with great interest. The Prime Minister has congratulated the Indian Cricket team for an impressive performance and he said " they played well and made us all proud. Keep it going team India". The Prime Minister also complimented Pakistan for playing well.

3404. (24-9-2007) NEW DELHI : Five coaches of 9038 Avadh Express caught fire when the train, on its way from Gorakhpur (U.P.) to Mumbai, was passing through Bharuch district in Gujarat at 1.30 a.m. today. The Railway medical team along with senior Railway officers was immediately rushed to the spot. None of the passengers were hurt in the fire incident. The fire was noticed in one of its Sleeper Class coach (S-10) when the train was on its run between Lakodra-Palez section of Vadodara division in Western Railway. Immediately the train was stopped and all the passengers from the affected five coaches (S-8 to S-12) were cleared safely and shifted to other coaches. The train has since resumed its onward journey early this morning. The cause of the fire is not yet known.

3405. (25-9-2007) NEW DELHI : Congratulating the Indian cricket team on winning the Twenty20 World Cup, the Minister for Civil Aviation Shri Praful Patel today announced a number of measures to honour the members of the winning team. Addressing a press conference here, the Minister said that he was proud to welcome the team, six of who belong to the Air India family. Air India will be giving out-of-turn promotions to these six players immediately. Additional travel benefits will be given to them and their family members, other than what is permissible to them as being part of Air India. Captain M.S. Dhoni, Yuvraj Singh, Irfan Pathan, Harbhajan Singh, R.P. Singh and Robin Uthappa are part of the Air India family. The Minister also announced that Air India would provide a free travel package for five years, for all 15 members of the team and their families, including the manager and the coach of the team, in the Air India network. He added that Air India would do its best to encourage young players and talents across the country. It would also promote the Indian women's cricket team. Shri Patel along with the CMD Air India will be receiving the Indian team when it lands in India tomorrow morning.

3406. (25-9-2007) NEW DELHI : The President, Smt. Pratibha Devisingh Patil, has condoled the passing away of former Union Minister, Shri K. Jana Krishnamurthy. In a condolence message to his wife, Smt. Bhagyalakshmi, the President has said, "Shri K. Jana Krishnamurthy was a parliamentarian, Union Minister and a lawyer by profession. In his passing away the country has lost a veteran public figure." The President has also conveyed her condolences to the members of the bereaved family.

3407. (25-9-2007) NEW DELHI : It is indeed a matter of pride to be amongst air warriors of IAC-I, who are due to embark on a peace keeping mission in the

Dr. Congo. This 243 Air Warrior strong task force is being led by Group Captain NJS Dhillon and this motivated team will soon be part of the United Nations. The contingent will be based at Goma, located amidst dense tropical forests, active volcanoes and ocean like lakes adjacent to Congo-Rwanda Uganda border. Charter of this contingent will be to enforce peace and will entail support of the Mi-17 utility helicopters as well as the Mi-25 attack helicopters. The contingent will operate in a hostile environment dotted with inhospitable terrain in the north eastern part of Congo. IAF has established a good reputation in undertaking peace keeping duties in support of the United Nations. Incidentally, the first mission was also in Congo, nearly half a century back in 1961 when six Canberra bombers of No. 5 Squadron adorned with the IAF's saffron white-green roundels were inducted to restore peace. These bombers had a dramatic impact on neutralization of the mercenary-run Katangan Air Force. Later, IAF made substantial contribution to the peace keeping effort in Somalia and Sierra Leone by undertaking some daring missions. In 2003, IAF was once again called upon by the UN to operate its attack and utility helicopters for wide-ranging operations to control the turbulence in Congo. The Democratic Republic of the Congo (DRC) has been afflicted by continuous strife ever since its independence in 1960. Located in Central Africa, it is a large country with a population of around 60 million with nearly 350 African ethnic groups. It is well endowed with natural resources including diamonds, gold and other minerals. Its people, however remain amongst the poorest in the world as the economy is in shambles. A vicious war is on for control of resources between the Government and the rebel forces.

3408. (25-9-2007) NEW DELHI : The Ministry of Health & Family Welfare, Government of India, in the public interest, decided to increase the number of MBBS seats in JIPMER, Puducherry from 75 to 100. However, due to administrative reasons, the enhanced admissions in this Institute will take effect from the Academic Year 2008-09 onwards.

3409. (25-9-2007) NEW DELHI : India got re-elected to the International Civil Aviation Organization (ICAO) Council on 23rd September 2007 during the 36th ICAO Assembly session being held at Montreal. India has been elected consistently to the ICAO Council since its inception and the elections are held once in three years. The 36th Assembly commenced on 18th September 2007 and will conclude on 28th September 2007. An Indian delegation headed by Shri Ashok Chawla, Secretary, Ministry of Civil Aviation and including the Director General of Civil Aviation, Shri K. Gohain, Chairman, Airport Authority of India, Shri K. Ramalingam and the Joint Secretary, Ministry of Civil Aviation, Shri R.K. Singh participation in the session. Dr. Naseem Zaidi is India's representative in the ICAO. The ICAO Assembly is assisted by four Commissions set up under the Assembly. These are the Technical, Economic, Legal and the Administrative Commissions. This year Shri R.K. Singh, Joint Secretary, Ministry of Civil Aviation has been elected the Chairman of the Economic Commission. It may be noted that the International

Civil Aviation Organization (ICAO), an agency of the United Nations codifies the principles and techniques of international air navigation and fosters the planning and development of international air transport to ensure safe and orderly growth. Its headquarters are located in the Quartier International of Montreal, Canada. The ICAO Council adopts standards and recommended practices concerning air navigation, prevention of unlawful interference, and facilitation of border-crossing procedures for international Civil Aviation. In addition, the ICAO defines the protocols for air accident investigation followed by transport safety authorities in countries signatory to the Convention on International Civil Aviation commonly known as the Chicago Convention. Presently there are 190 ICAO Contracting States and India is one of them. ICAO works in close cooperation with other members of the United Nations family such as the World Meteorological Organization, the International Telecommunication Union, the Universal Postal Union, the World Health Organization and the International Maritime Organization. Non-governmental organizations which also participate in ICAO's work include the International Air Transport Association, the Airports Council International, the International Federation of Air Line Pilots' Associations, and the International Council of Aircraft Owner and Pilot Associations.

3410. (25-9-2007) NEW DELHI : Following is the text of the statement of Finance Minister, Shri P. Chidambaram during the high level event on climate change convened by the Secretary General : "The future in our Hands Addressing the Leadership Challenge of Climate Change" at the Thematic Plenary on "The Challenge of adaptation-from vulnerability to resilience" in New York yesterday: "May I begin by expressing our appreciation for the initiative of the Secretary-General in convening this High Level Event. I am confident that this event will assist in moving the process forward in the UN Framework convention for Climate Change (UNFCC). Like many developing countries, India is an energy deficient country. In 2006-07, we produced 662 billion units of electricity from all sources for a population of over a billion people. Energy is the sine qua non of development. We are obliged to explore every option available to us to produce or procure energy. However, we are profoundly concerned about environmental degradation and climate change. Our per capita consumption of energy is 530 kgoe of primary energy compared to a world average of 1770 kgoe. Our per capita emission of CO2 is among the lowest in the world: it is approximately 1 tonne per annum as against a world average of 4 tonnes per annum. Currently, developing countries bear an inordinate share of the burden of climate change, though this is due to the high-level of emissions of developed countries. Developing countries are, therefore, obliged to significantly augment their capacity to cope with and adapt to climate change. We acknowledge the principle of common and differentiated responsibilities. We uphold the view that adaptation is the key for developing countries and that it needs to be adequately resourced without diverting funds meant for development. In any case, development is the best form of adaptation. Adaptation has been integral to India's development process. We are challenged constantly by climate variability. We spend every year over 2 per cent of our GDP in development measures with strong adaptation content like cyclone warning and protection, coastal protection, flood control, drought relief, and food security. In 2001, we passed the Energy Conservation Act. We have notified an Energy Efficiency Code for new commercial buildings. A new Electricity Act was passed in 2003.

3411. (25-9-2007) NEW DELHI : "India is not a significant contributor to green house gas (GHG) emissions, nor will it be so in the foreseeable future. Nevertheless in line with the principle of "Common but differentiated responsibility", India has taken important steps to mitigate GHG emissions and adapt to climate change impact. India has also strongly promoted the Clean Development Mechanism (CDM) under the Kyoto Protocol and has the World's largest number of CDM projects. Nevertheless, India is among the countries more vulnerable to climate change. Hence, government proposes to appoint an expert committee to study the impact of climate change in India and identify the measures that have to be taken in future" Finance Minister in his Budget Speech. The Sun's rays pass through Earth's atmosphere. Much of this energy is absorbed by the surface and the atmosphere. Some radiation is reflected back towards space. Reflected energy has longer wavelength that cause molecules of greenhouse gases in the 'Troposphere', the lowest layer of the atmosphere, to move more rapidly. The rapid movement of these molecules traps heat in the Troposphere, warming the planet, creating a greenhouse effect. Trapped heat radiates back towards the Earth. What are Greenhouse gases? The gases that are effected this way are called greenhouse gases. The main ones are Carbondioxide, Water Vapour, Methane and Nitrous Oxide. The higher levels of carbondioxidee, methane and other greenhouse gases, accumulating in the atmosphere increase the natural greenhouse effect, raising the global temperature. The UN Climate Panel which has a group of 2,500 scientists from more than 130 countries predicted more droughts, heat waves, rains and slow gain in sea levels that could last over 1,000 years. The panel said global warming is manmade and has called for urgent government action to prevent irreversible damage from rising temperatures. The Montreal Protocol allows developing countries to keep increasing the production of HCPC-22, the refrigerant used in air conditioners, until 2016. Evidence has shown that the refrigerant harms the earth's ozone layer and contributes to global warming. The Montreal Protocol however, said freezing of the production should be complete by 2040. This schedule was desired in the early 1990s. The Kyoto Protocol, is the main plan, for capping emissions of greenhouse gases until 2012 but it has been severely weakened since the United States, the top source of greenhouse gases pulled out in 2001. Emission by many backers of Kyoto are far over target. A big problem is that no one has agreed what should replace HCFC-22. Perhaps switching to new commercial refrigerants could help the environment.

3412. (25-9-2007) NEW DELHI : The Indian auto component industry has enhanced its productivity and achieved substantial improvement in quality as a result of the UNIDO Partnership Programme for the Indian Auto Component Industry, which is now in the third phase of implementation since its launch eight years ago, according to an Impact Assessment of the Programme by Price Waterhouse Coopers." The partnership programme enhanced the business performance as well as the operational performance of targeted domestic small and medium enterprises (SMEs). 15 of the 30 firms (for which data was available for the phase II of the programme which began in 2002), showed growth rates that beat the industry growth rate of 62 %", the study says. The programme, which is a partnership between the United Nations Industrial Development Organization (UNIDO), the Government of India and the Automotive Component Manufacturers Association of India (ACMA), was in recognition of the need for the Indian auto components industry to not only become globally competitive by adopting global best practices in their own operations as the sector gradually opened up to foreign competition, but also to vertically extend such practices to their sub-suppliers. Around 20 companies participated in the first phase in the western region; 40 companies in phase 11 and 58 companies in the current phase III of the programme at the national level. It aimed at strengthening the SME auto component suppliers to meet the requirements of automobile manufacturers and their first tier suppliers, and enhancing productivity and overall performance to enable their inclusion in the domestic as well as global supply chains. Referring to business performance in terms of productivity, quality, delivery, safety and cost, the study states that existing customers have placed additional orders, and firms have also acquired new customers in the course of the programme. "As per representatives of many participant firms, the interventions transformed the look and feel of their shop floors to such an extent that customers who would otherwise not be inspired to place an order with them felt confident that the firm could deliver to expectation.

3413. (25-9-2007) NEW DELHI : The Memorandum of Understanding (MoU) is an agreement between the government and the 'management' of a Public Sector Enterprise (PSE). It had its origin in France, which too has had a considerable presence of public sector enterprises. The Nora Committee (1967) is credited for having recommended to the French Government this approach of performance contract. It emphasised on increased autonomy to the management along with a realistic price of output for balancing the accounts of PSEs. The Nora Committee Report essentially favoured a level playing field to the public sector enterprises vis-a-vis the private corporate sector. Since the PSEs have been set up consequent to investment decisions made within the framework of 'a national plan', the French system of 'performance contract' has been in the nature of medium term agreements (3-4 years) between the government and the PSEs coinciding with the national plan. The MoU system as introduced in India (since 1988) was for a number of years similar to the 'performance contract' of the French model. The Arjun Sengupta Committee (1984), which recommended the MoU system in India also laid emphasis on medium term contract recommending for a 5-year agreement that may be reviewed annually. Moreover, since the planning exercise laid greater emphasis on the core sectors of steel, heavy engineering, coal, power, petroleum and fertilizers, the Committee favoured MoUs to be signed in respect to these enterprises only. Sometimes delay in approvals lead to cost overruns and technological obsolescence in enterprises. Recognising this aspect of large scale corporations, the Arjun Sengupta Committee laid emphasis on greater autonomy to the management of public sector enterprises, while making them accountable at the same time, through performance evaluation.

3414. (25-9-2007) NEW DELHI : The Government has taken up number of initiatives for the protection and welfare of the children but public private-partnership is must to get desirable results in this area. This was stated by Smt. Renuka Chowdhury, Minister for Women and Child Development here today in a function organized by 'CHILDSCAPE' an NGO to facilitate street children for their outstanding achievements. Ms. Chowdhury said that setting up of Child Right Commission is an important step in the direction of child welfare but education and information of children is also very important to make them enlightened youth. She urged the private sector to come forward and help in this endeavour. Awarding street children for outstanding achievement, she said that the Government is exploring various options for education, health care and training of the street children with the help of private sector. She said that all the children are the assets of the nation and it is the duty of every citizen to see that all possible opportunities are provided to the children for their development. On the occasion, the Minister awarded certificate and cash prizes to:-Mohd. Ismail: A rag picker at Saket, working actively for community teaching of street children.-Master Sankar: a rag picker at Basant Lok community. He not only goes to school, but also ensures that all 12 children from his slum attend school.-Master Malik: a student of childscapes Bansant Lok and has today got a job and is self-sustainable.-Master Ajay: a young enterprising student who has shown extreme dedication. He ensures that all the other fellow children do not miss the class.-Master Anwar: supports in counselling on drug abuse of fellow students.

3415. (25-9-2007) NEW DELHI : Power Finance Corporation (PFC) has bagged the prestigious "Golden Peacock Award for Excellence in Corporate Governance" (National Award category) for the year 2007. Dr. V.K. Garg, CMD, PFC received the award at a special function attended by business leaders, corporate governance experts and policy makers from 34 countries in London on 20th September, 2007. The Award scheme for Corporate Governance was instituted in January 2001 by "World Council For Corporate Governance" (WCFCG) and Centre for Corporate Governance (CFCG) to encourage initiatives in Corporate Governance globally and in India. Golden Peacock Awards are the highest accolades of corporate excellence in quality, corporate governance, corporate social responsibility, innovation, training, environment management, technological leadership and business leadership. They provide not only worldwide recognition and prestige but also a competitive advantage in operations. The awards are considered unique for they have meticulously defined and transparent selection criteria and is determined by highly elaborate and independent assessment process. The award winners also got an opportunity to present their Corporate Governance initiatives to the largest collection of corporate governance experts and business leaders at the '8th International Conference on Corporate Governance' held in London on 20th September, 2007.

3416. (25-9-2007) NEW DELHI : All tax deductors / collectors are required to file the TDS / TCS returns in Form No.24Q (for tax deducted from salaries), Form No.26Q (for tax deducted from payments other than salaries) or Form No.27EQ (for tax collected at source). These forms require details of all tax deductions with name and permanent account number (PAN) of parties from whom tax was deducted. However, it has been observed that in most of the TDS / TCS returns, the PAN of the deductees is either missing or incorrect. As the requirement of filing TDS / TCS certificates has been done away with, the lack of PAN of deductees is creating difficulties in giving credit for the tax deducted and collected. It has, therefore, been decided that TDS returns for salaries, *i.e.* Form No.24Q with less than 90% of PAN data, and TDS returns for payments other than salaries and TCS returns, *i.e.* Form No.26Q and Form No.27EQ respectively, with less than 70% of PAN data will not be accepted for the quarter ending on 30.9.2007 and thereafter. Tax deductors and tax collectors are, therefore, advised to obtain correct PAN details of all deductees and quote the same in the TDS / TCS returns, failing which the TDS / TCS returns will not be accepted and all penal consequences under the Income Tax Act will follow. Taxpayers liable to TDS / TCS are also advised to furnish their correct PAN with their deductors, failing which they will also face penal proceedings under the Income Tax Act. For and from the quarter ending 30.9.2007, in addition to government offices and companies, filing of TDS / TCS returns in electronic form is mandatory for (i) deductor / collector required to get his accounts audited under section 44AB of the Income-tax Act in the immediately preceding financial year, and (ii) where the number of deductees' / collectees' records in a quarterly statement for any quarter of the immediately preceding financial year is equal to more than fifty. TDS / TCS returns in paper form will no longer be accepted from such tax deductors / collectors.

3417. (25-9-2007) NEW DELHI : The President of India said that I consider it a privilege to participate at the inaugural function of the 53rd Commonwealth Parliamentary Conference. It is after a gap of sixteen years that we, in India, have the opportunity once again to welcome Parliamentarians from the Commonwealth nations to our country. On behalf of the people of India and on my own behalf, I take this opportunity to wish you all, a pleasant stay and a successful Conference. I am particularly pleased that the Conference has chosen to address the theme "Delivering Democracy and Sustainable Development", a very relevant topic on which undoubtedly Parliamentarians can provide very useful insights. I am equally pleased about the Commonwealth Women's Parliamentary Conference that was held yesterday. Women constitute nearly half of the world population and their participation in elected bodies is fundamental for the effective functioning of a democracy. Similarly, there can be no doubt that a woman's perspective is indispensable for a broad-based and a balanced development process. Women should be fully involved and brought to the forefront of sustainable development efforts. Harnessing their wisdom and expertise in various fields, could be of immense value particularly to the developing countries. Development programmes should be gender-sensitive and should specifically address issues and concerns of women in different sectors. Women continue to face the challenge of breaking through the "glass ceiling" but they have made some inroads and have proved to be highly successful professionals, in varied fields, as astronauts, doctors, lawyers, bankers, entrepreneurs etc. However, the fact remains that women's participation needs to be increased whether in public life or in economic activities or indeed in society itself. I hope that this Conference will focus on these issues in depth. The Commonwealth is a family of sovereign states, representing more than two billion people, with diverse languages, cultures and customs spread over several continents. But they are all held together by a common allegiance to the basic values of democracy, faith in the rule of law and cooperation among nations for peace and prosperity. Speaking about India's decision to join the Commonwealth, Jawaharlal Nehru, our first Prime Minister, said in 1949 and I quote, "it is necessary that we touch upon the world's problems, not with passion and prejudice?. but in a friendly way and with a touch of healing ?. We have begun this new association with a touch of healing." In our contemporary world, full of strife and conflict, there is an acute need for a healing touch, where the stronger helps the weaker and the developed, the less developed. India is one of the oldest members of the Commonwealth Parliamentary Association and represents the world's largest democracy with an electorate of more than 670 million. In India, the roots of democracy are firm and deep.

3418. (25-9-2007) NEW DELHI : The Vice President Mohd. Hamid Ansari Conveyed his hearty congratulations to the members of the Indian cricket team that took part in the Twenty-20 World Cup tournament. The Vice Present noted that the performance of the team was superb throughout the tournament and rached its climax in today's final match. The team deserves all appreciation for their outstanding contribution to the game of cricket.

3419. (25-9-2007) NEW DELHI : The Union Minister of Shipping, Road Transport and Highways, Thiru T.R. Baalu has approved a sum of Rs. 4907.57 lakh for strengthening and widening of 23 road stretches in different parts of the state of Gujarat for a total length of Rs. 253.33 km. The approval has been given under the Central Road Fund (CRF) Scheme of the Ministry of Shipping, Road Transport & Highways. An amount of Rs. 2639.52 lakh has been sanctioned for strengthening and widening various stretches of the State Highways for a total length of 99.8 km in the Districts of Amhedabad, Anand, Sabarkantha, Mehsana,

Banaskantha, Gandhinagar, Godhara, Bharuch, Surat and Navsari. An amount of Rs. 664.32 lakh has been approved for construction of Service Road parallel to NH-8C at Chiloda-Gandhinagar Section and another service road parallel to the same highway at Chiloda-Gandhinagar-Sarkhej Road. Further, an amount of Rs. 1603.73 lakh has been approved for strengthening various stretches of Major District Roads (MDRs) at a total length of 146.53 km in the Districts of Sabarkantha, Patan, Panchmahal, Dahod, Surat, Navsari, Valsad, Rajkot, Jamnagar, Bhavnagar and Amreli.

3420. (25-9-2007) NEW DELHI: Rahul Gandhi, 37, was on Monday appointed Congress general secretary and inducted into the Congress Working Committee (CWC) in an indication that the party is preparing for early elections and that the scion of the Nehru-Gandhi dynasty is being groomed for higher and heavier responsibilities. Party workers welcomed his appointment, bursting crackers and distributing sweets. Congress president Sonia Gandhi also revamped the Manifesto Committee with the appointment of heavyweights including Pranab Mukherjee, Arjun Singh, Veerappa Moily, Digvijay Singh, Mani Shankar Aiyar, Arjun Sengupta and P. Chidambaram. Signalling a generational shift in the party, Ms. Gandhi set up a new cell, 'Group to look into future challenges', in which several members of the "young brigade" have found a place. They include Mr. Rahul Gandhi, Jyotiraditya Scindia, Sachin Pilot and Sandeep Dikshit. Union Minister of State for Commerce Jairam Ramesh will be the convener. Following in his father Rajiv Gandhi's footsteps, who became general secretary after having been elected to the Lok Sabha in the 1980s, the young Amethi MP is now ready to play a "larger institutional role" in the Congress, a senior leader said. Mr. Rahul Gandhi has been given charge of the Youth Congress and the National Students Union of India. Several first-time MPs and three Ministers of State have been inducted into the All-India Congress Committee, triggering speculation of a reshuffle in the government. Sunil Dutt's daughter Priya Dutt, Jitendra Prasada's son Jitin Prasad, Ram Niwas Mirdha's son Harender Mirdha, Rajiv Shukla, Abdul Mannan of West Bengal, Kodikunnil Suresh of Kerala, Madhu Goud Yashki of Andhra Pradesh, Mehboob Ali Kaiser Alka Lamba and Meenakshi Natarajan of NSUI have been made secretaries. While Minister of State Ajay Maken, Arun Kumar of Andhra Pradesh and Bihar leader Ashok Kumar are the new faces in the CWC, permanent invitees Noor Bano, M.M. Jacob and Harikesh Bahadur have been dropped. Ahmed Patel continues as political secretary to the Congress president. Veteran Mohsina Kidwai has been appointed general secretary in charge of Kerala, Lakshadweep, West Bengal and the Andaman and Nicobar Islands, and the Mahila Congress.

3421. (25-9-2007) NEW DELHI : The Prime Minister said here today that it is a matter of great pride for India to host the 53rd Annual Commonwealth Parliamentary Association Conference. I deeply regret missing the opportunity of participating in this important Conference, which has brought together people from a large number of countries. I welcome all the Parliamentarians, delegates and officials to the Conference. We in India are honoured to have you here as our guests. India has been an active member of the Commonwealth and has contributed on every front where the organization has played a role. I look back on this long association with the Commonwealth with a sense of pride and fulfilment. I reaffirm once again our deep and abiding commitment to the ideas and ideals that the Commonwealth has come to be associated with. Of all the principles that have defined and motivated the Commonwealth, none is more important than our shared commitment to democracy, to an open society, to an open economy, to the rule of law and to Fundamental human freedoms. I do sincerely believe that many of us in the Commonwealth have much to share with other countries in the common human quest for freedom and democracy. We are all proud of our plural, multi-religious, multi-lingual, multi-ethnic and multi-cultural societies. In the 20th century the Commonwealth symbolized the peaceful transition from colonialism to freedom. In the 21st century the Commonwealth will come to symbolize the hopes and aspirations of all humanity to live in an open society and an open economy. Given the unique composition of our membership-spanning continents, bridging the North-South divide and including all races and religions we in the Commonwealth have the opportunity of creatively addressing the great challenges facing humankind today. The most important of these challenges is that of poverty, and the social, economic, political and ecological consequences of poverty. The Commonwealth is a storehouse of experience and knowledge and we must put these to good use to banish mass poverty in our lifetime. There are other issues of global concern such as terrorism, the threat of climate change and the preservation of our environment that need our urgent attention. I hope this Conference will address these important issues and impart new energy to the Commonwealth. As representatives of the people, you are best placed to reaffirm our shared commitment to the principles of democracy and to the equality of all peoples and nations that have come to define the Commonwealth. I wish the Conference all success.

3422. (25-9-2007) NEW DELHI : India has been elected as a Member of International Organisation for Standardisation (ISO) Council for the term 2008-2009. The council is the highest governing body of the International Standards Organisation. The Council decides on policy issues relating to formulation of ISO Standards, quality verification system, identifying needs of standardisation of developing countries etc. It has 18 members who are elected from the General Body of the ISO which has 158 Member countries. Bureau of Indian Standards (BIS) is a founder member of ISO and represents Indian interests on this international body. By becoming the member of the ISO Council, India would be at an advantageous position to influence the functioning of the ISO and effectively safeguard the interests of the Indian industry and the consumers. Earlier India represented in ISO Governing Council in 2002-2003. Elections were held during 30th General Assembly Annual Meeting of ISO at Geneva. The Indian delegation to the ISO General Assembly was led by Shri Y.S. Bhave, Secretary, Ministry of Consumer Affairs and consisted of senior officials of BIS including its Director General Shri Sayan Chatterjee.

3423. (25-9-2007) NEW DELHI : Work on the ambitious Rohtang tunnel will commence next financial year beginning April, 2008. Disclosing this on a visit to the proposed tunnel site in Manali the Minister of State for Defence Shri MM Pallam Raju said that the project costing over 1,300 crores would be completed by 2013, a year in advance. Eight joint venture firms, in partnership with a foreign company, have been shortlisted for the project added Lt.General KS Rao, Director-General Border Roads (DGBR). The tenders are under scrutiny with the Defence Ministry and a decision would be taken soon, Shri Raju said. The tunnel, which would be the highest in the world, will make the strategic Manali-Leh highway an all-weather road. It would also reduce the journey between Manali and Sarchu by nearly 50 kms. Presently, road link with Ladakh region remains cut off from the rest of the country for over six months between November and April. General Rao said the Rohtang tunnel would be wide enough to meet the future needs and even container-trawlers would be able to drive through it.

3424. (26-9-2007) NEW DELHI : RailTel Corporation of India, a public sector undertaking under the Ministry of Railways, plans to extend its Optical Fibre Communication (OFC) network from about 2900 railway stations covering 30000 route kms at present to 5000 railway stations in the country covering 45000 route kms to provide bandwidth and multi-media services. The seventh Foundation Day ceremony of RailTel was organized at National Rail Museum, New Delhi today. Speaking on the occasion Shri S.K. Vasishta, Managing Director, RailTel Corporation said that RailTel is now a profit-earning PSU, taking into account the provisional earnings during the first quarter of the current financial year. Shri Vasishta said that the objective of RailTel is to penetrate the corporate segment including banking and financial markets, manufacturing industries, research and educational institutions to,meet the fast growing demands of MPLS-VPN services, corporate leased lines and internet leased lines in these institutions. He said that Railtel's data connectivity at every railway station on the OFC route is enabling large scale opening of Passenger Reservation System (PRS)/Unreserved Ticketing System (UTS) facilities thus benefiting common people even at remote stations. RailTel which emerged as the major telecom service provider with a motto 'Connecting India with Fibers' has today announced, on the occasion of its 7th foundation day function, the launch of various innovative services including passenger amenities at railway stations. RailTel has a plan of setting up feature packed cyber cafes initially at 82 Railway stations under the brand name of "Cyber Express". These are next generation cafes with facilities for web browsing at broadband speed, e-mailing, Internet Gaming, Internet Telephony, Scanning, Printing, Photocopying, faxing and video conferencing – all under one roof.

3425. (26-9-2007) NEW DELHI : In the Press Release titled "Mobile Train Exhibition on 150 years of 1857 gets underway day after", second sentence please read "Human Resource Development Minister Shri Arjun Singh will flag off the train." and not as rendered.......

3426. (26-9-2007) NEW DELHI : Eight envoys presented their credentials to the President of India, Smt. Pratibha Devisingh Patil at a ceremony at Rashtrapati Bhavan here today. The Envoys who presented their credentials were:-His Excellency Mr. Marc Courte, the Ambassador of Luxembourg, His Excellency Mr. Jerome Bonnafont, the Ambassador of France, Her Excellency Ms. Ann Ollestad, the Ambassador of Norway, His Excellency Mr. Miguel Angel Ramirez Ramos, the Ambassador of Cuba, His Excellency Mr. Jean-Marie Deboutte, the Ambassador of Belgium, His Excellency Mr. Charles Richard Vernon Stagg, the High Commissioner of the United Kingdom, Her Excellency, Ms. Daniele Smadja, the Ambassador of the European Commission and His Excellency, Mr. Hardijs Baumanis, the Ambassador of Latvia. The President, during her interaction with the Heads of Missions, stated that India was committed to promote peace and prosperity in the world. Smt. Patil stressed on the need for the international community to unitedly combat terrorism. The President also said that India seeks friendly relations with all countries and would work towards further strengthening ties by increasing trade and investment, as well as through enhanced people to people contacts, student and cultural exchanges. The credential presentation ceremony was attended by the senior members of the diplomatic missions, senior officials of the Ministry of External Affairs and of the Rashtrapati Bhavan. *****NSK/JS

3427. (26-9-2007) NEW DELHI : Following is the text of Prime Minister, Dr. Manmohan Singh's remarks at the book release function of Dev Anand's autobiography 'Romancing with Life' here today: It is really an honour for us to have Shri Dev Anandji here with us on his 84th birthday. I join millions of his admirers and well-wishers all over the world in wishing him a long, healthy and even more creative life in years to come. At 84, he is not only young at heart, but also youthful to look at. I am sure that for several generations of his fans, he will always be remembered as a delightfully romantic and endearing artist. He is possibly one of the most enduring romantics in the last half century. It is only fitting, therefore, that Dev Anandji has titled his autobiography "Romancing with Life". However, it would be wrong for us to conclude, either from the title of his autobiography or from the delightful happiness of many of his films, that Dev Anandji's own youth was one of fun and frolic. Hailing from a middle class family of modest means, he lived through a childhood and youth marked by deprivation and dislocation. Like thousands of young men and women of his generation whose lives were disrupted by the trauma of Partition, Dev Anandji too was forced to migrate to free India from what is now Pakistan. I am aware that he lived a life of great difficulty when he first arrived in Mumbai in search of a new life. The trials and tribulations of those difficult years did not, however, warp his personality not did they stunt his talent. He soon discovered his true calling in the world of Indian cinema. And Indian cinema discovered the immortal Dev Anand. He rose to be one of the trinity who ruled the heart of every Indian – Raj Kapoor, Dilip Kumar and Dev Anand. He has possibly acted with every top heroine over five decades – from Suraiya and Waheeda Rehman to Madhubala and Zeenat Aman. The range of themes he has covered in his movies is extensive. Who can forget the challenging roles he essayed in Guide, Hum Dono and Prem Pujari? Dev Anandji's life is a tribute to the world of opportunity and creativity that the Indian film industry has come to represent. Many talented young men and women have been able to live their dreams and earn their livelihood and make their mark thanks to the creativity and enterprise of filmmakers like Dev Anand. I salute their creativity, I salute their sense of enterprise, I salute their sense of compassion and above all, their deep patriotism. The Indian film industry, especially the Hindi film industry, has shaped the psyche of post-Independence India in many ways. No other institution has been as successful in achieving the emotional integration of this vast and diverse land of ours as our film industry has been. It is not official Hindi, or Government Hindi, that unites the length and breadth of this country but in fact popular spoken Hindi, as popularized by our Hindi cinema. It is a unique language, a mix of shudh Hindi, of spoken dialects like Bhojpuri and Hyderabadi, and of spoken languages like Urdu and Marathi. This unique mix of conversational Hindi from across the country, popularized by the film industry, has become the thread that weaves us all together as Indians. I would, therefore, like to take this opportunity to pay tribute to the Hindi film industry and to its tallest leaders like Dev Anandji. I am not a regular movie-goer and cannot claim to know much about recent trends in Indian cinema. But, I do know for a fact that wherever I go in the world, the Indian film industry has made its presence felt everywhere. From the islands of the Pacific to those of the Atlantic, from the southernmost tip of Africa to the icy deserts of Siberia, from the towns of West Africa to the cities of East Asia, from the suburbs of North America to villages across Asia-around the world, across the globe, the sun never sets on Indian films. Hollywood may have more money invested in it, it may be a bigger business, but I am sure that more people across the world actually watch Bollywood movies! More people laugh and shed tears, more people sing and cheer watching an Indian film. We must, therefore, pay a special tribute to artists like Dev Anandji for their contribution to this great saga of creativity and enterprise that Indian film industry represents. I hope his autobiography will inspire newer generations of Indians to aspire for a life of even greater creativity. His is a classic rags to riches life, where those riches have been earned through dint of sheer hard work and dedication. Dev Anandji's life mirrors India's own progress.

3428. (26-9-2007) NEW DELHI : A delegation of AICC General Secretaries met the Prime Minister, Dr. Manmohan Singh today and requested that the coverage of the National Rural Employment Guarantee Act should be extended to the entire country. The delegation discussed the expansion of the National Rural Employment Guarantee Act to uncovered areas of the country. They mentioned that the National Rural Employment Guarantee Act is a landmark legislation of the UPA government. It is also one of the important promises in the Congress Party manifesto and a key element of the National Common Minimum Programme. The delegation highlighted that the passage of this Act and its implementation in many parts has been widely welcomed across the length and breadth of the country. For the first time, the poor people of the country have been given a legally enforceable right to get minimum employment for 100 days. The Act has provided relief to those in distress and made a significant difference to the lives of the rural poor who have used it to secure relief wherever they had no other source of livelihood. Its popularity can be assessed from the widespread demand to extend it to other parts of the country. The Act itself has an inbuilt commitment to roll it out to cover the entire country. Keeping in view the commitment made by the government under the Act and the need to provide this legal right to all citizens of the country, the delegation of the Congress Party requested the government to immediately extend the coverage of the Act to all uncovered rural areas. This would double coverage from the current level of 330 districts to over 600 districts. Such a measure, it added, would be in the interest of the aam aadmi, would reinforce this government's commitment to eradicating poverty and be widely welcomed as an important welfare measure. The Prime Minister assured the Congress Party delegation that their request would be given serious consideration. He further assured them that a decision on the matter would be taken shortly by the Government. The delegation consisted of Shri Rahul Gandhi, Shri Veerappa Moily Shri Ashok Gehlot, Shri Janardan Dwivedi, Shri Kishore Chandra Deo, Shri Mukul Wasnik, Smt Margaret Alva, Shri Prithviraj Chavan, Shri V Narayanaswamy, Shri Satyavrat Chaturvedi and Shri V Arun Kumar.

3429. (26-9-2007) NEW DELHI : "Grama Seva Kendra Realises Gandhiji's Dream" Far from His birth place in Gujarat, the ideals, visions and teachings of Mahatma Gandhiji, the father of Nation, take wings here at the Gandhi Smaraka Grama Seva Kendra(GSGSK)at S L Puram, Alappuzha District, Kerala. It is the district branch of the Gandhi Memorial National Trust, New Delhi and is celebrating its golden jubilee this year. On April 1, 1958 this branch was established in connection with the rehabilitation of leprosy patients of Mararikulam Leprosy Foundation Hospital and their families. Since then, the GSGSK has been engaged in building a new social order-a casteless and classless society with equal opportunities in development-in accordance with the wishes and aspirations of Mahatma Gandhi. The Kendra has added a new dimensions to village oriented social development fulfilling the aspirations of Bapuji who sensed the soul of India in the villages. The territorial jurisdiction of the GSGSK is Alappuzha district encompassing 71 gram panchayaths, 12 block panchayaths and 5 municipalities. The total population of the district is 21,05,349 (Census, 2001). The strategies adopted by the GSGSK to achieve the goals are multifaceted and interrelated. The people at the grass root level and upwards are organized and networked by inculcating in them the spirit of cooperation and self reliance. The centre continuously makes researches for the most appropriate technologies for its clients by establishing close liaison with reputed organizations, Government Departments and Universities. The major objectives of GSGSK includes national as well as international unity, peace and amity, communal and social harmony and brotherhood, eradication of communal and provincial distinctions, alcoholic and other narcotic drugs. It is also keen to promote Khadi, handicrafts and other village and cottage industries. Educational reconstruction through "Nai Thalim" or new education (Pre-basic, basic and post-basic) is another important aim of GSGSK. Adult education, education in health, hygiene, sanitation, organization of health service, promotion of the National language-Hindi and all other regional languages of India, promotion of the SHG for the progress of women and welfare of children. Social and economic equality of women and depressed class etc. also form the part of the major activities of the centre. The Kendra has adopted a holistic development approach towards crops, livestock and fishery of Alappuzha which has basically an agrarian economy.

3430. (26-9-2007) NEW DELHI : Council of Scientific and Industrial Research, CSIR today celebrated its 65th Foundation Day with great enthusiasm. Shri Kapil Sibal, Union Minister for Science & Technology and Earth Sciences gave away the CSIR Young Scientist Awards 2007 and the CSIR Technology Awards 2007 at a function organized in New Delhi to mark the occasion. In his address, the Minister said that CSIR has done well to build up the scientific and technological capability in the country and support industry in the past when the endeavour was for technological self-reliance. However, in this era of global competitiveness, CSIR has to be sensitive and alert to the changing needs of the industry and continuously reposition its programmes and operations to be cost-effective and responsive to the market, he emphasized. Shri Sibal suggested that with all the goodwill and support that CSIR enjoys today, it should forge ahead boldly with its programmes that apply the great prowess of science to meet the basic human needs of our people, generate research scientists in cross-disciplinary sunrise areas of S&T, build up competence, capability and technology options in the emerging areas like biotechnology, nanotechnology, new materials and IT, and partner in greater measure with Indian industry both small and big to enable it to compete globally. Emphasizing that the future lies in innovation – not only in manufacturing but also in agriculture, services and governance as well, the Minister said that there is a need to focus and concentrate on leveraging our strengths and opportunities to unleash India's innovation potential. Prof. MS Swaminathan, Chairman, MS Swaminathan Research Foundation, Chennai, graced the occasion as Guest of Honour. In his address he called upon CSIR to consider initiating a PAN-CSIR Project relating to the generation of opportunities for skilled, non-farm employment in rural India. He said there is a vast array of technologies in CSIR laboratories in relation to post-harvest processing and value addition, biomass utilization and efficient natural resources management which if transferred to the field will bring immense joy and benefit to rural families. Prof. P Balaram, Director, Indian Institute of Science, Bangalore, delivered the CSIR Foundation Day Lecture on "Measuring & Assessing Science". On the occasion the Shanti Swarup Bhatnagar Prizes for 2007 were announced by Dr. T Ramasami, Director General, CSIR. He also named the winners of CSIR Diamond Jubilee Technology Award 2007 and CSIR Award for S&T Innovation in Rural Development.

3431. (26-9-2007) NEW DELHI : The Mobile Train Exhibition, on celebration of 150 years of 1857 and 60 years of independence gets underway on September 28 from New Delhi. Human Resource Development Minister Shri Arjun Singh will flag off the train. The Exhibition will journey throughout the country for eight months and would conclude on May 15, 2008.During its journey, it would pass through 70 destinations across the country. In sojourn, it would be stationed at these destinations from 2-5 days each, when general public can visit it and experience the spirit of freedom movement through visual medium. The Exhibition depicts the crowning moments of the history of our struggle for freedom, captured in images. Through it, one can travel back into the days of patriotic fervour and the spirit of national struggle for independence. It also depicts the march of our democracy since independence and epoch-defining events of our modern history. The Exhibition would make depictions by means of photographs, diaroma, cut outs, scrollers and videos. It would have various sections giving a chronology of the last 150 years of India's history. Rise of the spirit of freedom, struggle to achieve it events leading to Quit India Movement of 1942, the Partition of India. The transfer of power and making of the Constitution are reflected through the Exhibition. The exhibition also includes various social movements like the indigo farmers issue, Champaran incidents, the rise of the nationalist press, patriotic literature, Bhoodan Movement of Acharya Vinoba Bhave and participation of the women in the freedom struggle. Books, cards and mementos on 1857 and freedom struggle themes will be available at special sale counters in Mobile Train Exhibition the visitors. The exhibition is expected to be an inspirational tool for the younger generation, by providing a peep into our freedom struggle and march forward to prosperity. A project of Directorate of Advertising and Visual Publicity (DAVP), Ministry of Information & Broadcasting, the Mobile Exhibition is part of celebrations commemorating the first war of independence and diamond anniversary of India's independence.

3432. (26-9-2007) CHENNAI: Chief Minister M. Karunanidhi on Tuesday said that communal forces were conspiring to create law and order problems in the State to stop the Sethusamudram project. The people of Tamil Nadu have had to wait till the United Progressive Alliance government came to power at the Centre to implement their long-cherished dream, the Sethusamudram project. Many had tried to implement the project but there were many hindrances. Though the Vajpayee government had issued an order for the implementation of the project and Bharatiya Janata Party Ministers signed it, there was no forward movement. Now when the project was being implemented and at a time when the people of the State were looking forward to reap the consequent economic benefits, some realised that if the project made progress the DMK and its allies would get credit for realising this dream. The opponents were desperately looking to stop the progress of the project and decided to inflame communal passions, he alleged. These elements sought to ensure that the project was not implemented and they had sought to unleash violence to achieve their goal, he said. He claimed that they planned to indulge in violence and were plotting to decide on whom to apportion the blame. Mr. Karunanidhi urged the allies and DMK cadres to be on the lookout for such elements and foil their designs. It was the duty of all to protect law and order. Since the DMK and its allies were in power both at the State and the Centre, these elements were trying to create a situation where the government would be blamed for law and order problems. It was as part of this that a leader had spoken about harming him. The allies should also create awareness among the people of how anti-social elements exploited the circumstances to create trouble, he said.

3433. (26-9-2007) NEW DELHI : The new Chairman of the Congress Media department, Shri Veerappa Moily, addressed the media today and introduced his team of media spokespersons. Present on the dais were Shri Abhishek Singhvi, Smt. Jayanti Natarajan, Shri Mohan Prakash and media secretary, Shri Tom Vadakkan. Shri Moily welcomed the mediapersons by saying that it is not altogether a new team. I am only new to this team. Our dear friends Shri Abhishek Singhvi, Smt. Natarajan and Shri Mohan Prakash and of course your constant company Shri Tom Vadakkan have been working with you. Often I used to meet you in different capacities. Now I have been given a new role as the chairman of the Media department of AICC. In that new responsibility I am new to you. All of them you know very well and have interacted with them. I have also interacted with you a number of times on various issues. Our secretary has been very close to you all and all of you have had a long innings. I propose to set an agenda for a pro-active Media department, which will be accessible to you 24X7. It will be accessible to you because the Congress Party believes in transparency and responsiveness and the role the Media has to play in this nation. He ended by saying that all my colleagues and I will be available to you 24 hours. Smt. Jayanti took over and addressed the Media. She reiterated Smt. Sonia Gandhi's statement congratulating the Cricketing team on winning the Twenty 20 World Cup. I would like to add here, on behalf of the Party, that just two days ago the Indian National Congress effected a major organisational reshuffle. The highlight of which was the induction of Shri Rahul Gandhi as General Secretary in-charge of Youth Congress and the NSUI. Along with him a number of young MPs and young Congress leaders have been inducted into the organizational structure. A vast majority of our country's population is young people. It is fundamentally important for the nation to hear the voice of youth and recognise their special needs of development. As we are all aware the youth have always been at the forefront of social and developmental change. The nation cannot forget that it was the determined and dynamic leadership provided by Shri Rajiv Gandhi which galvanized our country with the technological revolution and took us into the 21st Century as a technological superpower. The youth of today have their own needs, aspirations and vision of development and it is an important recognition of the potential of the youth that a young team led by Shri Rahul Gandhi has been inducted into the AICC. In the forthcoming days they will lead a youth revolution and push forward the message of development to the remotest corners of India. The new AICC team represents a harmonious blend of youth and experience. The Party will work as a cohesive and effective entity under the leadership of Congress President Shrimati Sonia Gandhi and Prime Minister Dr. Manmohan Singh. To a question whether Rahul Gandhi was being projected as a prime ministerial candidate, Shrimati Jayanti Natarajan said that I am only asserting that Shri Rahul Gandhi will be at the forefront of galvanizing the youth power in the Party and in the country just as his father did. To a question that there is a sonrise happening in the BJP also as BJP chief's son has been inducted to lead their youth wing is the BJP trying to imitate the Congress dynastic rule, Smt. Jayanti said first of all Shri Rahul Gandhi cannot be compared to the person you have mentioned because Shri Rahul Gandhi has been elected as a Member of Parliament by the people of Amethi in a democratic way. It's not a question of being inducted as a yuva morcha president. Why the BJP has done this is a question for them to answer. It is a matter of internal BJP dynamics and I would best leave it to them to answer this question.

3434. (26-9-2007) NEW DELHI : Prof. Saifuddin Soz, the Union Minister for Water Resources was presented a dividend cheque of Rs. 2.40 crores for the year 2006-07 by the CMD, WAPCOS Shri D. Dutta, here today. Water and Power Consultancy Services (India) Ltd. (WAPCOS) has declared dividend of 120 % of its paid up capital for the year 2006-07, highest ever since its inception in 1969. WAPCOS has performed exceedingly well consistently during the last four years and has been placed in the 'Excellent' category by the Department of Public Enterprises (DPE), Government of India for the fourth time in succession. WAPCOS is a "Mini Ratna", Government of India Enterprise under the aegis of Union Ministry of Water Resources. It provides consultancy services in the critical areas of water resources, power and infrastructure development. It has ongoing projects in Afghanistan, Cambodia, Zimbabwe, Bhutan, Ethiopia, Laos, Lesotho, Zambia, Uganda, Swaziland, Eritrea, Rwanda, Sudan and almost all States in India.

3435. (26-9-2007) NEW DELHI : The Minister of Social Justice and Empowerment, Smt. Meira Kumar presented the Annual Awards of the National

Trust here today. The National Trust Awards is given to individuals/volunteers, NGO's and persons with disabilities for achievements in the Disability Sector. Addressing the gathering, She said that it has been a pleasure to give out the Awards to all the young achievers. Each one has been an inspiration and a role model, not only for the people with disabilities, but also for all people. She further said that each one of you now has a duty to create more awareness and make people understand that disabled people can also do many things if given the opportunity. Each Award has been specially instituted to ensure that this forms a source of encouragement for all round progress. She informed that the National Trust is now focusing on creating a platform for ensuring skill development and capacity building of people with disabilities. Therefore, Awards for innovative design and best products, are important. It is heartening to see that the innovative design is to facilitate the education of profoundly disabled people. The National Trust has set up Samarth-a Respite Care and Prolonged Stay Project. At present, there are 105 projects, running. Even in these programmes, we have made a consistent effort to encourage the participation of the local community, she added. PSmt. Meira Kumar also inaugurated the newly designed website of the National Trust. The Secretary of Social Justice & Empowerment Ministry, Smt. Veena Chhotray and Chairpersons of the National Trust, Smt. Poonam Natarajan were also present on the occasion.

3436. (26-9-2007) NEW DELHI : The President Smt. Pratibha Patil, Vice President Shri Hamid Ansari, Speaker of the Lok Sabha Shri Somnath Chatterjee, Chairperson (UPA) Smt. Sonia Gandhi were among the first to greet Prime Minister Dr. Manmohan Singh on his birthday. Smt. Sonia Gandhi called on the Prime Minister at his residence this morning. Several other Senior Congress leaders, Cabinet Ministers and Chief Ministers sent their greetings to the Prime Minister. Among those who spoke to the Prime Minister on telephone and greeted him was Shri Budhadeb Bhattacharya, Chief Minister of West Bengal. The Union Minister for Culture and Tourism Smt. Ambika Soni has said that the Expert Committee appointed by the Ministry of Culture to make suggestions for improvement of the museums in the country has submitted its report and the Government is examining the same. Inaugurating the exhibition of Nizams' Jewellery in National Museum, Delhi today she said, there is an urgent need to change the profile of museums. She said, because of the paucity of space, the existing museums are able to display only 10% of their treasure. She said efforts should be made to set up more museums in the country. She also called upon the museum fraternity to involve youth and students in museum activities in a big way. For this, the museums have to adopt a new style of presentation, the Minister added. Dr. Karan Singh, Chairman, Indian Council for Cultural Relations in his address complemented the National Museum for organizing this exhibition. He said the museums should be more 'interactive' for the benefit of the techno-savi new generation. Dr. Singh said the museums have an important role to play to provide an insight into our Archaeological and Cultural Heritage.

3437. (26-9-2007) NEW DELHI : The Small and Medium Enterprises Development Bill 2005 was enacted in June 2006 and was renamed "Micro, Small & Medium Enterprises Development Act, 2006". It became operational from October 2, 2006. The salient features of the Act are: The earlier concept of 'Industries' has been changed to 'Enterprises'. Enterprises have been classified broadly into: (1) Enterprises engaged in the manufacture/production of goods pertaining to any industry; and (2) Enterprises engaged in providing/rendering of services. Manufacturing Enterprises have been defined in terms of investment in plant and machinery (excluding land & buildings) and further classified into: (a) Micro Enterprises – investment up to Rs.25 lakh; (b) Small Enterprises – investment above Rs.25 lakh & up to Rs. 5 crore; (c) Medium Enterprises – investment above Rs.5 crore & up to Rs. 10 crore. The Service enterprises have been defined in terms of their investment in equipment (excluding land & buildings) and further classified into: (a) Micro Enterprises – investment up to Rs. 10 lakh; (b) Small Enterprises – investment above Rs. 10 lakh & up to Rs. 2 crore; (c) Medium Enterprises – investment above Rs.2 crore & up to Rs. 5 crore.It defines 'Medium Enterprises' to facilitate achievement of economies of scale. It provides statutory basis to Purchase Preference Policy for goods and services provided by micro and small enterprises. It also strengthens the legal provisions to check delayed payments to micro & small enterprises. The Act provides statutory basis to the National Board for Micro, Small & Medium Enterprises. The cumbersome two-stage registration process of SSI has been substituted with an optional filing of memorandum by Micro, Small & Medium Enterprises. The Act aims at facilitating the promotion and development of small and medium enterprises in a competitive way. It seeks to empower the Central Government to notify programmes, guidelines or instructions for facilitating the promotion and growth of small and medium enterprises. One of its primary objectives is to make provisions for ensuring timely and smooth flow of credit to small and medium enterprises.

3438. (26-9-2007) NEW DELHI : The Vice President of India and the Chairman of the Rajya Sabha Shri Mohammad Hamid Ansari has expressed his heartfelt condolences at the passing away of Rajya Sabha member and former Union Minister, Shri K. Jana Krishnamurthy. In a condolence message to his wife, Smt. Bhagyalakshmi, the Vice President noted that Shri Krishnamurthy was "always admired by the people for his dedication, sense of public service and honesty". He said: "In his death, the country has lost a noted public personality who was always alive to the social concerns of our times". The Vice President has also conveyed his condolences to the members of the bereaved family and the wide circle of his admirers and friends.

3439. (26-9-2007) NEW DELHI : "Shilpotsav" the handicrafts exhibition was inaugurated by Smt. Meira Kumar, the Minister of Social Justice and Empowerment at Dilli Haat. On the occasion, she said that in addition to providing social justice to the people through economic empowerment, our corporations are doing their best to provide marketing platform to the artisans. This is a big achievement of the Ministry to organize such a grand event. These events not only create awareness about our developmental programmes but also provide an opportunity to the artisans for interaction with potential buyers and exporters. She hoped that it will further the cause of social justice for the weaker section of the society and specially empower the women economically. The exhibition will continue till 8th October at Dilli Haat. More than 200 handicraft and folk-artisans drawn from all over the country are displaying their products. The Shilpotsav has been organized by a collective of apex organizations of Ministry of Social Justice and Empowerment; NBCFDC, NSFDC, NHFDC, NSKFDC, NISD and National Trust. The exhibition offers a visual treat of products made from bamboo work, footwear, Kalamkari, Terracotta and wood inlay etc. Products have been showcased in this exhibition cum sale by artists all over the country.

3440. (27-9-2007) NEW DELHI : The Minister of Corporate Affairs, Shri Prem Chand Gupta launched a website of Investor Education & Protection Fund (IFPF), www.iepf.gov.in here today. The website, dedicated to the education and protection of investors, is free of charge. Speaking on the occasion, the Minister assured that protection of investors' interest is government's prime concern and every necessary step would be taken for the purpose. The month of September is being observed as "Investor Awareness Month" by the Ministry of Corporate Affairs. A large number of programmes aimed at educating the investors and spreading awareness amongst them have been organized throughout the country during the month. The Institute of Chartered Accountants of India, Institute of Company Secretaries of India and the Trade and Industries Associations have actively collaborated to organize these programmes. The response of the investors to these programmes was very encouraging and they have benefited significantly from the literature distributed on various themes. As a culmination of various programmes this month, a 'National Convention on Investor Awareness' was held here today. Besides the launch of IEPF website, the Minister also released "Handbook on Capital Market Regulations", a publication of the Institute of Charterd Accountants of India, during the convention. During his address, Shri Gupta emphasized the need for transparency in the functioning of the corporate sector to generate confidence of the people in the financial market. The Minister said that the Government has taken many steps towards this directon including, legislative and administrative reforms and introduction of information technology in delivering the services. Many more initiatives are in the process, the culmination of which will pave the way for better and smoother functioning of the corporates, he said. "New Company Law is one of such initiatives, the bill for which is in the final stages of preparation. We hope to introduce it in the coming winter session of the parliament. The new law is likely to strike a fine balance between the freedom and accountability. It will also provide for a much better and stronger mechanism for protecting the interests of investors", said the Minister.

3441. (27-9-2007) NEW DELHI : Rashtriya Ispat Nigam Limited, Visakhapatnam, has won the Prime Minister's Trophy for the best performing Steel Plant for the year 2005 – 06. The award carries one crore rupees in cash. Instituted in 1992, the companies are evaluated on a slew of parameters including saleable steel capacity utilization, efficiency of operations, financial performance, export performance, quality of products, customer satisfaction, environment management, enabling parameters and observations of judges during the plant visits. The evaluation is carried out by a panel of judges led by the Secretary of Steel with management experts, economists and representatives of customers as members. The Secretary Steel Shri R. S. Pandey who conveyed the message to RINL today, congratulated the management and employees for the excellent work done. He hoped the award will motivate them in achieving new benchmarks in efficiency and productivity.

3442. (27-9-2007) NEW DELHI : India has generated a tremendous interest amongst mineral industry world over and is being keenly watched as a happening place by investors in the mining sector. This was stated by Shri J.P. Singh, Secretary, Ministry of Mines while chairing the 42nd Meeting of Central Geological Board here today. Shri Singh expressed confidence over FDI inflow increasing sharply in coming days. Referring to the important role of Geological Survey of India (GSI) in exploring minerals in the country, he informed that many countries have shown interest in collaborating with GSI in prospecting natural resources. They are seeking GSI's support in training their manpower. In the light of changes occurring in the mineral sector and also the changes suggested in the proposed New Mineral Policy, Mines Secretary stressed that GSI needs changes in their ethos enabling itself to serve the country better. He called upon State Governments to be more proactive in exploring/prospecting minerals which are backbone of the development and growth. The Board reviewed the achievements of the projects undertaken during 2006-07 and discussed and approved the Annual Programme of GSI for 2007-2008. The CGPB consisting of representatives of Central and State Government, Public Sector Undertakings and some academic institutions, is the apex body at the national level to overview the programme of geoscientific activities including mineral exploration in the country. Highlights of the GSI achievements during 2006-07 include assessment of an additional resource of 2290.14 million tonnes of coal during 2006-07 (upto June 2007). It explored additional gold ore resource of 0.48 million tonnes in Tumkur district of Karnataka, 7.32 million tonnes in Banswara district of Rajasthan.

3443. (27-9-2007) NEW DELHI : The Prime Minister, Dr. Manmohan Singh has granted a one-time ex-gratia payment of Rs. 3 lakh to the next of kin of each fisherman being held captive in Pakistan. He has also sanctioned an out-right grant of Rs 30000/- for smaller fishing boats and a grant of Rs. 5 lakh for trawlers to the owners of each boat or trawler seized. The grant is being made to ameliorate the hardships caused due to the continued retention of bread winners in captivity and to address the livelihood problems due to seizure of boats. The assistance is to be provided from Prime Minister's National Relief Fund (PMNRF). The Marine Products Export Development Authority (MPEDA) will be designated as the implementation agency. The Finance Ministry shall also liaise with the implementation agency and the Department of Animal Husbandry to develop a suitable soft loan package for the replacement of fishing craft. The Prime Minster's relief package will be in addition to all existing benefits, including those made by the Gujarat Government. The Prime Minister had received several representations from Gujarat regarding the problems being faced by the families of fishermen held in captivity in Pakistan, along with a number of memoranda regarding the problems faced by the fishermen community due to the seizure of fishing craft.

3444. (27-9-2007) NEW DELHI : Following is the text of the Finance Minister, Shri P. Chidambaram's Wharton Leadership Lecture-Indian Business – From Local to Global at Wharton School, University of Pennsylvania, USA:-"There is a nice feeling when one is at a University. More so, when one is at this University's best known school, the Wharton School. I am grateful to the Dean, the faculty and the students for inviting me to deliver a talk as part of the Wharton Leadership Lectures. I noticed that in recent years you had invited the CEOs of some of the best known companies in the United States – Xerox and Starbucks, Microsoft and PepsiCo, and Tyco and McKinsey. What do these companies have in common that have made them successful as well as household names? Each one of them is the child of an innovative idea and a leader in its business. There are many Indian business leaders who would qualify on the grounds of innovation and leadership to take a place in this series. I am here to speak on their behalf but I hope that, in due course, you will invite one of the true business leaders of India to deliver a lecture. The India story is now too well known to you. What is not known is the fact that innovation and leadership in Indian business go back over a hundred years. India's most famous business house, the Tatas, started their steel mill exactly one hundred years ago. Even before that, Indian business leaders had ventured into cotton textiles, jute and banking. All the factors of production – land, capital, labour and organization – were present in India. Yet India missed the industrial revolution. The few who dared to cross over from trading to manufacturing were perforce constrained to remain local – producing locally for the local market. Why local? Before independence in 1947, the levers of the economy were in the hands of the British and they did not allow any Indian entrepreneur to grow except under the shadow of a British company. After 1947, the Indian preference for Fabian socialism expressed itself in the form of myriad controls. The first controls on foreign exchange were imposed in 1947. In 1955, export and import trade was severely restricted. Practically, nothing could go out and nothing could come in, unless one was willing to violate the law. There was an extensive licensing regime in the manufacturing sector that restricted capacity, production, product mix, marketing and prices.

3445. (27-9-2007) NEW DELHI : The Minister for Chemicals & Fertilisers and Steel, Shri Ram Vilas Paswan will release the National Policy on Petrochemicals here tomorrow. The policy is aimed at promoting investment in upstream in downstream industries, increase production and consumption, create infrastructure and promote research and development of plastic and synthetic fibres.The global shift in consumption of petrochemicals has provided immense opportunities for petrochemicals. India's comparative advantages are huge population, availability of skilled manpower at competitive wage rate and current low per capita consumption are the major drivers for growth. Government of India has brought out the National Policy on Petrochemicals in order to take advantage of the global shift in demand and production for petrochemicals, to channelise substantial investments in this sector to support the increase demand and to use the growth in this sector as a support the increase demand and to use the growth in this sector as a "force multiplier" for the overall GDP growth, a National vision in the form of a Policy document is needed.

3446. (27-9-2007) NEW DELHI : The Tourism Ministry has identified 15 tourist destinations to be developed throughout the country and is willing to contribute Rs. 25 crore for each. This was stated by the Minister of Tourism and Culture Smt. Ambika Soni on the occasion of World Tourism Day here today. The Minister said Indian tourism industry is undergoing rapid transformation. Public-Private Partnership for tourist infrastructure creation is crucial for transforming the industry. The State Governments are forthcoming and are actively involving in the process. She said that to achieve 8.8% growth rate over the next decade, large revenue generating projects are being undertaken. For this purpose various interest groups and different aspects of tourism are being taken care to offer the best to the visitors. She said that from being the 10th most preferred tourist destination in 2004, the 4th in 2006, India has now moved to the top in 2007 underlining the importance of Public-Private Sector partnership which has a long way to go in tourism industry. Later, she interacted with the media elaborating on various projects and schemes of the Tourism Ministry. Earlier, speaking on the occasion Ms. Leena Nandan, JS (Tourism) said that on the World Tourism Day the Ministry has decided to revive 150 historic bandstands in Mumbai. An add film, a Bharat Bala production "Incredible India" based on "Saare Jahan Se Achha" theme was previewed.

3447. (27-9-2007) NEW DELHI : The Rural Development Ministry has sanctioned the construction of remaining 54 road works in Sikkim under the phase-VI of Pradhan Mantri Gram Sadak Yojana (PMGSY). With this all the 93 proposals to construct 482.26 km road length under PMGSY amounting to an outlay of Rs. 211.92 crore forwarded by the State Government of Sikkim has been cleared. Till now road construction projects amounting to Rs.298.37 crore has been sanctioned against the initial Rs. 180 crore state share of Sikkim under PMGSY and Rs.212.60 crore has been released. The Union Rural Development Minister Dr. Raghuvansh

Prasad Singh has already assured the state government of all possible cooperation towards the implementation of rural development scheme. Under PMGSY the Central Government has directed all the concerned agencies to connect all the villages with more than 1000 population with all weather roads. Enough funds are available for this purpose. In order to achieve the Bharat Nirman targets, instructions to speed up preparation of DPRs, floating of tenders and acceleration of road construction works has been issued. To ensure quality work in the entire process, MPs, MLAs and other elected representatives have been authorised to monitor the projects through the respective district vigilance and monitoring committees.

3448. (27-9-2007) NEW DELHI : Pursuant to the discussions with the representatives of five Major Federations of Port & Dock Workers on 12th of this month following which the federations agreed to unilaterally withdraw the two references pending before the Chief Labour Commissioner (Central), the Union Minister of Shipping, Road Transport & Highways, Thiru T.R. Baalu has approved the proposal for enhancing the retirement age of employees of the Major Port Trusts and Dock Labour Boards from 58 to 60 years with effect from 30th of this month (*i.e.* 30.09.2007) benefiting 66,000 dock and port workers. The Chief Labour Commissioner (Central) has confirmed to the Ministry of Shipping, Road Transport and Highways that the Federations have agreed to withdraw unilaterally the strike notice and the relevant dispute pending with the CLC during the conciliation proceedings initiated by it.

3449. (27-9-2007) NEW DELHI : The Directorate General of Quality Assurance (DGQA) is celebrating its Golden Jubilee today. In a message on the occasion, the DG of DGQA Lt Gen G Sridharan has said Contemporary Quality Management Systems coupled with our inherent organizational capabilities of knowledge, skill and zest for maintaining highest quality standards will enable DGQA to meet the challenges of technological advancements in state-of-art equipment and stores being accepted by DGQA. He said, DGQA will strive to keep pace with advancing technologies and provide weapons systems, equipment and stores of high quality to the Armed Forces for sustaining their combat effectiveness. The organization was awarded National Award for Economics of Quality by the President of India in February this year. DGQA provided services beyond call of duty in extracting live ammunition with clinical precision from tank involved in accident due to fire, thereby, avoiding accidental injury to troops and civilians of that area. The Adventure Cell of DGQA conducted a multi-dimensional exercise in Thar desert for para gliding cum para sailing camp at Sambhar lake near Jaipur. A major automation plan worth Rs. 2.32 Crore to link all Technical Directorates, Adm Directorate and Units of R&S Directorates to provide online Quality Assurance Services to users and production agencies is in the final stage. The testing capabilities of various laboratories of DGQA are being strengthened. A Predictive technology lab to ascertain the remaining shelf life of ammunition is being established at

Controllert of Quality Assurance (Armaments) Pune. The testing facilities of night vision devices at Controllert Quality Assurance (Instruments), Dehradun are being strengthened. The DGQA has entered into Reciprocal Government Quality Assurance (RGQA) agreement with various countries. Similar agreements are in offing with other countries. This would be beneficial for DGQA to align its working with prevalent international Quality Assurance practices. Considerable savings have been achieved by revising proof schedules thereby cutting down proof expenditure. A Committee has also been constituted to further reduce expenditure on proof. DGQA traces its roots to Inspectorate of Armaments established at Ammunition Factory Kirkee in 1869. With the transformation in portfolio of Weapons & Equipments, the Organisation has undergone many changes over the decades.

3450. (27-9-2007) NEW DELHI : The Union Public Service Commission will hold the Combined Medical Services Examination, 2008 on 3rd February, 2008. The examination will be held at various centres across the country. For details regarding Eligibility Conditions, Syllabus and Scheme of the Examination, Centres of Examination, Guidelines for filling up the application form etc. aspirants must consult the detailed notice of the examination published in the Employment News/ Rozgar Samachar dated 22nd September, 2007. In case of any guidance/information/ clarification regarding their applications, candidature etc. candidates can contact UPSCs Facilitation Counter near 'C' Gate of its campus in person or over Telephone No.011-23385271/011-23381125/011-23098543 on working days between 10.00 hrs. to 17.00 hrs. The Commission also has a website at address: http:// www.upsc.gov.in over which the candidates can obtain details of the examination as well as information about registration of their applications, venue of the examination and results etc.

3451. (27-9-2007) NEW DELHI : In exercise of the powers conferred by clause (1) of article 224 of the Constitution of India, the President is pleased to appoint (i) Shri Asok Potsansgbam and (ii) Shri Pranoy Kumar Musahary, to be Additional Judges of the Gauhati High Court, in that order of seniority, for a period of two years, with effect from the dates they assume charge of their respective offices.

3452. (27-9-2007) NEW DELHI : 'Azadi Express'-the Mobile Train Exhibition, on celebration of 150 years of 1857, 60 years of independence and birth centenary of Shaheed Bhagat Singh begins its journey tomorrow from New Delhi. Human Resource Development Minister, Shri Arjun Singh will flag off the train in the presence of Minister of Information & Broadcasting and Parliamentary Affairs, Shri P. R. Dasmunsi. A project of Directorate of Advertising and Visual Publicity (DAVP), Ministry of Information & Broadcasting, the Exhibition will journey throughout the country for eight months and would conclude on May 15, 2008. During its journey, it would pass through 70 destinations across the country. In sojourn, it would be stationed at these destinations from 2-5 days each, when general public can visit it and experience the spirit of freedom movement through visual medium. Azadi Express takes one on a journey through time. It begins from an era when our country was one of the richest nations of the world, to a time when we were reduced to abject poverty. India fought back, emerged victorious and came firmly back on the road to achieve its past glory. The eleven coach Exhibition depicts the 150 years of our history by way of photographs, diaroma, cutouts, scrollers and videos. Each of the first eight coaches carries a specific epoch in the freedom movement and is titled as such. They carry exhibits under various themes; Kompany Raj; The Lightening – incidents and events related to Barrackpore and Merrut when Indian soldiers revolted against the British; Fire spreads – reflecting the spread of revolt across northern and eastern India; British takeover – showing the defeat of the revolutionary forces, revengeful British campaign against the leaders and masses who took part in the uprising; National Awakening section depicts the formation of Indian National Congress, Partition of Bengal and opposition thereto, Gandhiji's emergence on the scene, draconian Rowlatt Act and Jallianwala Bagh incident; Gandhiji leads – depicts the launch of Non-Cooperation Movement and Britishers ruthless repression, Civil Disobedience Movement, Dandi March; Quit India and Azadi sections show the climax of India's freedom struggle and its culmination into Free India. Last three coaches focus on the new dawn in our national history and march forward to prosperity and the strengthening of a vibrant democracy. The Exhibition also includes various social movements like the indigo farmers issue, Champaran incidents, the rise of the nationalist press, patriotic literature, Bhoodan Movement of Acharya Vinoba Bhave and participation of the women in the freedom struggle. Books, cards and mementos on 1857 and freedom struggle themes will be available at special sale counters in Mobile Train Exhibition. The exhibition is expected to be an inspirational tool for the younger generation, by providing a peep into our freedom struggle and march forward to prosperity.

3453. (27-9-2007) NEW DELHI : Attention of the Government has been drawn to a report published in a section of the Press, today, stating that in order to control IIMs a new law is being planned. This news item is far from truth and is not based on facts. The factual position in this regard is as follows:-The IIMs in the country function under their respective Memorandum of Associations (MoAs) and rules and regulations framed thereunder. They are societies registered under the Societies Registration Act. The IIMs are public institutions and are accountable to the Parliament. Their accounts are annually audited by the Comptroller & Auditor General and their Annual Reports along with the audited accounts are submitted to the Parliament. They enjoy complete autonomy as regards the academic matters and matters relating to fees, selection of faculty, introduction of new courses, incurring of expenditure in conformity with the prudence involved in public spending etc. Though it is a fact that the three IIMs at Ahmedabad, Kolkata and Bangalore are not dependent on government funds for their day to day operational expenses, this in no way compromises their status of being public institutions. However, funds are being proposed to be given to them for their future expansion.

The Government has been examining the issue of bringing the IIMs in the country under an umbrella legislation like the Institutes of Technology Act. It may be clarified that bringing the IIMs under the ambit of a Central law will in no way alter their accountability to the Parliament or their status of being public institutions, while it will empower the IIMs to award degrees to the students which they are not competent to do so at present.

3454. (27-9-2007) NEW DELHI : The Union Minister of State for Health & Family Welfare, Smt. Panabaka Lakshmi will lead an Indian Delegation to Budapest (Hungary) where besides inaugurating the International Conference cum Exhibition on Ayurveda on 29th September 2007 will have bilateral meetings with officials of Health insurance fund, National Institute of Pharmacy, Debrecon University and Business Environment European team, Brussels.

3455. (27-9-2007) NEW DELHI : Indian Railways and Konkan Railway Corporation Ltd. are hosting this year's International Railway Safety Conference (IRSC) in Goa from 1st to 5th October 2007. More than 150 representatives from 15-20 countries including USA, Canada, Australia, Japan, France, Germany, and UK etc. will be taking part in the conference. Railway safety practitioners and other experts from all over the world including India will be sharing global experiences and best practice on 'Emerging Dimensions for Railway Safety'. The Minister of State for Railways Shri R.Velu will inaugurate the conference at 9 a.m. on 1st October 2007 at Unicon Hall of Radisson Resort Goa. Shri K.M.Singh, Member of the National Disaster Management Authority, Shri V.N.Mathur, Member Traffic, Railway Board will also be present among others at the inaugural function. International Railway Safety Conference is an annual event attended by Railway Safety Managers, Safety Regulators and Accident Investigating Agencies from all over the world. It provides a platform to the delegates from various international railway systems to exchange ideas and information on the current safety issues faced by them. The first IRSC was hosted by East Japan Railway in 1990 in Tokyo, Japan and since then, this has been held every year by some railway or the other but it is for the some time that it is being held in India. Indian Railways' sustained efforts during the recent past have resulted in more than 50 per cent reduction in consequential train accidents which have come down with from 0.65 accidents per million train kilometres in 2001-02 to the order to 0.23 in 2006-07. This conference offers immense opportunities for the world Railways help formulate future possibilities. Thirty one technical papers will be presented during the conference to specifically dwell upon subjects like Integration of Safety Management in Development Planning, Impact of Safety Enhancement Systems and Diagnostic Technologies on Human Performance, Emerging Trends on Mitigation of Third Party Hazard, and Trends and Practices of Safety Regulation and Accident Investigation.

3456. (27-9-2007) NEW DELHI : The Director-General of World Health Organization (WHO), Dr. Margaret Chan in a communication dated 17th

September 2007 has expressed her congratulations to the Union Minister for Health & Family Welfare, Dr. Anbumani Ramadoss for getting the Polio Champion Award. Appreciating the critical role in leading the polio eradication efforts in the country, the Director-General expressed confidence that India will soon become polio-free and attain a historic milestone under the chairmanship of the Minister. The following is the text of the message sent by the Director-General: "I would like to express my congratulations to you for being recently awarded the "Polio Champion Award" by Rotary International in recognition of your critical role in leading the polio eradication efforts in India. Your personal commitment and the strong support of the Government of India for polio eradication have yielded significant results during the past six months – polio in India is now primarily restricted to a few districts in two states, Uttar Pradesh and Bihar, and there has been a sharp decline in the number of type 1 polio cases in 2007. I want to reassure you that the strategic focus on combating type 1 poliovirus, even while there is a focal outbreak of type 3 polio in some districts this year, has been effective. With your continued leadership and sustained political and financial support from the Governments of India, Uttar Pradesh and Bihar in 2007-08, I am confident that India will soon become polio-free and attain a historic milestone. The World Health Organization stands ready to assist the Government of India in its efforts to deliver a perpetual gift of a polio-free world to all its children".

3457. (27-9-2007) TIRUCHI: The City unit of the Communist Party of India (CPI) has urged the district administration to take immediate steps to issue house site pattas to those living in government, poromboke and temple lands. Nearly 2000 petitions have been given to the district officials through the party, a resolution adopted at the party's City Committee meet said. The party demanded expeditious completion of underground drainage works. It also urged the district authorities to ensure that there was no short-supply of essential commodities supplied through the public distribution system.

3458. (27-9-2007) NEW DELHI : Shri K.C.Jena, Chairman, Railway Board and Chairman, IRCON International Limited, a Public sector Undertaking under the Ministry of Railways, said that IRCON public sector continuously excelling on growth path by achieving a record turnover of Rs. 1543 crore during the year 2006-07, showing an increase of 39 per cent more than that of the previous year. Addressing the shareholders at IRCON's new, state of the art environment friendly, office premises here yesterday, Shri Jena said that IRCON's dividend contribution during 2006-07 stands at Rs.25.74 crore at the rate of 260 per cent of the paid up share capital, which is 34 per cent of its post tax profits. The company, which has already executed landmark construction works in both Railway and Highway sectors in India and abroad in the last 30 years, is pursuing large value projects in Algeria, Sudan, and Malaysia. In India, IRCON is executing projects of national importance like new broad gauge Rail Link in Jammu & Kashmir, Pradhan Mantri Gram Sadak Yojna, Rashtriya Sam Vikas Yojna, Golden Quadrilateral road project, Married Accommodation Projects for defense personnel.

3459. (28-9-2007) NEW DELHI : The sensational disclosure of Sten Lindstorm, Principal Swedish Investigator vindicates the BJP's assertion that the CBI on behest of the UPA Government has been instrumental in ensuring the acquittal of Quattrocchi. The revelation that the CBI did not cooperate with the Swedish Investigator reaffirms our charge that the Government had left no stones unturned in scuttling the Quattrocchi investigations, trial and extradition. The glaring complicity of the UPA government gets further strengthened by the remark of Sten Lindstorm who categorically stated that despite Quattrocchi having direct personal links with the Gandhi family, he was denied interrogation even once. The UPA government had clandestinely intervened in de-freezing the London Bank Accounts holding the Bofors kick back amount, and thereafter the failure of the Government as well as the CBI to disclose the arrest of Quattrocchi even after 17 days of his detention amply reconfirms the complicity of the UPA Government in Quattrocchi's wrongful acquittal. The categorical reply of Lindstorm to a specific querry whether kickbacks were paid in the Bofors deal stating "Yes, to several persons & to several organization and among that Mr. Quattrocchi absolutely" continues to haunt the mind of the nation. The BJP demands that the nation deserves to once and for all know the truth behind the Bofors kickback issue and the UPA government must come clean on all accounts about its alleged complicity in ensuring the wrongful acquittal of the Quatttrocchi. The complete subversion of the independence of the CBI by the government to protect the interests of one particular family is an unfortunate exposition about the sorry state of affairs in the country.

3460. (28-9-2007) NEW DELHI : A delegation of dentists called on the Prime Minister, Dr. Manmohan Singh to present a book on oral health and HIV-AIDS. Speaking to the doctors the Prime Minister emphasized the importance of providing affordable dental care to all sections of society. The Prime Minister said that he often heard complaints that dental care was not within the reach of the poor. The Prime Minister reiterated the Government's commitment to widen access to affordable health care to all sections of society and said that this is one of the key objectives of the Government's health policy.

3461. (28-9-2007) NEW DELHI : Following is the text of Prime Minister, Dr. Manmohan Singh's remarks at the book release "Mr. & Mrs. Dutt : Memories of our Parents" by Namrata Dutt Kumar and Priya Dutt here today: "I am truly delighted to associate myself with the release of this loving book on the late Sunil Dutt and Nargis Dutt – a book that is a labour of love and a symbol of affection, respect and gratitude. I compliment young Namrata and Priya and Sanjay Dutt for this unique tribute to the memory of their beloved parents, Sunil Dutt ji and Nargis ji. This is a historic day when we celebrate the life and work of two outstanding personalities of our time and I am very happy to have this opportunity to associate myself with this function. Shri Sunil Dutt and Smt Nargis Dutt were in every sense of the term extraordinary individuals. They were true professionals, humane and at the same time human. They were true citizens of our Republic, patriotic and secular and deeply committed to the value system inhabited by us through our freedom struggle. They were public-spirited artists, tremendously creative and tremendously concerned. I salute their memory. Their life and work meant a lot not only for the world of cinema but also for the cause of nation building, at a particularly important moment in our history after independence. Both of them ruled the hearts and minds of our people with their captivating charm and calibre as artists. They cast a spell on several generations and their romance and love touched every one of their innumerable fans across the country and indeed outside our country. The film that brought Sunil Dutt and Nargisji together was in itself a milestone in the history of Indian cinema – Mother India. This immortal film brought them together and became the bedrock of their marriage. Mother India was a turning point in their lives, in the history of Indian cinema and, indeed, in the life of our young nation. Mother India reflected the determination of a young newly independent nation to stand firmly on its feet and overcome adversity – as so aptly put in the song Dukh bhare din beete re bhaiyya. Their coming together as Mr. & Mrs. Dutt, in 1958 made them a loving symbol of our composite culture. It affirmed the unity of religions, the coexistence of diverse approaches and most importantly, the harmony of outlook and perspectives in this diverse society and nation that India is. It is rare to find a couple whose life of romance, love and exceptional artistic accomplishments was so deeply influenced by their larger vision of India. In fact, it became the guiding factor in the life of both Sunil & Nargis Dutt. The Ajanta Troupe established by them went to remote frontiers to entertain our brave men in uniform defending the frontiers of our nation. To think about others and care for the underprivileged was their abiding and overriding concern. Nargisji used to visit hospitals, especially cancer hospitals, to help those ailing from cancer. She also was the founder, if I am correct of the Spastic Society and the excellent work that society is doing owes a great deal to the pioneering zeal of Nargisji. Later, when she herself became a cancer-patient and was treated abroad, she wanted something to be done for those who could not afford costly treatment outside India. Both of them played a very important role in our parliamentary life. Nargisji was an active member of the Rajya Sabha and Dutt Saheb was, till his last breath, a true soldier of the Congress Party. When Rajiv Gandhiji invited him to contest the Lok Sabha elections, Dutt Saheb had said "I thought it would be a good launching pad to express my thinking about India's unity". His historic march from Mumbai to Amritsar in 1987 to promote the cause of communal harmony and his invaluable work for riot victims, brought out what he and Mrs. Dutt stood for till the very end of their lives. Given the deep commitment of Nargisji to our celebrated values of secularism, communal harmony and social justice, it is only appropriate that the Award for Best Feature Film on National Integration is named after her.

3462. (28-9-2007) NEW DELHI : The All India Consumer Price Index Number for Industrial Workers (CPI-IW) (base 2001-100) during August 2007 increased by one point to stand at 133 (one hundred and thirty three) points. The Rise/Fall in index varied from centre to centre. The index recorded an increase of 7 points in Faridabad centre and 4 points each in Kodarma, Munger-Jamalpur and Bokaro centres, 3 points each in 8 centres, 2 points in 10 centres and 1 point in 14 centres. The index during August 2007 decreased by 2 points each in Quilon, Godavirikhani and Mercara centres and by 1 point in 16 centres, while in the remaining 23 centres the index remained stationary. The increase of 7 points in Faridabad centre was mainly on account of increase in the prices of Wheat Atta, Mustard Oil, Onion, Vegetable & Fruit items and School Fees. The increase of 4 points in Kodarma centre is mainly due to increase in the prices of Rice, Wheat, Wheat Atta, Vegetable & Fruit Items and Country Liquor. In case of Monger-Jamalpur centre it is due to Rice, Wheat, Onion and Vegetable & Fruit items, while in Bokaro centre it is due to Wheat, Wheat Atta, Mustard Oil, Onion, Vegetable & Fruit items, Bus Fare and Washing Soap. The decrease of two points in Quilon centre is mainly due to decrease in prices of Fish Fresh, Coconut, Pan (Finished) etc., in Godavarikhani centre it is due to Groundnut Oil, Goat Meat and Vegetable & Fruit items, while in Mercara centre it is mainly due to Rice, Urd Dal, Poultry and Vegetable & Fruit items. The point to point rate of inflation, based on the CPI-IW on base 2001=100 has increased from 6.45% in July, 2007 to 7.26% in August, 2007.

3463. (28-9-2007) NEW DELHI : Government of India have announced the sale (re-issue) of "5.87 percent Government Stock, 2010" under Market Stabilization Scheme for a notified amount of Rs. 4,000 crore (nominal). Government of India have also announced the sale (re-issue) of "11.30 percent Government Stock, 2010" under Market Stabilization Scheme for a notified amount of Rs. 3,000 crore (nominal). The Government Stocks will be sold through price based auction using multiple price method. The auctions will be conducted by the Reserve Bank of India, Mumbai Office, Fort, Mumbai on October 3, 2007 (Wednesday) Up to 5% of the amount notified for the sale of stock is reserved for allotment to eligible individuals and Institutions on non-competitive basis as per the Scheme for Non-Competitive Bidding Facility in the Auction of Government Securities.

3464. (28-9-2007) GWALIOR: Central Bureau of Narcotics (CBN), Gwalior, Department of Revenue, Ministry of Finance organized a workshop on precursor control for importers, exporters and manufacturers of these chemicals in Gwalior, Madhya Pradesh today. The objective of this workshop was to generate a consciousness in the trade regarding the diversion potential of these chemicals. The workshop was chaired by Smt. Jagjit Pavadia, Narcotics Commissioner of India. In the Workshop both the trade and the department made presentations on the subject and discussed the strategy to control the diversion. The Workshop was attended by around 35 representatives from the Chemical Industry, and the Officers of CBN. The representatives from the industry consisted of top executives of major companies dealing in manufacture, import, export and trading in Precursor Chemicals. During the Workshop the Narcotics Commissioner initiated the concept of Precursor Watch Programme (PWP). The concept was aimed at encouraging the stake holders to report suspicious transaction to the regulating authority. The PWP would further involve regular interaction with the industry and adoption of a Voluntary Code of Conduct. It was also discussed how to extend this programme to spread awareness regarding use of various drugs in the out reaches of the society. PWP is intended to be a movement against drugs and to evolve a public private partnership and create greater awareness about the ill-effects of drugs and strategies for drug demand reduction. Drug abuse, now a days is not limited to natural substances like opium and cannabis. Of late synthetic and semi-synthetic drugs like Cocaine, Heroine, LSD, Methaqualone, Ecstasy etc. are also abused, especially by the youth. The chemicals required for synthesis of such drugs are therefore sensitive in nature and are commonly referred to as precursor chemicals. One of the strategies to suppress the use of Synthetic Drugs is to prevent the access of these chemicals to the drug traffickers for conversion into drug of abuse, like Heroine, Methamphetamine, Cocaine, LSD etc. These chemicals are not only prone to diversion within the country from licit channels but are attempted to be diverted in the course of international trade. C.B.N. is the designated Competent National Authority for regulating import and export under Article 12 of UN Convention against illicit traffic in Narcotic Drugs and Psychotropic Substances 1988. Central Bureau of Narcotics (CBN), Gwalior, Department of Revenue, Ministry of Finance is entrusted with various functions under the NDPS Act, inter-alia drug law enforcement activities, supervision over licit cultivation of opium poppy, regulating import and export of Narcotic Drugs & Psychotropic Substances and Precursor Chemicals, in addition to enforcement functions under the NDPS Act 1985.

3465. (28-9-2007) NEW DELHI : Chief of Naval Staff Admiral Sureesh Mehta took over as Chairman Chiefs of Staff Committee (COSC) from the outgoing Chairman General JJ Singh. In a solemn ceremony held in Defence Headquarters today, Gen Singh handed over the baton of Chairman COSC to Admiral Mehta. A former resolution placing on record a rich contribution made by the outgoing Chairman was also passed in the meeting. A large number of senior officials from the Army, Navy and the Air Force attended the ceremony.

3466. (28-9-2007) NEW DELHI : Sh. Abhishek Sanghvi announced that the Congress Party welcomes the imminent announcement of the scheme for the significant expansion of the National Rural Employment Guarantee Initiative. It is a unique initiative in post Independent India by the Congress Party. But more importantly it is an initiative of the people, by the people, for the people by this government, by this Congress Party. The Congress President started this phase of the UPA government with this historic announcement. This is the first time in the history of Independent India that such a remarkable, comprehensive scheme has been created. It is a scheme, which results in solid assets, it is a scheme which addresses rural districts. It is our Congress definition of inclusive democracy. It is the Congress' approach to what we might call the 3Es, E for empowerment,

E for empathy, E for efficacy. It is not a dole, it is not a charity. It combines the dignity of labour with those people who are the deprived sections of society and from roughly 300-330 odd districts we now have the significant expansion to roughly 593 rural areas in India. We might recall this scheme was started several years ago across the length and breadth of India without discrimination, without bias. If we look at the first phase of the scheme the maximum areas and rural districts chosen were districts in states ruled by non-Congress governments. Because where there is interest of the poor, interest of the aam aadmi, interest of the Nation the Congress does not believe in such kind of politics. This is a historic initiative because it changes the mindset, the way of thinking and looking at poverty removal. It provides what we can call livelihood security. It is important that the act itself contemplated the progressive expansion of the scheme to an all-India basis. The delegation led by General Secretaries which met the Prime Minister recently, made many suggestions not only for all-inclusive growth of the scheme but for an improvement in the quality of work. We are proud and happy that this is a jewel in the crown of the Congress Party, the UPA government and all the supporting UPA constituents. To a question on implementation of the scheme Sh. Singhvi said let us cease be doubting Thomases, let us not nit-pick on small irrelevant technicalities. Let us look at the substance. The substance is that this is being done. Why should we assume that it will not be done. Who will give the money? Today the Prime Minister, the Finance Minister and the Rural Development Minister have had a meeting. There is no resource problem. The resource problem is in the minds of our opponents and I sympathise with them, they are understandably jealous. In so many decades India has not seen this unique scheme. Let me assure you that instead of being doubting Thomases let us have pride in how we will do it, how soon we will do it. To a question regarding job cards being supplied Sh. Singhvi said, your question reflects the typical mindset of the Opposition to throw out the baby with the bath water. We in the Congress Party and the UPA are not deterred by the fact that any good scheme will have angularities and scope for improvement. Who has propounded the scheme? The Congress, the UPA. Who is suggesting reform in the scheme? The Congress and the UPA. Who is trying to make it better and better? The Congress and the UPA. When you try to improve something it does not mean that it is bad. It means that you think positive. Every attempt has been made from day one and the scheme started in 2004 is now in a much more comprehensive, inclusive and improved format in terms of ground-level monitoring. All the leakages are being plugged. Monitoring is improved, accountability is more, punishment is greater.

3467. (28-9-2007) NEW DELHI : The Minister for Steel, Chemicals and Fertilisers Shri Ram Vilas Paswan has said that Rs. 36,000 crore investment is likely to be made in the Petrochemical sector during next five years. The Minister was speaking after releasing "National Policy on Petrochemicals" here today. He said the investment will increase ethylene capacity, the basic raw material for the industry, from the current level of 2.7 million tonnes to 6.9 million tonnes. Expressing hope that the Policy will help India to become a major global sourcing centre in Petrochemicals and Plastics, the Minister said that the implementation of Assam Gas Cracker project with an investment of Rs. 5460 crore an ethylene capacity of 2.20 lakh tonnes per annum is being monitored by the Ministry. The Minister said that domestic petrochemical industry employs about 3.4 lakh persons both in upstream as well as downstream processing industry and has high potential to generate employment to the tune of 3.3 million more people during the 11th Plan. The Policy resolution aims to increase investments in the sector, capture a slice of resurgent Asian demand in polymers, creating quality infrastructure to ensure value addition and increase exports. The other objectives include to increase the domestic demand and consumption of plastics and synthetic fibres and to increase the use of petrochemicals in thrust areas. The existing per capita domestic polymer consumption of 4.7 kg is likely to be enhanced to 12 kg as compared to the existing world average of 25 kg. per capita. Earlier speaking on the occasion, the Minister of State for Chemicals & Fertlisers, Shri B.K. Handique said that petrochemical industry has made significant contribution in the economic growth and development of the country. He said that keeping in view India's advantageous position in Research and Development front, the global companies from developed countries may look to India for investment and outsourcing their research requirements and India must be ready to seize the opportunity.

3468. (28-9-2007) NEW DELHI : About 200 experts on steel sector form home and abroad will be participating in an international seminar here on 1st October 2007. The seminar on Iron ore beneficiation and Pelletisation is meant to create awareness for maximizing the use of indigenously available iron ores and fines by increasing pelletisatiion capacity. It will bring plant suppliers, technology suppliers and prospective entrepreneurs on a single platform. The participants from abroad include experts from Metallurgical Construction Corporation (MCC), Sino Steel Industry and Trading Corporation (SSIT) and Bao steel form China, All Mineral Gmbh from Germany and CVRD from Brazil. Experts from SAIL, TISCO, Essar Steel, JSW, JSPl, Bhushan Steel and Ispat Industries and researchers from NML, Jamshedpur and Institute of Materials and Minerals Technology (Formerly Regional Research Laboratory), Bhubaneswar will be among those attending the seminar. Availability of high-grade iron ore at internationally competitive price has been the strength of Indian steel industry. However, with continuous increase in domestic consumption of high grade iron ore and export of iron ore fines, there is an increase in the domestic price of iron ore. There are constraints in utilizing iron ore fines by the domestic iron and steel making units mainly because of limited sintering and pelletising capacity. The seminar is expected to give a boost to increase awareness for pelletisation in the small and medium capacity ranges. The seminar will be inaugurated by the Secretary Ministry of Steel, Shri R.S.Pandey and will also be attended by senior officials of the ministries of Steel and Mines.

3469. (28-9-2007) NEW DELHI : The proposal of the Total Sanitation Campaign (TSC) Project for Gumla District in Jharkhand has been under examination in the Department of Drinking Water Supply, Ministry of Rural Development. The project was revised on the basis of the recommendations of the National Scheme Sanctioning Committee (NSSC) of TSC. As per the said recommendation, an amount of Rs.208.27 lakh has been released under TSC for Gumla District vide sanction order dated 22.8.2007 of the Department of Drinking Water Supply towards the balance of the first instalment representing 30% of the Revised Central share of Rs.1548.23 lakh for Gumla District of Jharkhand under the Total Sanitation Campaign of the Central Rural Sanitation Programme. With this release, an amount of Rs.464.47 lakh of the revised GOI share stands released, under the scheme to the District.

3470. (28-9-2007) NEW DELHI : The Government has decided to extend the National Rural Employment Guarantee Act (NREGA) to the rural areas of all the remaining districts in the country. Disclosing this here today the Union Rural Development Minister, Dr. Raghuvansh Prasad Singh said that the decision has been taken in a meeting chaired by the Prime Minister, Dr. Manmohan Singh today itself. Under NREGA 200 most backward districts were notified on Feb.2, 2006. 130 additional districts were notified in the financial year 2007-08, bringing 330 districts under NREGA, till now. Notified on 7th Sept., 2005, the National Rural Employment Guarantee Act aims at enhancing the livelihood security of the people in rural areas by guaranteeing hundred days of wage employment in a financial year, to a rural household whose adult members volunteer to do unskilled manual work.The Act provides for extension to the entire country within five years of its notification on September 2005.

3471. (28-9-2007) NEW DELHI : A proposal for establishing Communication and Capacity Development Unit (CCDU) was submitted by the Govt. of Gujarat to the Ministry of Rural Development, Govt. of India, in 2005. The project cost for this proposal was Rs.3.05 crores for the first year. The CCDU has already been sanctioned for Rural Development Department of Gujarat State and it caters to the needs of rural sanitation. A request was again received by the Govt. of India for establishing a separate CCDU for drinking water sector in Gujarat State. While this matter was under consideration of the Govt. of India, the Working Group set up, as decided in the Conference of Ministers' In-charge of Drinking Water, recommended strongly the need for a separate CCDU for water supply in those States where two separate Departments are handling the subject of sanitation and rural water supply. Accordingly, the guidelines on the subject has been modified to permit two units in such States. The request of Gujarat for another CCDU has been accepted and the requisite funds are being released shortly.

3472. (28-9-2007) NEW DELHI : The area coverage of kharif crops as compared to 28th September last year has gone up as per data compiled by Agriculture

Ministry. The total coverage of kharif rice has gone up to 365.92 lakh ha as compared to 364.22 lakh hectare last year, the weekly Crop Weather Watch Group meeting of the Ministry of Agriculture was informed here today. Transplanting is at ending stage in almost all the states except Andhra Pradesh, Karnataka, Kerala, Orissa and Tamil Nadu where transplanting is at peak. The sowing of various coarse cereals has ended in almost all states. The area coverage under jowar, so far, is 34.40 lakh ha against 36.66 lakh ha during last year, under bajra 83.24 lakh ha against 91.82 lakh ha last year, maize 76.78 lakh ha against 72.45 lakh ha last year and total coarse cereals 216.09 lakh ha against 221.01 lakh ha during the corresponding period of last year. The area covered under cotton so far is 90.94 lakh ha against 87.48 lakh ha during the corresponding period of last year. Out of this 53.32 lakh ha is under Bt Cotton. The total coveage under sugarcane has been reported at 51.04 lakh hectare against 48.32 lakh ha during the corresponding period last year. The coverage under jute has been reported at 8.29 lakh ha against 8.18 lakh ha during the corresponding period of last year. Mesta has been sown in 1.47 lakh ha against 1.53 lakh ha during the corresponding period of last year. The total coverage of oilseeds so far has been 175.99 lakh ha as compared to 163.55 lakh ha on September 27, last year. Soyabean has been sown in 8 % and groundnut in 14% higher area as compared to that in 2006. Pulses cover an area of 124.79 lakh ha against 112.41 lakh ha up to this time last year.

3473. (28-9-2007) NEW DELHI : Climate change due to rising levels of Carbon dioxide in the atmosphere is one of the most serious environmental concerns of our time. General expansion of economic activity, increased population and use of fossil fuels are responsible for man made emission of Green house Gases (GHG). To address the problem posed by Climate Change the international community set up the United Nations Framework Convention on Climate Change (UNFCCC) in 1992, based on the principle of "common but differentiated responsibilities and respective capabilities of countries". The objective of UNFCCC is to stabilize GHGs concentration in the atmosphere to prevent dangerous anthropogenic interference with the climate system. Later in the year 1997, Parties adopted the Kyoto Protocol which sets legally binding targets for GHG reductions by industrialized countries during "first commitment period", 2008-2012, totalling 5.2% below their aggregate 1990 emissions. The projected climatic change indicates adverse impacts on developing countries in many ways resulting in changes in frequency, duration and intensity of extreme events such as heat waves and heavy precipitation events. Climate change would also increase the threats to human health due to increase in vector borne diseases. The impacts of climate change would fall disproportionately upon developing countries and would further exacerbate inequities in health status, access to food, clean water and other resources. India in particular is seriously concerned about the climate change because of its dependency on climate sensitive sectors like agriculture and forestry for livelihoods.

3474. (28-9-2007) NEW DELHI : "The present Indian Government is committed for the empowerment of women and has taken up several initiatives in the recent past in this direction". This was conveyed by Smt. Renuka Chowdhury, Minister for Women and Child Development during a meeting with Secretary of State of USA, Ms. Condoleezza Rice in New York today. Smt. Chowdhury told Ms. Rice that Indian women could boast of the achievements, which are still dreams for the women in some of the developed countries. India has a women as head of the State and its women are leading different fields whether it is education, business or science. Smt. Renuka Chowdhury is in New York to participate in the 3rd meeting of Women Leaders' Working Group convened by Ms. Condoleezza Rice to discuss women's empowerment issues such as education, political and economic empowerment and access to justice. The working group is comprised of about 40 women leaders including women heads of States and Ministers from across the globe. The meeting is being held on the margins of the UN General Assembly at New York on the theme of the 'Progress on Women's Empowerment'. Smt. Renuka Chowdhury apprised other participants also about challenges and opportunities before the Indian women and how they have succeeded in overcoming traditional hurdles and made significant achievements in various fields. The Women Leaders' working group was constituted in 2006 by Ms. Condoleezza Rice and it meets intermittently to discuss current challenges to women's empowerment and strategies to address them.

3475. (28-9-2007) NEW DELHI : 'Azadi Express'-the Mobile Train Exhibition, on celebration of 150 years of 1857, 60 years of independence and birth centenary of Shaheed Bhagat Singh was flagged off from New Delhi today by the Human Resource Development Minister, Shri Arjun Singh, in the presence of Minister of Information & Broadcasting and Parliamentary Affairs, Shri P. R. Dasmunsi. In his address, Shri Arjun Singh said that we have to take inspiration from our freedom struggle to guide our future course of action. He also said that I am honoured to be here to flag off the Azadi Express. Shri Arjun Singh said that the National Implementation Committee had decided that as part of the celebrations of 150th year of first was of independence, a train based Mobile Exhibition be organised to create awareness among the people of the events which constituted the bedrock of our freedom struggle. The Exhibition also aims to convey to the people the achievements of free India in various fields. He also reminded the new generation that today is the occasion when we all should take a pledge as to how best we can contribute to the nation and this pledge should be a sincere pledge like the true intention of Shaheed Bhagat Singh. Today his sacrifices only make us proud as countrymen of free India, he added. In his remarks, Minister of Information & Broadcasting and Parliamentary Affairs, Shri P. R. Dasmunsi exhorted the younger generation to revive the spirit of patriotism and follow the ideals of our martyrs like Bhagat Singh. They should be upright about the expression of their views on patriotism. The sacrifices of the freedom fighters who won us freedom and those at our borders who are making sacrifices even today to protect our hard earned freedom should always be borne in mind, he said."Azadi Express" have three sections covering (i) first war of independence 1857 and the events which led to it (ii) period of freedom movement and (iii) country's progress in post-independence period. The events are depicted through panels, graphics, dioramas, projection screen and through audio system. The Exhibition train comprises 12 non-A/C sleeper coaches depicting the exhibits.

3476. (28-9-2007) NEW DELHI : This year's World Habitat Day is being celebrated on 1st October. The United Nation has designated the first Monday in October every year as World Habitat Day to reflect on the state of human settlements and basic right to adequate shelter for all. It is also intended to remind the world of its collective responsibility for the future of the human habitat. The theme of this year's celebration chosen by the United Nation is "A safe city is a just city", is to reflect on the state of human settlements around the world. The United Nations chose this year's theme in order to raise awareness and encourage reflection on the mounting threats to urban safety and social justice, particularly urban crime and violence, forced eviction and insecurity of tenure, as well as natural and human-made disasters. One of the most significant causes of fear and insecurity in many cities today is crime and violence. UN-HABITAT has designated Dutch city of the Hague to spearhead the 2007 global celebration of World Habitat Day.In India, the national level celebration is being organised by the Ministry of Housing & Urban Poverty Alleviation at Vigyan Bhawan, New Delhi. On the occasion, Kumari Selja Minister of State for Housing & Urban Poverty Alleviation will release special publication of Housing & Urban Development Corporation Ltd. (HUDCO), Building Materials and Technology Promotion Council (BMTPC) and National Cooperative Housing Federation of India (NCHF). The Minister will also give away the prizes to the winners of NHB Essay Competition for 2007 and Painting Competition of physically & visually challenged children. The function would be attended by the Secretaries of State Governments, Union Territories, Senior officers from the Central Ministries, NGOs, UN-HABITAT and other agencies.

3477. (28-9-2007) NEW DELHI : The Prime Minister, Dr. Manmohan Singh is still recovering from the Prostate Gland Surgery he underwent last week. Doctors advised him to limit his activities for few more days. Consequently the Prime Minister's visit to Himachal Pradesh and Punjab has been postponed. Therefore, the Prime Minister is also unable to participate in the Shaheed Bhagat Singh Centenary celebrations.

3478. (28-9-2007) NEW DELHI : Following is the text of the address of the President, Smt. Pratibha Devisingh Patil at the inauguration of the 150th anniversary celebrations of the YMCA here today: "I am delighted to participate in the 150th Anniversary Celebrations of the Indian YMCA. On this occasion, I congratulate all members of the YMCA fraternity for their commendable work in rendering community service and for promoting youth development activities. Community service is essential for the building of better societies. It requires a spirit to work, not merely for one's own sake, but also for the welfare of others. Individuals and organizations involved in rendering social service should work selflessly for the betterment of society and should motivate the youth to do the same. A holistic approach towards the development of youth is extremely necessary for preparing them to undertake service towards humanity. India is a country of young people, with 54 percent of its population in the age group below 25 years. Youth are clearly destined to play a major role in the future of India. It is important to inculcate the right values in them and nurture the mental, physical and spiritual aspects of their personality. It is heartening to note that the YMCA seeks to build a balanced human being and in this context, is associated with promoting education, sports and cultural activities. Extra-curricular activities, particularly sports, are important to our youth for maintaining their physical fitness and fostering in them a sense of discipline. Sports encourage a team spirit and sportsmanship like qualities that enable the youth to face the success and failures of life with equanimity. Similarly, cultural activities help youth to appreciate the richness and diversity of our culture and imbibe our age-old values of truth, tolerance and respect for all. India is growing at a rapid pace but we need to make our developmental process equitable. There are large sections of our society, especially in rural areas and even in certain areas in urban centres, where the fruits of growth have not reached. Development should be seen as a joint task of the Government and society at large. Government is undertaking a number of schemes for poverty eradication, employment generation, rural development, education and health. Government efforts need to be supported by voluntary agencies and civil society. They can work with the Government, in the social sectors and with the less privileged sections of society as well as in the less developed areas of the country, to take India forward on the path of overall progress. In this context, I am reminded of the words of Swami Vivekananda, who said, and I quote, "go from village to village, do good to humanity and to the world at large." These words should be a source of inspiration for NGOs and voluntary agencies involved in community service. It is important that NGOs fully asses the needs of the communities that they work with and take up projects in accordance with the priorities of the community they work in. Projects of NGOs should be designed so as to make communities more productive and to make individuals self-reliant. The motto for NGOs should not merely be to give crutches to the less privileged but to make them independent, with capacities and skills that enable them to participate confidently in all activities of life. Development brings about societal changes and new social challenges.

3479. (28-9-2007) NEW DELHI : The President is pleased to appoint Shri B.N. Talukdar to the post of Director (Exploration & Development), Oil India Limited (OIL). His appointment will be effective from the date of assumption of charge on or after 01.12.2007 for a period of five years or till the date of his superannuation, or until further orders, whichever is earliest. Ministry of Petroleum & Natural Gas, Government of India New Delhi, Asvina 06, 1929/September 28, 2007.

3480. (28-9-2007) NEW DELHI : In a new endeavour, to provide new, modern and improved facilities to the passengers of the Indian Railways, a common countrywide train enquiry telephone No.139 for West Zone will be inaugurated by the Minister of State for Railways Shri Naranbhai J. Rathawa at Chatterapati Shivaji Terminus (CST), Mumbai on 29th September 2007. With the commissioning of this service which is known as Integrated Train Enquiry System (ITES): 'Rail Sampark', the basic enquiry services like train arrival and departure, PNR status, availability of accommodation, train fare etc, are to be made available for the general public of Maharashtra, Madhya Pradesh, Chhattisgarh, Gujarat, Dadar Nagar Haweli, Goa and Daman Diu with MTNL and BSNL subscribers. In addition to Hindi and English, enquiry services will also be available in Marathi and Gujarati for west zone. In the first phase, Zonal hub for North Region at Delhi and call centre at Noida was commissioned on 17th July 2007. Under the North Zone basic enquiry services are being made available for general public of Delhi, NCR, Punjab, Haryana, Himachal Pradesh, Jammu & Kashmir, Uttar Pradesh, Rajashtan, Uttarakhand state and Chandigarh with MTNL and BSNL as Telecom Service Provider (TSP).The services in other two zones *i.e.* East and South Zones will begin in the month of October 2007. Work of implementation of ITES is based on Public Private Partnership model. Indian Railways Catering and Tourism Corporation (IRCTC) in association with Centre for Railway Informatics System (CRIS) are responsible for rolling out this project across the country.. Execution of ITES is being done by Rail Enquiry Franchisee-M/s Bharat BPO and Bharat Sanchar Nigam Limited.

3481. (28-9-2007) NEW DELHI : Government has released 42 lakh tonne of non-levy (free sale) sugar for the quarter October to December, 2007. For the month of October 2007, the non-levy sugar quota released is 16 lakh tonne. In addition, a quantity of 2.29 lakh tonne has been released under levy for distribution in Public Distribution System. Thus, the total availability of sugar in the month of October, 2007 would be 18.29 lakh tonne which would be sufficient to meet the festival demand for sugar.

3482. (29-9-2007) NEW DELHI : It has been brought to the notice of the Government by West Bengal State Government and others that the permission holder of FM radio broadcasting station in the city of Delhi namely M/s Digital Radio (Delhi) Broadcasting Limited in their FM Radio channel named Red FM being aired on 93.5 MHz has carried a programme on 24.9.2007 in which a Radio Jockey has made derogatory remarks about the Gorkha Community consequent upon the selection of Mr. Prashant Tamang as Indian Idol in a Sony television channel show. Gorkha community has reacted strongly to the remarks by the Radio Jockey protesting the stereotyping as racist and insulting. General strikes have been called in several places like Darjeeling, Kalimpong and Sukna in protest and to maintain law and order Army and Para Military forces were required to be deployed. In Siliguri, it has led to violent clashes between communities leading to loot, arson and injuries to many persons. Police had to open fire and curfew has been imposed to bring the situation to normalcy.As per para 11.2 of the Grant of Permission Agreement M/s Digital Radio (Delhi) Broadcasting Limited were supposed to follow the programme code of All India Radio which prohibits any programmes attacking communities, anything defamatory, incitement to violence and anything against law and order. From the sequence of events it is prima facie evident that the remarks are in violation of the programme code of AIR and hence the permission holder has been given time till 4 P.M. on 1st October, 2007 to explain why action should not be taken against them.

3483. (30-9-2007) NEW DELHI : General Deepak Kapoor, till recently the Vice Chief of the Army has taken over the reins of the Indian Army from General JJ Singh, who retired at midday today. The change over of the baton was solemnized in a simple ceremony in the Army Chief's office, here today. This was preceded by a farewell guard of honour to General JJ Singh in the lawns of the South Block. Gen JJ Singh, also paid homage to the martyrs at the Amar Jawan Jyoti at the India Gate. General Deepak Kapoor, the 23rd Chief of the second largest Army in the world, brings with him vast and rich experiences in strategic thought; operational excellence and effective management of vast multi-technology and multi-disciplinary resources including vast financial and human capitals that the Indian Army employs. An alumnus of Sainik School, Defence Services Staff College, the Army War College and the National Defence College, General Kapoor's rise through the steep pyramidical hierarchy of the Army, to its very apex, has been a journey that saw him performing extra-ordinarily well in a large number of key prestigious appointments. Commissioned in the Corps of Artillery in June 1967, as a young officer, General Kapoor participated in the war for liberation of Bangladesh in 1971. In addition, he has represented the country as the Chief Operations Officer for all United Nations Forces deployed in Somalia from 1994 to 1995, for which, he was awarded the Vishisht Seva Medal in January 1996. During his service as a Brigade Commander deployed on the Line of Control in Jammu and Kashmir, the General was awarded the Sena Medal (Devotion to Duty) in January 1998. During OP PARAKRAM, General Kapoor commanded one of the most prestigious Divisions of a Strike Corps. He went on to command a Corps in the North East deployed along the Sino – Indian frontier. For his excellent command of the Corps, the General Officer was awarded Ati Vishisht Seva Medal in January 2006. On promotion as Army Commander, he commended the Army Training Command at Shimla. Thereafter, he commanded the largest and the most sensitive command of the Indian Army *i.e.* the Northern Command from September 2005 to December 2006. As a result of his sustained efforts, both the violence levels and infiltration came down appreciably in the State of J&K. For his efforts, the General Officer was awarded Param Vishist Seva Medal in January 2007.

3484. (1-10-2007) NEW DELHI : The Cabinet Committee on Economic Affairs today gave its approval for the following: (i) Peripheral towns of Panchkula and

SAS Nagar (Mohali) urban agglomeration will be included in the Jawaharlal Nehru National Urban Renewal Mission (JNNURM) city of Chandigarh as these towns are entirely in continuum to Chandigarh and in fact, are spill over of the growth of Chandigarh. (ii) Naya Raipur, a satellite city, will be included in the urban agglomeration of Chhattisgarh State Capital, Raipur, so that simultaneous cohesive development of Naya Raipur, alongwith existing city of Raipur, is possible. Presently, total area of Naya Raipur comprises 41 villages. With the inclusion of the above two in JNNURM, the following benefits will be reaped: (i) Infrastructure development of both Panchkula and Mohali, that are spillovers of Chandigarh would be possible through JNNURM funds along with JNNURM City of Chandigarh. (ii) Maya Raipur, a satellite city of Raipur, will also have access to JNNURM funds for its infrastructure development. JNNURM was launched by the government of India in December, 2005 to implement reforms driven planned development of identified cities in a Mission mode, with focus on efficiency in urban infrastructure / service delivery mechanism and basic services to the urban poor with community participation and accountability of Urban Local Bodies (ULBs) / Parastatals towards the citizens.

3485. (1-10-2007) NEW DELHI : Lt Gen JK Mohanty has assumed the appointment of GOC-in-C Army Training Command (ARTRAC) Shimla. An infantry officer, he is an alumnus of the National Defence Academy, Khadkwasla and was commissioned in the Dogra Regiment in 1969. Prior to taking over his new assignment, Lt Gen Mohanty was Commandant of Indian Army's premier officers training establishment for combat training, Army War College, Mhow (MP). Lt Gen Mohanty has held several coveted command, staff and instructional appointments. These include command of a unit in high altitude and counter insurgency in Jammu & Kashmir. During his tenure as Commanding Officer, his unit was awarded the three highest peace time gallantry awards in a single operation, ie Äshok Chakra, Kirti Chakra and Shaurya Chakra. For this operation he was decorated with the Sena Medal. An alumni of the CDM and the NDC, he successfully commanded a Mountain and an Infantry Brigade. After tenure as Military Attaché to the VCOAS at Army HQ Gen Mohanty commanded an Infantry Division at the Line of Control. He also held the appt of Additional Military Secretary at the Army HQ. For his outstanding services, he was awarded VSM in 2003 and UYSM in 2004. He also commanded a Corps from Oct. 2005 to Jan. 2007. He is Colonel of the Dogra regiment and Dogra Scouts since May 2006. ARTRAC is responsible for the coordination of various facts of professional and technical training in twenty seven training establishments of the Army. He has taken over the reins of ARTRAC from Lt Gen ML Naidu, who has since taken over as VCOAS.

3486. (1-10-2007) NEW DELHI : A group of senior citizens called on the President, Smt. Pratibha Devisingh Patil at Rashtrapati Bhavan on the occasion of International Day of Older Persons. Speaking to the group, the President said that the elderly in our society needs attention and care. Smt. Patil acknowledged the importance of the contributions that the elderly have made to society and felt that in turn the society should recognize the needs, particularly the emotional needs of the older citizens. Organisations that bring together the elderly must be commended as by bringing persons of the same age together, such people can give each other mutual support. During the discussions, the group of senior citizens felt that old age is not merely a physical condition but more of a state where a person is helpless and dependent. However, the group felt that the elderly could contribute to society. The group also welcomed the move by the Government to introduce a Bill in Parliament for the welfare of parents and senior citizens.

3487. (1-10-2007) NEW DELHI : The Bharatiya Janata Party National Vice-President Shri Mukhtar Abbas Naqvi declared that the BJP will register its strong protest on October 2- the Gandhi Jayanti Day against UPA government's move to injure national feelings by attacking Sri Ram and Sri Ram Setu with the recital of Ram Dhun – RAGHUPATI RAGHAV RAJA RAM, and the SUNDARKAND from Ramcharit Manas. Shri Naqvi stated that the Central Government's affidavit denying the existence of Lord Sri Ram, the Congress Party's ally Shri Karunanidhi's insulting comments about Sri Ram and taking no action against the Minister responsible for that disgraceful affidavit are the clear examples of perverse mind-set of the Congress Party and the UPA government. He added that the silence of the Prime Minister Shri Manmohan Singh, the Congress President Smt. Sonia Gandhi on the affidavit and Shri Karunanidhi's statement as well as the statement of the Congress government's several ministers go to prove that this entire anti-Sri Ram campaign has silence support of Smt Sonia Gandhi and the Prime Minister. Shri Naqvi added that this is a matter of grave concern that despite insulting and shameful comments of the DMK against Lord Sri Ram, the DMK party continues to be a component of the central government. The Karunanidhi government in Tamil Nadu is resorting to violent attack on Rambhakts and the central government by keeping silence on these developments is inciting the morale of such evil forces. Shri Naqvi observed that the Congress-led government is denying the existence of Sri Ram and talking of historical proofs about Lord Sri Ram whose inspiration and devotion helped the Father of Nation - Mahatma Gandhi in banishing the Britishers from India and in freeing the country from the clutch of slavery. This is a crime which cannot be condoned at all. Shri Naqvi added that the BJP with the recital of 'Ram Dhun' and 'Sundarkand' at all district headquarters across the country will strongly oppose the Congress Party's onslaught on Indian culture, faith and traditions and demand immediate dismissal of Karunanidhi government in Tamil Nadu.

3488. (1-10-2007) NEW DELHI : Shri Viswanathan Anand has become the World Chess Championship winning the global tournament in Mexico. Shri Mani Shankar Aiyar, Minister for Youth Affairs & Sports congratulates the winner. In a message he says: "I am pleased as all Indians are to hear of your thrilling win at the World Chess Championship in Mexico. Wrestling the championship from an array of stars and simultaneously passing the 2800-mark ELO rating is a brilliant achievement. This is an immensely proud moment for all Indians. I join millions of my compatriots in congratulating you on this momentous victory bringing glory to our nation. Please accept my good wishes for your continued success in the international arena."

3489. (1-10-2007) NEW DELHI : Complementarities in trade & business and mutual synergies have the potential of enhancing India-Thailand trade & commerce, and strengthen bilateral relationship between the two countries, said Mani Shankar Aiyar, Union Minister of DoNER, Govt. of India, today in Bangkok, Thailand. He was speaking at the Inaugural Session of the " North East India Trade & Investment Opportunities Week", being jointly organized by the Ministry of DoNER, the Ministry of Commerce, Govt. of India, and the Indian Chamber of Commerce (ICC). The Investment Week, which will be attended by over 300 Indian and Thai businessmen, Govt. officials and other dignitaries, has been organized to project the North East of India as a favourable investment destination to prospective Thai investors and businessmen, and to create meaningful bridges of cooperation between Industry representatives from the two countries. Commenting that the Investment Week will witness the largest ever high-powered delegation from India in Thailand, the Minister said India-Thailand business cooperation and exchange are reaching new heights, Shri Aiyar emphasized that the North-East of India must develop the necessary absorptive capacity to accept significant Thai investments in sectors of strategic importance like Infrastructure, Agro & Food Processing, Tourism, Handloom & Handicrafts, etc. Saying that the India-Thailand FTA is a great positive step towards an improved bilateral relationship, Shri Aiyar stressed upon the need for improving connectivity between the two countries, especially Air Connectivity. The Inaugural Session had H.E. Mr. Krirk-Krai Jirapaet, Hon'ble Minister of Commerce, Thailand as the Chief Guest. The Thai Commerce Minister had earlier visited 3 North Eastern states for identifying areas for mutual business tie-ups and investment, as part of a high profile Thai business delegation. Energy, Food Processing, Agriculture and Textiles are some of the sectors Thailand is interested to explore in the North East, said Mr.Jirapaet. The proposed Trilateral Highway Project, which would connect Thailand, India and Myanmar, would create new economic opportunities for both North-east India and South East Asian countries like Thailand, added the Minister. The 4-day mega Investment Week which will also have Exhibitions and Expositions on the North-East, is expected to generate concrete business between the 2 countries, which are emerging economic superpowers in new resurgent Asia. The Inaugural Session also witnessed the presence of Shri Ashwani Kumar, Minister of State for Industry, Govt. of India, Chief Ministers of Manipur, Mizoram, Arunachal Pradesh, Meghalaya, Nagaland, H.E. Smt. Latha Reddy, Indian Ambassador to Thailand, among other important Govt. and Industry dignitaries from both the countries.

3490. (1-10-2007) NEW DELHI : US Astronaut Sunita Williams called on the Prime Minister, Dr. Manmohan Singh and Mrs. Manmohan Singh here today. She was accompanied by her father. The Prime Minister told Ms. Williams that India was truly proud of her achievements and that she is a source of inspiration for all our young people. The Prime Minister announced that the Government of India will finance ten scholarships, five for girls and five for boys to promote the study of outer space. These scholarships will be called the Sunita Williams Scholarships for Higher Education in Space. (SWISHES). The Union Minister for Science and Technology Mr. Kapil Sibal will announce the details of the scholarship. Ms. Sunita Williams told the Prime Minister that she was overwhelmed by the love and affection she received in India and by the interest of young Indians in aeronautics and space exploration.

3491. (1-10-2007) NEW DELHI : Dr. Harjit S. Anand, Secretary, Ministry of Housing & Urban Poverty Alleviation has stressed the need for finding ways of making our cities more "inclusive" to check the increasing divide between the rich & the poor. Dr. Anand was speaking at the inauguration of the World Habitat Day celebrations here today. World Habitat day is celebrated on the First Monday of the October each year. The Habitat Day is celebrated to sensitize a cross-section of stakeholders to initiate suitable actions on a most relevant theme to promote sustainable, inclusive and equitable development of human settlements. The theme of this year's celebration is a "A Safe City is a just City". Speaking further, Dr. Anand said that the Habitat Agenda commits nations to improving living and working conditions on a sustainable basis, so that everyone is able to secure good quality shelter accompanied by a healthy environment. A secure habitat implies healthy, safe, accessible and affordable shelter adequately serviced by basic amenities combined with appropriate security of tenure for all, he added. He further stated that from town planner to policeman, the concept of an inclusive city is pluralistic and requires a dialogue between science and folklore as well as between society and state. He said we need to promote urban planning and governance with a social and grassroots' approach for strengthening safety of cities. Such an approach at the local level will strengthen both crime prevention and detection. Giving his views on this year's theme of World Habitat Day, Dr. Singh said it is of critical significance in relation to the quality of life in our cities. Crime is a serious problem in cities all over the world. Crime and the fear of crime are serious threats to the social climate of cities as well as for sustainable and economic development. The growth of urban crime is posing a threat to urban safety all over the world and is a matter of serious concern for both national and city governments. On the increasing high level of unemployment amongst youth in urban areas, Dr. Anand emphasized the need to undertake concerted action for developing initiatives that improve the livelihoods of youth and generate amongst them a sense of belonging to society. On the occasion Dr. Anand released special publications of Housing & Urban Development Corporation Ltd. (HUDCO), Building Materials and Technology Promotion Council (BMTPC) and National Cooperative Housing

Federation of India (NCHF). Dr. Anand also gave away the prizes to the winners of NHB Essay Competition for 2007 and Painting Competition of physically & visually challenged children. Ms. Shalini Dewan, Director, United Nations Information Centre read out the message of Secretary General, United Nations, Mr. Ban Ki-Moon.

3492. (1-10-2007) NEW DELHI : The government will consider any policy changes that may be required for optimum utilization of iron ore resources of the country. Delivering the inaugural address at the international seminar on iron ore beneficiation and pelletisation here today, Secretary in the Ministry of Steel, Shri R. S. Pandey said, the growth of the steel industry has been spectacular after 2000 with the global output rising over 50 percent. He said, the Indian steel industry has registered a growth of over 10 percent during the 10th plan period. With China and India recording high growth rates, the demand for steel is rising. Some of the global researchers are projecting a higher demand growth for steel over the next few years, he said, This, he said, is putting pressure on the global steel prices and spot prices reflect the trend. With reserves of high-grade iron ore being limited, there is urgent need for utilization of lower grade ores and fines. Shri Pandey said, the answer to this problem lies in beneficiation and pelletisation which has not got enough attention of our steel makers due to the availability of high grade ores. He said, the technology is now available for effective beneficiation and should be increasingly adopted to make steel and mining industry both sustainable. He said, if any policy changes are required in this context, the government would be willing to consider them. Speaking on the occasion the Chairman of Steel Authority of India Limited, Shri S. K. Roongta said, beneficiation is going to play an important part as it will reduce the input of iron ore, reduce expenditure and capital cost. He called upon the steel and mineral industry to collaborate for optimum use of this resource. Special Secretary in the Ministry of Steel, Shri A.K.Rath, Joint Secretary Shri Uday Pratap Singh and Industrial Advisor Shri A.C.R. Das were among those who addressed the opening session. About 200 delegates from home and abroad are attending the seminar to discuss various aspects of iron ore beneficiation and pelletisation.

3493. (1-10-2007) NEW DELHI : On the eve of the birth centenary of the Father of the Nation, Congress Spokesperson Shri Abhishek Singhvi said the Congress Party is proud that it is inextricably intertwined with India's GNP–Gandhi, Nehru, Patel. The Congress rededicates and revives the spirit, the thinking, the creed of Gandhism not only in India but globally. The Congress Party ceaselessly works for the installation of the Gandhian ethic as the operative watchword for good governance. Gandhiji's association with India's freedom movement—through India's oldest political movement the Congress—is well-known. No doubt Gandhiji belongs to India, he belongs to the world. I have no hesitation in saying that in point of time he belongs first and foremost to the Congress. Therefore, after Independence you are seeing the biggest mass movement organized at the initiative of the Congress President by the

Congress Party through India to rekindle Gandhian values, the Gandhian spirit and Gandhian thoughts. I have to remind that in January this year, at the initiative of the Congress President a huge international conference was held in New Delhi. Apart from ninetyone countries, 122 organisations also attended. It was decided to seek designation as international nonviolence day by the United Nations on Gandhiji's birthday. The Congress President followed this with her letter to the Prime Minister requesting further moves in this regard with the UN at the governmental level. And, finally in the middle of June this year, a resolution was moved and it was co-adopted and co-sponsored by over 143 countries of the world and unanimously passed to seek this status of UN day for this particular birthday. Therefore, for the first time tomorrow, at our initiative, at the initiative of the Congress President, the Congress Party, the Government of India, the Prime Minister of India we have the 2nd of October as International nonviolence day. The Congress President has gone especially to thank the world, to thank the community of nations, to thank the global leaders for this solidarity and unanimity shown, on this historic and momentous occasion which is a global tribute to the Father of the Nation. It is not only that the Prime Minister will flag off the peace march from the AICC Headquarters in the morning but there will be a mass movement all over India at every PCC, at every DCC, at every block level. There will be peace marches, non-violent marches and Gandhiji's movement will be taken by the Congress tomorrow to each doorstep. This is a unique initiative of the Congress President and the Congress Party. In doing so we celebrate and we applaud the consistency of the Congress Party which has always put Gandhi in the forefront whether it is the Satyagrah movement, its commemoration, whether it is the dandi march commemoration, whether it is any other historic event related to Gandhiji's life. That remarkable moment in history when Gandhiji started the Satyagraha concept in 1906 has been put in the forefront by the Congress Party. We are happy that even if belatedly there is a reawakening in some of our opposition political parties about Gandhiji. Even if by imitation, even if they have not been part of the freedom movement under Gandhiji's leadership, even if they have not always shown and reflected those ideals of which Gandhiji stood for, we are proud and happy that they are following the Congress lead in today paying obeisance to and celebrating Gandhiji's birthday. I must say ironically even if they celebrate it by adorning arms and lathis in some processions as has been reported, in respect of the RSS, which of course is an ironical manner of celebrating nonviolence day. The Congress Party and the Congress President as its leader have always stood for empowerment, enrichment and entitlement, which are the three Es which Gandhiji stood for.

3494. (1-10-2007) NEW DELHI : The Northeast India Trade and Investment Week begins in Bangkok today. Ministry of Development of North Eastern Region in their efforts to show-case the potential of the North Eastern Region of India and to attract investments have organized this 'North-East India Trade & Investment Opportunities Week' in Bangkok from 1st October to 4th October, 2007. The primary reason for taking this initiative is to attract investment from Thailand in various sectors in the region. The main sectors which have been identified for this purpose include infrastructure (road, rail, inland waterways, air connectivity and energy), food processing, tourism & hospitality, horticulture, handlooms & handicrafts, rubber and bamboo. These sectors are not exclusive and businessmen interested in tie-ups in information technology, private airlines and any other areas have been also invited to participate. The sector-wise interactive sessions in specific sectors and one to one interaction will take place with a view to have meaningful dialogue between the two sides and to have a fruitful outcome at the end of the event. Shri Mani Shankar Aiyar, Minister for Development of Northeast Region (DoNER) is leading the delegation. Dr. Ashwani Kumar, Minister of State for Industry and the Chief Ministers of most of the North Eastern States are participating in the event. The Indian delegation comprises of around 70 delegates, which include officials from the Central Ministries like Ministry of Commerce & Industry, Ministry of Civil Aviation, Ministry of Tourism, Ministry of Shipping, Road Transport & Highways, etc., all the North East States, specific Central Organisations/Public Sector Undertakings like National Highway Authority of India (NHAI), Inland Waterways Authority of India (IWAI), National Hydroelectric Power Corporation (NHPC), Power Grid Corporation of Indian Ltd. (PGCIL), North Eastern Electric Power Corporation ltd. (NEEPCO), Air India, Agricultural and Processed Food Products Export Development Authority (APEDA), Rubber Board, Spices Board etc. More than 150 businessmen/companies are also participating. Indian Chamber of Commerce (ICC), Federation of Industries & Commerce of North Eastern Region (FINER) and SHEFXIL (Shellac & Forest Products), Export Promotion Council, along with others are participating in the event in a big way. The companies who had evinced interest in investment in the North Eastern Region during the course of the 3rd North East Business Summit (April 2007) form a significant part of the delegation. Mr. Krik-Krai Jirapaet the Thai Commerce Minister and Mr. Piyabutr Cholvijarn, Deputy Minister Industry of Thailand along with more than 200 Thai Businessmen are participating in the various sessions with senior officials from the Ministries concerned. The Indian officials/businessmen will interact with the Thai counterparts and will be having one to one discussions on the specific areas of interest for exploring the possibilities of investment and trade in the North East. The event starts today with the Inauguration of an Exhibition which showcases the products from the North Eastern States. The Inaugural Session includes addresses by Minister DONER, Minister of State of Industry, the Thai Commerce Minister and the Chief Ministers of North Eastern States. On the day 2, an exclusive sectoral Session on Tourism and Hospitality is being organized. It will be followed by addresses by Minister DoNER, Thai Commerce Minister and Plenary Session on other Sectors, Interactive Sessions between participants.

3495. (1-10-2007) NEW DELHI : A three-day Conference of Directors General of Police and Inspectors General of Police begins here on Wednesday. It will be inaugurated by the Home Minister, Shri Shivraj Patil. The Prime Minister, Dr. Manmohan Singh will address the Conference on Thursday. The Conference will discuss issues pertaining to overview of national security, left wing extremism, security situation in the North East, emerging threats to VVIP security, new generation crimes, computerization, economic intelligence, enforcement of the NDPS Act and various police issues. 42 officers of the Intelligence Bureau would receive the Indian Police Medals for meritorious services and 15 would receive President's Police Medals for distinguished services. The main objective of the Conference is to provide a forum to the police leadership in the country to discuss various problems being faced by the police in their day-to-day functioning and work out solutions to such problems through exchange of ideas and sharing of experience and thereby make the police more effective, efficient and people friendly. Efforts are also made through this forum to devise ways and means for the police forces to confront the ever-increasing and newer challenges to law and order and national security including terrorism, insurgency, extremism and espionage. Sharing of ideas and caring for each other's problems also generates greater bonding and camaraderie among the various police forces in the country. The conference of DGPs/ IGPs in India is being organized by the Intelligence Bureau since 1920. The conference has been held regularly in New Delhi. The Director, Intelligence Bureau continues to remain the ex-officio Chairman of the Conference. This year's DGPs/IGPs Conference is the 42nd since Independence.

3496. (1-10-2007) NEW DELHI : The Parliamentary Committee on petitions has invited public suggestions on introduction of sex education in CBSE affiliated schools. These can be submitted through a written memoranda containing suggestions/ views/comments of individuals/institutions/organisations interested in the subject matter. The Committee on Petitions under the Chairmanship of Shri M. Venkaiah Naidu, M.P, Rajya Sabha is examining the prayer of the petitioners and has decided to undertake wider consultations with all the stakeholders including eminent educationists, sociologists, psychologists, sexologists, spiritual leaders, teachers and parents for generating a national debate on the subject. Those desirous of submitting memoranda to the Committee may send two copies (each in English and Hindi) thereof to Shri J. Sundrial, Joint Director, Rajya Sabha Secretariat, Parliament House Annexe, New Delhi-110001 and E-Mail: sundrial@sansad.nic.in} within 30 days indicating whether they would also be interested in giving oral evidence before the Committee. The memorandum submitted to the Committee would form part of its records and would be treated as confidential and therefore should not be printed, circulated or publicised by anyone, as such an act would constitute a breach of privilege of the Committee. There has been severe criticism from certain quarters on the recent move of the Ministry of Human Resource Development, Government of India to introduce sex-education in the form of Adolescence Education Programme (AEP) in the Central Board of Secondary Education (CBSE) affiliated schools all over the country. Two petitioners have prayed to the Council of States (Rajya Sabha) that there should be a national debate on the subject and a consensus arrived before introducing sex-education in CBSE affiliated schools.

3497. (1-10-2007) NEW DELHI : Shri Kamal Nath, Union Minister of Commerce and Industry, has called for achieving forward and backward linkages for a positive impact of export growth on the national economy. He was speaking at the CAPEXIL's Golden Jubilee and Export Awards function, here today. Earlier, Shri Somnath Chatterjee, Lok Speaker Speaker, inaugurated the function and appreciated the excellent work done by the exporters. While complimenting the export award winners, Shri Kamal Nath said: "I am aware that many products of Capexil have great employment potential as also the potential for higher asset growth. Along with increase in the export revenue, it would be in the overall national interest to concentrate on more employment generation and wealth creation for the country. Towards this end, Capexil should introspect and try to evolve a system whereby it can offer better services to the exporting community. It should be an information-based organisation and should disseminate information about the latest global developments so that members benefits by this value addition". Shri Kamal Nath stated that this year India is likely to achieve a GDP growth of 9% plus for the third year in succession. The manufacturing sector which is the main driver of the economy, continues to maintain a double digit growth rate and the figures available for the first three months of 2007-08 show that out of 101 sectors reporting production, 23 sectors recorded an excellent growth rate of more than 20% and another 27 sectors achieved a high growth rate of 10-20%, he added. The service sector has been growing in double digits over the last two years and it now constitutes 55% of our GDP, he further added. Capexil has under its umbrella 16 different types of heterogeneous product groups namely Iron Ore and other Minerals, Natural Stone, Processed Minerals, Rubber, Auto Tyres, Paints, Glass, Plywood, Ceramics, Cement, Paper, Books, Bones, Ossein, Graphite, etc. These diversified groups are both a strength and weakness. Strength because if all the 16 groups are fully active then sky is the limit. The weakness lies in the fact that 16 different types of interests have to merge their sectoral interests into a common interest.

3498. (1-10-2007) NEW DELHI : An Environmental Survey Vehicle (ESV), developed by the DRDO, was formally handed over to the Indian Navy here today. Scientific Advisor to Defence Minister and DRDO Chief Shri M. Natarajan handed over the ESV to Vice Admiral Nirmal Verma, Vice Chief of Naval Staff, at a function held at DRDO Bhawan. Defence Laboratory, Jodhpur has designed and developed this ESV for Indian Navy. ESV is a radiological laboratory on wheels and is equipped with the state-of-art instruments. It is capable of estimating radioactivity in field conditions in solid, liquids and air. The qualitative and quantitative assay will be helpful to certify the suitability of eatables, drinkables and inhaleables in the field conditions from radiation safety angle for coastal areas. It is capable to measure alpha, beta and gamma radiation quantitatively and qualitatively to even very low level of radioactivity thereby facilitating early detection of any unusual increase in radioactivity in the area. The ESV is also capable to detect any intentional or unintentional release of radioactivity in a marine environment. Needless to say, the capabilities of this vehicle will find increased utility in the changing security environment. Accepting the ESV on behalf of Indian Navy, Vice Admiral Nirmal Verma commended the DRDO for its efforts in completing the project in the stipulated time.

3499. (1-10-2007) NEW DELHI : BJP National President Shri Rajnath Singh today while speaking to the electronic media at the party headquarters in New Delhi highlighted the following points with regard to the situation in Tamil Nadu and observations of the Hon'ble Supreme Court: • Nations are administered through rule of law. Challenging rule of law marks the beginning towards anarchy. • The UPA Govt. is one sad string of continuous failures. A Union Cabinet Minister raising inappropriate questions against the observations of the Hon'ble Supreme Court and challenging the authority of the courts is a dangerous precedent marking a direct confrontation between the executive and judiciary. • Union Cabinet Minister Mr. T R Balu after his adverse comments on the judiciary ceases to have the constitutional right of remaining as a minister of the union cabinet. • I urge Prime Minister Dr. Manmohan Singh and UPA Chairperson Smt. Sonia Gandhi to immediately dismiss Mr. Balu from the Union Cabinet, in order to fulfil the constitutional obligation of the government. • If the Central Government is not ready to do so, then as per the Constitutional principle of collective responsibility of the Union Cabinet, the entire government is responsible. This will be a serious threat on the constitutional and federal structure of the country. • The situation is for all to clearly see. First the present UPA Government filed an affidavit denying the existence of Bhagwan Sri Ram. Then blasphemy by the DMK chief, a constituent party of UPA. This was followed by violent attacks on the offices of Hindu organisations and the BJP in Tamil Nadu. Then trying to impose fear of 'Bandh' by using the might of power. Now, finally the disobedience of the Supreme Court by the Tamil Nadu government and today's criticism of judiciary by a Union Minister is a matter of grave concern for entire the country. • This indicates that under the present UPA government the cultural, federal and constitutional fabric of the country is being jeopardized. • This is a test for preserving our constitutional framework. The Prime Minister must stand upright and display the courage and commitment to uphold the true sprit of our constitution.

3500. (1-10-2007) NEW DELHI : Exports during August, 2007 were valued at US $ 12686.38 million which was 18.91 % higher than the level of US $ 10668.78 million during August, 2006. In rupee terms, exports touched Rs. 51787.31crore, which was 4.31% higher than the value of exports during August, 2006. Cumulative value of exports for the period April-August, 2007 was US$ 59483.99 million (Rs. 243611.53 Crore) as against US$ 50255.50 million (Rs.230788.99 Crore) registering a growth of 18.36% in Dollar terms and 5.56% in Rupee terms during the same period last year. Imports during August, 2007 were valued at US $ 19569.31 million representing an increase of 32.64 % over the level of imports valued at US $ 14753.47 million in August, 2006. In Rupee terms, imports increased by 16.35 %. Cumulative value of imports for the period April-August, 2007 was US$ 91986.78 million (Rs. 376964.85 Crore) as against US$ 70181.41 million (Rs. 322203.73 Crore) registering a growth of 31.07% in Dollar terms and 17% in Rupee terms during the same period last year Oil imports during August, 2007 were valued at US $ 6022.74 million which was 19.52% higher than oil imports valued at US $ 5038.96 million in the corresponding period last year. Oil imports during April-August, 2007 were valued at US$ 25901.26 million which was 8.32% higher than the oil imports of US$ 23912.08 million in the corresponding period last year. Non-oil imports during August, 2007 were estimated at US $ 13546.58 million which was 39.57% higher than growth on non oil imports of US$ 9705.74 million in August, 2006. Non-oil imports during April-August, 2007 were valued at US$ 66085.52 million which was 42.85% higher than the level of such imports valued at US$ 46260.56 million in April-August, 2006. The trade deficit for April-August, 2007 was estimated at US $ 32502.79 million which was higher than the deficit at US $ 19925.91 million during April-August, 2006.

3501. (1-10-2007) NEW DELHI : Central Ground Water Board (CGWB) under Ministry of Water Resources has prepared a conceptual report entitled " Master plan for Artificial Recharge to Ground Water in India" bringing out the areas suitable for Artificial Recharge to Ground Water Reservoir, by prioritising the areas wherein the schemes need to be implemented as a first priority to ameliorate the water scarcity problems. A total area of 448760 has been identified in the country which needs Artificial Recharge to Ground Water. It is estimated that annually about 36453 MCM of surplus surface run-off can be recharged to augment the ground water. The Master Plan envisages construction of 2.25 lakh Artificial Recharge structures in rural areas at a cost of Rs. 19880 crore. In Jammu & Kashmir, Himachal Pradesh, Uttaranchal, North Eastern States, Sikkim emphasis has been given for spring development and 2700 springs are proposed for augmentation and development. The need for conservation of ground water has been emphasized in urban areas. The roof top rainwater harvesting is proposed both by augmenting the ground water storage as well as by storing it in specially built tanks. It is estimated that 37 lakh roof top rainwater harvesting structures are feasible in the country at an estimated cost of Rs. 4590 crore. The total cost of the Master Plan is Rs. 24500 crore. The actual implementation of the plan will be taken up in a phased manner.

3502. (1-10-2007) NEW DELHI : Dr. Michael Cullen, Deputy Prime Minister and Minister of Finance and Tertiary Education of New Zealand called on Shri Arjun Singh, Minister of Human Resource Development here today. The Ministers discussed issues relating to increasing bilateral links in Higher Education. Over

3000 Indian Students study in New Zealand. India would also like to see more students from New Zealand studying in India.

3503. (1-10-2007) NEW DELHI : The President, Smt. Pratibha Devisingh Patil, has greeted the people on the occasion of Gandhi Jayanti, which will be celebrated tomorrow. In a message she has said, "Gandhi Jayanti is an occasion for all of us to rededicate ourselves to the ideals of Mahatma Gandhi on peace and nonviolence. Mahatma Gandhi had said, "Non-Violence is the greatest force at the disposal of mankind. It is mightier than the mightiest weapon of destruction devised by the ingenuity of man..." The life and work of Gandhiji is an inspiration for all of us about tolerance and respect. Gandhiji believed that intolerance was a form of violence. It is significant that the United Nations has declared October 2nd as the International Day of Non-Violence. This year as the Nation celebrates the 60th Anniversary of Independence, it is an appropriate opportunity for all of us to gratefully remember and pay homage to the Father of the Nation."

3504. (1-10-2007) NEW DELHI : The Cabinet in its meeting held on October 1, 2007 has approved the Amendments to the payment of Bonus Act, 1965, which are as follows:-i) Amendment to Section 2(13): To raise the eligibility limit for payment of bonus from the salary or wage of Rs.3500/- to Rs.10,000 per month. ii) Amendment to section 12: To raise the ceiling for calculation purpose from the salary or wage of Rs.2500/- to Rs.3500/- per month, and; iii) Deletion of section 32(vi): To cover the employees employed through contractors on building operations.

3505. (1-10-2007) NEW DELHI : The Rail Coach Factory (RCF) produced 117 coaches during the month of August 2007. Chitranjan Locomotive Works (CLW), Diesel Locomotive Works (DLW) and Integral Coach Factory (ICF) produced 17 electric locomotives, 20 diesel locomotives and 106 coaches respectively. Rail Wheel Factory (RWF) produced 12065 wheels and 1893 axles during the same period. Except ICF, all other units have exceeded the target. The performance of Indian Railways in respect of loading has gone up from 288.81 Million Tonnes during April-August 2006 to 308.89 Million Tonnes during April-August 2007, registering an increase of 6.95 per cent. Freight earnings have also gone up from Rs.16266.60 crore during April-August 2006 to Rs.17852.22 crore during April-August 2007, registering an increase of 9.75 per cent. Passenger earnings have gone up from Rs. 6896.34 crore during April-August 2006 to Rs.7739.07 crore during April-August 2007, showing an increase of 12.22 per cent. The punctuality percentage of mail/express trains was 93.6 per cent in Broad Gauge and 99.5 per cent in Metre Gauge during the month of August 2007 compared to 93.8 per cent and 97.3 per cent respectively during the same period last year.

3506. (1-10-2007) NEW DELHI : The Prime Minister, Dr. Manmohan Singh, has congratulated Vishawanathan Anand on his becoming the undisputed World Chess Champion. The Prime Minister in his message said, "It brings great joy to me personally and to all Indians that you have won the World Chess Championship. It is indeed a moment of pride for the nation. I wish you continued success in the years to come."

3507. (1-10-2007) NEW DELHI : The President, Smt. Pratibha Devisingh Patil has congratulated Shri Vishwanathan Anand on his becoming the world chess champion. In a message to Shri Anand, the President has said, " We are proud that you are not only a Grandmaster but now the World Champion for the second time. Your feat has brought joy and pride to all Indians. I wish you further success in the future."

3508. (1-10-2007) NEW DELHI : The Union Cabinet today gave its approval for signing of an Agreement between India and Philippines on the abolition of visa requirement for the holders of diplomatic and official passports. The Agreement would be signed during the visit of the President of Philippines to India on 5th October, 2007. The salient features of the Agreement are as under : i) Visa-free travel for diplomatic and official passport holders while entering, transiting through and exiting from the territory of the other country. ii) A citizen of one country holding the said passport shall be allowed to stay in other country's territory for a maximum period of 30 days without a visa. iii) The Agreement does not exempt the holder of the said passport from the obligation of complying with the laws and regulations of the receiving contracting party. iv) Each country reserves the right to refuse the entry into, or terminate the stay in its territory v) Members of diplomatic Missions / Consulates of respective countries as well as their spouses, children and dependent parents would be granted with 30 days of their arrival, Similar Agreements exist with 35 other countries.

3509. (1-10-2007) NEW DELHI : The Union Cabinet today gave its approval for acquisition of a new research vessel as a replacement of aging research vessel-Samudra Manthan of Geological Survey of India at an estimated cost of Rs. 448 crores for carrying out seabed surveys and exploration of non-living resources. At present no single vessel is available on chartering basis that has multidisciplinary equipment systems to undertake detailed investigation for offshore survey. Further, in view of aspects of information security and the objective of addition to the national wealth, the acquisition of new RV vessel is considered advantageous. This decision will facilitate GSI to acquire a tailor made new multidisciplinary research vessel with state-of-the-art equipment for undertaking geological, geophysical and geo-chemical mapping of the seabed. Data generated will be useful for creating and updating national database in the field of earth-science, oceanography and offshore mineral resources.

3510. (1-10-2007) NEW DELHI : Smt. Meira Kumar, Union Minister for Social Justice and Empowerment flagged off the Walkathon on the occasion of International Day of Older Persons here today. About 2500 senior citizens and school children participated in the Walkathon. The function was organised by the Ministry of

Social Justice. Speaking on the occasion, Smt. Kumar said that the Government is very much concerned about the welfare and security of the older persons and it is our duty to extend all possible help to them. She informed that the Government would soon bring effective legislation to provide care, maintenance and protection of parents and senior citizens. She further said that the Ministry of Social Justice and Empowerment has already set up a National Council for Older Persons (NCOP) to advise and aid the Government on policies and programme on older persons. The Ministry also has set up an Inter-Ministerial Committee with the aim of effective implementation of the NCOP, she added. Emphasising the need to sensitise the society atlarge about the problems and needs of the older persons, the Minister stated that cooperation of NGOs and public, especially the youth was required to create an environment where older persons get respect, care and due affection. There is need to inculcate the feeling of respect and care for older persons in the minds of young generations, she stressed. October is observed all over the world as International Day of the Elderly. The basic idea behind the celebrations is to recognise the services rendered by the senior citizens and to reiterate the government's commitment towards the cause of the elderly.

3511. (1-10-2007) NEW DELHI : Lt Gen AK Nanda has taken over as new Chief of Border Roads Organisation. Lt Gen AK Nanda is an alumnus of National Defence Academy, Pune, Defence Services Staff College, Wellington, Army War College, Mhow and National Defence College. The General Officer was commissioned into Bengal Sappers in Dec 1969. In his 38 years of illustrious service in the Army, the General Officer has held varied command and staff appointments. These include the Command of an Engr Regt, an Engineer Brigade and General Officer Commanding 101 Area. He has held instructional appointments at College of Military Engineering, Pune and Defence Services Staff College, Wellington. Before taking over as Director General Border Roads, the General Officer was ADG (Engineer Staff) in E-in-C's Branch. Lt Gen Nanda succeeds Lt Gen KS Rao, who superannuated on Sep 30, 2007.

3512. (1-10-2007) NEW DELHI : Retail prices of essential commodities monitored by the Department of Consumer Affairs at four metropolitan cities have remained stable or shown mixed trend in the week ending 21.9.2007. Prices of rice, wheat, atta, gram, tur dal, sugar, groundnut oil, tea (loose) and salt were stable over the week. Prices increased in respect of mustard oil by Rs. 2 per kg at Kolkata, vanaspati by 2 per kg. at Mumbai and Chennai and Rupee 1per kg at Kolkata. Milk price rose by Rupee 1 per litre at Kolkata. Potato prices increased by 50 paise per kg at Mumbai and Rs. 3 at Chennai and onion by Rs. 2 per kg at Kolkata. In Delhi, prices of rice, wheat and atta remained steady over six months and that of sugar, groundnut oil, mustard oil, vanaspati, milk and salt remained steady over the month.

3513. (2-10-2007) NEW DELHI : The Power Ministry is celebrating the august occasion of the International Nonviolence Day by holding a two-day exhibition of books on the Mahatma. The exhibition consisting mainly of books at the library of the Ministry includes a set of collected works of Mahatma Gandhi. The exhibition that has been set up in the Committee Room in Shram Shakti Bhavan, New Delhi was today inaugurated by the Secretary, Ministry of Power, Shri. Anil Razdan. Senior officials and staff of the Ministry were present on the occasion. The exhibition is open from 10 a.m. to 4.30 p.m. on the 2nd and 3rd of October 2007. The 2nd of October this year bears a special significance being the Centenary of the Mahatma Gandhi's Satyagraha Movement in South Africa. The United Nations has adopted a resolution to observe Mahatma Gandhi's birthday henceforth as the "International Day of Nonviolence".

3514. (2-10-2007) NEW DELHI : The Prime Minister, Dr. Manmohan Singh administered a pledge to the nation and released a set of four commemorative postage stamps on the occasion of International Day of Non-Violence. Today, October 2nd the Birthday of Mahatma Gandhi is celebrated an International Day of Non-Violence by the United Nations from this year. At a function organized by the Ministry of Culture and Gandhi Smriti and Darshan Samiti at Vigyan Bhawan here, Prime Minister Dr. Manmohan Singh administered the following pledge: "I shall work for an India in which the poorest shall feel that it is their country, in whose making they have an effective voice, an India in which there shall be no high class and low class of people; an India in which all communities shall live in perfect harmony. There can be no room in such an India for the curse of untouchability, or the curse of intoxicating drinks and drugs. Women will enjoy the same rights as men. We shall be at peace with all the rest of the world. This is the India of my dreams." M.K. GANDHI. Speaking on the occasion, the Minister for Tourism and Culture, Smt. Ambika Soni said history has time and again shown that violence can never be countered by violence, wars never bring peace and hatred and intolerance get only multiplied and reinforced whenever confronted with counter intolerance and hatred. She said Gandhiji, a visionary that he was, showed us the way out from this vicious circle. He clearly saw the futility of violent means to resolve conflicts and realize peace. She said the declaration of October 2, Gandhi Jayanti, as International Day of Non-Violence by UN mooted by India and supported by 142 member states is a manifestation of the change of hearts. Quoting Mahatma Gandhi "the world will live in peace, only when the individuals composing it make up their minds to do so". Smt. Ambika Soni said this message can and should be practiced by all of us at individual levels if we want this world to be a better place to live.

3515. (2-10-2007) NEW DELHI : Minister of Information and Broadcasting and Parliamentary Affairs, Shri P.R. Dasmunsi today announced the special DAVP advertisement policy package for small and medium newspapers in regional and other languages. The new DAVP Policy is focused on the special efforts being made to increase support through DAVP to newspapers in languages like Bodo, Dogri, Kashmiri, Khasi, Konkani, Maithili, Manipuri, Nepali, Sanskrit, Santhali,

Sindhi, Urdu and Tribal language newspapers published in J&K, Andaman & Nicobar Islands and North Eastern States as well as those published in backward, hilly, border and remote areas.

3516. (2-10-2007) NEW DELHI : The Government of India have decided to confer the KABIR PURASKAR, for the year 2007 Grade-III on Shri Khalifa Gufran S/o Shri Haji Zahoor Ahmad, r/o 4/715, Gali Halwaiyan, Moh. Chowki Sarai, PS-Kotwali City, Saharanpur, Uttar Pradesh. Following a verbal duel on 8.8.2006 under PS Kotwali, Saharanpur district between Muslims and Dalits over a petty matter, a scuffle ensued in which members from both the communities indulged in violence. The situation had taken on a communal colour by then and the violence left many members from both communities injured. Seeing two injured Dalit youths being taken to the emergency ward of district hospital, an already infuriated mob of the other community captured both the youths. The timely arrival on the scene by Shri Khalifa Gufran with the district authorities stemmed further escalation of violence and saved both the youths from the clutches of the mob. In doing so, Shri Khalifa put his own personal safety at risk. In another incident on 24.11.2006 Shri Khalifa Gufran alongwith the district authorities and other persons of the locality averted a possible communal riot in Saharanpur under PS Janakpuri. Again, on 27.3.2007 persons of Hindu and Muslim communities collected at Mohalla Jatavnagar and started pelting stones on each other. Shri Khalifa Gufran reached there with his friends and helped the district authorities in restoring peace and normalcy. In the past also Shri Khalifa Gufran has been taking active part in promoting communal harmony and has been proactively assisting the district administration in maintaining peace and communal harmony during Hindu-Muslim festivals. Kabir Puraskar is a National Award instituted by the Government of India for recognizing the acts of physical/moral courage displayed by a member of one caste, community or ethnic group in saving the lives and properties of member(s) of another caste, community or ethnic group during caste, community or ethnic violence. The Award is given annually in three grades viz., Grade-I, Grade-II and Grade-III, carrying cash amount of Rs. 2,00,000; Rs.1,00,000 and Rs. 50,000 respectively.

3517. (2-10-2007) NEW DELHI : India was the recipient of the much coveted Pacific Asia Travel Association (PATA) 'Grand Award' for Marketing under the banner of a highly successful 'Incredible India' campaign, at a special awards ceremony in Bali Indonesia. India also bagged two Gold Awards for Cultural Tourism (Aranmula) and Marketing Brochure (Kumarkom) awarded to Kerala Tourism. Leveraging India's colour and cultural diversity and intelligent use of traditional and interactive media including micro-sites and online contests and targeted at the international visitor, the Incredible India campaign has helped drive strong double-digit growth rates in foreign visitor arrivals into India. "Excellent visuals and print material combine in a creative way to highlight the many little known reasons to visit India. And strong growth in visitor arrivals during the period proves that it has worked. "This is a memorable, evocative, emotive campaign", Judges commented. After accepting the Award, Mr. S. Banerjee, Secretary, Ministry of Tourism, Government of India said that PATA's recognition of our efforts was a great honour and encourages the Indian tourism industry to promote India as a destination for all seasons. Initiatives are under way for development of tourism infrastructure and facilities in the country and the work on the identified thrust areas has already been undertaken for enhancing the experience of the tourists. The Ministry of Tourism has undertaken a series of promotional and marketing activities during the year to position India internationally as a destination of choice, Mr. Banerjee added. India is the host country for PATA Travel Mart being held in Hyderabad in September next year. At a glittering invitation reception hosted by the Ministry of Tourism for PATA dignitaries and delegates in Bali yesterday, Mr. Banerjee highlighted the tourism preparedness of India for organising the Mart and invited members of this prestigious international body to visit India to have a delightful experience. While addressing the gathering, Mr. Brian Deeson, Chairman of PATA said that the enthusiasm for India was evident from the large turn out and the PATA members and the Board were looking forward to visit this most preferred tourism destination-Incredible India. A strong contingent from Andhra Pradesh led by the Minister of Tourism Shri A. Ramnarayan Reddy attended the PATA Travel Mart and the reception in which tourist destinations of Andhra Pradesh were showcased through a Kuchipudi dance recital by Ms Deepika Reddy and her students. This was followed by display of percussion music showcasing musical traditions of various parts of the country by Rajeev Mahaveer and his troupe of Ethenic Fusion group.

3518. (2-10-2007) NEW DELHI : The progress of execution of National Highway Works and the works relating to improvement of other roads approved by the Centre under various schemes and programmes of the Ministry of Shipping, Road Transport & Highways was reviewed at a meeting held at Guwahati recently. The meeting was chaired by the Secretary (Road Transport & Highways) Shri Brahm Dutt and attended by the Commissioners and Secretaries of Arunachal Pradesh, Assam, Manipur, Meghalaya, Mizoram, Nagaland, Sikkim and Tripura. The Chief Engineers of the PWDs of the States and officials from the Border Roads organization (BRO) and National Highways Authority of India (NHAI) also attended the meeting. Shri Brahm Dutt discussed the issues, which have adversely affected progress of East West corridor in Assam like non-completion of land acquisition, diversion of forestland, shifting of telephone and electricity lines and security threat to workers and engineers. The Additional Chief Secretary of Assam assured Shri Dutt that the possession of the balance 43% land would be given to the NHAI within a fortnight. It was decided that the State government would direct the ground level officers of various departments to complete the works concerning their respective areas like shifting of utilities etc. on war-footing and in the meanwhile, NHAI would indicate priority of the areas where it needs to start work immediately. Shri Brahm Dutt also directed the NHAI officials to ensure that the contractors speed up the construction work the ground as the working season is going to start now and also to ensure that the project is completed by April 2010 as targeted. The Special Accelerated Road Development Programme (SARDP-NE) for the North Eastern States, especially the construction of Phase 'A' of the programme and preparation of Detailed Project Reports for the roads included in Phase 'B' was also reviewed comprehensively at the meeting. The issues of coordination between BRO and the States of Nagaland, Manipur and Tripura were resolved after deliberations. It was also decided that the State level monitoring committee headed by the Chief Secretary would be set up in all the states to monitor the programme on monthly basis. Shri Brahm Dutt pointed out that the States have not been able to make use of the sanctioned funds for maintenance of the National Highways. The Chief Engineers and Commissioners of the States and also the officials of the border road organization assured him that the entire fund allocated for improvement and repair of national highways would be utilized satisfactorily with the onset of working season. The Secretary also laid emphasis on construction of quality roads and directed that proper system and procedure should be evolved to ensure that all the roads are constructed to international standards as government has approved projects with high per km cost of Rs. two crore and above under SARDP-NE.

3519. (2-10-2007) NEW DELHI : The Prime Minister today released a set of four commemorative postage stamps on the occasion of International Day of Non-Violence. Today, October 2nd the birthday of Mahatma Gandhi is celebrated as International Day of Non-Violence by the United Nations from this year. Speaking on the occasion the Prime Minister said that Gandhiji's message was not just for India. Nor was it just for the times he lived in. Mahatma Gandhi's message of love and peace, of nonviolence and satyagraha, of the equality of all people, of harmony between all religions, is a universal message. It is a message for all times, for all societies, for all peoples. Gandhiji's message is more important today than ever before since nations across the world continue to grapple with the threat of conflict, violence and terrorism. For as long as there is temptation to resort to violence in the human mind, the Mahatma's message of nonviolence will tug at our hearts. Dr. Shakeel Ahmad, Minister of State for Communications and IT, said that the Department of Posts is privileged to release a set of commemorative postage stamps to mark the Centenary of Satyagraha. This set of four stamps entitled Satyagraha: the Stirrings is dedicated to the spirit of Satyagraha and is an endeavour to reflect on how a colossal revolution took place based on the philosophy of non-violent resistance. It is an attempt to turn the search light on oneself to find an alternative to violence within, which threatens to destroy the very fabric of civilized existence.

3520. (2-10-2007) NEW DELHI : The Prime Minister, Dr. Manmohan Singh, administered a pledge to the nation and released a commemorative postage stamp on the occasion of 138th birth anniversary of Mahatma Gandhi and celebration of International Day of Non-Violence here today. Following is the text of Prime Minister's address on the occasion: We in India have observed this day for decades as a day of prayer and thanksgiving. Every Indian has, year after year, thanked the Almighty on this day for bringing into this world such a noble soul as Mahatma Gandhi. But, today the heart of every Indian, of every citizen of the world who has been touched by the message of Mahatma Gandhi, is filled with joy and gratitude. We are grateful to the world community for declaring this auspicious day as the International Day of Non-Violence. Mahatma Gandhi's message was not just for India. Nor was it just for the times he lived in. Mahatma Gandhi's message of love and peace, of nonviolence and satyagraha, of the equality of all peoples, of harmony between all religions, is a universal message. It is a message for all times, for all societies and for all peoples. We in India are proud and grateful that the international community has declared this day as the International Day of Non-Violence. This unanimous decision of the United Nation General Assembly originates in a declaration of the International Conference on Peace, Nonviolence and Empowerment: The Gandhian Philosophy in the 21st Century, a conference which was convened by Smt. Sonia Gandhi and that met some months ago in New Delhi. This conference, commemorating the centenary of the Satyagraha Movement launched by Gandhiji, underscored the universal relevance of Mahatma Gandhi's message of nonviolence and the fight for truth. The decision was truly historic and universally welcomed. We are truly grateful to all those who supported this magnificent idea at the United Nation. Gandhiji's message is more important today than ever before since nations across the world continue to grapple with the threat of conflict, violence and terrorism. For as long as there is temptation to resort to violence in the human mind, the Mahatma's message of nonviolence will tug at our hearts.

3521. (3-10-2007) NEW DELHI : The GEAC did not give permission to conduct Large Scale trials on Bt Brinjal hybrids SBJ 1 Bt, SBJ 2 Bt SBJ 4 Bt, SBJ 6 Bt, SBJ 7 Bt and SBJ 8 Bt expressing cry 1Ac gene. The Committee expressed the view the Bt brinjgal hybrids developed by M/s. Mahyco is still under review and therefore the present request can not be considered at this stage. Permission to conduct confined Multi Location Research Trial (MLRT) on 2 Bt cabbage hybrids namely SCB-3 Bt and SCB-7 Bt expressing cry1Ac gene by conducting Multi Location Research Trial (MLRT) during Rabi 2007 was taken up for discussion. As the Bt cabbage has no place in the 24 items approved by the GEAC during 1.5.2006 to 22.9.2006, this approval will be subject to the outcome of the Hon'ble Supreme Court's decision. This will depend on submitting the name of the Lead Scientists responsible for the trails before undertaking the trials, submission of an event specific test protocol duly validated/verified by ICGEB, New Delhi, maintenance of an isolation distance of minimum 200 m and MLRT shall not be conducted in farmer's field. For strip trial with transgenic tomato (cv. Pusa.Ruby) has been considered with certain conditions. They include strip trials for new events should be undertaken by the companies/institutions in their own premises/

research farms and a distance of 200 m should be maintained. The applicant also should submit a validated event specific test protocol before undertaking the trial. The Committee considered permission to commercial release/strip trials of Bt cotton hybrids with approve gene events. Says no to large scale trials on bTs. The Committee noted that the proposals for commercial release and strip trials have completed the requisite regulatory testing and evaluation process. The GEAC therefore approved this proposal. It was decided that this approval would be valid for Kharif 2008 only. The GEAC also gave permission for Bt rice and RB-transgenic potato lines. Permission has been given for extension of the period for conducting replicated confined Multi-Location Research Trial (MLRT) on Bt rice hybrid containing cry1Ac gene from Kharif 2007 to Rabi 2007 and to generate the biosafety data. Regarding RB-transgenic potato lines (SP-951) permission to extension of the period for conducting contained limited field research trial (strip trial) from kharif-2007 to Rabi-2007 by Central Potato Research Institute, Shimla has been granted. The trials of these items could not take place during Kharif 2007, the GEAC approved to conduct the same during Rabi 2007. The applicant also should submit a validated event specific test protocol before undertaking the trials. After detailed deliberations the GEAC approved the request for strip trials subject to the following conditions: The applicant should submit to the RCGM/GEAC the name of the Lead Scientist responsible for the trials before undertaking the trials. The applicant should submit to the RCGM/GEAC an event specific test protocol duly validated/ verified by ICGEB, New Delhi / NBRI, Lucknow or any other accredited laboratory before undertaking the trials. An isolation distance of minimum 200 m shall be maintained. In cases where the Seed Standards Certification mandates a larger isolation distance, the same shall be maintained. The Strip trials shall not be conducted in farmers' field. Strip trials should be undertaken by the Companies/Institutions in their own premises or research farms.

3522. (3-10-2007) NEW DELHI : Smt. D. Purandeswari, Minister of State for Human Resource Development has said that the number of out-of-school children in India was estimated to be about 39 million, since then, this figure has fallen steadily, and in November 2005 it was reported to be around 10 million. She said while delivering a keynote address at the 4th International Conference of Asia Education Foundation (AEF) and Field Work Programme at India Habitat Centre, here, today. The Minister said that a National Programme of Nutritional Support to primary education or the Mid-Day Meal scheme was launched on 15th August 1995 to give a boost to Universal Primary Education. The other main vehicle at present for providing universal education for all children is a comprehensive programme called Sarva Shiksha Abhiyan (SSA), which was launched in 2001-02. SSA is a time bound mission with the objectives of ensuring universalisation of elementary education and bridging of gender and social gaps by 2010. The Minister added that 100 per cent success in these schemes is yet to be achieved and assured that shortcomings and deficiencies in the functioning of these schemes are continuously being monitored. She said "the emphasis for us are the child centric schemes". 'The World Conference on Education for All held in Jomtien in 1990 set this process in motion by adopting that the goal of Universal Primary Education be achieved by 2000 AD. The World Education Forum in Dakar in 2000 reaffirmed and extended this commitment. Universal primary education with complete gender equity in primary and secondary education was affirmed again in the same year as Millennium Development Goal', she said. The Minister further elaborated that what is to be ensured now is that there should be a vocational bias at the end of secondary education in the absence of which, students are presently proceeding to higher education pursuing degree course in general education resulting in the creation of surplus manpower who do not fulfil the productive requirements of the country. Diversification of education at secondary level would reduce the pressure on higher education. Vocationalization and terminalization of education at the middle school level and secondary education level is essential to gear up educational development for economic growth. 'India is emerging on the world stage as the largest economically powerful, culturally vibrant, multi-ethnic and multi-religious democracy. With a population of over 1 billion people, an expanding middle-class of 300 million and GDP growth rate of nearly ten percent, India cannot be ignored', she said. Australian Government initiated this Conference to promote learning about countries of Asia in Australian Primary and Secondary Schools. 250 delegates from Australia which included teachers, Principals, Education Administrators and teacher educators have attended the conference, which is scheduled for 5 days. Other speakers included Australian High Commissioner to India, His Excellency John Mc Carthy, Mr. Sai Nath, Dr. Karthikeyan and Prof. Mishural Hussain.

3523. (3-10-2007) NEW DELHI : Shri S.Regupathy, Minister of State for Environment and Forests, said that our biodiversity is a part of rich natural heritage. The Government of India has concerted efforts for protection and preservation of wild flora and fauna. The Minister said that our country is endowed with variety of flora and fauna and is among one of 12 Mega Biodiversity Countries in the world. For its protection we have formulated a comprehensive national policy, wildlife conservation strategy and National Wildlife Action Plan, apart from comprehensive legislation for wildlife protection. Addressing Valedictory function on the eve of the Wildlife Week Celebrations, Shri Regupathy further said that for better management and protection of wildlife a large network of 606 Protected Areas comprising 96 National Parks and 510 Wildlife Sanctuaries has been created. This covers an area of 15.59 million hectare. Shri Regupathy informed that Project Tiger has been restructured and transformed into the National Tiger Conservation Authority with wider mandate and powers. Shri Regupathy said that in recent years greater emphasis has been given on the better management planning for protected areas, expeditious settlement of rights, improved habitat management and strengthening of enforcement infrastructure. Shri Regupathy added that recently focus has been given on eco-development and improvement of rural livelihood programmes which take care of entire landscape. The Minister said that mammoth task of protecting the wildlife, people's participation and their support are crucial for implementation of policies and programmes. Some of the individuals and organizations have created a long lasting impact due to their exemplary and outstanding achievements in the field of wildlife conservation. Distributing Rajiv Gandhi Wildlife Conservation Awards to Shri Mike Pandey for the year 2004 and to Shri Himmat Singh Negi for the year 2005, he expressed hope that the efforts of the Government and the support of people will go a long way towards wildlife protection and preservation. On the occasion of the Wildlife Week, a message from the Prime Minister was also read. The Prime Minister called upon all the countrymen to follow the example of Mahatma Gandhi's birth anniversary, which coincides with the Wildlife Week, to follow his example to pledge to protect our wildlife and biological resources for posterity. Ms Meena Gupta, Secretary, Ministry of Environment and Forests said that the nation celebrates the Wildlife Week, in the first week of October, coinciding with the birth anniversary of Mahatma Gandhi. It is an occasion for all of us to reflect upon the marvelous creatures and plants collectively known as wild life, the rich natural heritage that they contribute, the importance of preserving and conserving them, she added. Expressing concerns over steadily shrinking nature and wild spaces, the Secretary said that wildlife conservation is enormously difficult task in today's world. She added that with human beings converting nature to serve their own comforts, they are changing climate of this world, which was once a vast expanse of landscape and water spaces teeming with innumerable life forms, plants and animals. She said that in India the ethos of conservation are deeply ingrained in our national culture. Conservation Movements by people such as Chipko Movement in Uttarakhand and the Bishnoi Conservation of Rajasthan bear testimony to this. The story of the Dodo, a bird of Madagascer and Passenger pigeon in North America are such examples of extinction. In our own country we lost Cheetah and Himalayan Quail. The tiger, the lion, the elephant, the rhino and many other lesser-known species are seriously threatened due to loss of forest. At this hour, it is delighted to say that many children and NGOs are concerned about conservation and are present here to receive various awards for exemplary work in the field of conservation of wildlife.

3524. (3-10-2007) NEW DELHI : Spinning of khadi yarn will no more be a monotonous work. One can now listen to music while spinning Charkha and generate electricity that can be used when the power goes off. Khadi & Village Industries Commission (KVIC) has developed an e-charkha, that would be formally launched by the President of India on the 19th November, 2007. Giving a demonstration on the e-charkha before media persons in Mumbai yesterday, the Chairperson of the Khadi & Village Industries Commission, Ms Kumud Joshi said "The Charkha will be a boon to the spinners, who would be able to experience the fusion of economic activity with the pleasure of music while working on the e-charkha." The e-charkha has been developed by Shri Hiremath, a Bangalore based engineer, who has been active in the field of non-conventional energy resources. The Charkha has maintenance free lead acid battery fixed at the bottom, which functions as an inverter. Spinning the Charkha for about two hours will give back up power for about 6-7 hours of basic lighting and playing radio. The cost of the new age Charkha is approximately Rs 3,000. KVIC plans to induct two lakh pieces of e-charkha at Khadi weaving centres across the country.

3525. (3-10-2007) NEW DELHI : A delegation of farmers from Medak district in Andhra Pradesh met me last week to apprise me of a unique campaign that they had undertaken to highight the problem of kisan suicides in the Telangana region of the state. Four of them D. Vasant Kumar, G. Govind Reddy, K. Narayan Reddy and K. Ramulu had come to Delhi on a 'Kisan Azadi Pad Yatra', covering a distance of 1840 kms on foot in 54 days. They explained to me the numerous difficulties faced by farmers, especially sugarcane-growers, in their region, which were compounded by the faulty policies and callous attitude of the central and state governments. As is well known, thousands of debt-ridden farmers have committed suicide in the Telengana region of Andhra Pradesh. Many such cases have also been reported from Medak district. I complimented the young kisan activists on their arduous pad yatra and conveyed my best wishes for the dharna they had planned at Jantar Mantar, along with scores of kisans from Medak who were expected to join them the following day. Yesterday I learnt that Vasant Kumar and Govind Reddy had also begun an indefinite hunger strike to draw the attention of the government to the plight of farmers in Telangana. Their hunger strike has entered the sixth day today. Concerned about their health, especially in view of the fact that they have suffered the strain of walking continuously for nearly two months all the way from Medak to Delhi, I appealed to them to call off their hunger strike. I said they had already done enough indeed, more than what one would expect from a non-political organization of youngsters to highlight the problems of kisans in their state.

3526. (3-10-2007) NEW DELHI : The total import of sensitive items for the period April-July 07 has been Rs 6356 crores as compared to Rs 6301 crores during the corresponding period of last year thereby showing an increase of 0.9%. The gross import of all commodity during same period of current year was Rs 297081 crores as compared to Rs 253546 crores during the same period of last year. Thus import of sensitive items constitute 2.5% and 2.1% of the gross imports during last year and current year respectively. Imports of fruits & vegetables (including nuts), products of SSI, marble & Granite, Tea & Coffee and milk & milk products have shown a decline at broad group level whereas imports of cotton & silk, automobiles, rubber and Alcoholic beverages have shown an increase. In the edible oil segment, the import has increased very marginally from Rs.3547.51 crores last year to Rs 3551.15 crores for the corresponding period of this year. The import of crude oil has gone down by 1.7% and that of refined oil has gone up by 36.7%. There is significant growth in import of Crude palm oil and its fractions, which has gone up by 19%. Imports of sensitive items from Indonesia,

United States of America, Brazil, Germany, Japan, Thailand, Australia etc. have gone up while those from Argentina, China P RP, Cote D' Ivoire, Malaysia, Benin, Sri Lanka DSR, Egypt A RP etc. have shown a decrease.

3527. (3-10-2007) NEW DELHI : Development and strengthening of intelligence agencies should receive first priority in any plan for combating crime and terrorism. The Union Home Minister, Shri Shivraj Patil said this while inaugurating a Conference of Directors General of Police and Inspectors General of Police here today. He said that no weapon or device is going to be as useful as intelligence can be to control and contain crimes, violence and terrorism. The Home Minister called upon the States to equip their special branches with modern advanced gadgets and technologies. Shri Shivraj Patil said that crimes committed against weaker sections of the society should be handled with determination and constant vigilance. The demands of these sections to have a just share in the police should never be lost sight of while recruiting candidates for the police forces. The Home Minister said that without a sense of security prevailing in the states, investments by entrepreneurs will not be possible. The strength of policemen and officers in the States is not adequate to meet the growing requirements of policing. In fact, the number should go up. The police cannot afford to lag behind the criminals, in making use of new ideas, equipment, technologies, and training. About the situation in Jammu & Kashmir, the Home Minister said that it continues to show definite improvement. However, there is no scope for complacency when infiltration across the border continues and terrorist incidents are still taking place. About the North-Eastern Region, he said, the security situation in the States like Meghalaya, Mizoram, Tripura and Arunachal Pradesh has been comfortable. However, continued violence in Assam and Manipur and persisting factional clashes in Nagaland are causes for concern. On Naxal violence, the Home Minister said that in some States, it has been contained, but in some others, Naxal problem has become more difficult. Since the problem cuts across State boundaries, the States would need to pursue a coordinated approach to meet this challenge. The Home Minister also stressed the need for police reforms and reforms in the Criminal Justice System. He also drew attention towards the role of media in maintenance of peace and public order. The Home Minister gave away the Indian Police Medals for meritorious service. 42 officers of the Intelligence Bureau have received the medals. The Conference of DGPs/IGPs in India is being organized by the Intelligence Bureau since 1920. The conference has been held regularly in New Delhi. The Director, Intelligence Bureau continues to remain the ex-officio Chairman of the Conference. This year's DGPs/IGPs Conference is the 42nd since Independence.

3528. (3-10-2007) NEW DELHI : Congress Spokesperson Smt. Jayanti Natarajan said that the Congress President and UPA Chairperson Smt. Sonia Gandhi, while addressing the United Nations General Assembly on the occasion of Gandhi jayanti and the first International Day of Nonviolence, thanked the entire world community for having paid homage to one of the world's greatest man of all time and having made this very important recognition of Mahatama Gandhi and of acknowledging the relevance of Gandhiji's philosophy of satyagraha and ahimsa in this contemporary world. To a question whether the Congress Party had capitulated to the Left Smt. Jayanti reiterated Smt. Gandhi's statement that there is no cause for alarm and the words speak for themselves and there is no question of capitulating to anybody. The issue is that we are hopeful that we will be able to convince our allies and our supporters of the importance of this Nuclear deal for our country, especially in terms of civilian energy. To a question on the Congress Party's stand on the Karnataka crisis Smt. Jayanti said, As far as Karnataka is concerned, I am sure the General Secretary in charge of Karnataka will be able to tell you more. But the stand of the Party is that we really do not have a role at the moment. I am not here to second guess what the Prime Minister said. I am only saying that we do not have any role at the moment. Politics is a constantly evolving and changing dynamic. It's not a question of what somebody said three months ago. Today's situation will have to be evaluated, at the moment we don't have a role. It's between the JD-S and the BJP. I have no idea of the way the BJP mind will function. All that I know is that they are incapable of seeing reality or working for the welfare of the people of the country. We have a mind, a tradition of commitment to the welfare of the people of the country. The Congress action plan is not based upon the activities of the Opposition party, especially the BJP. Our action plan is a positive commitment based upon a common minimum programme and the welfare of the people. We would not wish anybody to supports the BJP which does have a communal agenda. We do not wish that anybody supports the BJP which is a communal party. To a question that because of Gandhi jayanti, the Congress Party has forgotten the birthday of Sh. Lal Bahadur Shastri, Smt Jayanti said, we did have a function in Delhi as well as in Mumbai and the Home Minister was present on the occasion.

3529. (3-10-2007) NEW DELHI : The Khadi & Village Industries Commission (KVIC), under the Ministry of Micro, Small & Medium Enterprises launched Gandhi Jayanti Special Sales Rebate Campaign here today. Smt. Sheila Dikshit, Chief Minister of Delhi was the Chief Guest at the Special Rebate launch programme. Ms. Kumud Joshi, Chairperson, KVIC presided over the function. Up to 30 per cent rebate will be given on all khadi and polyvastra products. It may be mentioned that three registered brands are being used by the KVIC, exclusively for products under the purview of KVI sector: (a) Khadi Brand: Mainly for premium and export oriented products, (b) Sarvodaya Brand: Products for consumption of middle and lower income group & (c) Deshi Aahar: For organic food items. KVIC takes part in international trade fairs and exhibitions also where, branded products, including khadi items, are widely exhibited. Delegations of Export oriented Units/Institutions registered with KVIC/State/Union Territory Khadi and Village Industries Boards (KVIBs) are also provided financial assistance to participate in the international exhibitions. During 2006-07, KVIC took part in 5 such exhibitions. Every year on the occasion of Gandhi Jayanti, Special Rebate Sales Campaign is undertaken by KVIC. This rebate will continue till mid-January 2008.

3530. (3-10-2007) NEW DELHI : Shri. Vayalar Ravi, Minister of Overseas Indian Affairs has said that the government will soon establish a 'Diaspora Knowledge Network'-an electronic platform to enable the Indian Diaspora to deploy its knowledge and skills and transform ideas into individual initiatives and community action in India. He was speaking at the Harvard University on 'The Indian Diaspora: It's contribution to India's Economic Development' on the occasion of "Mahatma Gandhi Jayanti'. He said that we live in turbulent times, in a world that is profoundly divided between the haves and the have-nots. A world, witness to considerable violence and acts of terror. These are times when the world must be inspired, once again, by the principles of Truth and Nonviolence that the great apostle of peace-Mahatma Gandhi lived and died by. Shri Ravi announced that Government will soon establish a 'Global Indian Foundation', to provide the Overseas Indian Community a credible window to lead Diaspora Philanthropy into deserving causes such as education, health and rural development in India. He further said that Overseas Indians are being engaged through the Overseas Citizenship of India scheme. This scheme is exactly similar to the Green Card of USA. And the newly established Overseas Indian Facilitation Centre, a not for profit trust, promoted by my Ministry can be the Diaspora's window to invest in and benefit from India. It will serve as a 'one stop shop', he added. He informed that the size, the spread and the growing influence of overseas Indians is truly impressive. Estimated at about 30 million in 130 countries, the Indian Diaspora is a significant economic, social and cultural force in the world today. They are a representation of India: its peoples, regions, religions, languages, values, cultures and histories. The Overseas Indians worldwide who are our brand ambassadors produce an economic output of about $ 400 billion. The Indian Diaspora is estimated to generate an annual income equal to about 30 percent of India's Gross Domestic Product. He also informed that India is already the highest recipient of remittances from overseas Indians at over $ 23 billion last year. What is less known though is the fact that nearly half of these remittances-about $ 12 billion annually-comes from just 5 million overseas Indians in the Gulf. The Minister said that India is a country of young people with 54 percent of its population in the age group below 25 years. By 2020, India will become the world's youngest nation with the largest workforce of 820 million in the working age group (18 to 59) as compared to 400 million today. This will be a time when it will have the potential to dramatically enhance labour supply and productivity. The Overseas Indians comprise one of the largest, most diverse, best educated communities wherever they reside has added to India's brand as a 'knowledge economy'. The Indian Diaspora can contribute in substantial measure.

3531. (3-10-2007) NEW DELHI : Press Information Bureau, Ministry of Information & Broadcasting, observed Hindi Fortnight from September 14 to 28, 2007. Competitions in Hindi language on essay writing, drafting, translation, comments, typing and official language Q&A were held during this period with a view to promote and recognize the use of Hindi in office working. The competitions were held in eleven different categories for officers and staff. Shri S. M. Khan, Dy. Director General, awarded certificates and cash prizes to the winners today.

3532. (3-10-2007) NEW DELHI : Lt Gen Milan Lalitkumar Naidu, till recently Army Commander of Army's Shimla based Training Command has taken over as the next Vice Chief of Indian Army. He replaces Gen Deepak Kapoor, who has since taken over as Army Chief. Lt Gen Naidu paid tributes to martyrs at Amar Jawan Jyoti here this morning. This was followed by a guard of honour in the lawns of South Block. Lieutenant General Naidu had his early education at St Joseph's Convent, Bhopal, and to continue his family tradition, joined the National Defence Academy, Khadakvasla, where he excelled in marksmanship (shooting). Commissioned in the Rajput Regiment in Dec 1967, he has had a long and chequered career having served in all sectors and terrains in India and abroad. As Commanding Officer of 5 Rajput he participated in Op PAWAN in Sri Lanka where he was awarded the Yudh Seva Medal. He has the experience of Commanding a brigade in the semi desert terrain, a division in the plains of Punjab during Op PARAKRAM and a Corps in the high altitude and glaciated region. Selected to attend the Defence Services Staff College Course in Canada, Lt Gen Naidu has also attended the Higher Command Course at the Army War College. He also holds a Post Graduate in Environmental and Ecological Sciences. Lt Gen Naidu's forte has been in the field on instruction. Having trained cadets and young officers at the Indian Military Academy and the Infantry School, he has also had the distinction of being the Commandant of Indian Army's premier officers' training establishment for combat-Army War College. Lt Gen Naidu has had varied operational staff experience at all levels including a stint at the Military Operations Directorate at Army HQ. He was also the Defence Attaché in Germany. He is a keen sportsman and formed part of the Services team in the National Skeet Shooting Championship in 1968. He also plays golf, tennis and cricket. Lt Gen Naidu is also the recipient of Ati Vishist Seva Medal for distinguished services. Lt Gen Naidu is married to Mrs Neeharika who is the daughter of Lt Col Awasthy, a veteran of World War II and 1962 Operations.

3533. (3-10-2007) NEW DELHI : Shri. Jaipal Reddy, Union Minister for Urban Development has said that it was essential for higher levels of government to empower Urban Local Bodies and build their capacities to manage the inevitable process of urbanization that the country in experiencing. Shri Reddy was speaking at the India urban Space 2007 Expo at Mumbai recently. Shri Reddy inaugurated the Urban Conference and Expo. Addressing over 1000 delegates at the inaugural function of India Urban Space (IUSP) 2007, Shri. Jaipal Reddy urged the city leaders-Mayors and Municipal Commissioners to rise to the challenge of urban change. Coming in the backdrop of implementation of the Jawaharlal Nehru Urban Development Mission (JNNURM), the event was organized by India Urban Space Foundation in partnership with the Ministry of Urban Development, Government of India. Shri. Jaipal Reddy complemented the India Urban Space Foundation,for providing this platform for city representatives, private sector and leading experts to interact on wide range of urban planning and project implementation issues. Discussions were held on issues related to spatial planning, water supply and sanitation issues, waste management, urban transport, urban finances and e-governance. Addressing the gathering, Urban Development Secretary, Shri. M Ramachandran, said that India Urban Space itself is a good example of public private partnership, not for building infrastructure projects, but as an event that forges partnerships for exchange of ideas, solutions and knowledge. The event brought out the energy and sense of pride and competition amongst city officials, hitherto unknown amongst our cities. Shri. Jaipal Reddy, also gave away the IUSP-IL&FS Urban Implementation Awards for excellence in implementation of urban infrastructure projects. The awards were given to the town of Suryapet from Andhra Pradesh for excellence in solid waste management; the city of Indore for public-partnership model in building city roads; and the town of Rampur from Uttar Pradesh for use of innovative trenchless technologies for building sewer systems in congested areas. Earlier, Shri. Jaipal Reddy inaugurated the Urban Expo. Over 30 cities from across the country participated at the expo, showcasing their city vision, flagship projects and urban development initiatives. Cities ranging from large metros like Ahmedabad, Kolkata and Mumbai to small towns like Ujjain and Nanded participated in the Urban Expo. About 50 private sector companies and other service providers showcased their technologies, products and services at this Urban Expo. The municipalities of Surat, Kolkata and Greater Mumbai received awards for the best city booths at the Urban Expo from India Urban Space Foundation. Over 1,200 representatives from cities comprising mayors, municipal councilors, municipal commissioners, engineers and officials participated in the event.

3534. (3-10-2007) NEW DELHI : Shri A.Raja, Minister of Communications and Information Technology has emphasized the need to develop telecom infrastructure at a fast pace as it goes hand in hand with the economic development. Poverty and Unemployment in the Rural Sector are major challenges our country is facing today. Companies while ensuring profits for themselves should also focus on how they can use new technologies to address these problems. The Minister was speaking at a function to release the Compendium on Next Generation Networks here today. India which is well known for its IT talent base could use ICT technologies to advantage, he suggested the Department of Telecom should form a focus group and deliberate on innovative methods to make an action plan to bring broadband connectivity to rural areas at a much faster rate than presently envisaged. New innovative technologies in NGN could be used to support ICT to accelerate the present rate of rural coverage. India could look at a model where engineers could become entrepreneurs and multiply the wealth of the country. We have therefore to ensure that the benefits of new technologies like NGN are delivered to rural masses and that they bring value-addition in their lives through increased agricultural production and make life easier for the rural masses, he added. Telecommunication Engineering Centre (TEC), a technical body for telecom technology, under Department of Telecom (DoT), has played a lead role over the past 50 years in laying standards driven robust telecommunication network in the country. Traditionally, the TEC has been assisting the incumbent operators in providing technical support to plan and set up reliable telecom infrastructure in every nook and corner of the country. After the sector was opened to private competition, there have been a number of new networks and tele-density has seen tremendous growth. With the government's target of 250 million telephones by 2007 likely to be achieved in advance, the industry has set a new target for itself of achieving 500 million telephones by 2010. As competition becomes stiff, the operators are not simply looking for voice traffic but are planning to rollout triple play services. Standards bodies are becoming the rallying point for industry to ensure that the products and services follow an accepted standard so that products that are manufactured by different vendors are inter-operable. In a highly competitive environment, when there are multiple operators and multiple technology choices available for a user, security, quality-of-service, end-to-end availability of seamless services across networks, number portability, availability of adequate IP addressees, and bridging the digital divide especially in rural areas become serious issues.

3535. (3-10-2007) NEW DELHI : The Prime Minister, Dr. Manmohan Singh, addressed the 66th Annual General Meeting of Indian Language Newspapers Association here today. He also gave away awards to the regional language/ publications for their outstanding contribution in the field of language journalism. Here is the text of the Prime Minister's speech on the occasion: "I am delighted to have this opportunity to meet a very celebrated group of journalists and newspapermen from Indian language publication. Each one of you has played and is playing an important role in the process of nation building. I compliment you and particularly those who have won the very prestigious awards of ILNA for the very impressive performance of Indian Languages papers in recent years. There is concern all over the world over that the growth of television and internet threatens the survival of print media. In many countries, readership of newspapers is declining. Even in India, there is a deceleration in the growth of English language publications. Despite these developments, I am very happy to note that Indian language newspapers have bucked this trend. I am heartened to learn that the readership and circulation of Indian language newspapers is growing rapidly. I commend you for your efforts. We have witnessed, in India, an unprecedented growth both in readership and viewership of media. Rising literacy rates, growing political awareness and rising levels of incomes, along with processes of urbanisation, have contributed to this phenomena. It may be no exaggeration to suggest that we are living through a golden era of Indian media. The expansion of your market has contributed to greater employment opportunities as well as the growth of other media related industries and services. I compliment you for your spirit of adventure, enterprise and creativity. This growth has also widened the choice available to your readers and viewers. There is much greater variety, today, in terms of opinion and coverage. Depending on one's outlook, income and interest, one can pick and choose a newspaper or a channel of one's choice. Such diversity is always good in a democracy. I am also impressed by the quality of printing and production in Indian languages publication. All of this, we must celebrate. I am sure your organisation has reasons to feel satisfied about these impressive aspects of the growth of your profession. On the other hand, I must draw your attention to certain issues and urge you to reflect on them. I have said in the past that the quantitative growth we have witnessed in Indian media has outpaced qualitative growth. This is understandable partly because demand has been outstripping the supply of well trained journalists. In the long run, I hope, as supply adjust this problem will get addressed. But it does need the attention of your industry. I sincerely hope that your Association will pay greater attention to the challenge of improving the quality of journalism in our country. You are the medium through which the message of modernisation, the message of development, the message of national integration and the message of social justice must go to the far corners of our country. You have to promote communal harmony and secular values, which are the bedrock of our nation. You have a vital role to play in the transformation of our society and our polity. This is no doubt an onerous responsibility placed on the shoulders of Indian language media. The vast majority of our people see the world through your eyes. They see changes happening in our country and in their own regions through your coverage. Their thinking is shaped by the opinions you express through your newspapers. The challenge before you, therefore, is to help take India forward by changing the mindsets of our population. Modernisation is not just about better infrastructure, not about mere more creative comforts or the way we dress and live. Modernisation in the final analysis is an attitude of the state of the mind of our people. In an ancient land like India, successful modernisation must be rooted in our enduring traditions and socio-cultural values. At the same time, we must adapt some of these values, some of these norms to suit the needs of changing time. For example, our attitude towards the caste, our attitude towards women and to manual work. These must change so that our people, particularly our women and the downtrodden sections of our society do feel that they are part of the processes of social change and our effective partners in processes of social and economic development. Modernisation is not westernisation.

3536. (3-10-2007) NEW DELHI : The total approximate earnings of Indian Railways on originating basis during the period 11th September-20th September 2007 were Rs. 1815.18 crore compared to Rs. 1595.37 crore during the same period last year, registering an increase of 13.78 per cent. The total goods earnings have gone up from Rs. 1052.49 crore during 11th September-20th September 2006 to Rs. 1173.79 crore during 11th September-20th September 2007, showing an increase of 11.53 per cent. The total passenger revenue earnings during the period 11-20 September 2007 were Rs. 578.23 crore compared to Rs. 531.19 crore during the same period last year, reflecting an increase of 21.34 per cent. The revenue earnings from other coaching amounted to Rs. 46.24 crore during this period compared to Rs. 43.36 crore during the same period last year, showing an increase of 6.64 per cent. The total approximate number of passengers booked during the period 11-20 September 2007 were 188.92 million compared to 183.91 million during the same period last year, showing an increase of 2.72 per cent. In the suburban and non-suburban sectors, the number of passengers booked during 11-20 September 2007 were 107.50 million and 81.42 million compared to 107.85 million and 76.06 million during the same period last year, registering a decrease of 0.32 per cent and an increase 7.05 per cent respectively.

3537. (3-10-2007) NEW DELHI : Union Minister for Agriculture and Food, Shri Sharad Pawar, today called upon the States to promote ethanol production from sugarcane with a view to tackle the glut in availability of sugar in the country. Addressing the State Finance Ministers and Ministers dealing with sugar and sugarcane, Shri Pawar highlighted that against domestic consumption of about 190 lakh tonnes a year, sugar production in the coming year is likely to be about 290 lakh tonnes. This, together with the closing stock of about 119 lakh tonnes of sugar from 2006-07, has resulted in a very large sugar stock in the country. The Minister stated that the Government has taken a number of steps such as creation of a buffer stock of 50 lakh tonnes, waiver of margin requirement on the buffer stock, and export assistance. However, these measures cannot liquidate such huge stocks. High availability and low prices in the international market also disfavour exports. Because of this, sugar companies are reeling under huge arrears to be paid to farmers. The answer to the cyclical problem faced by the Indian sugar industry probably lies in converting surplus sugarcane directly to the ethanol, the Minister said. Emphasising that ethanol production would succeed only if continuous and adequate demand for ethanol is ensured, Shri Pawar called upon the States to remove all impediments imposed on free and unrestricted movement of denatured ethanol and avoid imposition of State taxes. 'The best way to achieve this is by including "denatured ethanol of 99% strength" in the "list of special goods" under CST Act, 1956. Such a step will lead to many benefits from the point of the national objectives while improving the condition of a sugar industry and the sugarcane farmers to a large extent', he said. Shri Pawar also argued that fixing State Advised Prices (SAP) by different States over and above the Statutory Minimum Price (SMP) fixed by the Central Government is leading to huge cane price arrears. The gap between the SAP and SMP has been widening for some States quite drastically. This results in huge production of sugarcane and low sugar prices resulting in the sugar mills not being able to meet the cost of sugarcane and building up of cane price arrears. As compared to last year when there were practically no cane arrears, the arrears have risen to the tune of Rs. 3800 crore this year, affecting the entire sugar industry including the farmers, he said.

3538. (3-10-2007) NEW DELHI : The first summit team of Indo Australian to Mt Shivling (6543M) expedition has successfully summitted the peak in Garhwal

Himalayas today at 1630 hrs. This team comprised of five Indian members and two Australians. The Australian members are Lt Col Mathew David Rogerson and Trooper Max Jonathan Pemberton. Lt Col Rogerson is leader of the Australian climbers. The Indian Army personnel include Sub Neel Chandra, Naik Jagmohan Singh, Rifleman Amit Kumar, L/Nk Mangal Singh and L/Nk Gyaltsen. The second team is to attempt the summit on Friday.

3539. (3-10-2007) NEW DELHI : Introduced in 2004, Air Force Essay and Quiz Competition has become a part of the AF Day Celebrations. This year too, the Directorate of Education as part of the AF Day Celebrations-2007 had organized an Essay Competition in Hindi and English for PBORs (Personnel Below Officer Rank) and Quiz Competition for children of AF Personnel in classes VIII to XII. An Essay Competition, both in Hindi and English was conducted at each Station; including Command Units. The Competition was open to all PBORs including NCs(E) (Non-Combatants Enrolled). The Essays were limited to a maximum of 1000 words. The winners of Essay Competition were (For Hindi)-Sgt Ashik Kumar, JWO BC Kumar and Cpl Ravi Ranjan (For English)-JWO D Ukl, LAC S Marimuthu and JWO Santra A Quiz Competition for children of AF Personnel studying in classes VII to XII was organized at AF Auditorium on 02 & 03 Oct. 07. A total of eight teams representing seven Commands and Air HQ participated in this competition. Each team consisted of four participants. Four teams namely, Maintenance Command, Western Air Command, Southern Air Command and Training Command made it to the final round which was conducted on 03 Oct. 07. The Chief of the Air Staff Air Chief Marshal FH Major PVSM, AVSM, SC VM ADC was the Chief Guest and Mrs. Zareen Major, President AFWWA gave away the prizes. The competition had an overwhelming response and was very keenly contested. The function was attended by a host of other Air Force dignitaries and children from Air Force Schools. 'Wings Quiz-2007' was conducted by the famous Quiz Master Mr. Derek O'Brien. The winners of the Quiz Competition were HQ TC, IAF-Winner, HQ SAC, IAF-First Runners Up and HQ WAC, IAF-Second Runners Up.

3540. (4-10-2007) NEW DELHI : Shri Kamal Nath, Commerce & Industry Minister, Govt. of India, has decided today that the exports of onion, which was hitherto canalized through the designated Public Sector agencies, be restricted immediately. Accordingly, a Notification has been issued by the Government providing that the exports of onion shall herein after be restricted and permissible only under an export license through designated canalizing agencies.

3541. (4-10-2007) NEW DELHI : Director of the National Institute of Health (NIH) USA Dr. Elias A. Zerhouni along with six other experts from the institute had a meeting today with the Health Minister Dr. Anbumani Ramadoss. The NIH, a part of the U.S. Department of Health and Human Services, is the primary Federal agency for conducting and supporting medical research. Helping to lead the way toward important medical discoveries that improve people's health and save lives, NIH scientists investigate ways to prevent disease as well as the causes, treatments, and even cures for common and rare diseases. The discussions mainly centred on cooperation and collaboration in the area of health research, funding for bio-ethics, capacity building and technology transfer under drug research. Special emphasis was also given for research collaboration in the fields of ageing, vaccine development, maternal and child health care, special tools for disease surveillance and environmental health. Appreciating the efforts made by the ministry in strengthening the clinical research the members expressed confidence that with the setting up of a separate Department of Health Research in the ministry the needed technologies and resources can be enhanced and the collaboration between the National Institute of Health and Indian Council of Medical Research will get further strengthened.

3542. (4-10-2007) BANGALORE: After Tuesday's resignation by the Bharatiya Janata Party Ministers in Karnataka, the action has shifted to New Delhi. The State BJP leaders have been summoned to attend a meeting of the Central Parliamentary Board. The Political Affairs Committee (PAC) of the Janata Dal (Secular) will also hold a meeting on October 5 to decide on the power transfer. Chief Minister H.D. Kumaraswamy, the former Prime Minister and JD(S) president, H.D. Deve Gowda, and other senior leaders are leaving for New Delhi after the JD(S) State executive meeting on Thursday. JD(S) sources told *The-Hindu* that the party had not received any indication of support from the Congress. They were hopeful of securing it now that it was becoming increasingly clear that the BJP would snap ties with the JD(S) if power was not handed over to it immediately. On Wednesday, Mr. Gowda and Mr. Kumaraswamy held detailed discussions on the developments. Prior to this, the Chief Minister exchanged notes with JD(S) Ministers and senior leaders. All that Mr. Gowda would say was that the next course of action would be decided on Friday after the meeting of the nine-member PAC. Incidentally, this is the first meeting of the PAC after Mr. Kumaraswamy and 39 other legislators aligned with the BJP to form a coalition government. The PAC's decision is expected to be conveyed to BJP president Rajnath Singh on the same day either by Mr. Gowda or by JD(S) vice-president Bapu Kaldate. Meanwhile, a senior BJP functionary told *The Hindu*, "We are not ready to wait beyond a week even if the JD(S) tries to drag the issue. If there is no decision from the JD(S), we may withdraw support to the present government on October 8 or 9." Senior leaders Yashwant Sinha and Venkaiah Naidu, and some State leaders, including Deputy Chief Minister B.S. Yediyurappa, have left for New Delhi.

3543. (4-10-2007) NEW DELHI : The Prime Minister, Dr. Manmohan Singh, addressed the Conference of Director Generals and Inspector Generals of Police-2007 here today. The Prime Minister also gave away President's Police Medal 2006 to the police personnel for their distinguished services. Following is the text of the Prime Minister's speech on the occasion: "Let me, at the very outset, extend my heartiest congratulations to the recipients of the President's Police Medal for

Distinguished Service. This award is an acknowledgement of your dedicated contribution to the maintenance of law and order. I also take this opportunity to convey my deep appreciation of the police fraternity for their significant contributions in fighting the forces of terrorism and instability with courage and determination. And all this, I recognize has been achieved despite heavy constraints and scarce resources. A policeman-like a farmer, a worker and a teacher-is an essential pillar of a civilized society. I believe that a nation and a society can be judged by how it treats each one of these professions. A nation that has diligent and productive farmers and workers, dedicated and committed teachers and policemen, is a truly fortunate country. The rule of law is the bedrock of any modern society. And as the key instrument for enforcing this rule of law, the police is one of the vital institutions of the state. I assure our police personnel that we are fully committed to their welfare and professional development. In turn we expect our police forces to be fearless, dedicated, competent and tough. At the same time, we expect them to be fair, humane and honest. The internal security situation in our country continues to remain a cause of concern for both the Central and State Governments. I have often said that most of the challenges we face are at home. Among them, the internal security challenge is one of the key ones. As we scan the internal security scenario, we notice a large number of incidents which should alert us to the formidable challenges we face as a nation. Hyderabad was witness recently to a heinous act of terrorism in which many innocent lives were lost. It was committed with an intent to terrorise ordinary citizens and demoralize our security apparatus. Naxalites attempted to eliminate a former Chief Minister near Nellore. Violent incidents continue in some states of the North East, particularly in Assam, Manipur and Nagaland. The ethnic overtones of violent acts in Assam are particularly disturbing. While the situation in Jammu & Kashmir has shown some overall improvement, violent incidents keep recurring. And last but not least, we are seeing many incidents of vigilantism and citizens taking law into their own hands, particularly in state like Bihar. While some of it could be a result of personal frustration, some of it also arises out of dissatisfaction over the functioning of the law enforcement and justice systems. These incidents-and many others you are well aware of-should only strengthen our resolve to constantly improve our internal security machinery. We need better police forces-better in all senses-be it training, be it skills, be it equipment, be it resources, be it mobility or be it attitudes. We need superior intelligence capabilities which can alert us to the impending threats. We need greater discipline, lesser politicization and zero corruption. We are committed to supporting your efforts in this direction.

3544. (4-10-2007) NEW DELHI : Following is the text of the speech delivered by the Defence Minister Shri A K Antony at the Golden Jubilee Celebration of Directorate General Quality Assurance (DGQA). 'I am indeed pleased to be amongst you on this occasion. The organization has contributed immensely to the all-round progress and development of the defence sector over the years. Our Armed Forces are among the best in the world. However, as is widely known, it is the man behind the machine who matters the most. Though the dedication and commitment of our Armed Forces is unparalleled, the role of latest equipment in modern day wars is of crucial importance. Modern-day war machinery is intricate and the complexities will only increase with advancement in technology. Therefore, modernization of our Armed Forces is a must and a continuous activity. The onus, therefore, lies on DGQA, not only to provide quality assurance, but also to optimize the efforts to maintain the reliability throughout the life-cycle of the equipment. I am sure that you will accord top priority to enlarging and broadening the vistas of knowledge of all the personnel to equip them to handle future challenges. Human resource is a vital component of any organization. Human resource development therefore, has to be accorded top priority. The outlook and mindsets must change, in tune with the changing times. These days, effective communication within the organization and with its clients is one of the most crucial parameters of its effectiveness. Thus, imparting professional training is the need of the hour. Today, the defence sector is growing at a fast pace. The role of DGQA becomes all the more important in such a scenario. You must look ahead and devise future plans keeping in mind the fact that Asia is bound to become the hub of economic activity in our region. The coming years will witness a change in the equipment profile of our Armed Forces. As cooperation between nations in the defence sector increases, the DGQA's role will undoubtedly increase. The Government is already going ahead with Reciprocal Government Quality Assurance (RGQA) Agreements with other countries. The onus will be on all of you to attain international standards and strive to be among the best in the world. In today's world of intense competition, your performance on the international scale will be judged by the levels of transparency and responsiveness to the needs of global players. I wish to assure you that on its part, the Government will provide all the support you require in your endeavours. I am sure that you will continue to strive to be among the best in the world. I congratulate all of you for the Golden Jubilee celebrations and wish you the very best for your future endeavours.'

3545. (4-10-2007) NEW DELHI : The second International Flight Safety Conference, IFSCON-07 is being organised by the Indian Air Force in New Delhi on 09-10 October 2007 at the Air Force Auditorium, Subroto Park. The objective of this conference is to address global aviation safety issues. The conference will provide a platform for mutual interaction of around 60 foreign delegates from 30 countries and delegates from a host of national aviation organisations. The foreign participants include delegates from across the globe viz. Europe, Russia, Middle-East, South & South East Asia and the Americas. The number of delegate countries has more than doubled from the inaugural conference held last year. Apart from the participating delegations of different nations, defence attaches of these countries would also take part in the conference. National delegates include those from the Indian Army, Indian Navy, Coast Guard, Border Security Force, Directorate General of Civil Aviation, Hindustan Aeronautics Limited, Airports Authority of India, Rotary Wing Society of India, Indian Airlines, private airline operators and a number of other bodies associated with aircraft research and development, certification and Quality Assurance. The Hon'ble Raksha Utpadan Rajya Mantri, Shri Rao Inderjit Singh, has kindly consented to inaugurate the conference on 09 Oct. 07. This will set the tone for two days of stimulating presentations and panel discussions on aviation safety subjects of universal interest. In keeping with the global concerns of all aviating countries and organizations, the broad issues planned to be addressed in the conference include: New Concepts: An Overview, Accident Investigation & Safety Management, Human Factors and Environmental & Organisational Issues. The conference would serve as a forum for meaningful interaction of experienced Aviation Safety functionaries of a spectrum of countries and agencies, all with a common goal,-promoting aviation safety. This conference will serve to smoothen adoption of new concepts and methodologies of accident prevention and significantly shorten the learning curve for induction of modern safety schemes. In this context, the theme of the Conference, Aviation Safety-A Universal Language, by itself speaks volumes of the mindset of the IAF, which seeks cooperation for an integrated approach to generate synergy in the field of Aviation Safety. Aviation activity in South Asia is seeing a dramatic growth, both in military and civil aviation. The scale of induction of modern aircraft is unprecedented in numbers, technology, capability and cost. Precious national resources are being devoted for the purpose and it must be the endeavour of all stakeholders to ensure the preservation of aviation assets. This growth in aviation requires support both through infrastructure development and trained manpower. Modernization and rapid growth bring with them numerous challenges related to safe operations, which we need to be ready for. As aviation touches the lives of a larger percentage of the population year on year, the requirement to ensure safety assumes greater importance. The new challenges need to be assessed and addressed by an integrated approach. The IAF, through sustained and proactive measures, has successfully brought down its accident rate substantially, especially over the last three years. Accidents cause a loss of precious and expensive resources and must be avoided at all costs. Information sharing amongst the operators becomes crucial, as timely information flow on the cause of aircraft accidents can be instrumental in averting accidents from occurring elsewhere. There is hence an imminent need that organisations operating similar type of aircraft have a network and protocol to share accident related information. This conference is a step by the Ministry of Defence and the Indian Air Force towards promoting such free flow of information and experience to address a global problem.

3546. (4-10-2007) NEW DELHI : The Indian Railway Catering & Tourism Corporation (IRCTC), a Public Sector Undertaking, under the Ministry of Railways has introduced a 'Mahaparinirvan' special train for the Buddhist Pilgrimage from India and abroad particularly from the South Asian countries to promote tourism. This special train will be flagged off from Safdarjung Railway Station, New Delhi on 6th October 2007. The train covers the whole journey in eight days. The passengers will be taken to Gaya, Rajgir-Nalanda, Varanasi, Gorkhpur, Kushinagar, Lumbani in Nepal, Gonda, Agra and back to Delhi. The fare from October 2007 to March 2008 will be US$ 150, 105 and 88 for 1st AC, 2nd AC and 3rd AC respectively for per person per night on twin sharing basis. In other words, the total individual fair for seven days will be US$ 1050, 735 and 616 respectively. Tariff includes all the comforts of Rajdhani Express Air Conditioned train, which includes train journey, onboard/off board catering, house keeping, road transfer by AC vehicles, sightseeing, Darshan, visit to holy places, hotel stay in AC rooms and entrance fee at monuments. Indian passengers can pay in equivalent Rupee (INR) amount, at the exchange rate prevalent at the time of payment.

3547. (4-10-2007) NEW DELHI : Monitoring of ground water regime is an effort to obtain information on ground water levels and chemical quality through representative sampling. The important attributes of ground water regime monitoring are ground water level, ground water quality and temperature. The primary objective of establishing the water monitoring network stations is to record the response of ground regime to the natural and artificial conditions of recharge and discharge with reference to geology, climate, physiography, land use pattern and hydrologic characteristics. The natural conditions affecting the regime involve climatic parameters like rainfall, evapo-transpiration etc. and the artificial conditions including pumpage from the aquifer, recharge due to irrigation system and other manmade causes like waste disposal etc. Ground water levels are being measured four times a year during January, April/ May, August and November since 1969 by Central Ground Water Board through a network of about 15000 observation wells located all over the country. Ground water samples are collected through these observation wells once a year during the month of April/ May to create background information of ground water quality changes on regional scale. The database generated forms the basis for planning the ground water development and management programme. The ground water level and quality monitoring is of particular importance in coastal as well inland saline environment to assess the changes in salt water/fresh water interface as also the gradual quality changes in the fresh ground water regime. This data is used for assessment of ground water resources and changes in the regime consequent to various development and management activities. A perusal of depth to water level map of India during Pre-Monsoon (May 2006) reveals that in sub-Himalayan area, north of river Ganges, generally the depth to water level ranges from 2-10 meter below ground level (mbgl). In the eastern part of the country in the Brahmaputra valley water level generally ranges from 2-5 mbgl, except in isolated pockets where depth to water level is less than 2 mbgl. However, in upper Assam, isolated pocket of deeper water level, 5-10 mbgl has been observed. In major parts of Indus basin, depth to water level generally ranges from 10-20 mbgl. In the western part of the country covering states of Gujarat and Rajasthan deeper water level is recorded in the range of 10-20 mbgl. Depth to water level more than 40m has also been observed in Jodhpur, Churu, Jalore, Nagaur, Jhunjhunu and Jaipur district of Rajasthan In the west coast, water level generally ranges from 5-10 m. Western part of Maharastra recorded water level less than 5m. In the east coast *i.e.* coastal Andhra Pradesh and Orissa, generally the water level ranges between 2-5m. However, isolated pockets of water level less than 2m have also been recorded. Eastern most part of West Bengal recorded water level in the range of 5-10 mbgl. In central India water level generally varies between 5-20 mbgl, except in isolated pockets where water level is more than 20 mbgl. The peninsular part of country generally water level ranges between 2-10 mbgl except in pockets where water level is more than 10 mbgl. Isolated patches of deeper water level in the range of 20-40m and more than 40m have also been observed in various parts of the country. A perusal of depth to water level map of India during Pre-Monsoon (May 2006) when compared with decadal mean (1996-2005) reveals that there is general rise in water level in the range of 0-4m in the peninsular India, coastal Andhra Pradesh and Orissa. However, in isolated pockets, fall of water level has also been recorded. In Northern India there is general fall in Water level in the range of 0-2m. However there is rise in water level in the northern part of Bihar and Uttar Pradesh. In Central India there is mixed trend of Rise and fall in water level. In addition, isolated patches of rise or fall of water level in the range of 0-2m have been observed through out the country. A perusal of depth to water level map of India for the Post-Monsoon period (November 2006) reveals that in sub-Himalayan area, north of river Ganges, generally the depth to water level ranges from 2-5 mbgl. Isolated pocket of shallow water level less than 2m has also been observed. In the eastern parts of the country in the Brahmaputra valley water level generally ranges from 2-5 mbgl, except in isolated pockets where depth to water level is less than 2 mbgl. However in upper Assam isolated pocket of deeper water level, 5-10 mbgl is observed. In major parts of Northwestern states-Indus basin, depth to water level generally ranges from 10-20 mbgl. In the western parts of the country covering states of Gujarat, Rajasthan deeper water level is recorded in the range of 10-20 mbgl.

3548. (4-10-2007) NEW DELHI : The Indian Council of Medical Research (ICMR) is primarily responsible for medical research in India. During the last 97 years, the ICMR has responded effectively to the changing health needs of the country by developing infrastructure and has built capacities to meet newer challenges in health research and healthcare industry of global standards. The current health scenario in the country calls for a much closer interaction with health systems and disease control programmes supported by the continued utilization of the scientific and technological advances. The present structure of the ICMR does not facilitate meeting of some of the challenges to its fullest potentials. In order to build upon and effectively utilize the research capacity and capabilities to engage in effective health systems research, conduct research into social determinants of health and develop technologies and products that respond to national health priorities, the Ministry of Health & Family Welfare has now set up a separate department of Health Research. By setting up the new Department, the Ministry hopes to put research on the fulcrum of the Common Minimum Programme by setting up a Health Research System (HRS) as an overarching mechanism for coordination. The Department would provide leadership and support in generation of new knowledge, improve medical and health research in medical colleges and medical schools and help in providing inputs for operationalization of disease control programmes. It would address the manpower and infrastructure needs for medical and health research in India and assess the health technology and health sciences developed in the country and take these up at various levels of Government to translate the research results into policy and also better articulate the policies of the Ministry of Health and Family Welfare in furthering its programmes and policies. The Health Research Department will be able to interact effectively with the policy makers so that the health investment policies and interventions are based on scientific input. Inter-agency partnerships and coordination is expected to improve through better interaction with Secretaries of Scientific Departments like the Department of Science and Technology (DST), Department of Biotechnology (DBT), Department of Scientific and Industrial Research, Department of Agricultural Research and Education (DARE), Department of Space, Department of Atomic Energy, Department of Ocean Development and Department of Defence Research Development. This would enable smoother transition of technologies and products developed by other S&T agencies into the health sector and avoid fragmentation and duplication of efforts. The Department would be able to build stronger and effective partnerships especially those bridging public and private initiatives and create structures such as the Technology Development Board, and others for better public private interaction for health technology implementation.

3549. (4-10-2007) NEW DELHI : The Chairman and Managing Director of HSCC (India) Ltd., Shri V.C. Sharma presented a cheque of Rs. 10.40 million today to Hon'ble Minister for Health & Family Welfare, Dr. Anbumani Ramadoss towards final dividend of paid-up capital for the Financial Year 2006-07. A public sector undertaking under the Ministry of Health & Family Welfare, the company has already paid an equal amount as interim dividend in April 2007. HSCC is consecutively paying dividend for the last 22 years. HSCC is currently providing consultancy services under Pradhan Mantri Swasthya Suraksha Yojana projects for upgrading hospitals at NIMS-Hyderabad, SGPGIMS-Lucknow and KMC-Kolkata. The company is also working on a prestigious project of Trauma Centre at Kathmandu, Nepal. During the year 2006-07, the company has successfully completed many prestigious projects like Vardhman Mahavir Medical College at Safdarjung Hospital, Trauma Centre at AIIMS etc.

3550. (4-10-2007) NEW DELHI : Smt D. Purandeswari, Minister of State for Human Resource Development (Higher Education) Government of India will attend 117th Assembly of the Inter-Parliamentary Union (IPU) to be held at Geneva (Switzerland) from October 5-10, 2007. This 117th Assembly of the IPU will be discussing the following issues:-a) The role of Parliaments in National Security, human security and individual freedom and in averting the threat to democracy; b) Parliamentary over sight of State policies on foreign aid; c) Migration of workers, people trafficking, Xenophobia and human rights. IPU shares its objectives with United Nations and supports its efforts and works in close cooperation with UN. It also cooperates with the Regional Inter-Parliamentary Organizations, as well as with international inter-governmental and non-governmental organizations which are motivated by the same ideals. The Inter Parliamentary Union (IPU) Assembly is the Principal Statutory Body that expresses the views of the Inter-Parliamentary Union on political issues. The main objects of the IPU are-a) to foster contracts, coordination, and the exchange of experience among Parliaments of all countries; b) to consider questions of international interest and concern (expresses its views on such issues with the aim of bringing about action by Parliaments and their Members); (c) to contribute the defence and promotion of human rights; (d) to contribute better knowledge of working of representative institutions and to strengthening and development of their means of action. More than 140 National Parliaments are currently Members of the IPU. The main organs of the IPU are-a) The Assembly which meets twice a year. The Members of the Assembly have voting rights; (b) Governing Council, which is composed of three Representatives from each Member of the Union; (c) Executive Committee which is composed of the president of IPU, 15 Members belonging to different Parliaments and the president of the Coordinating Committee of the Meeting of Women Parliamentarians. (d) Secretariat of the Union.

3551. (4-10-2007) NEW DELHI : The Minister of External Affairs Shri Pranab Mukherjee will deliver the keynote address on October 7, 2007 at Guwahati at the inauguration of a conference on "India's Look East Policy-Challenges for Sub-Regional Cooperation". The Governor of Assam, Lt. Gen (Retd.) Ajai Singh and the Chief Minister of Assam Shri Tarun Gogoi will be present on the occasion. The Conference is being organized by the Public Diplomacy Division of Ministry of External Affairs in association with Omeo Kumar Das Institute of Social Change and Development (OKDISCD) and Indian Council for Research on International Economic Relations (ICRIER) on October 8-9, 2007 at Hotel Vishwaratna, A.T. Road, Guwahati. The Deputy Chairman of Planning Commission, Shri Montek S. Ahluwalia will address the inaugural session of the Conference on October 8, 2007. The Minister of DONER, Shri Mani Shankar Aiyar will deliver the valedictory address on October 9, 2007. The eminent academicians, think tanks, representatives of industry, intelligentsia, civil society and senior officials will share their views in the two-day Conference. The issues to be discussed relate to: a) India's Look East Policy-Political Economy Implication b) Governance and Social Issues and Role of the Civil Society c) Regional Connectivity and Infrastructure d) Competitive Business Investment, Informal Trade and Regional Integration e) Challenges of

Poverty and Human Resource Development in North East India The Public Diplomacy Division of MEA has been in contact with researchers, think tanks, academia, civil society and industry, both within India and abroad, to highlight the contours of Indian foreign policy, as well as initiate debate and discussion within the wider public about the key foreign policy issues confronting India. It is in furtherance of these objectives that this conference is being organized to discuss the opportunities and challenges confronting India with regard to the 'Look East Policy.'

3552. (4-10-2007) NEW DELHI : An Indo-US meeting on translational Health Sciences was held today in New Delhi. The meeting organised by the Department of Biotechnology, Government of India focused on sharing expertise of Indian and US scientists from public/private institutions to identify and conduct collaborative biomedical research to improve health care of our people. An agreement was signed between the National Institute of Biomedical Imaging and Bioengineering, USA within the National Institute of Health (NIH) and the Department of Biotechnology, Ministry of Science & Technology Government of India for the development of low-cost diagnostics and therapeutic medical technologies. The major focus will be on infectious diseases, trauma, maternal and child health and chronic diseases like diabetes, hypertension and cardiovascular diseases. The collaboration will include organization of workshops and meetings to share experiences and scientific information; direct links between appropriate centres of excellence, institutes and institutions in both countries and collaboration among scientists and engineers in centres of excellence in both countries to conduct research, research training and technology development. Addressing the meeting, Shri Kapil Sibal, Minister for Science and Technology and Earth Sciences stressed the need for availability of funds to the public institutes to pursue research activities for innovative solutions to the challenges in the public health sector. Dr. Elias A. Zerhouni, director, NIH, USA in his address spoke about the NIH roadmap for biomedical research and the paradigm shift in the focus of research over the years.

3553. (4-10-2007) NEW DELHI : Network expansion will be the focus of the future which would be greatly possible by penetrating into rural areas. Shri A.Raja, Minister of Communications and Information Technology was speaking after inaugurating the 13th India Telecommunications International Summit 2007 here today. The Minister said that the Universal Services Obligation Fund of the Department of Telecom will be asked to assist in the operational expenditure on this initiative. The Minister said that the Department of Telecommunications, under Bharat Nirman programme a Four Year business plan for rural infrastructure, is committed to providing telephone connections to 66822 villages that do not have telephone connections are covered by November,2007. The Ministry is also committed to providing connectivity to 14183 remote far flung villages through satellite phone terminals. Shri Raja said that his Ministry is committed to creating infrastructure for mobile services in rural and remote areas. I am very pleased to inform that USO Fund is already providing financial support for operation and maintenance of about 5,61,000 Village Public Telephones covering more than 90% of the eligible villages. The Ministry has targeted to reduce the urban-rural digital divide from current 25:1 to 5:1 by 2010, he added. The Minister said that the PSUs under DOT have also introduced the One India Plan, with single tariff of Re. 1/- per minute to anywhere in India. This tariff was enumulated by most of the private service providers also. This scheme has led to death of distance in telecom and is going to be instrumental in providing national integration further.In the area of FDI, during the period August 1991 to November 2006, FDI of Rs.41,551 crore were approved, which is second only to power and oil refinery sector. The actual inflow of FDI up to November 2006 was Rs.11,808.79 crore. Shri D.S.Mathur, Telecom Secretary in his address said that the growth of telephony has generated tremendous demand for equipment. Many companies have set up their facilities in the country not only to meet the local demand but also to export to other countries. The 13th India Telecommunications International Summit 2007 has been jointly organized by ASSOCHAM and Beacon from Hongkong.

3554. (4-10-2007) NEW DELHI : Direct tax collections maintained a growth of over 40 percent for the six-month period ended September 2007. Net tax collections stood at Rs.1,11,055 crore, up from Rs.79,208 crore during the same period last fiscal. Corporate tax recorded a growth of 41 percent at Rs.72,240 crore, up from Rs.49,813 crore during the previous fiscal. Personal income tax (including FBT, STT and BCTT) grew by 39 percent at Rs.40,744 crore, up from Rs.29,329 crore. The growth in Securities Transaction Tax (STT) was 48 percent and Banking Cash Transaction Tax (BCTT) was 17 percent. Fringe Benefit Tax (FBT) recorded a growth of 103 percent. In terms of payment types, advance tax increased by 30 percent and tax deducted at source (TDS) by 48 percent indicating all-round buoyancy in taxes. Self-assessment tax grew by 80 percent, indicating better tax compliance levels. Among regions, corporate tax growth was the highest in Bihar-Jharkhand at 265 percent, while it was lowest in Vidarbha at minus 34 percent. Personal income tax growth was the highest in Vidarbha at 83 percent, while it was lowest in the northeastern region at minus 17 percent. Mumbai region recorded a growth of 96 percent in corporate taxes and 40 percent in personal income tax. Delhi region recorded a growth of 8 percent in corporate taxes and 29 percent in personal income tax.

3555. (4-10-2007) NEW DELHI : Consequent upon announcement of revised funding pattern for implementation of Sarva Shiksha Abhiyan (SSA) programme during XIth Plan on 25.09.2007, greater financial flexibility will become available to the States/UTs in implementation of SSA programme with greater momentum. The revised funding pattern between the Central Government and States/UTs shall be in the ratio of 65:35 for the first two years of the XIth Plan *i.e.* 2007-08 and 2008-09; 60:40 for the third year *i.e.* 2009-10; 55:45 for the fourth year *i.e.*

2010-11; and 50:50 thereafter *i.e.* from 2011-12 onwards. For the 8 North-Eastern States, the fund sharing pattern between Centre and States shall be 90:10 under the programme with the Centre's share resourced from the 10% earmarked funds for the NE Region in the SSA's Central Budget. The above funding pattern shall become effective from 1.4.2007. The States/UTs shall provide their prescribed State share on the basis of the above funding pattern.

3556. (5-10-2007) NEW DELHI : To commemorate the 58th Anniversary of the Territorial Army. The Citizens Army has planned a photo exhibition "Territorial Army Down the Ages" which covers various aspects of Territorial Army since its inception. In addition, a grand and scintillating band display in the backdrop of historic India Gate is being organized from 05 to 07 Oct. 07 daily from 1900hrs to 2100 hrs in the presences of the citizens of the country, in the true spirit of the Citizens Army. The pipe bands of Territorial Army units, 103 Inf Bn (TA) SIKH LI, 109 Inf Bn (TA) MARATHA LI, 155 Inf Bn (TA) JAK RIF and 105 Inf Bn (TA) RAJ RIF in their colourful attires will play martial music to add colour, festivity and gaiety to the celebrations. The citizens will be afforded an unique opportunity to hear the melodious music of pipes and drums and witness the history of the Citizens Army through an exhibition and a slide show at the lawns of India Gate.

3557. (5-10-2007) NEW DELHI : The Government has concerted efforts for protection and preservation of wild flora and fauna. India is endowed with variety of flora and fauna and is among one of twelve Mega Biodiversity Countries in the World. For its protection, the government has formulated a comprehensive national policy, wildlife conservation strategy and National Wildlife Action Plan, apart from comprehensive legislation for wildlife protection. For better management and protection of wildlife a large network of 606 Protected Areas comprising 96 National Parks and 510 Wildlife Sanctuaries has been created. This covers an area of 15.59 million hectare. Also, Project Tiger has been restructure and transformed into the National Tiger Conservation Authority with wider mandate and powers. Kaziranaga National Park(KNP) is a legendary wildlife sanctuary and home of the extinct Asiatic one-horned rhinoceros. A World Heritage Site, it traces its origin back to the early years of the last century with the Calcutta Zoo authorities requesting the Assam Valley Chief Commissioner for a rhino for the zoo. When the forest officials concerned informed the Commissioner about the fast dwindling population of the extinct and rare species the Administrator seriously pondered over and finally Kaziranga was declared a reserve forest with about 57,000 acres of land area. Things never looked back after this and a succession of developments came up with the park being declared a reserved forest, subsequently a wildlife sanctuary and finally a National Park. The Park is a marvelous model success story because starting with just a few rhinos today it is teeming with about 1,700 of the species, no mean achievement. Situated at a motorable distance of 217 kilometres from Guwahati the land area of the Park today is above 430 square kilometres covering four ranges in all. An equal land area has also been adjoined with the original one for better facilities for the fauna. The nearest airports are Jorhat and Guwahati. Apart from the main tourist attraction other habitats of importance in flora and fauna include, elephants, hog deer, jungle cat, leopards, thousands of migratory birds that visit the park every season, wild boar, ducks, geese, heron, reptiles and many more rare and extinct species notified in the WWF Red Data Book. The recurring and devastating floods are emerging as a major problem for this century-old rhinoceros sanctuary. During floods every year the dedicated workforce of the Park along with some like-minded volunteers keep a vigil at specific intersection points on the National Highway passing through the Park. This is because during the floods many animals cross over from one side of the road to the other in search of higher grounds. Poaching of rhinos for their horns which is believed to be possessing some medicinal qualities has come down. Shortage of manpower, equipment like tents, are some of the problems plaguing the staff at the Park. Yet the dedication and zeal that drive these personnel in this sanctuary day-to-day must be seen to be believed. As Assam is synonymous with rhinos and this park is known all over the globe. A number of measures have been taken for protection of the environs and habitats. Due priority has also been given to conservation and protection of wildlife.

3558. (5-10-2007) NEW DELHI : Government of India have announced the sale (re-issue) of "7.99 per cent Government Stock, 2017 for a notified amount of Rs. 6,000 crore (nominal) through a priced based auction using multiple price method. Government of India have also announced the sale (re-issue) of "7.95 per cent Government Stock, 2032" for a notified amount of Rs. 4,000 crore (nominal) through a price based auction using multiple price method. The auctions will be conducted by the Reserve Bank of India, Mumbai Office, Fort, Mumbai on October 12, 2007 (Friday). Up to 5% of the notified amount of the sale of both the stocks will be allotted to eligible individuals and Institutions as per the Scheme for Non-Competitive Bidding Facility in the Auction of Government Securities. Bids in the prescribed form obtainable from the Regional Director, Reserve Bank of India, Mumbai Office (Public Debt Office), Fort, Mumbai-400 001 and RBI website www.rbi.org.in should be submitted to that Office on October 12, 2007. The NDS members should submit competitive as well as non-competitive bids in electronic format using Primary Market Operation (PMO) module of NDS. All bids should be submitted by 12.30 P.M. The result of the auctions will be announced on October 12, 2007 and payment by successful bidders will be during banking hours on October 15, 2007 (Monday). Both the Stocks will be eligible for "When Issued" trading in accordance with the guidelines on 'When Issued transactions in Central Government Securities' issued by the Reserve Bank of India vide circular No.RBI/2006-07/178 dated November 16, 2006.

3559. (5-10-2007) NEW DELHI : India is hosting three days International Conference from 8th to 10th October, 2007 to discuss child adoption issues in

New Delhi. Briefing the media about the agenda of the conference, Smt. Renuka Chowdhury, Minister for Women and Child Development said that the conference would provide a plateform to get feed back from the receiving countries about the adoption of Indian children. It would also apprise them of our concern regarding inter country adoption. She said that the Government wants to make the adoption procedure more transparent, hassle free with all safeguards. With this objective, it would soon come out with new guidelines on adoption. Speedy Redressal of grievances and centralize monitoring of the adoption procedure will be focus of the new guidelines, she added. Underlining the importance of family based care for the children in need of care and protection, she said that adoption is not one time event but a life long celebration which not only provide a family to a children but also a new meaning in the life of a family. The international conference being organized by Central Adoption Resource Authority (CARA), an autonomous body under the Ministry of Women and Child Development will discuss the draft UN guidelines on children without parental care and safeguards for children placed for inter country adoption. The issue of trans-cultural adoption and identity issues for children for international adoptions will also be taken up during the conference. Preparing the special needs children for inter-country adoption and their rehabilitation is one of the important subjects besides review of guidelines for inter-country adoption. The conference will be attended by more than 300 delegates including 150 delegates from across the world including Govt. representatives, national adoption agencies, social scientists and child-care experts.

3560. (5-10-2007) NEW DELHI : The mortal remains of martyr Maj D Raghu Raman of 34 Rashtriya Rifles (RR) were consigned to flames here today. A large number of serving and veteran officers, jawans and their families paid tributes to the brave officer. A wreath was placed on behalf of Army Chief, Gen Deepak Kapoor. Lt Gen KPD Samanta, Director General Rashtriya Rifles and Brig HPS Dhillon, Station Commander Delhi were also present. Officers from 34 Rashtriya Rifles, 19 JAT (parent unit of the officer), Army HQ and his course mates spoke about his life and achievements in glowing terms. Maj Raghu Raman was a company commander in 34 RR. On hearing about the initial contact he rushed to the site and engaged the militants, nine of whom were killed eventually in this encounter. A product of National Defence Academy, he is the son of an ex-serviceman. His only sibling, Surgical Lt (Miss) Aparna is a doctor serving the Navy at INHS Patanjali at Karwar. His wife, Mrs Latha is an employee of TCS and was on an assignment in London till recently. She is expecting her first child in two months time. On being injured, Maj Raghu Raman was evacuated by a helicopter to Army's Base Hospital at Srinagar. Till then in his senses, the brave officer told his Commanding Officer, Col Harjinder Singh that he should not let any terrorist escape. These were his last words. Veteran Sub Maj (Hony Capt) S Krishnamurty, his father said that while he was proud to be the father of a martyr, despite having lost his son in the service of the nation he would still advise his grand child, who is yet to be born, to join the Army and serve the nation.

3561. (5-10-2007) NEW DELHI : The area coverage of kharif crops as compared to 5th October last year has gone up as per data compiled by Agriculture Ministry. The total coverage of kharif rice has gone up to 369.32 lakh ha as compared to 366.62 lakh hectare last year, the weekly Crop Weather Watch Group meeting of the Ministry of Agriculture was informed here today. Transplanting ended in almost all the states except Andhra Pradesh, Karnataka, Kerala, Orissa and Tamil Nadu where it is continuing. The harvesting of various coarse cereals is progressing in almost all states. The area coverage under jowar, so far, is 35.78 lakh ha against 37.94 lakh ha during last year, under bajra 86.99 lakh ha against 92.86 lakh ha last year, maize 74.55 lakh ha against 68.44 lakh ha last year and total coarse cereals 219.86 lakh ha against 220.62 lakh ha during the corresponding period of last year. The area covered under cotton so far is 90.94 lakh ha against 87.48 lakh ha during the corresponding period of last year. Out of this 53.32 lakh ha is under Bt Cotton. The total coveage under sugarcane has been reported at 51.04 lakh hectare against 48.32 lakh ha during the corresponding period last year. The coverage under jute has been reported at 8.29 lakh ha against 8.18 lakh ha during the corresponding period of last year.Harvesting has ended in all the states. Mesta has been sown in 1.48 lakh ha against 1.53 lakh ha during the corresponding period of last year. The total coverage of oilseeds so far has been 176.05 lakh ha as compared to 164.72 lakh ha on October 4, last year. Soyabean has been sown in 8 % and groundnut in 14% higher area as compared to that in 2006. Pulses cover an area of 125.22 lakh ha against 112.86 lakh ha up to this time last year.

3562. (5-10-2007) NEW DELHI : BJP President Sh. Rajnath Singh today expressed his concern over the postponement of elections in Nepal. He said that the present parliament in Nepal has finished its term way back in October 2002. Since then the electoral process to form a constituent assembly is persistently delayed. Now the election of constituently assembly scheduled on 22nd November are postponed indefinitely under the Maoist pressure. The constituent assembly is a major part of the peace agreement under which the Seven Parties Alliance is running the government. The postponement of elections under the threat of street protest by the Maoists is a sever blow in establishing a democratic environment capable of reflecting peoples will in a free and fare elections. The looming political uncertainty for long provides the opportunity for fundamentalist forces to further strengthen their control in Nepal. This should be a matter of concern for India. Now the Maoists are forcing the interim Parliament for immediate abolishment of monarchy. Since, this was an integral part of the basic political and constitutional structure of Nepal, so any decision on this should not be taken by the interim parliament. Technically any such decision should only be taken by a properly elected constituent assembly. And in any case should not be forcefully taken under the threat of a violent street protest. Nepal is our close neighbour with open border. If the democracy is not established in its true spirit in Nepal, then any development in Nepal is bound to have reflection on India. This should be a matter of concern for all the citizens of India. Therefore, I ask the government of India to make its stand clear on the recent political development in Nepal.

3563. (5-10-2007) NEW DELHI : The President of India, Smt.Pratibha Patil will release a set of four commemorative stamps and First Day Cover with Special Cancellation on the Platinum Jubilee Celebrations of the Indian Air Force on October 8, 2007. The set of four stamps are also in the form of Miniature Sheet. The stamps depict Westland Wapiti, Airborne Warning and Control System, IL-78 and Advanced Light Helicopter-Dhruv showcasing the technological and professional expertise of Indian Air Force. Indian Air Force has made the nation proud with their distinguished services both in war and in peace times. Department of Posts pays its tribute through a set of commemorative stamps that the philatelists in general and aero philatelists in particular will be happy to have as a part of their collections. The stamps will be available for sale in Philatelic Bureaux, Parliament Street, New Delhi on the day of release and during working hours at the bureau and philatelic counters across the post offices of Delhi like Lodhi Road Head Post Office, New Delhi GPO, Delhi GPO, Krishna Nagar Head Office, Indraprastha Head Post Office, IGI Airport Post Office.

3564. (5-10-2007) NEW DELHI : A Chair on Consumer Law and Practice will be set up at National Law School of India University (NLSIU), Bangalore. An agreement to this effect was signed here today between Department of Consumer Affairs and NLSIU in the presence of Shri Sharad Pawar Minister for Consumer Affairs, Food & Public Distribution and Agriculture. Shri Sanjay Singh, Joint Secretary, Deptt. of Consumer Affairs and Dr. A. Jayagovind, Vice Chancellor, NLSIU signed the MoU. Speaking on the occasion Shri Sharad Pawar observed that with the signing of this MoU a new vista has been opened which would be effective in developing and incorporating perspective of academia in the initiatives of the Ministry. Consumer welfare and awareness is an area that impinges on the life of every citizen and the Government has been earnestly trying to ensure that these rights are not trampled upon, he added. The Department of Consumer Affairs will provide an endowment grant of Rs. 90.00 lakh to the NLSIU to meet the annual recurring cost of the Chair and also Rs. 15.00 lakh as cost for setting up the Chair during the first year of the award. The primary objective of the chair is to act as a think tank for the Research and Policy related issues on consumer law and practice and also develop Consumer Affairs as a distinct subject for study at the undergraduate and postgraduate levels.

3565. (5-10-2007) NEW DELHI : Presiding over the function organized for launching the new Department of Health Research of the Ministry of Health & Family Welfare, the Health Minister, Dr. Anbumani Ramadoss said that there is an immense need of synergy between the various governmental agencies which address health issues like Department of Science and Technology, Department of Biotechnology, Department of Scientific and Industrial Research, Department of Agricultural Research and Education, Department of Defence Research Development and the Indian Council of Medical Research (ICMR). He said a close networking between these agencies is needed for deriving the maximum benefit from the investments made in and by these agencies. Shri Kapil Sibal, Union Minister for Science & Technology and Earth Sciences, Smt. Panabaka Lakshmi, Minister of State for Health and Family Welfare, Prof. K. Kasturirangan, Member of Parliament (Rajya Sabha) and Director of the National Institute of Advanced Studies, Bangalore, Prof. N. K. Ganguly, Director General, Indian Council of Medical Research and Dr. Elias A. Zerhouni, Director of the National Institutes of Health, U.S.A. and his team Members were present on the occasion. The new Department was formally launched today by Shri Kapil Sibal, Union Minister for Science & Technology and Earth Sciences. The following is the summary of the Health Minister's speech: I am pleased to be with you all on the occasion of the launch of the new Department of Health Research in my Ministry and honouring Dr. Elias A. Zerhouni, Director, NIH, USA, at the Annual Day Celebrations of the Indian Council of Medical Research. Three years from now we would be celebrating 100 years of establishment of the ICMR. In 1911, a handful of British officers of the Indian Medical Service created the Indian Research Fund Association. The officers who founded the Indian Research Fund Association had the vision and foresight to create a medical research organization in India two years before the British Medical Research Council was set up. In 1950, soon after Independence, the Indian Research Fund Association was renamed as Indian Council of Medical Research. What started in a 3-room office with a staff of 5 people at the Headquarters has today grown into a vibrant network of 26 permanent Institutes and over 70 field stations in the country. It employs over 5000 people. Its annual budget has grown from Rs.5 lakhs to close to Rs.350 crores in 2006-07. During the last 97 years, the ICMR has provided critical research support whenever the health needs of the country demanded rapid responses *e.g.* SARS, HIV, influenza, and other new and emerging and remerging infections like Chikungunya, dengue, and co-morbidities (HIV-TB) and the emerging epidemic of life-style diseases. ICMR have played an important role in defining the rules that govern international collaborative research. The Council is one of the few research organizations in the world, which has canonized its principles for the conduct of ethical bio-medical research. It has also supported traditional and other systems of medicine and successfully brought to the front the value of these systems and their validation using tools of modern medical research methods required for clinical trials in traditional medicine.

3566. (5-10-2007) NEW DELHI : India and Sri Lanka today signed a Memorandum of Understanding (MoU) to finalise the procedural arrangements for operationalisation of Tariff Rate Quota (TRQ) for import of 3 million pieces of apparel articles covered under the India-Sri Lanka Free Trade Agreement (ISLFTA). The MoU was signed by Shri Qaiser Shamim, Joint Secretary, Ministry of Textiles on behalf of Government of India and Shri W.D. Jayasinghe, Additional Secretary, Ministry of Textiles Industries, Sri Lanka on behalf of Government of Sri Lanka. In pursuance of the ISLFTA that came into force on 1st March, 2000, it was decided that Sri Lanka could export to India, in one calendar year, three million pieces of apparel articles covered under ISLFTA, on duty free basis and without any restriction on entry points and sourcing of fabrics. Under the MoU, the Textile Quota Board and Department of Commerce of Sri Lanka has been designated as authority for issuance of quota and certificate of origin for the export of apparel articles from Sri Lanka to India and in the case of India, the Textiles Committee has been nominated to monitor the TRQ parameters.

3567. (5-10-2007) NEW DELHI : The annual water demand of India would be of the order of 1447 km3 by 2050 as estimated by the Central Water Commission (CWC) under Ministry of Water Resources. The average annual precipitation over India's landmass is estimated at 4000 km3 of which only 1122 km3 is actually utilisable. Thus, on the one hand, nearly two-thirds of the country's available freshwater is lost due to evaporation and run-off into the sea, and on the other, the demand for water is growing steeply due to developmental activities even as the available water remains the same. In the already industralised world, industry and urban households use over 70 per cent of the water resources, while agriculture gets the remaining 30 per cent. In our water economy, the reverse is true: agriculture consumes over 70 per cent of the water resources and industry and urban areas the rest. But as our cities grow, the competition for this water will grow. Their growing demand leads to pressure to source water from further and further away. Thus in turn puts pressure on already stressed resources and exacerbates tensions. In this scenario, augmenting water resources by capturing more of the rainwater in diverse ways both for direct use and for groundwater recharge is a critical need of the hour.

3568. (5-10-2007) NEW DELHI : Dr. Istvan Minister for Education and Culture, Republic of Hungary, who is presently on an official visit to India called on Shri Arjun Singh, Minister of Human Resource Development, here, today. An Educational Exchange Programme has been signed between India and Hungary in 2003. Both Governments are offering a number of scholarships to each other countries' students for higher studies. Scholars and academicians are exchanged on regular basis as part of the Programme. The Ministers expressed satisfaction at the progress in implementing the Exchange Programme.

3569. (5-10-2007) NEW DELHI : Congress Spokesperson Shri Abhishek Singhvi said that the Congress Party is extremely concerned that the state of Karnataka reflects an unholy cocktail of opportunism, hypocracy and misgovernance. The state has an alliance born out of opportunism based on deceit resulting in nothing but the sharing of loot. Both the major constituents of their alliance are equally responsible for this grave situation and confusion. The irony is that people in that state are swearing in the name of secularism after having conducted governance in non-secularism formations for years. I would like to ask you why, for example, is the BJP shedding crocodile tears? Why are they indulging in breast-beating and shouting? If they are dissatisfied with the situation, instead of making visits to the Governor, to make noises, they should withdraw support. Why these double standards? In the state of Karnataka we have a government without a majority. We have a government which has lost all support. It is therefore, an unethical and unlawful government. We therefore call upon the Governor to restrain that government from taking any major decisions since that government has forfeited the support of the people. It is not even a lame duck government, even a lame duck has some legs to stand upon. This duck is only a duck, one big zero. We saw, for example today, that supposedly the Cabinet in that state took several policy decisions relating to SEZs. It is of course interesting and ironic that there is no Industry Minister under whose portfolio the SEZ subject may fall. The Cabinet which must have taken the decision would not have half or many members in session. The Congress calls upon these irresponsible parties to stop indulging in mock battles, to end this blatant marriage of convenience. We are most concerned that these parties and that this government has failed the people of Karnataka, has betrayed the common man of Karnataka, has forfeited the faith of the people of that state. It is a government of the lobbyist, by the hypocrites for the vested interests. And this situation must stop immediately. To a question, whether the local Congress leaders will support the JD (S) government in Karnataka, Shri Singhvi said, don't go by your subjective perceptions. Individual views, opinions are all going to be taken into account. In a fast evolving, fast dynamic situation but what we will decide is for us to decide, for the Party to decide, for the top leadership to decide, therefore don't jump to any conclusions. All I can tell you is that we are keeping a close watch on the happenings in that state where unprecedented events are taking place. To a question that Congress Party will have no engagement with JD (S) now, Shri Singhvi said, the ball is in the court of the Karnataka government and the constituent units of the state. The ball is in play in a game which has made a mockery of Democracy. The Congress is not answerable for anything. We reserve our right to decide your question and all other questions at an appropriate time. Nothing can be ruled out, nothing can be said. But the point of the matter is that every citizen of India and every person of Karnataka has a right to be concerned about the unprecedented events happening in that state. To a question whether President's Rule can be imposed in Karnataka, Shri Singhvi said, President' Rule is not the remedy for all ills. That is a decision for an appropriate authority under an appropriate Article of the Constitution to take. But certainly as of today we are very clear that as far as the Congress Party is concerned that a formation which forfeited all support and all right to rule must be restrained from taking any major decision or from frittering away and squandering the resources of this important state.

3570. (5-10-2007) NEW DELHI : The Union Rural Development Minister, Dr. Raghuvansh Prasad Singh will be holding a two day Regional Performance Review Committee Meeting on 9th and 10th of this month at Guwahati. He will review the progress of various rural development schemes in the Northeastern region of the country during the two day meeting. The Ministers of state Shri Chandra Sekhar Sahu and Smt. Suryakanta Patil and Rural Development Ministers from all the Northeastern states will also be present in the meeting. The achievements and the progress of different Rural Development schemes so far in the Northeastern region will be discussed in the meeting at length by the Union Minister. The progress of National Rural Employment Guarantee Act (NREGA), Sampoorna Grameen Rozgar Yojana (SGRY), Indira Awaas Yojana (IAY) and Prdhaan Mantri Gram Sadak Yojana (PMGSY) in the region will be presented during the meeting. Dr. Singh will also review the water supply and sanitation programme in Assam on the very first day of the meeting. Later in the day the MRD will also address the press to brief about the progress of rural development schemes in the Northeastern region. He will also visit the rural areas of Bongaigaon, Kokrajhar, Dhemaji, Lakhimpur and Jorhat districts if Assam to have first hand information at grass root level.

3571. (5-10-2007) NEW DELHI : As a concomitant of ambitious capacity addition programme of 80,000 MW in the 11th Plan, the Ministry of Power today took stock of the requirement and availability of highly skilled manpower for the power sector. Addressing a Seminar in New Delhi on 3.10.2007, the Secretary, Ministry of Power, Shri Anil Razdan called upon all participants in the sector to gear up to bridge the gap between the requirement and the availability of highly skilled manpower. It was observed that during 11th Plan, capacity addition programme is likely to lead to the creation of about 10 lakh jobs. Out of this the requirement of skilled manpower will be of the order of 7.28 lakhs (4.96 lakhs technical and 2.32 lakhs non-technical). Given the number of graduates passing out of the existing schools, colleges and other institutions each year, it is expected that there will be no shortage of manpower in any category in the country. However there is a need to train them to meet the challenges of working in today's technologically highly sophisticated power industry.

3572. (5-10-2007) NEW DELHI : The Strategic Forces Command successfully conducted the user trial of Agni Missile A-I at Chandipur at Sea near Balasore in Orissa at 10.35 this morning. The performance parameters of the 700 km range missile were as expected and the desired objectives have been met.

3573. (5-10-2007) NEW DELHI : The Union Minister of Shipping, Road Transport and Highways, Thiru T.R. Baalu has said that the issue of smart cards for driving licences and registration certificates for vehicles and electronically linking of Regional Transport Offices of the States have been targeted to be completed by March, 2008. Thiru Baalu was addressing the 2nd International Road Federation (IRF) Regional Conference on Road Safety-Design, Construction and Operations of Roads here today. The Minister also informed that a Committee constituted for formulation of a National Road Transport Policy has recently submitted its report for giving direction for improvement of road transport as well as road sector, and this report is under consideration of the Union Government. Expressing serious concern over the rising number of road accidents in the country, he said that the as per the latest available data, the total number of accidents is to the order of 4,40,000 in which about 95,000 persons were killed during the year 2005. He said that the Government had set up a Committee on road safety issues which has recommended creation of a dedicated body on Road Safety and Traffic Management. The Committee's report is presently under consideration of the Government, Thiru Baalu informed. The Minister said that the States have also been requested to strictly enforce traffic laws, take effective measures to control overloading, and install unified check posts at the State borders. With the cooperation of all the State Governments, the road safety scenario in the country would improve, Thiru Baalu hoped. Thiru Baalu asked the participants to dwell upon the issues like development of an efficient system of traffic management involving coordination between multiple agencies and defining their roles; Scientific investigation of fatal accidents to find out their real cause for taking corrective measures to arrest recurrences of such incidents; and involvement and participation of public in enhancement of road safety, besides generating awareness. Giving a brief account of the government's ambitious national highway development programme (NHDP), Thiru Baalu said that these projects would involve an investment of about Rs.2,36,300 crore, *i.e.*, US $ 59 billion and are targeted to be completed by 2015. With this enhanced scope, the Government wants to increase the private participation to a significant extent and all future projects under the NHDP would be taken up primarily on the Public-Private Partnership (PPP) pattern, he informed the participants. The Minister also told the participants about the 'Special Accelerated Road Development Programme for the North-Eastern Region' for development of the National Highways, State Roads and Roads of Strategic Importance in that Region. He said that the modified programme has been approved by the Government only this week which provides for development of 8,737 kms of such roads for implementation in two phases. The estimated cost of the first phase is Rs.12,793 crores, *i.e.*, US $ 3.2 billion and this phase is targeted to be completed by 2012-13 and the entire programme by 2015-16, he further informed. Thiru Baalu also said that the action is also being taken simultaneously for improvement of the regional connectivity with the SAARC countries. The Chief Minister of Delhi, Smt. Shiela Dikshit also addressed the Conference.

3574. (6-10-2007) NEW DELHI : The Minister of Railways, Shri Lalu Prasad, has said that the Indian Railways will continue to play a major role in promoting tourism in the country. The Minister was speaking at a programme organized on the occasion of flagging off Buddhist Circuit Special Train "Mahaparinirvan" from Safdarjung station here today. Smt. Ambika Soni, Union Minister of Tourism & Culture, Shri Chandan Mitra, Member of Parliament, Shri Ashok Ahuja, MLA, Delhi, Shri K. C. Jena, Chairman, Railway Board and senior officers of Ministry of Railways and IRCTC were among those present on the occasion. The train has been introduced by Railway Catering and Tourism Corporation (IRCTC), a public sector undertaking under the Ministry of Railways. Shri Lalu Prasad said that this special train has been introduced for the Buddhist pilgrimage from India and abroad particularly from the South Asian countries to promote tourism. The train will take passengers to important destinations linked to the life of Buddha such as Bodh Gaya, Rajgir, Nalandha, Kushinagar, Lumbini, Sravasti. He said that the package includes train travel, road travel, all meals, deluxe hotel facilities, sight seeing, monument entry fees, security, insurance and guide services. The Minister informed that the travel related information for this train has been prepared in Japanese, Korean, Chinese and Thai languages for the convenience of international travellers. The Minister pointed out that IRCTC is already running a "Bharat Darshan" train with a nominal fare of Rs.500 per day. More useful tour packages will be introduced for the benefit of the tourists, he added. He thanked the Ministry of Tourism for their cooperation in the project. Speaking on the occasion, Smt. Ambika Soni, said that Railways in recent times have made tremendous progress and earned huge surplus. She pointed out that several passenger amenities introduced by Railways are helping in the promotion of tourism in a big way. She said that her department will continue to collaborate with Railways in the tourist sector. The train covers the whole journey in eight days. The passengers will be taken to Gaya, Rajgir-Nalanda, Varanasi, Gorakhpur, Kushinagar, Lumbani in Nepal, Gonda, Agra and back to Delhi. The fare from October 2007 to March 2008 will be US$ 150, 105 and 88 for 1st AC, 2nd AC and 3rd AC respectively per person per night on twin sharing basis. In other words, the total individual fair for seven days will be US$ 1050, 735 and 616 respectively. Tariff includes all the comforts of Rajdhani Express Air Conditioned train, which includes train journey, onboard/ off board catering, house keeping, road transfer by AC vehicles, sightseeing, Darshan, visit to holy places, hotel stay in AC rooms and entrance fee at monuments. Indian passengers can pay in equivalent Rupee (INR) amount, at the exchange rate prevalent at the time of payment.

3575. (6-10-2007) NEW DELHI : The National Investment Fund (NIF) was launched here today at a small function which was presided over by the Finance Minister, Shri P. Chidambaram. All the Secretaries in the Ministry of Finance and other senior officials were also present on this occasion. The launching ceremony consisted of the following two activities : (a) Signing of the Portfolio Management Services Agreement by JS (Disinvestment) & Chief Executive Officer (CEO), NIF (on behalf of the Government) and CEO, of Selected Public Sector Fund Managers viz. UTI Asset Management Company Pvt. Ltd., SBI Funds Management Pvt. Ltd. and LIC Mutual Fund Asset Management Company Ltd. Separate Agreements were signed with each Fund Manager. (b) Handing over of cheques to the CEO of three Asset Management companies. All proceeds from disinvestment of Central Public Sector Enterprises will be channelised into NIF. NIF will be maintained outside the Consolidated Fund of India and is to be professionally managed to provide sustainable returns to the Government, without depleting the Corpus. NIF will be operated by the selected Fund Managers under discretionary mode of the Portfolio Management Scheme, which is governed by SEBI guidelines. UTI Asset

Management Company Pvt. Ltd., SBI Funds Management Pvt. Ltd. and LIC Mutual Fund Asset Management Company Ltd., which manage the assets of the three largest Public Sector Mutual Funds have been appointed as the Fund Managers, initially for a period of two years, extendable on the basis of their performance subsequently.

3576. (6-10-2007) COIMBATORE: Divergent stands on issues taken by the Dravida Munnetra Kazhagam (DMK) and the Communist parties in the last three meetings of the Coimbatore Corporation Council seem to be pointing out that this is a divided camp. The All India Anna Dravida Munnetra Kazhagam (AIADMK) is happy with the turn of events, especially the way the Communist Party of India (CPI) and the Communist Party of India (Marxist) have opposed the fee for door-to-door collection of garbage that is supported by their allies DMK and the Congress. Sources in the Opposition also point out that even the CPI and the CPI(M) seem to differ on the levying of charges. And, there is a marked difference between the approaches of both the parties.

3577. (6-10-2007) NEW DELHI : Following is the text of the speech delivered by the Defence Minister Shri A K Antony at the inauguration of Molecular Imaging Research Centre in the Institute of Nuclear Medicine and Allied Sciences (INMAS) here today. "It gives me great pleasure to be with you this morning to inaugurate the state-of-the-art Molecular Imaging & Research Centre with Positron Emission Tomography (PET) facility. I understand PET is the fastest growing technology in Molecular Medicine, used both for clinical application in diagnosis, as well as for advanced research. I congratulate all DRDO and INMAS scientists for establishing this unique facility to undertake high-end research in the development of advanced life support technology. It will not only enhance the health and operational efficiency of our soldiers, but also provide spin-off benefits to all sections of our society. India is strongly emerging as a major regional and global player. Our vibrant economy has meant that our Defence Forces, armed with latest technology, have gone from strength to strength. Indigenisation is our primary concern. Though the pace of indigenisation has increased, a lot more needs to be done. Our long-term objective is to minimise foreign assistance. We must therefore, make all-out efforts to accelerate the pace of indigenisation. The coming age will be dominated by knowledge nations and knowledge societies. India is emerging as a major knowledge power, managing it and applying the knowledge for progress. I am sure the provision of such advanced R&D facilities like PET and Molecular Imaging will enhance the quality, as well as quantum, of new knowledge generation and make a global impact. Wars in the future will be high technology intensive and the soldiers will be required to use high-end weapons. The wars will be shorter in duration, but intense, demanding higher levels of endurance. The selection procedures and training methodology must be reoriented with the changing times. However, considering that low intensity conflicts are likely to be the order of the day, our Armed Forces will have to be ever prepared for a conventional war on a routine basis. DRDO and other organisations have contributed to keep the jawans fighting fit, even in places with extreme environmental and operational conditions. DRDO has a wide canvas of activities-devising latest procedures or recruitment of soldiers, providing adequate nutrition, provision of special clothing, making available protective gear to facilitate acclimatisation to extreme weather conditions, stress management and thinking of ways and means to enhance our overall defence preparedness. Though latest equipment for our Armed Forces is a must, I would urge all of you to pay equal and adequate attention to keep the most important component-our human resource, motivated and contented. All our investment in equipment and machinery will not yield the desired results, till the human resource is looked after well. Therefore, I wish to emphasise the urgent need to devise strategies to reduce the stress on jawans. You must continue to devise new strategies to augment the welfare of our soldiers. Our Government is committed to optimum transparency. Moreover, we are living in an age in which information is easily available at the click of a button. In such a scenario, too much of secrecy can only be detrimental to our long-term requirements and interests. It is my privilege to dedicate this facility to the nation. I am sure it will be used not only by scientists of DRDO, but also other organisations to develop new products and processes to enhance the well-being and welfare of our Armed Forces personnel. I also hope that in a larger context, the facility will also provide spin-off benefits to the society and nation.

3578. (6-10-2007) NEW DELHI : Government has been monitoring the situation arising out of the appreciation of rupee. The appreciation of the rupee is a reflection, in part, of the growing strength of the economy and has positive economic benefits by way of cheaper imports and subdued impact on prices. However, the rapid appreciation of rupee in recent weeks has adversely affected exporters who had contracted export orders earlier. In July 2007, government had announced a set of measures aimed at providing relief to exporters. These related to accelerated reimbursement of dues to exporters, reduction in the interest rate on pre-shipment and post-shipment credit, and revision in drawback rates and DEPB rates. The total financial relief of these measures was estimated at Rs.1400 crore. On 17/9/2007, Government had announced refund of service tax to exporters in respect of four services (Port Services, Transport of Goods, Transport by Railways, and other port service) for export purposes.

3579. (6-10-2007) NEW DELHI : The second International Flight Safety Conference, IFSCON-07 is being organised by the Indian Air Force in New Delhi on 09-10 October 2007 at the Air Force Auditorium, Subroto Park. The objective of this conference is to address global aviation safety issues. The conference will provide a platform for mutual interaction of around 60 foreign delegates from 30 countries and delegates from a host of national aviation organisations. The foreign participants include delegates from across the globe viz. Europe, Russia, Middle-East, South & South East Asia and the Americas. The number of delegate countries has more than doubled from the inaugural conference held last year. Apart from the participating delegations of different nations, defence attaches of these countries would also take part in the conference. National delegates include those from the Indian Army, Indian Navy, Coast Guard, Border Security Force, Directorate General of Civil Aviation, Hindustan Aeronautics Limited, Airports Authority of India, Rotary Wing Society of India, Indian Airlines, private airline operators and a number of other bodies associated with aircraft research and development, certification and Quality Assurance. The Hon'ble Raksha Utpadan Rajya Mantri, Shri Rao Inderjit Singh, has kindly consented to inaugurate the conference on 09 Oct. 07. This will set the tone for two days of stimulating presentations and panel discussions on aviation safety subjects of universal interest. In keeping with the global concerns of all aviating countries and organizations, the broad issues planned to be addressed in the conference include: New Concepts: An Overview, Accident Investigation & Safety Management, Human Factors and Environmental & Organisational Issues. The conference would serve as a forum for meaningful interaction of experienced Aviation Safety functionaries of a spectrum of countries and agencies, all with a common goal,-promoting aviation safety. This conference will serve to smoothen adoption of new concepts and methodologies of accident prevention and significantly shorten the learning curve for induction of modern safety schemes. In this context, the theme of the Conference, Aviation Safety-A Universal Language, by itself speaks volumes of the mindset of the IAF, which seeks cooperation for an integrated approach to generate synergy in the field of Aviation Safety. Aviation activity in South Asia is seeing a dramatic growth, both in military and civil aviation. The scale of induction of modern aircraft is unprecedented in numbers, technology, capability and cost. Precious national resources are being devoted for the purpose and it must be the endeavour of all stakeholders to ensure the preservation of aviation assets. This growth in aviation requires support both through infrastructure development and trained manpower. Modernization and rapid growth bring with them numerous challenges related to safe operations, which we need to be ready for. As aviation touches the lives of a larger percentage of the population year on year, the requirement to ensure safety assumes greater importance. The new challenges need to be assessed and addressed by an integrated approach. The IAF, through sustained and proactive measures, has successfully brought down its accident rate substantially, especially over the last three years. Accidents cause a loss of precious and expensive resources and must be avoided at all costs. Information sharing amongst the operators becomes crucial, as timely information flow on the cause of aircraft accidents can be instrumental in averting accidents from occurring elsewhere. There is hence an imminent need that organisations operating similar type of aircraft have a network and protocol to share accident related information.

3580. (7-10-2007) NEW DELHI : The UPA Chairperson Smt. Sonia Gandhi laid the foundation-stone of the National Institute of Food Technology Entrepreneurship and Management (NIFTEM) at Kundli in Sonepat district of Haryana today. This

Institute will be set up in a 100-acre campus at the cost of 245 crore rupees. It will have technical support form Cornell University, USA. Speaking on the occasion, the Minister of State for Food Processing Industries Shri Subodh Kant Sahai has said that the vision for NIFTEM is to be an international centre of excellence which integrates all facets of Food Technology Entrepreneurship, Research and Management. It is expected to be as the focal point for catalyzing the growth of food processing industry in India with respect to global scenario. He said the academic session of NIFTEM would start from 2009. Shri Sahai further said, the mission of NIFTEM is to produce world-class business leaders, develop globally competitive processes and technologies and international best practices in the area of food technology, entrepreneurship and management. NIFTEM would be the apex R&D institute in India and coordinate all R&D efforts in this sector in the country. It will carry out R&D in frontier areas, develop world-class technologies and assist the Government in Food Processing Policy. On this occasion, the Secretary, Food Processing Industries Shri P.I. Suvrathan has said, food processing has an important role to play in linking Indian agriculture to consumers in the domestic and international markets. He said NIFTEM is to be set up as a world class institution to cater to the needs of various stakeholders such as entrepreneurs, industry, exporters, policy makers, government and existing institutions. NIFTEM would work actively in assisting in setting food standards, business incubation and information sharing. Haryana Chief Minister Shri Bhupinder Singh Hooda, other distinguished persons from food processing industries and State Governments were also present on this occasion.

3581. (7-10-2007) NEW DELHI : The Vice-President Mohammad Hamid Ansari has condoled the sad demise of Dr. L. M. Singhvi. In his condolence message the Vice-President has said, " I am deeply grieved to learn about the sad demise of Dr. L.M. Singhvi, whom I had known personally for many years. He was a distinguished jurist, an eminent parliamentarian and a very successful High Commissioner to the United Kingdom. A man of great vision, Dr. Singhvi made great contributions to national life through his writings and association with various cultural institutions. I convey my heartfelt condolences to the members of the bereaved family and to the wide circle of his admirers and friends".

3582. (7-10-2007) NEW DELHI : The Prime Minister, Dr. Manmohan Singh has condoled the passing away of Dr. L. M. Singhvi. In his condolence message to his son Dr. Abhishek Manu Singhvi, Member of Parliament, the Prime Minister has said, "I was deeply grieved to hear of the shocking news of your father's passing away. Please accept my heartfelt condolences and convey to all members of your family our sentiments. Gursharan and I knew Shri L.M. Singhvi personally and have had the highest regard and affection for him. He was one of our most distinguished jurists, constitutional experts and legal minds. More importantly, he was a great scholar who had a deep understanding of our ethos, our culture and our civilisational values. He also proved to be a highly regarded diplomat and

Member of Parliament. His absence will be deeply felt in the world of public affairs. I hope you will face this tragedy with forbearance and courage. I am sure you will take your father's good work forward."

3583. (7-10-2007) NEW DELHI : The President, Smt. Pratibha Devisingh Patil has condoled the passing away of Dr. L.M.Singhvi. In her condolence message to his wife Smt. Kamla Singhvi, the President has said, "In the passing away of Dr. Singhvi, the nation has lost a prominent constitutional expert, eminent jurist, renowned scholar, able Parliamentarian and distinguished diplomat."

3584. (7-10-2007) NEW DELHI : The President, Smt. Pratibha Devisingh Patil has condoled the passing away of the former Chief Minister of Maharashtra, Shri Babasaheb Bhosale. In her condolence message to the Late former Chief Minister's son, Shri Justice Dilip Babasaheb Bhosale, the President has said, " I had a close association with Shri Babasaheb Bhosale, especially during the time when I was a member of his cabinet when he was the Chief Minister of Maharashtra. A committed nationalist, he took active part in the freedom struggle right from his student days. His personality was such that he was admired by all."

3585. (8-10-2007) NEW DELHI : The Minister of State for Women & Child Development, Smt. Renuka Chowdhury has called for transparency in adoption procedure and making it hassle free so that more and more destitute children are able to find families which love and care for them. Inaugurating the 2nd International Conference on Adoption being organized by Central Adoption Resource Authority (CARA) here today, she said that adoption is excellent opportunity for rehabilitation of orphan children. In view of large number of such children in the country we need more children in the adoption loop and more adoption agencies. At the same time all illegal adoptions need to be stopped, she stressed. Highlighting the importance of the non-government sector in child adoption, she said that while the Government is ready to provide necessary support by way of policies and guidelines, it is a non-government sector which necessarily plays a far greater role in such a sensitive matter. The children depend on them for not only their immediate physical and emotion needs, but also for ensuring that they are ultimately united either with their own biological parents or with loving adoptive families, she added. Briefing about the Government initiatives, Smt. Chowdhury said that Integrated Child Protection Scheme going to be implemented during the 11th Plan would give shape to essential child protection setup to deal with all vulnerable children including the orphan and abandoned. Besides this the State Governments have been asked to streamline the adoption procedure and existing guidelines in this regard have been simplified to bring more transparency in the procedure. She expressed the hope that the deliberations of the Conference would be meaningful to further improve the adoption programme in the best interest of the children. The three-day Conference is being attended by about 300 delegates including Central Adoption authorities across the world, State Governments, social scientists and non-government organisations.

3586. (8-10-2007) NEW DELHI : The President Smt. Pratibha Patil today released a set of four commemorative stamps and First day Cover with Special Cancellation on the Platinum Jubilee Celebrations of the Indian Air Force here today. The stamps are also in the form of Miniature Sheet. The Vice President Shri Hamid Ansari, the Prime Minister Dr. Manmohan Singh, UPA Chairperson, Smt. Sonia Gandhi were among the dignitaries who attended today's function. Speaking on the occasion, Shri A. Raja Minister of Communications and Information Technology said that the Department of Posts is privileged to release a set of commemorative stamps on this memorable occasion. This set of four stamps which depict the four aircraft Westland Wapiti, Airborne Warning and Control System, IL-78 and Advanced Light Helicopter-Dhruv is a tribute to the spirit and professional skills of the Indian Air Force and a recognition of its vital role in the life of our nation. The Indian Air Force also assists India Post in providing dedicated load for mail transmission to otherwise inaccessible areas of the country. India Post has also signed an MOU with Indian Air Force for delivery of AOG consignment all over the country, he added.

3587. (8-10-2007) NEW DELHI : At the threshold of 21st century, India is one of the world's most dynamic economies, yet the country has a large population of poor people. According to National Sample Survey's 61st Round for 2004-05 (the latest), roughly 22 percent people live below the poverty line. They are predominantly workers belonging to unorganized sector bereft of any worthwhile social protection. Social protection is central to any development agenda. Without it the talk of inclusive growth is meaningless. There has to be investment in schemes/programmes that help reduce vulnerability of people at risk, improve their health and create opportunities for self reliance. Mahatma Gandhi said," I shall work for an India in which the poorest shall feel that it is their country, in whose making they have an effective voice, an India in which there shall be no high class or low class of people...". Even after six decades of Independence, India of Gandhiji's dreams is yet to emerge. It took the country five decades of debate to evolve some basic social security measures for the poor. A bill for providing social security to workers in the unorganized sector was introduced in Parliament on the last day of the previous session. While law makers are yet to debate it, the government, announced three social security schemes and launched two of them, viz., "Rashtriya Swasth Bima Yojna" (Health Insurance Scheme) and "Aam Admi Bima Yojna" (Life and Disability Insurance Scheme) on the occasion of Gandhi Jayanti giving effect to two important commitments made in the National Common Minimum Programme of the UPA government. The Economic Survey (2006-07) says, "Healthcare is important not only for reaping the demographic dividend, having a healthy productive workforce and general welfare, but also for attaining the goal of population stabilization". The Survey further points out that India's position on health parameters compared to some of its neighbours continues to be unsatisfactory. In this scenario, the worst sufferers are the poor workers who, because of very low affordability take recourse to inadequate and incompetent medical treatment. This results in significant loss of earnings and progressive deterioration of health. Thus, bringing in the Health Insurance Scheme for unorganized sector workers who constitute 93 percent of the country's 400 million workforce. The scheme will go a long way in providing quality healthcare to poor workers. This, in turn, would improve their employability and productivity and help in poverty reduction. Given the vast number of workers to be covered, the Health Insurance Scheme (HIS) would be implemented in a phased manner. Initially workers living Below the Poverty Line (BPL) are to be covered in next five years. Launching the Scheme, the Finance Minister Shri P. Chidambaram said that in the first year of its operation in 2008-09, over Rs.750 crore would be allocated by the Centre. Each year 120 districts across the country would be selected by the State Governments on the basis of availability of hospitals/ health facilities as well as presence of potential intermediaries in such districts to ensure effective grassroots support to beneficiaries in various aspects of operation of the Scheme. The notable feature of the HIS is that the beneficiary can avail healthcare facility at any of the notified hospitals without any cash transaction up to Rs.30,000/ - per annum for the family comprising five members on floater basis. That too at no cost to the poor beneficiary as the estimated annual premium of Rs 750/ - to be paid to the health insurance provider would be shared by the Central and State Governments in 75:25 ratio. Each beneficiary would be issued a smart card for this purpose costing Rs 60/- . This cost would be exclusively borne by the Central Government. The card would be valid for availing the service even if the worker migrates from one state to another. The beneficiary would, however, have to pay Rs. 30/- per annum as registration/ renewal fee. The purpose is to inculcate a sense of participation in the scheme so that the beneficiary demands the service as a matter of right. The other notable feature of the Scheme is that all pre-existing diseases would be covered.

3588. (8-10-2007) NEW DELHI : Government of India have announced the sale (re-issue) of "5.87 percent Government Stock, 2010" under Market Stabilization Scheme for a notified amount of Rs. 4,000 crore (nominal). Government of India have also announced the sale (re-issue) of "11.30 percent Government Stock, 2010" under Market Stabilization Scheme for a notified amount of Rs. 4,000 crore (nominal). The Government Stocks will be sold through price based auction using multiple price method. The auctions will be conducted by the Reserve Bank of India, Mumbai Office, Fort, Mumbai on October 11, 2007 (Thursday). Up to 5% of the amount notified for the sale of stock is reserved for allotment to eligible individuals and Institutions on non-competitive basis as per the Scheme for Non-Competitive Bidding Facility in the Auction of Government Securities. Bids in the prescribed form obtainable from the Regional Director, Reserve Bank of India, Mumbai Office (Public Debt Office), Fort, Mumbai-400 001 and RBI website www.rbi.org.in should be submitted to that Office on October 11, 2007. The NDS members should submit competitive as well as non-competitive bids in electronic format using Primary Market Operation (PMO) module of NDS. All bids should be submitted by 12.30 P.M. The result of the auctions will be announced on October 11, 2007 and payment by successful bidders will be during banking hours on October 12, 2007 (Friday).

3589. (8-10-2007) NEW DELHI : Bharatiya Janata Party condemns the statement of Mrs. Sonia Gandhi calling those who oppose the N-Deal and present alignment of Setu Samundaram Project as enemies of development and peace. It is not only arrogant but smacks of intolerance and dictatorial tendencies. This is precisely the Congress character to call names to those, who oppose their policies, as the forces opposing the country's progress. Actually, it is the Congress, which has halted the progress of the country by slowing down on various development initiatives of NDA like North-South and East-West corridor and River Linking Project. Bharatiya Janata Party charges Congress of playing strategic subservience to US foreign policy by rushing through the N-Deal and doing so with collateral purpose. Nation has not approved the proposed Deal. The majority in Parliament is opposing this Deal and government has not addressed any of the concerns raised by opposition parties. If the Deal is about Energy Security the govt. must reveal the costs involved. 35,000 MW of Electricity over the period of 30 yrs at the investment of 50 $b (2 Lack Crore of Rs.) is not at all in the interest of the country. Even if Suhansiri project in Arunachal is completed it can generate 35,000 MW of hydel Power in next 3 years at much lower cost. Congress must ask the people whether they approve N-Power @ Rs. 15 per unit or hydel Power at Rs. 4 per unit. Govt. must also explain why they are not reaching out to Nepal on channelising perennial water resources for power generation? Congress must also answer why the govt. is not operationalising Fast Breeder Reactor Programme, which can open up possibilities of self-sufficiency. As far as Setu Samundaram Project is concerned blame squarely lies with Congress, which has not only hurt the religious sentiments of the people but is bent upon blowing up the Ram Setu. BJP demands that govt. should unequivocally declare that it would complete the project with other alignment and not by cutting through Ram Setu.

3590. (8-10-2007) NEW DELHI : The Government is planning number of initiatives for the development and protection of children. Setting up of Child Right Commission is a beginning in this direction. Addressing the national consultation on a legal framework for protection of rights of children in the 0-6 years age group organized by National Commission for Protection of Child Right, Smt. Renuka Chowdhury, Minister for Women and Child Development said that her Ministry had requested Planning Commission to consider significant increase for child nutrition under ICDS during 11th Plan. Under proposed integrated child protection scheme several protective and preventive checks are being planned for the protection and welfare of the children, she added. Stressing the need of monitoring of various child welfare programme at district level, Smt. Renuka Chowdhury said for effective implementation and desired results that it is very important. She said that the Government in partnership of private sector would take up a campaign for sensitization and awareness about the rights of the children. On the occasion Dr. Syeda Hameed, Member Planning Commission said that protection and welfare of the children would be the centre stage of the 11th Plan. Numbers of initiatives are being taken for the children in the age group of 0-6 years. She said that immunization; breast-feeding and nutrition should be treated as right of the children. The Government should consider extension of maternity leave to ensure mother's feed to the child upto 6 months. Briefing about the objective of the meeting, Chairperson of Child Rights Commission. Smt. Shanta Sinha said that there is need for legal instruments to provide all such essential services that enable children to have access to health, nutrition, care and protection. There should be law that guarantees protection of children of informal sector and migrant workers. She said that the meeting will discuss about the core sectors which are important for children of 0-6 years age group and made the recommendations to the Government to include them in existing legal framework. The two days meeting is being attended by representatives of Planning Commission, UN agency, medical experts, child experts and NGOs.

3591. (8-10-2007) NEW DELHI : Government of India had approved a plan for modernization of 35 non-metro airports. Airports Authority of India (AAI) was mandated to undertake development of these airports to world-class standards. The work on construction of new terminals and expansion/upgradation of runways, apron etc. is in full swing and several new terminals are likely to be completed during the current financial year. The maintenance and commercial exploitation of the new terminal buildings are proposed to be outsourced to credible private entities on a long-term concession so that these passenger amenities are maintained at world class levels. Besides the above many of these airports have surplus land that can be used for providing cargo facilities and passenger amenities such as hotels, restaurants, car parks, etc. The concessionaires chosen for commercial operation and maintenance of the terminal would also undertake such city side development. An RFQ has been issued by the AAI inviting Expressions of Interest from experienced and qualified parties to undertake the above activities at the Amritsar and Udaipur airports. AAI has developed the terminals at Amritsar and Udaipur at a cost of Rs. 112 crores and Rs. 125 crores respectively. These terminals have been built to world-class standards and are likely to be commissioned by March 2008.

3592. (8-10-2007) NEW DELHI : The 1500 MW Indira Gandhi Super Thermal Power Project on completion will be the biggest power station in the State of Haryana supplying power to the states of NCT Delhi and Haryana. The foundation stone of the project was laid by Smt. Sonia Gandhi, Chairperson, United Progressive Alliance (UPA) yesterday in Jhajjar, Haryana. The 1500 MW project shall be executed by Aravali Power Company Private Limited (APCPL) a joint venture of NTPC Limited, Haryana Power Generation Corporation Ltd.(HPGCL) and Indraprastha Power Generation Company Ltd.(IPGCL). Spread over 2200 Acres, the project shall have 3 units of 500 MW each. Scheduled to be commissioned by the year 2010-11 the estimated cost of the project is approx. Rs. 7892 crore. The other important features of the project are Drum Type Boilers with Single Reheat Type Steam Turbines to achieve higher efficiency. The project shall have closed cycle cooling water system with Natural Draft Cooling Towers. The height of the chimney shall be 275m.

3593. (8-10-2007) NEW DELHI : Shri L.K. Advani said here that I am pleased to be with all my sisters at this concluding session of the Study Camp. I gather from Smt. Kiran Maheshwari, president of the Mahila Morcha, that all the sessions at the camp have been fruitful, and that all the participants have shown great enthusiasm in the deliberations. I am sure that one of the main reasons for the participants' enthusiasm is the historic decision that the party's national executive took at its recently concluded meeting in Bhopal to introduce 33 per cent reservation for women at all levels within the organization. I am proud that ours is the first party and so far the only party to take this bold decision. I would like to congratulate Smt. Sushma Swaraj and all the other members of the committee that made this recommendation. I call upon all other parties to emulate the BJP in this regard. UPA's broken promise on women's reservation bill With this decision, we have shown that women's political empowerment is not merely an election slogan for the BJP, as it is for the Congress and the Communist parties. Today I would like to ask both Prime Minister Dr. Manmohan Singh and Congress president Smt. Sonia Gandhi: "The Common Minimum Programme of the UPA government had solemnly pledged to bring in legislation for 33% reservation for women in Parliament and State legislatures. What happened to this promise? Why haven't you introduced the bill even once during the past three and a half years that you have been in power?" The NDA government made sincere efforts to pass the women's reservation bill. We introduced it in Parliament, not once but twice. But it was opposed mainly by those parties (like the Samajvadi Party) that later either supported the UPA or (like the RJD) which joined the UPA government. The UPA government's betrayal of its promise on the women's reservation bill is only one of the numerous betrayals that have blotted its track-record so far. On price rise, protection of farmers' interests, employment for the youth on each of these and other issues, the UPA government has been an utter failure.

3594. (8-10-2007) NEW DELHI : Access, Equity and Quality are focus of new initiatives in Higher Education as per the meeting of the Consultative Committee relating to the Ministry of Human Resource Development which took place earlier today. The meeting chaired by Shri Arjun Singh, Minister for HRD, discussed new initiatives for the 11th Plan in the higher education sector. The Minister for HRD briefed the members on the proposals from the Ministry that had been discussed in the Full Meeting of the Planning Commission. Shri Singh mentioned that the proposed initiatives would not be ready for implementation till the formal approvals of the Planning Commission and the National Development Council (NDC).

Members were also informed that while the 10th Plan outlay for higher education, including technical education was approximately Rs.9500 crores, the Ministry was hopeful of getting an outlay several times higher for its Central Plan proposals. The 11th Plan objectives are aimed at increasing the Gross Enrolment Ratio(GER) (access rate) in higher education from the present 10% to 15% by 2012, while ensuring improvement in quality and enhancement of equity. Acknowledging that States' share in Plan outlay being roughly four times the Central plan outlay, co-opting States to contribute substantially would be critical to the achievement of the Plan objectives. The Ministry's proposal for the 11th Plan accordingly include incentives to States to allocate higher resources to colleges and universities, partial assistance to setting up of colleges of excellence in as many as 370 districts with low GER and less than four colleges per one lakh of population, special assistance for institutions in 88 minority concentration districts, substantially higher allocation for establishing women's hostels in order to rectify gender bias in enrolment, removal of regional imbalances through the establishment of 30 new central universities-sixteen of which would be in States which have no Central University at present. Members were informed that the Central Government has already approached the State Governments to suggest alternative locations in regard to the new Central Universities and the Ministry in consultation with the Planning Commission and the UGC was in the process of working out the concept of world 'class universities'. The proposals include higher level of assistance to State universities and colleges and also assistance from the UGC to the nearly 150 State universities and 6000 colleges which are not being assisted at present, in order to plug the quality gaps identified by the National Assessment and Accreditation Council (NAAC).

3595. (8-10-2007) NEW DELHI : Union Rural Development Minister, Dr. Raghuvansh Prasad Singh has exhorted on the Private Sector to help build up the rural economy through skill upgradation and entrepreneurship development among the rural masses by way of technological assistance and micro credit at reasonable rates of interest. Addressing the India Rural Business Summit here today organised jointly by the Federation of Indian Chambers of Commerce and Industry (FICCI) under the aegis of Ministry of Rural Development and the Department of Commerce, the minister emphasised the need of providing sustainable jobs to rural house holds in such a way that poverty and unemployment could be eradicated effectively. The biggest challenge in India today is to create income generating ventures for about 4.4 crore rural Below Poverty Line (BPL) families and majority of them have no start up capital or skills and lack credit worthiness as per banking perspectives and therefore, all forward linkages like activity choice, credit and market are required to be brought up to the doorstep of the rural beneficiary, the minister added. Dr. Singh said there is lack of markets in rural areas and lack of adequate awareness of market trends among the rural artisans. Moreover, rural entrepreuneurship in India is a dual scenario, combining market potential with the object of poverty alleviation. Hence there is a need for strong support systems and hand holding by the Government and other institutions. The minister said his ministry implements the Swarnjayanti Gram Swarozgar Yojana (SGSY) schemes, which is aimed at creating sustainable income generating activities for the rural poor in an effort to bring them out of poverty. Till now 26.59 lakh Self Help Groups (SHGs) have been formed and at a total investment of Rs. 18824.32 crore 88.5 lakh Swarozgaries have been given assistance. The minister lauded FICCI for taking an initiative in recognising the potentials of our vibrant rural economy as a crucial factor in the growth of national economy and asked the champions of Indian Industry to come forward for providing necessary training and finacial help to the rural entrepreneurs and artisans for the skill development. He said, the Government is providing all possible help to rural artisans in a bid to erradicate the poverty and unemployment from the rural areas and now it is up to the leaders Indian business community to do necessary market survey and share the feasibility report with rural entrepreneurs. It should also provide necessary technological assistance along with micro credit to them at reasonable rates. Assistance to them may be also given to them in the production of intermediate goods in the rural areas and the integration of rural products with the urban supply chain can be done by the private sector so that the rural masses could brave the challenges of Global economy in a successful manner.

3596. (8-10-2007) NEW DELHI : 839 units in various States have been categorized as 'over-exploited' out of 5723 assessment units in the country, *i.e.* the annual ground water extraction exceeds the annual replenishable resource and significant decline in long term ground water level trend has been observed either in pre-monsoon or post-monsoon or both. In addition, 226 units are 'critical' that is the stage of ground water development is above 90 per cent and within 100 per cent of annual replenishable resource and significant decline is observed in the long-term water level trend in both pre-monsoon and post-monsoon periods. It has been stated in the latest assessment of ground water resources carried out jointly by the Central Ground Water Board (CGWB) and the States. Although the total area classified as "dark area" seems a small per cent of the total number of blocks, a paper from the National Centre for Agricultural Economics and Policy Research says that 'dark' or critical' blocks increased at the rate of 5.5 per annum during mid-1980s to mid-1990s and even assuming the trend continues at the same rate, one-third of the blocks in the country would come in the 'grey' category within two decades. In 1995, over 50 per cent of dark blocks were located in six states namely Gujarat, Haryana, Punjab, Tamil Nadu, Karnataka and Rajasthan. India has a long tradition of using groundwater for agriculture, drining and other uses. But the advent of tube wells, the spread of irrigation and growth of cities, the state of groundwater deteriorate quickly. From the 1960s, intensive agriculture has led to the exploitation of groundwater to such an extent that in areas such as Mehsana in Gujarat and pockets of Haryana and Punjab, it is now common for farmers to drill tube wells to a depth of 500 metres. Furthermore, after boring so deep, farmers sometimes run into saline water that lies beneath freshwater aquifers. Thus while groundwater irrigation has been the mainstay of marginal farmers, water managers face an enormous challenge in ensuring sustainable use of groundwater. The over-depletion of groundwater is becoming a major problem in many parts of the country, especially in urban areas. Urban needs account for 8 per cent of total water consumption and water tables around almost every town and city are falling.

3597. (8-10-2007) NEW DELHI : The Union Public Service Commission will hold the Combined Defence Services Examination (I), 2008 on 17th February, 2008 for admission to Indian Military Academy, Naval Academy and Air Force Academy for the Courses commencing in January, 2009 and Officers Training Academy, Chennai for the Courses (Men and Women) commencing in April, 2009. For details regarding the Eligibility Conditions, Syllabus and Scheme of the examination, Centres of examination, Guidelines for filling up application form etc. aspirants must consult the Detailed Notice of the examination published in the Employment News/Rozgar Samachar dated 29th September, 2007. In case of any guidance/information/clarification regarding their applications, candidature etc. candidates can contact UPSC's Facilitation Counter near 'C' gate of its campus in persons or over Telephone No. 011-23385271/011-23381125/011-23098543 on working days between 10.00 hrs. to 17.00 hrs. The Commission also has Website at address: http:/www.upsc.gov.in over which the candidates can obtain details of the examination as well as information about registration of their applications, venue of the examination and results etc.

3598. (8-10-2007) NEW DELHI : The Central Board of Direct Taxes have extended the last date of filing of income tax returns due by 31st October 2007 to 31st December 2007 in the State of Bihar. The decision has been taken in view of the disruption caused by floods in the State.

3599. (8-10-2007) NEW DELHI : Shri V.K.Aggarwal, Managing Director, RITES Ltd, a consultancy organization under the Ministry of Railways, presented a dividend cheque of Rs. 40 crore for the year 2006-07 to the Minister of Railways Shri Lalu Prasad. RITES achieved a turnover of Rs 566 crore with profit after tax of Rs.118 crores for the financial year ending March 31, 2007. Dividend payment of Rs. 40 crore for the year 2006-07 on equity capital of Rs.4 crore, is the highest ever paid by the company. Recently, the Prime Minister, Dr.Manmohan Singh gave the "SCOPE Award for Excellence" for the outstanding contribution to the Public Sector Management in March 2007, which was received by Mr.V.K.Agarwal, MD (RITES). Meanwhile, Shri Ankush Krishan, Managing Director, IRCON International Limited, a Public Sector Undertaking under the Ministry of Railways, also presented a cheque of Rs. 5.63 crore to the Minister of Railways, Shri Lalu Prasad being the final dividend for 2006-07. This amount is in addition to the interim dividend of Rs. 20.04 crore already paid to the Ministry of Railway in February 2007, brining the total to Rs. 25.67 crore, which is 34 per cent of its post tax profits and 260 per cent of the share capital. Over the years

IRCON has paid a cumulative dividend of Rs. 187 crore to its shareholders against the paid up share capital of Rs. 9.898 crore. IRCON, a schedule 'A' Public Sector company has achieved a record turnover of Rs. 1543 crores during 2006-07, 39 per cent more than last year.

3600. (8-10-2007) NEW DELHI : Mr. Hartmut Schauerte, Parliamentary Secretary of State in the German Federal Ministry of Economics & Technology called on Dr. Chandrapal, Secretary, Ministry of Micro, Small & Medium Enterprises here today. Mr. Hartmut Schauerte evinced keen interest in Indian Micro, Small & Medium Enterprises (MSME) sector, especially cluster development programme. He said Germany could set up Information Centres on small and medium businesses in the line of their centres already opened in China, Indonesia and Singapore. Mr. Hartmut Schauerte said that his country could help India in upgrading technologies in the MSME sector. Appreciating the Rule of Law in India Mr. Hartmut Schauerte said Germany was uninhibitedly keen to bring advanced technology here as there was no threat to Intellectual Property Right violation. Welcoming the proposal, Dr. Chandrapal, Secretary MSME said, the Government had taken a number of steps to boost the MSME sector in recent months, including the enactment of the Micro, Small & Medium Enterprises Development Act, 2006. Explaining the provisions of the Act, Dr. Chandrapal said it aims at facilitating the promotion and development of small and medium enterprises in a competitive way. It seeks to empower the Central Government to notify programmes, guidelines or instructions for facilitating the promotion and growth of small and medium enterprises. One of its primary objectives is to make provisions for ensuring timely and smooth flow of credit to small and medium enterprises, especially the unemployed youth of our country. Citing specific example of Indo-German collaboration, Dr. Chandrapal said the Indo-German Tool Rooms set up in Ahmedabad, Indore and Aurangabad are still among the best in India. These Tool Rooms were established by the Government in technical collaboration with the Government of Federal Republic of Germany to fulfil the tooling and training needs of the Small Scale Industries in the field of Tool Design, Manufacture and training of technical personnel in these fields. He, however, said that India was now keen to have the next generation technology. Shri Jawhar Sircar, Addl. Secretary and Development Commissioner, MSME, Shri Sesh Kumar Pulipaka, Joint Secretary, MSME, were also present on this occasion.

3601. (8-10-2007) NEW DELHI : The Defence Minister said at Platinum Jubilee day of Air force that Marshal of the Air Force Arjan Singh; my esteemed colleagues Admiral Sureesh Mehta, General Deepak Kapoor; AOC-in-C WAC; former Chiefs; honoured guests, Air Warriors, ladies and gentlemen. I am privileged to greet you on the Platinum Jubilee of the Indian Air Force and delighted to share with you this historic moment. Parade Commander, Air Warriors on Parade that was a most impressive and spirited display-well done! I commend you on your turnout, precision and 'josh'. This demonstration reflects our professionalism and discipline. I compliment AOC-in-C WAC and AOC Hindon.

I congratulate all award-winners for your exemplary achievements. 75 years have been an eventful journey for us in the IAF-from a flight of 'Wapitis' in 1932, to the fourth largest, professionally acclaimed, strategic Air Force of today that is the guardian of our vital interests. With a mixed inventory, but home-grown tactics, the IAF has always fielded winning capabilities, from 1948 to Kargil. IAF's professional and prompt operations in peace time, at home & abroad and in peace-keeping, have earned many accolades. In recent years, we have enhanced cooperation with other air forces and exercised with some of the best, to sharpen talons, assimilate 'best practices' and strengthen ties of friendship all over the World-and that is a National priority. Today, the IAF has formal cooperation with six nations; exchanges with many others; teams and missions in 10 countries; and four widely appreciated UN missions in the Congo and Sudan. Over the last year, our operational preparedness has remained at an all time high. Numerous tasks that stretched our resources were effectively completed. It was also among our safest years. IAF offers to the Nation both the application and transportability of national power. To remain competitive and credible, it is imperative that the IAF imbibe modern technologies to achieve long-reach, precision, networked and space-enabled force capabilities. The changing global environment, Regional military capabilities and vital national interests, necessitate a transformational modernisation. I assure you, IAF is keenly conscious of the costs to the Nation. We therefore, seek only the requisite capabilities, but well in time. One year is too short a time for technological transformation, but progress is noticeable on all fronts. The process for acquisition of the MMRCA has begun. The Su-30 project is on track. The first of the Hawk AJTs arrive in a month and the AWACS will be with us next year. Additional Dorniers and VIP Boeings will join the fleet. Contracts will soon be signed for six Hercules C-130Js, 80 Mi-17 1Vs and 54 ALHs. Joint design and development for a 5th Generation Fighter and a Medium Transport Aircraft are being negotiated. The first LCA Sqn should be operational by 2010.

3602. (8-10-2007) NEW DELHI : The role of education in facilitating social and economic progress has long been recognized. Education is not only an instrument of enhancing efficiency but is also an effective tool of widening and augmenting democratic participation and upgrading the overall quality of individual and societal life. India has a population of around 225 million in the age group of 10-19 years. To capture this potential demographic dividend, there is a need to massively expand education within a relatively short span of about 10 years. From the Higher Education point of view, India's GER in higher education is only around 10-11% as compared to 21% in China, 54.6% in developed countries and the world average of 23.2%. The faster growth of the economy has thrown up shortages of technically qualified people. In view of the fast-changing domestic and global economy, the ever-growing importance of knowledge as the critical input in the process of development, and our improved prospects for rapid growth, country needs to pay attention to expanding higher education in a manner which ensures an adequate supply of technical work force and also greater inclusiveness of access to counter the regional and social imbalances.

3603. (9-10-2007) NEW DELHI : International flight safety conference 2007 (IFSCON 07) began at AF Auditorium in Delhi today with the inaugural address by the Chief of Air Staff, Air Chief Marshal Fali Major. The conference provides an important forum where participants of various global aviation organization, Air forces and aviation related organization such as DGCA, AAI, etc. come together to share their experiences to enhance flight safety globally. This year delegates from over 30 countries are attending IFSCON 07. The objective of this conference is to address global safety issues. In his inaugural address Air Chief Marshal Fali Major said "That aviation has inherent dangers is stating the obvious. The air is not our natural medium and it takes a most complex machine to reach there and operate in-therein lie the risks. Modern technology has however over the years made flying very safe, routine and convenient. Its key characteristics of speed reach and imperviousness to terain have made it very attractive transport-whether of passengers and goods or of national power. Consequently aviation is blooming all over the world, bringing with it the additional challenges of crowded skies and huge pressures of aviation infrastructure". He also said "modern day environment has more distractions for the people than earlier", further adding "it is always good to share ideas and strategies for mutual benefit". The delegates of IFSCON would be discussing and deliberating on topics such as, adoption of tri-services Pan Defence Aviation Regulatory & Safety Group, operational risk management, Accident Investigation techniques, pitfalls in Human factors and suggested remedies. It has been observed that 45% accident take place due to technical glitches, 45% due to human error and 10% are attributable to the flying environment. The global effort of IFSCON 07 would surely make aviation universally safe.

3604. (9-10-2007) NEW DELHI : The Cabinet Committee on Economic Affairs today gave its approvals for up-gradation and modernization of iron ore handling facilities at the Outer Harbour of Visakhapatnam Port at an estimated cost of Rs. 185.15 crores. This decision will enable the port to handle higher traffic leading to increased revenue for the port and will improve the productivity and efficiency in handling iron ore at the port.

3605. (9-10-2007) NEW DELHI : The Cabinet Committee on Economic Affairs today gave its approval to the continuation of the Rajiv Gandhi Grameen Vidyutkaran Yojana (RGGVY) in the XI Plan. It was noted that the Planning Commission had made an allocation of Rs.28,000 crore in the XIth Plan for the scheme.

3606. (9-10-2007) NEW DELHI : The Cabinet Committee on Economic Affairs today gave its approval for the procurement of long delivery equipments as a pre-project activity for four 700 MWe PHWRs at an estimated expenditure of Rs.1680 crore ahead of the project financial sanction. The procurement of long delivery equipment is a prerequisite for timely completion of the project. This ensures timely availability of equipment so as to take advantage of parallel progress of civil construction and equipment erection. The long delivery equipment are to be obtained from indigenous manufacturers. Two Boiling Water Reactors and fifteen Pressurised Heavy Water Reactors (PHWRs) with a total installed capacity of 4120 MWe are currently in operation. Three 220 MWe PHWRs and two 1000 MWe Light Water Reactors with a total capacity of 2660 MWe are under advanced stage of construction. Construction work has also been taken up on one 500 MWe Fast Breeder Reactor (FBR) at Kalpakkam, Tamil Nadu signifying launch of the second stage of the nuclear power programme. With the completion of these projects the total nuclear power capacity in the country will reach 7280 MWe by March 2011.

3607. (9-10-2007) NEW DELHI : The CCEA gave its approval to the following today : The Inland Waterways Authority of India (IWAI) to acquire six nos. Cutter Suction Dredging Units along with workboats and accommodation boats for National Waterway No.1 and National Waterway No.2 at an estimated cost of Rs.113.45 crores. The dredging requirement assessed for National Waterway No.1 (Haldia to Allahabad-1620 kms) is 15 lakh cubic meter per annum with a total of shoals length of 64.0 kms. This volume of work necessitates use of 11 units of which four are available with IWAI. Hence, there is a balance requirement of 7 nos. of which only 2 are proposed to be procured at present. Thereafter, the requirement of dredgers for the stretch Haldia to Varanasi (1383 kms) will be fully met. The dredging requirement assessed for National Waterway No.2 (Dhubri to Sadiya-891 kms) is 14 lakh cubic meter per annum with a total shoals length of 45.0 kms. This volume of work will require 8 no. of dredging units out of which one is already available with IWAI on NW-2. Hence, there is a balance requirement of 7 units of which 4 are to be acquired. After this acquisition the requirement of dredgers upto Dibrugarh (768 kms) will be met fully. The delivery of all the Cutter Suction Dredging Units along with workboats and accommodation boats will be received within 22 months from the date of award of contract to shipbuilders.

3608. (9-10-2007) NEW DELHI : Smt. D. Purandeswari, Minister of State for HRD has urged the developed countries to take lead in addressing "climate change" while making intervention from the Indian side on agenda item no. 4 "Parliamentary Campaign on Climate Change. She was representing the Indian Delegation at the 117th Assembly of the Inter Parliamentary Union on October 8 at Geneva." Minister has stated that India shares the concerns of the international community regarding the challenge posed by climate change and environmental degradation as they impact disproportionately upon developing countries which lack the resources to tackle it. She has pointed out that the challenge must be addressed through universal mechanisms such as the UN Framework Convention on Climate Change in a manner that protects the interests of developing countries by implementation of the principle of common but differentiated responsibilities. The environment cannot be protected at the expense of perpetuating poverty in the developing countries nor by sustaining excessive consumption patterns in the developed world. The Minister has stated that the countries with the primary responsibility for the present state of Green House Gases (GHG) concentrations in the atmosphere must shoulder the responsibility in addressing this global challenge. She has also emphasized that it is very important for the developed countries to take the lead in mitigating GHG emissions and make the critical clean technologies available and affordable for developing countries. Smt. Purandeswari mentioned that the key issue for India and other developing countries is developing the ability to cope with the adverse impacts of climate change and adapt to it. This requires technological and financial resources that can only come through development which is the best form of adaptation. Minister has pointed out that the time is not ripe for the developing countries to take on quantitative targets of emissions limitations. Minister has pointed out that India with 17% of the world's population has only 4% of the global GHG emissions. The energy intensity of GDP growth in India has in fact reduced from 0.30 kgoe per US$ GDP in PPP terms in 1972 to 0.16 kgoe per US$ GDP in PPP terms in 2003. Minister has reminded the forum that India is committed for not increasing the per capita GHG emissions beyond those of the industrial countries while pursuing economic growth. Minister has informed the forum that India has in place a comprehensive policy and legislative framework to address energy environment issues. Government of India has recently set-up Prime Minister's Council on Climate Change to coordinate national action for assessment, adaptation and mitigation of climate change. She has also pointed out that India has been constantly addressing climate variability concerns which together had to over 2% of GDP each year and in all the major energy intensive sectors, such as steel, fertilizer, cement, etc., levels of energy efficiency are at global level. Minister has also informed the forum that India is the largest global player in Clean Development Mechanism in terms of number of projects. The Indian national CDM authority has accorded host country approval to over 667 projects facilitating an environment of nearly Rs. 60,000 crores. Responding to the intervention made by Smt. D. Purandeswari, the Executive Director of UNEP, Mr. Achim Steiner has shared the same concern that the industrialized countries should feel the pressure and take up the responsibilities in addressing climate change. He also mentioned that the new technological innovations should lead to the energy efficiency in the developing countries. Mr. Achim Steiner, has appreciated the measures taken up by India to mitigate GHG emissions in spite the fact that she is an emerging global economic power as pointed out by Smt. D. Purandeswari. He opined that India should be emulated in this endeavour.

3609. (9-10-2007) NEW DELHI : The Government has taken up number of initiatives to combat trafficking, which include proposed amendments to the immoral Traffic Act to target the traffickers and other perpetrators of the crime. While making amendments the Government has also proposed to withdraw those provisions which revictimise the victims of trafficking, this was stated by

Smt. Renuka Chowdhury, Minister for Women and Child Development addressing the media here today on the eve of South Asia Regional Conference on Human Trafficking being organized by the Ministry of Women and Child Development in collaboration with Ministry of Home Affairs and United Nations Office of Drugs and Crime (UNODC). Expressing concern over trafficking of women and children, Smt. Chowdhury said that her Ministry is launching a comprehensive scheme for prevention of trafficking and rescue, rehabilitation, reintegration and repatriation of the victims including cross border victims. The Ministry has also set up a Central Advisory Committee to combat trafficking which include all concerned Ministries, State Ministries, enforcement agencies; International organizations and NGOs are its members. The Committee meets every quarter and deliberates on various aspects of trafficking. The Minister disclosed that the Government is also in the process of formulating a National Plan of Action for Combating Trafficking, with special focus on women and children in collaboration with Ministry of Home Affairs. She said that this plan of action would address all forms of trafficking. Emphasizing over early repatriation of cross border victims, Smt. Renuka Chowdhury said the issue of cross border trafficking had received considerable attention especially with regard to the safe, expeditious and humane repatriation of victims of trafficking. A major problem experienced was that even after identification of cross-border victims, the repatriation procedures took a very long time, which was traumatic for the victim and a family. She disclosed that Women and Child Development Ministry in Collaboration with the Ministry of Home Affairs is working on a joint plan of action and roadmap with Bangladesh counterparts for quick and safe repatriation of cross border trafficked victims of both countries. She expressed the hope the South Asia Regional Conference beginning tomorrow would provide an effective platform to generate awareness on various issues of trafficking and initiate a collaborative regional effort to tackle the problems. On the occasion, Minister of State for Home Affairs, Shri Manik Rao M. Gavit briefed the media about various initiatives taken by the Ministry of Home Affairs to check the trafficking of women and children which include setting up of working groups, training and capacity building for monitoring agencies. Mr. Gary Lewis of UNODC made the presentation of the occasion about the global initiative to fight human trafficking. The two days conference on human trafficking will be attended by the representatives of Governments, civil society, private sector leaders and UN agencies in order to draft strategies and adopt Delhi Declaration to check trafficking of women and children in the region.

3610. (9-10-2007) NEW DELHI : The Home Minister, Shri Shivraj Patil today met Vietnamese President Nguyen Minh Triet and Prime Minister Nguyen Tan Dung in Hanoi. He also visited the Police Academy in the city. The Home Minister held official discussions with Vietnamese Minister of Public Security, Le Hong Anh yesterday. The Mutual Legal Assistance Treaty on Criminal matters was signed by the two Ministers. A draft MoU on cooperation between the Ministry of Home Affairs and the Ministry of Public Security of Vietnam was also initialed at the official level. A formal MoU will be signed during the visit of the Minister of Public Security of Vietnam to India scheduled for early next year. The Home Minister today unveiled the bust of Smt. Indira Gandhi in Hanoi. After Lenin, Smt. Indira Gandhi is the only leader in whose name a public park has been named in Hanoi. The unveiling function was attended, among others, by the Vietnamese Vice Minister of Public Security, Gen. Col. Le The Tiem, Vice Chairperson of Hanoi People's Committee, Ngo Thi Thanh Hang, senior Government officials and the Indian community.

3611. (9-10-2007) NEW DELHI : Ministry of New and Renewable Energy signed a Memorandum of Understanding on Renewable Energy Cooperation today with the Government of Iceland. Under the Memorandum both the countries will decide upon project proposals related to design and development of various new and renewable energy technologies, identified areas of mutual interest and cooperation for systems, sub-systems, devices, components etc. and monitor and evaluate cooperation activities. Minister of New and Renewable Energy, Shri Vilas Muttemwar led a delegation to Iceland in June 2006. During this visit both sides agreed to explore cooperation in the areas of geothermal, hydrogen and fuel cells and wind energy. The MoU proposes to take forward cooperation in various areas of renewable energy technologies. Iceland and India cooperates in hydrogen and fuel cells under the forum of International Partnership for Hydrogen Economy (IPHE). Icelandic side will be fielding a trade delegation in November 2007 to establish industry level contacts in renewable energy.

3612. (9-10-2007) NEW DELHI : Development and beautification projects will take place in Nagpur soon. Shri Vilas Muttemwar, Minister of New and Renewable Energy and Shri M.M. Pallam Raju, Minister of State for Defence met yesterday at Nagpur to resolve long pending problems. Both the Ministers discussed issues relating to land swap between Indian Air Force (IAF) and Maharashtra Airport Development Cooperation Limited (MADC). Accordingly, Cargo Hub Project of Government of Maharashtra and Gajraj Project of IAF were the major subject of discussion. Besides, the Beautification and Development programme of Sitabuldi Fort, land transfer for development of Koradi Devi Temple Complex, Ganesh Tekri Temple Complex, Fly-over near Nagpur Railway Station and Kamptee Railway Station, Idgah land and Rubbani Food Ball ground were also discussed. Shri M.M. Pallam Raju, instructed IAF to ensure to reach MoU about land swap between MADC and IAF within next fifteen days. He also ensured that most of the issues will be sorted out amicably within a short period of time.

3613. (9-10-2007) NEW DELHI : The BJP said here that the nation is tired and indeed fatigued by the farce which goes in the name of United Progressive Alliance. It is now finally evident that an alliance of mutually hostile and antagonistic elements like the Congress and the Left based solely upon common hatred against the BJP is inherently unstable. The UPA ought to be characterised more appropriately as "Ulta-Pulta" Alliance which needed few sparks only to bring the divide sharply into the open. The two major fractious quarrelsome partners have brought a virtual paralysis in governance and vital decision making. Be it the issue of food security, compelling matters of national security or, pressing problems of "Aam Adami"; whose interest the UPA deceptively claimed to represent; all have been disturbingly relegated to the background. Major decisions on economic issues in a government led by the so called pioneer of economic reform Dr. Manmohan Singh have been pushed into the cold storage. An India rearing to leap foreword has become the victim of a paralysed central government. Now an inter-se competition goes on between the Congress and the Left as to who should be blamed for the impending mid-term poll. One notices political brinkmanship at its worst. One is surprised as to how parties of the Left failed to note that running a coalition government is not in the DNA of Congress. The Congress has a dominant arrogant character fuelled by the conviction that it has a sole monopoly to decide as to what is in India's interest. In its sheer opportunism the Left forgot its past where they have also been victims of Congress's arrogance. The impending demise of the UPA misadventure brings the inherent undemocratic character of Congress into sharp focus. The statement of Smt. Sonia Gandhi in Harayana that any one opposing the nuclear deal is against the nation, gave unmistakable glimpses of the theme slogan of the Emergency days in the seventies that the "history of Congress is the history of India" and "Indira is India" and those "who oppose Congress oppose India". Let Mrs. Gandhi note that the India of 2007 is not an India of 1975. The roots of democracy are much stronger in India. It is finally evident that it is the NDA led by BJP alone which can give a foreword looking development oriented stable coalition as demonstrated before the nation in its six years rules under Shri A. B. Vajpayee as the Prime Minister. The nation is sick of the UPA. A nation of more than a billion people is in a state of drift where governance is a casualty. Perhaps it is time to say for God sake UPA please go and spare India.

3614. (9-10-2007) NEW DELHI/KOLKATA: On the eve of the fifth meeting of the UPA-Left committee on the Indo-U.S. nuclear deal, CPI(M) general secretary Prakash Karat met External Affairs Minister Pranab Mukherjee at his house in New Delhi on Monday. Later, Mr. Karat and Sitaram Yechury, Polit Bureau member and MP, also met UPA chairperson and Congress president Sonia Gandhi. The subject of both meetings was the nuclear deal. Mr. Karat declined to comment on the meetings when asked by *The Hindu*. Earlier, talking to journalists in Kolkata, veteran Marxist leader Jyoti Basu said that in the event of the UPA calling for snap polls, the CPI(M) was "ready" to face the electorate but "it is better that elections are not held now and we [the UPA and the Left parties] stick together for some more time." He said he had spoken to senior leaders of his party to see whether it was possible to work out a "compromise" over the deal. On the remarks of Ms. Gandhi being construed as suggestive of the party being inclined to early elections, he said: "She spoke favourably [about those supporting the Congress-led UPA government] while in the United States recently but has been speaking differently here [since her return] and talking of elections and collapse of the government. This is not right." "But if they [the Congress] force elections we [the CPI(M)] are also ready," Mr. Basu said, adding that he "is not in favour of they being held soon as communal forces are still very much in existence, weakening in some places but gaining strength in others." On Sunday, Mr. Mukherjee had a meeting with Mr. Basu in Kolkata.

3615. (9-10-2007) NEW DELHI : Paddy procurement in the current kharif marketing season has reached 29.43 lakh tonnes today. Different agencies have procured 23.86 LT paddy in Punjab, 5.5 LT in Haryana, 5892 tonnes in Kerala and 1397 tonnes in Chandigarh. Agencies have also procured 75141 tonne coarse cereals in Haryana. As per data compiled by the Department of Food and Public Distribution, 33.35 lakh tonne paddy has arrived in various markets so far this year.

3616. (9-10-2007) NEW DELHI : The National Common Minimum Programme (NCMP) of the UPA Government envisages a strong and effective public sector and pledges to devolve managerial and commercial autonomy to successful profit making companies operating in a competitive environment. There is a need for appropriate public accountability of the Central Public Sector Enterprises (CPSE) managements regarding discharging of their duties and responsibilities keeping in view the fact that large public funds have been invested in them. Thus, it is imperative that ethics and probity are maintained in the functioning of CPSEs. Good Corporate Governance practices, therefore, should be built into the management systems of CPSEs. The Government has considered the above and approved the implementation of Guidelines on Corporate Governance for CPSEs. These guidelines have been formulated through a consultation process with various stakeholders and keeping in view the relevant laws, rules and instructions. These guidelines cover issues like composition of Board of Directors, setting up of Audit Committees, role and powers of Audit Committees, issues relating to subsidiary companies, disclosures, accounting standards, risk management, compliance and schedule of implementation, etc. These guidelines though voluntary in nature should be followed by all CPSEs as proper implementation of these guidelines would protect the interests of shareholders and relevant stakeholders. The compliance with these guidelines requires to be reflected in the Directors' report, Annual Report and Chairman's speech in the Annual General Meeting. The Department of Public Enterprises would also grade the CPSEs on the basis of their compliance of the corporate governance guidelines.

3617. (9-10-2007) NEW DELHI : India and Singapore signed an agreement today on a long-term arrangement for conducting joint training and exercises between the Indian Air Force and the Republic of Singapore Air Force. The agreement was signed by the Defence Secretary Mr. Vijay Singh and Singapore's

Permanent Secretary of Defence, Mr. Chiang Chie Foo as the two-day 4th India-Singapore Defence Policy Dialogue began here today. During the dialogue, both sides gave an update on India-Singapore defence relations and expressed the need to further intensify cooperation. Sub-groups reported progress made in respective fields including research & development. The regional security aspects, both from Indian and Singaporean perspectives, were discussed.

3618. (9-10-2007) NEW DELHI : Lieutenant General ET Motanyane, Commander, Lesotho Defence Forces, is visiting India from 07 Oct. to 12 Oct. 07. The visit assumes special significance in the light of enhanced defence cooperation between India and Lesotho. India has maintained good relations with Lesotho. Defence cooperation, as a part of defence diplomacy, has been an important tool towards enhancing this friendship. The defence cooperation between the two countries got a boost after signing of a MoU on Establishment of Training Team in 2001. Since then, the Indian Army Training Team is providing quality training to Lesotho Defence Forces and also provides valuable advice to them on various security related issues. Consequently, cooperation between the two armies has enhanced in the field of attendance on courses, exchange of observers in exercises and visits. Lieutenant General ET Motanyane and his four member delegation will be visiting Northern Command and various Army training establishments. The delegation will be interacting with the COAS, the Defence Secretary and various other dignitaries. Discussions on enhancing defence cooperation in the fields of training/courses, sports and adventure activities are likely during this visit.

3619. (9-10-2007) NEW DELHI : The services in India Government Mints, Kolkata, Noida (U.P.), Mumbai, Hyderabad, Cherlapalli (Ranga Reddy) will continue as a public utility service under the Industrial Dispute Act, 1947 for another six months with immediate effect. In a notification issued here, the Labour Ministry said that this has been done in public interest. The Central Government had earlier declared the services in India Government Mints as a public utility service for six months from 28th February 2007.

3620. (9-10-2007) NEW DELHI : Prime Minister Dr.Manmohan Singh has said that the Government is considering the idea of offering further incentives to States and cities that implement reforms on a faster track. The Prime Minister was speaking at a National Conference on Jawaharlal Nehru National Urban Renewal Mission (JNNURM) which he inaugurated here today. He urged the State and Local Governments to advance the timelines for implementation of reforms so that the Mission's objectives are met within the time specified. For example, the reforms pertaining to improving Urban Local Body Finances could be completed within the first three years of the Mission. This will enable these bodies to become viable and eligible to enlist institutional finance, he added. The Prime Minister said the sum of Rs.50,000 crore provided by the Government is hardly adequate for meeting the infrastructure investment needs of JNNURM cities and towns. States must leverage these funds and raise more from the market. To do so, the quality of projects and the fiscal health of Urban Local Bodies must be improved, he added. The private sector can be encouraged to invest in urban development through public-private partnerships. Urban infrastructure and services and low cost housing offer huge potential for such partnerships. He said that the State Governments and cities must provide the enabling environment for the private sector to participate. Speaking on the occasion, Shri Jaipal Reddy, Minister of Urban Development said that while JNNURM is a reforms linked investment programme, the Government is keen to not just incentivise, but also enable implementation of reforms. He urged the States and cities not to look at reforms narrowly as just a set of milestones and commitments. Urban reforms are not just about policies, legislation, process improvements and use of I.T, he added. A number of smaller municipalities, nor part of Mission cities, are showing similar aspirations and leadership the Minister said. Recognising that these small and medium towns too need more financial support, we are working closely with the Ministry of Finance and the Planning Commission to allocate more funds to the UIDSSMT scheme, he added. Kumari Selja, Minister of State for Urban Housing and Poverty Alleviation welcomed the gathering. Mayors of several Mission cities, State Urban Development Secretaries, Municipal Commissioners are participating in the Conference.

3621. (9-10-2007) NEW DELHI : The Prime Minister, Dr. Manmohan Singh, said that today, our policies are better informed and we have begun to see urbanization as an opportunity. All projections of the coming decade indicate that the process of urbanization would accelerate rapidly. If we can manage this transformation effectively, the physical and economic regeneration of urban India is well within our reach. While inaugurating the National Conference on Jawaharlal Nehru National Urban Renewal Mission here today, the Prime Minister said that India no longer lives only in its villages but increasingly in its small towns and cities and that the process of economic growth has unleashed dramatic changes in our cities. 'Cities have become major growth engines of our economy opening up unprecedented opportunities', he added. The Prime Minister also hoped that the National Urban Renewal Mission will help realize the dream of making urbanization ecologically sustainable, economically productive and socially equitable. Following is the text of the Prime Minister's address on the occasion: "I am happy to be present at this National Conference of Leaders of Local Bodies and State Governments to take stock of the work we began some 22 months ago through the Jawaharlal Nehru National Urban Renewal Mission. I compliment the Minister of Urban Development Shri Jaipal Reddyji and the Minister for Housing and Urban Poverty Alleviation Seljaji for taking the initiative in this matter and also leading from the front this major initiative for urban transformation in our country. At the outset, I wish to say that a systematic effort to improve our cities has been long overdue. India no longer lives only in its villages but increasingly in its small towns and mega cities. The process of economic growth has unleashed dramatic changes in our cities. Cities have become major growth engines of our economy opening up unprecedented opportunities. At the same time, this rapid urbanization has spawned its own set of problems. A large proportion of our urban population still lives in slums in unacceptable conditions. Urban housing stock, especially housing for the poor, has not kept pace with the expanding demand. As much as 30% of urban households live in single room units. This creates social and health problems. It affects the education of young children. The demand for civic services has shot up exponentially. We, therefore, need to facilitate and respond to this transformation through effective measures for improvement of city services, proactive creation of urban infrastructure and improved systems of public governance to match the requirements of the situation. Since its launch, the JNNURM has come to signify the agenda for urban transformation all over the country. It has brought about a uniformity of approach and strategy creating an umbrella framework involving almost all the stakeholders. Our approach of accelerating the implementation of urban sector reforms by linking these to support for large-scale capital investment for urban infrastructure, has been widely accepted. I sincerely hope the National Urban Renewal Mission will help us realize the dream of making urbanization in our country ecologically sustainable, economically productive and socially equitable. I commend both the Ministries as well as the representatives of the State Governments and Mayors of Municipal Corporations present here for their enthusiastic response to this initiative. 63 cities have already developed their "City Development Plans" and are in the process of preparing Detailed Project Reports to access funds. One positive feature observed in these plans is that about 60 per cent of the investment is going for improvement of essential basic services like water supply, sanitation and sewerage. We should ensure that those localities that today have minimal services gain the maximum from the new investments proposed. In fact, internal earmarking in city budgets for basic services to the urban poor has been made an important reform conditionality. I would urge the local bodies and the state governments to give this area priority attention to ensure that we do develop inclusive cities where every citizen has an entitlement to basic services. We are all agreed that governance reform is the cornerstone of urban renewal. Such reforms would ensure the long-term sustainability of the investments and greater transparency and accountability in urban planning and development. Hence the link between investment and reform. This will also be the approach to be adopted in the XIth Five Year Plan, which will further strengthen the JNNURM. Our Government stands committed to providing the requisite budgetary support to States and cities. I urge State and Local Governments to advance the timelines for implementation of these reforms so that the Mission's objectives are met within the specified time period.

3622. (9-10-2007) NEW DELHI : UGC is organising a National Conference of the Vice Chancellors of all central, state, deemed and private universities here on October 10-11, 2007. Sri Arjun Singh, Union Minister for Human Resource Development, Government of India, would inaugurate the Conference. Over 400 vice chancellors from all niversities from across the country are scheduled to attend the two-day conference. Valedictory address of the conference will be delivered by Shri Kapil Sibal, Union Minister for Science and Technology. To commemorate the completion of 150 glorious years of Modern University System, an exhibition is also being organized by the UGC, depicting through the exhibits, the journey of Higher Education from early 18th century onwards. This exhibition which will act as a prism to view the vision and horizon of Higher Education would also be inaugurated by the Hon'ble Union Minister for Human Resource Development, Shri Arjun Singh. This National Conference is a culmination of four Regional Conferences that the UGC had organised at Mumbai, Kolkata, Hyderabad and New Delhi in which a total of 218 vice chancellors, directors of the college development councils and secretaries/directors of higher education of different states, chairpersons of state councils of higher education had participated. The issues raised and recommendations made in the regional conferences would be deliberated upon in this National Conference and would revolve around the following six themes.

3623. (9-10-2007) NEW DELHI : The Cabinet Committee on Economic Affairs today gave its approval to the following: (i) To extend the moratorium on outstanding term loans as on 01.04.2005 announced in September 2005 for co-operative sugar factories, from 2 to upto 5 years (reckoned from 01.04.2005) and to include cooperative sugar mills, not included in the earlier package, for availing the benefits of earlier package. Interest subvention amount to be provided by the Central Government from budgetary support, to the banks for reduction in the rate of interest to 10% per annum on the restructured loans, has been increased from Rs. 560 crores to Rs. 600 crores; (ii) to consider conversion of outstanding loans on account of harvesting and transport charges and short margins on sugar stocks, as appearing in the books of the sugar mills on 01.04.2007 into term loans upto a maximum period of 5 years, without any reduction in the existing rate of interest; (iii) to approve making 5% blending of ethanol with petrol mandatory across the country, except in J&K, North-Eastern States and Island Territories and to make 10% blending optional from October, 2007 and mandatory from October, 2008, excepting in the areas mentioned above; (iv) to approve a uniform purchase price of Rs.21.50 per litre ex-factory for supply of ethanol which can be implemented all over the country for the next three years; (v) to give loans from the banks under special guidelines to the sugar mills-private, public sector and cooperatives-of an amount equivalent to the Central Excise duty actually paid by the sugar mills for levy and non-levy sugar during 2006-07 and an estimated amount of excise payable in 2007-08 and to provide interest subvention to the banks on account of this loan through budgetary provisions by the Central Government. Such Central assistance should be confined to the portion of arrears of sugarcane price which is relatable to SMP. Necessary guidelines will be issued by Department of Financial Services, Ministry of Finance in consultation with Department of Food and Public Distribution, based on the recommendation of GOM; (vi) to reduce customs duty from 7.5% to 5 % on "denatured alcohol" and from 10% to 5%

on molasses and to implement the same only when mandatory ethanol blending at 5% level is operationalized in the country; (vii) to permit sugar factories to produce ethanol directly from sugarcane juice to augment availability of ethanol and reduce oversupply of sugar; and (viii) to extend export assistance scheme continuing at present, by one more year from 19th April, 2008 to 18th April 2009 to target an additional export of further 3 million tons of sugar. The export assistance will be provided from Sugar Development Fund (SDF). These will enable the sugar factories to improve their financial position and make timely payment of cane dues and bank dues.

3624. (10-10-2007) NEW DELHI : NAFED, Mother Dairy, Kendriya Bhandar and Delhi Government's Food and Supplies Department would act in coordination with each other and continue their present market intervention measures for sale of onion in Delhi. This was decided in a meeting taken here today by Secretary, Department of Consumer Affairs Shri YS Bhave. The meeting was called to review the situation of availability and prices of onion and the extent of market intervention made by these agencies. It was decided that different agencies would take the price at which Delhi Government was selling onion through its outlets as the benchmark price. The sale price would not exceed Rs. 18 per Kg. Presently Delhi Government is selling onion through its outlet at the rate of Rs.17 per Kg, while Mother Dairy is selling onion at the rate of Rs. 18 through its 350 outlets. Kendriya Bhandar has agreed to start market intervention on a pilot basis at some of its outlets in Delhi. This agency would sell onion through its outlets where other agencies have no outlets in proximity. NAFED would assist Kendriya Bhandar in procurement of onion. It was decided to review the situation from time to time.

3625. (10-10-2007) NEW DELHI : India was described as a Hydraulic Civilisation by historians. Even when the British came to India about 250 years ago, India was urbanised and there were a number of towns, like Patna, Varanasi, Allahabad, built on riverbanks and other cities with tanks for water supply like Jodhpur, Jaisalmer and Bhopal. In south India, cities had temple tanks. Tens of thousands of water structures with diverse technologies, existed; more importantly, there were also management structures to share and distribute water equitably. One of the best examples of how ancient and rich is the Indian tradition of water harvesting, is from the recent excavations of the Indus Valley civilisation at Dholavira, in the Great Rann of Kutch, dating back to 3000 B.C. In an arid region with very little rainfall, devoid of any water sources from rivers, with poor quality groundwater, the people had created several huge reservoirs to collect rainwater. The design and technology was ingenious that allowed them to harvest all the rainwater and drain off excess water. Techniques of Water Harvesting A variety of techniques were developed, in an attempt to harvest every possible available form of water-from rainwater to groundwater, from stream water to river water and floodwater. In the hill and mountain regions people diverted water into channels or dykes to bring water for irrigation and they called them variously as kuls, guls or kuhals.

In the central highlands and western part of the country, people built small dams across small rivers so that the water so captured gets recharged into the soil and provides moisture for the post-monsoon crops, called pats and johads. In the arid desert of Rajasthan, every kind of structure was built from small ponds (nadis) to wells (kundis, baoris, jhalaras) to large tanks or talabs. In the south of India, where there are two monsoon seasons, the rulers built a large number of tanks, these tanks were built in a sequence sometimes of 25-30 tanks, which were fed by a stream. For instance, the ancient Palar dam system supplies water to 317 tanks. In the floodplains of Bihar, a system of canals and reservoirs diverted surplus flood waters to be used later. The structures are maintained by a complex and interconnected system of community discipline and fiscal responsibility. Water was never considered free, but rather a responsibility of the community. The rulers never constructed these structures for the public, but rather provided fiscal incentives like tax exemptions that would motivate individuals and communities to build water harvesting structures. For instance, in Jodhpur, the Ranisar, situated within the fort was only meant for nobility and the common people used the Padamsar that was fed by runoff form the Ranisar. Similarly, in Udaipur, the famous Pichola lake was built by the Banjara gypsies which is used by the public. Rainwater harvesting-the paradigm of the past-has in it as much strength today as it ever did before. It can be used in rural areas to drought-proof the country. It can be used in urban areas to make cities self-sufficient in water.

3626. (10-10-2007) NEW DELHI : Following is the text of the Defence Minister Shri A K Antony's address to the valedictory session of the International Flight Safety Conference-2007 here today: "Aerospace has reached a critical stage, as it finds increasing application and utility in peace time, as well as during conflicts. Aerospace has emerged as one of the most dominant factors in maintaining a balance on the geopolitical and economic fronts. With state-of-the-art equipment and upgraded technology being sought across the globe, higher costs of operations, maintenance and training have become key questions. Nations cannot afford to waste valuable resources. In recent times, significant progress has been made in the field of aviation safety in terms of developing new ideas, methods and techniques to prevent aircraft accidents and improve the investigation procedure. Aviation safety is today being treated as a management function, concentrating more on humans than on machines. Aviation organisations are accepting new programmes and fine-tuning them to meet their requirements. Our Air Force has to meet different challenges pertaining to aviation safety. Operation and maintenance of different flying machines, continuously degrading environment around populated centres and the problem of attracting suitable manpower, given the strong pulls of the private sector and MNCs are only a few of the challenges. Due to the various initiatives taken in the field of aviation safety, there has been a marked drop in the accident rates of our Air Force in the last three years. With the expansion of civil aviation activities, challenges in ground and air space management, commonality of languages and procedures have manifested themselves. In the years to come, the main challenge will be to keep pace with the fast-paced changes in the realm of technology. The emphasis will increasingly be on the ability of the personnel to handle multi-tasking effectively. Thus, understanding the abilities and limitations of the human element and minimising human failures would remain the true challenge for all of us. Our Air Force's recent experience has shown that awareness is the greatest tool to prevent accidents. Indeed, the process of 'learn and teach' is the best way to benefit the national and global aviation community."

3627. (10-10-2007) NEW DELHI : The North-East Region because of its remoteness and peculiar geographic situation has remained among the more backward regions of the country. The Region has remained insulated from the national mainstream. The N.E. State officials get little opportunity for quality training and they generally suffer from a lack of exposure to the latest development/ trends in the country. The lack of proper communication and administrative skills affects the delivery of services at all levels. There is a continuing need, therefore, to provide exposure to the officials of North East to the developments in rest of the country for improving the delivery of public services. The technical staff in the government is often poorly equipped for planning, preparation of DPRs, implementation and monitoring of the projects. As a result, the quality of implementation of projects suffers apart from delays and cost over-run. Most of the NE States have a high literacy rate. However, due to the lack of industry and tertiary sector as well as reduced employment opportunities in the Government sector, the problem of education unemployment is very acute. The Region does not have many institutes of high quality and even the few institutes that exist are often unable to attract the best faculty or technical manpower from outside. Although the Government is taking steps to set up appropriate institutes, this will take time. The only viable solution in the short terms is, therefore, to develop and upgrade the skills of the existing manpower, utilizing the best institutes in other parts of the country. Technical Assistance & Capacity Building to the North Eastern States is therefore a key requirement for sustainable development of the Region and its people. There is a strong need to bridge the gap in the technical and managerial skill requirements in the North Eastern Region. The basic strategy has been to select important developmental sectors, identify the gaps and select appropriate training institutes to build customized programmes as per training needs assessment, relevant to the North Eastern Region. The target groups include government officials, potential entrepreneurs, unemployed educated youth etc.

3628. (10-10-2007) NEW DELHI : The Backward Region Grant Fund is designed to redress regional imbalances in development. The fund will provide financial resources supplementing and converging existing development inflows into 250 identified districts, so as to: 1. Bridge critical gaps in local infrastructure and other development requirements that are not being adequately met through existing inflows. 2. Strengthen, to this end Panchayat and Municipality level governance with more appropriate capacity building, to facilitate participatory planning, decision making implementation and monitoring to reflect local felt needs, 3. Provide professional support to local bodies for planning, implementation and monitoring their plans. Improve the performance and delivery of critical functions assigned to Panchayats, and counter possible efficiency and equity losses on account of inadequate local capacity. Integrity development will commence with each district undertaking a diagnostic study of its backwardness by enlisting professional planning support. This will be followed by preparing a well-conceived participatory district development perspective plan to address the backwardness during 2006-07 and the period of the Eleventh Five-Year. The Panchayats at the village, intermediate and district level referred to in Part IX of the Constitution, will undertake planning and implementation of the programme, in keeping with the letter and spirit of Article 243 G, while the Municipalities referred to in Part IX A will similarly plan and implement the programme in urban areas in conformity with the letter and spirit of Article 243 W, read with Article 243 ZD of the Constitutions. The Programme has two components namely, a district component covering 250 districts and Special plans for Bihar and KBK districts of Orissa. A total provision of Rs.5000 cores had been made for the two components in the Budget of 2006-07. Out of this allocation Rs.1250 crore had been provided in the Demand for Grants of the Ministry of Finance for the Special Plans dealt with by Planning Commission. The remaining amount of Rs.3750 crore had been placed at the disposal of the Ministry of Panchayati Raj for District Component covering 250 districts. The allocation of Rs.3750 crore consisted of two funding windows (a) capacity building fund Rs.250 crore and (b) development grants of Rs.3500 crore for the financial year 2006-07. This allocation was revised to Rs. 1925 crore the Revised Estimates stage. The existing Rashtriya Sam Vikas Yojana (RSVY) has been subsumed into the BRGF Programme. The erstwhile districts under RSVY will receive their full allocation of Rs.45 crore per district as per norms of RSVY. Thereafter, they will shift to the BRGF mode of funding. As amount of Rs. 1925 crore was released under the BRGF programme during the financial year 2006-07.

3629. (10-10-2007) NEW DELHI : The terms of the Legislative Assemblies of Gujarat and Himachal Pradesh are normally due to expire on 26th December 2007 and 9th March 2008 respectively. By virtue of its powers, duties and functions under Article 324 read with Article 172(1) of the Constitution of India, Section 15 of Representation of the People Act, 1951, the Commission is under a constitutional mandate to hold general elections to constitute the new Legislative Assemblies in these States at any time within a period of six months before the expiry of the present term. In the case of Himachal Pradesh, there are 68 assembly constituencies. Out of them, there are 3 ACs namely, 1-Kinnaur (ST), 54-Bharmour (ST) and 55-Lahaul and Spiti (ST) located in higher reaches of the State. The passes in this area are officially closed on 15th November in view of winter and snowfall. In the past, whenever the General Elections were held during winter, though the elections were announced together for the entire State, invariably, the elections to these 3 ACs had to be postponed to a later date in May-June as the areas become snow bound and inaccessible. There was a demand that the elections to all the constituencies in Himachal Pradesh should be held together and there was a specific opinion against the elections to the above 3 ACs being held separately after the conclusion of the elections in the other constituencies. This matter also is being agitated before the Hon'ble High Court of Himachal Pradesh. The Election Commission had a consultation meeting with all the political parties on this issue and all the political parties were of the view that the elections to all the constituencies of Himachal should be held together, and expressed a specific opinion against the idea of elections to the 3 ACs being conducted after the election process is completed in rest of the State. Keeping all these in view, the Election Commission has decided to announce the election schedule for conducting general election to Himachal Pradesh.

3630. (10-10-2007) NEW DELHI : The Chairman of the Law Commission of India, Dr. Justice AR. Lakshmanan today submitted a Report on Dowry Death to the Union Law Minister, Dr. H. R. Bhardwaj. The question that has been examined by the Law Commission in this Report is whether Section 304-B of Indian Penal Code, should be amended to provide for more stringent punishment of death sentence to curb the menace of dowry death. This section provides for punishment of imprisonment for a term which shall not be less than seven years but which may extend to imprisonment for life. Although this section has come into force w.e.f. November 19, 1986 yet the incidents of dowry death have not shown any significant decline. This gave rise to demands for death sentence for the offence of dowry death in order to imbibe necessary deterrence in the law. The Commission examined Section 304-B IPC in the light of various judicial pronouncements and critically dealt with the substantive as well as procedural aspects of the subjects. The Commission finds that the offence of murder is not the same thing as the offence of dowry death. Though death of bride may be a common element in both the offences, the absence of direct connection between the husband and the death of wife distinguished the offence of dowry death from the offence of murder. Besides, the presumptive character of the offence of dowry death and cardinal principle of proportionality as well as the underlying scheme of the Penal Code go against the proposed prescription of death sentence in case of dowry death. It may be pertinent to point out that where a case of dowry death also falls within the ambit of the offence of murder, awarding death sentence may be legally permissible. The guidelines laid down by the Supreme Court for award of death sentence, especially, the dictum of rarest of rare case, will, however, have to be adhered to in such cases. The Commission found a lot of misgivings and misapprehension associated with the subject of dowry death. Dowry death is quite often confused with the offence of murder. There may be instances where the two may overlap with each other. This gives rise to demand for parity in the matter of sentence in both these cases. Nevertheless, the two offences are distinct and independent offences. The Commission has proceeded to spell out the finer nuances of the offence of dowry death for their better understanding and appreciation to dispel the ambiguity and confusion shrouding the notion of dowry death vis-à-vis murder. This will help in providing clarity on the subject for its correct understanding and appreciation to the concerned authorities while dealing with the cases of dowry death. The Commission has, there, not recommended death penalty for dowry death cases. However, the Commission has favoured the increasing of the minimum sentence from seven years to ten years in such cases.

3631. (10-10-2007) NEW DELHI : The Minister of Petroleum & Natural Gas Shri Murli Deora has directed all three CMDs of PSU Oil Marketing Companies (OMCs)-IOC, HPCL and BPCL to ensure adequate availability of cooking fuels-LPG and kerosene all over the country specially in view of the ensuring festivals. Addressing Parliamentary Consultative Committee attached to his Ministry here today he asked the Chief Executives-Chairman IOC Shri S. Behuria, CMD HPCL Shri Arun Balakrishnan and CMD BPCL Shri Ashok Sinha to set up full proof systems to meet the demand and to have a quick response to any breakdown in supply at local level that may occur. Simultaneously, the Minister has directed Petroleum Secretary to increase vigilance efforts to curb hoarding and diversion of these vital household fuels, specifically during this festival season. Earlier on 26th September, Shri Deora reviewed the situation regarding the supply of LPG and kerosene all over the Country in view of the forthcoming festival season. The Government has been taking necessary initiatives to ensure availability of these products to the genuine users as also checking their diversion/misuse. Referring to the sharp increase in the global oil prices, Shri Deora reiterated commitment of UPA Government to protect the interests of 'Aam Aadmi' (Commonman) by ensuring equitable burden sharing amongst all stakeholders. He informed that the Government is closely monitoring the prices of petrol, diesel, PDS kerosene and domestic LPG. Indian basket of crude oil touched a record high recently. There has been no revision in the prices of these products in spite of consistent rise in international oil prices whereas following softening of prices post August 2006 petrol and diesel prices were reduced on 30.11.2006 and 16.02.2007. He added that the under-recoveries of public sector oil marketing companies (OMCs) is expected to be about Rs. 52,500 crore during this fiscal. Shri Deora pointed out that the Government along with oil PSUs shared most of the burden of rising oil prices during 2006-07. Government issued oil bonds worth Rs. 24121 crore to OMCs to partly compensate them for under recoveries on these products while upstream companies shared to the tune of Rs. 20,507 crore. Shri Deora also elaborated other recent initiatives of the Government including approval to the proposal of Oil India Ltd. for fresh equity issue of 10 per cent of its paid up capital through "Initial Public Offer (IPO)". This would enable the company to get listed on the Stock Exchanges. Approval was also given for issue of additional 1 per cent of OIL's paid up capital to the employees along with divesting 10 per cent in favour of OMCs (IOC, HPCL and BPCL in the ratio of 2:1:1 respectively). Further, he informed that 46 oil and gas discoveries have already been made in the 162 blocks contracted under the first six rounds of New Exploration Licensing Policy (NELP). These discoveries are located in Cambay onland, North East Coast and Krishna-Godavari deep water areas for which development plans by the operators are in progress. In respect of gas discovery by RIL-NIKO in KG basin is likely to commence from June, 2008. Members made important suggestions to further improve working of the oil sector PSUs. These include suggestions for developing latest infrastructure to train oil & gas personnel, removing malpractice in distribution of domestic LPG along with ensuring its availability, streamlining the process of dealer selection, offering more blocks under NELP-VII from North East, initiative for gas supply in the eastern parts of the country, in encouraging R&D for alternative energy. The members landed excellent performance of oil sector in general and refining crude oil and exporting petroleum products in particularly. The members who attended the meeting are: S/Shri K. Samba Siva Rao, K. Manvendra Singh, G.V. Harsha Kumar, Jaswant Singh Bishnoi, Prof. Rasa Singh Rawat, Rajen Gohain, Dr. Arun Kumar Sarma, Hemlal Murmu, A.P. Abdullakutty, Lakshman Chandra Seth, Ramakant Yadav, B. Vinod Kumar, Ram Kripal Yadav, K. Yerrannaidu, Kiren Rijiju and Ms. M.S.K. Bhavani Rajenthiran, Ms. Paramjit Kaur Gulshan from Lok Sabha and Shri Nandi Yellaiah, Dwijendra Nath Sharmah, and Prof. Ram Deo Bhandary from Rajya Sabha. Shri Dinsha Patel, Minister of State for Petroleum & Natural Gas, Shri S. Sundareshan, Addl. Secy.(MoP&NG), Chief Executive Officers of Oil Public Sector Undertakings and senior officers of the Ministry & Oil PSUs also attended the meeting.

3632. (10-10-2007) NEW DELHI : Indian and Singapore armies will hold joint artillery exercises at Deolali, near Nasik in Maharashtra, later this month. The Singapore Army will be represented by an over 100-member contingent.

3633. (10-10-2007) NEW DELHI : The Indian National Congress expresses appreciation, and welcomes the step taken by the UPA Government to announce the highest ever hike in the minimum support price of wheat for the coming rabi season, thereby giving an incentive bonus on the support price of kharif rice. Government has also announced a very substantial hike in the support price of barley, mustard, sunflower and other commodities. A relief package for the sugar industry has been announced which will bring much needed relief to farmers, particularly because the moratorium on outstanding loans has been extended from 2 to 5 years. Apart from setting the minimum support price at Rs.1000/- as against Rs.850/- last year, an incentive bonus has also been announced of Rs.50/- a quintal. The Indian National Congress has always given very high priority to issues relating to the welfare and concerns of farmers and to the agriculture sector. It has been our continuing focus to encourage the development of this sector, and ensure that the farmers of this country are given as much support as possible. It is in keeping with this commitment to the welfare of farmers, that this step has been taken by the UPA Government. The latest announcement of government with regard to the welfare of farmers, follows upon several other important initiatives taken earlier, including a Rs 25,000 crore package for the agriculture sector and very high credit facilities for the agriculture sector. It is entirely due to the commitment of the Indian National Congress and the UPA government that growth in the agriculture sector has improved from negative during the NDA government to nearly 3.8% growth today. We are confident that our policies will ensure sustained and improved agricultural growth. Smt. Jayanti Natarajan said that the Indian National Congress welcomes the decision to impose President's rule in Karnataka. This was a decision taken in the highest traditions of democracy and in order to ensure that horse-trading and other unconstitutional activities do not vitiate the democratic polity in the state of Karnataka. To a question on the flurries of goodies for aam aadmi Smt. Jayanti said, it is a serious concern for the welfare of farmers and in-keeping with our commitments made in the common minimum programme. The Congress President has also made it clear that we would not like the interests of small traders, small farmers and small holdings to be affected and all steps will be taken to ensure that their problems are addressed. On the suicides by farmers Smt Jayanti added that it is nothing new. It is unfortunate and very regrettable and it is our primary focus to prevent such suicides amongst farmers but I have to point out it is not something which began during the UPA government. It has been happening even in earlier times. These may be due to many reasons. But certainly our focus is to improve the conditions of the farmers and prevent such totally avoidable suicide deaths. To a question on Mayawati's attack on both the nuclear deal and the Ramsetu issue Smt Jayanti said, as far as the nuclear deal is concerned our stand is very clear. She has a right to her opinion. We stand by whatever steps we have taken and we do believe the nuclear deal is very important for civilian energy. Our nuclear energy will be the answer to our energy crisis and problem. This is at the national level. We have certain dynamics and at the level of the states we have other dynamics. If this is the opinion of the Chief Minister of Uttar Pradesh, certainly she has the right to express it. We have our space and she has her space. I do not believe that the party of the stature of Indian National Congress should worry about any threat perception. Political activity is an ongoing and fluid dynamic process. We are aware of what is happening around us and we are very confident that our cadre will take our message to the people and that we will be able to convey our message to the people of India and to our allies. To a question on the suspended animation in the Karnataka Assembly Smt. Jayanti said, I cannot take any stand without reference to any particular circumstances. At this point of time we are welcoming the position of President's rule because it has prevented some highly avoidable horse-trading and a very anomalous situation. As and when developments continue to happen in Karnataka, our General Secretary and the High Command will take notice and necessary steps.

3634. (10-10-2007) NEW DELHI : The High Powered Committee to review the security preparedness of the Ports, Shipyards and other allied installations in the country presented its report to the Union Minister of Shipping, Road Transport & Highways Thiru T.R. Baalu here today. Thiru Baalu had constituted this Committee in April, 2007 under the Chairmanship of Chairman, Cochin Port Trust, Shri N. Ramachandran. The Committee was to review the security arrangements in these Organisations and assess the adequacy of their security arrangements in the context of the threats & recommend specific measures to be taken to make them adequate. The Committee deliberated upon the issues like extending the security scanning system in all container terminals with new scanning techniques, access control in Ports and Shipyards, issue of Identity Cards to fishermen using Port and Shipyard area, introduction of Automatic Surveillance System such as CCTVs, equipping CISF Units with Dog Squads and Bomb Disposal Units, periodic Security Audit by Home Ministry, strengthening of Infrastructure such as scanners etc. to implement International Ship and Port Facility Security (ISPS) Code and reporting by Merchant Vessels while passing near the coast of India. The High Powered Committee after visiting Major Ports finalised its report and has recommended wide ranging measures to improve security arrangements at the Major Ports and Shipyards. The recommendations include proposal to set up an apex agency for regulation of security issues on the lines of the Bureau of Civil Aviation Security which may prescribe security standards for ports and other stake holders, setting up of communication control centre as a single point of security issues at every port, smart card based tamper proof bio-metric ID cards for employees and deployment of a single security agencies like Central Industrial Security Force (CISF) at all the ports. Thiru Baalu directed that the Committee Members and officials should constitute a working group to identify the critical issues raised in the recommendations and these should be discussed threadbare with the concerned Departments and agencies before the recommendations are considered by the Government for decision. Apart from the Chairman, Cochin Port Trust, the other members of the Committee included Dy. Chairman, Chennai, Paradip, Jawaharlal Nehru Ports and Traffic Manager, Mumbai Port and representatives from the Intelligence Bureau and CISF.

3635. (10-10-2007) NEW DELHI : Smt. D. Purandeswari, Minister of State for Human Resource Development has informed the United Nations Conference on Trade and Development (UNCTAD) that India attaches significance to this Forum's quadrennial Conferences. She also expressed hope that the forthcoming conference of UNCTAD XII scheduled in Accra, Ghana in April 2008 will further consolidate the mandate of the Forum for the integrated treatment of Trade and Development and the interrelated issues. She said this while making intervention on Globalization for Development in the Forum's meeting on October 9, 2007, at Geneva. The overall theme for UNCTAD XII is 'Globalization for Development: Opportunities and Challenges'. The Minister has mentioned that for the developing countries poverty alleviation and elimination of exclusion can not but be an overriding priority as continued poverty, low incomes constitute a major impediment to the growth of global incomes, demand and consumption. She has noted with satisfaction that as the next Conference is taking place in Africa this will bring focus on the development deficit in that continent which is home to 34 of the world's 50 Least

Developed Countries (LDCs). Smt. D. Prandeswari has emphasized that in the era of liberalization developing countries have to address issues related to migration, over-subsidization of agriculture in developed countries that affect the livelihood of the small and marginal farmers in developing countries, food security, conventional agricultural practices which are recognized as contributors to the GHG emissions. She has urged that it would only be appropriate for UNCTAD to deliberate on such development issues in pursuit of consensus building from the development perspective in the run up to and at UNCTAD XII. The Minister noted that despite several notable achievements, UNCTAD had witnessed a slow devaluation of its role as an intergovernmental organization over the last two decades. Responding to the intervention made by Smt. D. Purandareshwari, Mr. Kobsak Chutikul Special Advisor to the Secretary General UNCTAD has shared the same concern and expressed the hope that the developed countries will increasingly take interest in the affairs and activities of UNCTAD. He has also acknowledged India's long association with UNCTAD and its active role in the affairs of UNCTAD.

3636. (10-10-2007) NEW DELHI : Based on her contributions to the deliberations to the plenary, Smt D. Purandeswari, Minister of State for Human Resource Development, has been nominated on the Drafting Committee of the recently established Inter Parliamentary Union Committee on UN Affairs on October 9, 2007. This Drafting Committee will be working on the modalities of the proposed cooperation between Inter Parliamentary Union and the United Nations.

3637. (10-10-2007) NEW DELHI : A delegation of Congress party leaders from Punjab led by Mrs. Rajinder Kaur Bhattal, including Union Cabinet Minister, Mrs. Ambika Soni, called on the Prime Minister, Dr. Manmohan Singh and complemented him for the various steps taken in the interests of the farming community. The delegation hailed the Government's decision to increase the Minimum Support Price for wheat by 33 % to Rs 1,000 per quintal. They also welcomed the decision to increase the procurement price for paddy. The delegation conveyed the gratitude of the farming community to the Prime Minister.

3638. (10-10-2007) NEW DELHI : Shri Arjun Singh, Minister for Human Resource Development has said that the time has come that the academic world of the country should come to terms with reality. He was inaugurating the two-day National Conference of Vice Chancellors on Development of Higher Education, here, today. Addressing the Vice Chancellors Conference, he said that the experimentation should be a key word for Higher Education reforms. The National Conference is a culmination of four Regional Conferences that the UGC had organised at Mumbai, Kolkata, Hyderabad and New Delhi. Terming higher education as a sick child of education, he said that higher education is not serving the cause of young people of India. He said 'as Vice Chancellors, you have opportunity and duty to find a way out for it. To prescribe is not my ideology. Let us now inscribe. Give the country a road map of higher education'. He advised VCs to keep in mind the rich and poor divide in the country and asked to work out the strategy with conviction and a national commitment to see India through. He exhorted the VCs to jointly define the parameters of higher education as to what should be the content, what should be the extent of higher education, what should be the methodology of teaching and what should be the basic ingredients of the syllabus etc. In the end, he said that India is not knocking at the doors of the world but the world is knocking at the doors of India. The Minister also inaugurated e-visit of Exhibition on 150 years of Higher Education. To commemorate the completion of 150 glorious years of Modern University System, the exhibition depicts through the exhibits, the journey of Higher Education from early 18th century onwards. In his address Prof. B. Mungekar proposed Five Point Action Plan for Higher Education Reforms in XIth Plan. He elaborated that the education has some how become divorced from the realities of the country. It should be in terms of the developmental goals set out in the Constitution of India. He, therefore, suggested drastic restructuring of the curriculum in higher education. His next proposal was inclusive education. By inclusive education he suggested expansion of University system as a system of excellence as seven IITs and seven IIMs are not enough to cater to the large number of students of the country and the access should be our watch word for providing egalitarian education. He also commented that the annual exam system has become irrelevant, therefore, one should now switch over to semester system. In the end, he suggested revision of fee structure and also scholarship to meritorious students. He also proposed Higher Education Loan Guarantee Authority for those educational institutions who have good academic records so that they can avail of the loan without any collateral security. He also suggested that the unfilled posts of teachers in the State colleges and universities should be filled up on priority basis. He said that our growing economy rests on robust qualitative education system and this system needs overhauling now so that it can support the growth of economy. Prof. S.K. Thorat, Chairman, University Grants Commission gave the glimpse of the Regional Conferences of Vice Chancellors and introduced the agenda of the present Conference. He said that the agenda centres around six issues viz. access, inclusiveness, support to needy colleges and universities, bridging the quality gap, focus on State colleges and universities, and the issue of finance. He said that the public funding has to be increased and therefore, the present fee structure needs revision. Mentioning the role of private sector, he said that several self financing education institutions have come up and also expanded and therefore, a regulatory framework is needed. Prof. Moolchand Sharma, Vice Chairman UGC gave the welcome address and flagged four current developments viz. information technology, managerial challenge, free flow of capital and human resources and the challenges of globalisation. He said that one can meet these challenges by reforming higher education in the direction of access, quality and equity.

3639. (10-10-2007) NEW DELHI : The Sainik Schools will hold an all-India entrance examination on Sunday, January 6, 2008 for the session 2008-09 for admission to classes Sixth and Ninth. Admission test will be held at various centres for all 21 Sainik Schools across the country barring Nagrota, Jammu and Kashmir, which will conduct a separate examination. Boys between the age of 10 and 11 years as on July 1, 2008 can apply for admission to Class VI while those between 13 and 14 years are eligible for Class IX. Necessary advertisements inviting applications are being issued by the respective Sainik Schools this month. The prospectus can be obtained by the candidates from the Sainik Schools where admission is desired on payment of Rupees 300/- (Rs.200/- for SC/ST) by crossed Postal Order in favour of the Principal. Last date for receipt of applications is December 10, 2007. Admission is made strictly on merit in the entrance examination and subject to medical fitness. Reservation will be made in admission for 15% and 7½% seats for SC and ST candidates respectively. Besides 25% seats are reserved for wards of service personnel, including exservicemen. Admission will also be made to Class XI subject to vacancy and criteria laid down by respective Sainik Schools.

3640. (10-10-2007) NEW DELHI : The Minister of Petroleum & Natural Gas Shri Murli Deora has approved a protocol to remove Light Diesel Oil (LDO) from the purview of Solvent Raffinate and Slop (Acquisition, Storage and Prevention to use in Automobile) Order, 2000. This will do away with the requirement of procuring licenses and other restrictions imposed in the said Order, thus facilitate smoother sale/business of LDO in the country. The present decision has been taken in view of favourable views provided by the industry and technical bodies like Indian Institute of Petroleum, Dehradun and Indian Oil R&D Centre, Faridabad. The Government had also received a representation from the Petroleum Products Dealers and Manufacturers' Association, Mumbai in this regard. LDO along with Furnace Oil (FO) was earlier brought under the purview of Solvent Raffinate and Slop (Acquisition, Storage and Prevention to use in Automobile) Order, 2000 through an amendment order dated 21.11.2001 as a substantial price difference between these two products and HSD offered an incentive for unscrupulous dealers for using LDO/FO as adulterants. Over the years, the price difference between LDO and HSD has come down to negligible levels while the price of FO is still about Rs. 10 per litre less than HSD. Hence, LDO does not enjoy any significant price advantage over HSD for adulteration. It is in this context that the Government has decided to remove LDO from the purview of Solvent Control Order. A notification in this regard would be issued shortly.

3641. (11-10-2007) NEW DELHI : The Vice President Mohd. Hamid Ansari has expressed shock and strongly condemned the blast at the Ajmer Sharif Dargah today, which has caused injuries and casualties. He has termed the blast that has been perpetrated at the shrine during the holy month of Ramzan as a despicable act. The Vice President has called on all citizens to maintain peace and harmony and work to frustrate all attempts to disturb social peace.

3642. (11-10-2007) NEW DELHI : The President, Smt. Pratibha Devisingh Patil met a delegation of the Members of the Akhil Bharatiya Aggarwal Sammelan at Rashtrapati Bhavan. The President described the founder of the Aggarwal samaj Maharaja Agrasen as a social reformer and a human being of the highest order. Smt. Patil felt that some of the practices established by Maharaja Agrasen nearly 5000 years ago were similar to the principles of socialism. Maharaja Agrasen, she said, was also a social reformer as he stopped animal sacrifices in rituals practiced in those times. The President further added that today the Aggarwal samaj was actively participating in the development and progress of the nation and nation-building. The Minister of State for Home Affairs, Shri Sriprakash Jaiswal was also present on the occasion.

3643. (11-10-2007) NEW DELHI : The Employees State Insurance Corporation (ESIC) met today under the Chairmanship of Shri Oscar Fernandes, Minister of State for Labour & Employment. The 140th meeting of the Corporation was called specially for considering provision of medical care by the E.S.I.S. hospitals to the workers in the unorganized sector under the Swasthya Beema Yojna being launched by the Ministry. Setting the agenda for the meeting Shri Fernandes observed that workers in the unorganized sector constitute about 93 per cent of the total work force but they do not have any social security cover. The E.S.I. Scheme being the premier social security scheme in the country must, therefore, come forward and make a beginning by participating in the Health Insurance Scheme for BPL unorganized sector workers by making available its vast network of Hospitals for providing medical care wherever the same are under-utilized. The Members of the Corporation deliberated the proposal to amend certain provisions of the E.S.I. Act, 1948 enabling opening of facilities in E.S.I.S. Hospitals to non-insured persons on payment of user charges and enabling the Central Government to notify separate schemes for different Sectors of Employment or Occupation with separate source of financing. The Ministry has formulated a health insurance scheme named "Swasthya Beema Yojna" with a view to provide Health Insurance Cover to Below Poverty Line (BPL) workers in the unorganized sector and their families. The scheme provides a cover of Rs. 30,000/- per BPL family, per annum and will provide health care which will include pre-existing diseases, hospitalization, surgical procedures which can be provided on a day care basis, transport allowance of Rs. 100/- per visit and pre and post hospitalization expenses for one day prior to and 5 days after hospitalization. The medical care under the scheme will be provided through Government Hospitals including E.S.I. Scheme Hospitals as well as through private hospitals.

3644. (11-10-2007) NEW DELHI : On the occasion of 58th Anniversary day of Territorial Army, Maj Gen VK Datta, Addl Dir Gen along with Officers, JCOs, OR and families of Terrier fraternity called on Her Excellency the President of India here today. This day has immense historical significance as it reminds us the contribution of Citizens Army in service of the country. Territorial Army has many achievements to its credit and besides supplementing the efforts of Regular Army during wars, Counter Insurgency, counter terrorist operations, aid to civil authorities, it has trained personnel to support national efforts in rail communication, oil & natural gas refining, medical services and telecommunication. The ecological task forces have also very successfully addressed the environmental concerns and have achieved praiseworthy results. On the occasion of the 58th Anniversary day the President, Mrs Pratibha Patil complimented the Territorial Army for performing its duties in a commendable manner.

3645. (11-10-2007) NEW DELHI : Media registration has begun for the 38th International Film Festival of India-IFFI 2007, to be held in Goa from 23rd November to 3rd December, 2007. This time all media accreditations will be carried out online. The online media registration form, along with terms and conditions can be accessed by logging on to Press Information Bureau website at www.pib.nic.in under sub-head 'Media Accreditation'. Accreditation is granted to experienced journalists / media persons, who have been covering film festivals for at least three years. Normally one accreditation is given for one media organization. However, for the main news agencies, upto four accreditations can be granted. For TV news channels, accreditation will be given for upto three teams comprising a reporter, a cameraperson and a technician. Eminent persons with ten years experience of film journalism will be accredited under the 'freelance' category. The last date for media registration is 15th November, 2007. For details S.Subramanian can be contacted at 011-2338 6602 or iffi-pib@nic.in In the meantime, Panaji, the capital of Goa is getting ready to play host to the 38th International Film Festival. Infrastructure is being spruced up at multiple venues. A new media centre with state-of-the-art communication facilities is coming up at the Food and Drug Administration building on Dayanand Bandodkar Marg. Deputy Director General of Press Information Bureau, New Delhi, Ms Esther Kar and Director of PIB, Mumbai, Manish Desai reviewed the press facilities along with Shri Narinder Singh, Joint Director and Shri Suryakant Jog, Media Officer of PIB, Panaji. The Media Centre and other facilities are likely to be ready for use by 10th November, 2007.

3646. (11-10-2007) NEW DELHI : Manganese Ores India Limited (MOIL), a public sector undertaking under the Ministry of Steel, has more than doubled its net profit during the first half of this financial year. During April to September this year the company earned net profit of Rs. 116.27 crore as against Rs.50.41 crore during the same period in FY 07. Presenting a final dividend cheque of Rs.4.57 crore to the Minister for Steel, Chemicals and Fertilisers Shri Ram Vilas Paswan here today the Chairman and Managing Director of MOIL Shri K. L. Mehrotra said that the turnover during the first six months has increased to 6.5 lakh tonnes from 5.5 lakh tonnes last year. He said, during the year turnover is expected to be about Rs. 600 crore. Shri Mehrotra said, the company is expanding its capacity keeping the growth of capacity in steel industry. He said, MOIL is planning to set up a plant in Bhilai at a cost of Rs.260 crore. The project will come up as a joint venture with Steel Authority of India Limited. Receiving the cheque the Minister said, the company has proved its strength and has stood up to the government's expectation. It has paid Rs.168 crore to the government revenue besides dividend. Shri Paswan said, the company is also taking up various projects as a part of its corporate social responsibility. Asked about the capacity expansion in the steel sector, the Minister said, the government expects the capacity to reach 80 million tonnes by 2010. The final dividend that is 20 per cent of the share value takes the total dividend paid to 100 per cent during the year. The Government of India holds 81.57 percent share in the company.

3647. (11-10-2007) NEW DELHI : To protect the interests of the common man, the Oil Marketing Companies (IOC, HPCL and BPCL) are selling petrol, diesel, domestic LPG and PDS kerosene at lower than international oil prices. The Indian basket of crude oil has averaged about $ 70 per barrel during 2007-08 as against the average price of about $ 62 per barrel last year. Due to the mismatch between the retail prices of the four sensitive petroleum products and the international oil prices, Oil Marketing Companies are facing financial under-recoveries of approximately Rs.54,935 crore this year. However, their physical performance continues to steadily improve as evident in the increase in both refinery throughput and domestic sales. To restore the financial health of the Oil Marketing Companies, the Government, as per the principle of equitable burden sharing among the different stakeholders and in line with a similar exercise undertaken last year, has decided that 42.7% of the total under-recoveries would be borne by the Government in the form of oil bonds. About 1/3rd of the under-recoveries would be shared by the upstream oil PSUs in the form of discounts on crude oil and products. Further, the Subsidies Schemes for PDS Kerosene and domestic LPG which were available till March, 2007 have been extended till March, 2010.

3648. (11-10-2007) PATNA: Leader of the Opposition in the Lok Sabha and senior BJP leader L.K. Advani on Wednesday predicted snap polls in the first half of 2008. "If there is anything certain, it is that the UPA government will not last its full term [till 2009]. Polls to the Lok Sabha will surely be held in 2008 and most probably in the first half." "Those who created the situation are aware that they'll not fare well in the event of snap elections and are now trying to avoid them," the former Deputy Prime Minister said. Earlier, speaking at the felicitation of octogenarian Kailashpati Mishra, Mr. Advani said that till about two months ago he had ruled out early elections. But the change in the situation was the natural fallout of an 'alliance' between opposite poles. "They don't see eye to eye on economic issues and on foreign policies." The only thing they had in common was the determination not to allow the BJP and the NDA to come to power. Bihar Chief Minister and JD(U) leader Nitish Kumar ridiculed the manner in which the UPA and its partners sought to avoid snap polls. "Till yesterday we read that elections were a certainty and today's papers tell us that they had agreed to put on hold their differences till October 22." He charged that the government was living on borrowed time.

3649. (11-10-2007) NEW DELHI : The Committee of Eminent Persons constituted by the Government of India on Sethu Samudram Shipping Channel Project held its first meeting on 11th October, 2007 in New Delhi in which all the Members of the Committee were present. The Terms of Reference of the Committee are to invite objections and suggestions from all concerned including the writ Petitioners in the court cases in the Hon'ble Supreme Court of India, having interest in the Sethu Samudram Shipping Channel Project and to consider all suggestions/ proposals/documents after giving them a personal hearing. The Committee comprises of :-i) Prof. S. Ramachandran-Chairman of Monitoring Committee on Environmental Impact Issues, of Sethu Samudram Ship Channel Project and Vice-Chancellor of University of Madras-Convenor ii) Prof. R.S. Sharma-Former Professor of History, Delhi University iii) Dr. M. Sakthivel-President of Aqua Culture Foundation of India iv) Prof. Dilip K. Biswas-former Chairman of Central Pollution Control Board, Ministry of Environment and Forest, Government of India v) Dr. J.R.B. Alfred-former Director of Zoological Survey of India, Kolkata vi) Dr. S.R. Wate-Deputy Director of National Environmental Engineering Research Institute (NEERI), Nagpur vii) Prof. P. Jagadeesan-former Vice-Chancellor of Bharatidasan University, Tiruchi, Tamil Nadu viii) Prof. Y. Vaikuntham-former Vice-Chancellor of Kakatiya University, Andhra Pradesh ix) Dr. K. Paddayya-Director of Deccan College, Pune x) Shri R.K. Jain, IAS-Managing Director, Indian Ports Association-Member Secretary The Committee after detailed deliberation on the matter referred to it, decided to invite objections and suggestions from all concerned including the writ Petitioners so as to reach at the following address of the Committee by 1700 hrs. on 31st October, 2007. Member Secretary, Committee of Eminent Persons on Sethu Samudram Shipping Channel Project The Tamil Nadu Dr. Ambedkar Law University, Post Graduate & Research Development Block, "Poompozhil", 5, Greenways Road, Chennai-600 028.

3650. (11-10-2007) NEW DELHI : The Government has considered and approved the National Policy on Rehabilitation and Resettlement, 2007, to replace the National Policy on Resettlement and Rehabilitation for Project Affected Families, 2003. In a meeting held here today the Union Cabinet has also decided to bring a legislation on the lines of the new Rehabilitation and Resettlement Policy, and to suitably amend the Land Acquisition Act, 1894. Necessary steps shall be taken in this regard as per the established procedure. A Gazette Notification will be issued shortly to bring into effect the new Policy. The new Policy and the associated legislative measures aim at striking a balance between the need for land for developmental activities and, at the same time, protecting the interests of the land owners, and others, such as the tenants, the landless, the agricultural and non-agricultural labourers, artisans, and others whose livelihood depends on the land involved. The benefits under the new Policy shall be available to all affected persons and families whose land, property or livelihood is adversely affected by land acquisition or by involuntary displacement of a permanent nature due to any other reason, such as natural calamities, etc. The Policy will be applicable to all these cases irrespective of the number of people involved. The benefits to be offered under the new Policy to the affected families include: land-for-land, to the extent Government land would be available in the resettlement areas; preference for employment in the project to at least one person from each nuclear family within the definition of the 'affected family', subject to the availability of vacancies and suitability of the affected person; training and capacity building for taking up suitable jobs and for self-employment; scholarships for education of the eligible persons from the affected famlies; preference to groups or cooperatives of the affected persons in the allotment of contracts and other economic opportunities in or around the project site; wage employment to the willing affected persons in the construction work in the project; housing benefits including houses to the landless affected families in both rural and urban areas; and other benefits. Adequate provisions have also been made for financial support to the affected families for construction of cattle sheds, shops, and working sheds; transportation costs, temporary and transitional accommodation, and comprehensive infrastructural facilities and amenities in the resettlement area including education, health care, drinking water, roads, electricity, sanitation, religious activities, cattle grazing, and other community resources, etc. The benefits expressed in monetary terms have been linked to the Consumer Price Index, and the same shall also be revised suitably at appropriate intervals.

3651. (11-10-2007) NEW DELHI : The Minister of State for Shipping Road Transport & Highways, Shri K.H. Muniyappa has deeply condoled the sad demise of Shri S. R. Bommai, former Chief Minister of Karnataka and former Union Minister. In his condolence message he said that Shri S. R. Bommai, a Law graduate was a freedom fighter and an eminent statesman, who plunged into politics through M.N. Roy's Radical Democratic Party. He was elected to the Assembly for the fist time in 1967 and became the Chief Minister of Karnataka in 1988 and served as Union Minister for Human Resource Development in the Central Government. He had also served the people of the country for over four decades. He also conveyed his heartfelt condolences to the members of the bereaved family and prayed to God to give enough strength to his family members to bear this irreparable loss.

3652. (11-10-2007) NEW DELHI : The Income Tax department has conducted a search on a business family on the basis of information that it is involved in unaccounted draft discounting. The search was conducted at 6 business and residential premises in Delhi. Investments in various properties and bank accounts have come to light, which is being investigated. It is clarified that there is no search in respect of Shri Gautam Gambhir, a member of the national cricket team of India.

3653. (11-10-2007) NEW DELHI : Uk sport and the ministry of youth affairs and sports, government of India signed a memorandum of understanding in new delhi today in the presence of Mr.. Mani shankar aiyar, the minister of youth affairs and sports, government of India, which marks the start of an international sports development partnership that will reach thousands of school children and communities throughout India. Mr. Aiyar observed that the present bilateral cooperation programme between the united kingdom and India has materialised at an opportune time when his ministry is in the process of finalising the new national sports policy. The minister added that, " i am glad that the united kingdom and India are embarking upon a joint initiative that leverages sports for youth-led national development. By virtue of the multiple benefits that sports generates in the areas of education, public health, social inclusiveness, cultural identity and recreation, this initiative is strategically placed to achieve this objective". The agreement brings together national and international experts in the fields of development, physical education, sports development and sporting excellence to provide access to quality physical education and sports at community level and the development of pathways to excellence for elite athletes. This new commitment between the two nations was sealed by Mr.. Richard stagg, british high commissioner to India, and Mr.. S. K. Arora, secretary of the ministry of youth affairs and sports, government of India. After signing the agreement on behalf of the ministry of youth affairs and sports, Mr.. Arora stated that "the government of India has taken recent initiatives, such as the proposed panchayat yuva krida aur khel abhiyan and the draft comprehensive national sports policy, to create extensive sports infrastructure in rural areas to provide universal access to children, adolescents and youth who have thus far been deprived of well-organised opportunities for participation in sports and games and to build a sports culture in the country. This will also help in spotting and nurturing talented sportspersons to achieve excellence. The mou with uk sports will help to refine the modalities on a pilot scale, which could then be extended to other areas." The partnership offers both parties a unique opportunity to share best practice methods and expertise, while also allowing those involved in sport in the uk to keep up to date with the latest international developments. Uk sport's head of worldwide impact, debbie lye, confirmed that as a sporting nation India has an important role to play internationally in youth development through sport and future legacy planning for the hosting of international sporting events: "this agreement is a fantastic opportunity for the uk to work in partnership with a dynamic country that recognises the importance of a youth-led sports development approach. For a long time there has been a mutual desire to work together and, as commonwealth games hosts, both countries will be able to share learning and expertise to ensure that a social legacy can be delivered through the hosting of international events."

3654. (11-10-2007) NEW DELHI : The Trade Marks (Amendment) Bill, 2007, introduced in the Lok Sabha on the 23rd August, 2007 and pending therein, has been referred to the Department-related parliamentary Standing Committee on

Commerce, with Dr. Murli Manohar Joshi, Member, Rajya Sabha, as its Chairman, for examination and report. The Committee has decided to invite memoranda containing views of the individuals/organisations, etc. interested in the subject-matter of the Bill and also to hear oral evidence on the subject. Those desirous of submitting memoranda to the Committee may send two copies (either in English or Hindi) thereof to Shri Surinder Kumar Watts, Director, Rajya Sabha Secretariat, Room No. 240, Second Floor, Parliament House Annexe, New Delhi (Tel: 23034240, Tele fax: 23013158, E-mail: watts@sansad.nic.in) within fifteen days, indicating whether they would also be interested in giving oral evidence before the Committee. The memorandum submitted to the Committee would form part of the records of the Committee and would be treated as confidential and would not be circulated to anyone, as any act contrary thereto would constitute a breach of privilege of the Committee. The Bill was published in the Gazette in India, Extraordinary, Part II, Section 2, dated the 23rd August, 2007. Its copies can be had on written request to the above-mentioned Officer or can be downloaded from the official web-site of the Lok Sabha (http://loksabha.nic.in), under the caption "Bills with the Committee".

3655. (11-10-2007) NEW DELHI : The Prime Minister, Dr. Manmohan Singh conveys his greetings to the followers of Maharaj Agarsen on the occasion of Maharaja Agarasen Jayanthi. He sends his best wishes to the All India Agarasen Samaj on this auspicious occasion.

3656. (11-10-2007) NEW DELHI : The Final Report of the National Family Health Survey (NFHS-3), 2005-06 released today by the Ministry of Health and Family Welfare offers a comprehensive picture of the health, nutrition and population in the country. Releasing the Report, the Mission Director, National Rural Health Mission, Ministry of Health and Family Welfare, Shri G. C. Chaturvedi, said findings from NFHS-3 have added substantially to the knowledge base about the health and family welfare situation of the country and will be a valuable source of information for making further improvements in health and family welfare policies and programmes. The national report paints a mixed picture of India's overall reproductive health status. On the one hand, women are having fewer children and infant mortality has dropped in the seven-year period since the last NFHS survey in 1998-99. On the other hand, anaemia and malnutrition are still widespread among children and adults. And, in an unusual juxtaposition, more adults, especially urban women, are overweight or obese than they were seven years ago. NFHS-3, the third in the NFHS series of surveys, provides information on population, health and nutrition in India and each of its 29 states. For the first time, NFHS-3 collected information on men and unmarried women. The survey is based on a sample of households that is representative at the national and state levels. It conducted interviews with around 200,000 women age 15-49 and men age 15-54 throughout India. NFHS-3 also tested more than 100,000 women and men for HIV and 215,000 adults and young children for anaemia. The data set on key indicators provides a trend that includes information on several new topics, such as HIV/AIDS-related attitudes and behaviour, male involvement in family welfare and attitudes about family life education for children in school.

3657. (11-10-2007) NEW DELHI : A 'cluster' may be defined as the agglomeration of enterprises producing same/similar products/services or engaged in the same line of manufacturing activities or services, located within an identifiable and, as far as practicable, contiguous area. Industrial cluster occupies the driver's seat for propelling economic activities in Micro & Small Enterprises (MSE) sector. The Ministry of Small Scale Industries (now Micro, Small & Medium Enterprises) laid special emphasis for development of cluster and launched a scheme Technology Upgradation and Management Programme called UPTECH in 1998. Although it was having a cluster based approach for development of MSE, but was mainly technology-focused comprising of diagnostic study, setting-up of a demonstration plant and organising workshops, seminars, etc. for quicker diffusion of technology across the cluster of small enterprises. Later, in August 2003, the scheme was renamed as Small Industry Cluster Development Programme (SICDP) and made broad based by adopting holistic pattern of development of the cluster encompassing marketing, exports, skill development, setting up of common facility centres, including technology upgradation of the enterprises, etc. Broadly, the Cluster Development Programme implemented till March, 2006 consisted of assistance mainly in "soft" areas, which encompasses activities like general awareness and trust building, counselling, training and capacity building, exposure visits, credit facilitation, market developments etc. SICDP guidelines were comprehensively revised in March, 2006 making the cluster programme more broad-based by facilitating substantial economics of scale in terms of deployment of available resources in the medium to long term. The Government of India's assistance under the scheme was enhanced upto Rs.8 crore to support soft as well as hard intervention, including setting up of common facility centres. As per the Promotional Package announced by the Government, SICDP was renamed as Micro & Small Enterprises-Cluster Development Programme (MSE-CDP) to make it more attractive, though basic features of this scheme have been retained as such. The proposals for setting up new clusters shall now be considered under MSE-CDP and the quantum of grant has been raised to 75% of the cost and the project cost has been raised from Rs. 5 crore to 10 crore. Raising the project cost to Rs. 10 crore and the central grant upto 7.5 crore is quite attractive and is expected to encourage the setting up of new clusters for micro and small enterprises. Cluster approach is different from the concept of development of Industrial Estates. The latter is largely based on infrastructure development and creation of new assets, whereas, cluster development aims at holistic development (covering diverse areas like marketing, export promotion, skill upgradation, infrastructure etc.) and may be designed to cover industrial estates as well as natural clusters, which may have evolved on their own historically at any place.

3658. (11-10-2007) NEW DELHI : The Union Cabinet today gave its approval for the National Policy on Rehabilitation and Resettlement, 2007, to replace the National Policy on Resettlement and Rehabilitation for Project Affected Families, 2003. A Gazette Notification will be issued shortly to bring into effect the new Policy. The Cabinet also decided to bring a legislation on the lines of the new Rehabilitation and Resettlement Policy, and to suitably amend the Land Acquisition Act, 1894. Necessary steps shall be taken in this regard as per the established procedure. The new Policy and the associated legislative measures aim at striking a balance between the need for land for developmental activities and, at the same time, protecting the interests of the land owners, and others, such as the tenants, the landless, the agricultural and non-agricultural labourers, artisans, and others whose livelihood depends on the land involved. The benefits under the new Policy shall be available to all affected persons and families whose land, property or livelihood is adversely affected by land acquisition or by involuntary displacement of a permanent nature due to any other reason, such as natural calamities, etc. The Policy will be applicable to all these cases irrespective of the number of people involved. The benefits to be offered under the new Policy to the affected families include; land-for-land, to the extent Government land would be available in the resettlement areas; preference for employment in the project to at least one person from each nuclear family within the definition of the 'affected family', subject to the availability of vacancies and suitability of the affected person; training and capacity building for taking up suitable jobs and for self-employment; scholarships for education of the eligible persons from the affected families; preference to groups of cooperatives of the affected persons in the allotment of contracts and other economic opportunities in or around the project site; wage employment to the willing affected persons in the construction work in the project; housing benefits including houses to the landless affected families in both rural and urban areas; and other benefits. Adequate provisions have also been made for financial support to the affected families for construction of cattle sheds, shops, and working sheds; transportation costs, temporary and transitional accommodation, and comprehensive infrastructural facilities and amenities in the resettlement area including education, health care, drinking water, roads, electricity, sanitation, religious activities, cattle grazing, and other community resources, etc. The benefits expressed in monetary terms have been linked to the Consumer Price Index, and the same shall also be revised suitably at appropriate intervals. The Requiring Bodies shall be responsible for development of designated areas on the periphery of the project site, and shall earmark funds for the purpose of such periphery development activities.

3659. (11-10-2007) NEW DELHI : The Union Cabinet today gave its approval for the following amendments / insertion of the new Articles in the existing Air Services Agreement between Government of India and Governments of Denmark, Norway and Sweden: (i) Article 9 (Capacity Provisions) has been amended by removing subsection 4 thereof which required advance agreement between the designated airlines of the contracting parties about their operational details etc. (ii) Article 10 (Tariffs) has been amended-As per this amended article, the designated airlines of the respective parties are free to decide the fares based on commercial considerations and are not required to file tariffs for international air services between the territories of the parties. (iii) Article 15 (Aviation Security) has been re-drafted as per our model standard clause. (iv) A new Article has been introduced with regard to safety provision. This is as per our model standard clause (v) A new Article has been introduced with regard to Co-operative Marketing arrangements, which would enable the designated airlines of both sides to operate code-share flights including third country code share. The amendments in the existing Air Services Agreement between Government of India and Governments of Denmark, Norway and Sweden has the potential to spur greater trade, investment, tourism and cultural exchanges between the two countries, besides bringing it in line with the developments in International Civil Aviation.

3660. (11-10-2007) NEW DELHI : The Union Cabinet today gave its approval to the following proposals : 1. Extension of existing subsidy schemes for a period of 3 more years from 1.4.2007. 2. 42.7% of the total under-recoveries for the current year (2007-08) may be borne by Government in the form of oil bonds. 3. The upstream companies may share about 1/3rd of the total under recoveries of OMCs. This decision will enable for continuing of subsidies on PDS kerosene and (dom) LPG; and sharing the burden of OMCs' under-recoveries on account of sale of sensitive petroleum products.

3661. (11-10-2007) NEW DELHI : The Union Cabinet today gave its approval to the following proposals for winding up of M/s. Bharat Yantra Nigam Limited (BYNL), Allahabad, a public sector holding company :-i) Waiver of GOI loan of Rs. 1.10 crore as on 31.3.07 ii) Waiver of interest of Rs. 4.14 crore accrued on GOI loan as on 31.3.2007, and any addition upto the date of closure. iii) Writing down of the share capital of BYNL to the tune of Rs. 2.31 crore. iv) Opening of Voluntary Retirement Scheme to enable the employee desirous of opting for an early separation before closure of the company. v) Budgetary support for the cost of closure of the company to the extent of Rs. 3.82 crore vi) Transfer of the assets and liabilities as on a cut off date of 31.3.07 of the company among the subsidiaries vii) Transfer of shares held by BYNL in subsidiaries to the GOI viii) Closure and winding up of BYNL, the holding company under the relevant provisions of Companies Act, 1956 after transfer of assets and liabilities to the subsidiary companies and transfer of shares of the Subsidiary held by BYNL to the GOI. Each Subsidiary will become separate Central Public Sector Enterprise. BYNL is a holding company of six subsidiary companies namely, (i) M/s Bharat Heavy Plate and Vessels Limited (BHPV), Visakhapatnam; (2) M/s Bharat Pumps and Compressors Limited (BPCL), Naini; (3) M/s Bridge and Roof Company India Limited (B&R), Kolkata; (4) M/s. Richardson and Cruddas (1972) Limited (R&C), Mumbai; (5) M/s. Triveni Structurals Limited (TSL), Naini; and

(6) M/s Tungabhadra Steel Products Limited (TSPL), Karnataka. The decision for winding up of BYNL will enable its subsidiaries to have an independent status which will improve their performance and profitability.

3662. (11-10-2007) NEW DELHI : The Union Cabinet today gave its approval for payment of Productivity Linked Bonus (PLB) equivalent to 70 days wages to eligible non-gazetted railway employees (excluding RPF/RPSF personnel) for the financial year 2006-07 on the basis of the formula approved by the Cabinet in their meeting held on 23.09.2000.

3663. (11-10-2007) NEW DELHI : The Vice President of India and the Chairman of the Rajya Sabha Shri Mohammad Hamid Ansari has deeply condoled the sad demise of Shri S. R. Bommai, former Chief Minister of Karnataka and former Union Minister. In his condolence message sent to his son Shri Basavaraj Bommai, MLA, the Vice President has said that Shri S. R. Bommai was an able administrator, parliamentarian par excellence and above all a committed humanist who always championed the cause of the poor and the deprived. As Chief Minister and Union Minister, he made valuable contributions for the development of our country. In his sad demise the country has lost an eminent public personality who shall always be remembered. The Vice President conveyed his condolences to the members of the bereaved family and the wide circle of his admirers and friends and paid his respectful homage to the departed noble soul and prayed to God to grant it eternal peace.

3664. (12-10-2007) NEW DELHI : The Vice President of India Mohd. Hamid Ansari has greeted the people of our country on the joyous occasion of Id-ul-Fitr, which marks the end of the holy month of 'Ramazan'. In his greetings, the Vice President said that the festival is celebrated with traditional gaiety and piety across the country. The spirit of generosity and charity associated with this festival promotes the feeling of brotherhood among people and help usher in a humane society. The Vice President said that on this occasion, the noble ideals of the festival fill our lives with peace, prosperity, and harmony and unite us all in a common brotherhood of all humanity.

3665. (12-10-2007) NEW DELHI : The President, Smt. Pratibha Devisingh Patil has congratulated the Intergovernmental Panel on Climate Change (IPCC) chaired by Dr. R.K. Pachauri for sharing this year's Nobel Peace Prize alongwith the former U.S. Vice President Mr. Al Gore. Smt. Patil has said the award is recognition for the crucial work done by Dr. Pachauri and his team members on the IPCC for the benefit of humanity and future generations.

3666. (12-10-2007) NEW DELHI : The Prime Minister Dr. Manmohan Singh called on the President Smt. Pratibha Devisingh Patil at Rashtrapati Bhavan today. The meeting lasted for about 25 minutes. They reviewed recent national and international developments.

3667. (12-10-2007) NEW DELHI : Government of India have announced the sale (re-issue) of "5.87 percent Government Stock, 2010" under Market Stabilization Scheme for a notified amount of Rs. 5,000 crore (nominal). Government of India have also announced the sale (re-issue) of "11.30 percent Government Stock, 2010" under Market Stabilization Scheme for a notified amount of Rs. 5,000 crore (nominal). The Government Stocks will be sold through price based auction using multiple price method. The auctions will be conducted by the Reserve Bank of India, Mumbai Office, Fort, Mumbai on Octob r18, 2007 (Thursday). Up to 5 per cent of the amount notified for the sale of stock is reserved for allotment to eligible individuals and Institutions on non-competitive basis as per the Scheme for Non-Competitive Bidding Facility in the Auction of Government Securities. Bids in the prescribed form obtainable from the Regional Director, Reserve Bank of India, Mumbai Office (Public Debt Office), Fort, Mumbai-400 001 and RBI website www.rbi.org.in should be submitted to that Office on October 18, 2007. The NDS members should submit competitive as well as non-competitive bids in electronic format using Primary Market Operation (PMO) module of NDS. All bids should be submitted by 12.30 P.M.

3668. (12-10-2007) NEW DELHI : The President, Smt. Pratibha Devisingh Patil will visit Amravati and Hyderabad from October 13 to 14. During her visit to Amravati on October 13, the President will participate in a felicitation function in her honour and also inaugurate the Amba Festival. The Governor and Chief Minister of Maharashtra, will also be present. Smt. Patil will declare the 4th Military World Games 2007 Open at the Gachi Bowli Stadium in Hyderabad on October 14, during her visit to the city. The President will return to New Delhi on October 14.

3669. (12-10-2007) NEW DELHI : In exercise of the powers conferred by clause (1) of article 224 of the Constitution of India, the President is pleased to appoint Shri Karam Chand Puri to be an Additional Judge of the Punjab and Haryana High Court for a period of two years with effect from the date he assumes charge of his office.

3670. (12-10-2007) NEW DELHI : Major General (Retired) Raajnish Gossain, CMD, Bharat Dynamics Limited (BDL), presented a dividend cheque of 23 crore rupees for the financial year 2006-07 to the Defence Minister Shri A K Antony here today. BDL is a mini-Ratna category-1 company and is amongst a few companies in the world having capabilities to produce state-of the-art guided weapon systems. The company has been regularly paying dividend to the government for over a decade. BDL has achieved a turnover of Rs 433 crores this year. This year the company was awarded the prestigious Raksha Mantri's award for excellence in design effort category for the year 2004-05, the Golden Peacock Innovation Award by the Institute of Directors, the FAPCII award for "Excellence in Research & Development (Silver Rolling Trophy)" by the government of Andhra Pradesh and the SODET award for technology development and innovation for the year

2005-06 in Silver Category. BDL has also received the Raksha Mantri's Award for Excellence for import substitution for the year 2005-06.

3671. (12-10-2007) NEW DELHI : The Central Government had imposed a prohibition of one month, with effect from 20.09.2007 to 20.10.2007, on transmission/re-transmission of JANMAT TV Channel for telecasting a sting operation, on Smt. Uma Khurana, Teachar, as the said sting operation was defamatory, deliberate, false and contained suggestive innuendos and half truths; incited violence and contained content against maintenance of law and order; it criticized, maligned and slandered an individual in person and it denigrated children. M/s Broadcast Initiatives Limited, distributor and uplinking applicant for Janmat TV Channel, vide their appeal dated 21.09.2007and 04.10.2007, inter alia, submitted that there was no deliberate attempt by the Channel to defame anybody by telecast of the said sting operation and that they had exercised all due diligence and care as per prevailing industry practice, it subsequently emerged that the reporter had misled them and unfortunately the sting operation telecast on 30.08.2007 took a different shape. And whereas they have requested the Ministry to reconsider the prohibition of transmission of the channel for one month which has put a question mark on the commercial viability of their channel. They have assured that they are committed to effectively using journalism in the best interests of the nation and society by following the highest standards of journalism and that they would be observing and minutely complying with all the relevant provisions of the Cable Television Networks (Regulation) Act, 1995 and the requisite license conditions. Therefore, the Central Government has now decided to revoke the prohibition imposed on transmission/re-transmission of Janmat TV Channel on all platforms with effect from 12.10.2007 midnight.

3672. (12-10-2007) NEW DELHI : The Asia Pacific Partnership (APP) is a group of six countries-Australia, China, India, Japan, the Republic of Korea, and the United States of America-cooperating to meet both their increased energy needs and associated challenges, including those related to air pollution, energy security, and greenhouse gas intensities. At the Partnership's inaugural meeting on January 12, 2006, in Sydney, Australia, Ministers agreed to a Work Plan setting out an innovative approach of using government-industry Task Forces to develop sustainable solutions to our shared challenges through bottom-up practical action. Public, private and research experts and leaders from each of the countries have focused on clean development issues in eight key sectors: (1) cleaner fossil energy; (2) renewable energy and distributed generation; (3) power generation and transmission; (4) steel; (5) aluminum; (6) cement; (7) coal mining; and (8) buildings and appliances. The PIC met Berkeley, California, on April 18-21, 2006 to initiate the work of the Task Forces. In all, about 300 representatives from government, industry, and research institutions from the six Partner countries met to begin their work. The PIC provided guidance to the Task Forces in undertaking their work while allowing them a significant degree of flexibility to develop projects and activities that fit the circumstances of their sector and theme. The eight Action Plans are the product of the Task Forces' initial stage of collaboration to formulate detailed Action Plans outlining both immediate and medium-term specific actions, including possible "flagship" projects. The Action Plans approved in Jeju provide a foundation for the Partnership's work, as well as an initial set of actions that Partners intend to implement. These activities represent a significant first step toward a more comprehensive set of actions to address clean development and climate goals. This initial portfolio of Partnership projects is weighted towards activities such as sectoral assessments, capacity building, identifying best practices and technology research and demonstration. Figure 1 below provides an approximate estimate of project types grouped by Task Force.

3673. (12-10-2007) NEW DELHI : The Union Minister of State for Health & Family Welfare, Smt. Panabaka Lakshmi launched today the Joint UN Programme on HIV and AIDS Prevention and Care in the North-Eastern States. This is a unique endeavour, which demonstrates a strong partnership between the Government of India, the UN system and the donors, the Governments of Australia and Sweden to improve the quality of and augment response to the HIV epidemic in North-East India. Shri Oscar Fernandes, Minister of State (Independent Charge) of the Ministry of Labour & Employment was also present at the function. As part of the programme, a NACO sub-office has been established in Guwahati to provide enhanced support to the programme in the North-East and strengthen a decentralized response. The sub-office will report directly to NACO and work in tandem with the National Rural Health Mission. The overall operations of the Joint UN Programme will be governed by a Programme Steering Committee, chaired by the Director General, NACO. It will include the Team Leader of the NACO sub-office, State AIDS Control Societies, Project Directors, UN Resident Coordinator, UNAIDS Country Coordinator, Chair of UN Theme Group and representatives from the Governments of Australia and Sweden. The Australian Government has made available AUD 10 million (approximately USD 8 million) for a period of over 5 years (2007-2011) for technical assistance. This will be delivered through the UN system for four North-East States (Meghalaya, Mizoram, Manipur and Nagaland) and for the establishment of the NACO sub-office in Guwahati, Assam. The Government of Sweden will provide USD 650,000 over the three-year period (2006-2008), through the UN system. This will primarily be used for capacity building of civil society organisations in the North-Eastern region.

3674. (12-10-2007) NEW DELHI : The South Asia Regional conference on Human Trafficking concluded here yesterday evening called for concerted efforts for effective enforcement of law so that offenders are punished quickly, certainly and severely in time bound manner for trafficking of children and women. The Conference was organized by the United Nations Office on Drugs and Crime in collaboration with the Ministry of Women and Child Development Ministry and Home Ministry. After three days deliberations, the conference adopted Delhi

Declaration which stresses on the role of youth for social and economic empowerment of women and to identify vulnerable areas including study of migration and trafficking trends to undertake focused programmes to target trafficking.

3675. (12-10-2007) NEW DELHI : The Cabinet Secretary, Shri K.M. Chandrasekhar has said that there is an urgent need to go further down the path of sustainable development in India, which encompasses the need for finding an acceptable balance between the priorities of economic development, social progress and environmental protection. Inaugurating a Seminar on 'Standards and Citizen: Contributing to Society' on the occasion of World Standards Day he added that we have to think in terms of meeting the needs of present generation without compromising the ability of future generations to meet their own needs. He stated that providing clean and green environment should be the top most priority of a nation. Through standards organisations ensure that their activities respect, promote and improve internationally recognized principles for citizen's rights and obligations. Shri Chandrasekhar pointed out that global warming has become a grave issue affecting the very basis of sustainability of the earth and humanity. Therefore, all organisations as well as individuals all over the world should address the issue of global warming, under a shared understanding since it will require changes in lifestyles. This can be achieved through compliance with environmental standards and safeguards by each one of us on this earth. Shri Yashwant Bhave, Secretary, Department of Consumer Affairs in his address suggested that there should be a single standards body in India to take care of national standardization needs and collaborate at international level. Proliferation of standards body would do damage to the need for unified standards at international level in the WTO regime, he added. Bureau of Indian Standards, the National Strandards Body of the country, organized the Seminar. World Standards Day is celebrated every year on October 14 to commemorate and recognize the contribution made by experts world over in the field of standardization in collaboration with the three international standards bodies namely International Electro-technical Commission (IEC), International Organisation for Standardisation (ISO) and International Telecommunication Union (ITU) so as to develop voluntary international standards that facilitate trade, spread knowledge and promote technological advancements and at the same time safeguard the consumers' interest with respect to safety, health, quality of the product and also protect the environment.

3676. (12-10-2007) NEW DELHI : The Department of Scientific & Industrial Research (DSIR) through National Research Development Corporation (NRDC) has announced awards for five meritorious inventions for the year 2007. Tax Free Cash Awards are given every year to those working in scientific and industrial fields for meritorious inventions, which are proved to be workable, useful and commercially viable to encourage inventive talent in the country. Dr. R. Chidambaram, Principal Scientific Advisor to the Government of India will give away the Awards in New Delhi on Monday, the 15th October 2007. The Corporation has also announced WIPO Gold Medals on behalf of the World Intellectual Property Organization (a Geneva Based UN sub-system). One medal is given for the outstanding invention of the year, which is considered to be a substantive contribution to the economic and technological development of the country. A separate WIPO medal is given to the best woman inventor of the year. This activity is carried out by WIPO to encourage inventors in developing countries.

3677. (12-10-2007) PATNA: Nationalist Congress Party and Rashtriya Janata Dal chiefs Sharad Pawar and Lalu Prasad on Thursday asserted here that there was no threat to the United Progressive Alliance government. The two had come to attend their party functions. The Union Ministers, who are members of the UPA-Left committee on the nuclear deal with the United States, were confident that the Left parties' "concerns" would be addressed to their satisfaction. Mr. Pawar said the discussions in the four meetings of the committee were good and he was confident that both sides would resolve the matter amicably. The issue would not impact the stability of the UPA government. He described as poor prophecy the observation of Leader of the Opposition in the Lok Sabha L.K. Advani that there would be a snap poll in the first half of 2008. Mr. Prasad said there was no remote chance of a mid-term poll, as talks with the Left were under way in the most cordial and amicable manner. The nuclear deal was for better power generation.

3678. (12-10-2007) NEW DELHI : In exercise of the powers conferred by clause (1) of article 224 of the Constitution of India, the President is pleased to appoint (i) Shri Mohinder Pal, (ii) Shri Harbans Lal, and (III) Shri Sham Sunder to be Additional Judges of the Punjab and Haryana High Court, in that order of seniority, for a period of two years with effect from the dates they assume charge of their respective offices.

3679. (12-10-2007) NEW DELHI : Congress Spokesperson Shri Abhishek Singhvi said that the Congress Party congratulates the Government of India and the Prime Minister for converting into reality the strong recommendations of the Congress President and the Congress Party to ensure maintenance of price on items like oil and oil products. That has been the strong consistent stand of the Congress Party, communicated at different times, on different occasions repeatedly and consistently by the Congress President and the Congress Party. Under the Congress President's leadership the Congress party considers this to be a historic, a landmark, a bold, innovative and pro-people decision. It is farsighted because it controls the cascading effect on other products if oil prices rise. It is a decision for India, by India, of India for the common man, for the aam aadmi. It is bold because it withstands huge international pressures which are inflationary in nature. It is innovative because it uses bonds to protect, to a large extent, the oil companies and yet holds the price for the aam aadmi. It protects, therefore, the vulnerable sections of society and is therefore basically pro-people. The Congress Party also welcomes the revolutionary safeguards for land acquisition for industrial development and the Congress President and the Congress Party had taken the initiative and the lead way back last year at the Nainital session to highlight and to show how the vital need for industrial development as also for protecting the farmers and the agriculturists to both go hand in hand. That was the first initiative by the Congress Party. We also welcome these decisions, both regarding oil, both regarding land acquisition because they are essentially in spirit and harmony and tuned with the Common Minimum Programme. In fact the safeguards on the land acquisition front are unique. They are unparalleled in the world. No where in the world you have such a comprehensive and mature scheme. And, most importantly they bear the footprint and the imprint of the philosophy of the Congress Party and we therefore welcome it. To a question on the Congress stand on the Nuclear deal Shri Singhvi said, the real point to be understood is that the relationship between the different constituents of the coalition is not unidimensional. It is not win or loose. It is not a relationship which is captured by a single issue or a single dissent or a single disagreement. The relationship is based firstly on ideology, secondly on a elective choice to get together to provide a government, thirdly on the CMP and in this holistic perception there are, no doubts, there are differences and disagreements. Nobody says that on such tough issues there are identical views. But since every effort is ongoing under our very eyes, every other week we are saying that to assume nemisses or to fake doomsday scenario, as occasionally happens in the Press, is not correct. I have already denied that there is any rethink, or u-turn or difference in perception. It is clear that the stand is the same. The stand is that energy, in all forms, including nuclear energy, is good for India. But equally the stand is that we have no doubt that our supporters, within and without the UPA, are fully engaged, fully interlocked in negotiations, discussions and understanding and we have absolutely no fear and doubt that there will be the emergence of an appropriate agreement. The Congress is as such[committed to good governance as to coalition dharma, the Congress is committed to energy for India and to consensus among allies, the Congress is as such committed to moving forward on all fronts while engaging fully all our allies.

3680. (12-10-2007) NEW DELHI : In exercise of the powers conferred by Sub Section (1) of Section 100-A of the Constitution of Jammu & Kashmir, the President is pleased to appoint Shri Jai Pal Singh, to be an Additional Judge of the Jammu & Kashmir High Court for a period of two years with effect from 4.10.2007.

3681. (12-10-2007) NEW DELHI : The Ministry of New and Renewable Energy is implementing a wide range of programmes for the development and deployment of new and of renewable energy. To encourage investment in the renewable energy sector, fiscal and financial incentives are being provided that include capital / interest subsidy, accelerated depreciation, concessional duties and relief from taxes, apart from preferential tariff for grid power being given in most potential States. Publicity and awareness on the need and usefulness of renewable energy systems / devices is created through print, postal and electronic media and special events like the Rajiv Gandhi Akshay Urja Diwas are being organised. District-level Advisory Committees have also been constituted in the states to facilitate effective coordination of renewable energy schemes. These apart, research, design, and development in new and renewable energy is being supported. The Expert Committee on Integrated Energy Policy in its Report (IEPR 2006) has estimated that by 2032, *i.e.*, 25 years from now primary commercial energy requirement in the country would need to go up 4-5 times the current level, electricity generation installed capacity 5.6-7 times the current level and oil requirement by 3-6 times the current level. The need to diversify energy supply options is brought out in the IEPR 2006. Accordingly, increased focus is being laid on the deployment of renewable power that is likely to account for around 5 per cent in the electricity-mix by 2032. This apart, alternate fuels, essentially bio-fuels, are proposed to be progressively used for blending with diesel and petrol, mainly for transport applications.

3682. (12-10-2007) NEW DELHI : The Prime Minister, Dr. Manmohan Singh, has addressed the Hindustan Times Summit-2007 here today. Following is the text of the PM's speech on the occasion:-"I am delighted to be back once again at this important gathering. As I have said before, these forums provide us opportunities to exchange views, to debate and shape the thinking of our people. Such public discourse is the life blood of a democracy. I compliment Shobhanaji for the interest she has taken to ensure that these summits are high quality events. You have, once again, an impressive gathering of speakers and participants. I hope the views and ideas expressed here are carried across the length and breadth of our country. These proceedings should be translated into all Indian languages so that our people get to know the thinking of the eminent personalities gathered here. I dare say, though, that one finds that on many issues, the people of our country are often ahead of their political and intellectual leaders! The people of India have shown time and again a remarkable capacity to keep in step with change and often, be the agents of the change they want to see. It is we-politicians, policy makers and opinion makers-who some times find ourselves lagging behind public opinion. This would be more so in a society of increasingly young people. India is going through a demographic revolution. We are a nation of young people, with a new generation entering the electorate at every election. Each generation has it's own dreams. Each generation "Imagines the India that can be". In a society of such rapid demographic and social change, new ideas and experiences capture the imagination of each passing generation. The India that we imagine that can be today, may well be obsolete by tomorrow. It is, therefore, of utmost importance that we remain in touch with this changing reality and understand the India `that is', even as we seek to imagine the India that `can be'. For us, here in India, this is not just a reality check, but also a way of renewing the basis of our nationhood, and our Republic. I say this because our Republic is itself the product of our collective imagination. It is often said that we are an ancient civilisation but a young nation. The "idea of India" draws inspiration both from our civilisational roots and from the social, political, intellectual and, above all, the emotional basis of our national movement. These define our collective imagination. A nation based on such diverse sources of human imagination-rather than on mere ethnicity, religion or language-has limitless possibilities. No static ideology can freeze or strait-jacket the creativity, the enterprise and the imagination of our people.

3683. (13-10-2007) NEW DELHI : The Panchayati Raj Minister Mr. Mani Shankar Aiyar has said that the Panchayats have to be empowered through participation right from the planning stage. The Panchayats should be involved in specifying requirements and defining priorities related to their village as they alone know what is required by them and is best for them. Mr. Aiyar was addressing the two day National Conference on District Planning under Backward Region Grant Fund(BRGF) here today. Mr. Aiyar expressed concern that out of the Rs.4000 crore that was to be given to panchayats across the country in the current financial year only Rs.222 crore has been given as panchayats could not meet the criterion required to utilize these funds which includes formulation of proper district plans. He said he wanted it to reach Rs.600 crore in this month and it could be done through proper district plans. As per the Indian Constitution a proper district plan has to be prepared without which funds cannot be disbursed to panchayats. Mr. Aiyar said that 53 districts have made plans of which only 31 meet the criterion and conform to guidelines. These districts are from various states and corners of the country. He said if district plans are made better, disbursing money would be easier and more effective. The Minister however added that only for the current financial year, funds could be made available to panchayats for the six activities without the district plans. The activities are; making Panchayat Ghar-a place for meetings, activities etc., rectify scarcity of staff, housing for poor, Aanganwadi strengthening, Education and Sports Facilities and functional facilities like kitchen etc. for Mid day meal scheme. He clarified that this exemption is only for the year 2007-2008. The Minister appealed to the participants that District planning Committees (DPC) should be set up where there are none and emphasized the need for making proper District plans. As of now there are no DPCs in Gujarat, UP, Punjab, Uttaranchal and Maharashtra. The BRGF programme covers 250 districts and the conference is being attended by delegates from these regions.

3684. (13-10-2007) NEW DELHI : The President, Smt. Pratibha Devisingh Patil, has sent her greetings to fellow countrymen on the occasion of Idu'l Fitr, which falls tomorrow. In a message, the President has said, "On the joyous occasion of Idu'l Fitr, I convey my warm wishes to all my citizens in India and abroad. As we celebrate this day as a day of forgiveness, fellowship, thanksgiving and moral victory, I hope that the occasion with its tradition of giving and sharing will infuse the spirit of unity and harmony in us."

3685. (13-10-2007) NEW DELHI : The President, Smt. Pratibha Devisingh Patil has congratulated the Intergovernmental Panel on Climate Change (IPCC) chaired by Dr. R.K. Pachauri for sharing this year's Nobel Peace Prize along with the former U.S. Vice President Mr. Al Gore. Smt. Patil has said the award is recognition for the crucial work done by Dr. Pachauri and his team members on the IPCC for the benefit of humanity and future generations.

3686. (13-10-2007) NEW DELHI : After keeping the nation on tenterhooks for over three months and precipitating the worst ever political crisis for his own government because of his intransigent stand over the Indo-US nuclear deal, Prime Minister Dr. Manmohan Singh has suddenly done a U-turn. "Even if the nuclear deal does not go through, it will not be the end of life," the P.M. has said. Smt. Sonia Gandhi has endorsed the P.M's volte face. A large majority in Parliament never wanted the flawed deal to go through. The Left Parties are against it just because it is an agreement with the U.S., and they would not like New Delhi to have any truck with Washington. The BJP's rejection of the proposed agreement was essentially on the grounds that the government was jeopardizing India's national security in the name of illusory energy security. Our view has been that it is a deal between unequals, in which India would have to accept a subservient status vis-a-vis America by surrendering its sovereignty and self-reliance in strategic security matters. This agreement amounted to a commitment by India that against the wishes of the U.S. Indira Gandhi may have done Pokharan I, and Vajpayee may have gone in for Pokharan II, but hereafter, there would be no Pokharans. Shockingly, thus, Dr. Manmohan Singh was assisting the United States to bring India into the NPT regime through the backdoor, even though every previous Prime Minister since 1968 (when the nuclear Non-Proliferation Treaty came into being) had refused to sign it. Neither rejection of the deal by the NDA and a majority in Parliament, nor widespread criticism from the community of scientists, security experts and foreign policy professionals had made the Prime Minister or the Congress president, who fully backed him, see reason. This is what Dr. Manmohan Singh told the country: *"It is not possible to renegotiate the deal. It is an honourable deal, the cabinet has approved it, we cannot go back on it. I told them (the communists) to do whatever they want to do, if they want to withdraw support; so be it...."* And this is what Smt. Sonia Gandhi said at a public rally in Haryana, as recently as on 7th October: *"Those who are opposed to the nuclear deal are enemies not only of the Congress but also of the nation's development. We should all join hands in giving them a strong response."* Therefore, when I now hear Dr. Manmohan Singh say, "Even if the nuclear deal does not go through, it will not be the end of life," all I can say is that this is certainly the end of whatever little legitimacy he had in the high office he occupies. If Dr. Singh and Smt. Sonia Gandhi have suddenly backtracked, they have done it not out of any principles, but purely due to a rude realization that going ahead with the deal would sink the government. Nevertheless, both of them owe an explanation to the nation as to why they caused virtual paralysis of their own government for the past three months. The extraordinary combination of ineptitude, arrogance, immaturity and lack of conviction that Dr. Manmohan Singh and Smt. Sonia Gandhi have displayed in the past three months shows that the thoroughly opportunist alliance that is the U.P.A., is unfit to govern India. The episode also confirms our party's evaluation that Dr. Manmohan Singh is the weakest Prime Minister of India has had. The UPA government is at its weakest point now since its inception in May 2004. From now onwards, its journey can only be downhill.

3687. (13-10-2007) NEW DELHI : The two-day National Conference on 'Climate Change and Indian Agriculture' which concluded here today made wide ranging recommendations concerning issues relating to climate change. Shri Sharad Pawar, Minister of Agriculture, Consumer Affairs, Food and Public Distribution, who addressed the valedictory session assured that the four parts recommendations *i.e.* strengthen research and assessment of the impacts, increase international collaboration, evolve and implement scientific and economic based policies, and invest in infrastructure to insulate agriculture from climatic vagaries would reach the highest level of policy decisions. These will be sent to the Prime Minister's Council as well as Planning Commission for further discussion and action, he added. Shri Pawar asked the scientific community to explore if climate change would benefit our agriculture system during any time period in future and anywhere in the country. He also suggested to Agriculture Ministry as well as related Ministries to come out soon with an appropriate action plan to increase our preparedness for climate change. The Minister complimented Dr. R.K. Pachauri, Chairman of Inter Governmental Panel on Climate Change for wining the Nobel Peace Prize. Dr. P.K. Mishra, Secretary, Department of Agriculture, Smt. M. Gupta, Secretary, D/o Environment & Forests and Dr. Mangala Rai, Secretary, DARE also addressed the session.

3688. (13-10-2007) NEW DELHI : The Prime Minister, Dr. Manmohan Singh, has greeted the nation on the joyous occasion of Id-Ul-Fitr. In a message, the Prime Minister said that the festival is being celebrated with gaiety and fervour at the end of the pious month of Ramzan. The festival symbolizes brotherhood, compassion, sharing and it also reflects the true spirit of our composite culture. He hoped that the festival would further strengthen the bonds of our composite society. May the Id-Ul-Fitr usher in peace, prosperity and happiness for all, the Prime Minister added.

3689. (13-10-2007) NEW DELHI : As a result of the overwhelming performance of the Indian Railways during the financial year 2006-07, the union Cabinet has approved the proposal of the Ministry of Railways for payment of Productivity Linked Bonus to the extent of 70 days wages for the financial year 2006-07. Productivity Linked Bonus is based on the productivity indices of the Indian Railways and this is the highest bonus ever paid on the Railways. This payment will benefit approximately 13.30 lakh non-gazetted eligible Railway employees.

3690. (14-10-2007) NEW DELHI : The Fourth CISM Military World Games, the biggest multi-sport international event of the year, got off to a spectacular start with a characteristic display of military pageantry, pomp and grandeur at the historic city of Hyderabad this evening. The President of India, Smt. Pratibha Devisingh Patil, who is also the Supreme Commander of the Indian Armed Forces, declared the Games open at the GMC Balayogi stadium, Gachibowli in the outskirts of Hyderabad. The President released three commemorative postage stamps and a First Day Cover capturing the spirit of the Games on this occasion. About 5000 military athletes from 101 countries are participating in the Military World Games, which is the biggest game after Olympics. This is the first time in the history of the Military World Games that more than 100 countries are participating to spread the message of the Game 'Friendship through Sport'. The uniqueness of the Games can be measured from the fact that some nations that are otherwise in conflict with each other have got together and will be competing in the true spirit of sportsmanship. A three-and-a-half hour grand opening ceremony marked the beginning of the week-long sporting extravaganza that concludes on October 21. A packed stadium of over 30000 spectators cheered and added to the festive spirit of Ramzan. Hyderabad also has the distinction of having hosted the 32nd National Games in 2002, and the 1st Afro-Asian Games in 2003. The Governor of Andhra Pradesh Shri N D Tiwari, the Defence Minister of India Shri A K Antony, the Chief Minister of Andhra Pradesh Shri Y S R Reddy, the Minister of State for Defence Shri M M Pallam Raju, the three Service Chiefs of the Indian Armed Forces, the President of CISM Brigadier General Gianni Gola were present on the occasion along with senior members of the armed forces from across the world. The ceremony began with a display of military bands of the three services. They regaled the audience with various military tunes after which they formed the pattern of MWG. This was followed by a spectacular display by Sarang helicopter display team of IAF. Led by Wing Commander Shashank Misra, the four Dhruv helicopter formation team displayed Diamond formation, Inverted Glass formation and INDIA formation followed by their signature 'Sarang Split' dedicating it to the sportsmen of the world. A Dhruv helicopter showered rose petals on the spectators ending their display. Spectators were then treated to a display in military precision drill by 28 Air Warriors of the IAF who in a synchronized pattern toyed around with their rifles while performing several drill patterns.

3691. (14-10-2007) NEW DELHI : India has entered into the quarterfinals in Football of the 4th Military World Games hyderabad today. In a do-or-die encounter, India defeated Afghanistan by 1-0 at AOC Ground. HAV NGURUILAL A scored the loan goal for India at the 5th minute. Apart from India, the other countries who entered the quarterfinals are Cameroon, Korea, Egypt, Guinea, Brazil, Qatar, and Ireland. The quarterfinal matches would be played from 16th October onwards at AOC and 1 EME grounds. In a one-sided match at 1 EME ground, tournament favourites Egypt beat Ireland 7-0. A Bassyonia of Egypt netted 2 goals. He is the maximum goal scorer in the tournament so far are with 5 goals in 2 matches.

Another favourites Qatar stunned Brazil by 3-1 at 1 EME ground. ANAS NASIR opened account for Qatar at 7th minute followed by ABDULQADIR ILYAS (67th minute) and MOUSSA ALBARAKA (77th minute). A MARCUS scored the only goal for Brazil at 78th minute. At MCME ground Guinea Republic defeated Canada by 4-0. In a well contested first half both teams could not convert good moves into a goal. In the 53rd minute, a beautiful header by M Mara of Guinea Republic floated into the Canadian goal. Three minutes later Bangura dribbled past the Canadian defence and shot a powerful right footer to which the Canadian custodian N Stankov had no answer. In the 72nd minute Soumah made no mistake in pushing the ball in from a cross he got from M Mara to take the tally up to 3-0. With barely 9 minutes to go, O Koulibaly was fouled by the Canadian custodian N Stankov in the goal area for which he was shown a red card and a penalty awarded to the Guineans. IS Conte made no mistake in increasing the tally to 4-0. Korea beat Germany by 3-1 at MCME ground. A tackle in the 24th minute by the German midfielder A Muller earned him a yellow card. The Koreans kept the pressure on the German defence and were soon rewarded in the 31st minute by S Han with a well angled shot that beat the German custodian to give Korea a 1-0 lead. With barely a minute for half time, Germany equalised through A Gerdes who toed in the ball from curving corner kick. A lightening move from the right flank in the 65th minute was headed into the goal by Y Kim to give the Koreans a 2-1 lead which was further consolidated in the 84th minute by K Kim to make the final tally 3-1 in favour of the Korerans. Women football league matches started today with Korea beating USA 4-0. U RI (28th minute), K RI (41) and Y KIM (61 and 87th minute) scored for Korea. In another match at Artillery grounds, Netherlands defeated Canada 4-0. TROMP LEONI (20), WMR1 M KELLY (53), NICOLLE TUEL (88) and WMR1 K JUDITH (90th minute) scored for Netherlands. Tomorrow, Germany women's football team will face USA and Netherlands will take on France.

3692. (14-10-2007) NEW DELHI : Following is the text of the Prime Minsiter, Dr. Manmohan Singh's condolence message on the passing away of Justice R.S. Sarkaria:-"I am deeply grieved to hear of the sad news of the passing away of Justice R.S. Sarkaria. Justice Sarkaria was one of our tallest and most sagacious constitutional lawyers. Starting his practice in the courts of Patiala in pre-independence India, Justice Sarkaria rose to the highest levels of our judiciary. He played a vital role in the evolution of the Indian Republic and our Constitution. A student of Government College Lahore, Justice Sarkaria was a erudite legal expert who translated our Constitution into Punjabi. He Chaired the Commission that has re-inforced the foundations of our Federal Republic. His wise guidance will for ever more be missed by our judiciary and constitutional experts. I join the nation in paying homage to the memory of Justice Sarkaria and I convey my heartfelt condolences to his family and his many admirers and disciples."

3693. (14-10-2007) NEW DELHI : Following is the Departure Statement of the Prime Minister, Dr. Manmohan Singh prior to his visit to Nigeria and South Africa:

"I will be visiting Nigeria at the invitation of His Excellency President Alhaji Umaru Musa Yar'Adua. Nigeria is the most populous country in Africa. It plays a leadership role in West Africa and within the African Union. It is an active member of the Commonwealth, NAM, G-77 and the UN. It is also a member of the Organisation of Islamic Conference. India's relations with Nigeria are historic and broad-ranging in nature. As two developing countries with a similar historical experience, we face common challenges of nation-building. Our relationship is marked by a convergence of interests and reflects our mutual commitment to South-South Cooperation. A vibrant Indian community in Nigeria contributes to the socio-economic development of Nigeria. I look forward to the opportunity of addressing the Joint Session of the National Assembly of Nigeria. I regard this as a great honour to India. My journey to Nigeria signifies India's desire to reinvigorate its ties not only with our friend and brother Nigeria, but also the continent of Africa. There is much that India and Africa have to do together for the betterment of our peoples. I also look forward to participating in the second India-Brazil-South. Africa (lSSA) Summit which is being hosted by President Thabo Mbeki in South Africa. The ISSA process has matured over time. It symbolises the coming together of like-minded countries of Asia, Africa and Latin America for the good of humankind. The Summit has a rich agenda. It will be preceded by an Academic Seminar, a Business Seminar, a Women's Forum and a Parliamentary Forum. Along with the leaders of Brazil and South Africa, I hope to review the substantial progress that has been made in expanding our trilateral cooperation, which now covers a wide range of activities. I expect the Summit to lead to concrete outcomes on both global and trilateral issues. I look forward to the opportunity of separately meeting President Mbeki and President Lula. India enjoys close and warm relations with South Africa and Brazil, which I will seek to further strengthen".

3694. (14-10-2007) NEW DELHI : Following is the Text of the remarks made by the Prime Minister, Dr. Manmohan Singh, at the Reception hosted by the High Commissioner of India. " Let me wish you all "Eid Mubarak" and in advance, "Happy Diwali". I hope the festive season brings each one of you and your families joy, success and happiness. My wife and I are delighted to be in Nigeria. Ever since our arrival we have been made to feel at home. The warmth of the reception and the graciousness of the hospitality have overwhelmed us. India and Nigeria share many commonalities. Our historical experience and common developmental challenges have brought us close together. We share common hopes and aspirations. India is the largest democracy in the world and Nigeria is the largest democracy in Africa. We are multi-ethnic, multi-religious and multi-lingual countries governed by system of plural democracy. India's partnership with Nigeria and with Africa is important for us. We now seek to build on the goodwill that exists between us to shape a strong contemporary partnership that is multi-faceted and mutually beneficial. During my visit, I look forward to holding extensive discussions with President Yar'adua and his colleagues, I have been given the honour of addressing the Nigerian Parliament and am looking forward to this opportunity. It will be our intention to place India and Nigeria on a higher and qualitatively new footing. Nigeria is India's largest trade partner in Africa. It also plays an important role in meeting India's quest for energy security. Indian companies, both public and private, have found willing homes in Nigeria. To our Nigerian friends present here today I wish to convey the warm greetings of the people of India. We greatly value your unstinting contribution to strengthening our traditional friendship and to diversifying our relationship in a meaningful manner. To members of our India community let me say that India is proud of you. You are our bridge that unites India and Nigeria. You have acquainted yourself most creditably. You have contributed to the development of friendship and goodwill between our countries. You have also contributed to the development of Nigeria by your initiative, enterprise and hard work. Indian teachers and doctors who came in the 1970s and 80s are still remembered fondly in Nigeria. I am told that Indian Industry and business is the second largest employer in Nigeria. Your contribution in the area of social work, especially in the health sector is widely appreciated. As people we value the virtues of tolerance and co-existence among cultures, language, religions, political and social views and different way of life. I believe that this background has something to do with the remarkable adaptability and resilience of India communities all over the world. While commending the success of India here, I would also like to pay tribute to the openness of the Nigerian society, which has created an enabling climate for our people to do well and to flourish. The government attaches the highest importance to the safety and security of our citizens living abroad. We have been assured at the highest level of the host government that this is a matter that is being given high priority. Our mission will offer all necessary assistance to our citizens in distress. We are engaged in efforts for the social and economic transformation in the framework of an open society and an open economy, committed to the rule of law and to fundamental human freedoms. Our success in combining will have a profound impact on the world. We are a rapidly growing economy and we are earning acclaim for the quality of our human resources. We are confident that in the coming years we can continue to sustain a growth rate of between 9-10 percent. We need this rapid growth to meet our socio-economic objectives and to rid our country of chronic poverty. India offers limitless opportunities and is looking to its overseas communities to contribute their might. India has entered an exciting new phase. It is a vibrant and self-confident nation. I invite you all to contribute your spirit, endeavour and enterprise in the service of your homeland."

3695. (15-10-2007) NEW DELHI : Damaris Changeiywo of Kenya created a new CISM Meet record at the 4th MWG in women's 10000 mtrs by clocking 32:32.44 Min. The earlier record was held by ZHOR EL Kamch with a timing of 33:01:29 Min. Kwambai Irene of Kenya and Nadia Alijufaini of Baharin also bettered the record with timings of 32:33:28 min and 32:36:41 min respectively. Another two athletes also bettered the earlier Meet record. In women's Hammer Throw final,

China's Zhang Wenxiu won the Gold by creating new Meet record with a performance of 72.25 mtrs. Russia's Gulfia Hanafeeva won the Silver with 69.28 mtrs and Bronze went to Italy's Ester Balassini (67.09 mtrs). Elena Bolsun of Russia won the Gold Medal in 100 mtrs Women Final at the 4th MWG, here this evening. She clocked 11.45 seconds while Moller Weissina Bettina of Austria won the Silver Medal (11.51 sec) and Rorcrynska Daria of Poland timed 11.54 seconds to clinch the Bronze. The Meet Record is held by Leshcheva Ekaterina of Russia (11.41 seconds). In Men's Triple Jump Savolainen Mykola of Ukraine won the Gold Medal with a jump of 16.93 mtrs. Russia's Punil Burkenya jumped 16.84 mtrs to win Silver Medal and Bronze medal went to Italy's Fabrizo Schembri for his jump of 16.23 mtrs. Slovenia's Kozmus Vrimoi won the Gold in Men's Hammer Throw with the performance of 75.98 mtrs. Italy's Nicola Vizzoni won the Silver with a throw of 74.96 mtr and Germany's Rautenkranz Jens threw 72.38 mtrs to win the Bronze. In men's Short Put event Miran Vodovnik of Slovenia was the Gold Medal winner with 19.93 mtrs. Al Suwaidi Khaled Habash of Qatar won the Silver with 19.74 mtrs and Siniarou Andrei of Belarus won the Bronze with a shot put of 18.73 mtrs.

3696. (15-10-2007) NEW DELHI : A Coffee Table Book titled 'Techno Warriors of the Indian Army: Corps of Electronics and Mechanical Engineers in Operations' was released by Gen Deepak Kapoor, Chief of Army Staff at a function held at Army Headquarters, New Delhi on 15 Oct. 07 on the occasion of the 64th anniversary of the Corps of EME. The unveiling of the book was carried out in the presence of Lt Gen SS Dhillon, Master General of Ordnance and Lt Gen Arvind Mahajan, Director General of EME. The book, which is a visual delight, captures the glorious and invaluable contributions made by the Corps of EME in various wars and operations fought by the Indian Army including counter insurgency operations and operations in aid to civil authorities. The Corps of Electronics and Mechanical Engineers has provided the cutting edge to the combat forces of the Indian Army, both in times of adversity and prosperity, with unparalleled commitment and dedication. The Coffee Table Book traces the lineage of the soldier craftsman, covers the formation of the Corps and highlights important facets of the growth of the Corps in every decade of its existence. The battle accounts encapsulated are hitherto untold sagas of personal and collective valour, dogged determination and sacrifice to keep the wheels of the Army moving and the guns firing.

3697. (15-10-2007) NEW DELHI : Russia and China showed their dominating streak in their ascent to the medals tally by winning a total of 9 (5-1-1) and 6 (2-3-1) medals respectively in the aquatics events on the first day of the Military World Games here at Hyderabad. In the male events, Russia won three Golds in 100 mts freestyle, 100 mts butterfly stroke and 100 mts breast stroke, while in the women events it won in 100 mts breast stroke and the 200 mts individual medley in which Darya of Russia set a new CISM record by clocking 2:15.92 sec, overhauling the timing of 2:17.40 sec set by China's Yiqi Pu Qi Hui

(1998-Rome) and Qi Hui (2001-St. Petersburg). In another women's event, Yafei Zhou of China improved upon her own CISM record in the 100 mts butterfly by clocking 59.05 sec improving her previous timing of 59.32 sec set in Catania in 2003.

3698. (15-10-2007) NEW DELHI : China defeated India in straight sets in Men's preliminary round of Volleyball at the 4th MWG here today. In a crucial pool B match at Yousufguda ground, China outplayed India 28-26, 25-22, 25-18. A strong Indian team started well and put up a good fight in the keenly contested first set which they lost narrowly 28-26. India took the lead in second set 13-10 however they faltered at crucial moments losing the second set 25-22 to let the Chinese go 2-0 up in the match. In the third set the Chinese side played superbly to take the set comfortably at 25-18. World and Olympic champions Brazil beat Latvia 3-1 in the fourth match of the tournament. The first two sets were taken (25-23 and 25-22) by the fancied Brazil with their magical touch. However they were in for a surprise in the third set which the Latvians took 26-24. However the Brazilians came back into the game to take the fourth set 25-16 earning a 3-1 victory in the match. In the first match of group A of the men's volleyball tournament on round robin basis at Yusufguda, the Republic of Korea defeated Qatar 3-1. Better teamwork helped Korea beat Qatar 23-25, 25-20, 25-17, 25-22. In a keenly contested match Netherlands defeated Canada by 3-1 sets with 25-20, 25-23, 23-25, 25-23. In women's preliminary round, China overpowered USA in straight sets 25-15, 25-11 and 25-7. In a close encounter Italy scraped through by beating Netherlands 25-9, 25-15, 25-20. Korea defeated Canada comfortably by 25-4, 25-8, 25-10.

3699. (15-10-2007) NEW DELHI : The preliminary rounds of Boxing on the first day of the 4th Military World Games had 25 bouts in five categories. All four Indian boxers made a winning start in the first day of the competition. In the first bout of the day, Havaldar P Narjit of India was simply too strong for his Namibian opponent Nampala Ruben in the 51-54 Kgs category and the referee had to stop the contest. In two other fights featuring Indian pugilists, Hav S Thoi Thoi defeated Benkhaoula Imad in 57-60 Kgs category (19-9) and Satya Raju defeated Filali Nasreddin in the 60-64 Kgs category (27-17) defeated their Algerian opponents while Hav Bhagya Rajan defeated Moejane Tello of Lesotho in the 60-64 Kgs category. In the other bouts in the 51-54 Kgs category, Yunhao Ma of China beat Ouadahi Amine of Algeria, Z Zhandybaev (Russia) beat Private Kikhtenko (Ukraine), Private H Ulugbek (Uzbekistan) beat D Nguyen Trong (Vietnam), in the 57-60 Kgs Private V Matviichuk (Ukraine) beat Private Mpotsang (Botswana), W O Yachmenev I (Russia) beat O Mehdi (Morocco), in the 60-64 Kgs category, Lance Corporal Nkabiti(Botswana) eat Soldier Abdulzahir (Afghanistan), Sergeant L Chun Suk(Korea) beat Mohamedabdel Rah (Qatar), Miguel Cobo(Ecuador) beat Lance Corporal A Mohamed Musabb (UAE), Cpl W Melis (Italy) beat Soi Yaser Khawaga (Sudan), Priv Y Ramashkevich (Belarus) beat Private A.aivazidi (Ukraine),

Sgt M Precious (Zambia) beat R Kamal (Morocco), L Cpl S Shawn (Jamaica) beat T Ho Van (Vietnam), in the 64-69 Kgs category WO B Kerin (Slovenia) beat 3rd Lt Hakan Ozyurt (Turkey), Pfc R Karimov (Germany) beat Pte Nick Abaka (Kenya), Cpl D Di Luisa (Italy) beat Mr. N Hakan Mursit (Qatar), Soldier D Ivanov (Russia) beat Sgt K Kemoko (Guinea Republic), Private H Rawshan (Uzbekistan) beat Cpt M Boyd (USA), Sgt M Alick (Zambia) beat Pte R Ricaroo (Jamaïca), in the 75-81 Kgs category Soldier S Kovalev (Russia) beat Konate (Mali), Spte Joshua Ndere (Kenya) beat Private M Farooh (Uzbekistan). In another bout in the same category, Gilbert Gonzalez (Ecuador) was disqualified and Ser T Zaur (Azerbaijan) was declared winner.

3700. (15-10-2007) NEW DELHI : His Excellency Dr. Manmohan Singh, Prime Minister of the Republic of India paid an official visit to Nigeria from 14-16 October 2007 at the invitation of His Excellency Umaru Musa Yar'Adua, President of the Federal Republic of Nigeria. During his visit, he held intensive and fruitful discussions with President Yar'Adua and addressed a joint session of the two houses of the Nigerian National Assembly. India and Nigeria are linked by common historical experiences and in the contemporary context are united in the desire to work towards democratic pluralism, tolerance, economic development and social justice. Both are multi-religious, multi-lingual and multi-ethnic societies with a vibrant media and civic society. They are both members of the United Nations, the Commonwealth, the G-77 and NAM and have a history and tradition of working closely together in regional and international organizations. The leaders of both sides reiterated the importance of ensuring socially inclusive economic growth in their countries. They agreed that exchange of experiences and programmes between the two countries with respect to poverty alleviation would be of great benefit to each other and to other countries in Africa. Nigeria is India's largest trading partner in Africa and the potential and opportunities for substantially enhancing trade and investment between the two countries are largely untapped. Both sides agreed to significantly enhance mutually beneficial trade and investment exchanges with each other's countries in sectors such as infrastructure (including railways), agriculture, food processing, small and medium enterprises, power generation, fertilizers, ICT, pharmaceuticals, automobiles, auto-components and other sectors. In this context, the two leaders desired that the fifth meeting of the Joint Commission be held within the next few months and should draw up a detailed roadmap for this purpose. The Indian side expressed its thanks to the Nigerian side for the rapidly growing partnership between the two countries in the energy sector. They confirmed the understanding that both governments would continue to encourage further cooperation between their companies in the oil and gas sectors of both countries.

3701. (15-10-2007) NEW DELHI : In men's handball matches played today at Saroor Nagar Stadium Lithuania beat Turkey 27-24. R Svedas of Lithuania scored 8 goals while T Kraucevicius scored 10 goals and Ergenc scored 9 goals. In pool

B Belarus defeated Latvia in a keenly contested match by 34-32. Pukhouski scored 15 goals while Vasilyeu scored 5 goals for Belarus. India lost to Korea in Pool A match by 29-40. In a pool B match Qatar beat UAE by 35-26.

3702. (15-10-2007) NEW DELHI : Dr. Shakeel Ahmed said that since this is my very first briefing as the AICC spokesperson, I welcome you all. First I would like to thank Congress President Smt. Sonia Gandhiji who has deputed me as the spokesperson and all media persons as when I was minister and MP and as a Congress worker you had projected my briefings in the proper perspective. I thank you all once again for the support given by you all. Dr. Ahmed said that I would like to brief you on two very sad incidents that took place, one in Gujarat where there was a stampede in a temple in which a dozen people lost their lives, and numerous others suffered severe injuries. The Congress Party and the Congress President have expressed their deep sorrow to the families who lost their loved ones. The second incident is the blast which took place in Ludhiana's cinema hall in which six people died and several suffered grievous injuries. It is a shameful act which should be condemned by one and all. The DGPs in all the states should take precautions so that such incidents do not take place again. The Home Minister and the State governments are in consultation on the law and order situation. Dr. Ahmed said that Shri Ramnarain Chaudhury, Rajasthan's Legislature Party leader, today handed his resignation which was accepted by the Congress President Smt. Sonia Gandhi. To a question that Shri Karunanidhi and his party are not comfortable with the nuclear deal Dr. Ahmed said, Shri Karunanidhi is a very senior leader of the UPA coalition and everybody and every political party has its own opinion on different issues. When we discuss these things on the negotiating table within the UPA framework, the Congress Party and our entire UPA under the chairpersonship of Smt. Sonia Gandhi we try to consider the viewpoints of all the parties who are partners of the UPA. I don't think there is any need to put more focus on this subject. And as far as U-turn is concerned whatever the Prime Minister and the Congress President have said is final and there is no question of adding or deleting anything.

3703. (15-10-2007) NEW DELHI : Brahmaputra Cracker and Polymer Limited (BCPL), a joint venture company with GAIL as the lead promoter, today signed the feedstock supply agreement with ONGC for Lepetkata gas cracker plant. The 2,80,000 tons per annum gas cracker plant is being set up at Lepetkata, Dibrugarh, Assam at the cost of Rs.5460 crore. Under the agreement Oil & Natural Gas Corporation Limited (ONGC) will supply 1.35 MMSCMD gas up to March 2012 and 1.00 MMSCMD thereafter to BCPL. Earlier BCPL had signed similar feedstock supply agreements with Oil India Limited (OIL) and Numaligarh Refineries Limited (NRL) last month in Dibrugarh. The existing LPG plant of GAIL at Lakwa will be modified to process gas for recovery of ethane and higher hydrocarbon fraction, which will be transported to Lepetkata through a pipeline. The agreement was signed by Shri RK Kashyap, Chief Operating Officer, BCPL and Shri J G

Chaturvedi, Executive Director and Asset Manager, Assam, ONGC in presence of Shri B K Handique, Minister of State for Chemical and Fertilisers.

3704. (15-10-2007) NEW DELHI : The Annual National Conference of Chief Registrars of Births and Deaths begins here tomorrow. Chief Registrars of Births and Deaths from the States / Union Territories, Principal Secretaries / Secretaries overseeing the work of registration of births and deaths, besides representatives of UNICEF, Plan India and officials of the Registrar General, India and Directorates of Census Operations in the States / Union Territories would be participating in the two day Conference. The National Population Policy, 2000 has mandated to achieve cent per cent registration of births and deaths by the year 2010. For achieving this, the National Conference would review the current status of registration of births and deaths across the States and discuss ways and means required to improve the current level of registration which is at 64% for births and 58% for deaths. The States which have achieved cent per cent registration of births would present their experience as well as innovative methods adopted by them to achieve it. The Municipal Corporation of Delhi is slated to make a presentation on the software, linking immunization with birth registration records (LIBRE) which has helped track the unregistered children. Generation of vital statistics from civil registration data in States having cent per cent registration has been an important issue for long. For the State of Kerala, it has been attempted. The experience will be shared to help other similarly placed States to generate data on vital indicators. India and Mauritius Seek New Avenues of Cooperation in Shipping and Road Sector

3705. (15-10-2007) NEW DELHI : The Union Minister of Shipping, Road Transport & Highways, Thiru. T.R. Baalu, reached Port Louis, the capital of Mauritius this morning on a 2-day visit and was received by Mr. E. Sinatambou, Minister of Information Technology and Telecommunications and the High Commissioner of India in Mauritius Mr. B. Jai Shankar. Later, he met the senior Mauritian leaders including the Prime Minister, Dr. Navinchandra Ramgoolam and the Deputy Prime Minister and Minister of Public Infrastructure, Land Transport and Shipping, Dr. Ahmed Rashid Beebeejaun. Thiru Baalu later also had a meeting with Mr. Madan Murlidhar Dulloo, Minister of Foreign Affairs, International Trade and Cooperation. The various issues of mutual interest were discussed at these meetings which included procurement of one oil tanker of 50,000-55,000 DWT capacity in collaboration with the Government of India through the Shipping Corporation of India; training of Merchant Navy Officers and allocation of four stand alone slots for the Merchant Navy officers from Mauritius in Indian Training Institutions; and procurement of equipment for the Maritime Training Institute in Mauritius. Earlier, in his meeting with the Mauritian Prime Minister, Thiru. Baalu said that Mauritius has managed to preserve exceptional social harmony in a multi-ethnic and pluralistic environment. He said that though Mauritius has brought about a successful economic transformation from a mono-crop agricultural colony to a vibrant economy, the level of economic and commercial ties between India and Mauritius has not been proportional to the richness and depth of their political and cultural relations. He stressed the need to strengthen the economic and commercial relations between the two countries. The Union Minister informed that the a Joint Working Group comprising of officers of both the countries has been formally set up a few days ago to explore areas of cooperation between the two countries in the area of shipping and road transportation in general, and to sort out the above issues in particular. The Joint Working Group will go through these issues and will submit its Report by November-December, 2007. Thiru. Baalu will be inaugurating the state of the art Mauritius Maritime Training Academy at Pointe aux Sables in Mauritius tomorrow.

3706. (15-10-2007) NEW DELHI : The Prime Minister, Dr. Manmohan Singh, addressed the joint session of the Nigerian National Assembly at Abuja, Nigeria today. Speaking at the occasionn the Prime Minister called for Indo-Nigerian Partnership in the 21st Century and added that for the partnership to flourish, we have to encourage and promote broad based exchanges covering all facets of our relationship. Dr. Singh said that the partnership will be based on the fundamental principles of equality, mutual respect and mutual benefit. Emphasizing that India and Africa have a shared destiny and a common future, the Prime Minister said: "I am deeply honoured by this opportunity to address you here today in this new temple of your democracy. I am also delighted to be in this beautiful city of Abuja, which symbolizes a dynamic Nigeria and a new dawn in the life of an ancient people. I stand before you to convey to the people of Nigeria the greetings and good wishes of over a billion Indians. We have been your brothers and friends of long standing. In the past, we have shared the pain of subjugation and the joy of freedom and liberation. We have worked shoulder to shoulder in the fight against apartheid and racial discrimination. We have worked together in the Nonaligned Movement to promote South-South cooperation for development. Today, we need to stand ever more united to meet the challenges of the new millennium. India is the largest democracy in the world. Nigeria is the largest democracy in Africa. We are multi-religious, multi-ethnic and multi-lingual societies. Our societies embrace modernity while preserving their traditions. There is a natural logic in ties between our two countries. The principal challenge before us remains the socio-economic development of our people. The information revolution and higher levels of literacy have raised popular expectations. Disparities are leading to social tensions. Economic growth has to be accompanied by a better distribution of its benefits. The success of diverse democracies like Nigeria and India is important. It will prove that democracy and development go hand in hand. We are approaching the fiftieth year of the establishment of our diplomatic relations. There can be no better occasion than this to launch a Strategic Partnership between India and Nigeria. It will be anchored in the past and look to the future. This is a partnership for economic growth. There are many complementarities in our rapidly growing economies. Nigeria is already India's largest trading partner in Africa, but we need to vastly expand and diversify our trade. There has been a surge in Indian investment abroad in areas such as Information Technology, energy, pharmaceuticals and auto components. We would like to see Indian investment expand in Nigeria. Nigeria has always provided a congenial home for Indian business. Our two countries can promote transfer of technologies in key areas of the knowledge economy like Information Technology and biotechnology. Small and medium industry can play a key role. Our partnership is for development. We need to share experiences on effective strategies for sustainable development, poverty alleviation, healthcare facilities and universal education. In this context, being largely agrarian societies, there is great potential for cooperation in agricultural research, soil and water management and food processing.

3707. (15-10-2007) NEW DELHI : Shri Arjun Singh, Minister of Human Resource Development would lead an Indian delegation to the 34th Session of the General Conference of United Nations Educational, Scientific and Cultural Organsation (UNESCO) to be held at Paris from October 16 to November 3. He would be leaving for Paris tonight along with two Members of Parliament *i.e.* Shri Sachin Pilot and Ms. Supriya Sadanand Sule, Secretary (Higher Education), Secretary (School Education & Literacy) and other Members of the delegation. HRD Minister will attend the Plenary Meeting and the General Policy Debate being held from October 16-20, and will address in the General Policy Debate in the afternoon session on October 19. He will also be addressing the Ministerial Round Table on 19th October, on "The right to education and the right to development". Minister will also be attending the Bilateral Meetings with the Ministers of Education of Afghanistan, Belgium, Brazil, France, Indonesia, Mexico, Nepal and South Africa. Shri Arjun Singh, HRD Minister would be hosting a reception on October 17, for the key participants of the Conference and a lunch in the honour of Mr. Koichiro Matsuura, Director General, UNESCO on October 20.

3708. (15-10-2007) NEW DELHI : With the introduction of third phase of the high-tech train enquiry system called Integrated Train Enquiry System (ITES); 'Rail Sampark' of the common country-wide Telephone No. 139 in the southern parts of the country today, this significant passenger friendly initiative is now available for general public of sixteen states and five union territories. In Chennai, the Minister of State for Railways, Shri R.Velu today inaugurated the third phase of 'Rail Sampark' Train Enquiry No. 139 for the South Zone Hub, which will cover Andhra Pradesh, Karnatka, Kerala, Tamil Nadu and Pondicherry. Earlier, the North Zone Hub covering Delhi & NCR, Punjab, Haryana, Himachal Pradesh, Jammu & Kashmir, Uttar Pradesh, Rajasthan, Uttarakhand and Chandigarh was inaugurated in July 2007 while the West Zone Hub covering Maharasthra, Madhya Pradesh, Chhattisgarh, Gujarat, Goa, Daman & Diu, Dadar & Nagar Haveli was opened in September 2007. The final East Zone Hub will become operational later in this month. Under this system, the MTNL and BSNL subscribers in the covered area may make a local call at telephone No. 139 (without requiring STD facility) to get basic enquiries pertaining to train journey like arrival/departure of train, status of availability of seats, train fare etc. Highly skilled and trained customer care executives have been deployed at this Call No. 139 to provide 24X7 Customer Care Services. This service will ultimately also be made available to all general public in the country who may subscribe to any telecom service provider irrespective of the type of telecom service (basic, mobile, WLL). In addition to Hindi and English, enquiry services will also be available in regional languages. The work of implementation of Integrated Train Enquiry System (ITES) is based on public-private partnership (PPP model). Indian Railway Catering & Tourism Corporation (IRCTC), a PSU under Ministry of Railways along with another Railway PSU, Centre for Railway Information Systems (CRIS) are responsible for rolling out this project across the country. Execution of ITES in the country is being done by M/s Bharat BPO and BSNL.

3709. (15-10-2007) NEW DELHI : Canada has formally joined Asia Pacific Partnership today at the Second Ministerial Meeting on Asia Pacific Partnership (APP) on Clean Development and Climate. The former Group AP6 has been thus expanded now. Announcing this, Shri Namo Narayan Meena, Minister of State for Environment and Forests informed the august gathering that this was proposed in yesterday's Ministerial Preparatory Session, where all Members endorsed this decision. Canada has shared the vision of the partners and also worked through bilateral and multilateral mechanism hence is most welcome in this fold. Giving inaugural address to the session, Shri Pranab Mukherjee, Minister of External Affairs welcomed Canada into this fold. He said that their request for Membership underscores the credibility this partnership has attained. The Minister said that this world is seized today with the issue of climate change. There is near unanimity that the United Nations framework convention on climate change is the only framework for negotiations. This was also reaffirmed at the major economies meeting in Washington recently. He added that our efforts are consistent with the principles of the UNFCCC and complement the Kyoto Protocol. He informed that India has 7000 MW of installed power, the forth largest wind generating electricity capacity in the world. Giving details of other clean development efforts, Shri Mukherjee said introduction of CNG for transports, introduction of Metro Rail as well as major bio-diesel programme and blending of ethanol in petrol are few of our clean developments. Shri Mukherjee suggested for collaborating research and development among Member countries and their R&D Institutions. Appreciating the support of the Federation of Indian Chambers of Commerce and Industry and the Confederation of Indian Industry to promote the aims of this partnership and progress of 8 Task Forces, he said we have achieved a lot in a very short time. All the Member countries presented their country statement and many of them congratulated the World's top Environmental Scientist Dr. R.K.Pachauri, who is heading United Nation's Inter-Governmental Panel on Climate Change for getting this year's noble peace prize. The members felt that with this award the world's awareness on Climate Change has reached its apex. Leader of Australian delegation,

DFAT, Ambassador for Environment, Ms. Jan. Adams said that their work in APP represents cooperation of an entirely different sort. She said it is cooperation of considerable importance, giving the fact that the APP countries account for half the world's GDP and produce about 65 per cent of the World's coal, 48per cent steel, 37 per cent aluminium and 61 per cent of the world's cement. These projects are real, practical and commercially relevant. The technology developed by Australia's CSIRO has potential to capture 95 per cent of CO2 emissions from power stations. She said that development of technology and dissemination will help to achieve our goals.

3710. (15-10-2007) NEW DELHI : The Defence Minister Shri A K Antony leaves New Delhi tomorrow on a four day official visit to Moscow to attend the 7th India-Russia Inter Governmental Commission on Military Technical Cooperation. He will be accompanied by a high level delegation of officers of the Ministries of Defence and External Affairs. This visit is a part of structured mechanism that exists between the two countries for Defence Cooperation as per Agreement between the Government of India and Russia on establishing the Indo Russian Inter Governmental Commission on Military Technical Cooperation (IRIGC). The meetings of the Commission co-chaired by the Defence Ministers of Russia and India are held once a year alternatively in Delhi and Moscow to review the progress of military-technical cooperation between the two countries. The 6th meeting of the IRIGC was held in Delhi on January 24, 2007. During his stay in Moscow, Shri Antony will hold discussions with the Russian Defence Minister Mr. Serdyukov Anatoly Eduardovich and visit important Defence Installations including the Tactical Missiles Corporation (TMC) and the Federal State Unitary Enterprise NPO Mashinostroyenia (NPOM). The Defence Minister will lay a wreath at the Tomb of Unknown Soldiers in Alexandrovsky Garden and visit the Kremlin Museum. The visit is indicative of the commitment of the leadership of both countries to consolidate and strengthen the excellent defence relations that exist between the two countries. A wide range of issues relating to Defence Cooperation between the two countries are to be discussed between the two sides. The discussions will culminate into a Protocol to be signed at the end of the IRIGC session.

3711. (15-10-2007) NEW DELHI : China started their campaign in style by winning the first gold medal of the tournament in Track & Field event this morning. Cui Zhide of China won the 20 km walk (Men) in 1:23:43 while Trotski Ivan of Belarus won Silver in 1:25:23.7 and Toth Matej of Slovakia won Bronze with a timing of 1:25:42.7. The world record for the event is in the name of Bernado Segura of Mexico with timings of 1:17:25.6 and the Meet record is held by A Fadejevs of Latvania with timings of 1:21:42.

3712. (15-10-2007) NEW DELHI : The Ministry of Tourism (MOT) gives special importance to improve the quality of tourism infrastructure all over the country. The Ministry has sanctioned several projects allover the country. These projects propose to create high class tourism infrastructure and facilities which will provide an opportunity for unique experience to the visitors. The Ministry of Tourism extends Central Financial Assistance to the State Governments/UTs for Product/ Infrastructure Development of Destinations and Circuits. During the XIth Five Year Plan period a double-pronged strategy of upgrading the tourism infrastructure and vigorous marketing under the banner of 'Incredible India Campaign' was followed to position India as a global brand. During 11th Five Year Plan (2007-2012) Ministry of Tourism propose to continue supporting creation of world class infrastructure in the country so that existing tourism products can be further improved and expanded to meet new market requirements and enhance the competitiveness of India as a tourist destination. In consultation with the State Governments and UTs the Ministry of Tourism have identified several tourist circuits and destinations for integrated development. During the current financial year the Ministry has sanctioned so far Rs.323.00 crore for various projects throughout the country. This is an all time record and will facilitate timely execution of projects during the working season.

3713. (15-10-2007) NEW DELHI : A delegation of Afro-Asian Rural Development Organisation (AARDO) led by its Secretary General Mr. Abdalla Yahia Adam called on Shri Kanti Lal Bhuria, Minister of State for Agriculture, here today and held discussions to explore the possibilities for resumption of collaborative arrangements with Indian Agricultural Research Institute (IARI). Shri Bhuria expressed India's willingness to accept the offer extended by AARDO for organizing training courses on water management, post-harvest technology and farm implements and tools. He further stated that once the collaboration agreement is finalised IARI could work out the details of the training programme in consultation with AARDO. IARI had organized training programmes on 'farm implements and tools' for AARDO during 1986-92 although Department of Agricultural Research and Education and ICAR do not have any institutional arrangement with AARDO.

3714. (15-10-2007) NEW DELHI : The strength and vitality of a nation emanates from its literate populace. Literacy begins from home and takes a formal shape in schools that lies in public domain. The schooling and elementary education are, thus, the edifice on which the pillars of a healthy society are built. Sarva Shiksha Abhiyan (SSA) is the main vehicle at present to provide elementary education to all children in the age group 6-14. The programme seeks to open new schools in habitations which do not have schooling facilities and strengthen existing school infrastructure through provision of additional class rooms, toilets, drinking water, maintenance grant and school improvement grant. The approach is community-oriented and village education plans, prepared in consultation with Panchayati Raj Institutions, form the basis of district elementary education plans. Existing schools with inadequate teacher strength are being provided additional teachers under the programme and capacity of existing teachers is built through extensive training including support for teaching-learning material. The SSA lays special focus on:-

educational needs of girls, and children of Scheduled Castes and Scheduled Tribes; ensuring the quality of construction; involvement of the local community in construction; creating a child friendly school environment. Many States have drawn up innovative designs, effective convergence for clean water and toilets. Approximately 5 lakh class rooms alongwith 59000 drinking water facilities and 57,327 toilet blocks have been sanctioned in 2006-07. Education think-tank National University of Educational Planning and Administration, has developed an Educational Development Index to track progress of States towards Universal Elementary Education (UEE) for primary and upper primary levels as well as for a composite look at Elementary Education. The EDI ranking, it is expected, will encourage the states to improve their performance and have a closer look at both the inputs and the outputs of the parameters that affect elementary education. It is also hoped that the EDI will also enable more effective targeting of Sarv Shiksha Abhiyan (SSA) to the most backward districts. The Educational Development Index (EDI), has been developed keeping in mind four broad parametres-access, infrastructure, teacher related indicators and outcomes. The index takes into account 22 variables for calculating EDI. These variables are-access-percentage of habitations not served, availability of schools per 1000 population; Infrastructure-average student-classroom ratio, school with student-classroom ratio greater than 60, school without drinking water facilities, schools with separate toilets for boys and girls as required; Teachers-Percentage of female teachers, pupil-teacher ratio, school with pupil-teacher ratio greater than 60, single-teacher schools-in schools with more than 15 students, percentage of schools with less than three or less teachers, teachers without professional qualification and outcome-gross enrolment ratio overall, scheduled castes : gross enrolment ratio, schedule tribes : gross enrolment ratio, gender parity index enrolment : repetition rate, drop-out rate, ratio of exit class over Class I enrolment-primary stage only, percentage of passed children to total enrolment, percentage of appeared children, passing with 60 per cent and above marks. Chandigarh has done well in providing facilities like infrastructure and teachers at the elementary education level in comparison to the surrounding States.

3715. (15-10-2007) NEW DELHI : Shri Vivek Desai of Ahmedabad has bagged the first prize for both sections (Black & white and Colour) in the 20th National Photo Contest organized by the Photo Division, Ministry of Information and Broadcasting, Government of India. To commemorate the 150 years of First War of India's Independence and 60 years of Independence, Photo Division organized a unique Photo Contest on the theme "Spirit of Independent India". A total of 1157 photographs were received from 294 participants from 16 States (Andhra Pradesh, Chandigarh, Chattisgarh, Gujarat, Haryana, Jharkhand, Karnataka, Kerala, Madhya Pradesh, Maharashtra, New Delhi, Orissa, Rajasthan, Tamil Nadu Uttar Pradesh, and West Bengal). Shri Anirudha Pal and Shri Supriya Biswas of Kolkata got the second prize and Shri Girish J. Kingar and Shri Upendra Upadhyay of Indore got third prizes in black and white and colour section respectively. Ten Commendation

Awards for black and white photographs have been announced for S/Shri T.Srinivasa Reddy of Andhra Pradesh, Hemendra A.Shah of Ahmedabad, Prasenjit Dhar of Asansol, R.V.Shiddhaye of Mumbai, Puranjit Gangopadhyay, Chinmoy Bhattacharjee, Dines Mukherjee and Avijit Datta of Kolkata and O.P.Soni of Indore. The Commendation Awards in colour section have been announced for S/Shri Nitin Khatri of Indore, Subhashis Basu, Partha Pratim Das, Jayanta Shaw, Partha Samal, Supriya Biswas of Kolkata, Devendra Sharma of Ratlam, Pravin Barnale, Ashu Patel, of Indore and Ambuj Soni of Dewas, Madhya Pradesh. The first prize carries a cash prize of Rs. 20,000/-, the second prize Rs.15,000/- and the third prize Rs. 10,000/- while the commendation prizes carry Rs. 2,000/- each alongwith a citation and a memento. The Jury Members selected 83 prints from Black & White and Colour in addition to the 26 award winning pictures for display in the exhibition.

3716. (15-10-2007) NEW DELHI : India Telecom 2007 will be held in New Delhi from December 12 to 15, 2007. The four day Conference will have sessions on a wide range of subjects. There will be five sessions in all. The Conference will be inaugurated on December 12, 2007. Session I will be on Accelerating the Growth of Broadband. Session II will dwell on Delivery of Cost Effective Voice and Data Services in Rural India. Session III will be on Investments in Indian Telecom Sector, Sector IV will cover the Growth of Value Added Services (VAS) Segment and Session V will be on Enabling Regulator Framework for Achieving the Desired Goals. On Day 4 *i.e.* December 15, 2007 there will be an Open House Session with senior officials from DoT, TRAI and DIT on Policy and Regulatory issues. The Valedictory Session will be on the same day. A curtain raiser function will be held in New Delhi on October 16, 2007.

3717. (15-10-2007) NEW DELHI : The Union Minister for Science & Technology and Earth Sciences, Shri. Kapil Sibal Today inaugurated the National Tsunami Early Warning System that has been set up at the Indian National Centre for Ocean lnformation Services (INCOIS), Hyderabad. Chief Minister of Andhra Pradesh, Dr. Y. S. Raja Sekhar Reddy graced the occasion. Recognizing the imperative to put in place an Early Warning System for mitigation of Oceanogenic Disasters that cause severe threat to nearly 400 million of our population that live in the coastal belt with devastation of life and property, and further driven by the national calamity due to the lndian Ocean Tsunami of December 26, 2004, the Ministry of Earth Sciences (MoES) has taken up the responsibility of establishing the National Tsunami Early Warning System. The Warning System has been established by MoES as the nodal ministry at a cost of Rs.125 Crore in collaboration with Department of Science and Technology (DST), Department of Space (DOS) and the Council of Scientific and Industrial Research (CSIR). The National Tsunami Early Warning Centre has been set up at INCOIS, Hyderabad. Tsunamigenic zones that threaten the Indian Coast have been identified by considering the historical tsunamis, earthquakes, their magnitudes, location of the area relative to a fault, and also by tsunami modelling. The east and west coasts of India and the island regions are likely to be affected by tsunamis generated mainly by subduction zone related earthquakes from the two potential source regions, viz., the Andaman-Nicobar-Sumatra island arc and the Makran subduction zone north of Arabian Sea. The Indian Tsunami Early Warning System comprises a real-time network of seismic stations, Bottom Pressure Recorders (BPR) and tide gauges to detect tsunamigenic earthquakes and to monitor tsunamis. The Early Warning Centre receives real-time Seismic data from the national seismic network of the Indian Meteorological Department (IMD) and other International seismic networks. The system detects all earthquake events of more than 6 Magnitude occurring in the Indian Ocean in the less than 20 minutes of occurrence. BPRs installed in the Deep Ocean are the key sensors to confirm the triggering of a Tsunami. The National Institute of Ocean Technology (NIOT) has installed 4 BPRs in the Bay of Bengal and the2 BPRs in Arabian Sea. In addition, NIOT and Survey of India (SOI) have installed 30 Tide Gauges to monitor the progress of tsunami waves. Integrated Coastal and Marine Area Management (ICMAM) has customized and ran the Tsunami Model for 5 historical earthquakes and the predicted inundation areas. The inundated areas are being overlaid on cadastral level maps of 1:5000 scale. These community-level inundation maps are extremely useful for assessing the population and infrastructure at risk. High-resolution Coastal Topography data required for modelling is generated by the National Remote Sensing Agency (NRSA) using ALTM and Cartosat Data. INCOIS has also generated a large database of model scenarios for different earthquakes that are being used for operational tsunami early warning. Communication of real-time data from seismic stations, tide gauges and BPR's to the early warning centre is very critical for generating timely tsunami warnings. A host of communication methods are employed for timely reception of data from the sensors as well as for dissemination of alerts. Indian Space Research Organisation (ISRO) has made an end-to-end communication plan using INSAT. A high level of redundancy is being built into the communication system to avoid single point failures. A state-of-the-art early warning centre is established at INCOIS with all the necessary computational and communication infrastructure that enables reception of real-time data from all the sensors, analysis of the data, generation and dissemination of tsunami advisories following a standard operating procedure. Seismic and sea-level data are continuously monitored in the Early Warning Centre using a custom-built software application jointly developed with MIS Tata Consultancy Services (TCS) that generates alarms alerts in the warning centre whenever a pre-set threshold is crossed. Tsunami warnings watches are then generated based on pre-set decision support rules and disseminated to the concerned authorities for action, following a Standard Operating Procedure. The efficiency of the end-to-end system was proved during the large undersea earthquake of 8.4 M that occurred on September 12, 2007 in the Indian Ocean. The National Early Warning Centre will generate and disseminate timely advisories to the Control Room of the Ministry of Home Affairs for further dissemination to the Public. For the dissemination of alerts to MHA a satellite-based virtual private network for disaster management support (VPN DMS) has been established. This network enables early warning centre to disseminate warnings to the MHA, as well as to the State Emergency Operations Centres. In addition, Messages will also be sent by Phone, Fax, SMS and e-mails to authorised officials. In case of confirmed warnings, the National Early Warning Centre is being equipped with necessary facilities to disseminate the advisories directly to the administrators, media and public through SMS, e-mail, Fax, etc. The cyclone warning network of IMD and electronic ocean information boards of INCOIS could be effectively used for dissemination of warnings directly to the public. Periodic workshops will be organized for the user community to familiarize them with the use of tsunami and storm surge advisories as well as inundation maps. Easily understandable publicity material on earthquake, tsunami and storm surges has been generated and will be distributed to the general public.

3718. (15-10-2007) NEW DELHI : For the first time, Eastern Railway is running a special train branded as "Howrah-Delhi Dollar Express". The Howrah-Delhi super fast bi-weekly 'Puja' special train (0231 Up) was flagged off by Shri Jayanta Kumar Saha, Additional Divisional Railway manager, Eastern Railway from Hawrah Station on 13th October 2007. This train will stop at Asansol, Dhanbad, Koderma, Gaya, Sasaram, Mughalsarai, Vindhachal, Allahabad, Kanpur and Delhi on both ways. M/s Bhawani Textile Ltd. having its office at OM Tower, 12th Floor, 32, J.L.Nehru Raod, Kolkata has been given a branding right for this trains. A total of 22 'Puja' special trains will run between Howrah and Delhi upto 19th November 2007.

3719. (16-10-2007) NEW DELHI : After testing their shooting skill the battling soldiers of Military pentathlon were set for the toughest of the events. The day started with Women-obstacle run. Two women competitors based on draw were to complete 500 meters long obstacle course of 16 obstacles. Forssten of Finland along with Tian Limna of China clocked 2 minutes 19.8 seconds were jointly adjudged the best women players of the event. The second position was also bagged by Chinese player who clocked 2 minutes 20 seconds. Team of China stood first in the event. Men competitors had to brave the conditions under scorching sun and sweltering heat to negotiate 20 obstacles. Frank of Germany clocked 2 minutes 16.8 seconds to be adjudged the best player of the event. HE Shugai of China with 2 minutes 20 seconds and Second Lieutenant Wang by finishing the race in 2 minutes 22 seconds were at second and third position. Over all Equador team scored first position. Women Judoka of China floored their opponents with skill and offensive spirit. In different weight categories, overall team championship with Gold was won by China. Italy won the Silver medal while Bronze medal was jointly won by Poland and Russia.

3720. (16-10-2007) NEW DELHI : Francis Samuel of Qatar became the fastest man at the 4th Military World Games, here today. He created the new CISM record in 100 mtrs men final by clocking 10.10 seconds. The earlier record was 10.18 seconds held by his country-mate T Mansoor. Italy's Simone Collio bagged the Silver with 10.29 seconds and Chyla Lukasz of Poland got the Bronze medal with 10.39 seconds. In the men's 400 mtr final Sudan's N Ali Bab Bakar clinched the Gold with 46.00 seconds. Dabrowski Daniel of Poland with 46.36 seconds and Amarasekara PS of Sri Lanka with 46.48 seconds bagged the silver and bronze medals respectively. Soudi Arabia's Hawsawi Edrees A I won the Gold in 400 mtrs hurdles with 50.26 seconds. De Jesus Sales Thiago of Brazil and Jeetender of India won the silver and bronze medals with the timings of 50.98 seconds and 51.70 seconds respectively. Slovekia's Brigita Langerholc bagged the Gold in 800 mtrs women final with 2:04.05 Min while Uzbekistan's Sidorova Anna won the silver with 2 : 04.70 Min. The Bronze went to Dziadkova Natallia of Belarus with the timing of 2 : 05.85 Min. In Men's Ple Vault final, Germany's Suerth Florian won the Gold with a jump of 5.20 M. Gensic Paul of USA won the Silver (5.10 M) and Matteo Rubbiani of Italy won the Bronze (5.00 M). A new Meet Record was created in Men 's Discus Throw by Malachowski Piotr of Poland with a throw of 65.87 M. The Silver medalis Kovago Zoltan of Hungary also bettered the Meet Record with a throw of 64.38 M. The Bronze went to Qatar's Al-Dossari Rashid Shafi (60.03 M). The earlier Meet Record in the category was held by A Seelig of Germany (63.52 M). Devetzi Chrvsopigi of Greece won the Gold in women's long jump with 6.69 M while Anna Pyatykh of Russia won the Silver medal with a jump of 6.23 M and Juravlyova Anastasiya of Uzbekistan won the Bronze with 6.21 M.

3721. (16-10-2007) NEW DELHI : In a closely contested team match for 50M Rifle Prone Chinese Women kept their winning streak securing the top spot in the team rankings by scoring 1775 points, 9 points today at Hyderabad University Shooting Range. Republic of Korea won the Silver by securing 1766 points. Ukraine came third with 1765 points. India finished fifteenth in the event. Chinese shooters [women] had maintained the lead throughout the three relays of 50M. In 25MTR Pistol shooting event for both men and women, only half matches were played today, in which Chinese seemed to be leaving only scraps for the opposition. This is an indication to the world that China is preparing itself well ahead for the forthcoming Olympics in the year 2008. The final tally of the results will be available after completion of the other half of the matches which would be played tomorrow. As per schedule for tomorrow, 300M Rifle [Men] for individual positions, 50M [Women] for individual positions and 25M Pistol {Men & Women} for team positions will be held.

3722. (16-10-2007) NEW DELHI : Russian wrestlers started their campaign.by winning one Gold and three Bronze medals in the 4th MWG at Lal Bahadur Shastri stadium here today. In Greeco Roman-Men 66kg category, Kovalenicd Seregy won the Gold while Kim Kumchol of D P R Korea won the Silver. Soomin Kim of Republic of Korea and Lebrus Mammadov of Azerbaijan were the Bronze medalists. In Greeco Roman-Men 56 kg category, Ennchul Park of Republic of Korea won the Gold and Vugar Ragmov of Ukraine got the Silver. Maksim Kazarski of Belarus and Mankiew Nazir of Russia were the Bronze medalists. Mehmet Ozal of Turkey bagged the Gold in Greeco Roman Men 96 kg category and Gergios Kaoutsioumpas of Greece won the Silver. The Bronze went to Ezerskis Mindaugas of Lithuania and Aslambek Khshto of Russia.

3723. (16-10-2007) NEW DELHI : The Juries for the Indian Panorama Section of International Film Festival of India (IFFI)-2007 today recommended 21 feature and 15 non-feature films for screening at International Film Festival at Goa in November 2007. Lenin Rajendran's Ratri Mazha (Night Rain-Malayalam) and Samir Chanda's Ek Nadir Galpo (Bengali) will represent the country at the Asian African and Latin American Competition of the 38th International Film Festival of India in Goa next month. The two juries for feature and non feature films headed by renowned film makers K S Sethumadhavan and Arun Khopkar respectively submitted their reports to the Secretary, Ministry of Information and Broadcasting, Smt. Asha Swarup. Ore Kadal (Malayalam), directed by Shyamaprasad will open the Indian Panorama feature film section, while Bagher Bacha (Bengali) directed by Bishnu Dev Halder will open the non-feature section of the prestigious Indian Panorama. The selections were made out of 119 feature and 149 non-feature films. The members of the feature film jury were Smt. Manju Borah, film maker from Guwahati, Shri Leslie Carvalho, film maker from Bangalore, Shri Abhijeet Dasgupta, film maker from Kolkata, Dr. Mrunalinni Patil Dayal, film maker from Mumbai and Smt. Shubhra Gupta, Film Critic from Delhi. The non-feature film jury comprised of Shri Pankaj Butalia film maker from Delhi, Smt Kavita Chaudhary, film maker from Mumbai and Shri Gautam Saikia, film maker from Guwahati.

3724. (16-10-2007) NEW DELHI : The march of technology has diminished distances and transformed the world into a global village. Internet and mobile revolution is sweeping across the country which allows one to be in touch with dear and near ones or to undertake professional decisions, just by a click of the mouse or a tap on the keyboard of a mobile phone. However, neither is the Department of Posts nor the era of letters have ceased to exist. Department of Posts was set up in the year 1854 and had 701 post offices. Rechristened as India Post recently. It has more than 150 thousand post offices, more than 26,000 departmental outlets and over 128,000 branch outlets and handles more than 15 billion mail pieces daily. This makes Indian postal system one of the largest in the world. The system covers rural areas with more than 89 thousand post offices. While the efforts are on to connect the villages by use of the latest technologies- the postal department too has been transforming itself to meet the challenges both in the urban and rural areas. The Postal department stands tall against the private courier service. Both in the rural and urban areas, postman has a personal bond in the locality, a strong human element that cannot be replicated by the courier service. One of the latest examples of innovation, a business opportunity and commitment to serve the society by the postal department is collection of traffic challans (fines) of Delhi Traffic Police through Postmen. Initially the project has been started in Delhi circle, but based on the success it could be replicated in other parts of the country. Delhi circle has signed an agreement with the Delhi Traffic Police for collection of Challans from defaulters effective from August 9, 2007. Aimed at simplifying the procedure of paying traffic fines, the postman will bring the challan along with money order form and a receipt book, the defaulter can pay the amount of challan to the postman then and there with a small service charge of Rs 5/- . This is aimed to make the payment of challan more public friendly. Another innovative scheme is the Bill Mail service that offers a huge benefit to utility service providers like power, telecom and water. Yet another customer oriented service is the Logistics Post for sending parcels and large consignments, across the nation and around the world. This service manages the entire distribution side of the logistics infrastructure from collection to distribution, from storage to carriage, from order preparation to order fulfilment. It is an ideal service for sending large consignments including multi-parcels, just-in-time parcels, bulk-break consignments and goods of any weight. While Parcel Post offers weight up to 35 kg, in respect of Logistics Post, there is no weight limit.

3725. (16-10-2007) NEW DELHI : Dr. Chandrapal, Secretary, Ministry of Micro, Small & Medium Enterprises has urged the young men and women to take the benefit of various programmes and schemes offered by the Central Government. He was inaugurating the National Conference on Employment through Entrepreneurship Development and launching the Entrepreneurship Development Scheme of the Ministry of Micro, Small & Medium Enterprises here today. Dr. Chandrapal said the Ministry of Micro, Small & Medium Enterprises was taking a number of steps to help the teeming millions of our country through three premier National Entrepreneurship Development Institutes. These are: National Institute for Entrepreneurship & Small Business Development (NIESBUD), National Institute for Micro, Small & Medium Enterprises (NIMSME) & Indian Institute of Entrepreneurship (IIE). He said these institutes strive to achieve the avowed objectives through a gamut of operations ranging from training, consultancy, research and education to extension and information services. The primary objectives of these institutes are to evolve standardised material and processes for selection, training support and sustenance of potential and existing entrepreneurs. These institutes also provide vital information and support to trainers, promoters and entrepreneurs by organising research and documentation relevant to entrepreneurship development. Besides, they offer consultancy nationally as well as internationally for promotion of entrepreneurship and small business development. They also work as a platform to share experience and expertise in Entrepreneurship Development across national frontiers. Dr. Chandrapal also said that the banks had been asked to provide collateral free loan upto Rs. 5 lakh to the entrepreneurs, which should motivate them to initiate small businesses.

3726. (16-10-2007) NEW DELHI : National Fertilizers Limited (NFL), a Public Sector Undertaking under the Ministry of Chemicals and Fertilizers today presented a dividend cheque of Rs.51.58 crore to the Govt. of India for the year 2006-07. The cheque was handed over to the Minister for Chemical & Fertilizer and Steel Shri Ram Vilas Paswan here today by Shri G S Mangat, Chairman and Managing Director, NFL. Minister of State for Chemicals and Fertilizers Dr. Shri B K Handique and Secretary Department of Fertilizers Dr. J S Sarma were also present on the occasion Recording 103.7% capacity utilization, NFL produced 33.51 lakh MT of urea during 2006-07. The company's sales turnover was Rs.3865.68 crore during 2006-07 as compared to Rs.3590.53 crore during 2005-06.It earned net profit of Rs.176.10 crore in2006-07.

3727. (16-10-2007) NEW DELHI : The two-day National Conference of Chief Registrars of Births and Deaths began here today. Inaugurating the Conference, the Registrar General of India, Shri D.K. Sikri complemented the Chief Registrars of different States and Union Territories on the good work done by their offices and hoped that it would be possible to achieve the target of 100 per cent registration of births and deaths by 2010 as mandated by the National Population Policy, 2000. The current level of registration is 64% for births and 58% for deaths. He informed that Himachal Pradesh, Kerala, Punjab, Tamil Nadu and West Bengal have achieved 100 per cent registration of births. Shri Sikri also outlined some of the reasons for low level of registration of births and deaths such as lack of awareness among people about the need and importance of registration, low priority accorded to this work and low utility of registration certificates, etc. The participants at the two-day Conference include Chief Registrars of States and Union Territories and representatives from UNICEF, Plan India, health department of different States, Office of Registrar General of India and Directorates of Census Operations in the States and Union Territories.

3728. (16-10-2007) NEW DELHI : Shri Sharad Pawar, Union Minister of Agriculutre & Consumer Affairs, Food & Public Distribution has said that the Right to Food Approach complements food security in terms of food availability, accessibility and utilization with human dignity and cultural acceptability. Addressing the World Food Day celebrations here today, he said the country is committed to ensure food security for every citizen. We have been following a twin-track approach in this regard to strengthen productivity and livelihoods at one level and implementing social safety nets for those unable to provide for themselves at another level, he added. Keeping in view the challenges of growing population and the need for food security, two major programmes have been launched recently to augment food production and availability in the country. The first one is the 'National Food Security Mission' targeted to push both production and productivity of stable food grains such as wheat, rice and pulses on a mission mode. The other programme 'Rashtriya Krishi Vikas Yojna' provides for additional assistance by Central Government as 100% grant to incentivize States to take up agriculture development on priority and in a comprehensive manner with definite action plans. He expressed the hope that with such major initiatives, there will be enough production to take care of the country's food security requirements. Shri Pawar stated that towards ensuring social safety net for food and nutritional security for our citizens, the States interventions cover the Targeted Public Distribution System. Under this, subsidized food grains are being distributed to the poorest of the poor families under the Antyodaya Anna Yojna. Under various welfare schemes, more than 50 lakh tonnes of food grains were distributed last year. To ensure that there is no adverse impact on food security in the country, the Central Government maintains the required buffer stock of food grains as per norms, procures food grains at minimum support prices from the farmers and also imports wheat when required from abroad. The Minister pointed out that the Central Issue Prices of food grains distributed under the targeted public distribution system have not been increased over last six years. Shri Kantilal Bhuria, Minister of State for Agriculture, Dr. Daniel Gustafson, Country Director, FAO and Dr. P.K. Mishra, Secretary, Department of Agriculture, Dr. Mangla Rai, DG, ICAR also addressed the gathering. World Food Day is observed every year as an International Day on 16th October, the founding day of Food and Agriculture Organisation. The theme for this year is 'The Right to Food'.

3729. (16-10-2007) NEW DELHI : The Union Minister of Shipping, Road Transport & Highways, Thiru T.R. Baalu called on Sir Anerood Jugnauth, President of the Republic of Mauritius today and discussed issues relating to shipping and port sectors. Later, he inaugurated the state of the art Mauritius Maritime Training Academy at Pointe aux Sables in Mauritius today. The function was organized by the Ministry of Public Infrastructure, Land Transport & Shipping of the Republic of Mauritius. Speaking on the occasion, Thiru T.R. Baalu said that this Training Academy would act as a bridge to further augment the bilateral cooperation between the two countries. He said that in due course, apart from having experienced trainers, this Academy would have to conduct training for even deck and engineering officers and would also have to install a large number of training equipments such as lifeboats, life rafts and various types of simulators etc. To equip the Academy with all these necessary facilities, there would be need for tangible cooperation between India and Mauritius, Thiru Baalu added. Stating that the Mauritius is in the hands of a visionary and progressive leadership, the Minister said that it could be clearly seen that policy makers are aiming to create a world-class infrastructure for Maritime Training. The Mauritius Maritime Academy will be undertaking various courses such as training for efficient deck hand, seafarers forming part of a navigation or engine room watch, safety training for personal direct services to passengers, proficiency in crisis management etc. Narrating the Indian experience in maritime training, Thiru Baalu said that the Maritime Training was privatised in India in 1998 and resultantly, it has now about 130 Maritime Training Institutes located across the country, as compared to only four Government-controlled Institutions in 1998. The privatisation of training had a multiplier effect as it has resulted in enhanced access to the maritime education & employment to remote parts of the country, the number of employment opportunities as seafarers increased substantially and a large pool of trained manpower has been created for taking over as teachers, surveyors and other professionals associated with Maritime Industry. The Minister said that due to high quality of training and stringent controls, the Indian seafarers, especially in those in the officers' category are well regarded all over the world and consequently, only about one-third of these seafarers work on the Indian ships and the remaining two-thirds get employment on the foreign flag vessels. He said that we are in the process of rationalizing of our employment conditions, and wage structure to attract and retain talent in this sector.

3730. (16-10-2007) NEW DELHI : The Government has sanctioned a Special Education and Book Grant to about 16,000 workers of 13 closed tea gardens of North Bengal. A cheque for Rs.1.7 crore was handed over to Shri R. Ranjit DM, Jalpaiguri by Shri Pranab Mukherjee, Minister for External Affairs, for disbursement to the beneficiaries. Speaking on the occasion, Shri Mukherjee reiterated the commitment of the UPA government for transforming the tea industry in the country and in North Bengal in particular. He highlighted the steps already been taken by the Tea Board to launch a special fund for replantation and to create new markets abroad. He congratulated the Tea Board for this humanitarian gesture keeping in view the distress being faced by workers and their families in North Bengal. He urged the Tea Board to strengthen its research and extension system in North Bengal. Shri Jairam Ramesh, Minister of State for Commerce, informed about the priority being given to opening of closed tea gardens, to address the concerns of ailing tea gardens and to create infrastructure for value-addition. He also underscored the social and economic significance of small tea-growers who now account for about 25% of North Bengal's tea production but who are in need of greater financial and technical assistance. The Centre for Tea Engineering being launched by the Tea Board at IIT, Kharagpur will develop new, cost-effective processing technologies for small tea growers. He stated that there are about 12,000 small tea-growers in North Bengal but just about 2500 are registered with the Tea Board. "The goal must be universal registration so that all small tea growers can derive benefit from Tea Board's schemes and programmes. The Tea Board has catalysed the formation of 19 Self Help Groups (SHGs) of small tea growers with a total membership of around 1200. The formation such SHGs is key to seaming a better deal for small tea growers", Shri Ramesh added. Shri Jairam Ramesh also informed that the allocation for labour welfare in the Tea Board's programmes has gone up from Rs.5 crore in the X Plan to Rs.50 crore in the XI Plan. He further mentioned that efforts are on to see, how central programmes being implemented by panchayat bodies can benefit tea garden workers who are covered separately under the Plantation Labour Act. The Tea Board had issued show-cause notices to all owners of closed tea gardens in Kerala, West Bengal and Assam on October 4th asking them to respond within ten days as to why Section 16(E) of the Tea Act, 1953 should not be invoked against them. This Section empowers the central government to take over, without any investigation, any tea garden lying closed for more than three months for purposes of finding a new owner. As of now, just 3 of the 13 closed tea gardens in North Bengal have responded to the show cause notice. In Kerala, 4 of the six remaining closed tea gardens have responded.

3731. (16-10-2007) NEW DELHI: Even as the first fragments of forensic evidence of the Shringar Cinema bombing in Ludhiana have begun to trickle in, Punjab police investigators find themselves with a mounting list of suspects — and, as yet, little hard evidence to work with. National Security Guard experts have determined that the bomb which ripped through the theatre was built around a core of Research Department Explosive, but officials said its final composition and construction would be known only after final results were available. Punjab police sources said they were focussing on the possible role of the Babbar Khalsa International (BKI)—the last Khalistan terror group believed to have credible offensive capabilities. Officials note that the globally-proscribed BKI, which frequently targeted migrant workers from Bihar during the past, has been desperate to register success. "Ever since the Inter-Services Intelligence started to choke off funding to the BKI in 2005, its Lahore-based chief Wadhawa Singh has been seeking to mount a major operation to raise funds from sympathisers in Europe and the United States of America," a New Delhi-based intelligence official told *The Hindu.* Only last month did the Punjab police seize 3.5 kg of RDX from a car owned by Jagraon resident Gurpreet Singh, son of a former terrorist. Investigators say Gurpreet Singh, who is absconding, met Wadhawa Singh earlier this year, after travelling to Lahore through Kuala Lumpur. Last year too, the Punjab police found evidence that the BKI was seeking to mount offensive operations. Four BKI terrorists, linked to a module controlled by the absconding Beant Singh assassin Jagtar Singh Tara, were arrested on March 21, 2006, and one kg of RDX was recovered. Just a day earlier, the Delhi police held the BKI operations chief Paramjit Singh Bheora and associates. Four kg of RDX was found in the terrorists' safe-house near Karnal. In 2005, the Delhi police arrested top BKI operative Jagtar Singh Hawara after his organisation bombed two movie theatres in New Delhi to protest what they claimed was its anti-Sikh politics. Hawara, architect of the 1995 assassination of Chief Minister Beant Singh, escaped from Chandigarh's Burail Jail in 2004. He was sentenced to death earlier this year. But intelligence officials also said the evidence available so far did not justify making a determination on which terror group most likely carried out Sunday's strike. Islamist terror groups have hit targets in Punjab before—a fact of significance given the spate of recent attacks nationwide. Among the largest terror strikes conducted by the Islamist terror groups in Punjab was the March 1997 bombing of a parking lot outside the Jalandhar City Railway Station. Six people were killed and 13 injured. An ammonium nitrate-based bomb packed in a still can was used to fabricate the device used in the explosion. New Delhi resident Amir Hashim, a Lashkar-e-Taiba operative, who operated under the code-name Kamran, was later convicted for his role in the bombing, as well as a series of prior strikes in Punjab, Haryana and the national capital.

3732. (16-10-2007) NEW DELHI : Shri A.Raja, Minister of Communications and Information Technology has said that in the past decade, the Indian telecom sector has gone through a total transformation. India now has the fastest growing telecom sector adding more than seven million subscribers every month and have almost reached 250 million subscribers three months ahead of the target date. Shri Raja was speaking at Curtain Raiser Ceremony of India Telecom-2007 here today. The growth momentum has shifted in a big way to small towns and rural areas. What lies ahead is far greater and far tougher than the road that travelled so far, he said. The Minister said that while we have been keeping pace with the latest technological advances in telecommunications, the indigenous value addition in our networks has been on a much lower side. A close look, however, reveals that we are far from reaping the benefits of the potential that exists. Rapidly changing technology along with a liberalised import regime has led to a situation where most of the equipment is currently imported. While the increasing size of Indian telecom market has encouraged most of the global telecom players to set up their manufacturing facilities in India, there is certainly a lot of scope to adopt the technology and undertake further indigenous value addition to meet the day to day need of the common man and India specific requirements. In such a situation, setting up of these Centres of Excellence was long overdue. Therefore, we have put them in place in a record time of only 9 months, Shri Raja said. These COEs being established in Public Private Partnership mode at the top most academic institutions of the country are needed to embolden the R&D efforts and enhance the much needed talent pool. COEs can play a catalytic role in our endeavours. It would be good idea for these COEs to develop telecom and IT solutions for rural areas of India at an affordable price, the Minister said. Two MoUs were signed today in this regard. The first between IIM Ahmedabad, IDEA and DoT and the second between IIT Kharagpur, Vodafone Essar and DoT. He congratulated IDEA, Vodafone-Essar, IIM Ahmedabad, IIT Kharagpur and the industry associations for this initiative. The other proposed COEs are not far behind, he added. The remaining 5 COEs will be set up progressively in the first half of 2008. He urged the COEs to focus on niche areas. In his key note address Shri D.S.Mathur, Secretary, Department of Telecommunication said this is a historic day for the Department and commended the academic institutes and the telecom service providers along with their industry associations for their initiative and enthusiasm in nurturing and promoting the concept of setting up of Telecom Centres of Excellence.

3733. (16-10-2007) NEW DELHI : On the second day of the Round Robin in men's volleyball today at Yusufguda Indoor stadium, India comfortably outplayed Latvia 25-17, 25-19, 25-16. A confident Indian team beat Latvia in straight sets gaining the first points of the tournament. Maintaining a lead right from the beginning the host team was in a commanding position at 23-13 and went on to take the first set 25-17. In the second set, Indians took the early lead after which the Latvians closed in but could not stop Indians from taking the set 25-19. In the third set the teams were at equal level 8-9 till halfway but the Indian aggression came through enabling them to sail through 25-16 in style. The Indians were better placed technically and put the pressure on the opposition at crucial moments in the match. In the other Pool B match, China upset fancied Brazil in straight three sets 25-23, 25-21,25-22. In the first set China took an early lead winning it by a narrow margin. In the second set the Brazilians geared up for an early lead but could not sustain the tempo and the youthful Chinese team overpowered them to take the set 25-21.In the third set scores were level at 20-20. But China edged past with better play in the last stages taking the set 25-22.

3734. (16-10-2007) NEW DELHI : Shri A.Raja, Minister of Communications and Information Technology will present awards to the winners of the Fourth Computer Literacy Excellence Awards for Schools-2005 on October 18, 2007 in New Delhi. The Computer Literacy Excellence Awards Scheme for schools in an attempt to bring the nation's children at par with young achievers of the world. While demonstrating outstanding competence, the 51 State/UT level awardees have created a benchmark or excellence in computer education for the rest of the schools across India to follow. There are two category of awards-one for Private/ Government aided school Category 'A' and Government/Municipal School as Category 'B'. The Department of Information Technology, Ministry of Communications and Information Technology in the year 2002 has instituted an Award Scheme for Excellence in Computer Literacy and Information Technology in schools at State and National level to create IT awareness among schools and to encourage Computer Literacy among students in early stage of schooling. All recognized schools in India, Government and Private, teaching computers and information technology in their schools are eligible to compete for the award.

3735. (16-10-2007) NEW DELHI : In women's volleyball at the 4th MWG at 1 EME Centre Indoor stadium today, Netherlands defeated Canada 25-15; 25-27; 25-18; 26-24. Netherlands having won the first set 25-15 could not hold on to the lead, because of some wonderful spiking and blocking by the Canadian players. This helped Canadians win the second set 27-25. In the fourth set the Canadians were leading 5-0 at early stage.. However the Netherlands kept the momentum to take the set 26-24. Meanwhile DPR Korea beat USA. In the first set, USA took the lead 5-0. Koreans came back strongly showcasing skills in all spheres of the game. Ok Sim Han with some good smashes got the first set in favour of DPR Korea. It seemed that USA gave up after the first set and lost meekly in the other two sets. The final scores were 25-16, 25-09 and 25-11 in favour of DPR Korea. The first match between China and Italy was a one sided affair with the Chinese women outplaying the Italians in all aspects of the game. The Chinese were led by their captain and Olympion Ms Song Nina to outwit the Italians taking the match 25-07, 25-12, 25-14.

3736. (16-10-2007) NEW DELHI : Indian boxers had yet another fine day's outing in the ring with all four boxers emerging winners in their respective bouts on the second day of the qualifying rounds at the World Military Games in Hyderabad today. Chief Petty Officer AL Lakra, a Commonwealth and National Games champion defeated DPR Korea's First Lt Won Il Kim (19-13) in the Featherweight category. Havaldar HK Belwal, a four-time National champion in the Flyweight category totally outclassed D Youssouf of Guinea Republic and the referee had to stop the contest in the second round itself. In other two bouts featuring Indians, Satya Raju in the Light Welterweight category defeated Herbert Nkabiti of Botswana (33-11) while in the Middleweight category Havaldar Amarjit Singh overwhelmed Martirosian Arsen (14-8) of Ukraine.

3737. (17-10-2007) NEW DELHI : Trailing by 14 points behind World Champions China, the Indian shooting quartet of Chandra Kumar Choudhary, Vijay Kumar, Pemba Tamang and Hambir Singh helped the hosts win a silver medal in the 25M Centre Fire pistol (Men) team event at the Military World Games here in Hyderabad, today. The Chinese tally of 1758 included the best three performances of Zheng Gao (587), Yadong Liu (586) and Yongde Jin (585). The Indians tallied 1744, Vijay Kumar (590), Choudhary (577) and Hambir (577). The bronze was taken by Russians with a tally of 1740, Sergey Polyakov (582), Mikhail Nestruev (581) and Anton Guriyanov (577). In the Women 50M rifle prone individual event, China was matchless and made a clean sweep of the three medals. First Lieutenant Jiao Yi struck gold while First Lieutenant Yin Wen and Cadet Wan Xyangyan took the silver and bronze respectively, all scoring 595 points each. In the 25M women rifle sports team event, China secured gold with 1730 points, Korea Republic the silver with 1719 points and Belarus the bronze with 1705 points.

3738. (17-10-2007) NEW DELHI : Two days All India Editors' Conference, jointly organized by Press Information Bureau and Government of Jammu & Kashmir commenced here today. Inaugurating the two-day Conference, Jammu & Kashmir Chief Minister, Ghulam Nabi Azad stressed the need for adequately publicizing massive developmental activities in the social sector across the country. He said that in the present era of 24 hour TV news channels, it is generally negative news that is preferred and positive news particularly developmental activities are ignored. He urged the media that they should have balanced outlook and give developmental activities proper share of coverage. Referring to Jammu & Kashmir, the Chief Minister said that there has been overall improvement in the situation and the State Government has taken several initiatives for speeding up developmental process. He also said the Government is giving top priority to prevent human right violations and this year there has been no custodial disappearance. The Chief Minister also enumerated the steps taken by Government to curb the corruption, improve work culture and enhance public welfare. He referred to amendment in anti-defection law, down-sizing of the Ministry and double shift system in construction activities. Union Minister for Rural Development, Dr. Raghuvansh Prasad Singh said that there has been 48 percent hike in spendings on rural developmental schemes in the last three years and the plan size for rural developmental schemes in Eleventh Plan will be to the tune of 225 lakh crore rupees. He said that Government wants to ensure that employment is available to the rural population and they have all basic facilities like road connectivity, safe water and healthcare. He said that National Rural Employment Guarantee Act is land mark step and the scheme which was initially introduced in 230 districts across the country will be implemented in all the districts from April 2008. Referring to Jammu & Kashmir, he lauded the efforts of Chief Minister in enhancing capacity of the State to spend funds available under centrally sponsored schemes and pledged to help from Centre in making Jammu & Kashmir the model State. After the inaugural session today on day one there were three interactive sessions dedicated to rural development, education and railway. In the first session, Dr. Raghuvansh Prasad Singh interacted with the visiting editors and local media persons about the various rural developmental schemes and overall scenario in rural developmental sector. In the second session, Minister of State for Human Resources Development, Shri M.A.A. Fatmi interacted with the media and implementation of Sarva Shiksha Abhiyan and Midday Meal Scheme. He announced setting up of 51 Kastoorba Gandhi Awasi Vidhayalas on the pattern of Kendriya Vidhyalas.

3739. (17-10-2007) NEW DELHI : Congress Spokesman Dr. Shakeel Ahmed said the Election Commission has directed that some officers in Gujarat be removed from their posts. He said these changes are rather cosmetic changes and are not enough. Lots of complaints were made earlier and even now number of complaints are being made regarding the misuse of machinery being used in elections officers, be they in the Civil Services, IPS or other services that are related to electioneering. These officers, whose integrity is suspect, should be removed immediately from taking part in any election work and the Election Commission should take a sterner stand in the removal of these officers. On the nuke-deal issue Dr. Ahmed said that Shri L.K. Advani has recently commented that the deal is not in public interest and is undesirable and is not in the interest of the nation. We do not agree with his statement because this deal is surely in the interest of the nation. The nation will benefit in terms of power generation which, as we all know, is essential for the progress of the nation in many ways. Dr. Ahmed said that when the NDA was in power, it was their leaders who said it was in furtherance of the process that was started by the NDA and the Congress Party should not take the credit for it. Today the NDA has the cheek to say that the nuke deal is not a good deal. Second, the NDA was ready to sign the CTBT and it was Shri Advani who went to the CIA office for the same and whether the prestige of our country was or was not lowered then, it is for Shri Advani and his partymen to explain to the nation. To a question whether the PM is not happy with the alliance partners and that he and the party are willing to step down Dr. Ahmed said, that these are rumours and neither the party nor the PM have issued any such statements. In fact the PM has full confidence in the alliance partners. To a question that technically, the Congress Party has subjugated the authority of the Prime Minister Dr. Ahmed said, the Prime Minister is as competent, as powerful as he was when the Government was formed. Of course we have a coalition government. There are issues which we have discussed among ourselves and it is the duty of the government to take into confidence all the alliance partners and that is exactly what we are trying to do and for which we are meeting on the 22nd of October. To a question that Shri Sharad Pawar, Shri Karunanidhi and Shri Lalu Prasad Yadav are of the opinion that the N-deal is put on hold Dr. Ahmed said it is absolutely wrong to say that the deal is in cold storage or on hold. It is very much in the offing and we are discussing among ourselves to narrow down the differences between our alliance partners and we are pursuing it and we are all for the deal. If there is any concern of any of our allies we are duty bound to discuss it again and take a final decision which again depends on the meeting which is to be held on 22nd October. As far as timeframe is concerned, the Director General of IAEA has said there is no timeframe, the Assistant Secretary of State, Asian Affairs Shri Boucher has also said there is no timeframe. Therefore we will discuss and come to a decision. Dr. Ahmed added that American President George Bush and Prime Minister Manmohan have discussed the issue and that they are not that ignorant of the facts.

3740. (17-10-2007) NEW DELHI : India sailed into the top four of the men's volleyball by beating Brazil 3-1 at the Yusufguda Volleyball Stadium in Hyderabad, today. After three rounds of matches in Pools A and B-Korea Republic, India, Qatar and China are the teams who are into the top four teams of the tournament whereas Netherlands, Latvia, Canada and Brazil will fight for 5th to 8th positions. In a spirited performance the Indian youngsters rose to the challenge by beating the mighty South Americans in a four set thriller. Brazil started well leading in the first set by a good margin. However, the Indians were fighting tooth and nail. The Brazilians were matched by the Indian youngsters point by point. However they lost the first set which Brazil took 25-23 taking 1-0 lead. Not taking it easy the Indians took the early lead in the second set and went on to take the set 25-17. A jeering crowd present in large numbers at the Kotla Vijay Bhaskar Reddy Stadium danced and cheered Indian team to the tune of 'Chak De India'. In the third set the roar from the crowd started reaching a higher level as India took an 8-4 lead. Indians were putting the pressure on the Brazilians forcing them to make mistakes. India took the decisive third set 26-24 to go up 2-1 in the match. The Brazilians fought back but the Indians were not in the mood to give any quarter. In the set the pressure was showing on the Brazilians as they argued with the umpires several times who was mostly not convinced. The fourth set was won by India convincingly 25-17 taking the match 3-1 as the crowd set the stadium on fire with their enthusiasm and victory chants. In another match this morning Qatar made a clean sweep of Netherlands beating them 3-0.Qatar dominated the first set winning it 25-22. The second set saw a close fight being given from Netherlands but the set was taken by Qatar 27-25. In the third set the Dutch lost 16-25. The overall slackness on part of the Netherlands team showed on the field and the result. In the other two matches Korea Republic beat Canada comfortably in three straight sets. The Korean domination started from the beginning and they pocketed the first set 25-17 before the Canadians could settle in the game. In the second set Canadians could only do marginally better and let the Koreans take the set 25-20. In the third and deciding set the Koreans won 25-18. In the fourth match in the evening China surpassed Latvia 3-0. The first set was taken by the Chinese 25-20. The Latvians resisted but the Chinese were more skilled and had their winning plans well chalked out. The second set also saw some resistance being put up by the Latvians but they rarely had the answers to the Chinese smashes to let the Chinese take it 25-17. In the third set Chinese had easy walkover winning the set 25-12. In tomorrow's fixtures in the second round of Round Robin league India plays Korea Republic (at 2 pm) whereas Qatar plays China (at 4 pm) and Netherlands faces Latvia (at 10 am) and Canada takes on Brazil (at 12 noon).

3741. (17-10-2007) NEW DELHI : Following is the text of the Closing Remarks of the Prime Minister, Dr. Manmohan Singh at the 2nd India-Brazil-South Africa (IBSA) Summit meeting in South Africa today: "I am happy to say that our deliberations today were most fruitful. We have discussed ways of pooling our strengths and limited resources to maximum benefit. This gives me confidence that the IBSA process is moving into a phase where our trilateral collaboration will show concrete results. IBSA is a unique model of trans-national cooperation. Our three countries come from three different continents but share similar world views and aspirations. If we can make a success of our model of cooperation based on collective self-reliance, it will serve as an example for all developing countries. We have today found a renewed convergence of interests on major international issues of contemporary importance. We need to forge the closest cooperation possible, so that we can together ensure a more equitable international political and economic order. The world is already looking upon the IBSA framework as a significant step forward in the emergence of a global partnership for development. We had a constructive discussion on the Doha Round of trade talks. This has emerged as an important issue facing the international community, in which each of our countries has an important stake. We committed ourselves to working towards securing a balanced and successful outcome of the talks. The IBSA process has enabled parliamentarians, civil society, academia, mass media, women and other segments of society to engage with each other. We greatly value their contribution in reinforcing the efforts of the three governments. Over a period of time, IBSA should emerge as a peoples' movement. The high level involvement of business and industry in IBSA is particularly encouraging. Governments can only do so much. We should leverage public-private partnerships to fill funding gaps and increase efficiency in key sectors of our cooperation. The agreements and the Declaration that we will be signing will provide a new impulse to our cooperation. They reflect our emerging priorities. The implementation of the decisions we have taken should be carefully monitored, and a regular system of feedback should be put in place. I am confident that under the Chairmanship of South Africa, our joint efforts in the framework of IBSA will acquire even greater resilience and dynamism. I am most grateful to President Mbeki for the warm and generous hospitality we have received during our stay in this beautiful country."

3742. (17-10-2007) NEW DELHI: After voicing its stiff opposition to the India-U.S. civilian nuclear deal, the Left on Tuesday took up the issue of price rise and collapse of the Public Distribution System (PDS) that have hit the common people hard over the recent months. Communist Party of India (CPI) leaders, including its general secretary A.B. Bardhan, national secretary and MP D. Raja, national secretariat member Amarjeet Kaur, and party workers held a demonstration at Jantar Mantar and courted arrest. The protest was against rising prices, continued hoarding and black marketing of essential commodities. "The nuclear deal might have been pushed back, but the danger to the government still remains. Now the issue is of price rise which is affecting the common people. We might have to reconsider our decision to support the United Progressive Alliance if adequate steps are not taken in this regard," Mr. Bardhan said while addressing the protesters. "Our support is based on the Common Minimum Programme (CMP) which says that the PDS will be streamlined and also that prices would be kept in check but the CMP is not being followed," he said. Criticising the move to opening agri-retail segment to the big corporate houses and multi-national retail chains such as Wal-Mart, Mr. Bardhan said that some farmers might benefit in the beginning but everything would turn out to be a sham. Mr. Bardhan said the Prime Minister had claimed that it was not an "one-issue" government but key issues such as price rise, food security, plight of unorganised workers have always been there. "Though belatedly, good sense prevailed upon Prime Minister Manmohan Singh and what exactly will happen to the nuclear deal will be known on October 22 when UPA negotiators will talk to the Left parties," the CPI general secretary later told reporters. "The government claims it is the government of the aam admi, but in practice it is not taking adequate steps to control price rise," said CPI leader D. Raja.

3743. (17-10-2007) NEW DELHI : Republic of Korea, Belarus, Lithuania and Latvia entered the semifinals of the Handball at Yousufguda stadium here today. The day started off with Greece beating India in the first match by 32-27. Both India and Greece could not qualify for the Semifinals. Indians were leading in the first half. Later in the second half two Indians players were suspended for two minutes. Greece used this opportunity to take the score to 27-21. They maintained the lead to finally beat India 32-27. India is yet to play Lithuania tomorrow, which will decide India's standing in the last three. India's captain, Petty Officer INC Singh of INS Satavahana, Vishakhapatnam, a confident shooter and a promising player of international standard scored 30 goals and is one among the top goal scorers of the tournament. " We generally play on mud courts. In the Para flex courts the game is faster which we lack " says INC Singh. One of the contenders, Belarus beat UAE 34-30. Belarus was found playing easy today as they did not want any player to get injured as they play semifinals on October 19th. The highest scorer of the tournament till now is B Pukhoski who scored 44 goals. Today he scored 16 goals. The match between Latvia and Qatar ended in Latvia beating Qatar by 28-19 to enter the Semifinals. The most interesting match was between Korea Rep and Lithuania. The match was tough as both teams were equally competitive. By half time Korea leading with the score at 12-10. Korea Rep finally beat Lithuania 29-24, to reach the semifinals.

3744. (17-10-2007) NEW DELHI : Following is the text of the Remarks of the Prime Minister, Dr. Manmohan Singh during his intervention at the 'Social Development Strategy for India-Brazil-South Africa' in South Africa today: The importance of social development was recognized by us as far back as in the Brasilia Declaration of 2003. Subsequently, we had constituted a Working Group on Social Development. We had also decided that the IBSA Fund for Alleviation of Poverty and Hunger will work in close cooperation with this Working Group. In addition, other Working Groups have been established on subjects like education, health, culture, human settlement, environment and skills development. Most recently, we have also set up a Women's Forum. South Africa recently hosted a seminar of practitioners to exchange experiences on our respective social development strategies. Social development has both national and international dimensions. An effective Social Development strategy has to ensure synergy between these two dimensions. It is a happy coincidence that it was South Africa that hosted the World Summit on Social Development in 2002. We thus have a rich menu of political declarations and initiatives. The question is what we-as India, Brazil and South Africa-can bring to the table based on our own real life experiences. We are pluralistic democracies, developing economies and aspire for rapid economic growth. I am aware of President Lula's Bolsa Familia programme and President Mbeki's programme for Accelerated Skill Development. India's current 11th Five Year Plan has been formulated on the basis of a political mandate for inclusive growth. Based on this vision of an equitable and prosperous world, we have in the last few years, put in place programmes which can accelerate the processes of development in an equitable, fair and all-encompassing manner. Based on our common experiences, I would like to suggest that a Social Development Strategy could emerge from the IBSA process having some of the following eight elements: Rapid Economic Growth: It is only within the framework of a rapidly expanding economy can we generate the necessary resources for investing in social development. We have to have faith in the creativity and enterprise of our people and create favourable conditions for these to have full play. Inclusivity: Economic growth cannot happen in isolation. Unless all sections of society derive benefits from such growth and develop a stake in the growth process, we will courting social and political instability. Disparities of any type-regional, gender, inter-community, inter-group-harm the growth process in the long run. However, addressing this aspect is easier said than done. All of us have diverse experiences which we need to share and learn from. Human Resource Development: While growth processes may be favourable, it is essential that people are empowered and enabled to become active participants in these processes. The key to this is education and skill development. Adequate resources need to be committed to education and skill development at all levels. Focus on equitable infrastructure: Often, the infrastructure needs of the poor are neglected. But they are important facilitators of growth. There must be adequate investment in rural infrastructure and connectivity, clean drinking water, sanitation facilities, health care and social welfare.

3745. (17-10-2007) NEW DELHI : Following is the text of the Remarks of the Prime Minister, Dr. Manmohan Singh during his interaction with the India-Brazil-South Africa Business Council in South Africa today: "I am particularly happy that the Business Forum has become an integral part of the IBSA process. A strong trade and economic partnership is essential for the success of IBSA. India, Brazil and South Africa are amongst the most dynamic developing economies of the world. We have obvious complementarities and strengths that we ought to share and build upon. We have set ourselves a modest target of 15 billion dollars by 2010 for trade among our three countries. My suggestion to our business leaders would be to aim to achieve this by 2009 and then go on to double that by 2012. Business must be pro-active. We in government assure you that we will endeavour to create the necessary environment for closer intra-IBSA trade and investment. We also hope that the Business Forum will work actively to create awareness of the opportunities that our three large markets provide. Each of us has strengths in Science & Technology. I would urge the business leaders present to look at innovative approaches to exploit these strengths including through joint R&D projects, particularly in sectors such as manufacturing, pharmaceuticals and ICT. Energy security is a major challenge confronting us. We should use synergies in this area to our common benefit. Brazil has comparative strengths in ethanol and bio-fuels; South Africa in Coal to Liquid and Gas to Liquid technologies. India has strengths in wind and solar energy. We need to look at how trilateral ventures in these areas can be made viable business models. Business also has a social responsibility. Within IBSA, we are in the process of elaborating a common Social Development strategy. We would welcome inputs from the business community to shape an effective public-private partnership in this area. Let me conclude by emphasizing how important it is for our business and industry to come together if we are to realise our objective of integrating our economies."

3746. (17-10-2007) NEW DELHI : The Committee of Eminent Persons constituted by the Government of India on Sethu Samudram Shipping Channel Project has already started functioning at Malligai, No.30/95, P.S. Kumarasamy Raja (Greenways) Road, Chennai 600 028. Eleven objections/suggestions have been received up to 16th October, 2007 by Registered AD/delivered against an acknowledgement. The Committee has invited objections and suggestions from all concerned including the writ Petitioners in the court cases in the Hon'ble Supreme Court of India having interest in the Sethu Samudram Shipping Channel Project. The Committee will consider all suggestions/proposals/documents after giving them a personal hearing. It is reiterated that the objections/suggestions have to be submitted either through Registered AD or delivered at the above address against an acknowledgment on all days up to 31st October 2007 from 1000 hours to 1700 hours except on 21st October, 2007. The Committee will also give personal hearing from 29th October, 2007 to 6th November, 2007 (all days including holidays) at the above address between 1000 hours and 1700 hours. Out of these days, the period from 4th to 6th November, 2007 has been kept for giving personal hearing to the Petitioners, who can come on any of these days as per their convenience. To participate in the hearing, proof of having submitted the objections/suggestions in the form of an acknowledgement of the Committee or Postal receipt have to be produced by all concerned except the Petitioners.

3747. (17-10-2007) NEW DELHI : Shri Arjun Singh, Minister of Human Resource Development is leading a delegation of parliamentarians and officials to the 34th General Conference of United Nations Educational, Scientific and Cultural Organisation (UNESCO) which commenced in Paris yesterday. The Minister who will address the Conference on Friday is also scheduled to have bilateral meetings with Ministers of South Africa, Afghanistan, France, Pakistan and other countries with whom India is engaged in strengthening links in the field of education. The General Conference comes at a time when UNESCO, which has recently completed 60 years, faces resource constraints and continued challenges of illiteracy, low quality education, lack of teachers, etc., around the world. The Conference is expected to approve a biennial budget for 2008-2009 for approximately US$630 million.

3748. (17-10-2007) NEW DELHI : A total of 45 films will compete for the top award in the International Competition and twenty for the award in the Asian Panorama in the forthcoming International Children's Film Festival, THE GOLDEN ELEPHANT-15, taking place in Hyderabad next month. Over 300 films were submitted from about forty countries for the Festival, which is organised by the Children's Film Society, India, and the Information and Broadcasting Ministry in collaboration with the state Government of Andhra Pradesh. The Festival, which takes place every second year, will be held from Children's Day November 14 which marks the birth anniversary of the country's first Prime Minister Jawaharlal Nehru and will continue till November 20. An international jury headed by renowned short filmmaker Mike Pandey will judge the films in the International competition. The international jury also includes veteran filmmaker V G Samant, producer Mathew Horrocks, Andi Spark of Griffith film School, Toon Boom CEO Joan Vogelesang, and Toronto International Children's Film Festival Director Jane

Schoettle. The Asian Panorama jury is headed by eminent broadcaster Chris McDonald and other members are Poland's Izabela Wierzbinska, Bulgaria's Tsvetomira Niikolova, and India's Mrinal Kulkarni. In addition, a children's jury will be set up to judge the films from the perspective of the young.

3749. (17-10-2007) NEW DELHI : India has a major role in the future of global food business as it has a strong base in agriculture and provides a large and varied raw material base for food processing industry. It is a country of over 1.10 billion consumers and there is a largely untapped domestic market of 1000 million consumers in the food processing sector and two hundred million more consumers are expected to shift to processed food by 2010. This was stated by Union Minister of State (Independent Charge) for Food Processing Industries, Shri Subodh Kant Sahai at the opening of Indian Pavilion in the Trade Fair "Anuga-2007" of International Food Sector at Cologne, Germany from October 13-17, 2007. The fair has been jointly organised by Ministry of Food Processing Industry (MFPI) and Federation of Indian Chambers of Commerce Industry (FICCI), Agriculture Products Export Development Authority (APEDA) and Industry Associations. The Minister said that there are many areas for investment in this sector which include Mega Food Parks, Agri-Infrastructure, Supply Chain Aggregation, Logistics & Cold Chain Infrastructure, Fruit and Vegetable Products, Animal Products, Meat and Dairy, Fisheries & Seafood, Cereals, Consumer Foods/Ready to Eat Foods, Wine and Beer, Machinery/Packaging. He said that Indian Government is giving priority to this sector. The Government has set up a National Institute of Food Technology, Entrepreneurship and Management (NIFTEM) at Kundli, Haryana as an Apex knowledge centre in the field of latest Food Technology. The Minister pointed out that the "Food Parks" are being set up in different parts of the country as part of the strategy to develop food processing infrastructure. It will help small and medium entrepreneurs in a big way. Shri Sahai also informed that Indian government has enacted the Food Safety and Standards Act, 2006 to consolidate multiple laws relating to food and to set up an independent Food Authority. Underscoring the salient features of Indian economy, the Minister said that India is the fourth largest economy in terms of purchasing power parity and is a fastest growing free market democracy. He said that the strategic geographic location like its proximity to markets in Europe and Far East, South East and West Asia has made India the hub of operations for most of the major global players in the industry today. The wide spread road and rail network along with well developed infrastructure and distribution network make India a good place for investment, he added. Pointing out the vision 2015 of the Government of India for the Food Processing Sector, the Minister said that enhancing and stablising the income level of the farmers, providing choice to consumers, promoting a dynamic food processing industry and making the sector attractive for both domestic and foreign investors and having a transparent and industry friendly regulatory regime are some of the highlights of this vision strategy. Later speaking at the "Indian Tastes" organised during the same Trade Fair, the Minister said that the event represents the growing

Indian Food Industry's appeal across the globe with its uniquely flavoured products, tastes and distinctiveness. He said that there is rising awareness and demand in the global market regarding ethnic Indian food products.

3750. (17-10-2007) NEW DELHI : The Union Public Service Commission will hold the National Defence Academy and Naval Academy Examination (I), 2008 on 20th April, 2008 for admission to Army, Navy and Air Force Wings of NDA for 121st Course and Naval Academy for 41st 10+2 (Executive Branch) Course commencing from 30th December, 2008. For details regarding the, Syllabus and Scheme of the examination, Centres of examination, Guidelines for filling up application form etc. aspirants must consult the Detailed Notice of the examination published in the Employment News/Rozgar Samachar dated 13th October, 2007. In case of any guidance/information/clarification regarding their applications, candidature etc. candidates can contact UPSC's Facilitation Counter near 'C' gate of its campus in persons or over Telephone No. 011-23385271/011-23381125/ 011-23098543 on working days between 10.00 hrs. to 17.00 hrs. The Commission also has Website at address: http:/www.upsc.gov.in over which the candidates can obtain details of the examination as well as information about registration of their applications, venue of the examination and results etc.

3751. (17-10-2007) NEW DELHI : The Bharatiya Janata Party holds the UPA government squarely responsible for today's blood bath in the capital market. The BJP also charges the UPA government of actively triggering extreme volatility in the capital market by making unwarranted utterances about policies in the absence of any clear direction. The earlier announcement by SEBI about its intention to regulate the PN followed by a late clarification by the Finance Minister only on following day after the crash, clearly exemplifies the complete mishandling of the situation by the government and its related agencies. The extreme volatility in the capital market also points towards the existence of a nexus between various persons and institutions who stand to gain from the volatility of the capital market. The BJP demands a JPC probe to investigate this nexus and mismanagement. It must also be investigated as to who actually has benefited from short selling during this fall? The Finance Minister owes an explanation as to why he waited for the market to fall by 2000 points before coming out with a clarification. The BJP wants to remind the country that under the UPA, this is the third occasion when the market has had to be closed down due to such a flip-flop from the government and the market regulator. The extreme volatility witnessed during the last few sessions, was not based on logical fundamentals and became a case of pure and excessive speculation. The sudden spurts in the market confused the ordinary investor as to the direction of the market and in turn resulted in hurting the small investors and is also rattling their confidence. Orderly financial market is the need of the hour and it is a definite responsibility of the government to protect the interest of the millions of stake holders. The PN route should have been checked much earlier as money without the knowledge of the source is systematically being pumped in by this method for some time. 51% of the assets under custody of all FIIs totalling Rs. 3,53,484 crores are through the PN route. This is a dangerous figure. In fact the NDA had in 2004 itself, laid down a clear road map for phasing out Participatory Notes. Even the Lahiri Committee had recommended the same set of action one year ago. But the UPA government did not act upon it well in time. The PN route has acquired the proportion of hot money, which may contain laundered Swiss Money, Drug Money and Terror Funds. The BJP had earlier demanded a complete ban or total regulation of such flows. The ordinary investor has to furnish all details for entering the market but the PN route has become a shelter requiring no explanations.

3752. (17-10-2007) NEW DELHI : Ahead of his discussions and the Seventh Meeting of India-Russia Inter Governmental Commission on Military Technical Cooperation, the Defence Minister Shri AK Antony today expressed confidence that a major breakthrough is likely to be achieved on key projects under discussion between the two countries. Speaking to reporters shortly after laying a wreath at the Tomb of the Unknown Soldiers at Alexandrovsky Garden in Moscow today, he said 'relationship between India and Russia is special' and his visit will further expand the scope of cooperation between the two countries. He said his visit will prepare the groundwork for the visit of the Prime Minister Dr. Manmohan Singh to Moscow next month. Asked to compare the Indo-US relationship with Indo-Russian relationship, Shri Antony said that India has cordial relationship with many countries including the United States. 'The improvement in our relations with the United States is not at the cost of our old friendship with Russia', Shri Antony said. He stressed that New Delhi's relations with Moscow in general and specially defence cooperation in particular are set to grow.

3753. (17-10-2007) NEW DELHI: Despite the nuclear deal with the United States having been virtually put on hold, India said it would continue with its efforts to integrate with the mainstream civil nuclear community. Minister of State for External Affairs Anand Sharma said the government would also scout for alternative energy sources to reduce its dependence on fossil fuels. The alternatives include renewable sources such as wind and solar, bio-fuels and even nuclear based energy. Sidestepping questions on whether the nuclear deal had been put on hold, the Minister said that putting an end to the country's isolation from global civil nuclear trade was "in supreme national interest." Mr. Sharma said: "India will continue to seek full integration with the global mainstream in the civil nuclear field. This [the nuclear deal] is not one narrow issue. We have to look at the larger picture of India's energy security. There is another aspect to the deal. We also want cutting edge technology that has dual use, including areas such as medicine and agriculture. "India is an emerging power. In the chapter of India's renaissance, we surely cannot be isolated from the global mainstream. It is going to hurt.

3754. (17-10-2007) NEW DELHI : Following is the text of the Opening Remarks of the Prime Minister, Dr. Manmohan Singh at the Plenary Session of the 2nd

Summit of India-Brazil-South Africa (IBSA) meeting in South Africa today: "I am delighted to be in South Africa for the Second Summit meeting of IBSA. I express our deep appreciation to the government and people of South Africa for hosting this Summit. I am happy that fruitful discussions have taken place at the Academic Seminar, the Business Seminar and the newly instituted Women's and Parliamentarians' Forums. When I had the privilege of meeting the Foreign Ministers of IBSA last July, I said to them that it is important to consolidate our gains. We should focus our time and resources to ensure productive outcomes in agreed priority areas of trilateral cooperation. Out of the several Working Groups that we have set up, only those on ICT and Trade and Investment have met thrice. We can agree today that by the time of the next Summit all the Groups should complete one cycle of meetings in each of our countries. At the next Summit, we would then be in a position to take stock of the areas we should concentrate on and where cooperation is proving useful. I am particularly pleased that discussions have begun on the India-SACU-Mercosur FTA. This is a bold initiative to give an impetus to our trading ties and we will work sincerely to bring it to fruition. With regard to global issues we are increasingly consulting each other on the margins of major international meetings. We should encourage this so that we can have common IBSA positions on important international issues. Last year we had agreed that assisting other developing countries should be one of the thrust areas of IBSA cooperation. I propose that we work on one big flagship IBSA project using the Fund for Poverty and Hunger, which will convey our commitment in this area. All developing countries face the challenge of balancing the need for more rapid growth with the need to address the problem of social inequality. Each of our countries has attempted innovative solutions to bring about inclusive growth. I am happy that we will discuss the issue of social development later on, including how to share experiences. The lack of adequate connectivity continues to hamper our cooperation. We should reflect on how to encourage air and maritime links, which may not be commercially viable to begin with. I look forward to having substantive and productive discussions today on strengthening the IBSA process. If the IBSA movement is to catch the imagination of our people we should move from a declaratory phase to one of time bound action. We all recognise the immense potential of IBSA. With the necessary political will and an outcome-based approach, I have no doubt that we will be able to realise this potential."

3755. (17-10-2007) NEW DELHI : Prof. Saifuddin Soz, the Union Minister of Water Resources has said that it is necessary for us to preserve our environment and the process of development must follow the fundamental rule of sustainability. Addressing the 10th Inter-Regional Conference on "Water and Environment (ENVIROWAT 2007)-Ensuring Water and Environment for Prosperity and Posterity" here today, he said that we have instances of over-exploitation of the resources in some areas resulting in adverse effect. This is definitely not desirable. Our National Water Policy emphasizes the importance of sustainable development of water resources. It states that water is a scarce and precious national resource to be planned, developed, conserved and managed as such, on an integrated and environmentally sound basis keeping in view that socio-economic aspects and needs of the States. The Minister emphasized that the objective of comprehensive and integrated planning for development and management of water resources can be achieved only when all the stakeholders join hands. We can derive optimum benefits from the most previous gift of the nature *i.e.* water and also ensure the benefits for our future generation only by adopting integrated approach in planning and management through mutual cooperation. All sections of the society-government agencies, planners, users, non-governmental organizations, academia, industries etc. have to play their role in this endeavour. Prof. Soz mentioned that the Ground water is one of the important sources of drinking water. It is also being used for irrigation purposes. In some areas, its excessive use has led to lowering of the ground water table. This has also resulted in deterioration of water quality in certain areas. Government of India has constituted the Artificial Recharge of Ground Water Advisory Council for popularising the concept of artificial recharge of ground water. The Government has also initiated Farmer's Participatory Action Research Programme in about 5000 villages and training one water man and one water woman in each village with the objective of ensuring more crop and income per drop of water. The underlying idea is to ensure that the development is sustainable and also to ensure participation of all stakeholders in the development of water resources.

3756. (17-10-2007) NEW DELHI : The Monopolies & Restrictive Trade Practices Commission (MRTPC) has held that the DLF Universal Limited indulged in unfair trade practice and came under the scrutiny of section 36-A of the MRTP Act by not disclosing to the complainant, Shri K.P. Jain, the basis of carpet area calculations thus prejudicing the interest of consumers. The MRTP Commission held that suppression of norms by DLF Ltd. in calculating carpet area has a flavour of misrepresentation. An agreement was entered into with the DLF Ltd. for purchase of office space. According to this agreement the complainant would have a super area of approximately 101.46 sq. mtrs., which includes carpet area of 74.88 sq. mtrs. (approx.), which works out to carpet area of 73.80% of the super area. The complainant was under the impression that the carpet area would be equal to floor area without including the thickness of the bounding walls. DLF Ltd. contended that carpet area would be floor area of the shop plus the thickness of its bounding walls. The respondent kept this view to itself without disclosing the same to the petitioner at the time of agreement. The petitioner relied upon the norms recommended by BIS. DLF rejected the idea of applying BIS's norms as they are not statutory in nature. The Commission pointed, " In such a situation when norms are not defined statutorily, it was all the more necessary for the respondent to define carpet area in terms of the norms understood by it and not to keep the same with itself to surprise the complainant". The Commission has directed DLF Ltd. to raise a fresh demand calculating the carpet area on the basis of the BIS standards.

3757. (17-10-2007) NEW DELHI : In consultation with the Reserve Bank of India and the Securities and Exchange Board of India, Government proposed to take certain measures to moderate capital inflows. These measures are in the overall interest of the economy and of the market and investors. The proposed measures include some kind of restrictions on issue of offshore derivative instruments by FIIs and their sub-accounts in relation to their exposure in market. Neither do these suggest nor is there any intention to ban issue of such instruments by FIIs. These proposed measures have been put on SEBI website for public comments based on which a view would be taken by the authorities.

3758. (17-10-2007) NEW DELHI : Continuing their fine form Indian boxers had yet another fine outing in the ring by winning four of the six bouts today keeping alive the hopes of anticipated medal haul as they enter the quarter-final stage in the ongoing Military World Games at Hyderabad. Havaldar P Narjit Singh beat 1st Lt. Ma Yunhao of China 9-1, Havaldar S Thoi Thoi Singh beat Russia's Yachmenev Ivan in a close contested fight in the fourth round 18-16, Havaldar Mahinder Thapa beat A Mursal of Sudan 26-5 and Havaldar Bhagyarajan D beat Hane Lei of China 18-14. Indian Sanjay Kolte however, lost to Korean Seungh Hyeok 20-24 and Amarjit Singh was outclassed by Vesialov Micalai of Belarus 12-4.

3759. (18-10-2007) NEW DELHI : India and Russia today signed a landmark Intergovernmental Agreement for the joint development and joint production of the Fifth Generation Fighter Aircraft (FGFA), marking the beginning of cooperation in the development of state of the art new technology major weapon systems. The agreement was signed by the Secretary Defence Production Mr. KP Singh and Deputy Director of the Federal Service for Foreign Military Cooperation Mr. Vyacheslav Dzirkaln in the presence of the Defence Minister Mr. AK Antony and his Russian counterpart Mr. Anatoly Serdyukov in Moscow today. The watershed agreement was signed at the conclusion of the Seventh Meeting of the India-Russia Intergovernmental Commission for Military and Technical Cooperation. Mr. Antony and Mr. Serdyukov also signed a Protocol which envisages a 'new strategic relationship' based on greater interaction at various operational levels. Speaking to reporters shortly after the signing ceremony, Mr. Antony said the two countries have agreed to strengthen and expand relations in all areas especially in the areas of joint exercises and greater cooperation in the field of Research and Development. "Now the frequency and level of exercises will be higher", Mr. Antony said. He said talkswith Russia have started to extend the Military Cooperation Agreement beyond 2010. The pact had been signed during the Russian President Mr. Vladimir Putin's visit to India in 2000. The Defence Minister described the Agreement on FGFA as a 'major landmark' and said that the Indo-Russian relationship is on a trajectory to reach new heights. He hoped that the two countries would soon sign an Intergovernmental Agreement on co-development and co-production of Multi-Role Transport Aircraft. Mr. Antony expressed satisfaction at the outcome of discussions on other important projects *e.g.*, supply and licensed production of T-90 tanks, SU-30 MKI aircraft and other strategic issues. He admitted that there has been a delay in the delivery of the repaired and refurbished aircraft carrier Admiral Gorshkov alongwith supply of deck-based fighter aircraft MiG-29-K and said it was decided that some more studies by technical groups would be done to go through the details. He appreciated the efforts made by the Russian side to resolve issues relating to life cycle support of equipment of Russian origin. On the question of Integrity Pact, he said, "the objective is neither to create problems for anybody nor to favour anybody. What India wants is transparency in all defence purchases. In the past, there have been a lot of controversies. We want to avoid it. We want speedy modernisation but with transparency. Integrity Pact is one of the safeguards for transparency". The Defence Minister returns home tomorrow.

3760. (18-10-2007) NEW DELHI : Indian spikers couldn't live up to the expectation with a crashing defeat from Korea today at Yusufguda Volleyball Indor Stadium. Korea Republic defeated India 25-15,25-23.25-19 in three straight sets in second round of men's volleyball. The Koreans took an early lead in the first set. This lead was narrowed midway through the set by the Indians. However Koreans were better at the nets and the Indian blocking could not prevent the opposition attack. In the second set Indians fought back hard to equalize the score at 19-19. The hard fought set was taken by Korea by a small margin lowering the enthusiasm of the cheering Indian crowd. In the third set Koreans displayed better play and maintained the lead to take the set comfortably. India have two more matches to play against China and Qatar in Pool C and need to beat either one of them to be in the reckoning for a medal in the tournament. In another match, the Chinese beat Qatar in three straight sets to take two points in Pool C. China won 25-23,25-14,25-20. In other two matches of the tournament, Netherlands defeated Latvia 3-1 whereas Brazil made short work of Canada 3-0 in Pool D. The Pool D comprises the above four teams fighting for the last four places. In the Dutch Latvia encounter the Latvians gave the wake up call to the Dutch when took the first set 25-18.However the Netherlands team gathered its wits and fought it out winning the next three sets 25-19.25-15 and 25-19 to wrap up the match. The Brazil Canada match was a one sided affair with the former winning in three straight sets 25-19, 25-16,25-16.

3761. (18-10-2007) NEW DELHI : Greece defeated Turkey 32-26 in the Men's Handball today at Saroornagar Indoor stadium, Hyderabad. Lieutenant Zaravinas Georgios, an Olympian from Greece, led the team from the start to take his team to a score of 31-21, by half time. Turkey now stands at 9th and the last position in the championship. India today played well with Lithuania during the second match of the day. By half time India was trailing 9-12. India will play Qatar tomorrow.

3762. (18-10-2007) NEW DELHI : In 25 meter Pistol Women individual Fire, China's Cadet Ding Xiaoxu won the Gold by scoring aggregate 584 points (289 in precision and 295 rapid stage) at Hyderabad University Indoor Shooting ranges today. Germany's Cpl Dorjsuren Munkhbayar with 583 points and Sergeant Martin Monica with 580 points clinched Silver and Bronze, respectively. Chinese shooters also dominated 25 mtr Centre Fire Pistol Men individual by staking claim on Gold and Silver. Major Lin Yadong scored 297 points in precision and 98 in rapid stage aggregating to 588 pts. Cadet Gao Zheng of China got 293 pts in precision and 294 in Rapid stage aggregating to 587 pts. Maj Trachor Oleg of Ukraine won Bronze with 585 points. Tomorrow, 300 mtr Military Rapid-Fire team match will be played at Lake view stadium at 9AM while 50 mtr Women Rifle 3 positions team match and 25 mtr Pistol Women Military rapid-fire (team) match will be played at Hyderabad Varsity Campus.

3763. (18-10-2007) NEW DELHI : The government has clarified that there is no threat of pests entering India with the fruit being imported from the USA and that procedures in consonance with the international convention are being followed before permitting import of apples into India. 'There are no reports of interception of any quarantine pests from the imported apple consignments from USA nor any non-compliance of Indian plant quarantine regulations,' the Ministry today clarified. This is in response to media reports stating that apples being imported from the USA are not being quarantined properly and are thus carrying pests to India. As per the procedure for quarantine of plant material entering India, the exporting country has to provide necessary phyto-sanitary certificate and the exporter has to meet certain conditions to ensure that no infestation enters India. Once at Indian ports of arrival, the consignments are inspected and approval is granted only after the consignment has passed through an established procedure.

3764. (18-10-2007) NEW DELHI : "There is every possibility that the US Government is moving once again to publicly list handmade carpets as products of child labour", said Shri Jairam Ramesh, Minister of State for Commerce, while inaugurating the 3rd India Carpet Expo in Varanasi yesterday. Shri Ramesh explained that on 1st October, the US Department of Labour issued a public notice seeking comments on "procedural guidelines" for the development of a public list of goods from countries produced by child and forced labour in violation of international standards. This action is in response to a law passed last year by the US Congress that instructs the US government to carry out "additional activities to monitor and combat forced labour and child labour in foreign countries". Government and industry will have to work closely together effectively to deal with this new development which could be used by groups hostile to our interests, Shri Ramesh said. In 2006/07, India's exports of handmade carpets of all varieties were around $ 800 million, with the US market alone accounting for 50%. Germany was the other big market accounting for another 20%. There are about 2 million artisans directly employed in carpet making that is concentrated in UP (Varanasi, Mirzapur, Bhadohi and Shahjahanpur), J&K (Srinagar and Jammu), Rajasthan (Jaipur) and Haryana (Panipat). India accounts for about 35% of world trade in handmade carpet and last year, it occupied the top spot amongst all handmade carpet exporters ahead of China, Iran, Pakistan and Turkey. Shri Ramesh complimented the carpet industry on its export performance over the past two years and exhorted it to invest in new designs and technology by way of improved looms that hold the key to enhanced productivity and competitiveness. The 3rd India Carpet Expo has attracted 250 overseas buyers showing the popularity of Indian carpets and the versatile capabilities of the industry. Shri Ramesh called upon the Carpet Export Promotion Council to carry out an independent social audit every year to convince NGOs and others that incidence of child labour has indeed come down significantly over the past two decades. He recalled that ten years back, there was an effort by the US Congress to put a ban on exports of handmade carpets from India on the child labour issue. But the combined efforts of the government and industry were successful in ensuring that this ban did not fructify. Now, Indian exporters are in a position to give their buyers the "Kaleen" certificate to certify that carpets exported do not use child labour in any way. The greater use of "Kaleen" would also help in combating adverse propaganda against India not only by foreign countries but also by our own NGOs and civil society groups. The central and state governments must also step up their verification and monitoring campaigns to ensure that anti-child labour laws are implemented in every way. Speaking on the occasion, the Chairman of the Carpet Export Promotion Council (CEPC), Shri Ashok Jain highlighted the adverse impact that the appreciation of the rupee vis-à-vis the dollar is having on the competitiveness of Indian handmade carpets in overseas markets and called for urgent measures to protect Indian exporters since employment will be the casualty. He also called for greater subsidies on export credit in order to meet with growing threats from countries like China and Pakistan.

3765. (18-10-2007) NEW DELHI : The Vice President of India Mohd. Hamid Ansari was presented a traditional Pankha by the members of the Anjuman Sair-e-Gul-Faroshan at a function at Vice President House here today.A number of dignitaries including Shri Salman Khurshid were present on the occasion. Many States send their Pankhas in this three day festival of Hindu-Muslim brotherhood beginning on 25th October 2007. This annual festival was revived by late Shri Yogeshwar Dayal in 1961. Addressing on the occasion the Vice President said that the 'Phool Walo ki Sair' is a symbol of composite culture of Delhi but its message of peace unity and prosperity should be spread nationwide. He said that this festival bring peace, prosperity and happiness in our lives. He wished this festival a great success.

3766. (18-10-2007) NEW DELHI : Department of Science & Technology in coordination with UNDP has taken an initiative to impart skills in the new and innovative vocations leading to generate employment. GOI-UNDP project, called, 'Skills and Knowledge for Improved Livelihoods and Living Standards' (SKILLS) is being implemented for promoting new training curriculum and facilities in the emerging technology skills for the benefit of the unemployed youth. The SKILLS project was initiated in 2004-05. The implementing institutions are: Tiruchirappalli Regional Engineering College-Science & Technology Entrepreneurs Park (TREC-STEP), Trichy; Vivekananda Institute of Bio-technology, Nimpith; JSS Academy of Technical Education-Science & Technology Entrepreneurs Park (JSSATE-STEP), Noida; and Agnel Technical Education Complex, Goa ICT (Information & Communication Technologies) are today recognized as very powerful enablers of knowledge dissemination. One of the important deliverables under the SKILLS project was to use the world wide web through a portal to provide a repository of information that can be accessed by all the stake holders of a vocational training eco-system.

3767. (18-10-2007) NEW DELHI : Shri Arjun Singh, Minister of Human Resource Development, currently in Paris for the UNESCO General Conference, held bilateral meetings with Ministers of Education from Indonesia and South Africa yesterday. The Indonesian Minister, Prof. Bambang Soedibyo, expressed considerable interest in India's advances in the field of higher education and sought to strengthen links between universities in both countries. He also hoped that the two countries would be able to encourage the teaching of Indonesian language, Bahasa, in India and of Indian languages in Indonesia. The training of English language teachers was also discussed as a possible area of cooperation. The South African Minister, Ms. Naledi Pandor, spoke warmly of the ties between India and South Africa. The countries have signed an Educational Exchange Programme in October 2006 and are planning for collaborative activities in teachers' training and curriculum development, university level exchanges and the use of IT in education. Shri Arjun Singh has invited Indonesian Minister, Prof. Bambang Soedibyo and South African Minister, Ms. Naledi Pandor to visit India.

3768. (18-10-2007) NEW DELHI : Direct tax collections maintained a growth of over 40 percent for the period 1st April to 15th October 2007. Net direct tax collections stood at Rs.1,21,950 crore, up from Rs.86,751 crore during the same period last fiscal. Corporate tax recorded a growth of 40.29 percent at Rs.75,549 crore, up from Rs.53,853 crore during the previous fiscal. Personal income tax (including FBT, STT and BCTT) grew by 41.13 percent at Rs.46,320 crore, up from Rs.32,821 crore. The growth in Securities Transaction Tax (STT) was 48.05 percent (Rs.3,784 crore as against Rs.2,556 crore) and Banking Cash Transaction Tax (BCTT) was 20.22 percent (Rs.284 crore as against Rs.236 crore). Fringe Benefit Tax (FBT) recorded a growth of 87.92 percent (Rs.2,326 crore as against Rs.1,238 crore). Growth of over 49 percent in direct taxes deducted / collected at source is a strong indicator of increasing employment, employee compensation and private investments; while growth of about 30 percent in advance direct tax collections is indicative of better profitability and improved cash-flows in businesses-particularly in the core, consumption and financial sectors. Increase of 64 percent in self-assessment tax confirms the trend of better tax compliance.

3769. (18-10-2007) NEW DELHI : The Chief Minister of Orissa Shri Naveen Patnaik called on the Union Minister of Shipping, Road Transport and Highways, Thiru T.R. Baalu here today and discussed the various ongoing road projects in the State. On a request from the Chief Minister for improving and strengthening of National Highway 215 (Panikoili to Rajamunda), Thiru Baalu informed Shri Patnaik that the technical sanction of Rs. 95 crore would be granted immediately It may be recalled that the entire length of 269 kms of NH-215 has been included under NHDP Phase III and preparation of DPR for four-laning upgradation by NHAI is under way. Meanwhile, in order to improve the deteriorating condition of the National Highways in Orissa, the Ministry would allocate additional Rs 45 crore. Thiru Baalu indicated to Shri Patnaik that the menace of overloaded trucks has taken its toll on NH 215 and the road condition has deteriorated rapidly. He urged the State Government to take immediate measures to control the plying of over-loaded vehicles on NHs. In order to curb the practice of overloading and to ease the problem of traffic congestion, Thiru Baalu desired that the State Government should organize a meeting with all the stakeholders in which Union Shipping and Road Transport & Highways Secretaries should also participate within a fortnight for finalizing the modalities for strengthening of National Highway 215 which is suffering from the menace of over-loading. Regarding the Vijayawada-Ranchi Road, Thiru Baalu told the State CM that the Government of Orissa will have to expedite the finalization of the Detailed Project Reports (DPRs) for remaining 600 km of this route in Orissa. The Minister desired to have a detailed presentation on this project as it comprises of National Highways, State Highways and the Village Roads. Thiru Baalu said that he would also be interacting with the State Governments of Andhra Pradesh, Orissa and Jharkhand to expedite finalization of the modalities for this Project. Regarding the Road connectivity to Paradip Port (NH 5A), the Union Minister told Shri Patnaik that land acquisition for NHDP in general and Paradip Port in particular is required to be expedited by the State Goverment. He also emphasized for immediate identification of alternate service roads and parking places for easing the traffic congestion near the Port area.

3770. (18-10-2007) LUCKNOW: With the Uttar Pradesh Assembly session scheduled to begin on October 30, Chief Minister Mayawati on Wednesday expanded her Cabinet by inducting six new Ministers, including four of Cabinet rank. Besides, three Ministers of State (independent charge) and a Minister of State were elevated as Cabinet Ministers. With the latest expansion, the size of the Mayawati Ministry has gone up to 53. The number of Cabinet Ministers has increased to 27. While first-timers Nand Gopal Gupta Nandi, Kamla Kant Gautam, Chandradev Ram Yadav and Ashok Kumar have been inducted as Cabinet Ministers, Bhagwati Prasad Sagar and Jaiveer Singh have been designated Ministers of State with independent charge. Mr. Nandi was instrumental in defeating the former Bharatiya Janata Party president and former Vidhan Sabha Speaker, Kesari Nath Tripathi from Allahabad South in the last UP Assembly elections. The three other

Cabinet Ministers have been rewarded for their loyalty to the Chief Minister and to the cause of the Bahujan Samaj Party. Of the two Ministers of State (independent charge), Jaiveer Singh had been a Minister in the Mulayam Singh regime. He was among the first Samajwadi Party ministers who pledged their loyalty to Ms. Mayawati in 2006 and later returned to the BSP fold. Mr. Singh subsequently lost his membership of the last Vidhan Sabha following a petition moved by the Samajwadi Party. He was a member of the Loktantrik Bahujan Dal, the breakaway faction of the BSP. The three Ministers of State with independent charge who have been elevated to Cabinet rank are Badshah Singh, MoS for Small Industries and Export Promotion; Rangannath Mishra, MoS for Rural Engineering Services; and Anant Kumar alias Antu Misra, MoS for Medical and Health. State Minister for Agriculture, Foreign Trade and Agri Exports, Abdul Mannan, has also been made Cabinet Minister. Antu Misra, a close relative of Satish Chandra Misra, the Minister attached to the Chief Minister, was elected from Farrukhabad in an Assembly by-election defeating Vijay Singh of the Congress. He was not an MLA when he was made the Minister after Ms. Mayawati came to power in May this year. Mr. Misra had lost the Assembly elections. Among those who have missed the bus are Kazim Ali Khan and Haji Yaqub Qureishi. They were in the Bahujan Samaj Party when Ms. Mayawati became Chief Minister for the third time in May 2002, but switched their loyalties to Mr. Mulayam Singh through the Loktantrik Bahujan Dal route when the latter came to power in August 2003. They returned to the BSP when Ms. Mayawati became the Chief Minister in May this year. Mr. Khan, who was elected from Swar Tanda on Samajwadi Party ticket in the May Assembly polls, resigned his seat and won the by-election from the same constituency on BSP ticket. Son of former Congress MP from Rampur, Noor Bano, Khan's name was being mentioned in the corridors of power on the eve of the expansion as a possible Cabinet Minister.

3771. (18-10-2007) NEW DELHI : Shri A.Raja, Minister of Communications and Information Technology presented awards to the winners of the Fourth Computer Literacy Excellence Awards for Schools(CLEAS)-2005 here today. Addressing the gathering he said that educational institutions are the nurseries wherein our future work force is being imparted the necessary skills to handle the challenges that lie ahead. Shri Raja said the focus of the Ministry is to "Catch Them Young" to inculcate IT knowledge and skills at school level itself. This, he hoped, would ensure that creativity and innovation are nurtured at a young age and in the long run would lead to the quality levels of graduates and post-graduates coming out of higher educational institutions. Emphasising the importance of awards he said they are for giving recognition to the leading schools. This, he said, would motivate the teachers and students of the schools and maintain a healthy competition among the various schools and motivate the management of these schools to provide more incentives to the teachers and students. The Computer Literacy Excellence Awards Scheme for schools is an attempt to bring the nation's children at par with young achievers of the world. While demonstrating outstanding competence, the 51 State/UT level awardees have created a benchmark of excellence in computer education for the rest of the schools across India to follow. There are two category of awards-one for Private/Government aided school and another for Government/Municipal school. Following is the list of award winners:

3772. (18-10-2007) TSHWANE (PRETORIA): Prime Minister Manmohan Singh on Wednesday indicated that the government had not given up persuading the Left parties on the nuclear deal with the United States. "Well, the process of evolving a meaningful consensus is still on," he said at a joint press conference with South African President Thabo Mbeki and Brazilian President Luiz Inacio Lula da Silva at the end of the IBSA (India-Brazil-South Africa) Summit here. Dr. Singh did not elaborate this one-sentence statement. He was responding to a question how he would balance the sentiments on civil nuclear cooperation expressed at the summit with domestic political constraints and compulsions. An IBSA Summit Declaration noted that the three heads of government "strongly emphasised" the need for ensuring the supply of safe, sustainable and non-polluting sources of energy to meet the rising demand.

3773. (18-10-2007) NEW DELHI : Bharatiya Janata Party will take high level delegation to the Prime Minister to demand immediate hike in Minimum Support Price for paddy from Rs. 725 to Rs. 1,000 per quintal. The disparity between MSP of wheat and paddy has increased phenomenally to Rs 275 per quintal after government's decision to increase MSP of wheat without commensurate increase in MSP of paddy. If course correction is not done at the earliest, the farmers of summer paddy might switch over to wheat and this could result in a crunch. The Food Security Mission as envisaged in 11th Plan has put a target of 10 million tones of additional production of rice. BJP charges the UPA government of having biased view against paddy. In many reports and statements government has expressed its opinion against the crop on the ground of its high water intensity. But this is true only where it is under irrigation. The major paddy crop in Andhra, Tamil Nadu, Maharashtra, Orissa, West Bengal, Karnataka, Kerala, Chattisgarh, Jharkhand is rain fed Kharif crop. The government bias is also reflected through its method of calculating the cost of production, which is showing downward trend though the ground reality is different. BJP warns that if this step motherly treatment continues for the paddy, it will result in a demand supply crunch sooner than later. UPA government must come clean on the embarrassment faced by External Affairs Minister Mr. Pranab Mukherjee on his inter governmental commission visit to Russia. Reports about Foreign Minister of Russia not meeting Sh. Mukherjee and his frisking at the airport do not gel well for the country. The country must know whether this is displeasure by the host country or bad handling of MEA visit by our government.

3774. (18-10-2007) NEW DELHI : Amidst loud cheering from a rapturous audience, the bright spark for India to go five up in the medal tally of the Military World Games at Hyderabad was ensured by five boxers who sailed into the semis today. Hari Krishan Belwal (51 kg), P. Narjit Singh (54 kg), Satya Raju (57 kg), D. Bhagyarajan (69 kg) and Mohinder Thapa (81 kg) all won their respective bouts that can fetch five medals at a single event for India at the games. Thoi Thoi Singh and Lakra who were favourites to win however, lost their bouts. The semi-final bouts will be fought tomorrow amidst a packed indoor stadium as boxing continues to attract the maximum crowd.

3775. (19-10-2007) NEW DELHI : The President, Smt. Pratibha Devisingh Patil has greeted the people in her message on the occasion of the festival of Durga Puja, which is being celebrated tomorrow. In her greetings, the President said that on the auspicious occasion of Durga Puja, I extend my warm wishes to everyone for their success, happiness and prosperity. The President said that on this occasion, the Durga Puja celebration symbolizes the triumph of good over evil. Let this occasion inspire us to dedicate ourselves to all causes that are good and noble and work for the betterment of humanity at large.

3776. (19-10-2007) NEW DELHI : India's P Narjit Singh kept alive the hopes of Gold in Boxing by reaching final of the 52-54 kg category today at Hyderabad. With the entire stadium rooting for him, Narjit Singh convincingly defeated Jang Kwan Sik of Korea by a margin of 18-13. Playing cleverly he didn't give an inch to his opponent and kept the pressure throughout the three rounds. Indian spectators brought the stadium down with chanting of 'Chak De India' and 'Bharat Mata ki Jai'. But the other four boxers in the fray could not live up to the expectations of the spectators and gave in meekly to their opponents. H.K.Beliwal went down to China's Gao Linzhi by 15-7. Satya Raju was defeated by Ramashkevich Yauheni of Belarus by 21-5. Bhagyarajan D lost to H Rawshan of Uzbekistan by 24-9, whereas Mohinder Thapa was defeated by Dymakavets Aleh of Belarus by 18-2.

3777. (19-10-2007) NEW DELHI : Russia and China took top two positions in 25 mtr military rapid fire pistol men team event with total aggregate of 1752 points and 1750 points respectively. Korea Republic got Bronze by scoring 1735 points in aggregate. India got 5th position by lagging behind from Korea by 5 point. DPR Korea and Belarus clinched Gold and Silver medals in 25 mtr rapid fire pistol women team event by scoring 1732 points and 1727 points respectively. Russia had to content with third position by scoring 1722 points, 5 points lesser then Belarus. In 50 mtr Rifle three positions Women Relay Team event China won the Gold with 1745 points. Ukraine (1729) and Russia (1727) bagged the Silver and Bronze respectively. Tomorrow's events are 300 mtr men military rapid fire individual match at Lake view Ranges while 50 mtr rifle 3 positions women Individual match, 25 mtr rapid fire men individual match and 25 mtr rapid fire women individual match will be played at Hyderabad University ranges.

3778. (19-10-2007) NEW DELHI : Russia won three Gold medals in Parachuting event today at the IAF Hakimpet station. Russia's Maksimov won the Gold with individual accuracy of 0.01 in men's event. His country-mate Lepezina clinched the Gold in women's event with individual accuracy of 0.01. Russia took Gold in women's Team event with accuracy of 0.25. German men's team bagged Gold with an accuracy of 0.19. In men's accuracy Slovenia and Czech Republic are tied with 0.20 and it will be resolved through single jump by each of five members tomorrow morning. Germany, which was, in the third position till 18th October overtook Slovenia, Czech republic and Russia in the last two rounds. India did not qualify for semifinal round that saw participation of first 15 teams. In individual men's accuracy also Erjavec of Slovenia and Gecnuk of Czech Republic are in tied position with 0.02 accuracy and they will take a jump each tomorrow to decide for Silver and Bronze medals. India did not qualify in semi final. The medal winners have maintained their position throughout the competition. China bagged Bronze in women's team accuracy followed by Belarus with accuracy of 0.36 and 0.44. Slovenia's Sajovic won the Silver and China's Ye took Bronze in women's individual accuracy.

3779. (19-10-2007) NEW DELHI : The Prime Minister, Dr. Manmohan Singh has written to Pakistan Peoples Party leader Benazir Bhutto and President Musharraf. The Prime Minister has conveyed his condolences on the loss of lives in the Karachi blasts and condemned terrorism and extremism in all its forms.

3780. (19-10-2007) NEW DELHI : The President, Smt. Pratibha Devisingh Patil urged a group of women and girls from Jammu and Kashmir who met her at Rashtrapati Bhavan today to spread the message of the importance of education of the girl child when they return to their homes after their visit to Delhi. The President was speaking while interacting with a group of 34 women and girls from the districts of Rajouri, Doda and Poonch who are currently on a visit to Delhi, Ajmer and Jaipur under the Indian Army's 'Operation Sadbhavana'. The Operation is part of the Army's efforts in providing succor to civilians of Jammu and Kashmir and to enable them to have a feel of the rich traditions of the other parts of the country. The ladies will be felicitated by various Army formations enroute to instill a feeling of belongingness and unity. The women and girls are in the age group of 18 to 50 years. The group arrived in the capital today. The theme of the tour is, "Nari Shakti Shanti Path Par". Two lady officers of the Army are leading the group. During the interaction with the President, the group said they were very happy with the work being done by the Army for them in their districts and also are happy that the tour has given them an opportunity to travel outside their district and state, to see the development and progress that has taken place in the country. Smt. Patil was very keen to know from the group what professions they were pursuing. They told her that some of them are involved in agriculture while others have taken up tailoring and stitching for which the Army has helped them. The President said the women in the group were brave as they have been facing up to terrorism and she also urged them to help the Army in its efforts to fight terrorism in the state. The President emphasized on the need to educate the girl child. Smt. Patil said, "The education of the girl child is as important as the education of the boy child".

3781. (19-10-2007) NEW DELHI : China emerged on top in both men and women Military Pentathlon today in the 4th Military World Games at Hyderabad. The final of the five events Military Pentathlon, Cross-Country race was contested at the picturesque Sarvatra Stadium. First it was Women Cross Country race over 4 Kms tortuous track running through hilly and jungle stretches. DPR Korea's Pvt Ya Un Jong came first with a timing of 14.36 minutes. Her compatriot DPR Korea's Pvt Pak Hyang Soi was second with 14.37 minutes and Cadet Liu Kum of China captured the third place with the timing of 14.38 minutes. Team championship in Cross Country race was won by team of DPR Korea with 3232.1 points, second place was secured by China with 3221.4 points and Russian women team came third with 3176 points. Overall Military Pentathlon of women was won by China with 16195.9 points, DPR Korea stood second with 15779.4 points and Russia was third with 15735.8 points. In men 8 kilometer long cross country race, Cadet Hequan Zhang of China came first with time of 25.57 minutes. Senior Officer Diego Elizondo of Argentina was second with 26.01 minutes and the third place went to Major Andrei Kudzin of Belarus with 26.18 minutes. Team championship in Cross Country race was won by team of Belarus with 4195.3 points, second place was secured by Germany with 4102.02 points and Chinese team came third with 4097.07 points. Overall Military Pentathlon of men was won by China with 21488.01 points, Belarus came second with 21408.06 points and Germany was third with 21348.09 points.

3782. (19-10-2007) NEW DELHI : Latvia beat Korea Rep in a close encounter to enter into the final of the Handball at the Saroornagar Indoor Stadium in Hyderabad today. In the other semifinal, Latvia defeated Belarus. Initially Latvia played offensive to take the lead 9-5. Both Mehtap Simsek and Pinar Unlu, the women Turkish referees were strict with players. But Latvia kept scoring to take the lead with 16-12 at half time. Janis Glusaks of Latvia was shown the red card just after half time. With their speed, strength and height, the Latvians overpowered the Koreans 37-30. The second semi final between Belarus and Lithuania who have figured consistently in the finals of World Military Handball championship also saw tough fight. Belarus was leading Lithuanians with 19-10 by half time. The Lithuanian goalkeeper, Sarunas Miciulis saved many attempts made by Belarus's Pukhouski Barys. Greece beat UAE by a solitary goal in another match today. UAE gave a tough fight to Greece but lost the match 33-34. Abdulla Al Saffar of UAE scored 8 goals and was the highest scorer during the match. In another match, Qatar beat India 35-27. Qatar raised a wall of defenders to restrict Indians from scoring. At half time Indians were trailing 13-21. During the second half, Qatar started widening the margin after Havaldar Bikram Singh was retired hurt during the clash with Al Hajri Hamad Abdulla. This was followed by Naib Subedar Kumar Praseed going out of the court retired hurt and Qatar's Mauadi Hamed Mohammed was given red card. However Qatar finally beat India by a comfortable margin of 37-27. India will now play with UAE tomorrow.

3783. (19-10-2007) NEW DELHI : Government of India have announced the sale (re-issue) of"5.87 percent Government Stock, 2010" under Market Stabilization Scheme for a notified amount of Rs. 3,000 crore (nominal). Government of India have also announced the sale (re-issue) of "11.30 percent Government Stock, 2010" under Market Stabilization Scheme for a notified amount of Rs. 3,000 crore (nominal). The Government Stocks will be sold through price based auction using multiple price method. The auctions will be conducted by the Reserve Bank of India, Mumbai Office, Fort, Mumbai on October25, 2007 (Thursday). Up to 5 per cent of the amount notified for the sale of stock is reserved for allotment to eligible individuals and Institutions on non-competitive basis as per the Scheme for Non-Competitive Bidding Facility in the Auction of Government Securities. Bids in the prescribed form obtainable from the Regional Director, Reserve Bank of India, Mumbai Office (Public Debt Office), Fort, Mumbai-400 001 and RBI website www.rbi.org.in should be submitted to that Office on October 25, 2007. The NDS members should submit competitive as well as non-competitive bids in electronic format using Primary Market Operation (PMO) module of NDS. All bids should be submitted by 12.30 P.M.

3784. (19-10-2007) NEW DELHI : Government of India have announced the sale (re-issue) of "7.27 per cent Government Stock, 2013 for a notified amount of Rs. 4,000 crore (nominal) through a priced based auction using multiple price method. Government of India have also announced the sale (re-issue) of "8.35 per cent Government Stock, 2022" for a notified amount of Rs. 4,000 crore (nominal) through a price based auction using multiple price method. The auctions will be conducted by the Reserve Bank of India, Mumbai Office, Fort, Mumbai on October 26, 2007 (Friday). Up to 5% of the notified amount of the sale of both the stocks will be allotted to eligible individuals and Institutions as per the Scheme for Non-Competitive Bidding Facility in the Auction of Government Securities. Bids in the prescribed form obtainable from the Regional Director, Reserve Bank of India, Mumbai Office (Public Debt Office), Fort, Mumbai-400 001 and RBI website www.rbi.org.in should be submitted to that Office on October 26, 2007. The NDS members should submit competitive as well as non-competitive bids in electronic format using Primary Market Operation (PMO) module of NDS. All bids should be submitted by 12.30 P.M.

3785. (19-10-2007) NEW DELHI : In appreciation of the persistent requests of the State / UT Governments for increased allocations for APL category for current festival season, an ad-hoc festival allocation of about 1 lakh tonne of wheat (0.98 lakh tonne) has been made by the Government of India to all the States / UTs at the rates applicable for Above Poverty Lane (APL) families. Another ad-hoc additional allocation of about 1 lakh tonne of wheat (0.98 lakh tonne) per month has also been made by the Govt. of India for the months of November & December 2007. This will help in cooling down of price of wheat and wheat products. The State Governments / UT Administrations have been requested to keep strict vigilance to ensure that the above APL allocations of wheat are distributed as per the procedure under TPDS to the ration cardholders through FPS network so that no leakage / diversion of foodgrains take place.

3786. (19-10-2007) NEW DELHI : Dr. Manmohan Singh's tirade against the BJP yesterday is not only unfortunate, but also outrageous. It shows how rattled he is by his own abysmal failure to look Prime Ministerial on an issue, which until last week, he made the point of utmost prestige for his government. In fact it clearly exemplifies the image of a much weakened Prime Minister hitting all around, when cornered and unable to explain his turnarounds on core issues and his gross failure in politics and governance. Let us accept one stark fact. Dr. Manmohan Singh, who began as a teacher and then as a civil servant is a late entrant in politics. In fact his entry into politics itself was more by accident than by design as was his elevation to the office of Prime Minister. Conviction and commitment have never been the characteristics of his politics, which is marked more by convenience, a reality which frequently manifests itself in his career profile. He claims to be the pioneer of economic reform, which too has become a complete casualty since he has become the PM. He had staked his personal reputation on the Indo-US nuclear deal for the last two years, but had no difficulty in taking an astounding U-turn by stating that Life does not come to an end if the deal does not go through. His recent actions have confirmed once again that he is the weakest Prime Minister since 1947 commanding no authority in the Cabinet or, enjoying any support within his Party, or support of the parties propping up his coalition. A powerless PM, whose crumbling government has begun its rapid journey downhill has resorted to creaking and unbecoming comments. He also suffers from selective amnesia, because, he conveniently forgets the catalogue of sins, which was heaped on the nation during Congress regime. However, Dr. Singh is sadly mistaken if he thinks that he can retrieve his "lost legitimacy" to remain in high office by diverting attention to the Congress Party's target of attack – the BJP. 1) If the description of unfortunate communal violence in Gujarat is "holocaust" which is indeed shocking, then how would Dr. Singh describe the mass targeted killing of thousands of Sikhs in Delhi and around in 1984 with clear governmental connivance? Dr. Singh then was holding some important office but maintained a conspicuous silence then and remains vacillating now. 2) What is further shocking is that the CBI, directly under his charge has recently closed the case against Shri Jagdish Tytler, one of the prime accused in the 1984 anti Sikh carnage. 3) Dr. Singh has lost his sense of balance when he describes the Agra-Summit as a fiasco. It was the Vajpayee government's uncompromising stand on cross border terrorism and refusal to agree to General Musharraf's description of Pak sponsored terrorism in J&K as freedom struggle that was responsible for non issuance of a joint statement. 4) It was the persistence of the Vajpayee government that finally forced General Musharraf to agree in Jan. 2004 that it shall not permit any part of Pakistan including territory controlled by it for terrorist activity. In a single stroke of supreme diplomatic blunder, Dr. Manmohan Singh completely frittered away all these initiatives by describing Pakistan as a "victim of terrorism". Dr. Singh, who has committed the fiasco – you or the BJP? 5) Our armed forces effectively replied to the Kargil misadventure by Pakistan and the aggressors were forced to beat a complete retreat. Pakistan was also exposed before the world. On the contrary, territories which we lost in the 1948 war with Pakistan in Jammu & Kashmir or to China in 1962, when the Congress was in power, is yet to be recovered. From J&K to North-East to the misadventure of our forces in Sri Lanka in the eighties to infiltration to patent sadistic communalism to pandering of the patrons of terror for the sake of vote bank politics and sacrificing national security in the process, the sins of the Congress are littered at every corner. The nation continues to pay a very heavy price for all these even today. Dr. Singh why don't you ever remember these?

3787. (19-10-2007) NEW DELHI : In order to check the prices of edible oils during the festival season, it has been decided to take the following steps: (i) STC, MMTC, PEC and NAFED have been asked to import 1.25 lakh tonnes of edible oils during the festival season. They have already placed import orders for 38,500 MT of edible oils. (ii) NAFED has been asked to sell upto 5000 MT of mustard seeds per day for the next 20 days. This is in addition to the crushing of mustard seed for selling the oil in the market which NAFED has been doing at the rate of about 50,000 tons per month.

3788. (19-10-2007) NEW DELHI : The Prime Minister, Dr. Manmohan Singh has congratulated the Inter-Governmental Panel on Climate Change and its Chairman Dr. R.K.Pachauri on winning the Noble Prize for Peace for the year 2007. Following is the text of the Prime Minister's message dated 13th October 2007: "It is a matter of great delight and honour to know that the Inter-Governmental Panel on Climate Change headed by Indian environmentalist Dr. R.K. Pachauri has won the Nobel Prize for Peace for the year 2007 jointly with Mr. Al Gore, the former Vice President of the USA. It is a historic moment for Dr. Pachauri and India. Never before has a UN body headed by an Indian been awarded the Nobel Peace Prize. This exceptional honour is recognition of the extraordinary work of Dr. Pachauri and his team at IPCC. They have done yeoman service in awakening our consciousness about the dangers of global warming and the measures that need to be taken urgently to address the serious challenges posed by it. This Award is a big boost to the efforts of Dr. Pachauri and his team of scientists, climate experts and economists to carry forward their work which will eventually promote the welfare of mankind. I have great pleasure in extending my hearty congratulations to Dr. Pachauri, his Panel and all those associated with this effort for being recognized for their efforts through the prestigious Nobel Prize. I am sure that it will encourage them to work with renewed vigour towards a more sustainable future."

3789. (19-10-2007) NEW DELHI : The Board of Approval of the Special Economic Zones (SEZs) has recommended grant of 10 formal and 3 in-principle approvals here today. The Chairman of the Board, while informing the members stated that so far, formal approvals have been granted for setting up of 395 SEZs. He further informed that out of these, 156 SEZs have been notified and investment of Rs.50,906 crore has taken place in these notified SEZs providing direct employment to over 72168 persons. Prominent among those recommended are: Formal approvals for an IT/ITES SEZ by Tata Consultancy Services Limited in West Bengal; Bio-technology Park SEZ by Saloni Business Park Pvt. Ltd at Maharashtra; IT/ITES SEZ by Rakindo Kovai Township Pvt. Ltd at Tamil Nadu; IT/ITES SEZ by Malwa IT Park Ltd at Madhya Pradesh; and Free Trade Warehousing Zone SEZ by Jafza Chennai Business Parks Pvt. Ltd at Tamil Nadu. In-principle approvals for setting up of multi-product SEZ by Privilege Power and Infrastructure Pvt. Ltd. at Maharashtra; Electronics & Electrical products SEZ by Sriperumbudur Ventures Pvt. Ltd at Tamil Nadu; and Multi-product SEZ by Sengadu Projects Pvt. Ltd. at Tamil Nadu.

3790. (19-10-2007) NEW DELHI : Gen Deepak Kapoor, COAS in presence of Lt Gen PR Gangadharan, Colonel of the JAK LI Regiment and Mr. Pawan Munjal, Managing Director, Hero Honda and Mr. RS Settia, DGM of Indian Oil Corporation, flagged in the 'Flags in the JAK LI mountaineering expedition to mount nun and Imphal-Siachen-New Delhi Motor Cycle Expedition' in New Delhi The Jammu and Kashmir Light Infantry Regiment, an illustrious Regiment of the Indian Army is celebrating its Diamond Jubilee this year. To mark the occasion the Regiment undertook a Mountaineering Expedition to Mount Nun, 7135m and a Motor Cycle Expedition from Imphal to New Delhi via Siachen (Base Camp). The Jammu and Kashmir Light Infantry Regiment was raised on 15 Apr 1948, out of volunteers who took up arms to defend their motherland. The volunteers were subsequently organized into a Militia Force of fourteen battalions. The gallantry of the Militia Force was recognized by.the Nation by redesignating it as "THE JAMMU AND KASHMIR LIGHT INFANTRY" in 1972. Mount Nun is an extremely hazardous and difficult peak which has challenged climbers over the yrs. The expedition led by Col Vinay Khosla braved bad weather and vagaries of the terrain to successfully summit the peak on 15 Sep 2007 under Maj Randeep Singh. Two subsequent attempts led by Col Vinay Khosla, the expedition leader and Maj Amit Soni created a record ascent by having 20 mountaineers summit the peak. The Regiment and the Red Shield Division undertook a Motor Cycle Expedition from Imphal to New Delhi via Siachen Base Camp. A distance of over 8000 Kms across the breadth of the country covering 12 states involved crossing of three passes; Rohtang 13360 ft, Tanglang-La 15055 ft, Khardung-La 18380 ft and Zoji-La 12535 ft. The aim of the expedition was to promote the spirit of adventure and to spread the theme of national integration, peace and harmony as the Indian Army and JAK LI Regiment is known to be the epitome of 'National Integration'. The expedition was supported by Hero Honda and Indian Oil Corporation. Gen Deepak Kapoor lauded the achievements of the Regiment for being one of the most decorated Regiments of the Indian Army post independence having been awarded four Battle Honours, three Theatre Honours, six Unit Citations, a Param Vir Chakra, two Ashok Chakras and a large number of other gallantry awards. He also congratulated both the expeditions and their leaders on their outstanding feat.

3791. (19-10-2007) NEW DELHI : Domestic and international traffic have seen an acceleration of growth in recent years. In the 12 months to 31 March, 2007, airlines carried 35 million domestic passengers (up 39.5% year-on-year) and 22.4 million international passengers (up 15.1%). This follows domestic traffic growth of 28% the previous year and 20% the year before. Domestic traffic has consequently doubled in the space of three years. The Centre for Asia Pacific Aviation, a special consulting and research practice, projects domestic traffic will grow at 25-30% per annum and international traffic at 15%, until 2010. The domestic market size is expected to cross 60 million and international traffic 40 million by the end of 2010.

3792. (19-10-2007) NEW DELHI : Shri Arjun Singh, Minister of Human Resource Development (HRD) has said that the Government of India is committed towards Education For All (EFA) and has been making strenuous efforts to increase domestic funding of its core programmes. Addressing the 34th session of the General Conference of UNESO, the Minister has said that the General Conference must set the tone for the discussions of the High Level Group on EFA in December 2007. He said, 'We are targeting to increase Gross Enrolment Ratio for higher education from the present 10% to at least 15% in the next five years. We are also working towards increasing the public expenditure on education to the level of 6% of GDP over this period. We have in recent years taken several affirmative actions to extend the benefits of education to the underprivileged and deprived sections of the society. He further added that India is organising several major UNESCO conferences in the near future-the IVth International Conference on Environmental Education in Ahmedabad, Regional Conference on Global Literacy and the meeting of the Forum of Ministers of Social Development of South Asia in February 2008.

3793. (19-10-2007) NEW DELHI : Japan International Cooperation Agency (JICA) presented the final study report on Dedicated Freight Corridor (DFC) to the Ministry of Railways here today. The final report was handed over to Shri K.C.Jena, Chairman, Railway Board by Mr. T. Fujii, Resident Representative, JICA India along with Mr. Tetsuya Masuzawa, Deputy Team Leader, and other members of JICA Study Team in presence of other Members and senior officials of Railway Board.. Speaking on the occasion, Shri Jena said that the DFC projects are the flagship projects of Indian Railways and are certainly one of the most ambitious infrastructure projects in the country. The project is a very vital for the Indian Railways for capacity creation to meet the ever-growing traffic requirements, he added. He said that the implementation of this project requires massive resources and is also a challenge for our engineers in more ways than one. Shri Jena further said that the completion of JICA study is the culmination of an initiative which originated in April 2005 in the Joint Declaration by the Prime Ministers of India and Japan. The study was agreed upon by the Governments of the two countries and is a good example of Indo-Japanese cooperation. He expressed his confidence that this study is only the beginning of the cooperation between India and Japan on the DFC project. Development of DFC for carrying additional traffic is essential in view of high growth in demand. Railways have proposed a 2700 kilometre long railway line project (Eastern Corridor-1279 kms. and Western corridor-1483 Kms.) as an augmentation of capacity of Indian Railways network to handle the large increase in volume of traffic over the coming years.

3794. (19-10-2007) NEW DELHI : The Vice President of India Mohd. Hamid Ansari has greeted the people of our country on the joyous occasion of Dussehra, which is celebrated across the country with religious fervour and enthusiasm. In his greetings, the Vice President said that the festival celebrates the epic victory of the forces of good over evil. The mood of jubilation is reflected in the festivities. This festival reaffirms our faith in all that is good, noble and virtuous in life and promotes the feeling of harmony in the society. The Vice President said that on this occasion, the festival fill our lives with peace, prosperity, and harmony and unite us all in a common brotherhood of all humanity.

3795. (19-10-2007) NEW DELHI : "Given the central aim of NTP 99 to ensure rapid expansion of tele-density" and the objective "to transform in a time bound manner, the telecommunications sector to a greater competitive environment in both urban and rural areas providing equal opportunities and level playing field for all players", the recommendations of TRAI that there should be no cap on the number of access provider in any service area has been considered by the Government and has been accepted. The Unified (Telecom) Access Services (UAS) licenses are technology neutral and the licensees are required to provide access services and meet the stipulated roll-out obligations using wireline and / or wireless technologies by utilizing network equipment that meets the prescribed standards. The allocation of radio-spectrum and grant of Wireless License shall be subject to availability. In case UAS Licensee is not allocated spectrum due to non-availability, the Licensee shall endeavour to roll out services using wireline technologies. It has also been decided that the roll out for wireless services shall be reckoned from the date of spectrum allocation. This will also apply to those licensees who are awaiting initial spectrum allotment. TRAI had recommended to enhance the subscriber link criterion for allocation of frequency spectrum to UAS/CMTS licensees and to set up a committee to study further allocation of spectrum. Government has accepted the TRAI's recommendation of enhanced subscriber linked criterion for frequency allocation and has set up a committee in Telecom Engineering Centre (TEC) to further study and give a report to the Government. In order to further enhance the penetration of access services for rapid expansion of tele-density, it has also been decided that the existing private UAS Licensees may be permitted to expand their existing networks by using alternate wireless technology *i.e.* the present UAS Licensee who is using GSM technology for wireless access may be permitted to use CDMA technology and vice-versa. The spectrum for the alternate technology, CDMA or GSM (as the case may be) shall be allocated in the applicable frequency band subject to availability after payment of prescribed fee. Allocation of spectrum for the alternate technology may be done to private UAS Licensees on payment of prescribed fee, which will be an amount equal to the amount prescribed as entry fee for getting a new UAS licence in the same service area. The existing UAS Licensees, who have already applied for allocation of spectrum for the alternate technology shall also be considered for allocation of spectrum in alternate technology from the date of payment of prescribed fee. BSNL and MTNL being incumbent operators shall be permitted usage of alternative technology and allocated spectrum for the alternate technology without paying the prescribed fee. For the purpose of payment of licence fee and spectrum charges, the stream wise revenue of different technologies shall be considered. At the time of further allotment of spectrum in any technology, allotment will be subject to the condition that in case the eligibility of the licensee for allocated spectrum in other technology falls below the criterion set for spectrum allotment in the specified technology for the last consecutive six months then corresponding chunk of spectrum in that technology will be surrendered by the licensee before any further allotment of spectrum is considered. The Access Services providers shall endeavour to use more efficient methods and optimum technologies for spectrum utilization. In order to encourage Licensees to use all available methods for efficient spectrum utilization, the "Spectrum Enhancement Charge", in addition to annual spectrum charges based on revenue share, may be levied at the time of additional spectrum allotment to licensees beyond 10MHz for GSM and 5MHz for CDMA. For each additional 1 MHz or part thereof "Spectrum Enhancement Charge" @ Rs 16 Crore, 8 Crore, 3 Crore for Metro/ Category 'A', Category 'B', Category 'C' service areas respectively may be charged. SACFA clearance should be given in a stipulated time frame of 60 days unless there are circumstances to the contrary.

3796. (19-10-2007) NEW DELHI : The Union Minister of Shipping, Road Transport and Highways, Thiru T.R. Baalu has approved a sum of Rs. 30.22 lakh for consultancy services for feasibility study and preparation of the detailed project reports (DPRs) for construction of bypasses in three towns in the state of Tamil Nadu. An amount of Rs. 12.35 lakhs has been approved for feasibility study for construction of bypass to Pullyanpatti town at Km 202/0-210/0 of NH-209. This town is a major industrial and agricultural market centre. Besides there is lot of tourist activity because of pilgrimage centre "Bannari Amman Temple" in its vicinity. There are numerous dangerous zig-zag curves in this section which are prone to the fatal accidents. The road stretch is very congested and to maintain the free flow of the traffic, it is necessary to provide a bye-pass to this town. Thiru Baalu also approved an amount of Rs. 10.68 lakhs for feasibility study and preparation of DPR for construction of bypass to Annur town at km 189/0 of NH-

209. This important road is the major route for the hilly towns like Thalavadi Ansanur, Kollegal and surrounding villages to nearby market centres in Coimbatore and Erode. Therefore, the construction of a bypass would improve the flow of the traffic and resolve the problem of continuous congestion on this stretch. Further, the feasibility study has also been approved for construction of bypass to Pollachi town at km 115/0-122/0 on the same highway by Thiru Baalu for a cost of Rs. 7.19 lakh. This is an important town with the tourism centres such as Valparai, Aliyar and Top Slip being situated around it. Educational Institutions and Industries are located on Pollachi-Karur road and Palladam-Avinashi-Pollachi-Meenakarai road. During festival time and summer vacation time large number of tourists and devotees arrive here. Hence it becomes very difficult to cope up with high intensity of traffic flow and therefore a bypass road to Pollachi town is expected to great relief to the people living in Pollachi and the adjoining towns.

3797. (19-10-2007) NEW DELHI : The government has approved a new Coal Distribution Policy which seeks to facilitate supply of assured quantities of coal to various categories of consumers at pre-determined prices in a regime of enforceable obligations on the part of both the suppliers and consumers of coal. The new policy takes into consideration the regulatory regimes in which various sectors of the economy are functioning for classification of consumers and prioritization of coal supplies in terms of quantities. This policy also envisages an enlarged role for state governments in the supply of coal to a large number of small and medium industries. Under this policy, e-auction sale of coal will be re-introduced with certain modified features to encourage emergence of proper coal market in the country. The new Coal Distribution Policy has been evolved based on the extensive discussions held by the Committee headed by Secretary (Coal) with all the stake holders. The Committee comprised of representatives from the Ministries of Power, Steel, Law, Finance, Small Scale Industries, Department of Industrial Policy and Promotion, Planning Commission, Coal India Limited and Coal Mine Planning and Design Institute Limited.

3798. (19-10-2007) NEW DELHI : The total approximate earnings of Indian Railways on originating basis during the period 1st October-10th October 2007 were Rs. 1864.64 crore compared to Rs. 1510.18 crore during the same period last year, registering an increase of 23.47 per cent. The total goods earnings have gone up from Rs. 1025.23 crore during 1st October-10th October 2006 to Rs. 1203.91 crore during 1st October-10th October 2007, showing an increase of 17.43 per cent. The total passenger revenue earnings during the period 1-10 October 2007 were Rs. 546.89 crore compared to Rs. 430.71 crore during the same period last year, reflecting an increase of 26.97 per cent. The revenue earnings from other coaching amounted to Rs. 47.41 crore during this period compared to Rs. 39.62 crore during the same period last year, showing an increase of 19.66 per cent. The total sundry earnings have gone up from Rs. 14.62 crore during 1-10 October 2006 to Rs. 66.43 crore during 1-10 October 2007, showing an increase of 354.38 per cent. The total approximate number of passengers booked during the period 1-10 October 2007 were 191.00 million compared to 176.33 million during the same period last year, showing an increase of 8.32 per cent. In the suburban and non-suburban sectors, the number of passengers booked during 1-10 October 2007 were 111.12 million and 79.88 million compared to 100.73 million and 75.60 million during the same period last year, registering an increase of 10.31 per cent and 5.66 per cent respectively.

3799. (19-10-2007) NEW DELHI : India is one of the ICAO's founder members, having attended the Chicago Conference in 1944, and has since been a member of the council of the ICAO, including the Provisional ICAO between 1944 and 1947. India has maintained a permanent delegation at the headquarters of ICAO in Montreal. India is fully committed to the aims and objectives of the ICAO and has participated in ICAO's organizational and governance activities in a very cooperative, constructive and positive manner.

3800. (19-10-2007) NEW DELHI : The Union Minister of Shipping, Road Transport & Highways Thiru. T.R. Baalu was presented a Demand Draft for Rs.19,79,79,300/- (Rs. 19.79 crore) here yesterday towards the final dividend for 2006-07 by Capt. S.S. Tripathi, Chairman and Managing Director of the Dredging Corporation of India (DCI), a Public Sector Undertaking under the administrative control of the Ministry of Shipping, Road Transport & Highways. At the 31st Annual General Meeting held on 28th September 2007, the Members of the Company declared dividend @ 150% (including 60% interim dividend paid in March 2007) on the paid-up capital of the Company for the year 2006-07. This is the same as that paid for the previous year 2005-06. The final dividend payable would be 90% *i.e.*, Rs.25.20 crores. Out of this, an amount of Rs.19,79,79,300/- (Rupees nineteen crore seventy nine lakh seventy nine thousand and three hundred rupees only) is payable to the President of India as final dividend for the year 2006-07. The paid-up capital of the Company is Rs.28.00 crores divided into 2,80,00,000 equity shares of Rs.10/- each of which 78.56% *i.e.*, 2,19,97,700 shares are held by the President of India. The Dredging Corporation of India (DCI) was established in 1976 to provide integrated dredging service to the Major Ports of the country. The DCI is a Mini Ratna category-I Public Sector Undertaking under the administrative control of the Ministry of Shipping, Road Transport & Highways, Department of Shipping, Government of India. The Company has been upgraded to Schedule 'B' from 'C' during the year 2002. The clients of the Company include Major Ports, non-major ports, Indian Navy, State Governments, etc.

3801. (19-10-2007) NEW DELHI : Gen Deepak Kapoor, COAS in presence of Lt Gen PR Gangadharan, Colonel of the JAK LI Regiment and Mr. Pawan Munjal, Managing Director, Hero Honda and Mr. RS Settia, DGM of Indian Oil Corporation, flagged in the 'Flags in the JAK LI mountaineering expedition to mount nun and Imphal-Siachen-New Delhi Motor Cycle Expedition' in New Delhi The Jammu and Kashmir Light Infantry Regiment, an illustrious Regiment of the Indian Army is celebrating its Diamond Jubilee this year. To mark the occasion the Regiment undertook a Mountaineering Expedition to Mount Nun, 7135m and a Motor Cycle Expedition from Imphal to New Delhi via Siachen (Base Camp). The Jammu and Kashmir Light Infantry Regiment was raised on 15 Apr 1948, out of volunteers who took up arms to defend their motherland. The volunteers were subsequently organized into a Militia Force of fourteen battalions. The gallantry of the Militia Force was recognized by the Nation by redesignating it as "THE JAMMU AND KASHMIR LIGHT INFANTRY" in 1972. Mount Nun is an extremely hazardous and difficult peak which has challenged climbers over the yrs. The expedition led by Col Vinay Khosla braved bad weather and vagaries of the terrain to successfully summit the peak on 15 Sep 2007 under Maj Randeep Singh. Two subsequent attempts led by Col Vinay Khosla, the expedition leader and Maj Amit Soni created a record ascent by having 20 mountaineers summit the peak. The Regiment and the Red Shield Division undertook a Motor Cycle Expedition from Imphal to New Delhi via Siachen Base Camp. A distance of over 8000 Kms across the breadth of the country covering 12 states involved crossing of three passes; Rohtang 13360 ft, Tanglang-La 15055 ft, Khardung-La 18380 ft and Zoji-La 12535 ft. The aim of the expedition was to promote the spirit of adventure and to spread the theme of national integration, peace and harmony as the Indian Army and JAK LI Regiment is known to be the epitome of 'National Integration'. The expedition was supported by Hero Honda and Indian Oil Corporation. Gen Deepak Kapoor lauded the achievements of the Regiment for being one of the most decorated Regiments of the Indian Army post independence having been awarded four Battle Honours, three Theatre Honours, six Unit Citations, a Param Vir Chakra, two Ashok Chakras and a large number of other gallantry awards. He also congratulated both the expeditions and their leaders on their outstanding feat.

3802. (19-10-2007) NEW DELHI : Commander R Mahesh and Giridharlal Yadav of Indian Navy created history by winning the first Gold Medal in 'Sailing' for India today in the 4th CISM Military World Games-07. France and Spain won the Silver and Bronze medal respectively. Having established a clear lead in four races out of total eight races conducted at the Indian Naval Watermanship Training Centre, Colaba, Mumbai the Indian crew were well ahead with 10.9 points. Pauchet Nicolas and Besson Billy of the French Team were placed second with 19 points and Francisco Javier Soto Loureiro and Jose Medina Ruiz of the Spanish team third with 25 points. On the concluding day of the Sailing Competition, Indian team was well ahead of their nearest rival France and Spain from the beginning of the race. Finnland and Russia are placed fourth & fifth respectively. For both the Indian crew winning in major championship is no surprise. Both Cdr Mahesh and Yadav were confident from the very first day of the competition having won the first two races on the opening day itself. Although on Thursday the Russian team won both the races and gave a big surprise maintaining the trend of different country winning the race on different days. Cdr Mahesh having secured

Gold & Bronze medal in the Asian Games has also won Bronze medal in recently concluded Sailing Competition in Russia this year Having won 40th Military Sailing Championship conducted during the same period last year (14 to 21 Oct. 2006) at the same venue in Mumbai, Indian crew were most favourite during this Competition.

3803. (19-10-2007) NEW DELHI : The Prime Minister said here that I am aghast at the news of the terrorist attack last night on the convoy of Benazir Bhutto in Karachi, within hours of her return from her eight-year-long exile abroad. The reported deaths of more than 125 persons in two bomb blasts show that the perpetrators of this barbaric act wanted to inflict maximum damage on an event that held the promise of the return of democracy in Pakistan. I am relieved that Ms. Bhutto has survived this bid on her life. It is an irony that, at a time when tall claims are being made about Pakistan's democratization, one former Prime Minister, Mr. Nawaz Sharief, was recently prevented from returning to his own country and another former Prime Minister, Ms. Benazir Bhutto, has been 'greeted' by a terrorist attack on her arrival. I have always been of the view that Pakistan's stability and progress, as also the normalization of India-Pakistan relations, are best guaranteed by the establishment of genuine democracy in that country, combined with a resolute fight against religious extremism and terrorism. Last night's shocking incident in Karachi leaves no doubt whatsoever that the battle for democracy and the battle against terrorism are interrelated.

3804. (20-10-2007) NEW DELHI : China dominated in swimming by winning 4 Gold medals on the last day of the aquatic events in the 4th Military World Games at Hyderabad. Two new CISM records were created today in 200 M back stroke women and 1500 M free Style men. Tianlongzi xu of China clocked 2:12.87 in 200 M back stroke women to win the Gold. The old record was 2: 13.68. In 1500 M free style men's event Spyridon Gianniotis of Greece clocked 15:16.50 to win the Gold. The old record was 15:24.31. New World & CISM record holder in 50 M back stroke (W), Yang Li today won her second Gold in 50 M free style by clocking 25.62 secs.

3805. (20-10-2007) NEW DELHI: Prime Minister Manmohan Singh on Friday wrote to the former Pakistan Prime Minister, Benazir Bhutto, and Pakistan President Pervez Musharraf, condemning the blasts in Karachi on late Thursday. Dr. Singh conveyed his condolences to the families of those killed and condemned terrorism in all forms. "Such acts of violence and terrorism are totally unacceptable in any civilised society," he said. Minister for External Affairs Pranab Mukherjee conveyed his sympathies through India's High Commissioner to Pakistan Satyabrata Pal to the families of those killed. Ms. Bhutto, speaking to Mr. Pal, thanked the people of India and Dr. Singh and others for expressing solidarity with her and condoling the death of many of her party workers and sympathisers.

3806. (20-10-2007) NEW DELHI : Boxer P Narjit Singh brought second Gold for host country India today in 4th Military World Games at Hyderabad. He beat

Pte Schneider Marcel of Germany by 12-8 in Men's 51-54 kg category. The entire stadium clapped and cheered for Indian Boxer who displayed his combination of left hook and right jam to prevail over his opponent. Even though he trailed in the first three rounds, Narjit Singh mixed attack and defence in an effective manner. With spectators waiving Indian Tri-colour, Narjit Singh improved his game in the final round to finish the match in a clinical manner.

3807. (20-10-2007) NEW DELHI : Russia continued their domination of wrestling ring by overpowering opponents in freestyle events today. Ramaaan Saritov beat Namia Sovdumov of Azerbaijan to take Gold in 60 kg category. Yom Jong Min of DPR Korea and Damir Zakhardinov of Uzbekistan were the joint winners of Bronze medal. In 84 kg category, Russia's Sazhid Sazhidov defeated Radoslaw Horbik of Poland to win the Gold. Du Soo Lee of Korea Republic and Abdul Ammaev of Uzbekistan were the joint winners of the Bronze medal. Gamedov Kurama of Russia won the Gold in 120 kg category beating Recep Kara of Turkey. The Bronze medal went to Fadin Mnesoumi of Iran and Serhii Priadun of Ukraine. Turkey's Ahmet Gulhan won the Gold in 74 kg category by beating Aliaksandr Matyl of Belarus. Germany's Peter Weisenberger and Russia's Tsargush Denis were the joint winners of the Bronze.

3808. (20-10-2007) NEW DELHI : Russia emerged on top in Parachuting by winning 3 Gold medals in the 4th Military World Games at Hyderabad today. Russia's Maksimov won the Gold in men's individual accuracy event while Russian women's team won the Gold in team accuracy. Russia's Lepezina won the Gold in women's individual accuracy event. In men's formation skydiving Belgium came on top winning Gold followed by USA (Silver) and Switzerland (Bronze). USA took the top honours in women's formation skydiving by winning Gold. Norway and Franc got the Silver and Bronze respectively.

3809. (20-10-2007) NEW DELHI : In a spirited display India today defeated Qatar to bag the Bronze medal in men's volleyball in 4th Military World Games at Hyderabad. At Yusufguda indoor stadium, the first set was a neck-to-neck tie in which Indians showed their aggression to get past Qatar by 25-21. Indians took early lead in the second set and went on to take it by 25-21. Having pocketed two sets, the confident Indian team took good lead in the third set to wrap it up 25-21. The Indian Captain Shijas Mohammed was well supported in smashing by P.K.Dinesh. Kumar Sharath's placements on short passes also won India crucial points. The final match turned out to be one-sided affair with China beating Korea Republic in three straight sets to clinch the Gold. The Koreans who looked better than the Chinese in most of the matches could not raise level in the crucial match against their Asian rivals. The first set which normally sets the tempo for the match was at one stage leveled at 23 points each. They won it 26-24 narrowly. Chinese later dominated the second and the third set 25-15, 25-20 without too much of a fight from their opponents. Brazil beat Netherlands 3-2 in the toughest of fights to take the 5th position. The first two sets were taken Brazil 28-26, 25-19 and they looked in comfortable position. However they had a surprise in store when Dutch enhanced their play and took next two sets 25-23, 25-18. The fifth set was taken by Brazilians 15-13 relegating Netherlands to the 6th position. Latvia beat Canada 3-1 to occupy the 7th position whereas the Canadians had to be content with the 8th position. The Latvians won 25-22, 25-20, 18-25, 25-18 in the match.

3810. (20-10-2007) NEW DELHI : Shri Arjun Singh, Minister of Human Resource Development (HRD), called upon UNESCO to respond to the challenges posed by the continuance of poverty and illiteracy in a rapidly changing world. Shri Arjun Singh was addressing the 34th General Conference of United Nations Educational, Scientific and Cultural Organisation (UNESCO) at Paris, yesterday. The Minister addressed the World Body as the heart and the mind of the UN system and said that education is the core of UNESCO's mandate and therefore the organisation must continue its work in Technical and Vocational education, adult education and for removal of illiteracy within the framework of Education For All (EFA)'. In the area of Science, the Minister called attention towards science education and the popularization of science for the development of a scientific temper. Shri Arjun Singh also commended the World Heritage Centre and its activities. The UN has declared 2nd October, the Birthday of Mahatama Gandhi as the International day of Non-Violence. Referring to this, Shri Arjun Singh said that while this gesture has been widely appreciated in India, Gandhi belongs to the whole world and his message of truth and nonviolence is ever relevant. Shri Arjun Singh also addressed a Roundtable on the theme of "Right to Education, Right to Development". He stated that in a democracy, economic growth can be sustainable only if it is accompanied by equity and justice. Development of human resources depends not only on expansion of educational opportunity but also on ensuring that education is inclusive. He announced that India is taking up an impressive programme of expanding secondary and tertiary education. India is also initiating far-reaching measures of positive discrimination. Shri Arjun Singh has also held bilateral meetings with the Education Ministers of Pakistan and Sri Lanka.

3811. (20-10-2007) NEW DELHI : The Government has accorded its approval to notify the EPF rate of interest for the year 2006-07 as 8.5%. All the RPFCs have been instructed to immediately give effect to the above and issue annual statement of accounts for the year 2006 at the earliest possible time. The Chairman CBT, EPF and Minister of State (Independent Charge), Labour and Employment has directed that issue of annual accounts for the year 2006-07 is required to be done on war footing. The EPF(Employees' Provident Fund) Scheme, 1952 requires that the interest shall be credited to the account of each member at such a rate as determined by the Central Government in consultation with the Central Board of Trustees (CBT). The CBT which met on the 23rd of July 2007 to consider the proposal for determination of rate of interest payable to the members for the year 2006-07 had recommended interest at 8.5%.

3812. (20-10-2007) NEW DELHI : The President, Smt. Pratibha Devisingh Patil, has sent her greetings to her fellow citizens on the occasion of Dussehra, which falls tomorrow. In a message, the President has said, "On the auspicious occasion of Dussehra, I send my greetings and good wishes to all my fellow citizens in India and abroad. May peace, goodwill and prosperity abound in the country and may we all work for the unity and well being of our nation".

3813. (20-10-2007) NEW DELHI : The Prime Minister, Dr. Manmohan Singh, has greeted the nation on the occasion of Dussehra and Durga Puja. In a message, the Prime Minister said that Vijayadashmi is a festival amass the length and breadth of the country, signifies the triumph of good over evil. It is an occasion to foster goodness within and to radiate peace and harmony. May the festivals of Dussehra and Durga Puja bring health, happiness and prosperity to all, the Prime Minister added.

3814. (20-10-2007) NEW DELHI : DPR Korea clinched Gold in Women's football today in 4th Military World Games at Hyderabad. They thrashed Germany 5-0 in the final at Artillery Stadium. K Kim scored started with a goal at 22nd minute followed by a goal by K Ri at 33rd minute. The next minute K Kim netted her second goal of the match making it 3-0 for DPR Korea. In the second half, C Mun scored fourth goal for her country and Y Kim made it 5-0 at 63rd minute. Germany had to content with Silver. France defeated Netherlands in the morning by 1-0 to take Bronze medal. M Cizac scored the solitary goal for France at 77th minute. Egypt beat Cameroon in the Men's Football final by 2-0. Soldier Ossama Hossni scored the first goal at 2nd minute. Soldier A Abdo netted second goal at 92nd minute.

3815. (20-10-2007) NEW DELHI : Belarus bagged the Gold in Handball today by beating Latvia in the 4th Military World Games at the Saroornagar Indoor Stadium, Hyderabad. Latvia began the match with the first goal followed by Belarus in the first two minutes. Towards the end of the first half, Belarus overtook and was leading by 17-14. The goalkeeper captain of Belarus saved many goals for his country. In the second half, Belarus got into the top gear to score on regular basis. Siamionau Yauheni of Belarus and Edgars of Latvia were shown the red card in the dying moments of the game. The excellent team effort and outstanding performance of the goalkeeper especially made Belarus win the Finals with a score of 33-29 against Latvia Lithuania won the bronze medal. During the last World Military Handball championship held at Riga-Latvia, Latvia had won the gold, Lithuania the silver and Republic of Korea the Bronze. Earlier in the day, India was pushed to the bottom of the tally. UAE defeated India by 34-32 to push latter to 8th position in the event. In the first half, India was leading 16-15. Indian captain INC Singh scored 9 goals. UAE fought back in the second half with Ibrahim Sanqour Qambar Mubarak scoring 10 goals leading his team to victory by 34-32. Lithuania beat Korea Republic 37-27 to take Bronze while Greece defeated Qatar 35-32 to take 5th position.

3816. (21-10-2007) NEW DELHI : The grand finale showcasing a blend of tradition and modernity marked the conclusion of the weeklong sporting extravaganza-the Fourth CISM Military World Games in Hyderabad this evening. The Defence Minister of India, Shri A K Antony declared the Games closed at the GMC Balayogi stadium. The closing ceremony was a four-hour long celebration adding to the festive mood of Vijayadashami, the Dussehra. Thousands of spectators filled every inch of the stadium to join the celebrations of the Games in which nearly 5000 athletes from 101 countries participated. This was the biggest International multi-sport event of the year, the motto of which was 'Friendship Through Sport'. Russia emerged on top of the Medal Tally with 42 Gold, 26 Silver and 28 Bronze medals. China, second with 36 Gold, 22 Silver and 13 Bronze while Germany came a distant third with 7 Gold, 10 Silver and 13 Bronze. India won 10 medals including 2 Gold, 1 Silver and 7 Bronze, its largest haul ever in the two editions of the Games that it participated in. The successful conduct of the Games brought together few nations who are otherwise in conflict and yet competed in the true spirit of sportsmanship. In the Games, 3 world records and 27 CISM records were either set or overhauled. Of these 17 were set alone by women athletes. A record 49 countries won medals during the competitions, the highest ever in any edition of the Games. The evening began with a performance of a classical Bharatnatyam dance by Sonali Sharma. Gayatri sang an ever-popular composition highlighting the unity in diversity of India 'Mile Sur Mera Tumhara'. Fusion dance of Bharatnatyam and contemporary jazz performance by students of Trapeze received huge applause from the spectators. Like the opening ceremony, Akashganga skydiving team and Sarang Helicopter display team exhibited their daring and breathtaking formation display. In an enthralling band display, Indian Armed Forces Bands played tunes to signal the march past by the competitors from participating countries. One after another, the countries followed in their immaculate military uniform waving to the cheering spectators. Indian contingent led by Captain Tushar Tomar received loudest applause and cheers from the audience. Defence Minister A K Antony congratulated the Indian Armed Forces for the successful conduct of the Games and said that these Games would usher in new era not only in the Indian subcontinent but also throughout Asia. CISM President Brigadier General Gianni Gola in an emotionally charged speech said that Military World Games have been a stupendous succeess. "This was the first Games outside Europe and that happens to be the best ever in India. Seldom has any country been successful in conducting such a wonderful organization of the Games", he said.

3817. (21-10-2007) NEW DELHI : Finance Minister, Sh. P Chidambaram will be on a three-day visit to Norway from 23rd October, 2007. During the visit he will hold bilateral discussions with his counterpart Ms. Kristin Halvorsen. The two Ministers had met earlier in March, 2007 during the visit of the Norwegian Finance Minister to India. As the main outcomes of the meeting, Ms. Halvorsen had indicated the possibilities of the Norwegian pension fund making investment in India (out of their corpus of over US$ 320 billion); suggested possibilities for utilizing our technical manpower strength; informed of a dedicated budget line for CDM projects in India; concurred with our views on climate change and on oil price rise (despite being a major oil producer), and appreciated the need to augment the bilateral trade and investment. During the visit the two Ministers are likely to discuss wide ranging issues of mutual interest particularly related to strengthening of bilateral economic ties in the sectors where either India or Norway have some advantage like information technology, Food processing, hydrocarbons, fisheries, shipping & ship building, hydro-electricity, tunneling and environment. Shri Chidambaram is also likely to call for policy changes by the Norwegian Government in order to facilitate investments in India from the corpus of the Pension Fund-Global. The Norwegian Minister for International Development, Mr. Erik Solheim will be calling on Shri Chidambaram for bilateral discussions on issues related to Bilateral Development Cooperation. Shri Chidambaram will also meet the Governor of the Central Bank of Norway, the Norges Bank. Norway's Pension Fund-Global which has a huge corpus of more than US$ 350 billion is being managed by the Investment Management (NBIM) division of the Norges Bank. NBIM is currently registered with SEBI in India and has started investments in India from July 2005 and as per SEBI, the purchase value of Norges Bank investments in India on 04.10.07 was Rs. 2107 cores ($ 533 million). While GPF-G investment in India has crossed half a billion dollar mark in two years time from its registration with SEBI in June, 2005, the figure is only 0.15% of the total corpus of GPF-G. Finance Minister's meeting with Governor of the Norges Bank is very important in this context. Shri Chidambaram is being accompanied by a Business delegation consisting of members of CII and FICCI, CMD of the Punjab National Bank and a representative of Shipping Corporation of India. An Investment Promotion Symposium is being organised hosted by NHO/NICCI/DNV (business and trade associations of Norway) to help promote bilateral investments which will be attended by Finance Minsiter and the entire Indian delegation. The Finance Minister is also scheduled to visit the prestigious Noble Institute at Oslo for delivering a keynote address on the topic "India's Socio-Economic Agenda: Development with Democracy". In addition Shri Chidambaram is scheduled to visit the Norwegian School of Management BI at Oslo, which is Europe's largest private business school, and will deliver an address on the topic "India's emergence as an economic power: Road travelled and the way forward". An IT outsourcing event is also being organised keeping in view India's strength in this sector which is likely to be attended by Norwegian business houses and also representatives from the India IT industry. Finance Minister will also be attending this event.

3818. (22-10-2007) NEW DELHI : The Sports Minister Shri Mani Shankar Aiyar has said that he will be organizing a programme to felicitate and honour Shri Vishwanathan Anand on his achievements of emerging at the World's No.1 Chess Champion, in Mayiladuthurai. In a letter to Shri Vishwanathan Anand, the Minister expressed his regrets for not being able to join the function being held in Chennai this evening for honouring Shri Anand. Shri Aiyar has not been well for the past few days. In his letter he said that due to my illness " I have to deny myself the opportunity of joining millions of my countrymen and women in congratulating you on your utterly remarkable achievement of emerging as the World's No.1 Chess Champion. For India, it is an achievement without parallel of precedent." The Minister also said that "as I am the Member of Parliament for Mayiladuthurai, I join all my constituents in felicitating ourselves on your having been born and brought up amongst us before you went into the wide world to secure fame and glory for our country. I trust we can make up for my not being with you this evening by organizing a felicitation in your honour in Mayiladuthurai." Expressing regrets for not being present in Chennai for today's function he said "My inability to be present on the occasion does not diminish one whit our pride and gratitude for the excellence of your achievement."

3819. (22-10-2007) NEW DELHI : The Minister of State for Defence Shri M M Pallam Raju released the Military Land Register (MLR) software at a function here today. The MLR is a step further towards digitizing Defence Land Records for all defence lands located outside notified cantonments. Speaking on the occasion Shri Pallam Raju called upon the Defence Estate officials to use the MLR for effective land management and safeguard the most important assets of the Defence Ministry, viz the land. The Minister pointed out that with the fast paced economy, the pressure on land has multiplied and it is now a precious commodity which requires judicious exploitation. In his address, the Director General of Defence Estates (DGDE), Shri C R Mohapatra pointed out that the task before Defence Estate was voluminous since the Defence Ministry is the biggest landholder in the Central Government. He said the Defence Estates officials are being trained in the new software at the National Institute of Defence Estates Management (NIDEM). Shri Mohapatra said that the digitization project has been delayed by over three months and is expected to be completed by March next year. He said that the Defence Estate is flooded with litigations over lands held by it across the country. The MLR, jointly developed by DGDE and National Informatics Centre (NIC), is in addition to the General Land Register (GLR) or the Raksha Bhoomi software, which maintains the entire land record for Defence Lands located within the notified cantonments. The GLR, released by Shri Pallam Raju in November, 2006, is in various stages of implementation in all 62 cantonments spread across the country.

3820. (22-10-2007) NEW DELHI : The Army Commanders' Conference, to focuses on key policy, conceptual and doctrinal issues in light of prevailing and developing security environment, will get underway in Delhi on Tuesday. The Conference is being chaired by the Army Chief, Gen Deepak Kapoor. All Army Commanders and senior officers of the Army will attend the same. The deliberations of the conference are to continue till 27 Oct. 07. The Combined Commanders' Conference, to be addressed by the Prime Minister, will be held on 24 Oct. 07.

The conference will take a holistic review of the security environment, status of operational readiness as also the appraisal of situation in the J&K and the North East. The aspects of force modernization including battlefield transparency, long range precision engagement and integral air-mobility will come up for in-depth discussions as part of the overall review as also the appraisal of the progress made in transforming the Army from platform centric to network enabled and finally to a fully network centric force. The senior Army leadership is slated to discuss a large number of important issues during the four-day deliberations. One critical issue on the agenda will be the Army's Space Vision 2020. The Army realizes the importance of space as a vital arena for future exploitation and has already established a "Space Cell" in the Army HQ to coordinate space based applications in a joint services operational environment. The deliberations during the conference will be aimed at ratifying the Army's space philosophy; concept of utilization of space at tactical, operational and strategic levels; desired operational capabilities and related ground and space assets. Space applications are expected to enhance functional effectiveness of the Army even in non-combat operations through use of space-based communications, weather forecasts, avalanche warnings and navigation. Towards this, the issue of consolidation and convergence of networks to cater to appropriate redundancies are also slated to be deliberated upon at length. The other issues that are expected to be addressed during the conference are effective management of ammunition and the ex-Servicemen Contributory Health Scheme (ECHS). As regards the ECHS, the focus is expected to be on expansion of the scheme for wider coverage as well as measures to make it more cost effective through enhanced outsourcing of health services.

3821. (22-10-2007) NEW DELHI : A 12 Member Indian Youth delegation led by Shri M.O.H.F. Shahjahan Minister of Transport, Information Technology, Fisheries, Education and Art and Culture, Government of Puducheery called on the Vice President of India Mohd. Hamid Ansari here today. The delegation comprising of Arabic scholars-v linguists, poets and literati as well as budding IIT Engineers and IT students, is visiting Saudi Arabia for 12 days from 24th October to 4th November 2007 under an Annual Exchange of Youth Delegation programme. During the visit of King Abdullah Bin Abdul Aziz Al-Saud, Custodian of the two Holy Mosques to New Delhi for Republic Day, 2006, an Agreement on Cooperation in the field of Sports and Youth Affairs was singed on 25.01.2006 in the joint presence of the Prime Minister of India and the Saudi King. The signatories were Shri Oscar Fernanades, the then Minister of State (I/C) of the Ministry of Statistics and Programme Implementation, Youth Affairs and Sports and Overseas Indian Affairs of the Government of the Republic of India and Mr. Lyad A. Madani, Minister of Culture and Information of the Government of the Kingdom of Saudi Arabia An annual exchange of youth delegation has been agreed. To begin with, the delegation will be limited to 12 young persons on either side to made a 12 day long visit.

3822. (22-10-2007) NEW DELHI: India and Pakistan are to discuss the modalities for exchanging information on terrorist acts in each other's countries. The issue will come up at the second meeting of the anti-terror mechanism (ATM) to be held here on Monday, according to official sources. New Delhi wants proactive assistance from Islamabad to help trace Pakistan nationals suspected of having had a role in terror attacks in India and bring them to book. It feels a good beginning has been made with the setting up of the ATM in March this year, and if meetings take place on a quarterly basis, the beginning of an institutional mechanism to exchange credible information will soon be in sight. Although the maiden ATM meeting resolved to meet every quarter, the second interaction will be taking place after seven months. India is of the opinion that the delay was more because of internal troubles in Pakistan. Officially, Pakistan maintains that the previous official nominated for the talks had retired and his replacement took time. This time India believes the climate is favourable for discussing the contours of an information exchange mechanism as the meeting comes close on the heels of Friday's bomb blasts in Karachi — an attempt to assassinate the former Pakistan Prime Minister, Benazir Bhutto. India will also seek to know the progress made in identifying a person suspected of having had a role in the Samjhauta Express bombing. At the previous ATM meeting, India handed over a photograph of the person, suspected to be a Pakistani national. India also believes persons of Pakistani origin are involved in a string of blasts that rocked several cities and killed or maimed civilians. This belief is backed by interrogation records of suspected militants who are understood to have "confessed" to the Pakistani link behind a few of the attacks. The Indian side's quest for Pakistan's assistance in this regard is backed by an agreement at the previous meeting that whenever possible both sides would seek and receive information about terror attacks. The two sides also agreed to immediately get in touch with one another in case either required urgent information on any terrorist issue. The Indian delegation will be led by Additional Secretary (International Organisations) in the Ministry of External Affairs K.C. Singh while the Pakistan team will be headed by his counterpart Khalid Aziz Babar.

3823. (22-10-2007) NEW DELHI : India is hosting the Second Meeting of SAARC Interior/Home Ministers preceded by the Second Meeting of SAARC Home Secretaries and Sixth SAARC Conference on Cooperation in Police Matters from October 23-25, 2007. As per SAARC tradition, India, as host, will chair the meetings. All member States will participate in these meetings. The newest member State of SAARC, Afghanistan, would be participating in the three meetings for the first time. These meetings will continue the exchange of apex level ideas/perspectives on issues of criticality and work towards enhancement of cooperation in security management and related issues. At the 14th SAARC Summit held in New Delhi, the Heads of Government emphasized the importance of increased cooperation in security related areas, especially the need to combat terrorism, narcotics and psychotropic substances, trafficking in women and children and other trans-national crimes. They had also expressed their commitment to take every possible measure to prevent and suppress, in particular, financing of terrorist acts and counter trafficking of narcotic drugs and illicit arms. Capacity building, institutional arrangements and multi-lateral agreements will be at the core of these deliberations at all three levels. The forthcoming meetings are, thus, expected to deliberate on among others, a network of cooperation amongst police chiefs, SAARC visa exemption scheme, a Draft Convention on Mutual Legal Assistance in Criminal Matters, greater strength to existing mechanisms of cooperation in drugs, terrorism and trafficking. As SAARC member States are signatories to the SAARC Regional Convention on Suppression of Terrorism and its additional Protocol and SAARC Convention on Narcotic Drugs and Psychotropic Substances, the deliberations are expected to witness increased dynamism within the existing and newly set up institutional mechanisms, namely, the SAARC Terrorism Offences Monitoring Desk (STOMD) and the SAARC Drug Offences Monitoring Desk (STOMD) flowing from these conventions.

3824. (22-10-2007) NEW DELHI : The 52nd meeting of the Central Wakf Council was convened in New Delhi. It was presided over by the Union Minister for Minority Affairs and Chairman of the Central Wakf Council, Shri A.R. Antulay. The Minister welcomed all the members to the meeting and discussed various agenda items. He expressed the hope that the deliberations of the meeting would be useful in improving the management and administration of the wakf properties through out the country. He said that the Central Wakf Council has to act as a guiding force to various State Wakf Boards to improve the management of wakf properties and also to get rid of unauthorized occupation of the properties in various parts of the country. The members of the Council emphasized on the need to early setting up of National Wakf Development Corporation and also to take appropriate steps for exemption of wakf properties from the purview of the various legislations as recommended by Rajendra Sachar Committee. The Minister assured the members that necessary steps have been initiated to set up a National Wakf Development Corporation and the matter is at various stages of implementation. He hoped that establishment of National Wakf Development Corporation will be possible in near future. As far as the exemption of wakf properties from the purview of certain acts, it was informed to the members that the Council is already on the job and is collecting various details of the laws as applicable in those areas and also to examine how wakf properties can be exempted from the purview of these laws with a view to make better management of wakf properties. Some of the States have responded in this regard and some are yet to respond. It was assured to the members that the matter will be expedited. The member was also informed that the Central Wakf Council will send its views on the proposed amendments in the Wakf Act, 1995 for which a JPC has already been constituted. For this purpose a special Committee was set up to formulate such views. It was also decided that a Conference of Chief Ministers and Wakf Ministers of various states will be convened on measures for survey, protection and proper development and management of wakf properties. It was also decided that Central Wakf Council will keep an eye on illegal transfers of wakf properties in any part of the country and will bring these to the notice of concerned authorities. The meeting was attended by Shri Syed Shahabuddin, former M.P., Shri Salman Khurshid, former Union Minister, Maulana Mohd.Fazlur Rahim Mujadadi and Justice (Retd.) Naseemuddin and other members of the Council.

3825. (22-10-2007) NEW DELHI : The All-India Consumer Price Index for Agricultural and Rural Labourers (Base 1986-87 = 100) increased by two points each during September 2007 to stand at 410 points for both the series. The rise and fall in index varied from state to state. In case of Agricultural Labourers 13 states reflected an increase in indices ranging between 1 to 10 points, in three states the declining trend in index ranged between 1 and 2 points while in four states the index remained constant. In case of Rural Labourers, 13 states reflected an increase in indices ranging between 1 to 12 points while in two states the index decreased by 1 and 2 points. The Index remained constant in five states. Haryana and Tripura experienced the highest increase of 10 points each for Agricultural Labourers. In the case of the Consumer Price Index Numbers for Rural Labourers, Tripura showed a steep rise of 12 points mainly due to increase in the prices of Rice, Wheat Atta, Milk, Onion, Vegetables & Fruits, Firewood and Allopathic Medicine/Anacin. On the other hand, the indices in respect of Madhya Pradesh showed a decrease of two points each for Agricultural Labourers and Rural Labourers mainly due to decrease in the prices of Rice, Maize, Moong Dal, Urd Dal and Vegetables & Fruits. Punjab with 446 points for Agricultural Labourers and 447 points for Rural Labourers figured at the top of the index table. Manipur with 360 points for Agricultural Labourers and 361 points for Rural Labourers remained at the bottom of the index.

3826. (22-10-2007) NEW DELHI : In one of the largest cases of central excise evasion detected in the recent past, the Central Excise Commissionerate, Rohtak, Delhi zone has registered a case of evasion of duty by M/s Som Sugandh Industries Ltd., Kundli, the manufacturer of popular brands of Gutkha namely Dilbagh, Talab and Tez. Acting on intelligence, the unit was kept under surveillance for a few days. Thereafter, a team of officers of Rohtak Commissionerate searched the factory premises and the residence of the Manager on 20th and 21st October. The searches revealed an evasion of central excise duty of Rs.15.15 crores, payable on account of production of only 19 days for the month of October, 2007. The modus operandi adopted by the party was that while they had declared to the Department only one shift, the factory, however, worked round the clock. The duplicate set of challans of such unaccounted production and clearances was kept in the personal custody of their Manager at his residence. This is the second case of evasion booked against this unit. The earlier case was detected in May, 2007, involving duty evasion of Rs. 9.64 lakh. This case is symptomatic of the large scale evasion taking place in the Pan Masala, Gutkha and chewing tobacco sector all over the country. The revenue from these commodities is far short of the estimated revenue that should be coming based on various parameters such as number of packing and filling machines, commodity manufactured and sold, estimates of consumption of raw materials such as Supari etc. The revenue from this sector has not been enjoying the growth which is expected, based on the growing consumption of these products amongst masses. The Chairman, Central Board of Excise and Customs had recently issued instructions to tackle the rampant evasion that is characteristic of this sector. Instructions have been issued to the field formations to verify the machines present in the factory, the number of such machines working, and for sealing of non-working machines. In the light of the detection of this case, the Chairman, has once again reiterated to all the Central Excise officials all over the country to gear up their anti-evasion activities and realize the revenue, the potential of which is very high going on the basis of this case which has unearthed evasion of over Rs.15 crores in a matter of 19 days only.

3827. (22-10-2007) NEW DELHI : Shri Kamal Nath has called for increasing the pace of economic engagement between small and medium enterprises based in Minnesota, USA and in India and establishing people-to-people contacts for achieving greater cooperation. Stating that India being a large importer and having a huge work force with an increasing manufacturing base offering vertical linkages offers an ideal platform for Minnesota based SMEs to establish business-to-business contacts with progressive Indian SMEs. He was welcoming Mr. Pawlenty, Governor of Minnesota here today. Shri Ajay Shanker, Secretary (IPP), senior officials from the Ministry of Industry and members of the business delegation from Minnesota were also present on the occasion. The Commerce & Industry Minister highlighted the increasing opportunities for business contacts available in various Indian states, which offer tremendous potential to SMEs based in Minnesota. The increasing commercial engagements would lead to greater people to people contact, the Minister observed. The Minnesota Governor articulated the interest of Minnesota based corporates in seeking greater Indian expertise for research in different sectors of manufacturing and engineering. This is the first-ever visit by a Minnesota Governor to India. Informing that it is one of the bigger and more economically vibrant states in US, Mr. Pawlenty stated that there is tremendous potential for our bilateral, commercial and economic relations.

3828. (22-10-2007) NEW DELHI : Shri Kamal Nath, Minister of Commerce and Industry, has called for replantation and rejuvenation of plantation crops in the country for the benefit of growers, workers and other stakeholders. Emphasising that the plantation sector is an important component of agrarian economy in India in terms of its contribution to its GDP, export potential and employment generation as the sector employs about 20 million people, the Commerce Minister informed that 15% of the total agricultural export earnings of India comes from crops like tea, coffee and rubber. Addressing a meeting of the Chairmen of the Commodity Boards and stakeholders of plantation sectors here today, Shri Kamal Nath also informed about the recent government efforts as regards the steps taken to benefit the growers and workers of the plantation sector in the country. Shri G.K. Pillai, Commerce Secretary; Shri O.P. Arya, Additional Secretary, Department of Commerce; senior officials of the Ministry and representatives from various Commodity Boards were also present on the occasion. The Commerce Minister informed the representatives present that a Special Purpose Tea Fund has already been set up in January 2007 for funding replantation and rejuvenation for improving the age-profile of tea plantations whereby an area of 2.12 lakh hectares with a financial outlay of Rs.4761 crore over a period of 15 years is proposed. A Rehabilitation Package was also announced for providing financial assistance to the closed tea gardens earlier this year and out of the 33 closed gardens, 9 gardens have already been reopened, the Minister further informed. As regards spices, Shri Kamal Nath informed that to improve upon the quality of spices exported and also to meet the requirements of importing countries, a state of the art laboratory has been set up at Cochin and similar laboratories are being set up at Guntur, Delhi and Mumbai. With a view to have a scientific processing and value-addition and to enhance quality standards of the product, government has decided to set up Spices Parks at 6 places *i.e.*, at Idduki, Guntur, Rai Bareili, Erode, Kota and Chhindwara where common infrastructure facilities for cleaning, washing, sterilization, packaging, warehousing would be available to provide high-end value-addition, processing, training on good agricultural practices and quality requirements of spices to farmers, traders, processors and exporters. Reacting to the demands of industry representatives, the Commerce Minister also agreed to look at the possibility of having a special risk policy for tobacco exports through ECGC and having a specialised institute for spices technology for coordinated research and market intelligence efforts.

3829. (22-10-2007) NEW DELHI : The food riots in West Bengal are a matter of serious concern. It is an anachronism to even talk of food riots in a country which is proud to flaunt a booming economy which rightfully seeks its true place in the community of nations. The riots reflect the enormous deficiencies in the availability, distribution, pricing and regulatory systems in that state. Those who profess concern for the poorest of the poor should immediately set their own house in order. They have to urgently address the legitimate concerns of the deprived and the needy. The Congress' concern is for that deprived segment and Congress and the UPA government is ever ready to extend all assistance and facilitation in that regard. But the State Govt. can neither abdicate nor transfer its vital role and responsibility in that regard. All other slogans, shibboleths and controversies are secondary compared to the basic food needs of the people of West Bengal. We hope and trust that an immediate healing touch is provided by those entrusted with this task. While on the issue of food, it is needless to add that Mr. Advani & the BJP are, as usual, fishing in troubled waters with a complete lack of understanding of agriculture. Mr. Advani's crocodile tears for enhancement of the MSP for paddy proves that he neither understands the plight of farmers nor speaks their language. During six years, form 1998 to 2004, the Govt. of which he was the Deputy PM, increased the MSP by approx Rs. 10 per quintal per year *i.e.* Rs. 60/- over 6 yrs. Between May '04 and now, the MSP has been increased by this Govt. by 300 Rs. Per quintal. This is the highest ever percentage increase. It shows that Mr. Advani's lament is opportunistic and hypocritical. The BJPs fake concern is also proved by the fact that just over the last year, this Govt. has increased the price by over Rs. 105 Per quintal – whereas the recommended increase by the Pricing Committee was Rs. 65/-. The PM and the Govt. then added Rs. 40/- as a bonus. Mr. Advani is making an untenable, unconnectable and totally illusory equation between wheat and rice in a facile and over simplistic manner. Some of you have heard yesterday the outpourings of hatred against the Congress President by imbalanced political entities like the Shiv Sena and its head, Mr. Bal Thackarey. Such persons and their parties represent the lunatic fringe of Indian politics. Whether it is Mr. Thackarey or Mr. Modi, who also used insulting words yesterday, they both represent the forces of intolerance and fascism in the country. Their remarks are condemnable, despicable, and deplorable. But they have done it earlier and we know that they will continue to do so. That is because they have nothing to say or show about their concrete achievements. Mr. Thackrey behaves like a leader but has no party left. He is searching amidst the wrecks and ruins of his rank and file. He has been punished by courts and rejected by the people but some persons never learn the lessons of history. Modi has been rejected even by his own partymen and is the embodiment of intolerance and demagoguery. He cannot even stand his own partymen and walks out of media interactions instead of engaging in discourse. What he cannot ignore, he is alleged to liquidate, as is clear from serious allegations regarding his own former Home Minister's death. Whether it is the Congress President or PM, such parties only believe in the politics of hate, the divisive approach and the idiom of insults. Each time they have done so, the Congress President and the PM have emerged stronger. Such imbalanced outbursts come from the Neros of Indian politics who fiddle and shout insults while their parties and their states burn.

3830. (22-10-2007) NEW DELHI : Higher education in India has expanded many folds during the past six decades. The number of universities in the country has increased from 20 in 1947 to 378 whereas the number of colleges, which were no more than 500 at the eve of Independence, has gone up to 18064. No less significant has been the increase in the number of teaching staff which has gone up from a meagre 15, 000 to nearly 4.80 Lakhs during the same period. The number of students enrolled in higher education too has gone up from 1 Lkah in

1950 to over 112 lakhs in 2005. Obviously, the institutional capacity of higher education has increased by several folds. This has, in turn, enhanced access to higher education as we find that the enrolment ratio has increased from less than 1 % in 1950 to about 10 % in 2007. These developments notwithstanding, the Gross Enrolment Ratio (GER) in relative terms compares quite poorly with 60% in USA and Canada, over 40% in several European countries and more than 20% in many developed and developing countries. International experience shows that no country has been able to become an economically advanced country, if its enrolment ratio in higher education has been less than 20%. The foremost priority must, therefore, be enhancing access to higher education such that the GER is raised to a minimum threshold level of about 20 percent for sustained economic development. In immediate term, the 11th Plan has set the target GER of 15 percent. Such a substantial increase in enrolment would require multi-pronged strategy. In order to ensure that the facilities for higher education are available in enough number for all who aspire to get it, we may have to establish new universities and the colleges in order to cope with the increasing demand for higher education. Some announcements have already been made in this regard. These include establishment of 30 new central universities and establishment of new IITs and IIMs. Besides, capacity increase will also have to be attempted by strengthening and increasing the intake capacity of exiting colleges and the universities through increase in seats of existing courses as well as by introducing new courses. In this process, universities and colleges in specific area of low enrolment ratio (lower than a all India average) and also districts falling in remote, hilly, border area, small towns, and rural area and districts with concentration of SC, ST, OBC and minority will have to be proactively supported. This may require enhanced additional development grants to existing universities and colleges and higher education being in the concurrent list, this will call for joint efforts by the union as well as the state governments. It cannot be overemphasised that expansion in higher education should be made in such a manner that it offers equitable access all. This will call for a conscious effort to ensure that the higher educational avenues and opportunities are made available to all and that the system does not suffer on account of disparities across region, gender, social groups such as scheduled castes, scheduled tribes, other backward castes, minorities, physically challenged and poor. The 11th Plan strategy will focus on the inclusiveness in higher education with schemes for inclusive education with a focus on regions and groups with lower enrolment ratio.

3831. (22-10-2007) NEW DELHI : The Union Minister of Shipping, Road Transport and Highways, Thiru T.R. Baalu has approved a sum of Rs. 475.01 lakh for road improvement works in the state of Tamil Nadu. An amount of Rs. 238.66 lakh has been approved for improvement of Riding Quality (IRQ) work at Km 3/200 to 10/000 of NH-49 between Madurai and Silaiman village. This is one of the important highways which connects Madurai and Dhanuskodi. In this stretch the intensity of vehicular traffic is very high. Due to stagnation of water, lot of vertical and horizontal crakes have been developed and lot of undulations have been formed on the riding surface. Hence it is necessary to take up the above stretch for repairs and improvement immediately. Thiru Baalu also approved an amount of Rs. 236.35 lakh for improvement of Riding Quality work at km 42/500-50/0 on the same highway between Usilampatti and Andipatti Kanavai Medu in Madurai district. This highway connects the temple city of Madurai and harbour city of Cochin. It is reported that this stretch of the road is sunken, undulated and potholes are formed due to recent monsoon. Therefore, for smooth and safe vehicular traffic, it is essential to improve the riding surface on this stretch of the National Highway.

3832. (22-10-2007) NEW DELHI : The Government of India has now extended the Mid Day Meal Scheme to the Upper Primary Stage of Education (classes VI to VIII) in 3479 Educationally Backward Blocks (EBBs) in 2007-08 and areas across the country from 2008-09. The programme has been extended as per State-wise list of EBBs attached in Annexure-A. The extension to the Upper Primary Stage in EBBs has already become effective from October 01, 2007. About 1.7 crore children at upper primary will be covered. The Government of India has released the Central assistance to the respective States for extension of Mid-Day Meal programme to upper primary stage. A sum of Rs.7324 Crores was provided in the Budget 2007-08 for the MDM Programme, representing 37% increase over the budget provision for 2006-07. The Expenditure as on 30-09-2007 is Rs.2231.12 Crores (30% of BE) including Rs. 422.94 crores towards cooking cost for upper primary stage. In addition, 3,22,785 MTs of food grain has been allocated to States/UTs for extension of coverage to upper primary stage (Annexure-B).

3833. (22-10-2007) NEW DELHI : The expansion of the telecom sector was further consolidated with an increase of 76.52 lakh in the number of telecom subscribers during the month of September 2007. As a result, the total number of telephones in the country is more than 2486.69 lakh, as compared to 1700 lakh as on September 2006. The GSM segment has shown an increase of 59.22 lakh during the month of September 2007, the CDMA segment of 18.84 lakh while the fixed segment continued to decline, with a decrease of 1.54 lakh during the month. The overall teledensity improved further to 21.85% in September 2007 as compared to 15.12% as on September 30, 2006. In the GSM segment, Tamil Nadu and Gujarat telecom circles added more than five lakh subscribers during September 2007. In the CDMA segment, Maharashtra circle added more than two lakh subscribers during the period. Andhra Pradesh, Gujarat, Karnataka, Maharashtra, Tamil Nadu and Uttar Pradesh (East) telecom circles have added more than five lakh subscribers each. The growth of broadband connections improved further and at the end of August 2007, about 25.15 lakh broadband connections were provided and coverage of broadband connectivity by public sector service providers has reached 1077 cities. Further, the total number of existing ISP licencees is 372. Under Bharat Nirman Programme, 686 VPTs were provided in the month of September 2007. Thus, out of the targeted 66,822 villages, a total of 50,520 villages have been provided with VPTs till September 2007. A total of 3551 VPTs have been provided in this financial year.

3834. (22-10-2007) NEW DELHI : Following is the text of oral intervention of Finance Minister, Shri P. Chidambram on 'Strategic Direction of the World Bank Group' Development Committee Meeting : 21 October 2007: "At the outset, I would like to congratulate Mr. Robert Zoellick on assuming office of the president of the World Bank, and welcome him to his first meeting of the Development Committee. I read with interest his speech the other day on completing hundred days in office and outlining his future vision of the Bank. His talk on 'inclusive and sustainable globalization' resonates with the challenges that we are dealing with in the development of our country. I am happy that the strategy outlined for the World Bank Group focuses on these important themes and that it includes the intent to refine the Bank's tool-kit of financial, knowledge and coordination products to meet the new challenges thrown up by globalization. The core mandate of the World Bank Group is 'Working for a world free of poverty' and we have an important development partnership with the four arms of this Group, especially IDA, in realizing this goal. A large proportion of global poverty is concentrated in Sub-Saharan Africa and South Asia. We welcome the focus of the Bank's activities in these regions, and within them, the fragile States. However, we need to acknowledge that even by 2015, there would be about 700 million people living on less than a dollar a day and nearly two billion living on less than two dollars a day globally. The challenge of achieving the Millennium Development goals is daunting and the global development community must rise to the occasion to keep its promises that have given hope to the poor and under privileged of the world. We look forward to working with the World Bank in its effort to foster inclusive growth. The Strategy paper recognizes that World Bank is one of the lead players in the global aid architecture, which is becoming increasingly fragmented and complex. The Bank has to remain competitive in this environment. In this context, we welcome the recent revision of IBRD pricing to bring it down to pre-Asian crisis levels. It also recognizes that IBRD is well capitalized, reflecting adequate room for growth. We look forward to continued simplification and transparency in not only the pricing of loans but also procedures involved in accessing these loans, what President Zoellick referred to as 'the non-financial costs of doing business with the Bank'. In addition, there is greater need for using country systems as well as being more innovative to provide cutting-edge solutions in key areas, such as infrastructure. In recent years, the Bank has been trying to reposition itself as an aid institution coupled with a knowledge bank. This is a welcome step. With various products in its menu, the Bank would be variously attractive to different countries; the poorest being more inclined towards the financial products, while the middle income countries would like more of knowledge and research products, along with financial services. We in India have been an active participant in contributing to sharing of development experiences. To keep the research more focused on the issues on the ground, we would urge the Bank to engage more actively with research institutions in developing countries, so as to make learning a two-way process. Among the many challenges that the World Bank Group needs to address is the one relating to the Global Public Goods (GPGs). In this regard, there are four concerns that I would like to highlight. First, the development mandate of poverty reduction and attainment of MDGs is the primary concern of the Bank compared to providing Global Public Goods, especially keeping in view the comparative advantage of other specialised agencies such as UNFCCC, WTO etc. Second, in its work on climate change, the Bank has to be mindful of issues relating to legacy of carbon emissions, energy equity and the principle of 'common but differentiated responsibilities'. Global burden sharing arrangements and national priorities of developing countries should not be disturbed. In this connection, I would recall the statement made by the Prime Minister of India, Dr. Manmohan Singh at Heiligendamm when he offered that developing countries will not increase their per capita carbon emissions above the level of the per capita carbon emissions of developed countries, and urged developed countries to reduce their per capita carbon emissions. Third, additionality of financial resources and availability of cost-effective clean technology is critical for developing countries. These have to be the core building blocks of any Clean Energy Framework that the Bank establishes. Fourth, while climate change is no doubt a matter of concern to all, we must not lose sight of other GPGs of concern for the developing countries such as orderly global labour mobility, technology transfer and intellectual property rights etc. Mr. Chairman, we welcome the strategy of the World Bank Group and look forward to working with the institution to convert the hopes of the poor into reality."

3835. (23-10-2007) NEW DELHI : Speaking at the 35th Convocation of the All India Institute of Medical Sciences (AIIMS) today, the Union Minister for Health & Family Welfare, Dr. Anbumani Ramadoss said that recognizing the importance of health as the backbone for growth and development in all spheres, the National Rural Health Mission (NRHM) was launched in 2005. To provide effective patient care services, healthy manpower is a pre requisite. There is ample scope for medical graduates for serving the underserved, poor and downtrodden through the NRHM. While Dr. Montek Singh Ahluwalia, Deputy Chairman, Planning Commission delivered the Convocation address. Prof. P. Venugopal, Director, AIIMS, Prof. R.C. Deka, Dean, AIIMS, Dr. Sandeep Agarwala, Registrar, AIIMS, and other members of the AIIMS Institute Body were also present at the function. The following is the text of the Health Minister's speech: "A Convocation is an extremely important day in the life of a student. You stand today at a new threshold in your life. Here, in this great institution, you have imbibed the values and skills needed to deal with the world outside. Today we are here in a good mood with a sense of pride and joy of achievements, both for the faculty and recipients of the degree and awards. It is a moment of glory for both, and feeling of accomplishment of academic pursuits for the students. I extend my felicitations to all the recipients of the degrees, awards and medals and wish them a bright future with a successful career of service to human beings. Each graduate and post-graduate of this institute is the best product that our country can offer to the medical sciences. How best you will be able to use this opportunity largely depends on the knowledge and expertise you have acquired so far, the values you have imbibed, the aims and ideals you have set for yourself and your dedication for the cause. Pursuit of excellence, commitment and enjoyment in the work are the key factors to real success in career. The All India Institute of Medical Sciences is well known for its academic excellence, modern patient care facilities and quality medical research. Reputation of AIIMS as an institute in the field of academics has spread beyond India and it has been sought as a valued collaborator by several nations all over the world. Established through an act of Parliament in 1956, this Institute is an example of Independent India's will to provide excellence in health care to the people and to ensure that the poorest of the poor can have access to the best treatment through its quality care services. I quote from NEWSWEEK INTERNATIONAL dated October 30th 2006, AIIMS-An Oasis for India's Poorest, "this is what it takes to be India's Best public hospital. The Government-run hospital, with about 2000 beds treated 3.5 million people, achieving mortality and infection rates comparable to the best facilities in the developed world-for fees that come to about $ 1 a day for inpatients"

3836. (23-10-2007) NEW DELHI : A six member delegation from Finland led by H.E. Mr. Paavo Vayrynen, Minister for Foreign Trade and Development called on Dr. Shakeel Ahmad, Minister of State for Communication and Information Technology yesterday. Dr. Shakeel Ahmad welcomed the Finnish delegation. Both the dignitaries exchanged views on the developments taking place in India in the IT and Telecommunications Sector. Dr. Ahmad said that he does not see any significant change in the policies of the Government in the telecom sector. If, there are changes, these are expected to be for the betterment for the industry and for growth, he added. The talks took place in a cordial and friendly atmosphere.

3837. (23-10-2007) NEW DELHI : The Committee of Eminent Persons on Sethu Samudram Shipping Channel Project held its second meeting on 23rd October, 2007 in its office at Malligai, Chennai. Seven Members were present in the meeting. The Sethu Samudram Corporation Limited made a detailed presentation on the salient features of the Project to the Members of the Committee. The Committee noted that 60 submissions have been received till 22nd October, 2007 by 'Regd. AD' or delivered in the Office of the Committee against an acknowledgment. In addition to these 60, the Committee has also received 3 submissions by 'Speed Post', 14 by 'Regd. Post' (without acknowledgement) and 58 by ordinary post including 'Under Postal Certificate'. The Committee reiterated that the objections and suggestions be sent by Regd. AD or delivered in the office of the Committee against an acknowledgement. The last date for receipt of suggestions/objections at the address of the Committee is 1700 hours on

31st October, 2007. The Committee will give personal hearing from 29th October, 2007 to 6th November, 2007 on all days including holidays from 1000 hours to 1700 hours at its office {No.30/95, P.S. Kumarasamy Raja (Greenways) Road Chennai 600 028} at Malligai, Chennai. Out of these days, the Committee has earmarked 4th November, 2007 to 6th November, 2007 for the personal hearing of the petitioners in the four court cases mentioned in the order dated 5th October, 2007 of the Cabinet Secretariat, Government of India. All such persons intending to be heard personally, except the petitioners, shall have to produce either acknowledgement issued by the Office of the Committee or the Postal receipt in token of the fact that they have sent their objections/suggestions to the Committee. Committee of Eminent Persons on Sethu Samudram Shipping Channel Project, Malligai, Chennai.

3838. (23-10-2007) NEW DELHI : In exercise of the powers conferred by clause (1) of article 224 of the Constitution of India, the President is pleased to appoint Shri Syed Ali Naqvi to be an Additional Judge of the Madhya Pradesh High Court, for a period of one year with effect from 18.10.2007. The President is also pleased to appoint Shri Subhash Chandra Vyas to be an Additional Judge of the Madhya Pradesh High Court, for a period from 18.10.2007 to 18.4.2008.

3839. (23-10-2007) NEW DELHI : The Committee on Infrastructure (COI) headed by the Prime Minister, on 18th April 2007 had directed the Constitution of an Inter Ministerial Group (IMG) under the chairmanship of Secretary (Civil Aviation) to recommend the principles, guidelines and licencing conditions for greenfield airports. This was done with a view to bridging the growing deficit in airport infrastructure. The anticipated investment in airport development during the Eleventh Plan is over Rs.40,000 crores, both from public and private sources, including for greenfield airports. It is, therefore, necessary to lay down the policy guidelines that would govern proposals for setting up greenfield airports, other than defence airports. An IMG under the chairmanship of Secretary (Civil Aviation) was constituted by the Ministry of Civil Aviation on 14th May 2007 with representatives from the Ministries of Defence, Home Affairs, Department of Economic Affairs, Planning Commission and officials of the Ministry of Civil Aviation. As per new draft policy, the mandatory approval of the Central Government for Greenfield airports should be dispensed with in all cases except in those where the project proposal is not in conformity with the policy. Certain functions to be performed at the airport such as air traffic services, security, customs, immigration etc. would be reserved to be performed by the central agencies. An airport company seeking a license would be required to obtain certain clearances from these central agencies. The guidelines of the respective agencies would be notified by them accordingly. State Governments desires of setting up a greenfield airport can either set it by itself or through any of its designated entity or a Joint Venture Company. The State Government would consider granting land (concessional or otherwise), real estate development right, airport connectivity and fiscal concessions to such an airport company. In case a private party is to be selected, it would be through competitive bidding. As per the draft policy, since the grant of a license for a greenfield airport involves several agencies, a Steering Committee is to be set up under the chairmanship of the Secretary (Civil Aviation) to coordinate and monitor the various clearances required for setting up a greenfield airport. As per the draft policy, greenfield airports to be set up by the Airports Authority of India would be preferably constructed through Public Private Partnership (PPP) and such airports would be financed substantially through PPP concessions. Land for such airports will have to be provided by the AAI and the concessions for development of greenfield airports would be awarded through open competitive bidding based on model bidding documents. Where it is not feasible to follow the PPP route, AAI could set up greenfield airports by itself, as may be approved by the Government on a case to case bases. Financing and development of any other airport would be the responsibility of the Airport Company seeking the license. Land for this purpose would have to be acquired by such airport company in accordance with the existing policy of the Government.

3840. (23-10-2007) NEW DELHI : Production of finished carbon steel during April-September 2007 was estimated at 24.80 million tonnes, recording a rise of 6.6 per cent over the same period last year. During April-September 2006, the production of finished carbon steel was 23.256 million tonnes. Production of Pig Iron recorded a rise of 7.9 per cent at 2.582 million tonnes. Steel Authority of India Ltd. (SAIL) produced 6.24 tonnes during April-September 2007 compared to 6.01 million tonnes last year while Rashtriya Ispat Nigam Ltd. (RINL) produced 1.203 million tonnes during the first six months compared to 1.307 million tonnes previous year. Import of finished carbon steel during the first six months, April to September 2007, was up by 28.2 per cent over the same period last year. During April to September 2007, the imports stood at 2.45 million tonnes compared to 1.911 million tonnes in 2006. Exports during the same period went up by 7.4 per cent, from 2.42 million tonnes in April-September, 2006 to 2.60 million tonnes this year.

3841. (23-10-2007) NEW DELHI : The Indian Air Force Commanders Conference began today at Air Headquarters (Vayu Bhawan), New Delhi. The week long commanders' conference commenced with the inaugural address of the Chief of Air Staff, Air Chief Marshal FH Major. Addressing the commanders in his inaugural address the Chief of Air Staff said "we must continue to adapt and evolve our operational orientations, strategies and capabilities to match the increasing demands of vital national interests, the widening spectrum of conflict and keep ahead of growing military capabilities within the Region". The Conference is attended by the top brass of the Indian Air Force comprising Air Officers Commanding-in-Chief of IAF commands and Principle Staff officers of Air HQ. During the commanders' conference, operational challenges before the IAF are discussed. Apart from this flight safety, maintenance, administrative and logistical issues are also taken up for discussions. During the present commanders conference the Air Officers Commanding-in-Chief of IAF commands would carry out a data based review. The Director General (Inspection and Safety) would also be presenting the data based review on flight safety. Discussions on Information warfare, placements of ex-air warriors and operational perspective on Garud force is also on the cards. The IAF Commanders would also be attending the Combined Commanders' Conference on 24 Oct. 07 before concluding on 26 Oct. 07.

3842. (23-10-2007) NEW DELHI : The twelfth Field Marshal KM Cariappa Memorial talk will be delivered by Gen SF Rodrigues, Governor of Punjab and Administrator of Chandigarh on "Resurgent India-The way Ahead" at DRDO Auditorium, New Delhi on Wednesday. The Defence Minister Shri AK Antony, will be the chief guest on the occasion. Gen Deepak Kapoor, Chief of Army Staff and other Service Chief's will also be present. The event is being organized by the Director General of Infantry, Lt General Rajender Singh and his team of officers from Infantry Directorate. Field Marshal KM Cariappa is an unforgettable name in the history of Indian Army. Born on 28th January 1900 in Mercara state, now part of Karnataka, he was amongst the first officers to receive the King's Commission in 1919. After an outstanding career, he became the first Commander-in-Chief of the Indian Army on 15 Jan. 1949. A hardcore Infantryman, Field Marshal KM Cariappa was a thorough gentleman who exhibited the highest standards of self discipline and compassion. He had been a legend in his life time and left an indelible impression that would inspire the people for a long time. He was bestowed with the highest rank of Field Marshal by the Government in 1983. He breathed his last in May 1993. In memory of this great son of India, the Infantry Directorate at the Army HQ has been organizing the 'Field Marshal KM Cariappa Memorial Lecture' every year, since 1995, as part of Infantry Day celebrations. Eminent speakers are invited to address issues of national importance as part of the Field Marshal KM Cariappa Memorial Lecture, Field Marshal Sam Maneksha, Lt Gen SK Sinha, Shri Jaswant Singh, Shri K Subramanyam, Shri Arun Shourie, Shri Yashwant Sinha, Shri NR Narayana Murthy and Shri Montek Singh Ahluwalia are some of the luminaries who have spoken in this premier event in the past.

3843. (23-10-2007) NEW DELHI : Annual Plan of Goa for the year 2007-08 was approved in a meeting, here today, between the Deputy Chairman, Planning Commission, Shri Montek Singh Ahluwalia and the Chief Minister of Goa, Shri Digambar Kamat, here today. The Annual Plan size was agreed at Rs.1430 crores, which includes additional Central assistance of Rs.25 crores for projects of special assistance to the State. In addition it was also agreed that Plan size could go up to Rs.1595 crores subject to certain Court Orders which could enable the State to raise another Rs.165 crores. Planning Commission complimented the State for achievements in literacy and poverty eradication. Compared to the national average of 27.5 per cent of poverty, the State has poverty ratio of 13.8 per cent as per Planning Commission estimates for the year 2004-05. Literacy rate also increased from 75.51 per cent in 1991 to 82.32 per cent in 2001. However, attention was drawn to declining sex ratio and gender gap in work force. Briefing the Commission on the performance and objectives of the State, the Chief Minister said the State Government was moving towards next state of development aimed at achieving standards of a developed nation by 2012. All requisite IT infrastructures were being established for moving towards knowledge economy. Efforts were on to create investment friendly climate leading to more employment avenues. 100 per cent literacy would be achieved by 2010. On fiscal initiatives, the Chief Minister pointed out that FRBM legislation has been enacted and revenue plus position achieved two years ahead of target. Fiscal deficit was also brought under check and sinking fund constituted to manage debt burden. Separate pension fund is being contemplated to take care of pension liabilities.

3844. (23-10-2007) NEW DELHI : Directorate of Film Festivals and Embassy of Arab Republic of Egypt is organizing an Egyptian Film Festival from October 24 to 26, 2007 in Siri Fort Auditorium-II. The three-day Festival will open with the Film 'Sleepless Nights' directed by Hani Khalifa. The other four films to be screened during the Festival are: 'Girls Secrets' (directed by Magdi Ahmed Ali), 'Egyptian Tale' (directed by Monir Rady), 'Women Love' (directed by Khalid El Haggar) and 'Free Times' (directed by Mohamed Mostafa). The opening film will be at 6.30 p.m. whereas the screening on the next two days will be at 5.00 p.m. and 8.00 p.m. Egypt has a strong cinematic tradition since the 1930s having the only major motion picture industry in the Arab world with Cairo its capital. The Egyptian cinema has a profound influence on the Arabs. The golden age of Egyptian cinema was in the 1940s and 1950s. during that period Omar Sherif emerged as a major international star and his former wife Fatin Hamama, reigned as the queen of Arab cinema. Directors such as Youssef Chahine have gained wide international respect and many of Egypt's leading literary lights including Tawfiq Al Hakim and Naguib Mahfouz, have written for the cinema. Today, the reigning superstar of the Egyptian cinema is the comedian Adel Imam, whose political satire has earned him the respect of serious filmgoers and occasionally the resentment of the government.

3845. (23-10-2007) NEW DELHI : In exercise of the powers conferred by clause (1) of article 224 of the Constitution of India, the President is pleased to appoint Shri Syed Ali Naqvi to be an Additional Judge of the Madhya Pradesh High Court, for a period of one year with effect from 18.10.2007. The President is also pleased to appoint Shri Subhash Chandra Vyas to be an Additional Judge of the Madhya Pradesh High Court, for a period from 18.10.2007 to 18.4.2008.

3846. (23-10-2007) NEW DELHI : Yesterday the nation witnessed the pathetic spectacle of the Prime Minister's office informing sections of the media that the Prime Minister was embarrassed and pained about the fiasco over the Nuclear Deal. The Congress Party later informed the nation that the Prime Minister was not resigning. Recent developments have thrown up several important questions in the mind of the people. The UPA Government is paralyzed by its internal contradictions. The Government has not taken any significant decisions in the recent months. The reality thrown up about the sad and helpless Prime Minister is a cause for national worry. Can a sad and helpless Prime Minister lead India ? India is a growing, youthful and a resurgent nation. It needs an enthusiastic leader, who is decisive, who can take decisions and implement them. The Prime Minister's speech at The Hindustan Times Summit that 'one has to live with disappointments but life must go on' is typical of an Indian condolence message. This speech displays the state of PM's mind. The nation needs to reflect on a question 'can a sad man lead a resurgent nation'. Neither the Prime Minister nor his office is doing the nation a favour by projecting the Prime Minister as a 'helpless leader.'

3847. (24-10-2007) NEW DELHI : The Interior Minister of Pakistan Mr. Aftab Ahmed Khan Sherpao met the Union Home Minister Shri Shivraj V. Patil today. Both the leaders discussed matters of mutual interests. Issues relating to maintaining peace and tranquility in the two countries and matters relating to SAARC were discussed. The two leaders felt that confidence building measures between the two countries should be increased. The meeting lasted about half an hour. The Interior Minister of Afghanistan Mr. Zarar Ahmed Moqbel also called on Shri Shivraj V. Patil, Union Home Minister today. The two leaders discussed issues of bilateral interest and SAARC related matters and measures to promote peace and tranquility in the South Asian region.

3848. (24-10-2007) NEW DELHI : There has been news in some sections of the media regarding diversion of funds collected for Prime Minister's National Relief Fund by Coal India Limited (CIL). Responding to these stories, Ministry of Coal has stated that it has taken serious note of the allegations made in this regard. The report of the preliminary inquiry indicates that out of Rs.48.06 crore collected since 1999 from the employees' wages by CIL and its subsidiary companies, CIL had deposited only Rs. 37.08 crore in the Prime Minister's National Relief Fund until a complaint was received in this regard. Rs. 7.34 crores were deposited subsequently. Clearly, there has been inordinate delay in depositing the balance fund. It has also come to light that an amount of Rs. 4.71 crore was deposited in several Chief Ministers' Relief Funds, besides payment for direct purchase of relief material for Orissa flood victims. A total of Rs. 49.13 crore has been remitted to PMNRF/spent on relief, which is actually more than the amount collected from the employees. The balance was paid from the internal resources of the company. Thus, it has been noted that funds collected towards PMNRF have not been siphoned off in any manner. The utilization has been done jointly by the workers' representatives and the management for the purposes directly related to disaster relief. 2. Therefore, although no case of misuse of funds is made out, the irregularities that have occurred merit action. Coal Ministry has directed the Chairman, CIL to undertake a detailed inquiry in the matter, identify individual responsibility for lapses and initiate appropriate action against the guilty urgently. 3. Ministry has also directed the CIL and its subsidiaries to ensure that in future the monies collected for the PMNRF are deposited with the Fund without any delay. 4. In view of the apprehensions expressed in the media by the person who had filed complaint regarding alleged misuse of funds, the Ministry has directed Chairman, CIL to ensure that there is no harassment to the employee and necessary measures are taken to ensure his security.

3849. (24-10-2007) NEW DELHI : The President of India has been pleased to appoint Dr. Shivinder Singh Sidhu, Governor of Manipur, to discharge the functions of the Governor of Meghalaya, in addition to his own duties, until regular arrangements for the office of the Governor of Meghalaya are made.

3850. (24-10-2007) NEW DELHI : Shri Kamal Nath, Union Minister of Commerce and Industry, while speaking at the Parliamentary Consultative Committee of his Ministry, here last evening, has said that plantations are very important from the point of view of development of remote areas, export earning, employment generation for poor and weaker sections of society and of course for creating large industrial base of processing industries. "We are largely dependent on agriculture as it forms the backbone of our economy. Despite rapid industrialization and increasing contribution of industrial sector in the GDP, agriculture still occupies a dominant place. 15% of the total agricultural exports earnings come from tea, coffee and rubber although the plantation crops occupy only 1% of the total agricultural area in the country", the Minister added. Highlighting the contributions of the plantation sector to the economies of southern, eastern and north/eastern States, the Commerce Minister said that tea is cultivated in remote, hilly regions and coffee is an integral part of the ecology of the Western Ghats. While the bulk of production of coffee, natural rubber and spices comes from smallholdings, in tea industry nearly 80% is accounted for by the corporate sector. The total number of people engaged in the plantation industry is about 20 million, he informed. Members who were present at the meeting include S/Shri Sambasiva Rao, Ram Singh Kaswan, Rajeev Shukla, Sharad Joshi, Shantaram Naik, Sudhangshu Seal, N.R. Govindarajar, M. Rajasekara Murthi, Abu Asim Azmi and Naresh Gujral. Shri G.K. Pillai, Commerce Secretary; Shri Ajay Shanker, Secretary (DIPP); senior officials of the Ministry of Commerce and Industry besides Chairmen of Tea Board, Coffee Board, Tobacco Board, Rubber Board and Spices Board were also present at the meeting. While Shri Naresh Gujral, MP, has sought benefits for the plantation sector, Shri Sharad Joshi emphasised the need to produce more organic spices in the country. Shri Sudhangshu Seal brought up the issue of Darjeeling tea being exported by some exporters by misleading the brand and also raised the issue of performance of SEZs in the country and desired to seek the progress made by some of these. As regards coffee, the Minister said, although we produce only 4.5% of world production, the Indian coffee has created a niche for itself in the international market, particularly the Robusta variety which is highly preferred for its good blending quality. India is perhaps the only coffee producing region whose coffees are fully shade grown, entirely hand picked and completely sun dried. Nearly 70% of the coffee produced in the country is exported. During the year 2006-07, 2.43 lakh tons of coffee valued at Rs.1958 crore was exported. "India ranks fourth in production and consumption of natural rubber in the world of which more than 80% comes from Kerala and Tamil Nadu. Rubber production of India is around 8.50 lakh tons which mainly meets the domestic requirement and about 50% of it is consumed by the tyre industry alone", Shri Kamal Nath said. While speaking about the spices, Shri Kamal Nath said that Indian spices are used in over 130 countries and their intrinsic quality in terms of taste, flavour, colour and fragrance has further increased the demand of Indian spices. Major spices and spice products exported from India are black pepper, cardamom, ginger, turmeric, chillies, seed spices, mint oils and oleoresins. During the year 2006-07, spices of the value of Rs.3575 crore were exported. With regard to the tobacco sector, he said, it is one of the most important cash crops in India, with an estimated 36 million people relying on it for their livelihood, both directly and indirectly. India is the second largest producer of all types of tobacco after China. India is the only country growing different types of tobacco in varied agro-climatic conditions. It is primarily grown in the states of Andhra Pradesh and Karnataka. "Tobacco is a significant source of foreign exchange with Rs.1723.42 crore being generated through export of tobacco & tobacco products export in 2006-07", he said. Shri Kamal Nath said that a number of new initiatives are being taken to ensure healthy growth and to improve the productivity of the plantation sector. "We have already set up a Special Purpose Tea Fund for replantation and rejuvenation of tea gardens. Similar packages, like the SPTF for tea are being put in place for spices, coffee and rubber for replanting and rejuvenation", the Minister added. For the benefit of growers and plantation workers of tea, rubber, coffee and tobacco a Personal Accident Insurance Scheme has been launched in January 2007, which provides insurance cover of Rs.1 lakh. The insurance premium of Rs.14 is to be paid by the Government and the beneficiary @ Rs. 7 each. The Minister informed that the scheme is proposed to be extended to spices as well.

3851. (24-10-2007) NEW DELHI : The IAF's communication Squadron; the official carrier of the President, Vice President, Prime Minister, visiting heads of the states and a host of other dignitaries is in the process of modernizing its fleet. The Squadron has turned sixty and celebrating its Diamond Jubilee. On this occasion, a first day cover has been released by The Chief of Air Staff, Air Chief Marshal FH Major, today in New Delhi. The acquisition of BBJ in Apr 08 is the next step in that process. The Boeing Business Jet is a specially configured aircraft for VVIP comfort. Its interiors create a working environment befitting the VVIP's official stature. It is more importantly equipped with the latest Self protection suit thus providing our VIPs the highest level of protection from any ground based or airborne threat. The IAF's communication Squadron has turned sixty and is celebrating its Diamond Jubilee this year. Formed in Jan. 1947 the Sqn has become synonymous with India's post Independence history. The Squadron over the last six decades other than flying the highest luminaries of the nation has also flown world leaders such as HO Chi Minh, Nikita Kruschev, Chou En, Tunku, Abdul Rehman, Jaqueline Kennedy, Shah of Iran, Tito, John Major, Bonis Yelstin, Princess Anne, Shri Premadasa, Nelson Mandela, Mother Teressa, Kofi Annan, Dalai Lama to name a few. The Squadron has since its inception flown twelve aircraft which have been on their inventory. It all started with the Airspeed Oxford to the Present trio of Mi-8, B-737 and Embraer-135 legacy. The personnel chosen to form the Squadron are the very best and understand the responsibility they shoulder when they fly the highest ranking dignitaries of our country. In 1962 President Dr. Radhakrishnan awarded the Sqn its Crest' the Pegasus and its Motto; Seva aur Suraksha. Later in 1984 President Gyani Zail Singh awarded the Squadron his standard. It was a proud moment that emphasised the glorious deeds of almost four decades. Aircrafts will change but what is timeless is the Squadron and its personnel, which made a unique system, a system that recognizes the stake and works with synergy. Where every man from loader through technician to Captain has a job to do and does it the only way he knows............... Flawless, Perfect, Anytime, all the time.

3852. (24-10-2007) NEW DELHI : Shri Kamal Nath, Union Minister of Commerce and Industry, has called for easing of Phytosanitary regulations with regard to export of floriculture and dairy products from India to European Union. During the bilateral meeting with the Dutch Minister for Economic Affairs, Mrs. M.J.A. van der Hoeven here today, Shri Kamal Nath informed that the floricultural consignments from India are subject to 50% mandatory checks which are carried out randomly while imports from countries in Africa are subject to only 2% checks. Similarly, the export of dairy products from India into the European Union is permitted only from approved list of plants. "We would appreciate if the Dutch could assist in helping to create a level playing field for our exporters on these issues at the EU level", the Minister stated. Shri Ajay Shanker, Secretary (DIPP); and senior officials from the Ministry of Commerce and Industry and business leaders from India and Netherlands were present on the occasion. Observing that Netherlands today is among India's top ten trading partners and, in terms of investments, the fourth largest foreign investor, Shri Kamal Nath stated that there is a lot of scope to increase bilateral trade, which is now US $ 3826 million (2006-07). He stressed that there is a great potential for cooperation between India and Netherlands viz., in the fields of agriculture & food processing, light engineering products, infrastructure etc. "We look forward to larger Dutch investments in India, particularly in the priority sectors identified by Government of India like agriculture, infrastructure, automotives, biotechnology, food processing and pharmaceuticals", the Minister said. The main exports to the Netherlands are: petroleum (crude and products); RMG cotton including accessories; electric goods; machinery items etc. and the main imports from Netherlands are: Metalifers ores* metal scraps, machinery except electric and electronic, organic chemicals, transport equipments etc. On the multilateral front, Shri Kamal Nath said: "India looks forward to the conclusion of the Round by the end of 2007 or at the latest by the early part of the next year. India has been engaging constructively and actively with other fellow member countries of the WTO towards this end. Such a conclusion can only be possible if we are faithful to the mandate and the outcome reflects a clear balance between market opening and the development needs of the majority of the membership. India will obviously show flexibility to achieve such an outcome but the onus for movement is clearly with the large developed countries". While speaking at the Indo-Dutch CEOs Roundtable, Shri Kamal Nath said that the FDI equity inflows in India were US $ 5.5 billion in 2005-06 and increased almost three times to US $ 15.7 billion in 2006-07 and now it is expected to double this fiscal to US $ 30 billion. The Minister said that there is steady increase in the presence of Indian companies providing technological services and software to Dutch companies to improve their global competitiveness. The Minister said that the private sector has been the biggest catalyst for India's growth over the last decade and a half. Some of the areas where private enterprises having major impact are, civil aviation, telecom, energy, banking, real estate and retail. They have also made inroads in both domestic and export markets in diverse sectors such as pharmaceuticals, automobiles, metals, cement and textiles. The share of top sectors attracting FDI inflows from Netherlands are: computer software & hardware-23.99%; services sector (financial and non-financial)-15.15%; chemicals (other than fertilizers)-11.23%; housing & real estate-6.94% and cement & gypsum products-6.28%.

3853. (24-10-2007) NEW DELHI : Oil India Limited (OIL) a PSU under the Ministry of Petroleum and Natural Gas handed-over a cheque for Rs.157.50 crore to Government of India, as the Final dividend @ 75% for the financial year 2006-2007. The cheque of said amount was handed over to Shri M.S.Srinivasan, Secretary to the Ministry of Petroleum and Natural Gas by Shri M.R.Pasrija, Chairman and Managing Director of Oil India Limited, here today. The Company had earlier paid first interim Dividend of 110% amounting to Rs.231.00 crore and a second interim dividend of 75% amounting to Rs 157.50 crore during the year. Thus, the total Dividend paid to the Government of India for the year 2006-2007 amounts to Rs.546.00 crore being 260% of the paid up capital of Rs.210 crore held by the Government. The Company recorded a total income of Rs. 6007.78 crore and profit after tax of Rs. 1639.99 crore for the year 2006-07. Net worth of the Company increased to Rs. 6849.07 crore up by 17% over the previous year's figure of Rs. 5848 crore. This is after providing for subsidy of Rs. 1993.75 crore on crude oil and LPG sales to share a part of under recoveries suffered by oil marketing companies(OMCs). OIL's proposed IPO, and issuance of shares to employees have been approved by Government of India. The Company informed that they are targeting the IPO during the 1st Quarter of 2008. During the year, OIL had bagged 8 exploration blocks (6 onshore blocks as operator and 2 offshore blocks as non-operator) under NELP-VI Round of bidding. OIL, in the process, has doubled the number of onshore blocks from six to twelve as operator in a single round. The company also said that lot of prospects exists in these blocks. OIL has participated in all the past six NELP bidding rounds concluded so far, and has now acquired total 21 blocks. Out of these 14 are onshore and rest 7 are offshore blocks located in the East Coast of the Country. The Company has overseas presence in six countries, Libya, Gabon, Nigeria, Yemen, Iran and Sudan. OIL has two Blocks in Libya, with an area of 9797 Sq.Kms, where OIL is the operator. These blocks are part of one of the most prolific basins in Libya. In Iran OIL has 20% PI in Farsi Block. Discovery of oil and gas in the block has been made which is being evaluated for commercialization. In Gabon, OIL has one block where the first phase of exploration is in progress. One of OIL's focus areas is to make a selective presence across the oil and gas value chain for balancing its risk portfolio. OIL has increased its stake in Numaligarh Refinery to 26%. OIL also has a 10% stake in the Assam Gas Cracker Project, recently named as Brahmaputra Cracker and Polymers Ltd. OIL recently signed an MOU with Total, Mittal Energy Investments Pte Ltd., HPCL and GAIL, for participation in the East Coast grassroot Refinery and Petrochemical complex at Visakhapatnam. In the area of services business, OIL is concentrating on the Pipeline sector-its area of strength. The Company is expected to complete the product-pipeline (NRL to Siliguri) by end of this year, which will generate additional gross revenue of about Rs 107 Crore per annum.

3854. (24-10-2007) NEW DELHI : The Indian National Congress condemns and rejects with contempt the vitriolic and highly unjustified attack made upon the Prime Minister of India, Dr. Manmohan Singh, by the BJP spokesperson Mr. Arun Jaitley. This vicious and petulant outburst is not only demonstrably false – but represents nothing more than an expression of the deep frustration and ideological and intellectual bankruptcy of the BJP, which, even after 3 years is unable to reconcile itself to the loss of power. Mr. Jaitley and the BJP would do well to reflect on their own leadership crisis now, and the utter shambles which their party finds itself in. The six years in government showed the BJP under Mr. Vajpayee and Mr. Advani was notorious for its devotion to opportunistic and unholy alliances. Its leaders were driven by venality and vaunting ambition. It developed a stake in big time corruption. It's sister organizations opposed its policies and state bosses worked at cross purposes. Indiscipline was rampant. It is the BJP which is a sad and defeated party and Mr. Vajpayee and Mr. Advani the Vikas Purush and Loh Purush who are disappointed and disillusioned leaders. In the ongoing battle for supremacy between Mr. Vajpayee and Mr. Advani, Mr. Vajpayee always used the threat to quit as his best weapon and also used this weapon with great success to score victories over Mr. Advani. The nation will not forget the words of the then PM Mr. Vajpayee, in response to criticism from his allies, and BJP itself on the UTI scam, the failure of the Agra summit and the botched up Naga cease fire. On July 31, 2001, Mr. Vajpayee said, "since I am Prime Minister, I am responsible. I cannot manage the NDA. I have grown old. I am also unwell. I shall leave the chair. That is why I have decided to resign". He also said he was unable to function in a coherent and disciplined manner and wanted to quit. Parliament came to a standstill. The nation was thrown into confusion. So it was Mr. Vajpayee who was a sad and defeated Prime Minister not Dr. Manmohan Singh who has led the country with great distinction with 9% economic growth, 25,000 crore package for farmers, NREGA, RTI and a host of other achievements. The BJP had the temerity to call Mr. Advani the Loh Purush and compare him to Sardar Patel. This was shameful disrespect to Sardar Patel who as the Iron Man was responsible for unifying all the states to create a strong India. What a stark contrast to Mr. Advani, who went to Pakistan and paid homage at the Samadhi of Mohammed Ali Jinnah who was responsible for the partition and division of this country. Mr. Advani also called Mr. Jinnah secular and then later, denied it. This Mr. Advani is not the "Loh Purush" but a Low Purush. The country will also remember how Jaswant Singh escorted the dreaded terrorists and freed them at Kandahar – the very terrorists who later came back to plan the terrorist attack on Parliament the highest edifice of our democracy. After being party to this shameful deed as 'home Minister' Mr. Advani later claimed that he had been against the decision. Truly a low purush. That is why Advani went to Pakistan and called Jinnah secular, only to come back and deny it. Then went out of the country to make the shameful statement that he had been against the release of the terrorist at Kandhar even though he was Home Minister of India at that time. Even out of power, the BJP continues its sad and defeated game on 30 Dec 2005, Vajpayee stunned his partymen by saying at a Mumbai rally to mark the silver jubilee of his party that he was bowing out of active politics. But on Sept 21, 2007, he sent a poem and letter to the party executives in Lucknow saying he will return soon to active politics, much to the horror or Advani supporters who were about to anoint him as Prime Ministerial candidate – Mr. Advani had publicly gone on record to say that he as leader of the opposition was Prime Minister in waiting. Advani was forced to welcome Vajpayee's return. Thus it is the BJP leaders Vajpayee and Advani, and indeed the entire BJP which is sad and defeated – both when they were in government and even when they had been swept out of power, they have failed to learn their lessons. They continue with their internal wrangling and bankruptcy of ideology. At this rate they will be swept out of the opposition, and even the political space in our democracy. The Indian National Congress and UPA allies stand like a rock behind the prime Minister and this UPA government will go down in history as a mature and stable government which ensured communal harmony, social justice and equity, primary concern for the aam admi, focus on all sectors of development particularly agriculture and a resurgent economy. Dr. Manmohan Singh is a successful dynamic, and respected Prime Minister and the nation will bear witness to that fact.

3855. (24-10-2007) NEW DELHI : The number of total operationalized private FM radio channels in the country has gone up to 120. Five more radio were commissioned during September 2007, taking the number of such stations to 120.

These are: MY FM (Synergy Media) for Ajmer, Radio Dhamal (BAG Infotainment) for Muzafarpur and Dhule, BIG FM (Adlabs Films) for Ajmer and Radio Mirchi (ENIL) for Kolhapur. The Government also received a same of Rs. 167.82 lakhs as license fee from private FM Radio Broadcasters during September 2007.

3856. (24-10-2007) NEW DELHI : Shri A.Raja, Minister of Communications and Information Technology has said that our IT exports which is around $37 billion today with an average rate of 30 per cent growth per annum will touch US $ 80 billion mark by 2011. The Minister was speaking at an awards ceremony of the Electronics and Computer Software Export Promotion Council here today. He said that his Ministry has a plan to connect the nation with a network of communication technologies using optic fiber and wireless connections and providing facility to interact in 22 local languages. The Ministry is in the process of implementation of an ambitious e-Governance project right across the country, which consists of 27 Mission Mode Projects. 100,000 broadband-enabled Internet Common Service Centres are being established across the country to connect the citizens of rural areas to the World Wide Web. These changes will have a direct bearing on the rural connectivity, governance, PC penetration, employment, quality of education for the underprivileged and those in the small towns and villages, artisans, craftsmen, farmers and more importantly on IT exports from the country, he added. With the range of telecom density that we have targeted to achieve, broadband connectivity of 20 million connections by 2010 and accelerated growth in Internet and PC penetration set at 40 million, we will have not only a groundswell of export capacities built into the system but also proliferation of ranks of knowledge leaders and workers. The Minister said that he forsaw tier two, three and four cities becoming IT hubs, which will help the industry to maintain the labour advantage and augment the supply of manpower. With the type of revolution that is taking place in the IT connectivity, one can set up a software unit in the remotest of the places and beat the cost push that has been experienced in the segment on account of spiraling real estate prices and wage level, he added. In a way, this would take the benefits of economic liberalization and higher development across the length and breadth of the country and help in empowering the masses. Electronic hardware is also going to be an equally significant export driver of the future. The Government is looking very closely at a strategy to build capacities in the hardware sector. Shri Raja said that the growth of hardware sector has to be augmented by focusing on R&D since technology changes are faster in this segment. On the rupee appreciation, which has considerably affected the margins, the Minister said that this was a challenge to face in the coming years. He said his Ministry was taking up the issue of continuance of exemptions available under 10A and 10B of Income Tax Act to IT companies operating under the existing scheme of the Software Technology Parks of India at the highest level. The Minister also gave away the ESC All India awards for Excellence in Electronics and IT Exports for 2005-06 and 2006-07. The awards are instituted by the Electronics and Computer Software Exports Promotion Council.

3857. (24-10-2007) NEW DELHI : The Central Warehousing Corporation (CWC) has declared a dividend of 27% for the year 2006-07. Shri N.K. Choubey, Managing Director, CWC handed over a cheque of Rs. 10.10 crore as dividend on the paid up capital of central government to Shri Sharad Pawar, Minister of Agriculture, Consumer Affairs, Food and Public Distribution here today. The CWC is a profit making PSU and has been declaring dividend to the shareholders for the last three decades. During the year 2006-07 CWC achieved highest ever turn over of Rs. 686.44 crore with the highest ever profit before tax of Rs. 133.80 crore. The profit after tax is Rs. 88.70 crore. Set up with the main objective of the providing scientific storage facilities for agricultural inputs and produce and other notified commodities, the CWC is operating 496 warehouses with a total storage capacity of 99.76 lakh metric tonne with an average utilization of 79%. The Corporation is also operating 95 custom bonded warehouses and 3 air cargo complexes. CWC in tie up with Indian railways has started a new concept of rail side warehousing complex. 22 locations in different railways zones have been sanctioned to the corporation for this purpose.

3858. (24-10-2007) NEW DELHI : The Finance Minister Shri P. Chidambaram, who is currently on a visit to Norway, met the Norwegian Finance Minister, Ms. Kristin Halvorsen. During the meeting the two Ministers acknowledged that the bilateral trade between India and Norway is below par its true potential and discussed various measures to improve the bilateral trade and investment. In this regard, the Finance Minister expressed willingness of the Government of India to set up a Joint Working Group on trade and investment. He also expressed hope that the Joint Study group set up to examine the possibilities of trade and investment between India and EFTA of which Norway is also a member, shall be able to submit the final report next month. He also conveyed the Indian Government's willingness to re-negotiate the Double Tax Avoidance Agreement, which was signed in 1986. Shri Chidambaram also welcomed the interest shown by the banks from both sides in opening up the branches in each other country. Shri Chidambaram also sought Norway's support in India getting the Observer status in the Financial Action Task Force. During the meeting, the two ministers discussed various subjects of global importance and of bilateral relevance, including Global economic trends, impact of rising oil prices on global economy, Climate Change issues, bilateral trade and investment matters, impact of sub-prime crisis on India, possibilities of Norwegian Pension fund's investment in India. On climate change issue, Shri Chidambaram informed that India's per capita emission of GHG is much lower than the global average and stated that the economic growth should be decoupled from the GHG emission. He suggested the possibilities of collaboration with Norway in sectors such as hydrocarbons, fisheries, shipping & ship building, hydro-electricity, tunneling and environment, where Norway has core competence. Shri Chidambaram also met Mr. Eric Solheim, the Norwegian Minister for International development and Environment. The two ministers exchanged their country's position on climate change issues. The Finance Minister is accompanied by a business delegation comprising IT, Banking, shipping and petroleum sectors.

3859. (24-10-2007) NEW DELHI : The following are the extracts from the Raksha Mantri, Mr. A K Antony's address at the Combined Commanders Conference here this morning. "At the very outset, I wish to pay my tributes to the dedication and professionalism of our Armed Forces. The nation is really proud of them and values the sacrifices made by them. We are living in a multi-polar world. It has often been said that the 21st century will be an Asian century. The Asian region has a geo-political and a strategic importance. However, while Europe and the Euro-Atlantic region are comparatively more peaceful, Asia has been plagued by several ongoing territorial disputes, low-key armed conflicts and tensions. As we develop as a regional and an economic superpower, our role and responsibilities are bound to increase too. Today, India is firmly on the centre stage of international geo-politics. Our defence and strategic partnerships bear testimony to this fact. As trans-border threats change in nature and scope, nations are becoming increasingly inter-dependent. In today's world, there is a need to carefully monitor the international environment and formulate flexible response options to emerging situations. Terrorism continues to be one of the major challenges facing us. As terrorists constantly modernize their communication network, there is an urgent need to continuously upgrade our own capabilities to successfully counter the threat posed by them. In this context, it must be said that the overall situation in Jammu & Kashmir and the North East has shown steady signs of improvement. As we accelerate the process of modernization of our Armed Forces, we must bear in mind that technology has compressed distances and times. At the same time, it has also significantly reduced response timings at every level. The urgent need of the hour is to change mindsets, in tune with the changing times-where transparency and fairness are the buzzwords. Steps like institutionalization of Defence Planning Process and refinement of Defence Procurement Procedure have added urgency in the methodology and transparency in functioning. Another instrument towards change is the delegation of powers and transition towards fusion of authority, responsibility and accountability. We have delegated significant financial powers from the Ministry of Defence to Services HQ. However, it must be ensured that these powers are put to best use. Jointness and integration is not merely a desire, but an urgent need of the hour. It is a process that is destined to grow. Synergy can produce only better results, than individual efforts. In conclusion, I wish to reiterate that the nation is proud of our Armed Forces. From this forum, I wish to convey our deepest appreciation and commitment, with which they perform the onerous duties and responsibilities given to them."

3860. (24-10-2007) NEW DELHI : A meeting of Hindi Salahkar Samiti of the Ministry of Steel was held in Vishakhapatnam yesterday under the chairmanship of Prof. Alka Balram Kshatriya, Member of the Rajya Sabha. The members of the committee held detailed discussions and made concrete suggestions regarding progressive use of Hindi in the Ministry of Steel and its Public Sector Undertakings. Apprising the members of committee of national level recognition of use of Hindi by the Steel Ministry, the Chairperson expressed happiness over the progressive use of Hindi in the ministry under the guidance of Samiti. The Ministry of Steel has been awarded with 'Indira Gandhi Rajbhasha Shield '(Third Prize) for the year 2005-06 for the progressive use of Hindi. National Mineral Development Corporation (NMDC), Hyderabad, a PSU of the Steel Ministry has been awarded "Indira Gandhi Rajbhasha Shield" (First Prize) for the year 2005-06 under the category of PSUs in region 'C' while Steel Authority of India Ltd. (SAIL) also bagged the First Prize in 2006-07 for publishing Best Magazine by the PSUs. Congratulating the Ministry of Steel for these achievements the chairperson hoped that the Ministry and its PSUs will continue to win such awards in future also. Senior officials from 11 Public Sector Undertakings and the Ministry of Steel participated in the meeting.

3861. (24-10-2007) NEW DELHI : The Bharatiya Janata Party rejects the government's claim that the rate of inflation has come down dramatically. The ground reality is diametrically opposite to the tall and false claims of the government. The prices of all essential commodities in general and food items in particular are on literally on fire. Though the government is claiming that inflation is just 3.6%, the reality is that prices have increased phenomenally over the last 3 months. The Consumer Price Index, (CPI-UNME) which is the real indicator, has galloped by 6.4% in one year since August, 2006 and food items have seen a steep rise of 9.11%. Prices of vegetables have shot up by well over 19.8%. The CPI-UNME for Delhi has increased from 430 to 522 during UPA regime of three and half years registering annual increase of almost 7%. The Government should have seen its own official statistics released by the Ministry of Statistics and Programme Implementation before making such false and misleading claims. The much touted Aam Aadmi of the Congress' election campaign is reeling under the pressure of continuous steep price rise. Refined Oils have seen an increase of Rs. 7-8 per kg. over the last 3 months. Prices of all varieties of rice have also shot up. Coupled with this price rise, the scarcity of Kerosene and Cooking Gas is causing further hardship to the common man. People have to either wait for one full month to get Cylinder and shell Rs. 27 for Kerosene or pay Rs. 500 for Cylinder in the black market. The government must consider changing its base of deciding the rate of inflation on only the Whole Sale Price Index. The Consumer price index represents the actual consumer basket of retail prices and includes day-to-day services used by the common man. Consumer Price Index is more relevant as it reflects what the consumer actually pays. The need of the hour is to develop a composite realistic price index, which will accurately reflect the true price situation. Instead of playing with statistic, fudging the figures and then making hollow and flase claims, the government must come out with an action plan to combat inflation and reduce the burden of the common man. The Bharatiya Janata Party also demands that the government must supply edible oil and pulses along with cereals through the PDS at reasonable price. Government must also strengthen the PDS by stopping large scale diversion amounting to Rs. 17,000 crores.

3862. (24-10-2007) NEW DELHI : The Vice President of India, Mohd. Hamid Ansari inaugurated the "First Briefing Programme of Indian Origin Parliamentarians" organized by the Public Diplomacy Division of Ministry of External Affairs here today. The Programme is being organized with a view to provide comprehensive presentations on different aspects on issues of concern and interest to the country. The objective behind such a programme is to provide the Indian origin Parliamentarians with upto date and detailed information on a canopic range of issues. The Indian Origin Parliamentarians from United Kingdom, the European Parliament and the United States of America attending this programme include : United Kingdom-Lord Bhiku Parekh (Labour), The Rt. Hon. Keith Vaz (Labour), Lord Adam patel (Labour), Baroness Sandip Verma (Conservative), Lord Mohd. Sheikh (Conservative), Lord Narendra Babubhai Patel (Crossbench), Baroness Usha Prashar (Crossbench), Lord Kamlesh Patel (Crossbench), Lord Karan Bilimoria (Crossbench), Lord Navnit Dholakia (Libdem), Lord Diljit Rana (Crossbench) and the Rt. Hon. Virendeer K. Sharma, MP; European Parliament-Hon. Ms. Neena Gill, Hon. Mr. David Geerts and Hon. Mr. Claude Moraes and United States of America-Hon. Swati Dandekar.

3863. (24-10-2007) NEW DELHI : The Union Minister of Shipping, Road Transport and Highways, Thiru T.R. Baalu has approved a sum of Rs.471.14 lakh for road improvement works in the state of Tamil Nadu. An amount of Rs. 275.73 lakh has been approved for improvement of Riding Quality (IRQ) work at Km 172/00 to 180/00 of NH-209 between Kurmba Palayam and Kunnathur in Erode District. This road connects Tamil Nadu and Karnataka States. This is one of the important road passing through cotton city of Coimbatore and popular pilgrimage centres Palani and Bannari. Since this road is the shortest route to connect Coimbatore with Mysore and Bangalore, vehicular traffic in this road is very heavy. Due to the heavy volume of traffic in this stretch, the existing pavement has been worn out badly and developed with ruts and potholes and also this stretch experience heavy rainfall during the recent monsoon season. Hence, in order to protect the pavement from further damages, it is proposed to improve the stretch. Thiru Baalu also approved an amount of Rs. 195.41 lakh for improvement of Riding Quality work at km 212/4-219/0 on the same highway between Nallur and Vinnappally in Erode district. This is an important road as it connects many agricultural industrial, tourist, textile and pilgrimage centres in its vicinity. A large number of patches are developed in the stretch due to incessant rains during the last monsoon. Therefore, it is essential to improve this stretch of the National Highway.

3864. (25-10-2007) NEW DELHI : The Light Combat Aircraft 'TEJAS' programme achieved the most significant milestone yet when it successfully test fired the Close Combat Missile R-73 today at the air to air range off Goa coast. The historic event marks the beginning of weaponisation, which is the focus of the current initial operational clearance (IOC) phase of the programme. Air to Air missile integration and testing especially on a fly by wire aircraft is a very complex task involving interfaces with aerodynamics, engine air intake, control laws, flight control system, avionics system, electrical and other general system of aircraft. Today's successful test firing is the culmination of preparatory work under the guidance of Mr. JJ Jadhav, DPD (Weapon Systems) and Mr. Balasubramanyam, AGM (HAL). Accordingly the main objectives of test firing were to validate: · Safe separation of the missile from the parent aircraft. · Effect of missile plume on engine air-intake · Functionality of store management system (SMS) including safety interlocks · Effect of missile plume on composites structures · Handling quality assessment during missile launch The historic flight was done on Tejas prototype vehicle PV-1, piloted by the Chief Test Pilot of the National Flight Test Centre ADA, Gp Capt. N. Harish. The test firing was done at 7 km altitude and 0.6 Mach. The flight test was conducted from the mobile telemetry vehicle where all the aircraft, systems and weapon data were closely monitored. Quick analysis of the data revealed that it was a 'text book' launch where the systems performance matched the predictions well. The event has proven the capability of the composite team comprising of designers, production agency, certification agency and Flight Test and the user agency (IAF) to integrate and flight test an advanced missile on an advanced fighter aircraft Tejas. INS Hansa of Indian Navy provided all support for this important flight trial. Photo chase aircraft Sea Harrier was flown by Capt. Yatish Saxena and Cdr. Dalip Singh. The successful missile firing was witnessed by Chief Controller (R&D) Dr. D. Banerjee, Programme Director ADA Mr. P. S. Subramaniam and Director LCA (IAF) AVM B. C. Nanjapa.

3865. (25-10-2007) NEW DELHI : The Prime Minister Dr. Manmohan Singh chaired the first meeting of the National Disaster Management Authority. The Prime Minister observed that the setting up of the Authority marks a "paradigm shift" in the Government's approach to disaster management from compartmentalized to integrated and from a purely response/relief-centric approach to a more holistic one, covering all aspects like prevention, mitigation, preparedness, relief, response and rehabilitation. The Prime Minister stressed the importance of citizen awareness in dealing with disaster management. He advised the Authority to develop as a high-level policy-making body capable of providing advice and assistance to states during times of disaster. It should be an efficient clearing house for relevant information, lead in capacity building at all levels and ensure that disaster management proceeds in an orderly and cost-effective manner. The objective is to provide focused attention to disaster management, bring to bear the best possible expertise and to generally professionalise the entire gamut of disaster management activities. The Prime Minister reviewed preparedness to deal with different types of terrorist attacks. The Authority took a number of important decisions to enable it to function better. It was decided to associate the Ministers of Agriculture, Finance and Home Affairs as well as the Deputy Chairman of the

Planning Commission with future meetings of the Authority. Immediate relief and response was assigned to the National Executive Committee. Certain categories of disasters need a broader approach and need involvement of other agencies. Therefore, it was decided to continue to have the existing arrangements under the National Crisis Management Committee for dealing with such crises. The Vice Chairman Gen (Retd.) N.C. Vij, Members-Shri B. Bhattacharjee, Lt Gen (Retd.) Dr. J.R. Bhardwaj, Dr. Mohan Kanda, Prof. N.V.C. Menon, Shri M.S. Reddy, Smt. P. Jyoti Rao, Shri J.K. Sinha, Shri K.M. Singh, National Security Advisor Shri M.K. Narayanan, Principal Secretary to PM Shri T.K.A. Nair and Cabinet Secretary Shri K.M. Chandrasekhar participated in the meeting.

3866. (25-10-2007) NEW DELHI : MTNL today presented a cheque for Rs.35.43 crore towards 10 per cent balance of final dividend for the financial year 2006-07 to the Minister of Communications and Information Technology, Shri A.Raja. In its 21st Annual General Meeting held on 28.9.2007, MTNL approved payment of final dividend @ 40 per cent (including 30 per cent interim dividend already paid) on the paid up equity capital of Rs.630 crore for the financial year 2006-07. This will involve an amount of Rs.63 crore in addition to Rs.189 crore already paid as interim dividend. Out of this, Rs.35.43 crore is payable to the Government of India towards the Government's share in the shareholding of the company. MTNL has paid dividend @ 40 per cent on its equity capital of Rs.630 crore last year also. During the last seven years, an aggregate amount of Rs.1921.50 crore has been paid as dividend to all the shareholders out of which Rs. 1080.78 crore has been paid to the Government of India on their shareholding of 56.25 per cent in the company.

3867. (25-10-2007) NEW DELHI : The first meeting of the Organizing Committee for IFFI-2007 was held today under the Chairmanship of Shri P. R. Dasmunsi, Union Minister of Information & Broadcasting and Parliamentary Affairs. The meeting deliberated on the various issues related to IFFI-2007 and reviewed the level of preparedness for Event. In his remarks, Shri Dasmunsi said that over the years the Festival has gone from strength to strength and our endeavour has been to make it still better. He lauded the role and suggestions of film industry in raising the standard of the Festival over time. The Organizing Committee took the under noted major decisions: The opening and closing functions will be simple and elegant in keeping with the practice in most of the prestigious international film festivals. The focus will be on the opening film and closing films. There will be no entertainment programme at these functions. The awards ceremony will be held at the closing function. This would be followed by the screening of the closing film. Two new theatres with a seating capacity of 300 seats are being built in the Festival Complex. Two public theatres are being upgraded and provided with the latest projection facilities thereby making another 400 seats available for the festival. The total number of delegates that may be registered has been fixed in proportion to the availability of theatre seats. The Government of Goa has been requested to screen the applications of local delegates and forward them to DFF for final approval. The registration system for all delegates has been made completely on-line. Delegate cards will be prepared well in advance so that there are no long queues at the registration counter. For the first time a ticketing system has been introduced whereby every delegate will have to book in advance for any films that he/she would like to see. A maximum of 3 tickets for every delegate and 5 for every media person will be issued. The delegate registration fee for late registration has been considerably enhanced to Rs. 1000/- . Students, will however, be given a concession of 50%. The Indian Panorama will have 21 features and 15 non-feature films selected by a peer Jury headed by Shri K.S. Sethumadhavan, and Shri Arun Khopkar respectively. Indian Retrospectives will showcase Retrospective on the films of Tapan Sinha and Vijay Anand. Homages section will focus on Cinematographer K.K. Mahajan, Actress Vanamala Devi and Music Director O.P. Nayyar. Among the highlights of foreign section are, 14 feature films from Asia, Africa and Latin America in the Competition Section. Cinema of the World will have About 60 award winning feature films from 40 countries. Master Classes, Technical Retrospective. Foreign Retrospectives and Country Focus will be the other features of IFFI-07. For the first time, two programmers from the Goa Govt. will be curating for IFFI with two separate sections called-India 60 which will celebrate India's 60th anniversary with three feature films and two documentary films and a retrospective package on Volker Schlondorff the eminent German film maker. The Film Market will be organized by NFDC with the participation of CII and FICCI. The NFDC is organizing a buyer's lounge and co production market. FICCI is organizing a seminar and master class on animation and visual effects. CII will organize 'The Big Picture' Conference. A new initiative is being undertaken by NFDC in partnership with DFF where international consultants and experts will advise and work with selected film makers to develop scripts of international quality. The meeting was attended, among others, by the Goa Minister for Water Resources and Forests, Mr. Philipe N. Rodrigues, Addl. Secretary, Ministry of I&B; Chief Secretary, Goa and Director, DFF.

3868. (25-10-2007) NEW DELHI : Army Gen Deepak Kapoor, presented the Annual Flight Safety Trophy for the year 2006-07 to 28 Recce and Observation Flight of Army Aviation. This trophy is awarded annually to the Army Aviation unit achieving the best flight safety record during the year. Flying more than 50,000 hours every year, Army Aviation helicopters are a lifeline for the far flung isolated posts, ferrying in men, material and evacuating casualties. One Army Aviation unit is also actively deployed in Congo as part of UN forces. The Corps has also rendered yeoman service to the nation in times of natural calamities. A host of awards, won by the officers and men of the Corps are a testimony of its gallant history.

3869. (25-10-2007) NEW DELHI : Rampur, 25 October 2007: Bharatiya Janata Party's National Vice President and In-Charge of its Central Election Committee,

Shri Mukhtar Abbas Naqvi, has said that the 'commercial break' provided by the dramatic tiff between the Congress and the Left, would be followed very soon by the 'breaking news' of the fall of the Central Government. Participating in a Jan Chaupal in Gram Matwali Dholsar in Shahbad Tehsil, Rampur, Shri Naqvi said that 'breaking news' of the demise of this government and announcement of fresh polls would be made after Diwali. He also said that whereas a weak, helpless and incapable Prime Minister is gifting the people of India, inflation, terrorism and corruption, the sad part is that the handing over of the control of our nuclear future, that was consolidated during the tenure of Shri Atal Behari Vajpayee, in the hands of the US, is also being counted as an accomplishment. The ordinary folk is being held hostage by people that are blind to national interests. Shri Naqvi further said that the BJP has completed the preparations for the Lok Sabha polls. "We have started giving the final shape of our panel of candidates. Party President Shri Rajnath Singh, and other senior central leaders, including Shri L.K. Advani, are keeping a close eye on the developments in the Centre." Shri Naqvi has said that with the announcement of polls, the list of NDA coalition partners would increase. Talks are at a final stage with several regional parties to join hands with the BJP and the NDA. Shri Naqvi also pointed out that the parties that are presently with the Congress are depressed and demoralized. The attitude and behaviour of the Prime Minister and the Congress Party has shown that the mentality of the Congress Party, which has always been against coalitions, has not changed. Shri Naqvi has said that to fulfil coalition dharma, what is required is honest politics, not merely good economics. The PM has proved him not only as an unsuccessful economist but also a poor political strategist. While on one hand the Congress brand of economics has resulted in inflation, unemployment and farmer suicides, on the other hand an ineffective and incapable Prime Minister has given the country a poor administration. He said that the 5 years spent by the BJP's in coalition at the Centre proved not only successfully, but was also crowned with several achievements. In the next Lok Sabha elections, BJP-led coalition would be successful and an NDA government would be formed in the Centre.

3870. (25-10-2007) NEW DELHI : The production of urea was estimated as 17.00 lakh tonnes during September 2007 as against the target of 17.40 lakh tonnes. The shortfall in production was caused by plants shutdown due to annual turnaround, mechanical problem in the plants and limitation of gas. The estimated production of DAP during this month was 3.61 lakh tonnes against the revised target of 4.45 lakh tonnes. The production of DAP was restricted due to limitation of rock phosphate, phosphoric acid and maintenance jobs. Besides these, during the month 6.08 lakh tonnes of Urea, 4.82 lakh tonnes of DAP and 3.26 lakh tonnes of MOP was also imported. On the availability front, approximately 23.71 lakh tonnes of both indigenous and imported urea was despatched to the states during September 2007. Availability of Urea during the month to the tune of about 38.51 lakh tonnes is reported to be satisfactory in all the states. The sale of Urea in the current season till 30.09.2007 recorded 9.62% rise at 124.58 lakh tonnes as compared to the 113.65 lakh tonnes in the corresponding period of previous year. The availability of DAP at 10.66 lakh tonnes and MOP at 5.11 lakh tonnes during this period had also been adequate to meet the demand of states.

3871. (25-10-2007) NEW DELHI : A salt lake or saline lake is a landlocked body of water which has a concentration of salts (mostly sodium chloride) and other minerals significantly higher than most lakes (often defined as at least 3,000 milligrams of salt per liter). In many cases, salt lakes have a higher concentration of salt than sea water. Salt lakes form when the water flowing into the lake, containing salt or minerals, cannot leave because the lake is endorheic or terminal. The water then evaporates, leaving behind any dissolved salts and thus increasing its salinity, making a salt lake an excellent place for salt production. High salinity will also lead to a unique flora and fauna in the lake in question. If the amount of water flowing into a lake is less than the amount evaporated, the lake will eventually disappear and leave a salt flat or playa (sometimes also referred to as salt pan).

3872. (25-10-2007) NEW DELHI : The Twelfth World Lake Conference-TAAL 2007 is being held at Jaipur from 28th October to 2nd November 2007. With its central theme of 'Conserving Lakes and Wetlands for Future', this five day conference will provide a unique platform for interaction between scientists, researchers, technologists and policy makers from different parts of the world. The Conference comprises of many plenary lectures, technical sessions, key-note addresses on various sectional things by eminent scientists, oral presentations, poster sessions and working group discussions, together with a programme of socio-cultural events. The Conference has selected five major themes which are: Science and Lakes; Conservation and Management; Special Group of Lakes; Socio-Economic Aspects and Special Sessions. Wide range of aspects will be covered in various sessions. They are bio-diversity and conservation, lake catchments, lake eco-system process, invasive species and wind control, lake wetlands and climate change, fisheries other use, Eutrophication and Modelling, Bio-remediation and Biomanipulation, Lake littoral Zone Management, Hydrology and Eco-hydrology, Community Participation, and Legal as well Regulatory frameworks. A biennial event, these Conferences are organized under the aegis of the International Lake Environment Committee Foundation (ILEC), Japan since 1985. The Ministry of Environment and Forests is hosting the Conference with support from Government of Rajasthan. Participants from Russia, Australia, Austria, The Neitherlands, China, Denmark, Zimbabwe, Italy, Canada, USA, Philippines, Czech Republic, Poland and Japan will attend the Conference.

3873. (25-10-2007) NEW DELHI : The Second Ministerial Council of Asia-Pacific Trade Agreement (APTA) will be held here tomorrow, 26th October 2007. The Council will be hosted by Shri Kamal Nath, Minister of Commerce & Industry. Over 30 delegates headed by the respective Ministers or Vice Ministers from the six APTA participating states (Bangladesh, China, India, the Republic of Korea, Lao PDR and Sri Lanka) will be attending the meeting. The most important task on the Ministers' agenda is the launch of the Fourth Round of Tariff Negotiations which when completed will deepen and widen trading relations among the six participating states. Ministers will also adopt the Agreement on Operational Rules for the Certification and Verification of the Origin of Goods, which is the first time that the economic powerhouses of China, India and Republic of Korea adopt a common set of operational rules. Together with membership expansion that is expected, to follow in the upcoming years, APTA is emerging as the only truly regional trade agreement that links east, southeast and south Asia, and is thus becoming an important platform for regional economic cooperation and integration.

3874. (25-10-2007) NEW DELHI : The Bharatiya Janata Party is deeply concerned at the lackadaisical and indifferent attitude of the UPA Government on the reported intrusion by the Chinese troops into Indian territory in recent times. This fact has also been categorically confirmed by the DG ITBP who has stated that over 140 such intrusions have taken place over the last one year in the regions of both Arunachal Pradesh and Jammu & Kashmir. The statement of the ITBP chief vindicates the assertion and claim of the party MP from Arunachal Pradesh Mr. Khiran Rijuju, who after extensive scouting in the inaccessible terrains, has repeatedly asserted the fact about Chinese incursions and has also raised it on all forums including the Parliament where it has been repudiated by the Government in general and the Home Minister Mr. Shivraj Patil in particular. While the Left and Congress party are both maintaining a deafening silence on this important issue of national security and sovereignty, both the CPM General Secretary Mr. Prakash Karat and UPA Chairperson Smt. Sonia Gandhi have instead of raising this issue have only confined themselves to congratulating Chinese President Hu Jintao on his re-election as the General Secretary of the ruling Communist Party in China. The BJP notes that the incursions are simply not the inadvertent misadventures of lost Chinese patrols but instead point towards the existence of a carefully designed strategy to undermine India's territorial integrity. In the absence of any strong governmental reaction on the issue, what is even more shocking is that in the meantime Smt Sonia Gandhi is all set to embark on a five day tour to China accompanied by her son Mr. Rahul Gandhi with an undisclosed agenda. The complete silence maintained by this high level entourage comprising even senior Ministers of the UPA Government is indeed shocking. The BJP aptly recalls the incident of refusal of Chinese visa to the Arunachal cadre IAS officers of the 1991 batch for a study tour sponsored by Government of India to Beijing & Shanghai. The Chinese claim was that since Arunachal Pradesh is a part of China, hence the officers in question were Chinese citizens who therefore required no visa. This has to also be viewed in context of earlier visa refusals to even State Ministers of Arunachal Pradesh. All these incidents are indicative of the fact that China rarely misses an opportunity to put forth its claim on Arunachal Pradesh. The BJP reiterates that the tactful diplomacy of the NDA government had compelled

China to forfeit its claims over the Indian state of Sikkim and had set a successful milestone in the direction of permanently settling all territorial disputes. The UPA government, seemingly under the pressure of its Left Front allies, is making camouflaged niceties to China in its attempt to placate the Left partners at home and in the process compromising the nation's territorial integrity.

3875. (25-10-2007) NEW DELHI : The Cabinet Committee on Economic Affairs today considered the Call Option Notice given by M/s. Sterlite Industries India Ltd. to acquire 10,81,06,005 equity shares held by Government of India in BALCO. CCEA has decided to constitute a Committee of Secretaries comprising Secretaries of Department of Legal Affairs, Department of Disinvestment and Ministry of Mines for finalizing government's position from time to time considering the legal issues as and when the need arises.

3876. (25-10-2007) NEW DELHI : For improving the quality of vocational training in the country and make it demand driven so as to ensure better employability of the graduates, the Cabinet Committee on Economic Affairs today gave its in-principle approval for Implementation of Central/Centrally Sponsored Scheme "Upgradation of 1396 Government ITIs through Public Private Partnership" for the XI Plan period and approval for implementation of the scheme for one year for the first batch of 300 ITI at a total cost of Rs.774.50 crore. Out of Rs.774.50 crore, Rs.750 crore shall be used for upgradation of 300 ITIs and Rs.24.5 crore shall be used for management, monitoring and evaluation of the scheme. Under the Public Private Partnership mode, for each ITI to be upgraded, an Industry Partner will be associated to lead the process of upgradation. The Industry Partner will be selected by the State Government in consultation with the Industry Associations. An Institute Management Committee (IMC) will be constituted for each selected ITI. The IMC will consist of following members: (i) Industry Partner or his representative, as the Chairperson (ii) Four Members from local industry to be nominated by the Industry Partner (iii) Five members to be nominated by the State Government (iv) Principal, ITI as ex-officio member Secretary of the IMC. After the approval, 300 selected ITIs will be upgraded through Public Private Partnership. Industry partner will be involved in all aspects of training from development of curriculum to trade testing. Academic and financial autonomy given to the ITIs will improve their internal and external efficiency. The demand driven and improved quality of training will lead to better employability of ITI graduates.

3877. (25-10-2007) NEW DELHI : India hosted the Second SAARC Meeting of Ministers of Interior/Home here today under the Chairmanship of Union Home Minister Shri Shivraj V. Patil. Today's meeting was preceded by the meeting of the SAARC Interior/Home Secretaries yesterday and the meeting of the Police Chiefs on October 23. Afghanistan attended the meeting for the first time after its induction into SAARC. The Home Ministers reiterated their commitment to the 14th SAARC Summit Declaration of moving from the declaratory to the implementation phase and reaffirmed their commitment to the need for a secure environment for facilitating economic growth, development and progress of the region. The Home Ministers also expressed satisfaction at the working of the institutional mechanisms within the ambit of the Home Ministries and urged enhanced coordination and networking among the police forces of the SAARC countries. The meeting noted that terrorism remains a serious threat to sustainable peace and development in the SAARC region, and called upon the Member States to strengthen institutional mechanisms with the aim to facilitate closer cooperation and more frequent interaction and regular exchange of information amongst the law enforcement agencies of the Member states to effectively combat the menace of terrorism and other related crimes such as drug trafficking money laundering, human trafficking, arms smuggling, counterfeit currency etc. The meeting considered the recommendations made by the Secretaries in the 2nd SAARC meeting of Secretaries of Interior/Home held yesterday, which, in turn, had considered the recommendations made by the Police officials in the Sixth SAARC Conference on Cooperation in Police Matters held on 23.10.2007. Considering the need for more frequent and higher level of interaction, the Ministers agreed that the SAARC Conference on Cooperation in Police Matters should be upgraded to the level of Police Chiefs and should be held bi-annually as against the present system of annual meetings. Pakistan has offered to host the next meeting at Islamabad in February 2008. The Ministers also agreed that the SAARC Terrorist Offences Monitoring Desk (STOMD) and the SAARC Drug Offences Monitoring Desk (SDOMD), located in Sri Lanka, need to be strengthened and operationally energized. The meeting noted the Indian offer to provide assistance in strengthening the infrastructure of these Desks. The implementation of the SAARC Regional Convention on Suppression of Terrorism and the Additional Protocol and SAARC Convention on Narcotic Drugs and Psychotropic substances was reviewed and progress appreciated, while reiterating the need for pro-active and sustained measures and mutual cooperation to combat these phenomena. With regard to the proposed SAARC Convention on Mutual Legal Assistance in Criminal Matters, it was agreed that the process should be accelerated and Legal Advisers from SAARC countries should meet for the second time by April, 2008 to examine the draft of the Convention. Sri Lanka's offer to host this meeting in early 2008 was welcomed. The Ministers also discussed the SAARC Visa Scheme. It was agreed to provide a special tenure-linked dispensation to the officials of the SAARC Secretariat. It was also agreed that retired Judges of Supreme Court/serving High Court Judges should be included in the Consolidated List of Entitled Persons. Later today, the Interior/Home Ministers are scheduled to proceed for a Retreat at Agra where informal consultations will he held.

3878. (25-10-2007) NEW DELHI : The Union Cabinet today gave its approval for making necessary amendments to the Labour Laws (Exemption from Furnishing Returns and maintaining Registers by Certain Establishments) Amendment and Miscellaneous provisions Bill, 2005 pending in Rajya Sabha. The newly amended

Bill would be called, Labour Laws (Exemption from Furnishing Returns and Maintaining Registers by Certain Establishments) (Amendment) Bill, 2007. The simplified forms to be introduced by these amendments will give relief to employers of establishments employing up to 40 workers in maintaining registers and submitting returns under various labour laws.

3879. (25-10-2007) NEW DELHI : The Union Cabinet today gave its approval to the promulgation of (i) the Daman and Diu Value added Tax (Amendment) Regulation, 2007; and (ii) the Dadra and Nagar Haveli Value Added Tax (Amendment) Regulation, 2007 by the President under article 240 of the Constitution. The Amendment Regulation will enable to refund the net negative tax to the assessee faster and to simplify the procedure.

3880. (25-10-2007) NEW DELHI : The Union Cabinet today gave its approval for signing the Agreement on Environmental Cooperation between India and Morocco. The Agreement would support and encourage the exchange of views and cooperation in the field of environmental protection and sustainable development between the two Governments, agencies, academic institutions and enterprises. The Agreement shall be effective for an unlimited period.

3881. (25-10-2007) NEW DELHI : The Union Cabinet today gave its ex-post facto approval for signing of the Convention. India signed the International Convention for the Protection of All Persons from Enforced Disappearance at the Special ceremony organized by the French Government in Paris on February 6, 2007 to open the Convention for signature. This was done with the approval of the Prime Minister.

3882. (25-10-2007) NEW DELHI: There is no indication that the Bharatiya Janata Party will shift from its stand on the nuclear deal with the United States that it should be re-negotiated; that it will adversely affect the country's strategic independence; that there should be a joint parliamentary committee to study it and that Parliament should vote on the deal. However, a senior BJP leader said that in the event of an advanced winter session and the deal coming up for discussion, the party may not stall Parliament altogether. "We cannot be seen stalling the House for a full 14 days or more," he said on condition of anonymity even as the BJP Parliamentary Party and the National Democratic Alliance leaders are yet to meet to finalise their strategy. Some senior leaders said that it would be in the party's interest to allow a discussion as it would clearly bring out the fact that the United Progressive Alliance did not have the backing of even its allies, not to speak of the supporting parties. What is clear is that if the deal is to come up for voting or if the sense of the House is taken, the BJP cannot be counted among the parties which will support the deal. "We are opposed to it. We have spelt out what parts of the deal we find objectionable," the leader said. The BJP leadership is keenly watching the standoff between the Congress and the Left parties on the deal and does not want to say or do anything that may bring them together. That was the reason cited by some senior leaders in the last parliamentary session for not bringing in a vote of no-confidence against the government. The BJP would like to see the UPA disintegrate as a result of the inner contradictions. At present the BJP is fully engaged in preparing for the electoral battle in Gujarat. Although in the last session of Parliament the party quietly accepted the Speaker's ruling against a discussion under a substantive motion entailing a vote, it has continued to reiterate its position that on a major issue such as the nuclear deal that would affect the country for decades, Parliament's approval in one form or the other was a must.

3883. (25-10-2007) NEW DELHI : The Union Cabinet today gave its approval for extension of the tenure of Short Service Commissioned Officers of AFMS upto 14 years and also for extending the time scale promotions to AFMS Short Service Commissioned Officers as applicable to permanent Commissioned officers owing to the extended tenure. This decision will help mitigate shortage of officers in the AFMS. It will bring about a parity with the existing time scale promotions available to the permanent Commissioned Officers and meet the career aspirations of AFMS SSC Officers.

3884. (25-10-2007) NEW DELHI : The Union Cabinet today gave its approval for setting up of two Indian Institutes of Science Education and Research (IISERs) at Bhopal and Thiruvananthapuram, at a total cost of Rs. 1000 crores (Rs. 500 crore per Institute). On the recommendation of the Scientific Advisory Council to the Prime Minister (SAC-PM), the Ministry of Human Resource Development (HRD) has set up three Indian Institutes of Science Education and Research (IISERs) at Pune, Kolkata and Mohali. Indian Institutes of Science Education and Research (IISERs), Bhopal and Thiruvananthapuram are the fourth and fifth in the chain of IISERs to be set up in the country by the Ministry of HRD. The Government of India has decided to create the IISERs with the unique objective of integrating undergraduate education, postgraduate education and research under the same umbrella. The basic idea of IISER is to create research universities of the highest caliber in which teaching and education will be totally integrated with the state of the art research. These universities will be devoted to undergraduate and postgraduate teaching in sciences in an intellectually vibrant atmosphere of research. One of the important goals of creating these universities is to make education and careers in basic sciences more attractive by providing opportunities in integrative teaching and learning of sciences and breaking the barriers of traditional disciplines. One other significant concept of the proposed IISER is to actively forge strong relationship with existing universities and colleges and network with laboratories and institutions, in order to share and complement faculty resources as well as research, library and computational facilities. IISERs at Bhopal and Thiruvananthapuram shall provide high-quality scientific manpower to government organizations such as the Department of Atomic Energy (DAE), Council of Scientific and Industrial Research (CSIR), Indian Space Research

Organization (ISRO), Defence Research & Development Organization (DRDO), teaching profession in other universities and other sectors of the society at large. They shall also cater to the growing research needs of the private sector. The IISERs shall have programmes of study called Schools in various interdisciplinary areas of Biological Sciences, Mathematical and Computer Sciences, Physical Sciences, Chemical Sciences and Materials Sciences. Each Institute is expected to have about 2000 undergraduate and postgraduate students and research scholars, and about 200 faculty members, across disciplines. The academic programmes will emphasise the spirit of research at an early stage of education.

3885. (25-10-2007) NEW DELHI : The Union Cabinet today gave its approval to the following decision : i) to reiterate the earlier decision dated 30.6.2005 of the Government that Purchase Preference Policy for Products and Services of CPSEs will be terminated with effect from 31.3.2008. ii) the preferential purchase policies framed for the specific sectors by the concerned Ministries / Departments within the relevant Act of Parliament or otherwise do not come within the purview of the decision at (I) above. The concerned Ministries / Departments may independently evolve / review preferential policies for the sectors of their concern, as per their requirement; and iii) to communicate the above decisions to the Supreme Court of India. This decision will result in a level playing field between CPSEs and private sector players and increase competition.

3886. (25-10-2007) NEW DELHI : The Union Cabinet today gave its approval for making necessary amendments in the Tyre Corporation of India Limited (Dis-investment of ownership) Bill, 2007 pending in Lok Sabha. The TCIL is a nationalized PSE and as per the advice of Ministry of Law and Justice, prior approval of Parliament is required for changing the nature of PSE from a government company to a non-government company. The Company can be revived on a sustainable manner only through joint venture for which change in nature of the PSE will be required.

3887. (25-10-2007) NEW DELHI : Shri A.Raja,Minister of Communications and Information Technology has said that the Government is cognizant of the fact that a key hurdle to the roll out of 3G services is the availability of spectrum. He said that an institutional mechanism has been put in place for early vacation by Defence. He said that we are hopeful that some spectrum for both 2G and 3G services will be vacated by the end of this year. The Minister hoped that this could pave the way for a roll out of 3G services by mid next year. Shri Raja was speaking at the Inauguration of 3G India Forum Organised by CNBC Network 18 here today. Shri Raja said that 3G offers an exciting opportunity for operators to provide innovative services, especially to the subcontinent's increasingly young, affluent and IT-literate urban population. As the world's second largest growing economy with rapidly rising income levels, India stands to gain enormously from a wide range of broadband mobile services from internet access to mobile TV. In a situation where telephone handsets are getting smaller and have become completely ubiquitous, and the market for 3G content is beginning to develop rapidly, operators and content providers have to concentrate their efforts on proposing contemporary content and services. Of course, the availability of cheaper 3G handsets is a major factor that will drive growth of 3G throughout India. 3G also offers vast potential to open the door to new social initiatives ranging from telemedicine and distance learning in rural schools to e-Government. TRAI in its recommendations has pointed out that Data applications as a significant driving force behind 3G will take some time. This observation is particularly relevant in the Indian marketplace, he added.With a current monthly addition of around 7 million subscribers in India, it is evident that there is still unmet demand for voice service.

3888. (25-10-2007) NEW DELHI : The Defence Minister Shri AK Antony will review the security situation in Jammu & Kashmir during a day's visit to the valley on October 27, 2007. He will hold meetings with Senior Army and State Government Officials. Meanwhile, the Ministry of Defence today increased the ex-gratia relief and assistance amount to the affected people inhabiting the areas adjacent to the ammunition depot at Khundroo to Rs. 26.75 crores to be disbursed by the Jammu & Kashmir State Government. It may be recalled that concerned by the loss of means of livelihood and property due to a major fire at the Army's biggest ammunition depot at Khundroo in Anantnag district on August 11, 2007, the MoD had released Rs 10 crores as an interim assistance to the J&K Government on August 28, 2007 to provide relief to the people. With today's sanction, MoD has fully met the amount requested by the State Government. It is hoped that the State Government will take urgent measures in disbursing the amount to the affected people. Shri Antony will also inaugurate the Silver Jubilee Celebrations of Jawahar Institute of Mountaineering and Winter Sports (JIMWS), Pahalgam and will attend the Executive Council and General Body Meetings of the Institute. Set up in October 1983, the JIMWS imparts theoretical and practical training in Mountaineering and rock climbing techniques. It also encourages and imparts training in winter sports.

3889. (25-10-2007) NEW DELHI : Following is the text of the Defence Minister Shri AK Antony's address at Naval Commanders Conference held in New Delhi today:-"I am happy to be present here today. At the very outset, I must complement the Indian Navy for the professionalism and dedication it has displayed in the preservation of our security at seas. The contribution of all Navy personnel has indeed been exemplary. Such occasions provide an opportunity to share views on important contemporary issues. The deliberations at this Conference will certainly provide crucial inputs in formulating a holistic strategy to meet the various challenges facing us. India is likely to become the third largest economy in the world by the year 2050. As a result, our energy needs are bound to grow rapidly. In fact, we will be one of the biggest energy consumers of the world in times to come. Major sea trade routes, carrying about 66% of the total world trade in oil, pass from close proximity to India. Moreover, the nature of maritime trade has changed drastically over the last decade. Today, the challenges are diverse, unpredictable and constantly evolving. To effectively meet these challenges, we must evolve strategies that deny or reduce the freedom of our enemies to exploit the maritime environment. To achieve this objective, the Services have to be developed into balanced and combat-ready forces. I wish to assure all of you that the Government is fully committed to modernisation and to provide the latest possible equipment to the Services. However, it is also your responsibility to ensure that the funds allocated are utilised judiciously and optimally. Time overrun of projects naturally leads to cost overruns, which in turn requires revised approvals, resulting in further delays. There is a critical need to institute suitable and adequate monitoring mechanisms to avoid delays in project implementation. I hope that the recent enhancement of financial limits in delegating financial powers will help in expediting procurement and execution of projects. The paradigm shift in military affairs today is driven by the merger of evolving high-end technology, which allows sifting and transfer of data in real time, enabling quick decision-making. Thus, our Armed Forces will have to evolve as a technology-intensive and networked force, ready to operate in an integrated manner. We need a special effort to identify and induct technologies that serve as force multipliers. However, these technological advances also pose a challenge-ensuring the security of information and data flow. I am sure that you will also be discussing ways and means to enhance cyber and network security during this conference. Along with modernisation, a related issue is that of indigenisation. All the stakeholders working to modernise our Armed Forces must work as a team, so that the R&D projects are completed in a time-bound manner. Our endeavour is to enhance the major capabilities of the armed forces through indigenous means, as far as possible. India is among the few countries that has built state-of-the-art ships and submarines. Earlier, the weapons and sensors fitted on these ships had to be imported, this trend has now been halted. I am confident that in the future, indigenous weapons and sensors will be inducted on the various facilities that are presently under construction. DRDO has been developing projects in collaboration with advanced countries. This will help in induction of high-end technology and also involve challenges in terms of system integration and intricate programme management. One factor that is often either neglected, or not given due importance is human resource management. The challenge before you is to not only to attract the best available talent, but also retain it.

3890. (25-10-2007) NEW DELHI : AROGYA, a comprehensive International Health Fair on Ayurveda, Yoga & Naturopathy, Unani, Siddha and Homoeopathy being organized by the Department of AYUSH, aims at projecting the capabilities and requirements of these systems in modern day health care, current research trends and exhibiting work of Research Institutions under this Department. The AROGYA Fair this year is being organized by the Department with the collaboration of India Trade Promotion Organisation from October 26-29, 2007 at Hall No. 7,

Pragati Maidan, New Delhi. The fair till 2004 used to be organized annually only at Delhi. However, on popular demand, since 2005 regional fairs have also been organized at Chennai in January 2005 and February 2006 at Hyderabad in November 2005 and at Dehradun in April 2007. This year regional fairs are proposed to be organized at Indore from 14th-17th December 2007 and at Amritsar from 7th-10th February 2008. This year for the first time 32 International Delegates from 16 countries will be participating in the AROGYA fair. These comprise of Regulators, distributors, consultants and academicians related with traditional medicine (TM) and natural products. An International meet of TM Regulators and Industry is being organized by PHARMEXCIL and Ministry of Commerce. The fair showcases participation by Drug Manufacturing Industry, Drug equipment manufacturing industry, publishers and booksellers of AYUSH, manufacturers of natural foods, Research Institutes, State Directorates of ISM&H, practitioners of AYUSH systems, medicinal plant nurseries and other stakeholders.

3891. (25-10-2007) NEW DELHI : Shri Arjun Singh, Union Minister for Human Resource Development will inaugurate the Conference on 'Social Exclusion and Inclusive Policy' on 26th October, 2007. Prof. B.L. Mungekar, Member, Planning Commission, would be the Guest of Honour. The Indian Institute of Dalit Studies, Delhi is organizing a two day National Conference on 'Social Exclusion and Inclusive Policy", on 26th and 27th October,2007 in New Delhi. This conference is being jointly sponsored by Indian Institute of Dalit Studies, Delhi and Princeton University, Princeton (USA). The main focus of this conference is to discuss the issue of social exclusion and discrimination faced by marginalized sections of the population such as SC,ST,OBC and religious minorities like Muslims and similar groups. The Indian society is characterized by social exclusion and discrimination of a number of social/cultural groups due to their social identity. This is the first conference of its kind which will discuss through presentation of papers the economic discrimination faced by discriminated groups in various market and non market transactions. This will include employment market in rural and urban areas, occupation and business, various factors market, services, and also education and health. Most of the papers are based on original research and will bring new insight on the theme of market and non market discrimination. In case of labour market discrimination,the conference will discuss the four studies conducted jointly by Indian Institute of Dalit Studies and Princeton University,USA,which have been published by Economic and Political Weekly in the form of a special issue. It will also discuss the discrimination in labour market and in occupation in rural areas of state of Haryana, Orrisa, and Gujarat. Besides, the conference will also discuss the discriminatory experiences of dalits in educational institutions and in seeking health services in primary health centre and private doctors. It will discuss for the first time the inequality in ownership of private enterprise by lower caste and higher castes. Some papers will discuss the discrimination faced by religious groups such as Muslims in economic spheres. This conference is of significant importance as it will address the most important problem being faced by vast section of population, namely SC,ST, OBC, religious minority like Muslim and women and currently being discussed in the academic and government circles. Based on the insights from the papers the conference will also discuss policies to overcome the discrimination.The discussion will centre on the various aspects of inclusive policy in the spheres of employment, education, health,business and other spheres both in public and private sector. The participants from various parts of the country will attend the conference. Besides, there are participants from Northern Ireland and USA.

3892. (26-10-2007) NEW DELHI : The Army Wives Welfare Association (AWWA) has given six ladies the prestigious AWWA Awards of Excellence. Mrs Deepa Singh has worked for empowerment of women and ex-servicemen, Mrs Dipanwita Das has worked for 18 years for the differently abled children and is Principal of Asha School. Mrs Sarita Chopra has worked for improvement in quality of life of soldiers and their families. Mrs Purnima Bakshi for establishing and successfully running a Candle Making women empowerment project for veernaris and differently abled, Mrs Trveen Dhillon for pre school education in army schools and Mrs Minu Lepcha for her commitment to the work as handicraft instructor. Mrs Kirti Kapoor, President AWWA pinned the badges of excellence of these ladies and gave a certificate in a grand ceremony held at NCC auditorium in the presence of all the regional AWWA Presidents. Later in her speech she complimented them and said these ladies are shining examples to others for their dedication and commitment to their work.

3893. (26-10-2007) NEW DELHI : Infantry Day is being celebrated on Saturday. Infantry; the queen of the battle, celebrates 27 October each year as the Infantry Day. On this historic day, sixty years ago in response to the first threat to the sovereignty and territorial integrity of our Nation, the first elements of the Indian Infantry landed in Srinagar and resolutely defended Kashmir from falling into the enemy hands. Pakistan staked claim on Kashmir being a predominantly muslim state and taking advantage of the procrastination of the ruler of J & K exploited the vulnerable situation by launching an attach with the help of raiders on 18 Oct. 1947. By 26 Oct. 1947, the situation turned grave as the raiders advanced along road Uri-Baramulla-Srinagar. On 27 Oct. 1947, a Battalion Headquarters with one company of Infantry were flown into Srinagar. These valiant soldiers fought a gallant action reversing the tide of the battle and saving Kashmir from being torn away by Pakistan. To commemorate this exemplary action of the Infantry in the nascent stage of our independence, 27 October is celebrated as the Infantry day. The Indian Infantry is one of the most battle hardened and combat rich forces in the world, Replete with the glorious history of warfare over a couple of centuries, the Infantry proudly continues to perform the primary and vital role in managing the security environment of the country. Any Army would be proud of the enviable reputation enjoyed by its foremost fighting arm and, in the Indian Army, the Infantry has earned for itself a unique place of pride. Indeed, the Army stood the nation in good stead through a difficult phase of its history, largely due to the selfless devotion to duty of India's gallant Infantrymen for whom sacrifice is a way of life. Infantry is the prime instrument of the nations efforts towards combating the most serious challenge to her security namely the scourge of terrorism. Infantry is fighting terrorism continuously both in J & K and North East in an exemplary manner. Besides zealously guarding the Nation's frontiers over sixty years of independent India's turbulent history, Indian Infantry battalions have acquitted themselves extremely creditably in internal security and counter-insurgency operations over prolonged periods. Through their dedication and disciplined professionalism, Indian Infantrymen have earned the respect and admiration of their counterparts the world over. Infantry is an arm of close combat, with the role of closing in with the enemy to capture or destroy him. While in defence, Infantry holds key areas of tactical and strategic significance and defends it to the 'Last Man Last Round'. This crucial role makes Infantry the most predominant, indispensable and decisive arm for achieving victory in war. Infantry comprises over one third of the Indian Army. They have an enviable combat record, having won 17 Param Vir Chakras and 33 Ashok Chakras out of a total 21 Param Vir Chakras and 34 Ashok Chakras, which have been awarded so far. Wreaths will be laid by serving and retired infantry officers at the AmarJawan Jyoti on Infantry Day on October 27 at 0900 hrs in the honour of the comrades who made the supreme sacrifice for the nation.

3894. (26-10-2007) NEW DELHI : The 10th Meeting of the India-France High Committee on Defence Cooperation (HCC) will begin in New Delhi on Monday, October 29th, 2007. The meeting will be co-chaired by the Defence Secretary Shri Vijay Singh and Mr. Thierry Borja de Mozota, Ministerial Representative of the French Defence Minister. Issues related to joint exercises and training, technology transfer and joint development of weapon systems will be discussed during the two-day meeting. Three sub-committees, formed under the High Committee, will also be meeting on the sidelines. The Sub-Committee on Military Cooperation will roll out the plan for service to service cooperation activities for the next year. The Sub-Committee on Defence Industry Procurement and Research and Technology will discuss matters of transfer of technology, joint development, production and research while the Sub-Committee on Strategic Issues will discuss matters of mutual strategic interest. The HCC was set up in 1998 following the Defence Cooperation Working Group which was set up under a bilateral MoU on supply of defence equipment signed in France in January 1982. The HCC meetings have been held every year, alternately in India and France. The 9th Meeting of the HCC was held on November 9-10 last year in Paris.

3895. (26-10-2007) NEW DELHI : The Directorate of Film Festivals, (DFF), M/o I&B and the Goa Government have signed a Memorandum of Understanding (MoU) on IFFI-2007. The MoU outlines the role and responsibilities between the DFF and the Goa State Government, for the IFFI, which is being organised in

Goa from 23rd November to 3rd December 2007. As per the major provisions of the MoU, signed yesterday, DFF would have authority in deciding all matters relating to entries of films in all the sections, selection and preparation of film programmes, inviting film personalities, film delegates, setting up of various functional units, all matters regarding issue of Delegate cards and be responsible for Media briefs on all matters. Director DFF would be sole recognized Festival Director of the event. The Goa Government would be responsible for making available all required infrastructure for the festival, including six theatres besides the Main Festival theatre, functional office space and the Media Centre with requisite paraphernalia. They would arrange hotel accommodation for delegates; arrange air tickets and local transport, and also assist DFF in providing local human resources for the smooth conduct of the Festival. Meanwhile, the first meeting of the Organizing Committee for IFFI-2007 concluded yesterday. The Meeting was presided by the Hon'ble Minister for Information and Broadcasting, Shri Priyaranjan Dasmunsi. The Goa Minister for Water Resources, Mr. Filip N. Rodrigues and other leaders from the Indian Film Industry and its related trade bodies attended the meeting. In keeping with a request from the Film Industry, Shri Dasmunsi announced that students of film schools would be registered as delegates free of cost, as against the past practice of fifty percent discount.

3896. (26-10-2007) NEW DELHI : The Ministry of Civil Aviation today reviewed the safety and security issues on the airside of the IGI Airport, New Delhi. The meeting was chaired by Shri K.N. Srivastava, Joint Secretary, Ministry of Civil Aviation. Representatives of the Directorate General of Civil Aviation, Bureau of Civil Aviation Security (BCAS), CISF and AAI were also present. The DGCA informed the gathering that from today walking in apron at taxiway in the airside areas of the airport will be strictly prohibited. There was consensus in the meeting for stricter enforcement of all rules and regulations. It has also been decided that violators of rules shall be strictly punished and may even lose their right to enter airport. The Ministry has passed on strict instructions regarding the security aspects of activities on the airside including vehicular movement, storage/placement of ground handling equipments, and movement of personnel-security staff, labour and service providers within the area. Strict instructions have been given to check the antecedents and background of the employees of contractors and sub-contractors of airlines and airport operators. They have also been asked to maintain strict surveillance of private contractors employees/staff providing various services to airlines and airport operators. Strict surveillance have also be maintained of movement of passengers and of crew-misuse of boarding passes for unauthorized entries. The stakeholders have been directed to be extra alert about the movement of screened cargo to and from aircraft, theft and pilferages of registered baggage, cargo etc., disposal of prohibited items detected in passenger baggage or on person and also about the maintenance of perimeter security. The Ministry has also called for adequate deployment of CISF personnel including female personnel in aviation security.

3897. (26-10-2007) NEW DELHI : Defence Minister Shri A K Antony has said that civilian employees of the Ministry of Defence have become a rich repository of information and knowledge which must be utilised optimally and gainfully. Addressing the Armed Forces Headquarters (AFHQ) Service Day Celebrations in New Delhi today, he said the contribution of civilian employees in various fields like manpower, finance, accommodation, materials management, general administration and human resource development should never be under-estimated. Referring to the challenges faced by the civilian defence employees, the Defence Minister said, 'I am aware that the civilian employees face some challenges. You have my full cooperation and I wish to assure you that the Government will do whatever is humanly possible to resolve the problems being faced by you'. There are about 1,40,000 civilian employees in the AFHQ cadre. The Defence civilian cadres were brought under a single authority in 1942 through the creation of the post of Chief Administrative Officer. They act as a bridge between the Service Headquarters and Ministry of Defence, both in times of peace and during war.

3898. (26-10-2007) NEW DELHI : The Indian Air Force has a long and chequered history of contribution to the United Nations Peace-Keeping operations. The process began when IAF sent a flight of Canberra bomber aircraft as part of United Nations Operations in Congo (ONUC) in 1962. This was followed by contribution of a Helicopter Unit in Somalia in 1993 and later at Sierra Leone in the year 2000. UN once again approached India to contribute an air element for its peace keeping operations in Democratic Republic of Congo (MONUC) in 2004. The IAF presently operates two avitation two aviation contingents at Goma and Bukavu. Additionally, the IAF has been tasked to operate an Indian Airfield Services Unit at (IASU) at Kindu. In the backdrop of internal ethnic strife in the Democratic Republice of Congo (DRC), the Eastern region of that country is volatile. The terrain and existing infrastructure in the region make logistics operations by air an imperative. The main airport in eastern Congo is at Kindu, which serves as a major support base for UN operaions. The IAF unit comprising of 120 personnel is manning Kindu base to support all UN air movements. The operations include airport management, ramp operations, crash and fire fighting services, cargo and passenger handling, medical support, meteorological services and communication. Contribution of IAF personnel has been repeatedly lauded by the UN authorities for dedication and professionalism. IAF missions have contributed wholeheartedly during crucial times which have facilitated the UN in executing its mandate. The trust that the UN places on India in general and the IAF in particular is symbolised by the UN requesting India to extend operation of ASU in Congo for another year. The IAF ASU is classified as a specialist unit by the UN. This places extremely high demands on the Unit. The unit personnel were given focused job oriented training coupled with training on general peace keeping operations and security. IAF contingent of 120 personnel includes a 27-member security complement of commandos from the IAF's Special Force Unit, the Garud Force. These men have undergone extensive training in both armed and unarmed combat with the Indian

Army and the NSG. It would be endeavour of every member of the contingent to undertake the assigned task in a professional manner. The contingent will also attemp to contribute whole heartedly in winning the goodwill of local populace through welfare activities. The preparation for the onerous task was taken as a challenge while planning a lean, compact and well trained contingent, Multi skilling, foeusd professional orientation, high morale and motivation would be the hall mark of this force in the months ahead Wg Cdr DV Wani VSM and his team emberk upon the mission to reinforce the faith and commitment associated with India in UN peace keeping operations.

3899. (26-10-2007) NEW DELHI : The government has allocated coal blocks for the power sector that is expected to add 68000 MW to power generation capacity. Twelve coal blocks, with geological reserves of about 6.4 billion tonnes, have been allocated to 18 Central/State Government Companies. This is expected to sustain power generation of approximately 30,000 MW. And 31 private companies have been allocated 15 coal blocks, with geological reserves of 3.6 billion tonnes to support additional generation of 16,000 MW. More than 900 applications were received for the allocation of these coal blocks. The allocation follows the decision of the Energy Coordination Committee, under the Chairmanship of the Prime Minister, to de-reserve such coal blocks that could not be taken up by Coal India Ltd and its subsidiaries for mining in the near future. 81 coal blocks with geological reserves of about 20 billion tonnes were identified by the Ministry of Coal for allocation to companies, both government and private, for permissible end uses. Out of these, 41 coal blocks, with geological reserves of about 15.7 billion tonnes, were earmarked for the power sector. The Government has also decided to facilitate the development of Ultra Mega Power Projects of about 4,000 MW capacity each under tariff based competitive bidding route using super critical technology. Four coal blocks, with geological reserves of 1857 million tonnes, have been allocated to two Ultra Mega Power Projects being set up in Orissa and Jharkhand. These will have a generation capacity of 8,000 MW. In addition two coal blocks have been earmarked for Ultra Mega Power Project of 2,000 MW capacity each in Chhattisgarh. Eight coal blocks, with geological reserves of more than 2650 million tonnes, are also to be allocated through competitive bidding route and will further enhance power generation capacity by 10,000 MW. The allocation of these coal blocks by the Government will support a power generation capacity of approximately 68,000 MW which will enhance energy security in the country.

3900. (26-10-2007) NEW DELHI : There has been more than a hundred percent increase in air services from Kerala-both to the Gulf Region as well as within India in the last three years. This is according to the figures available with the Ministry of Civil Aviation. Currently, the total number of flights per week from Trivandrum is 103 of which 47 are by Indian carriers and 56 are by foreign carriers. In 2004, the total flights per week from Trivandrum were 54-18 by Indian carriers and 36 by foreign carriers. Currently in Cochin there are total of 120 services per week-

62 by Indian carriers and 58 by foreign carriers. In 2004, there were 61 services per week-31 by Indian carriers and 30 by foreign carriers. In Calicut, there used to be 43 services per week in 2004, all of which were provided by Indian carriers. Now there are 90 services per week of which 82 are by Indian Carriers and 8 by foreign carriers. Presently, Air India Express operates 106 services per week to the Gulf Sector. 38 of these are from Calicut, 33 from Trivandrum and 35 from Cochin.

3901. (26-10-2007) NEW DELHI : Congress Spokesperson Smt. Jayanti Natarajan said that the, " the shocking and mind numbing revelations that have come to light as a result of investigative journalism by Tehelka prove beyond a shadow of doubt what the entire country has know since 2002. The Chief Minister of Gujarat has presided over, and extended both tacit and overt support to mass killing, and genocide, and also perpetration of the worst kind of human rights violation and murder. As we have been saying all along, the Chief Minister, and the entire Government at all levels, colluded in both the perpetration of these horrific acts, as well as the shielding of the perpetrators. At that time, even Prime Minister Vajpayee called the post Godhra killings as a national shame ad a black mark on our democracy. The response of the BJP to these serious revelations is even more shocking. There is deafening silence from senior leaders of the BJP, who have not come forward to condemn these horrific incidents. The official response of the BJP through its spokesperson is callous and irresponsible. To shrug off these heinous revelations, as the work of the pre-election dirty tricks department of the Congress party, is not just false and preposterous, but betrays the callous indifference of the BJP to these shameful truths. The BJP needs to come clean on this issue, and explain its position to the nation. Narendra Modi has lost all moral and constitutional authority to continue in office. We have said this before and will repeat it now. If the constitution of India is to be upheld, if we still call ourselves a civilized society, if the right to life has any meaning at all, if human rights are to be upheld, Narendra Modi should immediately step down from public office". To a question on the Centre's role regarding the Tehelka revelations Smt. Jayanti Natarajan said, we are now speaking about the incidents that the Congress Party has raised from 2002. There is nothing new in these revelations. These are proof that whatever we have been saying from 2002 is correct and therefore the BJP and Narendar Modi need to answer the questions raised and not talk about who's meeting whom. To a question why these revelations after five years and why not prosecute the guilty and what is the Centre doing Smt. Natarajan said, the matters are already pending before the Supreme Court of India and whatever the role therefore it is to the Court that we should appeal. All these incidents about which the revelations have come are all pending before the Supreme Court as you well know. And as regards the time taken (5 years), it is for the Court to take it up. Regarding the role of the Government, it can come in when the State Government agrees to a CBI inquiry which the State government under Modi has not agreed too. Any other chief minister who has any iota of principles will agree to an inquiry even if it's against him. It has been done in the past. And it can be done now. Therefore it is for Mr. Modi to agree to a CBI inquiry. To a question as to why the Centre does not dismiss Modi, impose President's rule and order fresh CBI inquiry Smt. Natarajan said, first of all we do not issue platitudes. This would be trivializing a serious incident about which Indian National Congress is deeply concerned. These are not platitudes. The Central government can act through the CBI. The CBI is an independent investigating agency and fortunately the hands of the CBI are tied. Unless the State government agrees and the State government has blatantly refused to accept a CBI inquiry, the matters are pending before the Supreme Court and it is totally wrong to accuse the Central government of inaction. And as far as banning a political organisation is concerned Smt. Natarajan said, the perpetrators should be punished and brought to book as murderers.

3902. (26-10-2007) NEW DELHI : Inaugurating today the comprehensive Health Fair on Indian Systems of Medicine, AROGYA 2007, the Union Minister for Health & Family Welfare, Dr. Anbumani Ramadoss said that with the changes in the lifestyle of people, it has become clear that chemical drugs alone cannot provide adequate solutions to lifestyle-related chronic and psychosomatic health problems. This is one of the main reasons why there is a global resurgence of demand for traditional medicines. Smt Panabaka Lakshmi, Minister of State for Health & Family Welfare, Shri Jairam Ramesh, Minister of State for Commerce, Smt Anita Das, Secretary (AYUSH), Dr. Sheela Bhide, Chairperson, India Trade Promotion Organisation and Shri Venkat Jaspi, Vice-Chairman, PHARMEXCIL were also present at the function. The following is the summary of the Health Minister's speech: On behalf of the Government of India and the Ministry of Health and Family Welfare, I heartily welcome you all to the AROGYA-2007. The Department of AYUSH have been organizing this comprehensive Fair and exhibition since 2001 showcasing developments in the AYUSH field and we have found a consistent rise in the public interest and attendance at the Fairs. For the first time this year, an International Meet of Traditional Medicine Regulators and Industry is also being organized and many foreign regulators, technical experts and consultants are registered to participate in the event. Buyer-seller meets have also been organized to discuss the market development of AYUSH products in India and abroad. This time the exhibition has an international dimension and I would like to congratulate the organizers-the Department of AYUSH, Ministry of Commerce, ITPO and Pharmexcil for having expanded the scope of the AROGYA Fair in this manner. New developments in technology now enable scientists to explore possible solutions from traditional medical knowledge. India is fortunate to have a long history of practice of the codified traditional medical knowledge systems like Ayurveda, Yoga, Unani and Siddha. These systems, which are officially recognized in India, have immense scope to provide solutions for diverse health problems. Even though AYUSH systems are gaining popularity, there are still doubts in the minds of some people that they are not evidence based, and therefore, not safe and efficacious. We need to address these issues and to dispel these doubts through research. There is increasing evidence of a global resurgence of interest in Indian systems of medicine all over the world. There is a great deal of demand for Ayurveda and Yoga in particular in many countries around the world, especially in the USA, Germany, Hungary, Italy, UK and Russia. During my tenure as Health Minister, a good number of foreign delegations have shown interest in bilateral cooperation in the area of Indian systems of medicine and have sought India's support for conducting collaborative educational and research activities. We are very happy about such initiatives and will provide all possible support for them. We are making all out efforts to push AYUSH products into the emerging global market for natural products and in order to achieve significant results, the Government of India is determined to make certain strategic interventions. To begin with, we have recently signed an agreement with the International Trade Centre (ITC) for a global market analysis for export promotion of Ayurveda, Siddha and Unani products. Once the report of ITC is received, we will take the measures necessary to implement its recommendations. It may be true that many aspects of AYUSH treatments and medicines cannot be tested with available scientific tools and technology. But it is also true that these systems have withstood the test of the time. However, there is no other option but to follow universally acceptable modes of evaluating safety and efficacy if we intend to certify the scientific basis of Ayurveda, Siddha and Unani treatments and medicines. As a medical professional and the Health Minister of the country, I feel that there must be an overwhelming commitment to R&D from all concerned both in the public and private sectors in order to achieve credibility and global acceptance for the Indian systems of medicine. The Department of AYUSH in collaboration with Indian Council of Medical Research (ICMR) and Council for Scientific and Industrial Research (CSIR) have initiated a Golder Triangle Project for scientific validation and development of R&D based Ayurveda, Siddha and Unani medicines for a variety of disease conditions for which there is no satisfactory treatment in conventional medicine. Way back in 1960s Pharmacopoeia Committees were constituted for these systems for laying down Pharmacopoeial standards based on modern analytical parameters. The work of laying down Pharmacopoeial Standards of crude drugs is almost over and now the work of laying down now Pharmacopoeial standards for compound formulations is currently underway. First volume of Ayurveda Pharmacopoeia Compound Formulations has been published. For technological upgradation of Ayurveda, Siddha, Unani and Homoeopathy drug industry it is proposed to develop common facilities for quality control, raw material standardization, sophisticated packing machines etc. in places where there is a cluster of 25-30 manufacturing units.

3903. (26-10-2007) NEW DELHI : Shri Arjun Singh, the Minister for Human Resource Development (HRD) has said, " Reservation of Other Backward Classes (OBCs) in Higher Education is very desirable. We should be able to convince the Supreme Court what India wants and the efforts in this regard have to be pursued with dedication". He was delivering the inaugural address on an ongoing National

Conference on Social Exclusion and Inclusive Policies (Oct. 26-27, 2007) organised by Indian Institute of Dalit Studies (IIDS) in collaboration with Princeton University (USA), here, today. Shri Singh said that the Conference is being held at an opportune time when the deliberations at the conference can help the policies to become inclusive, eventually giving a road map to further the commitment of removing discrimination in every sphere of life including social and cultural, economic and the political as well as extreme case of violence. He further added that policies formulated by our founding fathers of the Constitution to do away with the discrimination faced by marginalized sections of the population such as SCs,STs,OBCs, women and religious minorities such as Muslims have yielded good results in social and educational development but advancement made here is still falling short of the expectations of that section of the society. There needs to be done a lot. This is the time that India can or should stand up and face real issues of the Nation. He also shared his experiences at a recently held UNESCO conference at Paris and said that the time has come UNESCO should come forward with practical solutions and face the reality around the globe without any discrimination. The Conference is all about bringing together other studies undertaken by Indian Institute of Dalit Studies in the areas of education, health, food security and employment.The studies undertaken under joint Project by IIDS and Princeton University (USA) involve seminal work exploring discrimination in opportunities for employment for new graduates, hiring practices, attitudes, differences in earning private sector. The studies capture the discrimination in market and non-market transactions. The findings of these studies have been brought out by the Economic and Political Weekly in its latest issue of October 13,2007 that was released by Shri Arjun Singh. The two-day conference was also attended by Prof. Sukhadeo Thorat, Chairman UGC, Prof. B.L. Mungekar, Member, Planning Commission and Prof. Katherine Newmen, Princeton University (USA).

3904. (26-10-2007) NEW DELHI : The Prime Minister, Dr. Manmohan Singh, reviewed the implementation of various programmes taken up under the National Common Minimum Programme (NCMP) at a meeting here today. Among the issues discussed were: implementation of the recommendations of the Radhakrishnan Committee on agricultural indebtedness, Vaidyanathan Committee Report on cooperative sector and the Sachar Committee Report on empowerment of Minorities. The Prime Minister reviewed implementation of Mid-Day Meal Scheme, Integrated Child Development Scheme (ICDS), revamping of Public Distribution System, Implementation of Social Security Initiatives of the Government like old age pension, health insurance schemes for disabled persons. The Prime Minister also reviewed implementation of initiatives in education sector including announcements made in his Independence Day address. The Prime Minister expressed concern about the slow progress of infrastructure projects and has directed that a meeting of the Committee on Infrastructure be called to review progress in power, roads, ports, telecom and railway sectors.

3905. (26-10-2007) NEW DELHI : The Union Minister for Micro, Small & Medium Enterprises Shri Mahabir Prasad will lead a delegation to China tomorrow to attend a two-day ministerial meeting on Small & Medium Enterprises. He will speak at the third session on "Cooperation among and Development of SMEs" and will give special emphasis on cluster development. Accounting for more than 95% of all enterprises in most of Asia-Europe Meeting (ASEM) countries, SMEs act as a main driving force of technological innovation, expanding employment and boosting economic growth. ASEM members pay great attention to SMEs development. In the Hanoi Declaration on closer ASEM Economic Partnership adopted at Fifth ASEM Summit, ASEM members have strong political will to promote SMEs cooperation under the ASEM framework. Against this background, China proposed to host the ASEM SMEs Ministerial Meeting, which aims at deepening dialogue among governmental agencies of ASEM members in charge of SMEs, discussing policies and measures for better adapting to globalisation, creating sound SMEs social service policy and supporting system, improving SMEs capacity of innovation and competitiveness, enhancing cooperation among SMEs in ASEM members, strengthening regional cooperation of industrial clusters, and expanding mutual investment areas. The Minister is also likely to interact with the leaders of various ASEM countries regarding the development of SME sector. In India, the Small & Medium Enterprises sector has attracted worldwide attention in recent months. India has been a hub of activities for the development of Micro, Small & Medium Enterprises.

3906. (26-10-2007) NEW DELHI : The Union Minister of Shipping, Road Transport and Highways, Thiru T.R. Baalu has approved a sum of Rs.1254.61 lakh for road improvement work in the state of Karnataka. Thiru Baalu approved the proposal for widening of existing intermediate lane/single lane to two lane from km. 479.00 to 489.00 km on Sholapur Mangalore Section of National Highway-13. Earlier the road from Chitradurga to Shimoga was a Major District Road (MDR) and it used to cater the traffic volume, which was less compared to present traffic. The existing crust is inadequate to take the present traffic intensity of commercial vehicles carrying heavy loads. The surface is distressed at certain stretches and the overall riding quality of the reach is poor. Therefore, the approval has been granted for widening this 10 km stretch of National Highway.

3907. (26-10-2007) NEW DELHI : FCI Aravali Gypsum & Minerals India Limited (FAGMIL), a Public Sector Undertaking under the Ministry of Chemicals and Fertilizers today presented a dividend cheque of Rs.1,46,59,600 to the Govt. of India for the year 2006-07. The cheque was handed over to the Minister for Chemicals & Fertilizers and Steel Shri Ram Vilas Paswan here today by Shri Sunil Dayal, Chairman and Managing Director, FAGMIL. The Secretary, Department of Fertilizers Dr. J S Sarma was also present on the occasion. Engaged in mining of mineral gypsum and supplying it to Agriculture sector and others, FAGMIL sold 8.96 lakh tonnes of gypsum during 2006-07. It earned Rs. 11.51 crore profit before tax over sales turnover of Rs. 37.07 crore during the year. The company is planning to diversify into other minerals like Phosphate and SMS Grade Limestone.

3908. (26-10-2007) NEW DELHI : Finance Minister Shri P. Chidambaram delivered a keynote address on "IT Outsourcing to India" at a Seminar jointly organised by the Norwegian IKT Association and Embassy of India Oslo, Norway last evening. The meeting was attended by prominent IT stakeholders in Norway as well as India. Shri Chidambaram emphasised the unique fundamentals that had gone into making Indian IT industry among the world's best. He pointed out that Indian IT industry exports crossed US$ 37 billion last year and were likely to reach US$ 80 billion by 2011. The Minister said that the apprehensions about the jobs losses from IT outsourcing were unfounded. To the contrary, more jobs have been created as a result of IT outsourcing. He pointed out that IT outsourcing to India could improve Norwegian industries' competitivity and their capacity to adopt to the ongoing global trends. India has been Norway's first source of skilled professionals for past one year. During the seminar, acquisition of M/s SPAN, a Bangalore-based IT company by M/s EDB Business Partners ASA, Norway's largest IT company, was announced. Shri Chidambaram personally congratulated the two Managing Directors and wished them further success. This is the largest ever IT acquisition by Norwegian IT company in Asia involving over 500 IT professionals working with SPAN. In his welcome address IKT Director General Per Morten Hoff welcomed India-Norwegian synergy in IT sector and assured of his Association's patronage to this trend. Other companies outsourcing to India from Norway such as TCS and Accenture also made their presentations at the seminar. Finance Minister returned from his Norway tour this morning.

3909. (26-10-2007) NEW DELHI : Following is the text of the Fifth Convocation Address by the Vice President of India Mohd. Hamid Ansari at the Lakshmibai National Institute of Physical Education at Gwalior (Madhya Pradesh) today : "I am greatly honoured to be the Chief Guest at the fifth convocation of this prestigious and unique institution and to deliver the Convocation Address today. I am grateful to Minister Aiyar for inviting me to participate in this Convocation. I am greatly honoured by the Institute's decision to confer the Degree of Doctor of Letters (Honoris Causa) on me. It imposes a responsibility on me to further the cause of sports, a cause close to my heart. The Institute was established in 1957, the centenary year of the first war of independence, and located at Gwalior, where Rani Lakshmibai had laid her life for the cause of freedom. This year marks the 150th anniversary of 1857, and I feel privileged to be here in Gwalior today. Ladies and Gentlemen, the importance of physical education in the rise and fall of nations is an underestimated fact of history. In ancient Greece, Plato and Aristotle agreed that the right kind of person could be shaped through public education that stressed gymnastics to discipline the body and music to discipline the mind and soul. Indeed, ancient civilisations that could harness and impart physical education training on a systemic and institutional scale among their population could survive and thrive. The grammar and idiom of physical education has changed over the centuries-its essential role in human resource development, promotion of good health, recreation and social bonding remains unchanged. In India, the archaeological excavations of Mohenjodaro and Harappa, references in Vedic literature, Ramayana and Mahabharata and ancient Indian literary works attest the vital role of sports and games in our social and cultural life. The primacy of physical education and sports was best articulated by Swami Vivekananda who said: "Be strong my young friends, that is my advice to you. You will be nearer to heaven through football than through the study of the Gita." We have all heard the dictum of "a healthy mind in a healthy body". But indicators of national health are not very encouraging. The Third National Family Health Survey reveals that around 80% of children in the age group of 6-35 months are anaemic. Over 50% of married women and around 25% of married men are anaemic. Around 20% of children under three years of age suffer from acute under-nutrition or wasting. Around 38% of all children under three years face stunted growth, indicating chronic long-term under-nutrition. Public expenditure on health is around 1.2% of GDP and is low by any standards. Ladies and Gentlemen, at the outset, I wish to discuss the legal framework that guides sports and physical education in India. In the Constitution of India, in the Seventh Schedule, 'sports' comes under the State List clubbed with "theatres and dramatic performances, cinemas, entertainments and amusements". It is a supreme irony that while the Indian cinema and entertainment industry emerged as a global leader and is much feted and admired, sports in the country did not develop and prosper to the same extent. Under the Constitution, broad basing and increasing the popularity of sports and games is primarily the responsibility of States. In actual practice, allocation of resources to sports by state governments has been minimal. The question of inclusion of "Sports" in the Concurrent List needs to be pursued for effective involvement of all stakeholders in the development and promotion of sports in the country.

3910. (27-10-2007) NEW DELHI : At ministerial round table of member countries of UNESCO held on 26th October 2007 at Paris presided over by Shri Kapil Sibal, Union Minister for Science and Technology and Earth Sciences made a clarion call on UNESCO and member countries. He suggested that UNESCO may undertake a role in the development of a sustainable and global model for enrolling both technology sources and intergovernmental commitments for providing access to generic technologies to meet the developmental choices to large segments of global community based on the following: a) voluntary offer for free access to the needy, b) a formula of differential prices based on criticality of need and differentiated capacities to pay, c) deferred payment on loan basis to build global growth equity and d) conscious effort to render technologies affordable to many through North-South and South-South technology partnerships. He selected total of five areas of technology needs for meeting the developmental choices. They are, he said, solid waste management, safe clean drinking water, clean coal technologies, devices for solar power and mitigation of damages from natural disaster. Shri Sibal stressed the role of science and technology in bringing developmental values to the society. He observed that capacity building in science and technology is one of the most important needs of the world today. The Minister also stressed that such efforts to build capacities should take into account the differential levels of development and resource investment capacities and needs. Calling for innovative ways and techniques for bridging the differences between the cultures of science and industry through public-private partnerships, Shri. Sibal emphasized the need for greater interactions among the four pillars of development namely, industry, Government, research and academy. He also emphasized the need for grater autonomy to the university systems in developing world. The Minister observed that many member countries had noted the technology divides. There was a wide spread support to the proposal of Shri Kapil Sibal among the member countries for increasing the access to technologies in innovative ways. He concluded that among member countries, there was a large expectation in meeting the developmental challenges associated with poverty reduction, disaster management, desertification and pollution control. He expressed high hope that the leadership of UNESCO would meet the rising expectations. His chairmanship and leadership came to high praise among all member states and made India proud. The Director General, UNESCO paid high encomium for the extraordinary values brought to the round table by Shri Kapil Sibal.

3911. (27-10-2007) NEW DELHI : The Bharatiya Janata Party condemns the gruesome and brutal attack and killing of innocent political workers and others at Chilkadia Village in Giridih District late last night. The reckless and unmindful killing of Anup Marandi son of Sh. Babulal Marandi and other innocents by the naxalities is a shocking failure of Madhu Koda's government which is supported by Congress, RJD and others partners of the UPA. The UPA Government at Delhi whose partners have foisted a proxy government in the state of Jharkhand supporting an Independent as the CM are fully responsible for the total anarchy prevailing in the state. The BJP categorically reiterates that the UPA has to be squarely blamed for Naxal killings in the state. The BJP also takes note of the fact that the soft policies of the UPA government in Delhi with regards to Naxalism has resulted in a sharp decline in the internal security situation in the country with naxalism penetrating in more then 150 district across the country. In March this year Jharkhand Mukti Morcha MP Sunil Mahto was brutally killed near Ghatshila by Maoists wearing police uniforms while watching a Soccer match. There is a stunning similarity in the present attack in Giridih with that of killing of Sunil Mahto as the killers have apparently watched the cultural programme posing as policeman before striking. This instance clearly indicates a complete failure of the State as well as the Intelligence Agencies of Union alarmingly failing to pre-empt an attack, which has a stunning repetitive modus operandi. A mocked State Government which is run by an Independent MLA as the CM and assisted by a council of eight Cabinet Ministers who are also independents supported by UPA has resulted in an anarchic functioning of the state which is primarily focused on personal agenda of constituencies and individuals defying the basics tenets of Constitutional responsibility and commitment towards providing a safe state. On having learnt the heart rendering incident Sh. Rajnath Singh the National President of the Bharatiya Janata Party who is in Lucknow today conveyed his condolences to Sh. Babu Lal Marandi and others in a telephonic conversation this morning Sh. Arjun Munda, the former CM of Jharkhand Sh. Pashupati Nath Singh, the State President of BJP, several legislators and other senior office bearers have already reached the spot of the incident.

3912. (27-10-2007) NEW DELHI : The President of India, Smt. Pratibha Devisingh Patil will inaugurate the 12th World Lake Conference at Jaipur on October 29. The President will arrive in Jaipur on the evening of October 28 and return to New Delhi the next day after inaugurating the Conference. The Conference will be attended by experts from around the world and will discuss ways in which lakes can be conserved. This is the first time that this Conference is being held in the South Asian region. This will be the President's first visit to Rajasthan since she was sworn-in in July this year. Smt. Patil was the Governor of Rajasthan before she was elected as the President of India.

3913. (28-10-2007) NEW DELHI : The Bureau of the Asia Pacific Ministers' Conference on Housing and Urban Development (APMCHUD) at its 2nd Meeting at Amman, Jordan on October 27, 2007 has decided to set up its permanent Secretariat at New Delhi. Speaking at the meeting Kumari Saija, Minister for Housing and Urban Poverty Alleviation, Government of India and the Chairperson of the Bureau of APMCHUD said, India would look forward to working closely with the other member countries from the Asia-Pacific and other regional and global establishments like UN-Habitat, UN-Escap, ADB, etc. towards fulfilling the initiatives identified in the Delhi Declaration. She said the countries in the Asia-Pacific Region at large face common and similar challenges in their goal of achieving a better quality of life for the citizens. In their effort towards achieving sustainable, holistic and inclusive human development, the Asia-Pacific Region countries have recognized the fact that a synergic approach would go a long way in addressing these challenges of housing and urban development sector more comprehensively. The meeting was hosted by the Hon'ble Minister for Public Works and Housing, Government of Jordan, Hob'ble Mr. Hosni Abu Ghelda and was participated by His Excellency Mr. Manouchehr Khajedalcee, Vice Minister for Housing, Iran and representatives from China, Azabaijan and Malaysia The first meeting of the Bureau was held in Nairobi on April 15, 2007 wherein the framework of action to operationalise the APMCHUD was undertaken and it was decided to put in place an operational mechanism for the APMCHUD through establishment of a Permanent Secretariat of the Bureau. The second meeting was convened to draw up an action plan to take the initiative forward as envisaged in the 'Delhi Declaration'.

3914. (29-10-2007) NEW DELHI : The Union Public Service Commission (UPSC) regrets to announce that, inspite of the best efforts of the Commission, the Civil Services (Main) Examination, 2007 scheduled for 31st October, 2007 (Wednesday) is hereby postponed, due to some unforeseen eventualities beyond the control of the Commission. The UPSC, therefore, informs all the candidates appearing on 31st October 2007 for the subjects Public Administration/Political Science and International Relations to take note accordingly. A fresh date for the Examination of the said papers will be announced separately. Union Public Service Commission New Delhi, Kartika 7, 1929/October 29, 2007

3915. (29-10-2007) NEW DELHI : The Prime Minister, Dr. Manmohan Singh, reviewed the action taken by the government to counteract the erosion of the Majuli Island in the Brahamaputra River. The Prime Minister stressed the importance of Majuli as a site of great emotional and cultural significance to Assam given the presence of the Vaishnavite Satras. He said the issue must tackled on a war footing and the government should mobilize the best technical competence available to address this task. PM directed that the Action Plan be implemented on highest priority. He also directed that, in addition to technical professionals, civil society professionals should also be enlisted for the preservation of the Majuli Island. The Prime Minister also desired that an update on the work done on this matter may be sent to the PMO every three months. A Presentation was made on the gradual but steadyerosion of the Majuli Island in the Brahamaputra on account of high silt and sand content making it very erodible and the steps being taken to tackle the problem. The steps include the acceptance of a detailed project plan of Rs. 86.50 crores to be executed in three phases. Of these, Phase-1 of Rs.41.28 crores is now under implementation and is expected to be complete by March 2008. Phase-2 and 3 would be taken up and completed by year 2009. The meeting was informed that the measures taken up under Phase-1 has had some positive-impact on reducing further erosion, saving of crops and improvement of communications. The Minister of Water Resources will head a high level team for a field visit, soon after the monsoon, to assess the situation and take corrective action where required. The Ministry of Culture requested for accelerated action given the fact that Majuli is being sponsored by the Government of India as a site to be declared as world heritage. The meeting was attended by the Ministers of Water Resources and Culture, and the Secretaries of Water Resources and DONER, Chairman, Brahamaputra Board and Director General, ASI.

3916. (29-10-2007) NEW DELHI : On 27th October, 2007 the President has promulgated the Payment of Bonus (Amendment) ordinance, 2007 containing the following amendments:-i) Amendment to clause (13) of Section 2 of the Payment of Bonus Act, 1965 to raise the eligibility limit for payment of bonus from the salary or wage of Rs. 3500/- per month to Rs. 10000/- per month. ii) Amendment to section 12 of the Payment of Bonus Act, 1965 to raise the ceiling for calculation purpose from the salary or wage of Rs. 2500/- per month to Rs. 3500/- per month;

iii) Deletion of clause (vi) of section 32 of the Payment of Bonus Act, 1965 so as to cover the employees employed through contractors on building operations. Thus the employees, including those employed through contractors on building operations will be entitled to receive bonus as per the revised ceilings, for the year 2006-07 and onwards. The Ordinance shall be deemed to have come into force on 1st April, 2006. Ministry of Labour & Employment New Delhi, Kartika 07, 1929/October 29, 2007

3917. (29-10-2007) NEW DELHI : The Winter Session of Parliament shall commence from November 15 2007 and continue till December 7, 2007. The Cabinet Committee on Parliamentary Affairs, presided by Shri Pranab Mukherjee, Leader of the House and External Affairs Minister decided to send the recommendation for summoning the Winter Session of Parliament before the President, by tomorrow, with the above mentioned dates. Due to the Assembly elections in the States of Gujarat and Himachal Pradesh, it will be a short session of 17 sittings, covering 23 days. Before taking the decision in the meeting, the Minister of Parliamentary Affairs had also consulted the Speaker of Lok Sabha.

3918. (29-10-2007) NEW DELHI : The Vice President of India Mohd. Hamid Ansari has expressed his concern on the growing incidents of terrorism and naxalite acts in the country. He was addressing after releasing a book entitled " Political Violence and the Police in India " authored by Shri K.S.Subramanian (Retd. IPS) at a function here today. The Vice President said that the central government takes action on any political violence in the state only when the state government asks the centre to do so. This should be looked into. The Vice President said the book gives an overview of the role of various police organizations in tackling the terrorist activities and political violence. He congratulated the author for bringing out an informative book. A number of dignitaries were present on the occasion.

3919. (29-10-2007) NEW DELHI : The Committee of Eminent Persons on Sethu Samudram Shipping Channel Project has commenced hearings of persons interested in this project at its office at Malligai, No. 30/95, P.S. Kumarasamy Raja (Greenways). Road, Chennai-600 028 from 29th October, 2007 at 1000 hrs. The Committee reiterated that all persons interested in Sethu Samudram Shipping Channel Project, if they so wish, can appear before the Committee between 1000 hrs. to 1700 hrs. from 29th October, 2007 to 3rd November, 2007 at its office. All such persons intending to be heard personally, except the writ Petitioners in court cases mentioned in the Order dated 5th October, 2007 of Cabinet Secretariat, shall have to produce either acknowledgement issued by the Office of the Committee or the Postal receipt in token of the fact that they have sent their objections/suggestions to the Committee.

3920. (29-10-2007) NEW DELHI : The Central Government has decided to constitute a Committee on State Agrarian Relations and the Unfinished Task in

Land Reforms with the experts drawn from related specializations and fields. Disclosing this to media persons here today Union Rural Development Minister Dr. Raghuwansh Prasad Singh said that this committee will carry out required field surveys and studies, collate the necessary data and make its recommendations through the Ministry of Rural Development to the National Land Reforms Council headed by the Prime Minister. This committee would look into all related issues, including land reforms and will make specific recommendations on the policies related to land, speedier disposal of land related court cases and judicial forums relating to the latter. These recommendations would be considered by the Central Government for appropriate decisions and for making suitable recommendations and advise to the State Governments. The broad terms of reference of this committee would, among others, include detailed consideration of and making recommendations on the issues related to ceiling on land holdings, distribution of land to the eligible persons, including the landless and homestead landless and for ensuring their possession, speedier disposal of land-related court cases and necessary mechanisms for the same including setting up of fast track courts at various levels. This committee to be headed by the Minister for Rural Development as its chairperson would include persons eminent in the field of land reforms. The committee will comprise of both officials and non-officials. The recommendations of the committee would be advisory in nature and will also take into account the coordination and monitoring of the status in the field. The setting up of and finalization of recommendations of this committee will be in accordance with a clear time frame.

3921. (29-10-2007) NEW DELHI : Government of India have announced the sale (re-issue) of "5.87 percent Government Stock, 2010" under Market Stabilization Scheme for a notified amount of Rs. 3,000 crore (nominal). Government of India have also announced the sale (re-issue) of "11.30 percent Government Stock, 2010" under Market Stabilization Scheme for a notified amount of Rs. 3,000 crore (nominal). The Government Stocks will be sold through price based auction using multiple price method. The auctions will be conducted by the Reserve Bank of India, Mumbai Office, Fort, Mumbai on November 1, 2007 (Thursday). Up to 5 per cent of the amount notified for the sale of stock is reserved for allotment to eligible individuals and Institutions on non-competitive basis as per the Scheme for Non-Competitive Bidding Facility in the Auction of Government Securities. Bids in the prescribed form obtainable from the Regional Director, Reserve Bank of India, Mumbai Office (Public Debt Office), Fort, Mumbai-400 001 and RBI website www.rbi.org.in should be submitted to that Office on November 1, 2007. The NDS members should submit competitive as well as non-competitive bids in electronic format using Primary Market Operation (PMO) module of NDS. All bids should be submitted by 12.30 P.M. The result of the auctions will be announced on November 1, 2007 and payment by successful bidders will be during banking hours on November 2, 2007 (Friday).

3922. (29-10-2007) NEW DELHI : Mr. Sheikh Hamad Bin Khalifa Al-Thani, Emir of the State of Qatar, Mr. Abdullah Bin Hamad Al-Attiyah, Deputy Premier and Minister of Energy & Industry has assured Shri Murli Deora to consider Indian proposal for supplying additional quantities of LNG to India. In a meeting today morning at Doha, the two ministers emphasised the need for greater cooperation between India and Qatar in the hydrocarbon sector. Shri Deora evinced interest of Indian companies to participate including equity stake in the various opportunities and projects in the hydrocarbon sector in Qatar. He added that the Indian gas market is emerging as a mature market. In recent years, the Indian gas sector has received progressively greater attention from global companies and has made rapid strides on the upstream front. Speaking at the 6th Doha Gas Conference Shri Deora invited Qatari oil & gas companies and International Oil Companies (IOCs) present to actively participate in the next Indian Exploration & Production (E&P) bidding round which will be officially announced shortly. Shri Deora informed that a significant number of onshore, offshore and deep water blocks will be offered for participation. Shri Murli Deora is on a two day official visit to Qatar. He is accompanied by Petroleum Secretary Shri M.S. Srinivasan, CMD GAIL Shri U.D. Choubey, MD OVL Shri R.S. Butola and MD PLL Shri P. Dasgupta. Following is the text of Shri Deora's speech:-"Let me begin by thanking my friend His Excellency Al-Attiyah for his kind invitation to attend this Conference on Natural Gas. As "Oil" was the fuel which propelled human development in the 20th Century, the 21st Century, it is rightly said, belongs to "Natural Gas". 21st Century is also witnessing profound changes in the world economic order with the emergence of Asia, Africa and Latin America achieving equitable development and growth for their citizens. Fossil fuels will continue to provide the primary energy needs of this phase of economic progress in the foreseeable future. With our growing understanding of the environmental impact and costs of ever expanding use of hydrocarbons, we all are committed to an environment friendly use of fuels. We seek energy security with environment responsibility. The balance between the legitimate desire of growth and prosperity of countries across Asia and other developing countries is the quest for cleaner fuel with minimal impact on environment. The location of this conference provides us the way forward. Qatar is home to the world's largest gas fields by far, the Offshore North Field. With Qatar expected to achieve 77 MT of LNG capacity by 2010, it will become the largest exporter of LNG in the world. This extra-ordinary achievement of such a capacity creation within a decade is a tribute to the people and the Government of Qatar-and of course to my friend His Excellency Al-Attiyah.